PHAENOMENOLOGICA

COLLECTION FONDÉE PAR H. L. VAN BREDA ET PUBLIÉE SOUS LE
PATRONAGE DES CENTRES D'ARCHIVES-HUSSERL

76

THEODORE DE BOER

The Development of Husserl's Thought

translated by

THEODORE PLANTINGA

THE DEVELOPMENT OF HUSSERL'S TH

THEODORE DE BOER

The Development of Husserl's Thought

translated by

THEODORE PLANTINGA

1978

MARTINUS NIJHOFF
THE HAGUE/BOSTON/LONDON

Translated from the Dutch: De ontwikkelingsgang in het denken van Husserl,
Assen: Van Gorcum, 1966.

In Memoriam

PATER HERMAN LEO VAN BREDA O.F.M.

ISBN 90 247 2039 7

PRINTED IN THE NETHERLANDS

CONTENTS

PART TWO

PHILOSOPHY AS DESCRIPTIVE EIDETIC PSYCHOLOGY

Chapter II. PSYCHOLOGICAL AND TRANSCENDENTAL EPISTEMOLOGY

Chapter III. PSYCHOLOGY AND TRANSCENDENTAL PHENOMENOLOGY

FOREWORD TO THE ENGLISH EDITION

This book on the development of Husserl's thought is a translation of my dissertation, which was published in Dutch in 1966 by Van Gorcum of Assen. I have gone through the entire text once more, making changes, additions and deletions. In the process I have taken account of Husserl literature that has appeared since 1966 as well as some new insights of my own, while making a special effort to keep English-language readers in mind.

The publication of this new edition gives me an opportunity to express my appreciation to those who have helped make it possible. In the first place I must thank the translator, Dr. Theodore Plantinga, for his dedication, professional expertise and attention to detail. To Dr. Henry Pietersma I owe thanks for expert help in translating specific Husserlian terms. The Netherlands Institute for Advanced Study in the Humanities and Social Sciences (located in Wassenaar) has given me the opportunity to devote the necessary attention to the time-consuming task of preparing the text for publication and making last-minute corrections.

Now that the book is finally making its appearance after years of work, the chief figure who comes to mind is the late Father H.L. Van Breda, who took the initiative in arranging for the English translation. His interest and encouragement were instrumental in the successful completion of this project. All who enjoyed the privilege of knowing him personally treasured him for his warmth, his friendly manner, his interest in others, and his willingness to be of help. To his memory I dedicate this book.

TRANSLATOR'S PREFACE

Although this book is a translation from Dutch, the chief obstacle to be overcome was Husserl's (German) technical terminology. As I sought English equivalents for German phenomenological terms, I made thankful use of Dorion Cairns' *Guide for Translating Husserl* as well as existing translations of Husserl's works, especially J.N. Findlay's rendering of *Logische Untersuchungen*. Since the technical terminology in the various translations and English studies of Husserl is far from uniform, I had to devise my own system of equivalents for key Husserlian terms. As I translated the quotations from Husserl's works into English, I did consult the available translations and draw on them, but I endeavored to keep the technical vocabulary uniform – sometimes by fresh translations of the passages quoted and sometimes by slight alterations in the existing translations. I made these changes not so much out of any basic disagreement with other translators as out of a desire to keep the terminology uniform throughout the book.[1]

For the benefit of German and French readers not entirely at home with the English phenomenological vocabulary, I have included a small translation table in which my English equivalents for some central German terms are listed. Words with cognates or well-established phenomenological terms as their English equivalents have not been included.

Finally, I should like to express my thanks to Prof. Henry Pietersma of Victoria College (University of Toronto), who first suggested that I undertake the translation of this book, for his many valuable suggestions on technical terminology. The responsibility for any mistakes in the translation, of course, remains my own.

Theodore Plantinga

---

[1] See bibliography IV English Translations of Husserl's Works.

Jeder, der ernstlich Philosoph werden will, muß sich einmal im Leben auf sich selbst zurückziehen und in sich den Umsturz aller vorgegebenen Wissenschaften und ihren Neubau versuchen. Philosophie ist eine ganz persönliche Angelegenheit des Philosophierenden. Es handelt sich um seine *sapientia universalis,* das ist um sein ins Universale fortstrebendes Wissen – aber um ein echt wissenschaftliches, das er von Anfang an und in jedem Schritte absolut verantworten kann aus seinen absolut einsichtigen Gründen. Ich kann zum echten Philosophen nur werden durch meinen freien Entschluß, diesem Ziel entgegenleben zu wollen. Habe ich mich dazu entschlossen somit den Anfang erwählt aus absoluter Armut und den Umsturz, so ist natürlich ein Erstes, mich zu besinnen, wie ich den absolut sicheren Anfang und die Methode des Fortgangs finden könnte, wo mir jede Stütze vorgegebener Wissenschaft fehlt.

EDMUND HUSSERL, 'Pariser Vorträge' 1929.

Solche Überzeugungen des Verfassers haben sich in der Fortarbeit, in der Evidenz stufenweis aufeinander gegründeter Ergebnisse immerfort verstärkt. Hat er das Ideal seines Philosophischen Strebens praktisch auf das eines rechten Anfängers herabstimmen müssen, so ist er mindestens für sich selbst im Alter zur vollkommenen Gewißheit gekommen, sich einen wirklichen Anfänger nennen zu dürfen. Fast möchte er hoffen – wenn ihm Methusalems Alter beschieden wäre – doch noch zum Philosophen werden zu können.

EDMUND HUSSERL, "Nachwort zu meinen 'Ideen zu einer reinen Phänomenologie'" 1930.

INTRODUCTION

INTRODUCTION

Edmund Husserl is generally regarded as one of the most important philosophers of the twentieht century. Yet, despite the great influence which he has exercised, full agreement about the meaning of his work has by no means been reached. Husserl's appearance in the philosophical arena has called forth a number of interpretations. Even his own students were not agreed about the real intent of phenomenology. Many Husserlian schools came into existence, reproaching one another with not having "understood" Husserl. This was certainly a remarkable fate for a philosopher who already in his youth cherished the hope of putting an end to the "confusion" of philosophies and establishing the *one* philosophy.[1]

There have been many attempts to approach Husserl's philosophy on the basis of existing philosophical traditions. At first affinities between his phenomenology and certain themes in Scholasticism were noted, while later interpreters thought they had discovered close relations between Husserl and neo-Kantianism. At present Husserl is generally interpreted in an existentialistic way. Husserl himself protested repeatedly against such interpretations and uttered well-known complaints about the many misunderstandings to which his philosophy had been subjected because it had not been understood in its own intrinsic meaning.

A complicating factor was that Husserl's thinking never stood still. As a result he had to distantiate himself from his own students more than once and go his own way. Because of this constant development, there was considerable confusion about Husserl's intentions from the very beginning. The question 'What is phenomenology?,' which has been asked many times and answered in various ways, is still alive

[1] Nachwort, Id III 162.

today. This study was written in the conviction that only a thorough analysis of the development of Husserl's thought can clarify this matter. I hope to demonstrate that Husserl's phenomenology does offer points of contact for various interpretations based on existing philosophical tendencies, but that it must still be seen first and foremost as a unique philosophical achievement which must be understood on the basis of its own problematics. I will also try to show that the various students of Husserl can appeal with some justification to their teacher, but that they have tried to arrest and isolate his philosophy at a particular stage of its development. Husserl was usually far ahead of his students in diagnosing difficulties and following new paths.

Husserl's philosophical work does exhibit a distinct unity, even if it is only a unity of development. In his philosophy there is a definite major theme that is ever more consistently unfolded, and consequently the final phase of his thinking can be regarded as the culmination of all previous intentions. We shall see that it was Husserl's teacher Brentano who gave him the problems with which he was to concern himself throughout his entire career and which drove him to ever more radical solutions.

Throughout my analysis I have used a genetic method in which the text of Husserl's work as historically dated is accepted as the only authority. Thereby I hope to avoid all anachronistic interpretations – even if they stem from Husserl himself. As I see it, the well-known slogan 'to the things themselves' (*zu den Sachen selbst*) is itself in need of a historical and philologically justified interpretation. The procedure I have chosen makes it possible to understand the early work as a preparatory stage vis-à-vis the later work, and the later work as a response to the problematics of the earlier work.

Thus an extensive and sometimes detailed investigation into the genesis of particular themes is essential. The phenomenological precept that one must be able to exchange his bank notes for coins, which Husserl so often impressed upon his students, holds for the historian of phenomenology as well. Only then will we be able to grasp the key to the many difficult problems with which Husserl's phenomenology presents us (e.g. the meaning of his transcendental idealism and the problematic relation between psychology and transcendental phenomenology). Even the famous reduction, long a *crux interpretum*, can be understood in a genetic investigation on the basis of the inner necessity of a particular phase.

I will follow Husserl's career as far as his transition to transcendental idealism, which must be regarded as the high point of his development. I am well aware that this end was at the same time a new beginning for Husserl. He himself realized that it was "the true beginning" of any philosophy which, as Kant put it, "would count as a science." In methodological respects Husserl's thinking definitely reached a certain completion. From then on the transcendental reduction was the gateway to true philosophy. To use Husserl's own metaphor, the "promised land" (transcendental consciousness) had been discovered, but it was still in need of cultivation.[2]

Important themes from Husserl's later philosophy (e.g. time, embodiment, intersubjectivity, the "life-world," and philosophy of history) will be discussed only summarily. I hope to return to them in another study, in which I will argue further in defense of my conviction that Husserl never gave up his idealism and his unique conception of philosophy as a "rigorous science."

In the course of the exposition, I will repeatedly defend Husserl against his critics and interpreters. Husserl's complaints about superficial interpretations were not unjust. "Never write a critique until you have understood what you are criticizing in its straightforward sense," he remarked bitterly in this connection.[3] But my defense of Husserl should not be taken to mean that I myself am a transcendental idealist or that I share Husserl's philosophical intentions in other respects. It is my conviction that criticism is in order only after an honest attempt has been made to understand Husserl on the basis of his own aims. In this study I view such an understanding as my primary task. Marginal notes critical of Husserl will be made only in exceptional cases; for the rest I will follow Husserl's advice not to argue with the guide about the road

[2] Id III 159, 161. On the occasion of this English translation I must again emphasize that this study is not a treatment of the whole course of Husserl's development. In this work I will analyze Husserl's writings up to 1913, including Ideen II and III. Some reviewers of the original Dutch edition have incorrectly assumed that I was treating the entirety of Husserl's work and have then gone on to remark – rightly – that Husserl's development did not end in 1913. I fully agree that 1913 only represents a milestone in Husserl's development and not the end. Husserl's thought would even have continued to develop – as he himself remarked – if he were to live as long as Methuselah. But this is not to say that the transcendental idealist standpoint defended by Husserl in Ideen was later given up. It remained the basis for his further development. An extensive elucidation of this matter will have to wait for a future publication. In this study I will make only occasional references to the works that appeared after 1913.

[3] Id III 45, see also LU III, VI, where Husserl complains about Moritz Schlick's critique and appeals to the "eternal laws of literary conscientiousness."

we are following while we are still underway.[4] Husserl once said that
the path to transcendental phenomenology is "long and thorny."[5] In
the years that I have been occupied with Husserl's philosophy, I have
gradually come to see how true this remark is. And at the same time I
have seen how necessary it is to take this path if we are to understand
Husserl's phenomenology. I have tried to follow Husserl to the end of
this path and to chart the route taken.

[4] Krisis 440.
[5] Id I 180.

PART ONE

PHILOSOPHY AS DESCRIPTIVE PSYCHOLOGY

INTRODUCTION

In the first part of this study I will deal with the publications of Husserl's first period, i.e. *Ueber den Begriff der Zahl* (his "Habilitationsschrift" or Inaugural dissertation of 1887 which would qualify him as a University Lecturer), the *Philosophie der Arithmetik* of 1891 (the first four chapters of which are virtually identical in content with *Ueber den Begriff der Zahl*), and a number of articles on algebraic logic. This period closes with an article of 1894 entitled "Psychologische Studien zur elementaren Logik." Not long after the appearance of this article (in a "Selbstanzeige" published three years later), H appears to have changed his views on essential points.[1]

Throughout the years I have studied Husserl, I have become more and more convinced that the influence of Brentano on Husserl was of decisive importance. Thus, in order to present the work of the early Husserl in the proper perspective, it will be necessary to go back repeatedly to the work of Brentano. It is not my intention, however, to give Brentano's work an independent treatment. Passages on Brentano will be included only insofar as they are necessary as a background to Husserl's own work.

In the first chapter the most important themes of Husserl's descriptive psychology will be analyzed. In the ssecond chapter these themes will be placed in the broader framework of the opposition between descriptive psychology and genetic psychology. The next two chapters will deal with the connection between descriptive psychology and the priori sciences. The fifth chapter places the early Husserl against the background of the development of Brentano's philosophy and the two tendencies present in it. The last chapter contains conclusions.

[1] This change concerns the theory of perception and the founding of the *a priori* sciences, see below 133ff, 234ff.

CHAPTER ONE

ACTS, CONTENTS, AND THE RELATIONS BETWEEN THEM

In this first chapter the theme of intentionality in the early Husserl will be discussed. As Husserl himself pointed out later in Ideen I, "The name of the problem that encompasses all of phenomenology is intentionality."[1] Because of the central place which intentionality already occupied in the thought of the early Husserl, and because of the universal significance which it was later to assume, an analysis of this theme is an excellent way to get into the genesis of phenomenology. I will discuss in turn the intentional relation of consciousness to its objects, the mode of being of intentional objects, and the relation between these objects and acts of consciousness.

SECTION ONE.
THE INTENTIONAL RELATION TO THE OBJECT

This section begins with an analysis of Brentano's definition of intentionality, to which Husserl refers in his PA (Paragraph 1). Against this background I will investigate what the intentional relation meant for Husserl himself with reference to his analysis of acts of a higher order (Paragraph 2). Finally, I will discuss the important change in Husserl's concept of intentionality which first manifests itself in the article of 1894 (Paragraph 3).

PARAGRAPH ONE. THE DISTINCTION BETWEEN ACT AND CONTENT

At a central point in the argument of PA, Husserl for the first time makes use of the terms 'physical phenomenon,' 'psychical pheno-

---

[1] Id I 303.

menon,' and 'intentional inexistence,' thereby associating himself with Brentano. Thus he distinguishes two fundamentally different areas, i.e. that of primary contents or physical phenomena and that of acts or psychical phenomena. In a footnote on this point he remarks: "As to the meaning of the terms 'physical' and 'psychical' phenomenon and the fundamental distinction underlying these terms, which is indispensable for the considerations immediately following, see F. Brentano's *Psychologie vom empirischen Standpunkt*, Vol. I, Book II, Chapter I."[1] Husserl does not leave us in the dark about the nature of the fundamental distinction on which this division is based: in a following footnote he refers to *intentional inexistence*, which is the first and "most basic characteristic whereby psychical phenomena are distinguished from physical phenomena."[2] Husserl thus affirms this division of Brentano without criticism. Before analyzing Husserl's views more closely, I must devote some attention to this doctrine of intentionality as we find it in Brentano himself. Against this background I will then try to answer the question what this theme contained for the early Husserl.

"The entire world of our appearances can be divided into two large classes, i.e. into the classes of *physical* and *psychical* phenomena." With these words Brentano begins the first chapter of the second book of PES. In the rest of the chapter he tries to provide a fuller foundation for this division of phenomena (of which he had already made use in the first book), for there was little agreement on the question what is physical and what is psychical. A clear demarcation between these two areas is necessary if the corresponding sciences (i.e. physics and psychology) are to be properly distinguished. Brentano believed that he had succeeded in making this division clear. He listed a total of six properties that distinguish psychical phenomena from physical phenomena. The fourth of these six distinguishing characteristics is intentionality. For Brentano it is the most important criterion: "Without doubt, the distinguishing characteristic which characterizes psychical phenomena best of all is intentional inexistence."[3]

Utitz, who himself comes from the school of Brentano, is correct in remarking that this doctrine of intentionality, "as hardly any other, has been fateful for the further development of philosophy."[4] Here is the

[1] PA 71 note 3.
[2] PA 74 note 1.
[3] PES (edition Kraus) I, 137.
[4] E. Utitz, 'Franz Brentano,' 224.

relevant passage from Brentano's PES: "Every psychical phenomenon is characterized by what the Scholastics of the middle ages called the intentional (and also mental) inexistence of an object and what we would call – although not in entirely unambiguous terms – relation to a content, direction toward an object (which is not to be understood here as something real), or an immanent objectivity (*Gegenständlichkeit*). Each psychological phenomenon includes something as object within itself, although not always in the same way. In a presentation something is presented; in a judgment something is affirmed or denied; in love something is loved; in hatred something is hated; in desire something is desired, etc."[5]

In this definition we find five typifying expressions, three of which are fully synonymous, i.e. 'intentional inexistence,' 'mental inexistence,' and 'immanent objectivity.' In addition Brentano speaks of "direction toward an object" and "relation toward a content." The first series of expressions characterizes psychical phenomena by pointing to the fact that they include a content. This content is more precisely defined as intentional or immanent or mental. The second series of expressions points to the directedness (*Richtung, Beziehung*) toward a content.

These two aspects, which are mentioned in the same breath in Brentano's definition, do not cover the same ground and must be carefully distinguished. The immanence of the object and the direction of consciousness toward the object are entirely different things. This is evident from the fact that Brentano was later able to abandon the doctrine of the immanent object while continuing to maintain "direction toward an object" as the distinguishing characteristic of all psychical phenomena. Only the latter of the two conditions, then, is maintained by Brentano throughout his career.

What strikes the modern reader immediately is that Brentano uses the term 'intentional' as an adjective describing a content. It has the same meaning as 'mental' or 'immanent.' The terms 'intentional' and 'intentionality,' which now denote familiar concepts in modern philosophy (thanks to Brentano and Husserl), normally lead one to think only of the second aspect mentioned above. Does intentionality as a property of consciousness not mean that direction toward an object is the most basic distinguishing characteristic of consciousness? Is is not the case that the new element which these two thinkers have brought

[5] PES I 124f.

into modern philosophy is intentionality as the "turn toward the object"?

Given this modern development, it is important to emphasize that in the definition of 1874 cited above, Brentano uses the term 'intentional' not as an adjective for "direction toward an object" but as a characteristic of the content of consciousness. As he himself says, he concurs here with the Scholastic usage. 'Intentional' means immanent and stands opposed to 'real.' That Brentano does indeed understand the term 'intentional' in this way is apparent from a footnote in which he says that 'intentional' means the same as 'objective,' a term that the Scholastics used more often than 'intentional.' Both terms refer to the mode of being of the object in the knower, which is to be distinguished from the "real" object outside the mind. But Brentano prefers to avoid the word 'objective' because of the misunderstandings to which it gives rise: in modern philosophy it means exactly the reverse, i.e. really existing. It refers to a real existence outside the mind as opposed to mere subjective appearance. For the Scholastics, by contrast, 'esse objective' means the being in consciousness which the cognitive image or species enjoys.[6]

To the extent that Brentano is aware of his dependence on the Scholastics, the similarity has to do with this aspect of his definition. He speaks of the "intentional" or "objective" mode of being of the cognitive image in the knower. Later in this chapter the relation of Brentano's conception to the Scholastic conception will be discussed further. It will then be shown that a real and major difference in views is hidden behind the terminological agreement.

Be that as it may, it is important to establish that the term 'intentional' does not have one meaning only (i.e. direction toward an object), but that for Brentano, who follows the lead of the Scholastics here, it refers first of all to the mode of being of an object immanent to consciousness. We shall see later that this way of speaking is not limited to Brentano but also appears in Husserl. He too uses the term 'intentional' partly in this sense and, like Brentano, refers to Scholasticism in this connection.[7]

[6] PES I 124, note 3 and II, 8, note 2. In Scholasticism this is expressed as follows: "Cognitum autem est in cognoscente secundum modum cognoscentis" (see further below 18 and 40).

[7] Id I 185 (see below 194 and 427). Like the Scholastics, Husserl opposes 'intentional' to 'real' (and 'wirklich'). The older meaning of the term 'intentional' remained alive in the entire development of Husserl's phenomenology.

Nonetheless the modern meaning of 'intentionality' is also part of Brentano's definition, for he does speak of "direction toward an object." Spiegelberg rightly remarks that this is the most important element in the definition and points to the fact that this characteristic of psychical phenomena is a permanent feature of Brentano's thought, whereas the doctrine of the immanence of the object was abandoned after the so-called "crisis of immanence" of 1905.

Spiegelberg further remarks that it certainly was not Brentano's purpose that this direction toward an object should become linked with the old term 'intentionality.'[8] But one might ask whether Spiegelberg is correct on this point, for Brentano also speaks of "intentional relation": in USE (1889) he writes that the feature common to all psychical phenomena is a "subjective attitude" or "intentional relation."[9] Thus it was Brentano himself who used the term 'intentional' in connection with the expression 'direction toward.' It is this meaning of the term 'intentionality' that has survived in our modern philosophical terminology. When so used, the term does not refer to the mode of being of an object within the knowing mind but to a property of consciousness, i.e. direction toward an object. Brentano is generally awarded the honor of having discovered the "object-relatedness" of the psychical.[10] Later I will look into the question whether this relatedness to an object in Brentano may be conceived of as a "turn toward the object," a breaking out of the Cartesian immanentistic philosophy of consciousness.[11] For the present we may take it that Brentano saw direction toward an object as an essential characteristic of consciousness and used the term 'intentional' in connection with this direction.

Still to be discussed is Brentano's relation to Scholasticism with regard to the second element of his definition. It has been established that his initial use of the term 'intentional' (i.e. as meaning immanent or objective) is derived from Scholastic authors. But his definition of psychical phenomena in terms of relatedness to an object, on the contrary, is generally regarded as an original discovery on his part. This

---

[8] *The Phenomenological Movement* 40f.

[9] USE 16ff; Kategorienlehre 222, 244, 259, 282f.

[10] See, for example, Spiegelberg, " as far as I can make out, this characterization is completely original with Brentano" (op.cit. 41). Husserl too honours Brentano as the discoverer of the intentional directedness of consciousness, LU II, 364ff; FTL 231, 217; CM 79.

[11] See below 18 and 45.

is strange in view of the fact that the word 'intentio' is derived from 'intendere' or 'tendere,' which denote the psychological act of striving after. Thomas Aquinas speaks of an "actus mentis qui est intendere." Thus it appears that Brentano's direction toward an object has also been taken over from medieval Scholasticism. The term 'Vermeinen' (grasp putatively), which Husserl uses to refer to the intentional activity, appears to be a translation of the Latin 'intendere.'

Simonin, who has carried out an extensive and minute investigation of the concept of "intentio" in Thomas Aquinas, has shown that Thomas does use 'intentio' in this sense, as "in aliud tendere," but that this intending is an act of the *will*. "Intentio," according to Thomas, "est proprie actus voluntatis." With regard to Thomas's usage of the term 'intentio,' we must distinguish carefully between the cognitive order and the conative order. In the conative order 'intentio' means a striving after, an impulse, but in the cognitive order it can refer only to the specific mode of being of the object possessed by the mind.[12]

Hence Brentano's originality consists in this, that he uses the concept of "intentio" as "tendere in" to refer to a property of cognitive acts or – to use his own terminology – acts of presentation and judgment. Because these acts are the basic acts on which all others rest, this direction toward an object is the most fundamental property of consciousness.

Also original, in any case, in Brentano's noteworthy attempt to draw a definite boundary between psychology and natural science by using the old theme of intentional inexistence. In doing so he placed this theme in a totally new context, i.e. not in a theory of knowledge but in a preparatory chapter of a work on psychology in which he had set for himself the task of delimiting the area with which psychology is to deal. The fact that the theme of intentionality arises in this context seems to indicate that Brentano was not directly interested in a "turn toward the object" when he presented this definition. He was seeking a criterion to distinguish psychical phenomena from physical phenomena, and what he found was direction toward an object. It is not necessary that the object toward which consciousness is directed be a physical object; it could just as well be an act.[13] In the latter case the intentional relation would be purely intra-psychical.

[12] H. D. Simonin 'La notion d'"intentio' dans l'oeuvre de S. Thomas d'Aquin' 451ff. See also A. Hayen *Lintentionnel dans la philosophie de Saint Thomas* 194f, 244.
[13] PES I 48, 140, 142, 204f, 116, 119; II, XX; see also Oskar Kraus *Franz Brentano* 29; WE 17f.

PARAGRAPH TWO. ACTS OF A HIGHER ORDER

In the previous paragraph we saw that Husserl follows in Brentano's footsteps by distinguishing between physical phenomena and psychical phenomena. Yet this division of phenomena is mentioned in a very specific context. Husserl's concern is not to classify phenomena as such but to classify relations. In connection with his analysis of the concept of plurality, he tries to gain a deeper insight into what we call relations. A plurality comes about when a number of things are bound together by way of a so-called collective relation, and this is indicated by the use of the word 'and.' Because Husserl cannot appeal to a well-founded theory of relations, he is forced to include a few observations "concerning this very dark chapter of descriptive psychology." It is in this context that he makes reference to intentional inexistence. By applying it as criterion, we can classify not only phenomena but also relations. In the case of the latter, the result is an "essential division," i.e. into physical and psychical relations.

In the case of any relation, we can speak of foundations (relata) that the relation embraces. The *manner* in which relations embrace their relata does, of course, differ in fundamental respects from one relation to another. In the case of psychical relations, the relata are embraced *intentionally*, "that is, in that specifically determined way in which a psychical phenomenon (an act of observing, wishing, etc.) embraces its content (that which is observed, wished, etc.)." The collective relation is such a relation. Alongside these are relations of the character of physical phenomena. These include, for example, the relations of equality, continuity, connection, metaphysical connection (e.g. of color and extension), and logical connection (e.g. of the genus color with the species red). A relation of this sort is a physical phenomenon and is on the same level as the relata in the content of a presentation.

We recognize no psychical relation in the content itself. Wherever there is a psychical relation between contents, the contents are bound only insofar as they are observed in one psychical act. Thus the relation is first presented in an act of *reflection*.[1] The psychical relation which embraces its contents intentionally is therefore a special act; indeed, it is an act "of a higher order." The analysis of these acts is the original contribution of Husserl's PA to descriptive psychology. In collective

[1] PA 70, 72, 77.

connection one kind of act is built upon another. First, a lower psychical act is necessary to embrace each of the contents to be collected, and following this there is a higher act which encompasses all these acts and encloses them within itself.[2] These acts "of the second order" are acts that "are again directed toward psychical acts and only extend to primary contents through the mediation of these acts." Thus a unitary apprehension that takes in all the separate acts comes about.[3]

Acts of the second order, therefore, embraces their objects only *in*directly. These objects are direct contents of some act of the first order, and only by the mediation of such an act do they become contents of an act of a higher order. The mere fact that a number of contents comes to awareness in one embracing act creates a psychical relation between them according to Husserl. In these acts of a higher order we encounter an important Husserlian theme. In later publications it was worked out more fully: in LU we find it again in the doctrine of *categorial perception*, and in Ideen I, where Husserl makes reference to PA, we find it in the doctrine of polythetic acts.[4] In a note to the second edition of LU Husserl says, not without bitterness, that his first publication remained largely unnoticed. He adds that it is "the first work which attached importance to acts and objects of a higher order and investigated them thoroughly."[5] We shall see later that this remark is not entirely justified, for Husserl did speak of *acts* but not of *objects* of a higher order.

Husserl speaks only of these acts of a second order in the context of the subject under discussion. For further givens about his conception of intentionality, we are therefore referred to what he says about these acts. First, we note that Husserl, like Brentano, uses the word 'intentional' in two senses. He speaks of plurality as the intentional object of these acts.[6] Here 'intentional' is an adjective for the content. In a later paragraph I will answer the question whether 'intentional' is synonymous here with 'immanent' or 'mental.' In addition Husserl speaks of an "intentional embracing" of the object. In this case we must think of the directedness of the act toward its objects.

---

[2] PA 80.

[3] PA 45, 49, 99f.

[4] Id I 246 note 1.

[5] LU II 282 note 1. On this question, see also a remark made by Kraus in PES vol. III, XXIII.

[6] PA 45, 175.

PARAGRAPH THREE. SYMBOLIC OR NON-GENUINE
PRESENTATIONS

1. In Philosophie der Arithmetik

The acts of the first and second order discussed thus far are all
genuine or perceptual acts. In addition to these, Husserl distinguishes a
category of non-genuine or symbolic presentations. Here too he is
dependent on Brentano. Husserl begins the second part of PA, just as he
had begun the first part, with a quotation from Brentano that bears on a
central point in the argument: "In his university lectures F. Brentano
always laid the greatest emphasis on the distinction between 'genuine'
and 'non-genuine' or symbolic presentations. I am indebted to him for a
deeper understanding of the eminent importance of non-genuine
presentation for all of our psychical life, a point which no one before
him had grasped, to the best of my knowledge."[1]

Husserl defines a symbolic presentation as a presentation through
signs. When a content is not given to us directly as what it is but only
indirectly through signs which characterize it clearly, we have only a
non-genuine, symbolic presentation of it. When we see a house, we have
a genuine presentation of it. But when someone gives us the description
'the house on such-and-such a corner," we have a symbolic presentation. The house is given indirectly via a sign. This sign presentation – and this is essential for Husserl in PA – tends to replace the
real presentation. We make judgments about the sign which we later
carry over to the real object – thanks to the unequivocal correspondence. The symbolic presentation becomes a temporary or
lasting substitute for the real presentation.[2] Although originally the
real thing is presented indirectly through a sign, what finally comes
about is that the sign is directly presented while the real thing vanishes
completely from our attention.

In PA Husserl is interested particularly in non-genuine presentations
in which signs function as representatives, as in the system of number. (I
will return to this point in Chapter 3.) What concerns me particularly
here is the first phase of the non-genuine presentation of large numbers,
where there is still mention of a directedness toward that which is

---

[1] PA 215 note 1. According to Husserl's Erinnerungen 157, Brentano took up the
distinction between genuine and non-genuine presentations during the years that Husserl
attended his lectures.
[2] PA 216.

presented in a non-genuine way. Husserl gives the name 'intention' to this directedness. Because our minds are limited, this intention is not carried out. Only a few elements of the quantity are separately observed and collected. The intention to actually carry out this collecting remains a "mere intention."[3] We are speaking here of a presentation which has a real content (the actually collected contents) but includes something more via the content. In PA Husserl says nothing about the role which the mediating genuine content plays and the manner in which we are aware of it. Later he wrote: "I had already hit upon the distinction between that which a presentation 'means' and that which it contains itself, but I did not know what to do with it."[4]

II. In "Psychologische Studien zur elementaren Logik"

In an article of 1894 entitle "Psychologische Studien zur elementaren Logik," which appeared shortly after PA, Husserl made a special study of this non-intuitive presentation.[5] In this article he distinguishes many forms of this mere intending, the most important of which is mere intending via a word. The analysis of this phenomenon leads to an entirely new concept of consciousness. Husserl gives the following definition: "mere intending" means the same as "aiming, by a way of some contents or other given in consciousness, at others not given, meaning them, pointing to them in an understanding way, applying them in an understanding way as representatives of those not given." Over against this stands normal intuition. Intuitions are acts which not merely intend their objects but "actually embrace them within themselves."[6]

In PA these two forms of consciousness are distinguished as genuine and non-genuine presentation. But Husserl now discovers a dangerous ambiguity in speaking in both cases of "presentation." In mere intending we have to do with a totally different mode of consciousness, and therefore it is not correct to include both this consciousness and intuition under one concept. In place of non-genuine presentations he now speaks of "representations."[7]

[3] PA 218, 239, 245, 249.
[4] Entwurf 127, see also PSL 189.
[5] Published in *Philosophische Monatshefte*. According to Entwurf 127 note 3, this article was finished in 1893.
[6] PSL 174f.
[7] PSL 186, compare title 168.

What is the new aspect? I will try to bring it into focus by way of a closer analysis of the representing act. In a certain sense, these acts of representation have two contents, a representing immanent content and a represented non-immanent content. What, now, is the relation of the act to these contents? As far as the relation to the representing content is concerned, Husserl raises the question whether we can say that we intuit this content. That we do intuit it would appear obvious, for the content, after all, is immanent, and thus we could say that the act *really embraces* the content. Yet Husserl answers this question in the negative. This denial forms the "main thesis" of the whole article, as he himself points out. [8]

What we encounter here is an entirely new "mode of consciousness": "A sharp descriptive distinction with regard to modes of consciousness ('mental states', psychical interest) divides representations from intuitions." These "modes of consciousness" play an important role in LU. What Husserl means to say can best be illustrated by means of an example which he himself uses in this context and also appears in LU, i.e. a case in which we first see an arabesque purely aesthetically, as an ingenious figure, and then suddenly see it as a word, or a case in which we hear a strange word first simply as a sound complex and later – after we find out its meaning – "understand" the word and use it in our own speech. In both cases we are aware of the same sign in entirely different ways. Thus there is a "different manner of working psychically with or on contents." A content is intuited at first, but later we are aware of it in a different manner. We do indeed see it, but "we have not focused on it; we do not intuit it." The "psychical posture" is totally different. [9]

It is characteristic of these representing acts, then, that they are directed toward *non-immanent* contents by way of immanent contents. The former are "merely intended." Husserl also speaks of "aiming at," "meaning" and "pointing to" in place of intending. What does this signify? Up to this point, we have seen that only an immanent content can be in consciousness (in two ways). In what way, then, are we aware of these non-immanent contents? Husserl speaks here of a highly interesting function which, in many respects, "gives rise to amazement." How can one content refer to another which "is in no way in

---

[8] In an author's abstract of this article *Archiv für systematische Philosophie*, VOL. II 226.

[9] PSL 182. Intuition of the sign comes about only in the case of arithmetic, where the sign takes the place of that which is signified (*stellvertretende Anschauung*).

consciousness" and is therefore called a "non-existent content"? In one way or another, we do appear to be aware of it, for "while we are concerning ourselves with the representing contents, we believe that we are occupying ourselves with the represented objects themselves."[10] Thus Husserl wavers in his expressions. We are not aware of the intended content in any way, and yet "in a certain way" we are aware of it.

It is possible that this mere intending, in which we are directed toward an object in a peculiar way without actually embracing it (i.e. having it immanently present) passes over into an intuition of the object. In such a case we speak of a "filled intention." An "intuitive illustration," which Husserl also calls a "fulfillment," takes place.[11] The intention that could not be realized at first has attained its end. The aiming at or meaning or pointing to becomes a "realizing."

Here for the first time Husserl describes the "transitional experience" between two acts and thereby touches on the theme of the synthesis of acts, a theme which was later to undergo great development.[12] Intentionality creates a bond between acts. The unfilled intention forms a unity with its fulfillment and, conversely, refers the intuition in which a representation terminates back to its "empty" intention. This synthesis of acts is the reverse side of the *identity* of the object in both acts. Husserl's analysis of representative presentation has shown that in one way or another we are occupied with the signified object itself in such presentation – despite the fact that this object is not present "in

[10] PSL 179, 187.

[11] PSL 172, 175f.

[12] See below 146. In the Nachwort to Ideen I, Husserl criticizes Bretano for failing to provide an analysis of synthetic consciousness. Descriptive psychology must also describe how we can be aware of the same object in different modes of consciousness, see e.g. ZBW 149. For Brentano these changes are not possible, for he has a static conception of intentionality. In his theory of judgement, for example, he denies that degrees of evidence are possible (USE 72). A judgement is evident (in inner perception) or not evident (in outer perception). There are no intermediate stages. This conception of evidence was later sharply criticized by Husserl, see e.g. FTL 249ff.

On this question see also L. Landgrebe's "Husserl's Phänomenologie und die Motive zu ihrer Umbildung" in: *Der Weg der Phänomenologie* II, 15, 17. I cannot agree with Landgrebe's view that the new concept of intentionality and the concept of synthesis already come to the fore in the PA. The origin of the concept of constitution must be sought *after* 1891. Landgrebe's view appears to be bound up with an anachronistic interpretation of the doctrine of the acts of a higher order (see below 26, note 14). Husserl himself *Krisis* 237 (E 234) places the discovery of the concept of synthesis in the LU.

consciousness." If this is so, we can regard a perception of this object, a perception in which the object is bodily present (as Husserl was later to say), as an act which coincides with it or covers it.

This analysis of representative presentation is of great importance for descriptive psychology, for it leads ultimately to a basic modification of the concept of intentionality. It was a startling discovery that filled Husserl's own mind with a sense of wonder. The language he uses gives us the impression that he did not know just what to do with his new discovery.

Perhaps I can best explain this new development in the concept of intentionality by comparing it with Brentano's position. Brentano also recognizes various modes of presentation. The same object can be presented *in recto* and *in obliquo*, clearly and in confused way, etc. The completely new aspect of Husserl's "mode of apprehension" is that it exercises an influence on the mode of appearance of the object – in such a way that we are aware of a new object. The sound becomes a word; the arabesque becomes something written. Consciousness directs itself via one object which serves as a sign toward another – and this entirely because of a change on the side of the subject. The signified object is "present" to consciousness in a new and different way which is as yet mysterious. Correlated with the change on the side of the subject, thus, there is a change on the side of the object. Brentano, by contrast, emphasizes strongly that the difference in apprehension concerns one and the same object and involves only a change in the subjective awareness of that object.[13]

For Husserl, a particular physical thing takes on meaning and refers to another object through a different attitude or "interest" on the part of the subject. What Husserl discovers here is that certain contents are not simply *in* consciousness (as things are in a box, as he was later to put it), but that their significance is dependent on the attitude which consciousness takes toward them, the "sense" which it gives. In other words, here we encounter the *birth of the concept of "constitution"* understood as "sense-giving," which makes correlative analysis possible – in principle, at least. By way of a new mode of consciousness, a mere sound complex changes into a sense-bearing expression. When

---

[13] See Kraus in the Introduction of PES II, XIIV, XL; A. Kastil 'Die Philosophie Franz Brentano's,' 51, 55, 107, 165; ZBW 380 (E 36f).

Husserl expounds his new concept of intentionality in LU, he appeals to this passage in the article of 1894 and uses the same examples.[14]

It is no accident that Husserl discovered this sense-giving on the level of language, of "significative presentation," as he calls it in LU. This fact is relevant to the history of the concept of constitution. When Husserl later goes on to call perception a sense-giving, the concept of sense he uses is taken over from language to the level of perceptual consciousness, a transfer of which he was indeed well aware.[15] In significative consciousness we are occupied with the signified object "in a certain way," even though it is not given and we are therefore "in no way aware of it." Husserl's wavering is understandable. He continues to cling to the presupposition (which he later ascribed to Locke) that something which is *given to* consciousness must be *in consciousness*. He continues to see perception as an act that actually "embraces its object within itself." To this extent he remains true to the "principle of subjectivity" (*Satz der Subjectivität*).[16]

As Husserl describes this new mode of consciousness, he nonetheless discovers that in one way or another we can be consciously occupied with a transcendent content not immediately present. In this way too he prepares the way for the new concept of perception that comes to the fore in LU. Then perception too is a directedness toward a transcendent (i.e. interpreted as transcendent) object. The analogy with sense-giving on the level of language seems to have prepared the way for the new theory of perception. What Husserl has now discovered is that consciousness is not a concept with one meaning only. We cannot be satisfied with the simple view that contents are "in" consciousness. There are, after all, great differences in the attitudes which consciousness adopts in relation to contents. The task and future of descriptive psychology is to be sought in an analysis of the various forms of consciousness.

SECTION TWO.
CONTENTS

In this section I will deal with three topics. In the first place, I will raise the question to what extent the earliest publications of Husserl share

[14] LU II 384, see below 131.
[15] Id I 256; LU III 21, see below 138.
[16] See below 21.

Brentano's standpoint with regard to the immanence of contents. Second, I will take up the distinction between abstract and concrete contents. In the third paragraph of this section, I will discuss the so-called categorial properties that correspond to acts of a higher order. Because many point to this doctrine as the origin of both the concept of constitution and correlative analysis, it will require close attention if we are to get a proper view of Husserl's development.

PARAGRAPH ONE. THE IMMANENCE OF CONTENTS

I. In Brentano's Thought

Brentano's definition of psychical phenomena contains two elements: intentional or mental inexistence and direction toward an object. It has already been pointed out that Brentano is dependent on the Aristotelian tradition with regard to the first of these elements. As Brentano points out, Aristotle himself had already spoken of "psychical inhabitation."[1] In his inaugural dissertation (Habilitationsschrift), entitled *Die Psychologie des Aristoteles*, Brentano explains this "objective" being of things in the knowing mind in Aristotle's philosophy. There he contrasts physical existence with intentional existence.

Thus when Brentano speaks of the immanent object as "physical" in PES, he departs sharply from the Aristotelian terminology. We must not be misled by the term 'physical phenomenon,' for it refers not to a real object but to an immanent object. All the physical phenomena which Brentano cites as examples (e.g. color, sound, warmth) have only an immanent existence; they exist "only phenomenally and intentionally."[2] In Section 3 I will return to the difference between Brentano

---

[1] PES I 125, note 1. For a historical survey of the immanent object in Brentano's school, see A. Marty, *Untersuchungen zur Grundlegung der allgemeinen Grammatik und Sprachphilosophie*, 385. According to Marty, the immanent object is also called 'the presented as such,' a phrase that recurs in H. Kasimir Twardowski, another follower of Brentano, who is also an adherent of this doctrine, Zur Lehre vom Inhalt und Gegenstand der Vorstellungen, 29f, 40.

[2] PES I 129, 132. There are great dangers attached to the use of the term 'physical phenomenon.' It is strange to speak of an immanent object of perception as physical, see below, 40. It is even more dangerous to speak of an object of imagination as a physical phenomenon, as Brentano does, PES I, 112, 120; see also 42, 44, 109, 140. His division of phenomena into physical and psychical forces him to do so. Even a concept is a physical phenomenon; the example Brentano always uses is "the thinking of a general concept" 111; see also USE 17.

Husserl prefers the term 'primary object,' PA 37ff, 42, 46, 71f, 74, note 1, 91. The act is a

and Scholasticism on the question of the function of the intentional object.

II. In Philosophie der Arithmetik

I must now raise the question whether the early Husserl shares this standpoint with regard to immanence. That he does is suggested by his adoption of the term 'intentional inexistence.' This supposition is further supported by numerous passages. First, there is the way Husserl uses the term 'consciousness.' He uses it in a narrow sense in which it is like an act but also in a broad sense such that the physical phenomenon can likewise be called a state of consciousness. Together with the act, the contents than form a "psychical whole."[3] Husserl speaks of contents as "belonging" to consciousness. In a relation there is a "togetherness" of the relata in consciousness.[4] This presupposes the being-in-consciousness of the separate relata.[5] Husserl also uses the expression 'being at hand' (Vorhanden) in consciousness or in the presentation.[6] Consciousness is called the whole (a "whole of presentation") and the contents the parts. This is the case with regard to acts of a higher order.[7] The expression 'state of our consciousness as a whole' can also embrace both acts and contents.[8]

The immanent character of contents furthers the confusion about the use of the word 'presentation' (*Vorstellung*), which is used for both the act and the content of the act. We know that Husserl distinguished carefully between the two, as did Brentano, who repeatedly warned against this confusion (contra James, among others).[9] Nonetheless, Husserl was careless here in his choice of expressions. He says, for example, that the collective act connects the presentations, when he means the presented contents. He speaks of the intentional object of an act of a higher order not as the plurality but as the presentation of plurality. The connected parts he calls subsidiary presentations (or part-presentations,

"secondary object" (LU II first edition, 11). In LU he distinguishes the two types of phenomena as "primary object" and "content of reflection," LU III, 180; see also Id I 72, note 2.

[3] PA 70, 78, note 1.

[4] PA 17f, 38.

[5] PA 22, 53, 112.

[6] PA 20, 23.

[7] PA 21, 24, 77, 83, see also 15, 82.

[8] PA 18f; PSL 159; see also LU II 345, where this expression includes both acts and the material of sensation, i.e. contents.

[9] PES I 112, 119, 196, 249f; Unters. z. Sinnespsychologie 96.

Teilvorstellungen). In another place he speaks of intuition when he means the object of the intuition.[10]

It was probably this factor that misled Frege in his criticism of Husserl. Frege's review of Husserl's PA (the only review to go deeply into the book)[11] is worth examining all the same, since Husserl later agreed with a certain point in Frege's criticism and made his agreement public.[12] Thus it is of interest to examine the review to see where Frege hits the nail on the head and where he misses the mark. He is mistaken in his criticism of the concept of presentation. He points to the equivocal use of this term with these words: "By including something subjective and something objective in the word 'presentation,' the boundaries between the two are blurred, with the result that here a presentation in the genuine sense of the word is treated as something objective, and there something objective is treated as a presentation. Thus in our author, the aggregate (the set, plurality) appears sometimes as a presentation (15, 17, 24, 82) and sometimes as something objective (10 and 11, 235)." Frege thus maintains that Husserl is erasing the boundaries between the subjective and the objective, with the result that something objective is treated as a presentation. He sees this reduction to a presentation as *the* error of psychologism. "Finally everything becomes presentation." "The objects are presentations. Thus John Stuart Mill, with the approval of our author, allows objects (whether physical or mental) to exist as a state of consciousness, to form parts of this state of consciousness. In psychologism the expression 'moon' is reduced to – or at least, not clearly distinguished from – the expression 'presentation of the moon.'" With reference to this point Frege asks sarcastically: "But would not the moon... weigh somewhat heavily on the mind?"[13] The value of this criticism of Husserl, on my view, is that it points out the ambiguous character of his terminology. Contents are sometimes referred to by Husserl as "external world" but more often as presented content or simply as presentation. But this does not signify, as Frege appears to believe, that Husserl identifies these three. In the first place, it is clear that Husserl does not regard the world as a content immanent to consciousness.[14] Furthermore – and this is what interests me at present – within consciousness in the broad sense, Husserl makes a very sharp distinction between contents and acts, even though he does speak of both as presentation. What Frege misjudges here is exactly what typifies Husserl's theory of consciousness, i.e. the distinction between the act and the immanent object. Later we will see where Frege's criticism of Husserl does hit home.[15]

---

[10] PA 15, 19, 38, 45, 74 note 1, 88, 175; BZ 14.

[11] There were other reviews by: A. Elzas, W. Heinrich and Franz Hildebrand (see bibliography). The PA was also discussed by Jules Tannery in his book *Science et Philosophie*, 79–87.

[12] LU I 169 note 1.

[13] Frege op.cit. 316ff, 329.

[14] See below 47.

[15] See below 28.

III. In "Psychologische Studien zur elementaren Logik"

Husserl's standpoint with regard to perceived contents did not change essentially in the article of 1894. It is true that there too he speaks of non-immanent contents, but this has no bearing on the contents of intuition. The latter are immanent. The other, merely intended contents are *destined to become immanent*, i.e. by the fulfillment of the intention.[16] The interchangeable use of the terms 'content' and 'object'[17] and also 'experience' (*erleben*) and 'apprehend'[18] also suggests indirectly that objects are immanent. Husserl was later to distinguish sharply between the immanent content (that which is experienced) and the transcendent object (that which is apprehended).[19] Although by 1894 Husserl had already discovered sense-giving on the level of language, it did not yet influence his theory of perception. For Husserl as for Brentano, perception is a possession of immanent contents.

On the one hand acts and contents form "strikingly different and heterogeneous areas,"[20] but on the other hand both fall within consciousness. The distinguishing characteristic of intentional inexistence divides consciousness in the broad sense into two domains, as it were. We understand the term 'conscious' in a broad sense that takes in both areas: physical and psychical phenomena. The object of perception, even when it is an outer perception, remains immanent to consciousness. It is in this context that we must understand the broad use of the term 'psychology': Brentano and Husserl also apply it to the description of contents.[21]

[16] Psl 169f, 178f: see also ZBW 141.

[17] PSL 174 et passim.

[18] PA 10, 28, 232, 234, 236; PSL 160, 170, 178. This has been criticized in the LU II, 394 note 1; III, 243 note 1.

[19] LU II, 216 note 1, 217 note 1, 225, 228, 231, 234, 236, 239 note 1.

[20] PA 14, 77; BZ 55.

[21] Brentano does say that we must not assign the contents of imagination to psychology, PES I, 41f, 109, 140, any more than the contents of perception, but he nevertheless speaks of a "psychology of sensation," as Spiegelberg observes *The Phenomenological Movement*, 57. Stumpf, who originally spoke of 'psychology of sound' – sound is a physical phenomenon! – later corrected this, see below 43. Husserl himself assigned the entire doctrine of relations to psychology – including, therefore, relations between contents. The article of 1894, the first part of which deals entirely with contents, bears the title "Psychological Studies ..." The term 'association of ideas' is used with regard to such contents as colour and roughness PSL 163; see also PA 237. This doctrine of the relations between contents can be regarded as part of a psychology of association, see below 34, note 5. Perhaps this also explains why Husserl sometimes speaks of contents as objects of reflection BZ 55; PA 14, 77; PSL 163.

PARAGRAPH TWO. THE DIVISION OF CONTENTS – ABSTRACT
AND CONCRETE CONTENTS

The realm of contents can be divided in various different ways. Here the
distinction between abstract and concrete contents will be discussed,
for this distinction plays a role in Husserl's theory of abstraction
(Chapter 3) and in the problematics of a priori judgments (Chapter 4).
In PA Husserl makes this distinction in the context of a discussion of
physical relations. These relations are abstract moments, and their
foundations or relata are absolute contents.[1] Yet not only relations but
also properties can be called abstract. The concrete, then, is that which
has this or that property; it is the bearer of the property.[2]

This distinction between the abstract and the concrete (or absolute)
was further worked out by Husserl in his article of 1894. He tried to
trace it back to the difference analyzed by Stumpf between independent
and non-independent contents. Stumpf demonstrated this difference
with regard to contents in general. Husserl's thesis is that this very
difference recurs in contents that form a whole (*Ganzes*). In such a
whole, the concrete parts are independent, and the abstract parts are
non-independent. An independent content is a content with respect to
which we possess evidence that it can remain unchanged throughout a
change in all the other contents given with it in intuition. The head of a
horse, for example, can remain unchanged while we arbitrarily change
all the other parts. The independence of such a content is not a matter of
fact but of necessity. Contrasted with this independence is the dependence of non-independent contents. As an example, Husserl
mentions the intensity and quality of a tone. A change in the quality
necessarily brings about a change in the intensity, and vice versa. Here
too we have to do not with a "mere fact" but with an "evident
necessity."[3]

Applied to the parts of a whole, this means that abstract moments are
non-independent and concrete parts independent. In the case of the
latter we can speak of pieces. The color and extension of a thing, for

---

[1] PA 74, note 1, 14, 237. For the term 'absolute content,' see PA 37, 40, 56, 139. Husserl
also uses the term 'absolute concretum' PSL 165.
[2] PA 83f, 151.
[3] PSL 160 f, 163, 171.

example, are abstract,[4] while the physical parts of a table, the leaves and stem of a plant, etc., are independent.[5]

All the distinctions which Husserl makes here are expressed in a priori judgments. In later publications Husserl continued to uphold this analysis in the main but placed it under the heading of analysis of *essences*. The distinction between the independent and the non-independent, for example, is further discussed in the third of the logical investigations and also in the first section of Ideen I (under the title "Essence and Knowledge of Essence"). The doctrine of the "intuition of essences," which came along later, stems from the problematics of a priori judgments. In Husserl's earliest writing, these a priori distinctions à la Stumpf pose a problem to which the doctrine of the intuition of essences in the answer.[6]

PARAGRAPH THREE, FORMAL OR CATEGORIAL PROPERTIES—OBJECTS OF A HIGHER ORDER?

Formal or categorial properties is a subject central to PA, for the purpose of this work is to analyze the origin of the concept of plurality. The concept of plurality is used to refer to certain groups of objects. What, now, is common to such quantities and thus able to serve as the basis for abstraction in the concept of plurality? It cannot lie in the concrete content of the collected things, for there is no limit to the variation in content. Any objects whatever can be connected to form a plurality; an angel, the moon and Italy can together be regarded as a concrete plurality, as can certain trees, the sun, the earth, and Mars.[1]

That which is common to all such concrete collections can only lie in the fact that these objects are joined by a particular act of the subject.

---

[4] So-called 'figural moments' are a special sort of abstracta. Husserl gives an analyses of them in PA 227ff, see also PSL 161f. He means by them the same as what Ehrenfels meant by 'form-qualities' and Meinong by 'founded contents.' In the LU he uses the term 'moment of unity' II, 234 or 'quasi-quality' instead. A quasi-quality, for Husserl, is one which arises from the fusion of absolute contents PA 237 or of relations PA 234. It is a directly perceivable property, a 'sensible quality of the second order' PA 225. He calls such qualities figural moments because they generally arise out of the fusion of spatial relations, e.g. a row of trees. Over against Ehrenfels, see PA 236, note 1 and Cornelius and Meinong LU II 282, note 1, Husserl claims priority in this discovery, see also LU II 234, note 1, 243, note 1, 281 and Husserl's letter to Kraus, PES III, XXIII note 2.

[5] PA 77; PSL 173.

[6] See below 85.

[1] PA 11, 67, 79.

"An aggregate comes about when a unitary interest – and in and with it, at the same time – a unitary observing embraces various contents and sets them off for itself." Thus this relation is not a part of the content but owes its exisɩence to a particular act, i.e. an act of a higher order. It is a *psychical* relation. The basis for abstraction in the case of the concept of plurality can only be found in reflection. "Thus the collective connection too can only be grasped through reflection on the psychical act by means of which the aggregate comes about."[2]

Husserl also calls the concept of plurality a formal concept or category. Categories are "the most general and emptiest in content of all concepts." In addition to plurality and number (as the specification of plurality), Husserl regards such formal concepts as identity[3] and unity[4] as among the categories. What explains their all-embracing character is that "they are concepts of attributes which originate in reflection on psychical acts, which can be directed toward all contents without exception." Hence the connection is very loose. The relata are endlessly variable, and thus one could almost speak of a certain "relationlessness." It is clear that the term 'plurality' is a *predicate of reflection*. Its origin can only be found in reflection of (connecting) acts. Husserl also characterizes the collective relation as a *psychical* relation. Everything points to this, and even "inner experience" (the final authority for Husserl) testifies that "collective unification is not given intuitively in contents of presentation, but that it has its existence only in certain psychical acts which enclose the contents in a unifying manner...."[5]

The relation brought about by the act of a higher order exists exclusively on the side of the subject. We could also express this as follows: *there is no object of a higher order corresponding to the act of a higher order*. It is true that this act is directed toward a number of objects, but these cannot be called its *Gegenstand* (object) in a strict sense. They are objects of acts of the first order – the constituent acts in which the act of a higher order is founded. The act of a higher order is related to these objects only in a secondary sense, i.e. insofar as it is built

---

[2] PA 79, see also 45.

[3] PA 66, 91.

[4] The concept 'unity' together with the concept 'something' originates also in reflections on an act, PA 86, 141, 162, 170, 173.

[5] PA 79, 81, 91.

upon acts which intend these objects in a primary way. The act of a higher order *as such* has no correlate of its own.[6]

At this point my interpretation conflicts with Husserl's own testimony, for in a footnote to the second edition of LU, he remarks by way of complaint that his PA attracted little attention despite the fact that it was "the first work which attached importance to acts and objects of a higher order and investigated them thoroughly."[7] As I see it, this is only true in part. PA does recognize acts of a higher order, but not objects corresponding to them. Husserl here projects a later standpoint on to his PA. In LU it is his view that *every* act has a correlate, a view which is bound up with his new concept of intentionality. Even formal or categorial concepts find their origin in objective properties. The doctrine of these formal properties falls under the heading "theory of objects," which was later – in *Ideen* I – to be called "ontology."[8] It is a formal ontology whose judgments are not founded in the content of the objects in question and can therefore be called analytic a priori judgments.[9]

The idea that these concepts originate in reflection is combatted by Husserl in LU as a Lockean presupposition.[10] They find their origin not in acts but in objects of acts. Thus categorial properties can also be perceived. It is true that they are not perceived in a sensory perception. (To this extent H still subscribed to his position in PA.) They are perceived in a *categorial* perception founded in sensory perception, a perception in which we perceive "ideal" objects.

That Husserl already recognized objects of a higher order in PA is also maintained in Fink's article in "Ziegenfuss." Fink contends that in PA we already encounter the typical correlative manner of consideration characteristic of phenomenology.[11] This eisegesis has quite a

---

[6] See also LU II 401ff. In the PA Husserl does not yet endorse the view which he was later to emphasize in LU: "Whatever the composition of an act out of constituent acts may be, if it is an act at all, it must have a single objective correlate." That every act relates itself to an object is true of both simple and compounded acts. This is implicit self-criticism on Husserl's part.

[7] LU II 282, note 1.

[8] Id I 23, note 3; see also Entwurf 320f.

[9] LU II 251ff. See below 83.

[10] LU III 139. That these concepts originate in reflection is a 'natural but quite misguided doctrine, universally put about since the time of Locke.'

[11] Ziegenfuss, *Philosophenlexicon*, 570. According to this lexicon, the article was written by Husserl. In a letter to Marvin Farber, Husserl claimed that the article was written by Fink but that it is nonetheless a correct account of his development, Farber, *The Foundation of Phenomenology*, 17.

history. It also appears in Farber, who speaks of Husserl's "dual mode of analysis."[12] For Biemel, this interpretation of PA is the point of departure for reflection on Husserl's development. He sees the origin of the concept of constitution in the doctrine of acts of a higher order. According to Biemel, it is there that we first encounter typical phenomenological analysis, which seeks to clarify objects by going back to the source of their "significance" in productive consciousness.[13] This interpretation is probably partly inspired by Husserl's self-interpretation in FTL. His PA, he there explains, is a first attempt "to go back to the spontaneous activities of collecting and counting, in which collections ('sums,' 'sets') and cardinal numbers are given in the manner characteristic of something that is being generated originaliter, and thereby to gain clarity with regard to the proper, authentic sense of the concepts fundamental to the theory of sets and the theory of cardinal numbers. In my later terminology, therefore, it was a phenomenological-constitutional investigation; and at the same time it was the first investigation that sought to make "categorial objectivities' of the first level and of higher levels (sets and cardinal numbers of a higher ordinal level) understandable on the basis of 'constituting' intentional activities, as whose productions they make their appearance originaliter...."[14]

This is a self-interpretation stemming from a later period. In this later period, "analysis of origins" means not only the clarification of the concept on the basis of the object of the concept or "Begriffsgegenstand" (the basis for abstraction), as in PA and LU, but a clarification of that concept by way of a description of the acts that bring forth the object of the concept.[15]

In the "Entwurf einer Vorrede zu den LU" we find a view of Husserl's own past that is more reliable from a historical point of view. This

---

[12] Farber, op.cit. 58.

[13] W. Biemel, "Les phases décisives dans le développement de la philosophie de Husserl," 39.

[14] FTL 76, see also 73 note 3. Also Landgrebe, who admits that this is an interpretation of the PA on the basis of a much later perspective, is nonetheless of the view that Husserl is right in characterizing his first work in this way. He too sees here in germinal form the concept of intentionality in the sense of 'vermeinen' (grasping putatively), as a 'producing activity,' *Der Weg der Phänomenologie*, 14f, 17; compare above 15. Landgrebe is among those who seek the origin of the concept of constitution in the analysis of acts of a higher order.

[15] See below 72.

sketch stems from 1913 but was never published by Husserl; it was finally published by Fink in 1939. In this sketch Husserl writes of his PA: "The presentation of a 'set' was supposed to result from the activity of connecting (the awareness of unity characteristic of apprehending something as a group, grasping all the members of the set at once), and there is certainly some truth in this. The collective is not something real, a unity grounded in the contents of the collected things. According to the school model which I have been taught, which holds that everything must be grasped intuitively as either 'physical' or 'psychical,' it could be nothing physical. Thus the concept of collection had to arise from psychological reflection in Brentano's sense, from 'reflection' on the act of collecting, and the concept of unity likewise had to arise from reflection on the act of positing as something." Husserl immediately goes on to say: "But in that case, is the concept of a cardinal number not something essentially different from the concept of collecting, a concept yielded only by act-reflection? In the earliest beginnings I was already disturbed – indeed, plagued – by such doubts, and they extended to all categorial concepts (as I was later to call them) and ultimately in another form to all concepts of objectivities of whatever kind."[16]

In this passage the standpoint of PA and the difficulties inherent in it do indeed come to expression in a striking way. Reflection on an act of a higher order can only give us the concept of a collecting act. When the concept of number is formed by abstraction from acts, arithmetic becomes inseparable from psychology.[17] Here we should not feel obliged to accept the later remarks of Husserl at face value, for Husserl, after all, is not the ultimate authority on the *historical* interpretation of his thought. The textual analysis of PA would be advanced more by a

[16] Entwurf 127. Something that Husserl wrote in his diary during the crisis of 1908 is closer to the truth: "I did a good deal of reading in PA. How unripe, how naive and even childish this work seemed to me. Thus it was not for nothing that my conscience tormented me when I published it. At the time of publication, I had actually gone beyond it already. It stems essentially from the years 1886–87. I was a beginner without a proper acquaintance with philosophical problems, without the proper training of philosophical 'capacities,'" 'Persönliche Aufzeichnungen' 294.

[17] The "numbers in themselves" of which Husserl speaks are not objective entities, as Farber believes (op.cit. 56), following Frege (op.cit. 331), (who sees this as an inconsistency in Husserl's otherwise subjectivistic conception). Numbers in themselves are psychical acts of a higher order that are actually carried out in contrast with acts that are only symbolically presented, see PA 252, 254, 258f, 264, 268, 270, 272, 291, 294f. See below 64.

dissection of the "scholastic" pattern that governed his thinking at the time. This will also provide an opportunity to reconstruct the doubts and hesitations that already disturbed Husserl in "the earliest beginnings."

From the outset Husserl's analysis was governed by the alternative which he faced. The collective connection cannot be an objective property. Why not? Because in outer perception only sensory contents are given, i.e. contents that are visible and tangible.[18] Among them are absolute contents and abstract moments, including primary relations and "form-qualities." At the beginning of his book, Husserl already comes out against certain views of John Stuart Mill, who saw number as a physical property.[19] Number is not outwardly perceivable; it is not a physical phenomenon. Husserl notes the same error in Lange, Locke, Aristotle, Brix, Bain, and Kroman.[20] His teacher Brentano could also be mentioned in this context.[21] All these thinkers who see number as a "positive part-content" are accused by Husserl of extreme empiricism.[22] It is a view that is also characteristic of the more naive consciousness of primitive civilizations.[23] For them number is an "inner quality of outer things."

Husserl owes the insight that this view of number is mistaken to Sigwart, who refuted the "physical" abstraction theory and pointed out the proper path for an analysis of number.[24] What is this proper path? Here the presupposition that we can only perceive sensory contents in outer perception becomes operative. Inner perception is then left over as an alternative. As Husserl says in his Entwurf of 1913, the origin does not lie in outer perception and *therefore* had to lie in inner perception. Husserl does indeed reason this way in PA,[25] thereby becoming guilty of an error condemned by Frege, i.e. regarding as real only that which is perceivable via the sense and declaring that everything else is subjective. The result is a "psychologistic" founding of arithmetic. With regard to this point, Husserl ultimately had to recognize that Frege's attack was

[18] PA 11, 112, 179 note 1.
[19] PA 11f, 33, 155, 165, 225, 229.
[20] PA 31, 33, 49, 91f, 167.
[21] VE 53. See below 78.
[22] PA 167, 31.
[23] PA 279 note 1.
[24] PA 92.
[25] For example, PA 76 and 79. Husserl there poses two possibilities. The collective connection is present either in the content of presentation or in the psychical act. After demonstrating that it cannot be the former, he chooses for the latter.

justified.[26] He finally overcame this "sensualism" in LU, where he recognized a categorial perception alongside sensory perception. This categorial perception, which in turn paved the way for the "intuition of essences,"[27] offers a solution to the difficulties with which Husserl was already preoccupied in PA.

The view that number finds its origin in a perception of acts causes tensions which come to expression in the course of the argument itself. This can be seen from two sides.

(A) It appears, that a concept analyzed on the basis of an act denotes a property of a physical content! This we gather from an observation about abstract and general names, a distinction derived from Brentano[28] and closely bound up with the distinction between abstract and concrete contents. An abstract name indicates an abstract content or attribute; a general name indicates the bearer of that attribute. Some words can fulfill both functions. Thus 'color' can serve as an abstract name and indicate the property of color as an abstract moment. But we can also speak of 'colors' or 'a color'. In that case we mean "something that has the property of color."[29]

'Collective connection' is an abstract name denoting an attribute. But 'plurality' is a general name, for it denotes "something that this abstract moment of collective connection possesses."[30] In other words, the collective connection is seen as a property of a concrete group of physical objects. The relation of the collective connection to the concrete quantity of contents is like that of an attribute to be bearer of the attribute. One would expect that a concept abstracted from an act would denote a property of an act. But Husserl uses this concept to denote not the act (i.e. the collecting) but the collective.

The nature of the subject-matter here resists the explicit doctrine about it, as it were; it is stronger than the doctrine. According to Husserl, although the collective relation is not a part-content of the

---

[26] Frege *Grundgesetze der Arithmetik*, XIII, XVIII; PA 130 note 1; LU I 169 note 1; see also below 280.

[27] Categorial perception is not the same thing as intuition of essences. Husserl does treat these two together, for both represent a perception of that which is beyond the senses LU III 147. The categorial "object of a higher level" is "ideal" in nature, LU III 145, 156. See below 90 and 151.

[28] Compare L. Gilson, La psychologie descriptive selon Franz Brentano, 159ff.

[29] PA 151ff.

[30] PA 83.

physical phenomenon, it can nonetheless be called a property of the phenomenon, i.e. an "outer" or "relative" property.[31] But it is not a genuine property, for the object has the property only in relation to the act.[32] Hence Husserl also compares it to a negative property.[33] He expressly warns against afterward projecting into the contents themselves such concepts which have their origin in reflection.

(*B*) The same ambiguity is present in Husserl's explanation of the process of abstraction leading to the concept of collective connection. On the one hand, he makes it clear more than once that the basis for abstraction is an act. But on the other hand, contents play a role here.

We may not without further ado place the abstraction of this concept (and of all other categorial concepts) on a par with the abstraction of such concepts as judging, wishing, etc. The latter are concepts which are simply abstracted from psychical acts. But when it comes to categorial concepts, there can be no mention of pure reflection, for the object of the act must be held fast and at the same time must be related to reflection. Husserl speaks here of the following noteworthy difficulty, that on the one hand we reflect on an act while on the other hand the collected contents must not disappear from consciousness.[34] In a certain sense, then, the contents themselves serve as the basis for abstraction.

What was explained above with regard to the concept of plurality holds also for the concept of number. This follows a priori from the fact that numbers are nothing but specifications of the general concept of plurality.[35] The concept of number also originates in reflection. In opposition to Wundt, Husserl remarks that in the case of the concept of number, the act does not serve only as the bearer of the concept in the sense that the act abstracts the concept. (This is the case with regard to *all* concepts.) In addition, the act serves as the *content* of the concept.[36] Despite this clear statement, we again find the restrictions that apply in the case of the concept of "plurality." Here too a concept abstracted from an act is applied to particular concrete pluralities Husserl even devotes a whole chapter to showing that the concrete collection has the property of number.[37]

The difficulties bound up with this psychologizing of number come to the

---

[31] PA 15, 41, 45, 74, 79.
[32] PA 86, 158.
[33] PA 61.
[34] PA 84.
[35] PA 9, 87, 147.
[36] PA 94.
[37] Cap. IX "Der Sinn der Zahlenaussage" 179ff; see also PA 45, 126, 162, 182, 202.

fore in a striking way in the following passage: "It is true that numbers adhere to no objects as attributes, and to this extent, objects are not their bearers; but they are their bearers nonetheless in another, more correct sense. Number owes its origin to a certain psychical process which establishes a connection with the numbered objects and in this sense is 'borne' by them."[38] Thus at one and the same time, number is a property of contents and not a property of contents. It is not borne by objects, yet is it "borne."[39]

All of these difficulties flow from the presupposition that a concept arises either from outer sensory perception or from inner perception. Husserl had not yet broken free of the grip of this pattern of thought. Insofar as we seek the historical truth, we must not follow Husserl in his understandable inclination to project into PA a standpoint later achieved. Not only does this lead to a mistaken understanding of the earlier standpoint, but it also makes it impossible to understand the later stage on the basis of the intrinsic difficulties of the earlier period. The ultimate result is a blurring of the entire course of Husserl's development. Therefore the view that in PA Husserl had already discovered the constituting activity of consciousness must be combatted. Such a view cannot appeal to an alleged correlation between the act of a higher order and its object, for the simple reason that there is no such object. Husserl first came upon the sense-giving function of consciousness in 1894, in the analysis of language, in the understanding and reading of written signs. This was a clearly noted discovery.

But Husserl's analysis of acts of a higher order nevertheless represents an important side of his development. The line that originates here leads not to sense-giving constitution but to categorial perception and thereby to the intuition of essences.

[38] PA 182.

[39] Another difficult point for Husserl is that a material moment (the figural moment) must serve as the sign of a psychical process, in the non-genuine presentation of plurality, PA 220, 244. This is also the case with regard to the symbolic presentation of number, in which this function is assumed by a visible numeral. These tensions likewise appear in the concept of "something," a concept that arises from an act of "treating as something" on the one hand and is applied to contents on the other, BZ 63; PA 85; Entwurf 127. The concept of "unity," which also arises from reflection, is nonetheless applied to contents, PA 151, 170.

SECTION THREE.
THE RELATION BETWEEN ACT AND CONTENT

In the previous sections of this first chapter, acts and contents were discussed separately. The relation between them will now be examined.

PARAGRAPH ONE. ARE ACTS CREATIVE?

In his discussion of Lange, Husserl makes a few clear remarks about the possibility of acts being creative in character. Lange sees the synthesis of number as a spatial or material synthesis. This material synthesis is the product of a creative act of the understanding. With regard to this point, Lange is dependent on Kant, who sees all connections as products of the understanding, including the connections seen by Husserl as relations not purely formal in character.

Against this theory of creative acts, Husserl remarks: "Inner experience – which alone is determinative here – teaches nothing of such creative processes. The activity of the mind does not *make* the relations; they are simply there and are noticed through the proper directing of interest, in the same way as any other content. A creative act in the genuine sense, which produces some new content as a result different from itself, would be a psychological absurdity." The view that there are such acts is "psychologically untenable."[1]

In the case of acts of a higher order, the question is somewhat more complicated, for here we can speak of an "operation of the understanding" (to use Kant's term) resulting in new relative or formal properties.[2] Actually the properties are not positively perceivable part-contents; they are comparable to negative attributes. They belong to

---

[1] PA 42f and BZ 37. Despite these clear statements, Frege thought that Husserl did speak of a creative consciousness, see above 20. In connection with the confusion of the expressions 'moon' and 'presentation of the moon' which he had criticized, Frege remarked: "Is it not at bottom a completely innocent diversion to call the moon, for example, a presentation? Yes – as long as one does not imagine that it can be changed at whim or produced through psychological means." He then concludes: "Yet this conclusion is all too easily drawn," op.cit. 317f. This interpretation results from Frege's identification of content and act. The acts are created by us, but not the contents. Acts are not creative themselves. Frege makes two mistakes: Husserl does not reduce the external world to an immanent content and – *a fortiori* – not to an act.

[2] See above 24.

contents only in virtue of a particular act in which they are apprehended. I have already pointed to the typical difficulties to which this led in arithmetic.

This difficulty is also reflected in Husserl's hesitation in speaking of creation in the case of acts of a higher order. In BZ he denies that numbers are purely mental creations and calls this view "an exaggeration and misrepresentation of the true state of affairs." But four years later in PA he says: "... this is actually correct."[3] Indeed, numbers are creations on the one hand, and on the other hand they are not. They are mental creations insofar as the spontaneity of the mind plays a role here; we create the acts in which the relation of number originates. On the other hand, to say that we create numbers is still an exaggeration, for these acts do not themselves produce new primary contents. "In the case of outer activities, of course, we do separate the activity from the work which it produces and which can continue to exist after the activity has long since ceased. But the psychical activities which ground the concepts of number do not produce in them any new primary contents that can be found in space or in the external world separate from the generating activities."[4]

All the formulations finally come down to this, that the act of a higher order *qua* act of a higher order has no content of its own. Such acts have contents only indirectly; that is to say, their contents are borrowed from the acts in which they are founded. The relations between contents which they establish can be perceived only in reflection. This is a view that Husserl later combatted in LU as a Lockean presupposition – without mentioning that he had once held this view himself.

PARAGRAPH TWO. THE CORRELATION BETWEEN ACT AND OBJECT

Certain expressions in PA make it necessary to discuss once more in an explicit way the question of the correlation between act and object. The relations between these two is of importance in connection with the later "correlative manner of consideration," in which object and act are investigated together in close relation to one another. In Ideen I Husserl speaks of a noetic/noematic parallelism. This mirroring between act and object is basic to phenomenology. Spiegelberg correctly says of the insight that "there is a parallelism between the

---

[3] BZ 36f; PA 46.
[4] PA 18, 45, 64; BZ 37; see also PA 167 for Kroman, who sees number as a part-content and thus a self-produced object.

structures of the subjective act and of its objective referent" that it
"pervades the whole of Husserl's work," and he adds: "including even
his early and supposedly altogether psychologistic *Philosophy of
Arithmetic.*"[1] Is this last remark justified? On my view, it is not. I do not
base my conclusion on passages where Husserl rejects the notion of a
relation of pictorial similarity between act and object.[2] What Husserl
opposes in this case is the extreme empiricism discussed earlier, which
sees categorial properties as part-contents of things.[3]

What does the text of PA teach? We have already seen that the
problem of correlation cannot arise in the case of acts of a higher order.
In the case of acts of a lower order, there is likewise no trace of such a
correlation. We must of course assume that acts are differentiated
according to their objects. In this sense we find mention in Brentano of a
specification of acts according to their objects. As Kraus remarks:
"Consciousness is different depending on whether it has white or black,
a color or a sound, a sphere or a person as its object."[4] It is important to
note that this differentiation of acts never became thematic.[5] *The theme
of correlation could only be developed after the discovery of the sense-
giving function of consciousness.* Before that discovery, it was and
remained a simple claim to the effect that acts differ in accordance with
the objects with which they are concerned. After the discovery of
constitution, the appearance of the object becomes partly dependent on
the attitude of the subject. There is then an active relation between act
and content, whereby the object appears in the way that the act
"apprehends," "apperceives," "interprets," or "indicates" it. Thus
there is a parallel between the appercipient sense or the material on the
side of the act and the objective sense on the side of the object.[6] In Ideen
I Husserl speaks of the parallelism between the noesis and noema.[7]

    ¹ Spiegelberg, *The Phenomenological Movement*, 103.
    ² PA 36, 41, 92, 139.
    ³ See above 28.
    ⁴ PES II, XII.
    ⁵ This is not the case, for example, in the doctrine of association. As developed by the
British psychologists – Brentano names Mill in particular, PES I 17ff, 155, 166 – it
concerns contents. Brentano introduces the correlation only in that we can draw a *per
analogiam* conclusion about acts from contents, PES I 41f, 44, 109, 140. He does the same
in the case of the Fechner-Weber law, which also has to do with contents, PES I 17, note 2,
101, 169; compare 140, 193 and II 66.
    ⁶ See below 141 and 319.
    ⁷ See below 437. When Husserl discusses this parallelism extensively in Ideen I, he still
denies the relation of a pictorial similarity, 162. He does so on account of the difference in

When in later publications he discusses intentionality as it functions in Brentano, he mentions that a shortcoming of Brentano's analysis is that it is not correlative.[8] This reproach is rooted in the new conception of intentionality, the first traces of which appear in 1894.

PARAGRAPH THREE. PERCEPTION AND EVIDENCE

As we have seen, the doctrine of immanent contents is to be found in Brentano as well as in his student Husserl. It is noteworthy that one and the same conception appears to lead to two opposed views of outer perception. From the fact that contents are only phenomenal and intentional, Brentano draws the conclusion that outer perception is not trustworthy. Actually, perceiving is not a "Wahrnehmung" (which means, literally, taking as true) but a "Falsch-nehmung" (taking as false). But Husserl speaks of adequate perception and final fulfillment with reference to outer perception. How is this paradox to be explained?

I will discuss Husserl's views against the background of Brentano's standpoint.

(*A*) Brentano speaks of *outer perception* as a "Falschnehmung" because its contents do not actually exist; that is to say, they do not exist in reality outside us. He calls them merely phenomenal. Thus term 'phenomenon' is thus used to refer to that which does not actually exist.

The contents of outer perception are sensorily perceivable qualities, such as color, sound, smell, warmth, and coldness. Locke had already shown that warmth and coldness are not in the water but in our hands. Furthermore, pressure on the eye can cause the same appearances of light as the rays emanating from a colored object. Likewise, two spatial relations sometimes appear to us to be similar, when in fact they are not similar, and vice versa. In these considerations Brentano already sees "the full proof of their falsity."[1] But the most important of the arguments against the veridical character of outer perception is that borrowed from physics. Physics recognizes no colors but only molecular movements or vibrations of ether.[2]

mode of temporality between noesis and noema. The noema is within a cosmic, measurable time, while consciousness is within immanent time, see below 462. It is for this reason that Husserl hesitates to use the term 'mirroring' in Ideen I, 266, see also PSW 312f.

[8] Nachwort 156; Enc. Brit. Art, Husserliana IX 268; FTL 231.

[1] PES I 13.

[2] PES I 66, 132; II 136; see also the notes of Kraus I, 268 note 7, 270 note 14, 271 note 18 and the introduction, LXXIX, LXXXIV.

Inner perception is true perception, for its objects really exist. They are perceived with immediate inward evidence.[3] We should note that for Brentano, the term 'perception' has a different meaning with regard to evident inner perception than with reference to outer perception. This is apparent from a discussion which Brentano carried on with Comte and others who denied the possibility of inner perception. Brentano responds to their objections by declaring that observation (*Beobachtung*) is indeed impossible. Inner perception is not observational but is an additional consciousness (*Bewusstsein nebenbei*). At the same time that we are perceiving an outer object, we have an evident perception in inner consciousness of this outer perception. The outer object is then the primary object of the act, and the act itself is the secondary object.

Comte's argument is that the subject cannot divide itself. We cannot perceive the object and our presentation of it at the same time. Brentano in fact agrees with this. He opposes Comte here only in that he insists that an additional consciousness is possible. While we are perceiving, we are aware of our act of outer perception. But this secondary perceiving is not an attentive perceiving. Therefore it cannot serve as an instrument for scientific analysis. Real observation is only possible in memory. Spiegelberg correctly points out that the realm of this inner perception is infinitesmally small, being limited to the strict present, and that the psychologist's approach to the psychical phenomenon is by way of memory and therefore is not illusion-proof.[4] Brentano borrows the doctrine of additional consciousness from Aristotle. Secondary consciousness is of an accompanying character; it is not a self-sufficient act. If it were a self-sufficient act, this secondary consciousness would itself be perceived in turn, for every act is also secondarily perceived. This introduces endless complications, even in the case of a single perception.[5]

The inward evidence of inner perception requires no further proof, for every proof presupposes it. We must not say that this perception is evident because in its case – as opposed to the case of outer perception – we are able to compare the known intentional object with the real object. For this to be possible, the real object would first have to be known, and thus we would be involved in a circle. The inward evidence of inner perception needs no proof simply because it is evident. It is the

---

[3] PES I 129, 137; see also the polemic against Kant 223, 245, who also sees the inner phenomenon as "illusion" (*Schein*).

[4] PES I 41ff, 50, 63, 61; Spiegelberg op.cit. 39.

[5] PES I 179ff, 180, 189.

ultimate foundation of our knowledge. We can, of course, inquire into the ground of the possibility of this inward evidence. It rests on the unity of secondary consciousness and its object. Inward evidence would not be possible if the perception of the act and the act itself were two separate acts. Knowing the act is an aspect of the act itself.[6]

(B) Like Brentano, Husserl distinguishes in the case of *outer perception* between the transcendent object and the phenomenal immanent object. Yet he does not speak of outer perception as "Falschnehmung." He does not pursue the question of the transcendent object, for the simple reason that it has nothing to do with psychological investigation, which concerns itself only with the act and its object. Precisely because the object of the act is immanent, adequate perception is possible, i.e. a perception of the content *as* immanent content! Here Husserl is more consistent than his teacher. Brentano maintained that it is actually not proper to speak of "outer" perception.[7] This way of speaking stems from the time when people believed that colors, sounds, etc. exist outside us and that we perceive them. At that time one could really speak of outer perception, i.e. perception of something outside us. It is noteworthy that in his appraisal of outer perception, Brentano still takes the old view as his point of departure. It is only when perception pretends to perceive something outside us that it becomes a "Falshnehmung," but it is not a "Falschnehmung" if we regard the immanent object as criterion. If one adopts the view that the real object of perception is the immanent intentional object – and we shall see that this, in opposition to Scholasticism, is what Brentano and the early Husserl chose to do – there is no longer any reason to speak of "Falschnehmung." The intentional object is perceivable as such.[8] In a later paragraph we will see that Husserl's standpoint on this question is closely bound up with the descriptive-psychological point of departure. In limiting himself (on methodological grounds) to the givens for psychological investigation, he is more radical than Brentano.

Husserl recognizes the object-oriented distinction between inner and outer perception, but on his view it does not coincide with the

---

[6] PES I 196, 198, 249; for the later Brentano, see PES III 6, 98.

[7] PES I 140. For Brentano's standpoint after the "crisis of immanence," see PES II 136.

[8] See also LU III 239 where Husserl says that Brentano, should also have spoken of adequate perception in the case of physical phenomena that are experienced immanently.

distinction between evident and non-evident perception. In 1894 Husserl maintains – in agreement with his dynamic conception of intentionality[9] – that outer perception can be either adequate or inadequate and that there are intermediate stages, i.e. degrees of evidence. Our perception of the side of the thing facing us is adequate, whereas our perception of the other side is not adequate. Ultimately, one could say that the entire thing is adequately given, provided that we understand the perception in question to be a perception that includes every side of the thing in a series of acts. The thing-presentation here finds its final fulfillment.[10] Husserl is in fact already operating with the criterion for adequate perception that he later formulated expressly in LU: a perception is adequate if it intends nothing more that it actually "experiences" (erlebt).[11] According to this criterion, outer perception can also be adequate within certain limits – and thus evident.

When we operate with the same criterion in the case of *inner perception*, important consequences ensue. To bring about a real *adequatio*, it is not necessary that subject and object coincide. Just as in the case of adequate outer perception, *observation* is possible – without detracting from the evidence is any way. In LU Husserl rejects Brentano's equivocal use of the term 'perception.' (what the term means for Brentano depends on whether he is concerned with inner or outer perception.) In both cases, for Husserl, the term has the same meaning, and therefore it must not be used in some places in the sense of observation and in others in the sense of additional consciousness. Husserl rejects this as an artificial theory which cannot be justified on phenomenological grounds.[12] There are various indications that Husserl also rejects this theory in PA.

(1) He distinguishes between a "psychical occurrence" and a psychical act. The former cannot be perceived inwardly and falls outside the realm of reflection. The latter can be perceived but is not always perceived. This doctrine is incompatible with Brentano's standpoint, for he holds that every act is accompanied by a consciousness of it.[13]

(2) In PA Husserl replaces the term 'psychical phenomenon,' which he used in BZ, with 'psychical *act*.'[14] The latter is indeed more correct, for an act is not

---

[9] See above 15.
[10] PSL 178 and 187.
[11] LU II 354f.
[12] LU II (ed. 1) 334 (compare ed. 2, 356); LU III 232f; ZBW 473 (E 162ff).
[13] PA 66.
[14] PA 58, compare 73.

automatically a phenomenon. For Brentano, however, every act is a phenomenon.

(3) By inner perception Husserl means reflection in the sense of Locke. Locke did not mean by reflection a merely accompanying consciousness. That Husserl does not mean this either is apparent from his characterization of psychological analysis as intuition (*Anschauung*).[15] For Brentano it is an immanent remembering (as observation).

(4) Finally, additional perceiving has a different function for Husserl. He views it as something that appears *on the edge of normal perception*. Alongside its chief content, every perception also has an additional content. This distinction rests on inner experience and is not a psychological construction.[16]

Thus Husserl believes that he can uphold the evidence of inner experience without the use of an additional perceiving. For him this evidence puts an end to all contradiction.[17] Furthermore, it concerns not only acts but also immanent contents. Without further ado, the term 'inner experience' is then used interchangeably with 'experience.'[18]

Finally, I should like to touch on a point that is of importance for the later development of Husserl's theory of perception. Brentano had taught that it is one of the distinguishing characteristics of psychical phenomena that they are not spatial. Our speaking of a pain in the arm or a "desire that pervades the entire body" rests on a confusion of psychical and physical phenomena. Psychical phenomena cannot be localized.[19] All the objects of outer perception, by contrast, are spatially extended. Husserl adopts this view in PA. The psychical is non-spatial and cannot be localized, whereas contents are extended.[20] The ques-

---

[15] PA 66; PSL 170f, see also LU III, 230 note 3.

[16] PSL 181; PA 18.

[17] PA 20, 34, 42, 61f, 66, 69, 79, 98, 168; PSL 181, 183.

[18] PA 38, 40, 115, 228. In Ideen I the possibility of such an inward evident perception is expressly defended against objections *à la* Comte. Husserl admits that the spontaneous "experience" (*Erlebnis*) changes through reflection. Anger, for example, "blows over" when it is perceived, 130, see also PSW 306. Nonetheless, a perception of one's own experience is possible, thanks to retention, Id I 183, 145, 150f; ZBW 471ff (159ff). Husserl argues that the denial of the possibility of reflection is absurd in the sense in which any scepticism is absurd; that is, it contradicts itself, compare Id I 37, 155 and LU I 110. Anyone who raises doubts about reflection is speaking about his doubts, and this is only possible in reflection. Whenever one argues on the basis of the modification which consciousness undergoes in perception, he presupposes a knowledge of the experience *before* the modification, which is just what is being denied. Finally, every struggle against reflection presupposes a knowledge of reflection – and that by way of reflection.

[19] PES I 122f, 134 note 1.

[20] PA 32. That everything psychical is localized is completely untenable; regarding the

tion one might raise in this context is: how can an extended content be immanent to a non-extended act? Husserl's theory gives us no satisfactory answer to this question.[21]

PARAGRAPH FOUR. THE RELATION TO THE "REAL" OBJECT AND THE "INTENTIONAL" OBJECT

The relation between the "real" object and the "intentional" object, on the one hand, and the relation of consciousness to both, on the other, play a central role in the thought of both Brentano and Husserl. The terms as such stem from Scholastic philosophy. Therefore I will compare the view of Brentano and Husserl not only with each other but also with the Scholastic view.

I. Brentano

For Brentano, the real object is the object of physics. This physical thing (the molecular movements, etc.) is not the physical phenomenon.[1] We can however say – given a certain qualification – that physics is the science of physical phenomena. The qualification is that physics only takes physical phenomena as its *point of departure*. What it investigates, after all, are transcendent causes which give rise to physical phenomena in us. To use a somewhat paradoxical formulation, we could say that physics concerns itself with physical phenomena only insofar as it shows that they do not exist!

In order to explain physical phenomena, physics operates with the hypothesis of a world existing outside us. The laws which we establish about this hypothetical world explain the otherwise incomprehensible succession and coherence of our perceptions.[2] This presupposed world, furthermore, is not spatial but "space-like." Thus it manifests relations which are analogous to the spatial relations which we perceive. We know nothing about the absolute nature of this world. We can only take it that there are "forces" and "physical stimuli" that cause perceptions. The effects or physical phenomena do not give us a corresponding image of the stimuli. They are only "signs" that there is something by

act as something spatial is a pure absurdity, 41, see also 47. Acts take place in time, PA 14, 20ff, 28, 235.

[21] See below 164.

[1] PES 138 and 151. For the term 'physical phenomenon,' see the critical remarks above 18 note 2.

[2] PES I 13, 153, 184.

which they are caused. "We could say that something is at hand when it becomes the cause of this or that sensation under these or those conditions; we could also show that relations similar to those manifested by spatial appearances (magnitudes and shapes) must come to the fore in such a case. But this is as far as we could go. In and of itself, that which truly exists is not in the appearance, and that which appears does not truly exist."[3]

We see, then, that Brentano accepts a split between the *intuited phenomenon* within (i.e. the sensorily perceivable qualities) and the *theoretically postulated thing* outside (i.e. the object of physics). We could also express this in another way, relying consciously on terms used by the later Husserl, by saying that the "life-world," the world of colors, is within, while the "thing of physics" is outside us. It is not correct, therefore, to assert that Brentano recognizes sensory qualities existing outside us independent of the subject. Vollenhoven mistakenly sees the preponderant subjectivism of modern philosophy as taking a new turn in Brentano; he regards Brentano as recognizing the extramental existence of objects. We find the same mistake in his student Taljaard.[4] The latter appeals to a text in which Brentano says that there is no contradiction in the concept of a "color that is not perceived." It is true, of course, that it cannot be proven in an a priori manner on the basis of concepts that there are no colors that are not perceived. But Brentano leaves no doubt that it has been shown *in fact*, i.e. on the basis of natural science using inductive-empirical methods, that there are no such colors.[5]

It was probably Brentano's sharp distinction between act and content that gave rise to this misconception. The act is intentionally directed toward its content. But this does not mean that the content exists outside us. To do justice to Brentano, we must recognize three terms: the physical (which is the object of physics), the physical phenomenon, and the act. This can be represented as follows:

[3] PES I 28, 87, 110, 173, 196.
[4] D. H. Th. Vollenhoven, Geschiedenis der wijsbegeerte I, 237; J. A. L. Taljaard, Franz Brentano as wijsgeer, 40.
[5] PES I 30, 130f, 140, 172, 177f, 186, 250.

I		II		III
the act	→	physical phenomenon or immanent object	←	hidden cause
e.g. hearing		e.g. the sound		object of physics

The arrow pointing to the right is the arrow of intentionality. It only extends to the immanent object, not the the "thing in itself." The arrow pointing to the left is the stimulus, which proceeds from the hidden outer world and causes the phenomenon of sound. In his commentary Kraus rightly lays heavy emphasis on the fact that Brentano is not a phenomenalist *à la* Mach, for he accepts a reality behind the phenomenon.[6] It is in comparison to this reality that the phenomenon is "only phenomenal."

It is necessary to devote considerable attention to this question at this point, for the distinction between the perceived phenomenon and the postulated physical thing was to play a large role in Husserl's development. The overcoming of this problematics is in part the background of the famous transcendental-phenomenological reduction.[7] Two points in particular require our attention. First, physical concepts play a role in *explanatory* science. They are theoretical *constructions*. The content of such concepts as atom and electron (vibration of ether!) does not fall within the realm of perception – in contrast to the intuited phenomena which they must explain and which are the objects of a *descriptive* science. Second, physics is furthermore an *empirical* science which reaches only provisional results. The phenomena, on the other hand, are the objects of an *a priori* science which achieves apodictic insights.

In a later chapter we will see what an important role this distinction plays in Brentano and Husserl, for these two kinds of sciences are representative of two two philosophical outlooks which we could speak of as positivistic and "phenomenological." In the later Brentano and the early Husserl, these two outlooks still stand *alongside* one another. But this was not to remain so.[8] Without trying to anticipate what must come later, I would already point out that the physical thing is the basis for a philosophy that seeks to explain all of reality in a causal way, i.e. not just the physical phenomenon but also the psychical phenomenon –

---

[6] PES I 270 note 16; PES III, XXXI note 1.
[7] See below 416.
[8] See below 111.

thus the person as a totality. Human consciousness, after all, is founded in a body, and the latter is also a "thing of physics."[9]

Finally, we should take a look at this problematics from the standpoint of Stumpf, who was keenly aware of the dangers of the term 'physical phenomenon.' Physical phenomena, he pointed out, do not form the field of investigation of physics but only its point of departure. On the other hand, he was not willing to assign these phenomena to psychology either. It is true that he spoke of a *psychology* of sound, but he himself recognized that this term is not entirely correct, for psychology investigates not the sound but the hearing of the sound. Stumpf made a terminological distinction between physical objects and "appearances." The adjective 'physical' can be applied only to physical things in the genuine sense, i.e. atoms, molecules, vibrations. Over against physical objects and appearances stand "functions" or psychical acts, which form the field of investigation of psychology.

I		II		III
functions	→	appearances	←	physical objects
psychology		phenomenology		physics

Stumpf reserved a separate science (which he called "phenomenology") for appearances, for they form the field of investigation of neither physics nor psychology. He calls phenomenology a neutral "pre-science." It is neutral because it is neither physics nor psychology. It is a *pre*-science because it precedes both sciences and presents them with their material. Phenomenology *describes* what the other two sciences explain. Its objects are given immediately. Furthermore, this science formulates a priori laws which are founded in the dependence of these phenomena on one another. The sciences that come after this description investigate the dependence of these phenomena on *factors other than the phenomena themselves.*[10]

As Brentano correctly points out, the doctrine of the immanent intentional object stems from Scholasticism. We also encounter this doctrine in Brentano's inaugural (Habilitationsschrift) on Aristotle. The intentional object is the object as *present in the knower*. Intentional or objective being is contrasted with real or physical being. What the doctrine was to explain, then, is how the knower can in a certain sense be the object which it knows, without becoming like that object "physically." Since the known object in this physical reality is not present in

[9] This term is borrowed from the later Husserl, see e.g. ZBW 428 (E 98).

[10] C. Stumpf, 'Zur Einteilung der Wissenschaften,' 16, 20, 26. Compare H. Spiegelberg, *The Phenomenological Movement* I, 53, 56–61. See also Husserl about Stumpf, Id I 178.

the knower, it is necessary that there be an *image* as its *representative* in the knower. This representative image is called the species. This species is also called the "intentio." In sensory perception, then, we must distinguish between the real color outside us and the intentional color, which is an image or representative of it. The species *mediates* in the knowing process. It makes possible an "unio intentionalis" of the knower and the known object.

In Scholasticism, thus, intentionality is a *mode of being*. "Esse intentionale" is opposed to "esse naturae" or "naturale"; the intentional order is opposed to the natural order. Knowledge is only a *particular instance* of this.[11] A case of something intentional being present in something else is a case neither of separation nor of identity but of an incomplete identity. Thus light is the intentional presence of the sun in the sky. The user of an instrument is likewise intentionally present in that instrument. What first strikes us when we compare the Scholastic teaching with that of Brentano is that for Brentano intentionality is completely separated from its ontological foundation. Although intentionality has to do with all levels of reality for Thomas Aquinas, for Brentano it has to do only with consciousness. What is a metaphysical-cosmic principle for Thomas is narrowed down by Brentano to a psychogical principle.

The Scholastic doctrine of intentionality testifies to the intrinsic connection between reality and the knower who aims at knowledge of the object. Reality is potentially intelligible. It is the task of the soul, because of its connection with the material of nature, to actualize this potential intelligibility. This is explained by Brentano himself in his *Psychologie des Aristoteles*. The affinity between perception and the perceived object is for Aristotle a proof of the corporeality of the "anima sensitiva." The sensorily perceiving soul cannot be immaterial or immortal if its object is material and transitory.[12] In Brentano's PES there is no mention of such an interrelation. The soul is not only immortal but also non-corporeal. Brentano consciously turns away from the Aristotelian theory which sees sensory perception as an act of a corporeal organ and speaks of extension in connection with the soul.

[11] H. Spiegelberg 'Der Begriff der Intentionalität in der Scholastik, bei Brentano und bei Husserl' 78, see above 18; Edith Stein 'Husserls Phänomenologie und die Philosophie des hl. Thomas v. Aquino' 335; A. Hayen, *L'intentionnel dans la philosophie de St. Thomas*, 1942, 18f, 253, 256.

[12] Psychologie des Aristoteles 99f, see also 128.

Thomas too is criticized for viewing sensory perception as an act of the body.[13]

In Scholasticism, then, there is an inner relation between the real object and the intentional object; there is an essential bond between the color as it exists outside me and the color in me. It is even maintained that sensory perception is not subject to illusion, as Brentano himself points out in his book on the psychology of Aristotle.[14] But in Brentano's thought, the connection between the real object and the intentional object is completely broken. When we perceive a color, there is a "vibration" outside us. Even spatial relations, which still counted as primary qualities for Locke, cannot be said to exist outside us just as we perceive them. We can only presuppose by way of hypothesis that there is a space-*like* world. That which really exists does not appear and that which appears does not really exist, according to Brentano. Outer perception is not misleading *per accidens* but *per se*; it is a "Falschnehmung." Neither is the immanent object called an "imago" by Brentano; it is not a corresponding image.[15] The immanent object is a "sign"; it is only an indication that there must be something which causes this phenomenon. There can be no thought of an "adequatio rei et intellectus."

Finally – and this is closely related to the preceding – Brentano conceives of the relation to the real object in a different way. In Scholasticism the intentional object is a means used in knowing; it is an instrument and not an obstacle.[16] We know the real object via this medium, and the object is indeed what we actually know. In other words, what we know is not the species: *through* the species we know the real object. The species manifests itself, but it is not known. In the perception of the real object, we are unaware of the species. It is an "id *quo* cognoscitur," an "imago vicaria" *in* which the real object is known.[17] For Brentano, on the other hand, the intentional object is the end term of perception. It is an "id quod cognoscitur." There is no thought of being directed toward reality via the phenomenon. The term 'phenomenon' itself contradicts such a notion. This means that the

[13] PES I 37, 123, 176, 236; II, XVII.
[14] Psychologie des Aristoteles 83, 85.
[15] PES 13, 110, 140, see also 45 and 173.
[16] Rabeau, *Species, Verbum*, 73. "These intermediaries are not obstacles but instruments, and this is why St. Thomas does not hesitate to say that the conception has its basis immediately in the thing."
[17] Rabeau, op.cit. 287.

intentional object no longer has a mediating function. The intentional object is not an instrument but the only object known. Thus for Brentano, "direction toward an object" is unmediated and direct. The object known in this manner is not the real object but the immanent object. Therefore this intentionality has no epistemological significance – insofar as epistemology tries to account for our knowledge of the real object. This gives rise to the typically modern problematics of the thing in itself, of which Scholasticism (Thomas Aquinas) knows nothing.[18]

I have already pointed out that Brentano's doctrine of the intentional object occurs in an entirely different context than that of the Scholastics: it comes up not in a theory of knowledge but in a preparatory chapter of a psychology. It is a means for defining psychical phenomena.[19] The question whether a real object exists must be answered by physics (physiology). Thus, the doctrine of intentionality is not intended at all to serve as a bridge between consciousness and reality, the inner and the outer. This bridge is built by causal reasoning, by a "causal deduction"![20] By way of this deduction, we reach an external world that really exists. Landgrebe is right when he speaks of an epistemological realism in connection with Brentano, for behind the phenomena lies an existing reality.[21] But it must be emphasized that this is a *realism not based on the theme of intentionality*. It rests on reasoning independent of the doctrine of intentionality. This conclusion will be important later in criticizing the epistemological position of LU.[22]

II. Husserl

That contents are immanent for Husserl has already been established. Husserl lets it be known a few times that there is a transcendent

---

[18] See A. Hayen, op.cit.287.
[17] Rabeau, op.cit. 44, 49f.
[19] That Brentano frees this criterion from the context in which it stands in the thought of Thomas can also be illustrated as follows. Because every phenomenon that embraces an object in an intentional manner is psychical, these phenomena – from the Scholastic standpoint – also include a number of phenomena that Brentano calls physical. Color is present in the sky in an intentional way. This is the "color in aere" (color in the air) over against the "color in pariete" (color on the wall). (see Spiegelberg 'Der Begriff der Intentionalität in der Scholastik, bei Brentano und bei Husserl,' 84) Thus, the sky, in any case, is a psychical phenomenon!
[20] PES I, 184, 196.
[21] Landgrebe, *Der Weg der Phänomenologie*, 12.
[22] See below 196.

object, which is to be distinguished from the contents. In the article of 1894, he says that the concept of a transcendent thing is scientific in character and is foreign to natural thought.[23] It presupposes that in psychological reflection one has become aware of the subjectivity of knowing. That Husserl must accept some sort of transcendent thing follows from his observation that creative acts are psychological absurdities. Contents are passively taken in. In opposition to Kant, he says that primary relations are not brought forth by the mind but are simply encountered; they are "simply there." The same is true, *a fortiori*, of absolute contents.

If contents are conceived of as passive, the question where they come from naturally arises. Must there be some cause, a stimulus that evokes them in us? Nowhere does Husserl answer this question. But we must not interpret his silence as an argument *e silentio* for an idealist conception. We would then be forced to interpret him in Frege's sense, i.e. as maintaining that the moon is identical with the presentation of the moon – *esse* is *percipi*. But this cannot be what Husserl means, for he opposes this formula of Berkeley (albeit implicitly).[24] The question, then, is whether Husserl's silence on this point can be explained. I will begin by asking whether the real thing is the thing of physics, as in Brentano.

In Husserl's early publications, I have encountered only one passage in which he alludes obliquely to this question.[25] It occurs in the first half of the article of 1894, where he develops his theory of abstract and concrete parts. The passage falls under the heading of a priori pre-science in the sense of Stumpf, to whose theory of independent and non-independent contents Husserl subscribes. Like Stumpf, Husserl makes a distinction between two kinds of relations of dependence with reference to contents. In the first place, there are *necessary* relations *between contents themselves*. Secondly, phenomena are also dependent on other factors, i.e. causal relations between objective things. The latter are the origin of non-a priori relations between contents.[26]

---

[23] PSL 178; see also above 21.

[24] PSL 166.

[25] PSL 159. There are probably more givens to be found in Husserl's not available inaugural lecture at Halle in 1887, which dealt with the "goals and tasks of metaphysics." (In PA 216 Husserl mentions as an example of a non-genuine presentation of color: "so-and-so many billion vibrations of ether per second.")

[26] See above 43.

Thus Husserl's standpoint here is completely analogous to that of Stumpf. There is a descriptive pre-science which lays bare the structural laws that have to do with phenomena. One of the results of this pre-science, for instance, is the distinction between independent and non-independent contents. Alongside this pre-science there is also a science which explains the phenomena. Its starting-point lies in the causal relations between contents, which are a sign of the causal relations in the external world. The contents which *in themselves* form the object of an a priori descriptive science are the *point of departure* for an empirical explanatory science (i.e. physics). Because of the analogy with the thought of Stumpf and Brentano, we may conclude that Husserl's view is similar. The transcendent thing is the thing of physics.

This conclusion is indirectly corroborated by a passage in Husserl's "Prolegomena to Pure Logic" in LU, in which he says that some science require certain metaphysical investigations to be complete. The sciences that concern themselves with "actual reality" (*reale Wirklichkeit*) are the ones that make use of metaphysical presuppositions. "Such presuppositions are, e.g., that an external world exists, that it is extended in space and time, its space being, as regards its mathematical character, three-dimensional and Euclidean, and its time a one-dimensional rectilinear manifold, that all process is subject to the causal principle, etc."[27] This passage is reminiscent of Brentano's remarks about a natural science that must proceed on the basis of certain hypotheses. Husserl himself cites Brentano extensively on this point in an appendix to LU. He does so in a description of Brentano's standpoint, which he commends for its acuity and clarity. Phenomena are the point of departure for explanation. In such explanation, natural science makes use of "explanatory metaphysical hypotheses."[28]

In the introduction to the second volume of the German edition of LU, Husserl says that he wants to avoid all metaphysical presuppositions. Examples of metaphysical problems are: whether we must accept psychical and physical realities separate from our own ego (by which he means the sphere of experiences), "what the essence of these realities is and to what laws they are subject, whether the atoms and molecules of the physicist are part of them, and so on." "The question as to the existence and nature of 'the external world' is a metaphysical question."[29] Husserl speaks here of metaphysical hypotheses. This way of speaking should not surprise us, for metaphysics is regarded by Brentano as an inductive explanatory science that seeks to explain physical as well as psychical phenomena. Thus it is all-embracing.[30] Consequently, we can

---

[27] LU I, 11.
[28] LU III 228, 230 note 4.
[29] LU II (ed. 1) 20 (compare 2nd ed. 20); see also PSL 166.
[30] PES I 9, 27; WE 20. See also Husserl's critical sketch of a positivistic metaphysics, PSW 298 and L. Gilson, *Méthode et Métaphysique selon Franz Brentano*, 62ff.

speak of metaphysical hypotheses in place of natural scientific and psychological hypotheses. In Husserl's introduction to the second volume of LU, these terms are interchangeable.

The preceding suggests the answer to the question why Husserl is silent about the causal origin of contents and about their relation to the external world. This question is simply out of place in a descriptive psychology, for such a psychology limits itself to describing contents and their structural relations. The task of explaining these contents is passed on to physics (and physiology). What is true of contents is also true of acts, for they too are only described in a descriptive psychology. Their explanation is a task for genetic psychology.[31] Just as we refrain from using physical hypotheses in the case of contents, we stay away from psychological hypotheses in the case of acts.

Here for the first time we encounter a form of the *epistemological* reduction. The real object is left unconsidered. Landgrebe correctly writes of Brentano that all questions having to do with the real object, which ultimately corresponds to the intentional object, are deliberately eliminated at the outset in descriptive psychology.[32] This is true *a fortiori* of Husserl, who, as we saw in the preceding paragraph, is more consistent in this matter. Later we will see that the problematics of the later Husserl is closely bound up with this first form of the reduction. The exclusion in question must not be taken to mean that there is no real thing but only that for *methodological* reasons it is not discussed. The epistemological problem is not solved but only temporarily eliminated.

What was said by Brentano with reference to the end term of the intention holds in like measure for the early Husserl. The intentional object is no longer a stage on the way to knowledge but the terminus; it is an "id quod," not an "id quo." As we have seen, Husserl is actually more radical here than Brentano. The perception of the immanent content *as immanent content* is just as complete as the inner perception of the act. Thus, this theory of perception can really be called a theory of knowledge, i.e. a theory of our knowledge of the immanent object. We must then understand the term 'theory of knowledge' to mean a descriptive theory of knowledge, i.e. a theory of knowledge that places

---

[31] See below 55, 60.
[32] *Der Weg der Phänomenologie*, 12.

the question of the real object "between brackets." Husserl uses the term 'theory of knowledge' in this sense in LU.[33]

In summary we can draw the following conclusions. First, neither for Brentano nor for Husserl is the "intentional object" a medium. Intentionality is a direct relation to the object. This makes it possible for Husserl to use the term 'intentional object' in the sense of intended object in post-1894 writings, something that was not possible for the Scholastics.[34]

Second, for Brentano and the early Husserl, this object is an immanent object. Thus it is particularly misleading to speak of a "turn toward the object" in the sense of a turn toward the external world.[35] If Brentano and Husserl had maintained the Scholastic conception of the intentional object as an intentional presence that points beyond itself, such an interpretation would be justifiable.

Third, this doctrine of the immanent object leaves unresolved the problem of the relation to the external world. The relation of the intuited phenomenon to the hypothetical, theoretically constructed thing of physics is a question that long occupied Husserl's attention.

SUMMARY OF CHAPTER ONE

We encounter the theme of intentionality in the earliest writings of Husserl (as well as in the writings of his teacher Brentano) as the

[33] See below 177. One could speak of Husserl's immanent object, like the Scholastic species, in terms of 'representation.' But this must then be conceived of literally. This representation does not refer to the represented object but takes its place. It is a case of representation (*Stellvertretung*) in the sense in which Husserl comments on this concept in LU II 178, see also BZ 13 note 1. The Scholastic conception of representation can best be compared with the concept of representation that Husserl developed in 1894. In the case of a sign-presentation, e.g. the understanding of a word, we are indeed directed toward that which is represented via the representative. Our mental attention is focussed entirely on that which is represented, and we do not see – or hear – the word as sound. We live "through" it. What Scholasticism regarded as characteristic of perception holds true only for presentation via a sign, on Husserl's view. The "representations" refer to an intuition as to their fulfillment, and this intuition has nothing to do with an intermediary. It is a direct perception of an immanent object.

[34] See LU II 97 Anmerkung.

[35] See, for example P. von Schiller, *Aufgabe der Psychologie*, 71. Husserl himself appears to have been well aware of the difference between the Scholastic doctrine of intentionality and that of Brentano. In any case, he speaks of Brentano's "adaptation" (*Umwertung*) of the Scholastic conception of intentionality, PP. 247.

distinguishing characteristic of psychical phenomena. Husserl shows
that intentionality can also be used as a criterion for classifying
relations.

For Husserl as for Brentano, contents are immanent. Furthermore,
they are exclusively contents of sensory perception. Properties that are
not sensorily perceivable, such as categorial properties, owe their
existence to an act of a higher order. There is no object corresponding to
this act of a higher order. We have seen what difficulties this pattern of
though causes in the theory of numbers. From here runs a line to
Husserl's theory of categorial perception and indirectly to the intuition
of essences.

"Direction toward an object" can be more precisely described as a
possession of immanent contents. These contents are not brought forth
by consciousness but passively taken in. As yet there is no mention of
creation or sense-giving. Therefore, the theme of correlativity could not
yet be developed.

According to Husserl, an adequate perception of the immanent
content as immanent content is possible. This does not require that the
subject and object coincide.

The immanent object is the direct object and the end term of
perception. It does not refer to a reality beyond itself. For methodological reasons, the relation to the extra-mental object is not considered.

Although Husserl did not alter his theory of perception in the article
of 1894, we do find the beginning of a new concept of intentionality. In
this article consciousness is no longer a passive possession of contents
that are "simply there." What attitude consciousness takes toward
contents is of the greatest importance. In this discovery of sense-giving
activity on the level of language lies the point of departure for an
important theme of the later Husserl. It was to become ever more clear
to him that consciousness plays a role in the appearing of the object,
and that this process of constitution must be described in a correlative
analysis. In 1894 Husserl had not yet come this far. The new concept of
intentionality can only be developed when it is applied to perception
and so becomes of universal significance for the relation between
consciousness and the appearing world.

CHAPTER TWO

GENETIC AND DESCRIPTIVE PSYCHOLOGY

The themes discussed in the previous chapter all pertain to descriptive psychology. In this chapter I will show that Husserl attached himself to a certain tradition inaugurated by Brentano. The problematics embedded in the duality of genetic and descriptive psychology can perhaps be regarded as *the* driving force in the thinking of Husserl; after 1907 it finally led him to distinguish between descriptive psychology and transcendental phenomenology.

In my concluding chapter, I will trace the position which the two psychologies occupied in the whole of Brentano's philosophy. In this chapter, however, I will limit myself to an analysis of the characteristic differences between the methods of the two psychologies. The two are characterized by three pairs of oppositions: genetic psychology is explanatory, empirical-inductive and psycho-physical, whereas descriptive psychology is descriptive, a priori and "pure."

PARAGRAPH ONE. GENETIC AND DESCRIPTIVE PSYCHOLOGY IN BRENTANO'S THOUGHT

I. Genetic Psychology

In PES, Brentano writes that the purpose of explanatory psychology is the formulation of laws of coexistence and succession.[1] The method whereby we discover these laws is that of natural science.[2] Following an *inductive* procedure, we must establish general laws as "general facts."[3] Brentano admits – and this is important for our discussion – that *induction can never reach absolutely certain results.* We can indeed speak

[1] PES I 17, 138 II, 68, 81.
[2] PES I 62, 66.
[3] PES I 102ff, 105; see also L. Gilson, *Méthode et métaphysique selon Franz Brentano*, 112–158; Hugo Bergmann 'Brentano's theory of induction,' 281–292.

of high probability and even of infinitely high probability, but never of absolute certainty. Certainty and probability are not to be equated. In the case of infinitely high probability, which is "practically" equivalent to certainty, Brentano speaks of "*physical* certainty," which is then to be distinguished from *mathematical* certainty.[4]

Genetic psychology is not only explanatory and inductive but also psycho-physical: it is dependent in certain respects on physiology. That Brentano takes this to be the case, in any event, is evident from the fact that he advances this consideration as an argument to explain why a scientific philosophy (read: psychology) was so late in developing. There is a hierarchy of sciences, in the following order: mathematics, physics, chemistry, physiology, psychology. Each science is dependent on the development of the preceding science and can therefore blossom only when that science has reached a certain level.[5] This does not mean that psychical laws can simply be derived from physiological laws. Hence Brentano does not regard it as entirely correct to speak of physiological psychology, as Wundt does.[6] He prefers to think of psychology as "psycho-physical" instead.[7] Between the domain of psychical phenomena and that of physical phenomena there is an ineffaceable boundary. When we turn our gaze within, psychical phenomena form a new world. Physical phenomena and psychical phenomena are completely heterogeneous; the analogies between them are vague and artificial.[8]

In discussing psycho-physical dependence, mention has been made thus far only of physiological contributing causes. This is correct up to a certain point, but now further differentiation is necessary. It is apparent from Brentano's definition of physics that the task of this science is to explain the coexistence and succession of the contents of perception, with the help of the hypothesis of the existence of the external world. Here we could speak of an external dependence on physical factors.[9] The stimulated sense organs are themselves physiological in nature. Every outer stimulus is received into the physiological organization of the body. Husserl was later to speak of the

---

[4] VE 84, 94, 95; L. Gilson op.cit. 149ff.
[5] PES I 34, see also 260 note 22; Letzte Wünsche 38; Zukunft 95.
[6] PES I 10.
[7] PES I 65, 67, 105.
[8] PES I 66, 67, 71.
[9] PES I 17 note 2, 134, 138.

body as the "Umschlagstelle" (the locus where the physiological is transformed into the psychological) and as the organ of perception that necessarily mediates and is operative in each perception of a thing.[10] This involves some complicated problems which I cannot deal with further at this juncture. For the present I will limit myself to pointing out that Brentano gives to the physiological a certain autonomous role in influencing the psychical. In addition to the outer stimulus, there is also a dependance on processes within the organism, on organic or brain processes.

What is noteworthy here is that Brentano also refers to the latter factors as "physical processes." This state of affairs deserves the closest attention, for it reveals an essential difficulty in Brentano's philosophy, a difficulty which was also to play a role in Husserl's thought. This noteworthy leveling is readily understandable when we realize that it is a necessary consequence of Brentano's method of classification. This method allows for only two kinds of phenomena (i.e. physical and psychical), which are delimited with reference to one another. This in turn implies that all physical phenomena are somehow to be regarded as the same, although in some way or other they serve as "signs" of "organic" processes as well as of "physical" processes.[11]

The fact that the criterion for classification is taken from (the relation of) perception is of particular significance, furthermore, for it opens up the possibility of *drawing conclusions about the relation to one's own body by way of the relation to the perceived thing*. Brentano already does this when he says that physical phenomena, i.e. objects of outer perception, are signs of organic processes. This state of affairs will require our attention again in connection with Husserl.[12]

II. Descriptive Psychology

To assess the importance of descriptive psychology in PES (1874), we must look more closely at the structure of this work. Brentano's original intention was to write a book in six parts. The last four parts never appeared. Thus we must take account of the noteworthy fact that we have only a methodological introduction and a preparatory description of phenomena. The actual substance of the work is missing. *This fact is significant for Brentano's development.* The second part of

[10] Id II 56, 161, 286.
[11] PES I 87, 89, 100.
[12] See below 384.

PES has become the center of attention, although that was not what Brentano originally had in mind. This part was intended to provide nothing more than a *description* of the phenomena that were then to be *explained* in the succeeding parts. It is this second part that contains the famous definition of intentionality; it has also become widely known because of other chapters (e.g. on the unity of consciousness). As I said, this part of PES really has only a preparatory function. The intent of empirical psychology is to establish laws which explain the phenomena. But such an explanation cannot be undertaken before the phenomena are properly described.[13] This duality of descriptive and explanatory science is also to be found outside psychology. Brentano borrowed the model for this idea from natural science, where we find descriptive sciences alongside explanatory sciences, for example, a descriptive geography (geognosy) and an explanatory geography (geology).[14]

The descriptive character of this psychology has an important consequence, namely, that *all its concepts can be checked against intuition*. In other words, there are no hypothetical concepts in descriptive psychology. But in genetic psychology such explanatory hypotheses are used, e.g. the postulation of "forces" to explain sensations. In descriptive psychology every concept can be verified through intuition and thereby "clarified." Descriptive psychology is therefore the domain of the *"analysis of origins."* An example of such analysis in PES is the attempt to classify psychical phenomena. Brentano often takes ordinary, everyday language as his point of departure. In such language we already find a certain classification of psychical phenomena: we distinguish, for example, between thinking and desiring. But we must not rely exclusively on classifications embodied in language, for this sometimes leads us into confusions, e.g. when we speak of both presentation and judgment as "thinking."[15] In

---

[13] PES I 63. Consequently Brentano prefers to eludicate the concept by way of an example rather than by way of a definition, 111.

[14] Zukunft 153 note 40, 154 note 44; Letzte Wünsche 34. See also Spiegelberg *The Phenomenological Movement*, 37.

[15] PES I 45, 63, 180; see also 141, 142 on various meanings of the term 'consciousness' also PES II 3, 14, 33, 73. During his final period, Brentano went very far in his critique of language, e.g. in the interpretation of a priori judgments, see below 81; see also Kastil *Die Philosophie Franz Brentano's*, 31. The analysis of origins only takes its point of departure in language. Furthermore, it is an analysis of the phenomena by which language is measured. This analysis is not a hollow scholastic analysis of words. This charge against phenomenology was laid to rest by Husserl in PSW 304. See below 244.

such a case we must track down the origin of the concept in inner perception, in order to give the concept unequivocal clarity. Other and different examples of concepts that originate in inner experience are given by Brentano in a lecture of 1889 entitled "Vom Ursprung sittlicher Erkenntnis" (On the Origin of Ethical Knowledge). As the title suggests, this lecture is concerned primarily with the origin of the concept of goodness. According to Brentano, such a normative concept, like all other concepts, originates in concrete, intuitive (inner) phenomena.

On my view, this lecture on the origin of ethical knowledge is evidence of an important turn in Brentano's thinking. In a concluding chapter this matter will be discussed further. For the present we can draw some conclusions about the evolution of Brentano's thought from the difference in the relation of the two psychologies to one another. What strikes the student of PES most about the later Brentano is the dominant position which he gives to descriptive psychology. Whereas in PES it was only a subordinate stage preparing the way for explanatory psychology, by the end of the 1880's it had become an autonomous and independent science.

Brentano was well aware that his later achievements lay in the area of descriptive psychology. When he prepared his lecture of 1889 for publication, he wrote in the preface: "What I have presented here is part of a 'Descriptive Psychology' which I hope to be able to publish in its entirety in the near future. This work will develop some of the views that were set forth in my *Psychology from an Empirical Standpoint* and will differ in fundamental respects from everything that has previously been said on the subject. My readers will then be able to see, I hope, that I have not been idle during the long period of my literary retirement."[16] The results of this reflection of many years are entirely on the level of descriptive psychology, as Brentano himself admits. According to Kraus, Brentano first worked out this new psychology in his early lectures in Vienna.[17]

---

[16] USE 3. These are results of 'later investigations.'

[17] PES I, XVII where Kraus writes: "As far as I have been able to establish up to now, Brentano first lectured on 'descriptive psychology' during the winter semester of 1887–88, and then again under the title 'psychognosy' during the winter semester of 1890–91 at the University of Vienna." In his "Erinnerungen," 153, 157, Husserl writes that he had already heard Brentano lecture on the descriptive psychology of the imagination and the intellect during the summer semesters of 1884–5 and 1885–6.

Although the term 'descriptive psychology' is of fairly late origin, what it names already appears in PES (1874) as a preparatory stage within genetic psychology. Spiegelberg is correct in observing that "it was only gradually and after the publication of his first volume that Brentano himself fully realized the newness of his own approach."[18] On this basis, an explanation of why the succeeding parts of PES never appeared becomes possible. It is likely that Brentano only realized later what he had actually done, thereby achieving greater clarity about methodology. (This sort of thing also happened more than once to Husserl.) But this would not yet explain the dominant position which descriptive psychology assumed by 1889. As I see it, the explanation is the *new purpose* which this psychology served. In addition to serving as a preparation for genetic psychology, this descriptive psychology now also played a role in the *founding of the normative sciences*. It not only laid bare the structural laws of consciousness but also founded norms. In this psychology Brentano thus found a weapon against the rising tide of relativism and historicism. This is already clearly evident in the lecture of 1889, for Brentano's purpose was to find the norm for the good, in order to be able to combat historicism in ethics and jurisprudence.

Thus the "analysis of origins" has two functions. First, in the descriptive, preparatory stage of genetic psychology, it gives concepts a clear content. This is the function it fulfills in PES. Secondly, in the case of the founding of the normative sciences, it investigates the origin of the concepts of truth and goodness;[19] that is to say, it tries to find a foundation for norms.

Excursus. The Name 'Phenomenology'

Spiegelberg, who had access to the papers left behind by Brentano, reports that Brentano already referred to his descriptive psychology as "descriptive (*beschreibende*) phenomenology" in the course given in 1888–89.[20] Previously it had been believed that this name for descriptive psychology was first used by Husserl in LU. In any event, Brentano was not consistent in his use of this name, for he also spoke of "psychognosy." Husserl gives a special reason for speaking of "pheno-

---

[18] Spiegelberg, *The Phenomenological Movement*, 36; see also Kraus in Zukunft XIX.

[19] USE 16, 53; WE 53; see also Kastil, *Die Philosophie Franz Brentano's*, 29 and below 106f.

[20] Spiegelberg, op.cit. 27 note 2, see also 9, 16, 17, 672.

menology," a reason that has to do with the second function of descriptive psychology.[21] The name 'phenomenology' again underlines the fact that this investigation does not aim at explanation.

Stumpf combatted the use of the term 'phenomenology' to refer to descriptive psychology. He regarded it as a needless innovation. He himself reserved the term for the study of "appearances" (*Erscheinungen*). Thus by 'phenomenology' he meant a "phenomenology of objects." This meaning of the term 'phenomenology' did not prove to be important in the history of the phenomenological movement.

On the basis of concepts which have an empirical origin, *a priori* laws are then established. These laws are "grounded purely in concepts." Descriptive psychology is not an empirical science but an a priori science.

I will return later to this doctrine of a priori truths which are not based on induction but which instead are evident without induction, which are made obvious (*einleuchten*) in one stroke.[22] Here we face the question of Brentano's development again, for the theory of a priori judgments in descriptive psychology originated after PES. The famous doctrine of a priori judgments in inner perception is first to be found in a worked-out form in the lecture of 1889 on the origin of our ethical knowledge. We do not come across this doctrine in PES (1874). Nonetheless, a priori psychological judgments are *in fact* to be found in that work. To take an example, it is a law of this sort, which is "made obvious" on the basis of concepts (indeed, on the basis of the concepts of presentation, judging and desiring), that serves as the second criterion by which psychical phenomena are distinguished from physical phenomena: all psychical phenomena are presentations or are founded in presentations. Such a law is not established inductively but is an a priori certainty.[23] To this one example we could add many others; the well-known definition of intentionality, according to which every psychical phenomenon has an immanent content, likewise, is not an empirical, inductive proposition. The same holds for the law that we

---

[21] LU II (ed. 1) 18; See also K. Kuypers 'Ursprung und Bedeutung der deskriptiven Methode in der Phänomenologie.'
[22] Below 77.
[23] PES I 112, see also the notes of Kraus 268; 276 note 7; Zukunft XIX.

cannot "observe" any psychical phenomenon,[24] as well as the law that all psychical phenomena are secondarily perceived in an "additional consciousness" (*Bewusstsein nebenbei*).[25] Here we encounter another manifestation of a tendency noticed earlier, namely, that it is only afterward that Brentano gives an account of what he in fact does. A priori judgments are already fully present in PES, and therefore Spiegelberg properly remarks that the content of this "psychology from an empirical standpoint" might well "surprise the empirical psychologist in today's sense."[26] Here too the new function which descriptive psychology has assumed plays a role, for the founding of the normative sciences, in which a priori judgments play a central role, forced Brentano to reflect more deeply on this matter.

Spiegelberg calls descriptive psychology "a 'pure' psychology, i.e., a psychology free from non-psychological admixtures."[27] It is a psychology that is independent of physics and physiology. Kraus uses the term 'pure' (*rein*) in the same sense in this context. He calls descriptive psychology a "pure mental science" (*Geisteswissenschaft*). It does not treat man as a corporeal-mental being. It is the only pure mental science, "for it concerns itself with nothing outside consciousness, whereas the psychology that explains in a causal manner has to do with the physiologically conditioned 'coming about, enduring and passing away' of states of consciousness."[28] I have not come across the term 'pure psychology' in Brentano's own writings.[29] Be that as it may, what has been established thus far entails that descriptive psychology is a pure psychology in this sense, for it described only psychical phenomena. *This description does not require bringing in physiological laws.* This was only necessary in genetic psychology, since causal processes are partly influenced by physiological factors. Descriptive psychology is free of such dependence, and this explains why important discoveries have been made in this field even in the past, while physiology (particularly the physiology of the brain) is still in its infancy.

[24] PES I 41, 181.

[25] PES I 179.

[26] Spiegelberg, *The Phenomenological Movement*, 36.

[27] Spiegelberg, op.cit. 38, 50.

[28] O! Kraus, 'Geisteswissenschaft und Psychologie,' 500; see also PES I 260 note 22; Zukunft, XVIII, XIX and Kastil, *Die Philosophie Franz Brentano's*, 29.

[29] In PES, Brentano does use the term 'pure' in his definition of natural science. There too purity is a result of *abstracting* from causal factors (in this case, psychical factors). Contents must be grasped purely, i.e. apart from any conditioning by psychical factors, PES I 138.

That descriptive psychology is independent of physiology means, among other things, that when we describe contents (insofar as they are assigned to psychology), we can abstract from their possible causes in the external world.[30] Furthermore, as far as the founding of these normative sciences is concerned, purity means that we are not dependent on the development of the empirical sciences or the progress of their research, for in moral matters, as Descartes already observed, we cannot wait for the results of future research. Action cannot be postponed.

PARAGRAPH TWO. GENETIC AND DESCRIPTIVE PSYCHOLOGY IN
THE THOUGHT OF THE EARLY HUSSERL

Both PA and PSL (1894) are examples of descriptive psychology. In a "Selbstanzeige" of 1897, Husserl characterizes the latter work as pure descriptive psychology.[1] I will give one example of Husserl's procedure drawn from each work.

In PA Husserl opposes analysis that appeals to the unconscious. Brentano already regarded the unconscious as a hypothesis of explanatory psychology[2] – which hypothesis he rejected, in any event. Husserl admitted that the unconscious could perhaps explain the occurrence of a particular phenomenon, but how could an unconscious cause contribute anything to the clarification of a concept? Only "inner experience" can do this.[3]

In describing the concept of representation, Husserl also rejects all reference to the unconscious or to that which is not observed. The difference between intuited contents and represented contents is sometimes explained, for example, by the presence of accompanying contents that are not observed. In connection with this point, Husserl remarks that the unobserved contents might well condition the observed contents, but that this does not alter the fact that they are not themselves the differences perceived by us between the observed contents.[4] "Inner experience" here teaches clearly that the pheno-

---

[30] PES I 17 note 2; see above 21 and 49.
[1] Archiv für systematische Philosophie 1897, 225; see also PA 70 and PSL 182, 184, 190.
[2] PES I 151.
[3] PA 62, see also 38f, 42, 220, 222f, 227, 289.
[4] PSL 183.

menon from which the concept of "representation" is abstracted is another manner of being taken into consciousness. All of this does not mean that Husserl rejects genetic psychology as such but only that it is unsuitable for the typical task of clarification.[5]

Husserl also mentions certain laws which we came across in Brentano as a priori. In addition to the criterion for intentional inexistence, he mentions the structural law that all psychical phenomena are presentations or are founded in presentations. The latter is the case with regard to emotional acts and judgments.[6] Husserl was to take over both laws – albeit in corrected form – in LU, where they are expressly called laws about "essences." The justification of these a priori judgments later posed great difficulties for Husserl and led him to his doctrine of "ideation" or "intuition of essences." In the following chapters I will go further into the concept of analysis of origins and the problem of the a priori sciences.

[5] PSL 183, 187f.
[6] PSL 183, 187; Archiv für systematische Philosophie, 1897, 226 note 1.

CHAPTER THREE

PHILOSOPHY AS ANALYSIS OF ORIGINS

In the preceding chapter we have seen that Husserl's earliest philosophical publications must be viewed against the background of
Brentano's descriptive psychology. Husserl's agreement with this form
of analysis inaugurated by Brentano was determinative for his idea of
philosophy, which differed in basic respects from that of the early
Brentano. In the latter's PES of 1874, philosophy is the same thing as
psychology, which is in turn conceived of in a natural scientific sense.
Thus, philosophy = genetic psychology.[1] Toward the end of the
1880's, Brentano's views on this matter underwent a change, and
descriptive psychology came to the fore as an autonomous science. The
heart of philosophy now lay in a descriptive clearing up of the
fundamental concepts of the normative sciences (aesthetics, logic,
ethics). The normative pronouncements of these sciences, which are
made on the basis of their fundamental concepts, thereby receive a firm
foundation.

Husserl's early philosophy (including LU) also follows this line of
thought. The task of philosophy is to clarify the fundamental concepts
of the sciences. When Husserl attempted to provide a particular science
with a philosophical foundation, his choice was determined by his own
academic studies. His original interest was philosophy of mathematics,
particularly philosophy of arithmetic. Mathematics in turn awoke in
Husserl an interest in logical problems. LU, his second important
work, is devoted to the clarification of the fundamental concepts of
logic. But when Husserl published this work, his philosophical views
had undergone a basic alteration, an alteration bound up with a
problem that remained unresolved in his earlier work (and also

---

[1] See below 103.

remained unresolved in the work of Brentano), i.e. the problem of the justification of a priori judgments.

The course of my further exposition in Part I will be as follows. In this chapter I will look into the question what analysis of origins actually is and what significance it has for arithmetic. Then, in the following chapter, I will raise the problem of a priori judgments especially in the foundations of logic. I will devote a separate paragraph to the application of this problem to logic.

PARAGRAPH ONE. THE ANALYSIS OF ORIGINS IN ARITHMETIC

Philosophy of arithmetic has a double purpose: Husserl strives for an analysis of the fundamental concepts of arithmetic and for a clearing up of symbolic methods in arithmetic.[1] This philosophical analysis presupposes that arithmetic is incomplete in itself: it needs a philosophical complement.[2] Here we encounter Husserlian philosophical criticism of the sciences in its first form – an enterprise which was to play a very important role in phenomenology. Mathematics has blossomed in recent centuries, says Husserl, despite the fact that its practitioners were not agreed about the fundamental concepts employed. One might conclude from this that philosophy is superfluous, but this would be a mistake. The lack of clarity with regard to fundamental concepts has led to some wrong turns in mathematics itself. Proceeding from the existing science, Husserl proposes to go back to the sources, to the phenomena from which the very first concepts arise. In principle, this could be done in either of two ways. We could take the highest and most abstract concepts as our point of departure and work back to the primordial phenomena, or we could do the reverse, beginning the analysis with the fundamental concepts and then ascending to the highest results in the formation of symbolic concepts. Husserl in fact chooses the latter way. There are three stages on the path which he follows. He wants to show (1) that the fundamental concepts originate in intuition, (2) that symbolic concepts are founded in genuine concepts, and (3) that signs have their basis in symbolic concepts.

(1) The analysis of the fundamental concepts of arithmetic was already discussed in Chapter 1. We have seen that Husserl defines

---

[1] Vorwort PA and 119, 131, 151, 174; Selbstanzeige of PA in 'Vierteljahrschrift für wissenschaftliche Philosophie,' 1891, 360; see also LU I, V.

[2] See below 221.

number as a specification of the concept of plurality, and that he believes he has found the origin of the concept of plurality in the inner perception of the collecting act.[3] He traces the concept of a unity as a component of the concept of number – according to Euclid, a number is a "multitude composed of units" – back to reflection on the act of "treating as something." Husserl's analytical talents, indeed, all that is characteristic of his philosophizing, come to the fore particularly in his analysis of the concept of a unity. The analysis of origins is intended to eliminate ambiguity by checking concepts against intuition. Thus in PA, Husserl distinguishes eight meanings of the concept of a unity.[4]

(2) Symbolic concepts were perhaps even more of a philosophical problem for Husserl than fundamental concepts. He testified that all the logic of his time failed him on this point.[5] The first question that arises here is that of the justification of symbolic concepts, such as the concepts of all numbers above twelve (i.e. the numbers that cannot be checked by way of experience). Is it not absurd, Husserl asks, to base arithmetic, the most certain of all sciences, on such concepts?[6] This can only be done if the formation of these symbolic concepts is based on genuine concepts. Husserl shows that this is indeed the case. The symbolic concepts are formed by the repeated addition of one unit to an existing collection of units. We represent this via the following signs: $1 + 1 + 1 + 1$, etc. This natural series of numbers is then transposed into the systematic series.[7] Such a formation of symbolic concepts is valid – and therefore squares with any actual counting in which we might engage – because in actual collecting too, we repeatedly add one unit to that which is already there. This intuitive process – the number "in itself" – founds the symbolic process that we carry out only in thought.[8]

(3) We are even farther removed from the intuitive foundation once we have made the transition from the formation of symbolic concepts to a mechanical operation with signs. The *forming of signs* in the

---

[3] See above 23 and 30. The act of a higher order also serves as the basis for the abstraction of the concepts more and less PA 97 and of the arithmetical operations of addition and division PA 202, 203.

[4] PA 169; in LU, Husserl distinguishes thirteen meanings of the concept of presentation or "Vorstellung," LU II 505.

[5] PSL 189; see also PA 212, 292, 298; see also LU I, V.

[6] PA 214.

[7] PA 259, 268.

[8] PA 252, 258, 264, 268, 270, 291, 294.

systematic series of numbers is founded in a particular formation of concepts. The signs mirror the formation of concepts. What we should note in this connection is that in counting we can disregard this formation of concepts and operate solely with signs. Thereby *mechanical* counting originates. The concepts and rules of operation are now replaced by signs and rules about the equivalence of signs. These rules tell us how to replace complicated combinations of signs with simpler signs. (In the decadic system, for example, 10 + 1 + 1 is replaced by 12, 10 + 10 by 20, 10 × 10 by 100, etc.). The signs serve as "counters" (*Spielmarken*) with which we operate in accordance with certain rules of the game.[9]

How do we justify this technical use of "mere signs"?[10] How does it come about that the result agrees with reality when we "interpret" (*auswerten*) it, i.e. translate it back into real quantities?[11] This operating with signs is possible because the formation of signs exactly parallels the formation of symbolic concepts. Calculation by means of signs is founded in thinking by means of concepts.[12] Because signs mirror the formation of concepts, we can abstract from the process of thought. This allows an enormous saving of energy.[13] The formation of symbolic concepts already involved a saving of energy because it enables us to forego carrying out the formation of genuine concepts. Now we can also lay aside this founding formation of symbolic concepts and operate exclusively with signs.

This practical gain brings with it a loss in intuitive insight; something of the genuineness of arithmetic is lost, for we have lost sight of the source, which lies in intuition. If we wish to understand this technical operation, we must go back to the founding concepts as the "logical sources"[14] – and from these symbolic concepts we must again go back to the intuitive concepts. Only in this way is their logical justification to be achieved. Husserl wanted to emphasize very heavily that operating

---

[9] PA 269f.
[10] PA 300; see also 291, 292. In LU II 69 Husserl corrected this expression. Arithmetic is concerned not with the mere sign but with the sign taken in a certain operational value or "games value." It is not that the sign replaces the concept but that a certain games value replaces the original arithmetical sense, see also LU I 199.
[11] PA 270, 293, 300.
[12] PA 298f, 304.
[13] PA 271, 304, 323.
[14] PA 199, 290; see also LU II 70.

with signs is not the same thing as drawing conclusions from the concepts that form the basis of such operation.

Such symbolic methods are used not only in arithmetic but also in *logic*, in the so-called symbolic logic or algebraic logic that flourished in Husserl's time. Husserl had a deep knowledge of this logic and wrote an extensive discussion of Schröder's *Vorlesungen über die Algebra der Logik*. In this review he presented some serious criticisms of algebraic logic. This has given rise to the view that Husserl did not recognize the value of such a logic and even warned against it,[15] but this view is based on a misunderstanding. Husserl learned a great deal from mathematical logic. Thanks to this algebraic logic, he came to the realization that there is no essential difference between algebra in arithmetic and in logic.[16] Both involve a calculatory method which is founded in purely formal deductive reasoning. Formal logic and formalized mathematics are therefore identical in essence.[17] Husserl was later to work out this view more fully. In an article entitled "Die Folgerungscalcul und die Inhaltslogik" (The Deductive Calculus and Intensional Logic), he tried to show that such a calculus could also be applied to the content of concepts, and hence that it need not always make a detour through the logic of classes or extensional logic. In a certain sense, then, Husserl himself made a contribution to this algebraic logic.[18] Consequently it is a mistake to think that he rejected the idea of such a logic. In order to do so, he would also have to reject arithmetic, for it rests on a similar principle!

It is not difficult for the reader of PA to understand Husserl's objection to algebraic logic. He has nothing against the method as such; his objection is rather against calling this method a *logic*, for it is no more a logic than is arithmetic. Logic, after all, is the theory of correct thinking, but the calculus of logic is a method intended to spare us the trouble of thinking. The rules which it prescribes are not rules for how

[15] See A. Voigt. 'Zum Calcul der Inhaltslogik. Erwiderung auf Herrn Husserl's Artikel,' 504ff and 'Was ist Logik,' 289ff.

[16] PA 293f and 309; LU I, VI, 252, 253, Id I 20.

[17] In both cases we are dealing with pure determinations, whether of "states of affairs" or of "characteristics." These determinations can be worked out algebraically, see A. Voigt's 'elementare Logik' 120 and FTL 65.

[18] 'Der Folgerungscalcul und die Inhaltslogik,' 173; see also "Voigt's 'elementare Logik . . . ,'" 112, 113 and Literaturbericht Palàgyi, 288.

one *must* think but for how one *can* think.[19] Calculating is not thinking but a substitute for thinking.

The validity of calculation is based on the parallelism between the formation of concepts and the formation of signs. One of the tasks of logic is to point out this parallelism and thereby to found the logical justification of the calculus. If the algebraic method is to have sense, it must first be founded by logic. Like arithmetic, algebraic logic needs a logic justification. Far from being itself a logic – to say nothing of being *the* logic – algebraic logic, the "logical calculus," needs its own "logic of the logical calculus."[20]

Thus we must understand Husserl's opposition to the term 'algebraic *logic*' on the basis of his continual quest for that which is original. Algebraic logic fails to appreciate the fact that signs have meaning only as reflections of concepts. Scholastic logic, on Husserl's view, had already degenerated into a technique for drawing and evaluating conclusions. No logical laws were formulated; the logician simply pointed out how conclusions could be worked out mechanically. This was not a theory of deduction but the art of making deduction superfluous.[21] Logic and algebra are completely different theoretical fields. Thus it is possible for one and the same person to be a good algebraic technician but only moderately successful as a philosopher of algebra: the devising and application of a calculus might well be accompanied by a lack of insight into its essence and its cognitive value.[22]

My reason for devoting considerable attention to this analysis of algebra and the symbolic method is that it illustrates a tendency operative in Husserl's thinking, namely, the return to the sources in intuition. This is Husserl's "intuitionism." It is no accident that the most symbolic and indirect science (i.e. arithmetic) became the point of departure for Husserl's philosophizing. This manifests a deep dissatisfaction with the logical game of mathematics. Although Husserl certainly possessed the abilities necessary to become a good "logical technician" – his dissertation and other academic accomplishments testify to this – he chose philosophy instead. But this by itself does not

[19] SAL 246f.
[20] 'Der Folgerungscalcul und die Inhaltslogik,' 169 note 2; "A. Voigt's 'elementare Logik ...,'" 111, 119 note 1: see also LU I 10, 23, 24; LU II 70, see below 92.
[21] SAL 247; 'Der Folgerungscalcul und die Inhaltslogik,' 173, 176.
[22] SAL 260; PSL 188f; PA V.

detract from his appreciation of the achievements of mathematicians and practitioners of symbolic logic; Husserl repeatedly warns against such a misunderstanding.[23] Yet for the philosopher, such technical operation is a "meaningless activity" which is "empty of content" unless it is accompanied by insight into the logical foundation. Operating with signs is an "empty sign-game."[24]

In Husserl's earliest period, then, we already find the protest against the "emptying of sense" (*Sinnentleerung*) which the sciences have undergone. In the Krisis, Husserl's last work, this complaint is expanded into a principal critique of all the sciences that have contributed to science's loss of function by forgetting their origin in the concrete "life-world." At this point I cannot go into the significance of Husserl's theory of science in the Krisis. But an analysis of the second part of PA is of special interest because it is the only place in the writings prepared for publication by Husserl himself where we find a detailed explanation of the emptying of sense which he later diagnosed in all sciences with their "calculative thinking." The "original sense-giving of method" which Husserl calls for in the Krisis is actually carried out in PA.[25]

PARAGRAPH TWO. WHAT IS ANALYSIS OF ORIGINS?

An analysis of the origin of a concept is a description of the way in which a concept originates. Husserl presents two characterizations of this analysis of origins. The two partially coincide. One is a delineation of the process of abstraction that leads to the concept,[1] and the other is a description of the phenomena on which the abstraction is based, i.e. a description of the basis for abstraction.[2] The latter can be viewed as an application of the former, for what is important is not so much the process of abstraction itself, which is in principle the same for all

---

[23] "A. Voigt's 'elementare Logik ...,'" 119 note 1; 'Der Folgerungscalcul und die Inhaltslogik,' 169 note 1.

[24] PA 192, 197.

[25] Krisis 5, 45 ff (E 47); see also Id III 96, 97. Husserl's objection is against the one-sidedness of calculative thinking, which does teach us how to master the world but does not help us "understand" reality. He calls this the "destitution" (*Notstand*) of reason, "something which can only be overcome by going back to the origin, see below 503.

[1] PA 10, 12, 14, 131.

[2] PA 16, 28, 130, 131.

concepts, but pointing out the concrete phenomena from which the concept has been abstracted.

The important fourth chapter of PA is entitled "Analyse des Anzahlbegriffes nach Ursprung und Inhalt" (Analysis of the Concept of Cardinal Number with Regard to Origin and Content). This analysis must be conceived of as a clarification of the content via an analysis of the origin. An analysis of the content or "meaning" (*Bedeutung*) is a logical analysis. What is really at issue is not an analysis of the content but a clarification of it – and that by means of a description of the phenomena from which the concept has been abstracted. If these phenomena are psychical in nature, as they are in the case of number, the analysis is of course a psychological analysis.

What Husserl means becomes clearer when he contrasts the analysis of origins with definition. He attaches little value to definition. Euclid, he points out, gave a definition of number: a number is a multitude or plurality of units. But this definition is of little use to us, for we do not yet know what a plurality is and what a unit is.[3] When we raise the question what pluralities and units really are, we find the most diverse answers. Husserl presents many of these answers as specimens. There are various views of the concept of a unit, for example. What, then, is meant when we speak of a plurality of units? The answer to this question can only be found by going back to the concrete phenomenon from which the concept has been abstracted. Here we can no longer define but only "point out" (*aufweisen*).

Only that which is logically compounded can be defined. In the case of such ultimate and elementary concepts as quality, intensity, place, and time, definition is impossible. "What one can do in such cases is simply this, to point out the concrete phenomena from which or out of which they were abstracted and to make clear the manner of this process of abstraction." The same is true of such elementary relations as part and whole, equality, and unity and plurality. The collective connection on which the concept of plurality of based cannot be defined. It is an elementary fact which can be described only by reference to the phenomena. This description must be of such a nature that the reader will be in a position to see the basis for abstraction himself and thus to abstract the concept.[4]

[3] PA 8, 16.
[4] PA 97, 130, 131, see also Entwurf 336. According to Husserl, one must read the psychological description as a "zoological or botanical description about the object

Husserl therefore opposes the efforts of mathematicians who want to give a definition of every term. The concept of number, for example, is sometimes defined by way of the concept of equivalence. But this is an artificial construction whereby something familiar is obscured by something remote and strange.[5] What is in fact done in such a case is that a concept whose extension is identical with that of the concept of number is formed. But there is no difficulty with regard to the extension, for we already know what the extension is, i.e. the concrete pluralities. The important question is: what is the basis for the abstraction of the concept of plurality?[6] "The difficulty lies in the phenomena, in their proper description, analysis and interpretation (*Deutung*). Insight into the essence of the concept of number can be achieved only when we consider the phenomena."[7]

The analysis of origins is a recapitulation, as it were, of an original process of abstraction. We proceed from an existing fund of concepts. No new concepts are formed, but existing concepts are clarified. This procedure thus moves between two poles, i.e. the general concept on the one hand and the concrete phenomenon on the other. The latter is the basis for abstraction, the point of departure for abstraction, while the general concept is the point of departure for the analysis of origins. In the following paragraphs, both poles (i.e. the concept and the basis for abstraction), and the relation between them will be further analyzed.

PARAGRAPH THREE. THE BASIS FOR ABSTRACTION – THE ORIGIN

The analysis of origins need not always be an analysis of acts. Concepts can arise from outer perception as well as from inner perception. We have already seen that in a certain sense, the description of contents can also be assigned to descriptive psychology.[1]

As far as *external abstraction* is concerned, it is important to note that there is an ambiguity in the concept of an abstractum. In the

itself..., consequently, as an expression for something that is intuited and can only be really understood in an originary way through direct intuition." Wundt's mistake in his criticism of LU is that he looks for definitions rather than descriptions. "It is no wonder that he was continually disappointed. Does he perhaps look to a Sven Hedin for definitions of the settlements, tribes and deserts in Tibet? Surely he expects only descriptions" 339.

[5] PA 103, 107, 114, 123, 127, 129.
[6] PA 10, 67, 137.
[7] PA 142.
[1] See above 21.

analysis of contents, it appeared that an abstractum is a non-independent property of a concrete whole.[2] It is important to distinguish this abstractum from the concept that results from an abstracting activity, i.e. the concept as meaning. This is necessary especially because Husserl also speaks of the abstractum in the former sense as a concept. The attribute is then called the concept, and the bearer of the attribute is the "object of the concept" (*Begriffsgegenstand*).[3] If we take the concept in the sense of meaning, then either the concretum or the abstractum could indeed be the "object of the concept." Therefore we distinguish between abstract and concrete concepts according to whether the basis for abstraction is abstract or concrete.[4] In the same way we can speak of abstract and concrete intuition, for either an abstract content or a concrete content can occupy our attention in perception.[5]

Reflective abstraction yields specific psychological concepts, such as presentation, affirmation, denial, loving, and hating.[6] The same is true of the concepts of collective connection and unity.[7] We have seen that there is something special about the latter concepts: They do originate in reflection, but in one way or another, the contents must still remain present in consciousness.[8]

The concept of *origin* can have various meanings. It is necessary to distinguish clearly between them. Many an interpretation of Husserl's thought has gone astray because of a mistaken grasp of the concept of origin.[9] First of all, we can distinguish between a phenomenological (i.e. descriptive-psychological) concept of "origin" and a causal concept of "origin." Within phenomenology, the term 'origin' can also refer to various different things.

(1) *The origin of the concept.* What we must first understand by 'origin' is the origin of the concept, the basis for abstraction. Analysis of

---

[2] See above 22.

[3] PA 151. This ambiguity recurs in LU, see LU II 134.

[4] PA 159, 186 horse is a concrete concept; 93, 151 colour and redness are abstract concepts; PSL 166, 172; see also Id I, 28, 29, 133 where Husserl speaks of concrete essences and sciences of concrete essences. Concrete, for Husserl, is not the same as individual.

[5] PSL 167.

[6] PA 66.

[7] Husserl also speaks of psychological origin in the case of number, PA 138, 174, 227.

[8] See above 30.

[9] See below 283, 295.

origins is a description of these phenomena. Husserl uses the term 'analysis of origins' in this sense in both PA and LU.

(2) *The origin of the object*. It is also possible that what is meant by 'origin' is the origin of the object, e.g. when the object is constituted by consciousness. It is in this sense that consciousness is the origin of everything for the later Husserl. Using a phrase borrowed from Goethe, he speaks of transcendental consciousness as the "mothers."[10] Consciousness might be conceived of as "making something appear" or as creation, but in either case it can be called the origin (i.e. of the "sense" of being or of being itself). It is clear that if we are to achieve a proper view of Husserl's development, the two conceptions of the origin must be kept separate. The rise or origin of the concept from the "object of the concept" (*Begriffsgegenstand*) is something completely different from the rise of the object itself from consciousness in so-called constitution.

This constitution is of importance, however, for the analysis of origins. What characterizes phenomenological analysis (after the change in the concept of intentionality) is that object and consciousness are described in relation to one another. In other words, the clearing up of the concept with reference to the object is only possible by *describing at the same time the achievements of consciousness* that constitute this object. Conversely, the analysis of the act must be led by the object as the "clue" (*Leitfaden*). Thus the analysis of origins can well go together with a philosophy of constituting consciousness.[11] But it is not necessary for the two to go together; in PA they do not.[12] (We will see later that even in LU, the analysis of origins is not yet correlative.)

As I indicated, furthermore, we can also speak of origin in the sense of genetic psychology. All acts are caused and therefore have a *causal* origin. Thus we could speak of the origin of concepts in this sense as well. The process of forming concepts is subject to many causal factors, both psychical and physiological. The tracing of the origin of concepts

[10] See below 357.

[11] In FTL 76, Husserl himself interprets PA as a phenomenological-constitutive analysis which clarifies the concept of number on the basis of spontaneous acts that constitute numbers "in the manner characteristic of something that is being generated originaliter," see above 26. In this bringing forth, they possess the full "originality of their sense."

[12] Especially confusing in this respect is vague talk about the "origin of pre-sentations," for 'presentation' can mean either the content of a concept or simply a concept. It is likely that Frege was misled by this.

in this sense means something diametrically opposed to what Husserl had in mind. It was because of the question of the *validity* of concepts that Husserl was interested in the founding of a concept in its origin. The genetic explanation of concepts has an entirely different purpose and leads rather to a reverse result. In the area of ethical concepts, we need think only of the "genealogy of morals." This too is a method of finding the "origin of our ethical knowledge," but it is a method entirely different from what Brentano had in mind.[13] Husserl too later found it necessary to warn repeatedly against confusing genetic explanation with the logical clearing up of concepts.[14]

PARAGRAPH FOUR. THE GENERAL CONCEPT

The concept is a non-intuitive presentation or "representation." It is an intention supported by a sign (the word). A concept is the same as the meaning (*Bedeutung*) of a word. The speaking or understanding of a word can be accompanied by intuitive presentations, but it need not be so accompanied, and in most cases it is not.[1] In many cases, an intuition of what we intend simply is not possible. This may be for contingent reasons, as in the case of a number that embraces more than twelve units. The cause of this impossibility is the limited nature of the human mind. In other instances, however, the intuition is principally impossible, e.g. "round square" or "transcendent thing."[2]

We must not confuse meaning with the object intended. Such an expression as 'round square' can well be understood, even though we can never perceive what it signifies. Husserl accuses Schröder of such a confusion. Schröder calls such an expression senseless, without mean-

---

[13] Brentano's distinction between descriptive analysis of origins and genetic explanation is analogous to Windelband's distinction between the critical and genetic methods, see his paper 'Kritische oder genetische Methode?' of 1883, which pre-dates Brentano's lecture on the origin of our ethical knowledge by six years and is included in *Präludien II*. See below 108. With reference to this theory of Bretano and Husserl, Lev Shestov remarks in a humorous vein: "What is true-is true. When inquiries into descent are dropped, the tasks of epistemologists and moralists looking for absolute truth and the absolute are significantly lightened and simplified. Genealogical investigations are always dangerous for pretenders to a throne." 'Potestas Clavium oder die Schlüsselgewalt' 337.

[14] PSW 307, 318, 325; LU I, 75, 205, 206; LU II, 114; Krisis 379 (E 370); see below 216. W. Heinrich, in his review of PA, does not take this distinction into account.

[1] PA 273; PSL 182ff, 187; 'Der Folgerungscalcul und die Inhaltslogik,' 258, 259.

[2] PSL 167, 171, 173, 178, 182; PA 214.

ing. But the question whether a name has meaning is actually separate from the question whether there is an object corresponding to that meaning. 'Round square' definitely has a meaning, even though there is no such object. Expressions like 'abracadabra' are without meaning.[3]

Not all concepts are general. Alongside words that signify something general, there are also words that signify something particular and individual (i.e. proper names).[4] In a general name, there is an intention directed toward something general. Thus the general name is founding in a general representing (= concept).[5] Husserl here opposes nominalism, which seeks universality exclusively in the word as a sensory sign. A general word without a conceptual substratum would certainly be a noteworthy discovery.[6] The general name points to an object via the general concept.[7]

The nominalistic view is furthered by an improper interpretation of mechanical counting. In counting, we focus attention not on founding concepts but only on signs, a procedure that save us psychical energy. Nominalism now concludes that these concepts do not exist. The signs are viewed purely as signs, as "strokes."[8] However, the concept of oneness does have such a foundation in a concept and via that concept in an object, namely, the "act of treating as something." Without this foundation, operations with signs would be completely senseless, for their basis in concepts is their "logical justification." All of Part II of PA is devoted to the logical founding of technical operations with signs, a founding in the logical sources that make up the "sense" and "meaning" of the signs.[9]

PARAGRAPH FIVE. ABSTRACTION

Every concept originates in an abstraction from concrete intuition. "A concept without a founding in concrete intuition is unthinkable."[1] In

---

[3] PSL 171, 174. 'Der Folgerungscalcul und die Inhaltslogik,' 250.

[4] PA 215 note 1; for the general name see 83, 151, 153 note 1; 169, 186; 'Der Folgerungscalcul und die Inhaltslogik,' 250.

[5] PA 16, 82, 152, 215 note 1; see also LU II 134.

[6] PA 48, 88, 190ff, see also 258, 264.

[7] PA 171, 193, 197 f., see also LU II 68. The Scholastic adage "Voces significant res mediantibus conceptibus" (words signify things by means of concepts) could be applied to Husserl's theory as well as to Brentano's, Kastil, *Die Philosophie Franz Brentano's*, 100.

[8] PA 128, 139, 165, 193.

[9] PA 141, see above 64f.

[1] PA 84; Vorrede BZ.

what way is the general concept abstracted from the concrete phenomenon? Husserl sees abstraction as a function of the concentration of
attention (*Aufmerksamkeit*). In a perception there are always a number
of contents observed "in addition" (*nebenbei*) as well as a content which
is the object of special interest.[2] Thus abstraction is nothing other than
an application of the attention at work in every intuition. This
abstraction has a negative side and a positive side. The term 'abstraction' is usually used in the negative sense, in the sense of looking away
from. Thus Husserl says: "To look away from something or to abstract
means simply to note nothing in particular about it."[3] This disregarding is the reverse side of a looking at, a making something stand out. In
this sense Husserl says that abstraction is "taking notice of something
for itself."[4]

This looking away from or abstracting, furthermore, can be understood in various senses. Among other things, it can mean the abstracting of every material determination. The concept of something is an
example of a result of such an abstraction. Husserl later speaks of such
abstractions as formalizing.[5] In the case of the formation of general
concepts, abstraction is a disregarding of differences. To locate the
foundation for the abstraction of a general concept, we must proceed
from the members of the extension of the concept – which is simply a
matter of record.[6] In the case of the general concept of plurality, these
members are the concrete pluralities.[7] We must pay special attention to
the common element in these "objects of concepts" (*Begriffsgegenstände*). Thus the foundation of the concept is found by comparison. In
this way we form such concepts as color, continuous connection, etc.
Husserl also speaks of the common element as "homogeneous"
(*gleichartig*) and makes mention of similarities between the things
compared. It is because of their similarity that both Hans and Kunz can
be called men.[8] The result of such a comparison gives us a collection of
characteristics which typify the object of a particular concept. The
property of rationality, for example, belongs to the concept of a person.

---

[2] PSL 179ff.
[3] PA 85, see also 131, 148.
[4] PSL 167.
[5] PA 91, 186; see also LU II 285 and Id I 26.
[6] PA 10, 67.
[7] PA 12, 14, 28, 85.
[8] PA 48, 88, 89, 137, 165, 232, 235, 238.

Thus the question how we find back in intuition the content of a general concept that we intend in a non-intuitive way is answered by Husserl as follows: we find it in the characteristics which a number of intuited things – in principle, an infinite number[9] – have in common. The common element could be called the universal, the "fundamentum in re."

---

[9] PA 249; see below 86.

CHAPTER FOUR

THE A PRIORI SCIENCES AND THE PROBLEM OF THEIR FOUNDING

According to Brentano, a priori truths can be derived from concepts originating in perception. Although the origin of such a concept is empirical, the judgment that ana-lyzes it is a priori. In Brentano's terminology, it is an ana-lytic a priori truth valid for experience. I will begin this chapter with an explanation of Brentano's teachings on the question of a priori judgments and judgments "grounded purely in concepts." The latter form the background to Husserl's problems.

PARAGRAPH ONE. BRENTANO'S THEORY OF THE A PRIORI SCIENCES

Alongside the empirical sciences, which follow the inductive method, Brentano also recognizes a priori sciences. Included among them are arithmetic, geometry, the pure theory of motion (phoronomy), parts of the theory of sensorily perceivable qualities, and finally, logic.[1] Brentano repeatedly uses the expression 'made obvious (*einleuchten*) purely from concepts' to characterize these sciences. This expression was also used by Husserl.[2]

In an article on Comte, Brentano points out the difference between *a priori* sciences and *a posteriori* sciences by way of two examples.[3] The following is true of the proposition "$2 \times 2 = 4$." (1) We can see the truth of this proposition *independently of experience*. We do not need a long series of inductive inferences, for this truth is obvious a priori from the concepts themselves. There is no place for wonder in such a case. We penetrate "inside" the matter, as it were, and grasp the how and

---

[1] VE 82; Vier Phasen 164; PES III, XXVI, see also Kastil, *Die Philosophie Franz Brentano's*, 198ff.

[2] See below 241.

[3] 'Auguste Comte und die positive Philosophie,' 1896 in Vier Phasen 118ff.

why. (2) This truth has absolute, universal validity. Although it does not rest on experience, it is valid for experience.

Over against such propositions stand empirical certainties about facts, e.g. that of the law of gravity. (1) These truths are dependent on experience. We can only ascertain the actual facts of the matter, without knowing why it is so. We have no insight into the "highest wondrous ways of causality."[4] Here there can be no talk of rational truth. (2) The general law that explains appearances is nothing more than a "general fact." The law is indeed more general than the fact to be explained, but it does not possess absolute, universal validity.

The two kinds of truths could also be characterized by way of the old names 'truths of reason' and 'truths of fact.' Brentano's way of speaking of the founding of these rational truths "purely in concepts" does indeed lead us to suppose that they are truths proper to the mind as such. In these truths the mind recognizes its own lawfulness, and therefore there is no place for the surprise which is occasioned by encounters with the world of facts. In this context Lucie Gilson also speaks of an intelligibility inherent in the mind.[5]

Now, what Brentano teaches is that apodictic judgments are derived from concepts and are in this sense *a priori*, but that these concepts themselves have an *empirical* origin. All concepts originate in intuition. Thus the judgments, but not the concepts themselves, are a priori.[6] According to Brentano, "the empirical origin of the concept of number is indubitable; it is even an origin that does not afford the slightest difficulties in investigation..."[7] Thus in Brentano we already find the attempt to reconcile elements of rationalism with empiricism. This is also characteristic of Husserl's later doctrine of the intuition of essences. Brentano shares with rationalism the belief in a priori sciences. At the same time he accepts the empiricist principle that all knowledge must be justifiable on the basis of experience. Husserl was later to speak in this connection of the phenomenological principle that

---

[4] Vier Phasen 120, 121.
[5] See L. Gilson, *Méthode et métaphysique selon Franz Brentano* 109, 111, 115, 139, 141ff., 148, 160.
[6] USE 82, 111; see also Kastil, *Die Philosophie Franz Brentano's*, 57, 199 and Kraus PES III, XXIX.
[7] VE 52, 53; see also PES I 261 note 1; see also L. Gilson, *Méthode et métaphysique selon Franz Brentano*, 68, 95.

only intuition may be accepted as a final authority.[8] This "intuitionism" is already to be found in his teacher Brentano. The difference between Husserl and Brentano is that the latter regards sensory experience as the only form of experience. This causes the characteristic difficulties in his theory of the founding of the a priori sciences, as we shall see later. Meanwhile, tying these judgments to experience has this advantage, that it provides an answer to the question how truths which are not dependent *on* experience can nonetheless be valid *for* experience. Brentano calls them analytic a priori judgments – because they are ana-lyzed from concepts[9] – but this does not mean that these judgments imply no cognitive claims. Within Brentano's theory this is easy to understand, for these judgments are based on concepts which are derived from reality itself. Thus they can also yield information about reality. We must grant that known reality is not only purely factual and contingent but also intelligible, that it has necessary structures with which we become acquainted empirically. One example of such a necessary structural law is that color is necessarily linked with extension. But it is purely contingent that particular colored surfaces are sometimes alike.[10]

This empirical founding of a priori judgments raises great problems. This problematics also plays a role in the thought of the early Husserl; it was to lead him to a fundamental revision of the empiricist theory of abstraction and to an acceptance of the doctrine of the intuition of essences. Here I must raise a question: how is it possible, on the basis of one individual perception, to form a concept which is valid for all exemplars of the class to which this individual thing belongs, so that we can go on to form an a priori, absolute, universally valid judgment? How do we know that 2 plus 2 *always* equals 4, that for *all* triangles the sum of the angles equals 180 degrees, that *every* sound has certain overtones, that *every* psychical phenomenon has an immanent object, etc.?[11]

---

[8] Compare Husserl's famous pronouncement: "With someone who will not and cannot see, one cannot reach an understanding" Entwurf 335.

[9] See also L. Gilson, op.cit. 81, 106 and C. Stumpf *Erkenntnislehre*, I, 201.

[10] See also L. Gilson, op.cit. 144.

[11] The examples are borrowed from VE 53, 82 and Kastil, *Die Philosophie Franz Brentano's*, 200; see also Spiegelberg, *The Phenomenological Movement*, 60 and, with reference to the triangle, PES III 112 and LU II 153.

That this is where the problem lies becomes clear when we compare *a posteriori* concepts with non-inductive concepts. Brentano may speak of an empirical origin in both cases, but it turns out that he does not mean the same thing in each case. The formation of the concept takes place in an entirely different way in the one case than in the other. When we form an inductive concept, we establish a general fact through a comparison of a series of perceptions. The concept thus formed is limited in its validity to the perceived instances. On the basis of this concept, of course, we can formulate a law – "purely from (inductive) concepts" – but such a judgment can never go beyond what is included in the premises, and if it should do so (e.g. in the formation of hypotheses), the judgment must ever and again be tested by experience.[12]

The concepts which found a priori judgments do rest on experience, but not on empirical experience. In the case of such concepts, we have an immediate insight into the universal ground of factual occurrence – on the basis of one individual perception. When in this context we make a judgment on the basis of concepts, we do so not on the basis of inductive concepts but on the basis of pure concepts, to use an expression of the later Husserl, who was to speak of judgments "purely from *pure* concepts."[13] Brentano himself says: "On the basis of a single clear observation, we have absolute certainty here as to the universal validity of the law, and as absolute, this certainty cannot in any way be further increased. There [i.e. in the case of inductive concepts] we have no absolute certainty, but we believe nonetheless that we ought to prefer the acceptance of the law to its rejection; this belief is strengthened by the repetition of the same observation in many other cases."[14]

My critical question is: how can the empirical origin of "pure" concepts be explained simply on the basis of an individual perception? How can the same perception be the source of two kinds of sciences, *a priori* and *a posteriori*? In his response to this question, Brentano avoided seeking refuge in a Platonizing theory, as Husserl was later to do. His judgment about all triangles is not founded in an inspection of *the* triangle. Universal things do not exist, as Aristotle correctly argued

[12] VE 54.
[13] EU 409, 410.
[14] VE 81; see also PES I, XVIII.

(contra Plato). Brentano accepts the Aristotelian theory of reality, which recognizes only individual, actually existing things.[15]

Against Brentano one could use the argument – as Husserl was later to do[16] – that a judgment about the universal also implies the existence of the universal. Such a view appears to result from Brentano's own theory of judgment. A judgment, according to Brentano, is always a "positing" (*Setzung*), a "belief" – or the opposite thereof – with regard to something that is simply presented in presentation. The judgment claims that what is presented in a presentation is – or is not. It is an acceptance or a rejection. Every judgment is therefore an existential judgment or can be reduced to such a judgment. A seemingly categorical judgment (e.g. "The man is sick") can be translated into an existential judgment (i.e. "The sick man is"). If this is the case, then one could maintain that the subject of the judgment "Color implies extension" presupposes an existential judgment to the effect that *the* color (as something universal) is. But Brentano rejects this conclusion. The universal, apodictic judgment is indeed equivalent to an existential judgment, but it is a *negative* existential judgment. With regard to its implications for individual existence, the apodictic judgments is really a hypothetical judgment. It says only that *if* colors exist, they have the property of being extended. The same judgment can be expressed as a negative existential judgment (i.e. "There is no color that is not extended"). It is like a particular negative judgment, even if it is affirmative in form.[17] Whatever one might think of Brentano's theory of judgment, it does appear that his claim that only a *negative* existential judgment can be derived from an a priori judgment is correct. An a priori judgment implies nothing about the actual occurrence of that which the judgment is about. *What is presupposed here is that actual, individual existence is the only form of existence.* Husserl was later to attack this basic Aristotelian conviction of Brentano. According to Husserl, another form of existence and of existential judgment is possible. I cannot go into this matter at this point;[18] what concerns me at the moment is whether Brentano's theory is inwardly consistent.

I still have not found an answer to the question how, on the basis of a

[15] PES II 199; PES III 89, 98; WE 154; Kastil, *Die Philosophie Franz Brentano's*, 54.
[16] See below 155.
[17] PES II 56, 57; PES III, XXV.
[18] See below 248.

perception of individual facts, an apodictic judgment is possible "in one stroke" without any induction. Can such a theory be reconciled with the Aristotelian ontology? Does Brentano not appeal here to sources of knowledge that go beyond sensory perception? One can well say that an apodictic judgment is equivalent to a negative existential judgmnet, but does a negative judgment about every color that might exist not presuppose some positive knowledge about *the* color? And if every concept has an empirical origin, then there must be a reality from which this concept arises. Brentano resolutely refuses to take as much as one step in a Platonizing direction which would force him to accept entities that on his view are fictive. In the noteworthy opening sentence of PES, he does speak of an "ideal intuition," which he regards as compatible with his empirical point of departure, but this concept is nowhere clarified; we find no further trace of it in the work itself.[19]

Thus there is clearly a gap in the theory of a priori judgments. Neither can Brentano take refuge in the doctrine of the *intellectus agens*, for although he accepts Aristotle's ontology, he does not accept his theory of abstraction.[20] The question how the concept in which the a priori judgment is founded can be based on perception (which is the only source of validity) is not answered in a satisfactory manner.[21] Brentano wants to save rationalism's rational truths and the principle of experience of empiricism. But it appears that the truths of reason must be sacrified. This, in any event, is how Husserl viewed this matter.

PARAGRAPH TWO. HUSSERL'S THEORY OF THE A PRIORI SCIENCES

Like Brentano, Husserl distinguishes between *factual* and *necessary truths*. He gives a few examples of each in his analysis of abstract and concrete contents. A concrete content can be presented "as such" and apart from all the contents connected with it. But an abstract content is

---

[19] See also Spiegelberg, *The Phenomenological Movement*, 35.

[20] Brentano regards abstraction as a constuction through association, PES III 89, 94; Kastil, op.cit. 53, 57; see also 'Psychologie des Aristoteles' 133, 144.

[21] Here I am disregarding Brentano's later doctrine that in perception we can perceive only the universal. On this point see O. Kraus, *Franz Brentano*, 34, 37 and PES I 262 note 3, 264 note 7; PES III, XXVII, XXVIII. This theory, which again has its own problems, is a very late development in Brentano's thought. In a lecture delivered in 1896 and published in unchanged form in 1907, Brentano still defends the earlier standpoint, *Untersuchungen zur Sinnespsychologie* 53ff. Husserl gives no indication of being acquainted with the later theory.

necessarily connected with others (e.g. intensity with quality). The one cannot be presented without the other. This is not just a factual impossibility but a necessary impossibility.[1]

The difference between factual and logical impossibility can be further illustrated by way of the concepts of a large number and an infinite number. That we cannot perceive a large number of units as such is a factual impossibility. The reason for this is simply the limited character of our intellect. At most we can actually form a presentation of ten or twelve units. But we can imagine a perfect being forming a presentation of a large number, or even a very large number. We form the idea of such a perfect being by idealizing our own minds.[2] It follows that such a perfect being would know no arithmetic, for arithmetic and the forming of symbolic presentations serve to overcome the imperfections of the intellect. "We could attribute a genuine presentation of *all* numbers only to an infinite mind, for the ability to unify a true infinity of elements in one explicit presentation would lay only in such a mind." (Therefore Husserl does not agree with Gauss's thesis "ho theos arithmétizei" but would replace it with "ho anthropos arithmétizei."[3])

But this does not apply to the concept of an infinite number. The thought of an actual collecting of an infinite number of units is logically impossible and therefore absurd.[4] What we encounter here, then, is not a factual impossibility but a logical impossibility. Thus it is completely in line with the course of Husserl's thinking to declare that God too is incapable of this. That God is also bound by laws about essences was affirmed many times by the later Husserl. Brentano had already expressed himself in this spirit: "God himself could not make it evident to us that red is a sound or that $2 + 1 = 4$."[5]

In Husserl's early period we also find the a priori sciences divided into *formal* and *material* (analytic and synthetic) sciences. He distinguishes between two kinds of "immediate evidence."

(*A*) First, there is purely analytic evidence. This is the evidence belonging to the formal theory of deduction, i.e. to logic. The laws of

[1] PSL 246, 247, 160, 161, 163, 171. See above 23.
[2] PA 246, 247, 251, 264, 272.
[3] PA 212, 213 note 1, see also O. Becker 'Mathematische Existenz,' 508 note 2, 751.
[4] PA 246, 249; see also LU II 168.
[5] According to Stumpf, in *Franz Brentano* of O. Kraus, 100, 101; see also Brentano's letter to Husserl, WE 157.

pure deduction constitute evidence of this kind. "More precisely expressed, it is the area of pure determinations between any judgments whatever, in which, because the judgments are 'pure,' we do not reflect on the content of the terms about which we are judging." Therefore we can replace the terms of a .judgment by general signs (i.e. variables), then draw conclusions in accordance with the pure laws of thought, and finally fill in the particular meaning again. We have then drawn conclusions from particular premises purely on the basis of their form.[6] Furthermore, Husserl is also of the opinion that the application of such a doctrine about purely formal determinations is not limited to judgments. When analogous relations appear in other domains, the formal laws hold also for objects, e.g. for collections or continua.[7] A year before the publication of PA, Husserl had already come to the realization that the integral number is one of these forms of objects, and that arithmetic is consequently nothing but a systematic development – indeed, in the form of a calculus – of the implications of such a form. Pure logic and mathematics are one in essence. They are two cases of the many possible theories of form.[8]

(B) In addition there is evidence that is dependent on the particular character of the contents about which we are judging. Of such a nature, for example, are the claims that a color cannot exist without something that has color and that intensity cannot exist without quality.

Evident truths are truths that are "grounded purely in concepts" in Brentano's sense. Our not being able to think the opposite does not follow from any fact or facts about our subjective thinking; it is objectively founded. It follows from the concept of color or the concept of number or the concept of triangle. These concepts too must have their basis in perception. Here we encounter the same difficulty as in Brentano. The general concept can have no other origin than an "empirical" origin, i.e. an origin in an individual fact. According to Husserl, the proposition "$2 + 3 = 5$" is "immediately obvious, with

---

[6] SAL 244, 245, 247.

[7] SAL 263ff; PA 293; "A. Voigt's 'elementare Logik ...,'" 119; 'Der Folgerungscalcul und die Inhaltslogik' 1891, 178; see also Farber, *The Foundation of Phenomenology*, 65, 87.

[8] See W. Biemel 'Les phases décisives dans le développement de la philosophie de Husserl,' 41, 42; LU I, V, VI, 248ff. 'Number' is one of the formal objective properties, ibidem, 172, 244, 246, 253; see also FTL 68f.

evidence."[9] The basis in intuition is actually to be sought in an individually perceived instance. That this proposition is true is ultimately founded in the fact that we can perceive the three quantities, and that when we do so, we see that the one is composed of the units of the two others. We perceive this as: $(..)(...)$ and $(..,...)$.[10] But how do we know that this holds for every quantity that falls under the concepts 2, 3, and 5?[11] Can this universal validity be reconciled with an *empirical* origin?

The problem is even clearer in geometry, a science operating with ideal figures that are never intuited. Geometrical concepts are "objectives of idealizing processes and, therefore, of conceptual processes," and they are *eo ipso* not perceivable. The figures drawn manifest a certain analogy with geometrical figures, but only an analogy.[12] "The signs are merely supports for conceiving of the actually intended concepts; sensory operations on the figures, likewise, are nothing more than sensory crutches for conceiving of the actually intended operations on concepts, or else on generally presented objects of concepts (*Begriffsgegenstände*)."[13] The case of geometry is illustrative because here Husserl admits that the basis for abstraction is not to be found in sensory perception. The discrepancy between the general concept and that which can be sensorily perceived comes to light more openly here than in the case of other general concepts.[14] It is this tension between the universality of the concept and individuality in intuition that was later to lead to a basic revision of the theory of abstraction and to the doctrine of the intuition of essences. In this paragraph I will make an attempt, finally, to reconstruct the course of thought that must have led Husserl to accept this intuition of essences.

We have seen that Husserl speaks of concepts as a "union of distinguishing characteristics (*Merkmale*)." Synonymous expressions are: 'content of a concept,' 'aggregate of distinguishing characteristics,'

---

[9] PA 213.

[10] PA 98f, 202.

[11] PA 202.

[12] PSL 173, 174, 184; On the concept of idealization, see PA 230 note 1, 246, 247, 251, 264, 272, 294.

[13] SAL 248f.

[14] The doctrine of evidence presented in PSL was later corrected by Husserl in the 'Selbstanzeige' of 1897, Archiv. f. system. Phil., 225 note 1; see LU 239 note 1; see also below 235.

and 'totality of (valid) distinguishing characteristics.'[15] Now, it makes a difference whether this sum of properties is intended in a non-genuine presentation or intuited in perception. Only in the former case, i.e. in connection with "meaning," is there a real intending of the universal. In perception we do not find the universal; we encounter it only in that in which a number of things agree. Using a later term of Husserl, we could say that in perception the universal is "dispersed"; we find it back as a "dispersed manifold."[16] Although the concept is one, the extension of the concept is a plurality, and in the case of universal concepts, it is even an infinite plurality.[17] In other words, the universal is present in perception in an individual form, as the universal *in re*, but it is not present in this way in the concept. All objects that have a particular property in common fall under one concept. Thus the content of the concept is not individual but universal.[18]

This tension comes to the fore indirectly in the polemic against Schröder, who identifies "the meaning of the name with the presentation of the object named by the name." If this were correct, Husserl writes, a striking consequence would present itself, namely, that all general names would be equivocal.[19] It is apparent from this remark that Husserl distinguishes between "object" and "meaning," and also that there is a certain incongruity between the two. The meaning points to the universal. On the side of the signified object, however, we find only a plurality of concrete things which resemble one another in a certain respect. Such are the differences between them that the general name would become equivocal if it were identified with the concrete things!

Illustrating this by way of the concept of redness, we could say that there is a difference between the general meaning 'red' and the many red things. If we identify the former with the latter, as Schröder does, 'red' becomes equivocal. It would mean something different in the case of this red thing than in the case of that red thing; it would differ in meaning from thing to thing. In another context Husserl speaks of the "error" which we make when we use a general name, for in using the name 'person' we refer to Hans as well as to Kunz.[20] Thus there is no general object corresponding to the general meaning (as in the later Husserl in the LU) but only many individual objects. We could then ask

---

[15] 'Der Folgerungscalcul und die Inhaltslogik,' 1891, 171f, 185; "A. Voigt's 'elementare Logik . . .,'" 510.

[16] LU II 113; see above 75f.

[17] PA 246, 249.

[18] PA 220f, 239.

[19] SAL 250, see above 73; we find the same argument in Bretano PES III 89 and 112; see also LU II 48.

[20] PA 165.

whether a real intuitive illustration of a general concept is possible. The relation between the general meaning 'red' and this red thing or these red things is not univocal; the relation between a proper name and that which it names, on the other hand, is univocal. The name 'Hans' finds its intuitive foundation, its "fulfillment," in the concrete figure of Hans.

The concept is called a "collection of distinguishing characteristics." In this concept of a distinguishing characteristic, there is a peculiar ambiguity, an ambiguity in which a problem is hidden. In non-intuitive signifying, the distinguishing characteristic is not the same as in intuiting or abstracting, for in abstraction it is part of a concrete thing. It is a "part-content." (Teilinhalt) If this property is non-independent and thus an abstractum (e.g. color), then there is a part-content that forms an indissoluble whole together with other contents. Husserl speaks of abstracta "inherent in concreta," for abstract and concrete properties together form a whole.[21] This is clear in the example mentioned, that of color, for Husserl speaks here (following Brentano) of a special relation which he calls logical. We find that this logical relation obtains between color and redness, for example. Color is then the logical part that we find back in redness and blueness.[22] Redness and blueness in turn form an indissoluble whole with extension. Brentano speaks of this connection as "metaphysical."[23] Thus, in all these cases, we have to do with a concrete whole of which the properties are part-contents.

But the distinguishing characteristic of the concept is not a part-content. The concept of a continuum, for example, is not "contained in the presentation of every concrete given continuum as a particular part-content observable as such."[24] Although the universal content is not contained in something concrete as a part-content, it is nevertheless "derived" from this concrete content.[25] How is this possible? Is there not a special sort of abstraction going on here implicitly, a universalizing, a procedure that cancels out individuality? Is there not a disregarding not only of differences but of individuality as well? And is attention capable of such an abstraction?

---

[21] PSL 165.
[22] PA 72f, 151.
[23] PA 15 note 1, 58, 72, 88, 76f, 151, 178; see also Twardowski, Zur Lehre vom Inhalt und Gegenstand der Vorstellungen, 58 note 1.
[24] PA 14.
[25] PA 42.

In Husserl's early works, there is no mention of such a possibility, although we do find the distinction between the general meaning and the concrete phenomenon. This is particularly clear in the passage in which Husserl says that we must distinguish carefully between the description of a phenomenon and the specification of its meaning. "The phenomenon is the foundation of the meaning, but it is not the meaning itself."[26] In this connection he presents the following example. There are philosophers (e.g. Kant) who regard succession as the foundation of the concept of plurality. In the collecting of a number of units, time plays a major role, for acts take place in time. Thus time is included in the basis for the abstraction of the concept of collective connection. When we describe this phenomenon, we must make mention of time. When someone collects A, B, C, and D, he can begin with A and end with D or vice versa. Where he begins and ends makes a difference to the phenomenon. "All these distinctions," however, "are canceled by logical meaning." Whether one says "a + b" or "b + a" makes no difference from a logical standpoint, although the one or the other may be necessary from a psychological standpoint.[27] Thus time has nothing to do with the content of a concept, although it does have to do with the substratum. The same applies to space.[28] Space is certainly a psychological condition of collective connection, but it is not a part of the content of the concept. The spatial position of the units counted is irrelevant. Thus we abstract from it. Now, time and space are the principle of individuation. In logical meaning, then, we abstract also from the "here" and "now."[29] Again we can raise the question how this is possible. Is attention capable of this? When we focus special attention on a property of a concrete thing, is the individuality of that thing thereby canceled? Can we focus attention on the universal as such? Clearly, we cannot.

If the concept as general concept cannot be checked against intuition, certain consequences for the theory of the a priori sciences ensue. These sciences are "grounded purely in concepts." How can a science

---

[26] PA 28, see also 83 on "meaning in the sense of logic," see Id. 1 256.

[27] PA 210. On the distinction between the logical substance of a concept and its psychological substance, see 10, 62, 138, 244, 245, 247; (logical = conceptual 294, 297, 309).

[28] PA 34f.

[29] Time and space are the principle of individuation for Brentano PES III 91, 99 (time); Kategorienlehre 24, 71, 117, 212, 218, 246 (space); and also for Husserl. LU II 102, 123, 141, 148, 159; ZBW 422 (E 90f).

explicating concepts be founded when these concepts, having no basis in intuition, cannot themselves be adequately founded? Intuition is the final source of validity for concepts: "A concept without a founding in concrete intuition is unthinkable." How can an individual phenomenon found a general meaning?

The results of this analysis can be summarized as follows.

It appears that in his early work, Husserl, like his teacher Brentano, makes a distinction between factual and necessary truths. The latter are recognized in an immediate evidence. Husserl is caught in a clear impasse with regard to the founding of these truths. They are rooted in the analysis of concepts. These concepts have an empirical origin: they arise from an abstracting perception of physical and psychical phenomena. But it is not clear how an individual phenomenon can serve as justification for a universal a priori concept. Husserl does recognize general conceptual presentations (contra nominalism) but not general perceptions. The general intention can only find fulfillment in that which a number of individual things have in common. This identical element is present in each individual thing as a part-content. But can an immediate evidence with regard to something general be based on the perception of an individual part-content? Can the abstractum in the sense of meaning find its origin in the abstractum in the sense of the individual, non-independent part-content?[30]

In Part II I will show that Husserl's doctrine of the intuition of essences arose out of such questions. The solution to these difficulties lay in the acceptance of an ideal being alongside real being and in the possibility of intuiting this ideal being. This was a big step for Husserl to take, for it involved breaking free of his sensualist theory of knowledge according to which we are to proceed solely from outer sensory perception and inner perception. This "empiricist" pattern of thought leaves room for only two possibilities: a concept arises either from outer perception or from inner perception. This scheme had already led

---

[30] In the "Selbstanzeige" of PSL Archiv. f. syst. Phil. 1897, Husserl recognizes that this is impossible. He writes that he now sees the essential difference between the abstract content as intuited part and as concept. 'Concept' here means species or essence, and evidence must be found in it. In LU, Husserl presents a criticism of Brentano's disciple Twardowski that is actually a self-criticism. According to Twardowski, the object of a general presentation is "a part of the object intended by an individual presentation, which stands in a relation of exact *likeness* to definite parts of the objects of other individual presentations." See below 235.

Husserl into difficulties in connection with his analysis of number, but a way out in the direction of inner perception seemed possible there. In his doctrine of general concepts, Husserl makes use of a theory of abstraction (probably borrowed from Mill) which claims that the universal can be grasped via concentration of attention and comparison.[31] In LU, Husserl appears to have recognized the untenability of this standpoint. From two sides, then, Husserl felt pressure to abandon the old schema. The analysis of numbers opened the first breach in this dogma. The tensions in this theory necessitated a recognition that we can also intuit contents that are not sensorily perceivable. Once this concession was made, the way was open, as it were, for the doctrine of the intuition of essences and for an entirely new founding of a priori judgments.

Applying these conclusions to the philosophy of arithmetic, we could say that there are two unresolved problems in PA for which Husserl in LU presents closely related solutions. First, there are the difficulties bound up with the lack of objective, formal relations. Categorial perception offers a solution to this problem. In addition there is a problem that was not mentioned in Chapter I, i.e. the problem of the founding of the a priori judgments of arithmetic. These difficulties led to the doctrine of the intuition of essences.

The two problems are overcome in two phases in LU: Husserl bases the analysis of number on a categorial perception of a collectivity *and* on an intuition of essences (categorial abstraction) founded in this perception.[32] Although the concepts of categorial perception and intuition of essences are not part of the same context and find their origin in separate sets of problems, it is nonetheless possible that categorial perception was the catalyst in the birth of the concept of intuition of essences. For Husserl, these two perceptions agree in a negative respect, namely, that they break through the "sensualist" prejudice. In Part II, I hope to be able to show that it is indeed possible to understand the development of Husserl's thought in this way on the basis of his own presuppositions.[33]

[31] See below 239.
[32] See below 251 and 279.
[33] See below 151, 154.

PARAGRAPH THREE. LOGIC AND PSYCHOLOGY

In this paragraph I will again raise the problem of a priori judgments, applying it this time to the question of the possibility of logic in the broad sense (including formalized mathematics[1]), for it was this problem that forced Husserl to alter his standpoint. The purpose of this paragraph is to reconstruct Husserl's earliest conception of logic, on the basis of givens stemming from the period before 1900. Once this is achieved, I will be in a position to indicate certain connections with a future problematics.

In the foreword to BZ, Husserl defines logic as the theory of the art (*Kunstlehre*) of correct judgment. In the article of 1894 he characterizes it as theory of science.[2] These two definitions complement one another in a certain sense. The former is derived from Brentano.[3] In "Prolegomena to Pure Logic" (the first volume of LU), Husserl regards this definition as too narrow, since it does not make it sufficiently clear that logic investigates scientific judgment. Every act of inner perceiving is a judging and thus a knowing (*Wissen*) – but not a science (*Wissenschaft*). In scientific knowledge, the judgments which logic analyzes form an ordered coherence. Husserl also expressed an appreciation of Scheiermacher's definition of logic as the theory of the art of scientific knowledge.[4] Hence we could summarize the two definitions above as follows: logic is the theory of the art of correct scientific judgment. This definition is in agreement with what Husserl in fact sees as the task of logic, even in his earliest work.

The notion of logic as theory of science can be interpreted in a narrower or a broader sense. It is interpreted too narrowly, according to Husserl, if it is limited to thinking or judging in the strict sense. Logic would then do nothing more than give us directions for strict logical reasoning or deduction, as the formal theory of the syllogism does, for example. Logic must have a bearing on all the logical activities in which we engage in a deductive science. Pure deduction is only one of these activities. "The deductive sciences do not only draw conclusions; they also perform operations, form constructions, and make calculations."[5]

---

[1] See above 66.
[2] Vorwort BZ; PSL 189.
[3] *Die Lehre vom richtigen Urteil*, 1, 2.
[4] LU I 14, 28.
[5] SAL 246.

It is also part of the task of logic to investigate and justify this mechanical calculation and operation. This is done by way of the "logic of the logical calculus."[6] We have already seen that Husserl does not regard the logical calculus itself as a part of logic – except perhaps as a very subordinate part.[7] The performing of operations and the forming of constructions is based on logical deduction, for which it is a substitute. The rules by which we *can* think must be founded in the rules by which we *must* think. The logic of symbolic methods is based ultimately on logic in the narrower sense, i.e. as the theory of correct thinking.

I will now develop the implications of the concept of a theory of an art (*Kunstlehre*). This way of defining logic is closely bound up with the problematics of so-called psychologism in logic or "logical psychologism," as Husserl later called it to distinguish it from other forms of psychologism.[8] Brentano, from whom this definition derives, presents an explication of the concept of a theory of an art; it corresponds to Husserl's own explanation of the concept in his Prolegomena. It is highly probably that Husserl was dependent on Brentano in this discussion too, although he does not mention him. Brentano's lectures on logic of 1884–85, which formed the basis for the publication of *Die Lehre vom richtigen Urteil*, already contained an introduction in which he distinguished between a theory of an art and a theoretical science. During that academic year, Husserl attended Brentano's lectures on logic.[9] All sciences, according to Brentano, form a connected totality of truths. There are various principles of unity that may be operative in science. The principle of unity of a particular science could be an inner affinity, in that all the truths are concerned with the same field of investigation, e.g. in the case of arithmetic and geometry. It could also be a purpose. The truths would then belong together because they all serve the same purpose, e.g. medicine or architecture. Here one would speak of a practical science.[10]

Logic, it turns out, is a practical science of this sort. Its goal is correct judgment, and it prescribes directives for attaining that goal. Now,

---

[6] Therefore the second part of PA is also called a "logical investigation"; see also LU I 10, 23, 29; see above 92.

[7] "A. Voigt's 'elementare Logik ...,'" 118.

[8] LU II, XIII; FTL 136, 137, 138.

[9] *Die Lehre vom richtigen Urteil* 309; LU I 236; see A. Roth, 'E. Husserl's ethische Untersuchungen,' 70, where this dependence on Brentano is confirmed; see also Erinnerungen, 153. In PA Husserl also used this distinction 291.

[10] *Die Lehre vom richtigen Urteil*, 4.

judgments are acts of a psychical nature. A judgment is an act which posits something which is "merely presented" in presentation. It is an act of belief (*Glaube*). This too Husserl takes over from Brentano.[11] Thus it is clear that logic has close ties with psychology. According to Brentano, the logician must turn to psychology in order to find out what a judgment is.[12] Husserl made it known that he had attended a lecture on elementary logic given by Brentano. Under this title Brentano presented "basic elements of a descriptive psychology of the intellect."[13] Husserl also regarded the descriptive study of psychical phenomena as of great importance and was himself the author of some "psychological studies toward an elementary logic." Logic is distinguished from psychology in that it deals with *correct* judgment. Such a view indeed presupposes a norm by reference to which the judgment can be judged. Husserl speaks of a "canon."[14] Where do we get this norm? Brentano answers – at least implicitly – that we get it from psychology, for the logical norm is derived from an analysis of *psychological* concepts. The attempt to found the norms of logic in psychology is called "psychologism." Husserl later became famous for combatting this psychologism in his "Prolegomena to Pure Logic." On his view, the roots of the laws of logic lie not in psychology but in pure logic as an ideal science.

But we must not assume without question that Husserl's arguments against psychologism were directed against his teacher Brentano and thus against his own earlier view.[15] It is important to distinguish between the various forms of psychologism.[16] In LU, Husserl understands by psychologism the attempt to base logic on *genetic* psychology. When Husserl combatted psychologism, he had in mind thinkers like Sigwart and John Stuart Mill, who regard logical laws as bound to the actual nature of the human mind. Thus Mill, for example, regards the principle of contradiction as a generalization of the empirical fact that opposed acts of "belief" cannot coexist.[17] Thus he

---

[11] PA 66, 47; Selbstanzeige PSL Archiv. f. system. Phil., 1897, 226 note 1.

[12] *Die Lehre vom richtigen Urteil*, 4.

[13] Erinnerungen, 153.

[14] SAL 247.

[15] After V. Delbos in 'Husserl, La critique du psychologisme et sa conception d'une logique pure,' 687 and R. Sokolowski, *The formation of Husserl's Concept of Constitution*, 40.

[16] See below 271, 300.

[17] LU I 79.

derives a universal, apodictically valid law from a fact of experience. The absurdity of this view was demonstrated at length by Husserl.[18]

Now, Brentano and especially his fervent apologist Kraus have tried to show that the rejection of this psychologism was really nothing new when compared with Brentano's own views. On this point there was a fair amount of misunderstanding between Brentano and Husserl. Brentano thought that Husserl's critique was directed partly against him, and he vigorously defended himself against it.[19] His defence was not without justification, for Brentano never maintained a psychologism à la Sigwart and Mill. In the lecture on the origin of our ethical knowledge, we already find Brentano combatting Sigwart. The truth of a judgment is not determined by a psychological law, and therefore evidence cannot be described as a "feeling of compulsion." It is entirely possible for me to feel compelled to accept the truth of a particular judgment, but this does not yet guarantee the truth of that judgment. A thinker who does not believe in indeterminism – and Brentano does not – must regard every judgment as necessary in a certain sense, but he need not regard every judgment as true.[20]

In his Versuch über die Erkenntnis of 1903, Brentano calls the attempt to base the principle of contradiction on induction an "astounding error."[21] In a letter to Husserl in 1905, he writes that psychologism comes down to Protagora's thesis to the effect that man is the measure of all things. The logical norm is made dependent on the contingent organization of the human mind. "I join with you in pronouncing my anathema against this."[22] In a note to the 1911 edition of PES, Brentano writes that he has always made a sharp distinction between law in the sense of law of nature and law in the sense of norm. "Indeed, no one before me and no one after me – not even Husserl – would have been able to express himself on this matter more clearly and with greater emphasis than I have done."[23] In the 1889 lecture on the origin of our ethical knowledge, Brentano laid great emphasis on the difference between the empirical sanction of a command (e.g. through custom) and the "natural" sanction attaching to a law of logic. This

---

[18] See below 217f. In PSW, Husserl compares it with making water flow from a rock (ex pumice aquam), 326.
[19] See also Spiegelberg, The Phenomenological Movement, 49.
[20] USE 66.
[21] VE 57f.
[22] WE 157.
[23] PES II 181 note 1.

difference was properly pointed out by Kant (among others), he claims, but unfortunately it "was not properly understood" on the part of many, "including many adherents of the empirical school to which I myself belong." He points to John Stuart Mill in particular as one of the members of the empirical school who made this error.[24] But such insights are actually much older. Brentano was *always* an anti-relativist. Stumpf claims that as early as 1869, Brentano concluded that what is evident for our understanding is evident for every possible understanding. "Thus he was many miles removed from the psychologism that seeks to derive logical necessity from psychological necessity."[25]

When Brentano derives norms from psychology, it is from *descriptive, a priori* psychology! The principle of contradiction is an example of an a priori law "grounded purely in concepts." Thus it is one of the laws that is a priori despite the fact that its formulation is grounded in a fact of experience. The concepts from which this judgment arises are the following: judgment, evidence, difference in the quality of judgment (affirmation and denial). The judgment which is formed on the basis of these concepts reads: if two judgments contradict one another, they cannot both be true. These concepts have an empirical origin in the inner, individual experiencing of an evident judgment. Yet on this basis I can make the following *negative apodictic* judgment: every judgment which conflicts with an evident judgment is untrue.[26] Brentano thus believes that he can maintain the objectivity of truth without taking refuge in a doctrine of ideal "truths in themselves," which he regards as fictitious. To use the terminology of Husserl's LU, a priori truths stem from the "psychological concept" and not from the "logical concept" (i.e. from the act and not from the eidos of the act).[27]

To speak of the standpoint of Brentano (and that of the early

---

[24] USE 13, 49.

[25] In O. Kraus', *Franz Brentano*, 101.

[26] Kastil, *Die Philosophie Franz Brentano's*, 200, 89, 90; USE 21, 70; *Die Lehre vom richtigen Urteil* gives the formulation of the period after the "crisis of immanence"; it is impossible that someone who denies something that another sees with evidence denies it justly 175, see also 192.

[27] Kraus claims that Brentano's standpoint is a synthesis of Plato and Protagoras. The norm comes from the subject (Protagoras), yet not from any subject whatever but only from a subject judging in an evident manner. Not man as such but man judging in an evident manner is the measure of all things USE XII; PES III, XXV, XXVII and I, LXI.

Husserl) as psychologistic is not at all to say that these two thinkers reduce logical laws to empirical psychological laws. Brentano is in full agreement with Husserl's demonstration of the absurdity of this position in LU. But when I speak here of psychologism from the standpoint of LU, this charge has to do with the *founding* of the laws of logic. It is proper to seek the origin of the concepts in which these laws are founded in an a priori descriptive psychology. In this respect Brentano is not being reproached. But in his reflection about the basis of these concepts, Husserl came to the conclusion that a distinction must be made between the individual fact and its essence. The real source of the concept lies in the inspection of the essence. In the case of the founding of logical laws, this means that we must distinguish between the psychical act and its eidos (or between the psychological concept and the logical concept).[28] In LU, then, it is Husserl's view that the laws of logic can be founded only in a descriptive *eidetic* psychology.

[28] See below 273.

CHAPTER FIVE

BRENTANO AND HUSSERL

In this chapter I will examine the philosophy of the early Husserl against the background of the development of Brentano's thought. Just when Husserl became one of Brentano's students, Brentano's thought took a new turn which provided the point of departure for Husserl's own development. Then, in Chapter 6, I will present a brief characterization of Husserl's first period, followed by a few critical observations about the literature on the early Husserl.

PARAGRAPH ONE. HUSSERL'S STUDENT YEARS – THE ENCOUNTER WITH BRENTANO

Husserl did not become acquainted with Brentano until his student years were almost over. In 1876 he came to Leipzig to study at the university there and stayed for three semesters. In addition to studying physics, astronomy and mathematics, he also attended lectures on philosophy given by Wundt, who had little to say to Husserl. In April of 1878 he transferred to Berlin, where he studied under Kronecker and Weierstrass. Through the influence of the latter, Husserl gave up astronomy and devoted himself completely to mathematics.[1] Kronecker, who also taught philosophy of mathematics, first aroused Husserl's interest in philosophy. Both of these teachers at Berlin regarded the integral number as the basic concept of mathematics – and we find the same view in Husserl's PA. The point of departure for Husserl's psychological observations was the clarification of the concept of an integral number, and he referred to both of these teachers

---

[1] The following givens are taken from A.D. Osborn, *The Philosophy of Edmund Husserl in its development from his mathematical interests to his first conception of phenomenology*, 1934. This work was reprinted in 1948 under the title *Husserl and his logical investigations*, 5, 15, 24.

in this connection. Husserl's awakening interest in philosophy was also due in part to Friedrich Paulsen, particularly his lectures on ethics.[2]

Husserl left Berlin in March of 1881 to work on a dissertation under Leo Königsberger at Vienna. He received the doctorate on January 23, 1883. The title of his dissertation was "Beiträge zur Variations-rechnung." He then returned to Berlin, where he spent the winter semester of 1882–83 as an assistant to Weierstrass. The latter was ill during the winter of 1883–84. Husserl then went to Vienna to study philosophy, and there he first met Brentano.[3] Husserl informs us that he originally went to Brentano's lectures only out of curiosity, for he wanted to see the man who had created such a stir. The impression that Brentano made on Husserl was overwhelming; Husserl testified to this eloquently in his "Erinnerungen an Franz Brentano." It was under Brentano's influence that Husserl came to see philosophy as his life's vocation. "At a time when my philosophical interests were on the rise and when I hestitated between remaining in mathematics as my life's vocation and devoting myself entirely to philosophy, Brentano's lectures settled the issue."[4] It was not only the fascinating personality of Brentano but also his method, the acuity of his way of posing problems and his clarity in solving them, that stirred Husserl. It was from this example that he drew the courage to make philosophy his life's vocation, for he now saw that philosophy too is a field for serious labor and could be treated in the spirit of a rigorous science. He very much admired the penetrating argumentation, "the analysis of

---

[2] Husserl spoke of the philosophical influence of Paulsen as "deep and lasting," see L. Kelkel and R. Schérer, *Husserl, sa vie, son oeuvre*. These authors worked from givens in the unpublished correspondence. Ziegenfuss writes of Paulsen's ethics that it paid tribute to the natural scientific way of thinking and quotes Paulsen as follows: "It seems to me beyond doubt that ethics, from the standpoint of its method, is related more closely to natural science than to mathematics, and that it is closest to the biological sciences." Thus ethics establishes actual coherent structures ascertained in experience. In the person of Paulsen, then, Husserl had already come into contact with natural scientific positivism. Also typical of the philosophical climate of Berlin is an anecdote told about Weierstrass. The philosophy of German idealism, in particular that of Hegel, had fallen into such disrepute that Weierstrass, who was Hegel's son-in-law, had to hang a sign in his office which read: "Hegel is not to be reviled her." A. de Waelhens, *Existence et Signification*, 9.

[3] Husserl himself says in his "Erinnerungen": "At that time (i.e. when he became acquainted with Brentano) I had already completed my university studies and was still a beginner in philosophy, which was my minor field for my doctorate in mathematics," Erinnerungen 153.

[4] Erinnerungen 153, 154; see also the passages on the choice of a vocation. It seems to me that these pages should be regarded as autobiographical, PSW 334.

equivocation, the tracing of all philosophical concepts back to the ultimate sources in intuition." He spoke particularly highly of the seminars which were continued long after hours in Brentano's home with a small circle of students. Brentano even took Husserl along on a summer vacation at the Wolfgangsee, where they took walks together and made boat excursions. Thus the contact between them was not only academic in character but also of a personal nature.[5]

Despite this close contact, there were few letters exchanged between Brentano and Husserl. Husserl's own explanation for this is important for the further development of their relationship. Despite Husserl's high regard for his teacher, it was not his lot to remain a member of his school. Brentano was very sensitive to any departure from his views. Husserl informs us that Brentano did become unreasonable toward him and that he found this very painful. Furthermore, Husserl hesitated to reveal new ideas that were not yet entirely clear in his own mind, especially to such a "logical master" as Brentano, who would often win out in a debate through his "masterly dialectic," but without satisfying his former student by his display of acuity. Thus, a certain distance on academic matters grew up between the two, although their personal relationship remained good. Husserl dedicated his PA to Brentano "in heartfelt gratitude."[6]

Husserl only attended Brentano's lectures for two years, including only two full semesters (the winter semesters of 1884–85 and 1885–86). In 1886 Husserl went to Halle to write an inaugural dissertation (which would qualify him as a university lecturer) under Stumpf. After becoming a Privatdozent (lecturer) in 1887, he visited Brentano once more during the summer vacation. After that the two did not meet again until the year 1908, in Florence.[7] On that occasion they also

[5] Erinnerungen 153, 156, 161ff.

[6] Erinnerungen 160, 163f. Husserl always held his teacher Brentano in high esteem. His good friend Stumpf writes: "Yet I know that Husserl, at least, who in his later works moved very far away from Brentano's ideas on the future and salvation of philosophy, was even farther removed from any underestimation of the power and fullness of the seeds scattered by his teacher." 'Erinnerungen an Franz Brentano von Carl Stumpf' in O. Kraus,' *Franz Brentano*, 144.

The dedication of PA to Brentano is itself a noteworthy story. Brentano discouraged it, on the grounds that it would bring the hatred of Brentano's own enemies down on Husserl. Husserl nevertheless went ahead with his intention, which Brentano only discovered fourteen years later. Husserl himself was also subject to philosophical absent-mindedness. In the article in Ziegenfuss written by Fink and authorized by Husserl, we read that LU was dedicated to Brentano. It was really dedicated to Stumpf.

[7] Erinnerungen 165.

talked a great deal about philosophy. Husserl tried to make his phenomenological method and his struggle against psychologism somewhat clear to Brentano, but the two did not achieve an understanding.

From Husserl's own testimony, it appears that two things in Brentano's method impressed him in particular, namely, Brentano's tracing of all concepts back to their basis in intuition and his sharp, dialectical manner of thinking and arguing a point. Yet we shall see that he did not value both in the same way. Although he was impressed more by Brentano's argumentative skill, it was the latter's intuitive analysis that really took root. On the basis of this principle of intuitive analysis, Husserl raises a cautious criticism of Brentano: however "deeply penetrating and often brilliant his analysis, he nevertheless made the transition from intuition to theory relatively quickly." We have already noted that Brentano was often able to suppress opposition by means of his skill in arguing, even though his opponent might be based on original intuitions.[8] As an example of an "artificial" theory of this sort, Husserl pointed in LU to Brentano's theory of "additional consciousness" (Bewusstsein nebenbei). In his theory of apodictic judgments, Brentano had also explained a phenomenon away, i.e. the perceiving of the universal. The same could be said of his analysis of time.[9]

Husserl was later to find fault with Brentano first and foremost for his "naturalism."[10] The ideal of rigorous science was oriented toward the exact natural sciences. Thus Brentano could have no appreciation whatever for German idealism; to him it was not science but mysticism. Husserl shared this view at first. It was only much later, he says, that he discovered that although idealism is not scientific, its motives are nevertheless to be highly appreciated. It was then his view that correct suppositions and intuitions were present in the thought of Kant and the post-Kantian German idealists. What they lacked was a scientific method. That Brentano did not see the greatness of these thinkers but regarded their philosophy as pure degeneration was a result of his special conception of rigorous science, according to Husserl.[11] When

[8] Erinnerungen 158, 160f; See also Stumpf, ibid. 93.

[9] LU II, (ed. 1) 14, 334; ZBW 378 (E 34f).

[10] For Husserl's view on Brentano, see PSW 304; Id. I 174; Id. III 59; Entwurf 339; FTL 217, 231; Nachwort 155; CM 79, 86 note 1, 115, 170; Encyclopaedia Britannica-article, Husserliana IX, 247, 249, 269. Like Husserl's 'Erinnerungen,' all of these statements stem from the transcendental-idealist period.

[11] Erinnerungen 159, see also 148.

Husserl wrote this comment in 1919, he regarded the transcendental-phenomenological method as the only rigorously scientific method. It is this method that can elevate the groping motives of idealism to the level of rigorous insights.[12] But this new idea if rigorous science has points of contact with Brentano's own motives, particularly with his "intuitionism."[13]

PARAGRAPH TWO. BRENTANO'S DEVELOPMENT

I. The Positivistic Period

Despite the fact that Brentano and Husserl went their separate ways in philosophy, there is an important similarity between their lives, namely, that both began with an awareness of the crisis in philosophy. This sense of crisis forms the background to their will to reformation and their consciousness of a mission. In 1930 Husserl wrote about the despair of someone who "has the misfortune to have fallen in love with philosophy and is already as a student and beginner faced with the confusion of philosophies and has to make a choice, but then becomes aware that he really has no choice, for none of these philosophies have sought a genuine presuppositionlessness and none have arisen from the radicalism of autonomous self-justification, which is the radicalism demanded by philosophy."[1]

Brentano's experiences were similar. In his youth he already got a taste of the chaotic state of philosophy in his day. He grew up at a time when the crisis of the classical German idealist systems was becoming ever more acute. It appeared to him that the philosophy of Schelling was nothing more than a "playground for wild fancies." Brentano called the speculation of Hegel "the ultimate degeneration of human

[12] Nachwort 139.
[13] The slogan 'philosophy as a rigorous science' must be interpreted *historically*. The same holds for the phrase 'to the things themselves.' These adages take on a different meaning in each phase of phenomenology. For Brentano, the latter originally meant "to the fact" (*Tatsachen*) – as opposed to the "wild fancies" of idealism. 'Phenomenon' thus means fact see the article on Comte, Zukunft, 112f, 158 noot 8. In PSW, Husserl says that the slogan 'to the things themselves' was first raised in the modern period in opposition to the hollow word analyses of Scholasticism. It was interpreted wrongly as meaning "to the facts" and as denying the existence of essences. In no case must the slogan be reed as a return to realism, as a reaction against a philosophy of subjectivity. What the slogan means is that we must direct ourselves toward the given. In LU, this given is primarily consciousness! Here "experiences" are the "things themselves," Entwurf 117. In Ideen I, the slogan indicates an analysis of transcendental consciousness, 180.
[1] Nachwort 163.

thinking."[2] He gave eloquent expression to this mood of despair in his inaugural lecture at Vienna in 1874, which dealt with "the grounds for discouragement in the area of philosophy." What is discouraging about philosophy is not only the division between philosophers but also the lack of any development. Brentano draws an unfavorable contrast between philosophy and the natural sciences, for the latter manifest a gradual progress. The success of these sciences has the effect – among others – of undermining confidence in philosophy. In the natural sciences, knowledge signifies power. But philosophy has shown itself to be completely fruitless in practice.[3]

Thus the situation in philosophy is characterized by two facts: the breakdown of idealist philosophy and the success of the natural sciences. Were these developments to bring about the end of philosophy? According to Stumpf, Brentano was already tormented by this question in his youth, but by the time he reached the age of 22, he had found the solution in principle. The solution lay in his discovery of analogous situations in the past. There too it had come about that philosophy, which was once held in high esteem, had gradually degenerated. This led to the idea of the four phases in the history of philosophy. This idea of the four phases proved to be an illuminating and saving idea for him.[4] What this theory boils down to, in brief, is that the history of philosophy represents a spiral movement. Each spiral begins with a period of bloom, which is followed by three periods of increasing decay. When philosophy reaches the depths of the most extreme decay, it is re-born and the cycle begins anew. History thus gives us reason to hope for a new period of bloom. That the philosophy of idealism has been discredited should not discourage us but should instead cause us to rejoice. It indicates that there is an awakening desire for genuine science. Furthermore, we may take it that the new period that is dawning will not again be followed by periods of decay, for philosophy has now found its *true method*. What is this true method?

The procedure by which Brentano hopes to deliver philosophy from its horrible state is as simple as it is effective. Philosophy has fallen into disrepute through the rise of the natural sciences. Well then, let philosophy take over the method of these sciences. Thus in 1866, on the occasion of his habilitation, Brentano already put forward the famous

---

[2] Vier Phasen 91, 23.
[3] Zukunft 87ff.
[4] Erinnerungen 89, 90; Vier Phasen 5ff.

thesis: "The true method of philosophy is none other than that of the natural sciences."[5] Just as within the sphere of the natural sciences, astrology and alchemy had to make way for genuine science, idealist philosophy will be replaced by a scientific positive philosophy. This philosophy must not seek to penetrate to the essence of things but must patiently observe appearances and in this way seek to arrive at universal laws. The philosopher does not possess an all-penetrating eye in the style of Schelling's intellectual intuition, whereby he is able to see what nature is in essence, by-passing the inductive method.[6] When philosophy follows the example of the natural sciences, all the objections now raised against it will fall by the wayside. The dividedness of philosophy will disappear and be replaced by the one philosophy, which will make the same gradual progress as the one natural science. The golden age of philosophy is not behind us but ahead of us.

The question arises whether philosophy would not then coincide with natural science. Would it still have a territory of its own? Brentano does not regard this as a major difficulty. He simply equates philosophy with psychology. Psychology is the basic philosophical discipline, of which all the other philosophical disciplines (ethics, logic, aesthetics) are subdivisions.[7] Like Comte, Brentano sees the relationship between the various sciences as hierarchical. There is an order of increasing complexity in the sciences, such that the development of the later sciences is dependent on that of the earlier sciences. The order is as follows: mathematics, physics, chemistry, physiology, psychology. Mathematics developed in antiquity, physics in the seventeenth century, chemistry still later, and physiology, according to Brentano, first begins in our era. It is no wonder, then, that it took so long before a genuinely scientific psychology was born. Thus it would be too early to expect this science to give us results significant for practice. These results will come in time: Brentano was fully confident of a brighter future in this regard. If psychology goes about its work using the methods of the natural sciences – by seeking universal laws on the basis of the perception of facts – a new future will dawn for mankind.

[5] Zukunft 137.
[6] Zukunft 89, 95, 119.
[7] See above 62.

Brentano speaks about this in PES, which appeared in 1874. This psychology from an empirical standpoint is of great value because it is the basic philosophical discipline. One of the results of a better psychology would be progress in art. Logic too is dependent on psychology for its development. Psychology must likewise lay the scientific foundation for educational theory as applied to both the individual and the community. "Thus it appears to be the basis condition for the progress of mankind. . . ."

Because psychological theories have never been applied in a thorough way in the area of politics – since politicians were not in possession of the knowledge required – one could say that history has not yet seen a great statesman, just as there could not have been great physicians before the development of physiology. Up to now political leaders have been "blind empirics." But great abuses in society could be corrected if proper psychological diagnoses could be made and the laws according to which psychical states change could be known. Only psychology can provide us with the wherewithal to combat the decline by which civilization is repeatedly threatened. The illnesses of nations have often turned out to be fatal because of the absence of good physicians. For the future, however, we may hope for the best. The social conditions that cry out for reformation – even more than the imperfections in shipping and railways – have directed all scientific attention toward psychology. Many investigators have set for themselves the goal of tracing psychical laws. Brentano concludes his hymn of praise to psychology and its possibilities with the declaration: "We could, as other have already done, characterize psychology in this sense as the *science of the future*, that is, as the science to which the future belongs (rather than to any other theoretical science), the science which will shape the future more than any other science, the science which all other sciences will serve in the future and to which they will be subordinated in their practical application."[8]

The thesis that the true method of philosophy is none other than that of the natural sciences has a clear programmatic significance. Brentano spoke of a universal revolution.[9] He could not disguise his pride when he testified to the response which students give his new method. When he first began to teach at Würzburg in 1866, the chair of philosophy was held by a follower of Schelling and Baader. "The lecture hall was empty, and on the door the word 'sulphur factory' was written in large letters, in the hand of a bold student." But as soon as Brentano began to teach these immature beginners, he aroused their interest, and by the time he left Würzburg six years later, no lectures attracted as many students as those in philosophy. "I still see the young people before me; they often sat so closely crowded together that their elbows got in the way as they wrote."[10] In Vienna it was no different; we can well imagine

8   PES I 6, 28, 30, 36, 259 note 17; PES II 68.
9   Zukunft 12.
10   Zukunft 15.

the young Husserl sitting between these students, listening to the esteemed master. The elevated sense of mission that Husserl encountered in Brentano was supported by his confidence in the new method. "his self-confidence was complete," Husserl testifies, and then adds: "I would almost characterize this simple conviction of his mission as the primal fact of his life."[11]

This reformation of psychology is comparable to what took place in the natural sciences in the seventeenth century, when scientists learned to discover and govern the regularities of nature not through abstract speculation but through exact perception and the formation of verified hypotheses. "Natura non nisi parendo vincitur." This maxim of Bacon from the beginning of the modern period could also be called Brentano's leitmotif, although for him it held not for nature in the narrower sense but for human nature: "Natura *humana* non nisi parendo vincitur." In psychology too, knowledge is power, a power that must be applied to the regulation of political relationships and the correction of social abuses.

The philosopher must play a leading role in human progress. Stumpf mentions Brentano's idea of "the higher calling of philosophy for the education of mankind." From philosophy Brentano expected – if not a new religion – at least a renewal of the religious consciousness of those who are educated and cultured, and through them a renewal of the religious consciousness of the masses.[12] In the later Husserl we encounter an equally powerful sense of high cultural calling. At the end of his life, Husserl was to speak of philosophy as the sustaining power in the "rational construction of a new humanity" and of the philosopher as the "functionary of mankind."[13] But what a difference there is in the means by which these two thinkers pursued this goal! One could read Husserl's entire Krisis as a protest against the method of Brentano, against the exclusive position claimed by the experiential sciences, against their preoccupation with "prosperity," against the positivistic narrowing down of the science ideal of the Renaissance, against the "superstition" of naturalistic ideals – in short, against making natural science a model for philosophy.[14] How such a

[11] Erinnerungen 160.
[12] Erinnerungen 116. Stumpf relates that it was originally Brentano's view that the philosopher should remain unmarried because of his high calling, but that he later broke with this self-made dogma.
[13] Krisis 4, 15, 356, 154 (E 6, 17, 151); see below 494.
[14] PSW 335f.

development was possible within the phenomenological movement is one of the intriguing questions which I will attempt to answer in this study. But before I can take up this question, I must examine the question to what extent this development arises out of motives in Brentano's own thought.

II. Phenomenological Tendencies

In Chapter 2 § 1 and in the beginning of Chapter 3, I already pointed to the turn in the thought of Brentano.[15] An indication of the change in his thinking is the autonomous position assumed by descriptive psychology. This psychology took on a new function, namely, the founding of the normative "Geisteswissenschaften" (mental sciences). I expressed my conviction that for Brentano, this new function was a means of combatting historicism, which was then on the rise.

That this is indeed the case is apparent from the context in which Brentano first published the new results in descriptive psychology. He did so in his lecture on the origin of our ethical knowledge. The topic of this address was the question of the existence of a so-called natural law. The original title was "Von der natürlichen Sanktion für recht und sittlich" (On the Natural Sanction for the Right and the Ethical). Brentano was responding to a lecture of Jhering entitled "Ueber die Entstehung des Rechtsgefühls" (On the Origin of the Sense of Right). Jhering had denied the existence of natural law. The problem was formulated by Brentano as follows: can there be a law which, in contrast with the arbitrary dictates which those in power may happen to lay down, is "known to be correct and binding in and of itself by virtue of its own nature"?[16] Brentano answers emphatically in the affirmative. On his view there is moral truth which is independent of any ecclesiastical or political authority and is taught by nature itself; there is a moral law which is "universally and incontestably valid – valid for men in all places and at all times, indeed, valid for any being that thinks and feels."[17] Natural law is then based on this natural moral law.

How can this moral law be known? How do we arrive at knowledge of that which is good in itself? Here Brentano points to descriptive psychology. The origin of the concept of goodness is to be found in

[15] See above 56.
[16] USE 7.
[17] USE 9.

inner perception. In inner experience we encounter judgments that are
evident in themselves. There is an analogy to this within the class of
emotive acts, namely, the phenomenon of "love characterized as
correct." Just as there are blind and evident manner of judging, there
are blind and correct manners of desiring. The correct manner is
characterized by an "inner correctness," an inner evidence, which is the
ultimate source of our knowledge of goodness. When we experience
this love within us, we know immediately what is good; we know this
"at one stroke without any inductive inference."[18]

I cannot go further into Brentano's theory at this point, but it is clear
from what has been said that he regards descriptive psychology as a
defence against the relativistic historicism of the so-called historical
school of law. In sharp reaction against the Englightenment, which has
proceeded from the postulate of a natural law valid for all times and
places, the historical school had directed its attention to the genesis of
law, which was at the same time regarded as the basis for the ethical
justification of law. When combined with nationalistic motives, this
approach could lead to a glorification of the power state. The basis for
authority was sought not in the right or in morality but in positive
dictates, as Brentano put it.

Through his defence of an a priori norm, Brentano became part of a
back-to-Kant movement – despite his critique of Kant's idealism, with
which the decay of modern philosophy begins.[19] I think here in
particular of neo-Kantianism, which (through the person of
Windelband) opposed the "genetic method" in the mental sciences. The
origins of the historical forms of morality and law can be explained or
understood by way of a genetic method – but not the ideal norm from
which they derive their sanction. In PSW, Husserl too raised objections
against the historical way of thinking. History can indeed tell us
something about the historical forms of law, morality and religion, but
nothing about their "idea."[20] In the same spirit, Brentano opposes the
genetic method in the mental sciences. Jhering had spoken of the
"Entstehung" (origin in the sense of genesis), but Brentano seeks the
"Ursprung"; that is to say, he does not seek a historical genetic

---

[18] USE 12, 13, 14, 82; see also VE 81, 82.
[19] USE 11 note 9, 12, 13.
[20] PSW 324f.

explanation but an origin in the sense of a "clearing up" (*Aufklärung*) that founds the validity of that which is being investigated. [21]

Does all of this mean that Brentano later abandoned his positivistic science ideal? This question comes up because it was in part the application of the inductive method that led to this crisis in the mental sciences. An inductive investigation of the actual coherence of factual phenomena can never yield universally valid norms. On the contrary, the powerful flow of historical investigation has manifested the relativity of all norms. Does this plea for a priori norms represent a denial of the inductive method? Is the descriptive method (rather than the inductive method) now the true method of philosophy, logic, ethics, and politics? [22]

We find an answer to this question in Brentano's lecture of 1892 on the future of philosophy. In this lecture Brentano polemicizes against an address given by Adolf Exner, rector of the University of Vienna, in which Exner warned against the application of the method of the natural sciences to the mental sciences. From the 1892 lecture, it appears that Brentano still supports fully his sensational claim of 1866. In the quarter-century that had passed since that time, it seemed to Brentano that the correctness of his claim had been ever more fully borne out. In the mental sciences too, the correct method is the observation of phenomena in order to arrive at universal laws via generalizations. Exner himself had in effect admitted as much, for he inquired into the causes of that which had come about historically in the moral-political arena. [23]

Thus far nothing in Brentano's position seems to have changed. But he added an important note to the published version of the lecture, and

[21] See above 73 and below 217.

[22] Kraus writes in his foreword to USE XIII, that only the knowledge of the good and the consciousness of ethical duty can be the condition for the regulation of social and international life. The sounds we hear there are markedly different from those of PES (1874), where genetic psychology is the "foundation of society," PES I 6. At the end of his lecture on ethical knowledge, Brentano says that the jurist and the politician must know *both* the genetic laws and the natural moral law. Then there will be light in the darkness of history. Then will come "the most significant dawn in the history of the world" 43; see also PES III, XXXVII.

[23] Zukunft 18, 46. Brentano also maintains the claim of 1866 in its application to psychology 35, see also 153 note 40 and 154 note 44. He is very clear on this point in "meine Letzte Wünsche für Oesterreich" of two years later. The natural scientific method, he writes, is the only true method for philosophy: "that much is agreed in our day" 32.

from it we learn that there is indeed something new. This note bears the title "Die Auswüchse, zu denen die öffentliche Meinung zu gunsten naturwissenschaftlicher Methoden auf dem Geistesgebiete Anlass gibt" (The Abuses to Which the General View in Favor of Natural Scientific Methods in Intellectual Matters Gives Rise).[24] Brentano had become aware of degeneration in the application of the natural scientifc method. He had already refuted some of these abuses in PES. He mentioned the effacing of the boundary between physical and psychical phenomena, whereby psychology is reduced to physiology. Another mistake is engaging in explanation before the phenomena to be explained are properly described. A third argument brings in a new element. The natural scientific method is sometimes accused of *confusing norms with laws of nature*, especially in such sciences as logic, ethics and aesthetics. It is then believed that scientific work can only begin when the inquiry into the "ought" (*Soll*) is replaced by inquiry into the "must" (*Muss*). Sciences like geometry, chemistry, and theory of electricity, after all, do not inquire into how things ought to be but into how they are. They seek a law in the sense of a general fact. Thus Exner is correct, according to Brentano, in pointing to such an instance of confusion when he announces that a school of jurists flourishing in Italy is transforming criminology into psychiatry.[25] We have already seen in Chapter 4, Paragraph 3 that Brentano pointed unequivocally to the absurd consequences to which this view leads in logic.[26]

When Brentano points out this error made by the practitioners of the natural scientific method, he is not arguing against their method as such but only against an abuse of it. We find such a degeneration not only in the naturalistic reduction of norms to laws of nature but just as much in the historicism mentioned above, which identifies norms with what has come about historically. In both cases norms are reduced to facts, and the inquiry into the ought is replaced by the inquiry into actual origins. Against this relativism (in the two forms of naturalism and histo-ricism), Brentano pleads for the eternal validity of norms.

As far as the question of the development of Brentano's thought is concerned, what I have established above does not mean that he gave up the positivistic science ideal but only that he became aware of its limitations. The possibilities of inductive investigation are bounded. It

[24] Zukunft 75.
[25] Zukunft 76.
[26] See above 94.

cannot show us the way in individual and intersubjective practice. Positivistic science no longer rules alone; it governs only a limited domain. An autonomous place has been given in addition to the descriptive method. Brentano's attitude toward the natural scientific method can best be described as a relative acceptance. The inductive method provides information about the laws of nature and history, but in no respect can it tell us how we must live. For Brentano as for Kant, the question what I must do is not less important than the question what I can know. Both questions must be answered by philosophy. Because of the urgency of the question what I must do, we can speak of a primacy of practical reason in Brentano.

It is typical of Brentano's "rationalism" that the failure of the positivistic approach to science does not lead him to take refuge in some sort of irrationalism. Practical decisions must not be founded in dictates of will – and definitely not in a romantically glorified state power. Practical *reason* must be subjected to rational norms. Brentano finds these norms in an a priori, descriptive analysis of consciousness. It is not his view that the positivistic approach to science must be limited in order to make room for the "faith" of a "worldview." Positivistic reason must make room for *reason in a new form*. Alongside the inductive road to knowledge, Brentano points out another road which is no less scientific, i.e. descriptive, a priori analysis. This is the first form of the new ideal of "rigorous science," which was later to be further developed by Husserl.

When Husserl later wrote his essay "Philosophy as a Rigorous Science" (PSW), he showed himself to be a follower of Brentano in many respects. Like Brentano, he looked to philosophy to give leadership in human life. The idea that an ethically responsible life is only possible through science was regarded by Husserl as the basic idea of the civilization of the West. This ideal, which stems from the Greeks and was renewed in the Renaissance era, took on an unfortunate form in positivism. Through the influence of modern natural science, the term 'science' came to mean natural science exclusively. Like Brentano, Husserl showed that the founding of the normative sciences via the positivistic approach is impossible – and even absurd. Such a founding is only possible via a priori analysis; this analysis was deepened by Husserl and eventually developed into the doctrine of the intuition of essences. The irrational alternative to the natural scientific science ideal, which at that time appeared under the name 'philosophy of worldviews,' is also rejected by Husserl. Positivism is a falsification of scientific philosophy, but historicism is a *denial* of it. Husserl saw it as a renunciation of the ideal of the Renaissance and the Enlightenment. What is to be rejected is not reason itself but the mistaken path which reason has followed under the influence of natural science. Husserl saw the flight toward an irrationalistic historicism – as a reaction to the failure of naturalism – as a symptom of the "softening and weakening of the scientific impulse," and thus as something against which a warning must be raised in the name of reason.[27] We will see later that when Husserl wrote this essay, he had already arrived at a more thoroughgoing critique of positivism than Brentano had ever produced. Husserl's fuller critique included more than a limitation of the competence of the natural scientific method.[28]

III. Some Problems

What characterizes the thought of Brentano as well as the thought of the early Husserl (including the period of LU) is the *juxtaposition* of two conceptions of science. The natural scientific method is placed alongside the phenomenological, and each is allowed a limited validity. The problem inherent in this becomes acute in the juxtaposition of a natural scientific psychology and a descriptive psychology.

Brentano's picture of the world is typical of what Husserl was later to call the "natural attitude" (natürliche Einstellung), which he himself did not overcome definitively until 1908. The world of Brentano is the "natural world." It is a system governed by causal lawfulness. Even psychical phenomena form part of this system; that is, they form only a higher stratum of this reality. This comes out clearly in Brentano's theory of the hierarchy of the sciences. Descriptive psychology, of course, can abstract from this causal dependence, but this would only be an artificial and provisional abstraction. Description must be followed by explanation. The same psychical phenomena that are subject to an absolute norm are at the same time subject to the laws of nature. From the standpoint of the norm, only some judgments are necessary, but in relation to the laws of nature, all judgments are necessary. Brentano was well aware of this difference, but he never saw a problem in combining the two points of view.[29]

---

[27] PSW 292f and 338.

[28] See below 390, 486 and 502.

[29] See his letter to Husserl of January 19, 1905: "Anyone who judges in a truly evident

On the basis of what Brentano has written about determinism and the problem of free will, we may conclude that the naturalistic outlook dominates his thought. According to Brentano, the inductive method presupposes a universal causality. At this point I cannot go into Brentano's intensive investigation of the principle of causality; he was finally driven to an attempt to demonstrate the a priori character of this principle. He wanted to prove that everything that happens, happens necessarily.[30] When Brentano speaks of probability, he means only a probability-for-us, i.e. in relation to our incomplete knowledge. This probability has nothing to do with the inherent character of reality. For a divine mind à la Laplace, everything is necessary and thus intelligible.[31] Furthermore, the existence of such a God would imply that everything is necessary and would exclude contingency. Thus Brentano concludes a chapter in his ethics bearing on this matter with the exclamation: "Indeterminism is atheism!"[32]

I will now draw attention to two aspects of Brentano's theory of causality, i.e. its ontological character and its undifferentiated application. On the ontological concept of cause, we are to understand causality as an agent which exercises an influence such that it imparts existence to something. Over against this stands the modern concept introduced by Hume, which recognizes only conditions. It was Brentano's view that Hume "strayed from the true concept of causality" when he conceived of causality as "antecedant without exception" instead of as efficient cause. Gilson correctly points out that causality is not only a connection of succession but a connection of production: that is to say, the antecedent "not only precedes the consequent but brings about its appearance." It is a "productive efficacity."[33] Perhaps for these reasons, empirical psychology is called *genetic*.

It is also Brentano's view, in opposition to Hume, that we really perceive the causal bond between two phenomena – and not just their succession. He gives two examples, one borrowed from logic and the other from ethics. When we think deductively, we perceive that the conclusion follows from the premises. The latter not only precede the conclusion but are perceived by it as causing the conclusion. The same is the case when we desire something because of

way truly *knows* and is certain of truth. And this has nothing to do with the fact that as judging . . . he is caused and is dependent in particular on the organization of the brain . . . Anyone who believes that this is contradictory is deceiving himself," WE 156f.

[30] See also L. Gilson, *Méthode et métaphysique selon Franz Brentano* I 159ff.

[31] VE 168 (this text dates from 1916), 154, 174; Vom Dasein Gottes 198; see also Gilson op.cit. 194.

[32] *Grundlegung und Aufbau der Ethik* 293. In the later history of phenomenology an opposed conclusion was drawn from the same thesis (Sartre).

[33] VE 114; Gilson, op.cit. 169, 192.

something else: "we the notice not only that the one desire precedes the other but also that – through the co-operation of a certain reflection – it produces the desire in us."[34] These two examples also make it clear that the universal causal principle is applied by Brentano to psychical phenomena. Thus it is definitely not the case that Brentano recognizes any difference in the application of this principle to physical and psychical phenomena respectively.

With regard to the freedom of the will, Brentano declares that it is not the determinists but the indeterminists who deny freedom. According to indeterminism, it is possible that a particular effect not be determined by a cause. What does this imply for the process of willing? It involves the loss of the effective exercise of freedom, according to Brentano, for it leaves open the possibility that all the conditions for a particular action – we must think here of reflection in advance and so forth – might be present while the effect, i.e. the action willed, fails to follow: an entirely different action might conceivably follow, which could be the very opposite of what was intended. Thus we would lose all power over willed actions. This power, after all, rests on knowledge, i.e. our knowledge of the laws of the process of willing. On the indeterminist view, I am not the author but the observer of my own deeds, and therefore I am not free but unfree.[35] This "solution" is typical of Brentano's way of thinking and represents a beautiful illustration of "Natura *humana* non nisi parendo vincitur." The process of willing is regarded as a natural process, and the well-known adage "Savoir pour prévoir, prévoir pour agir" is then applied to it.

Here I have a critical question: who is the victor in this process? Do we not discern a curious identity between victor and vanquished? Is the former not part of *natura humana*? If so, must it not in turn be overcome? How is it to be vanquished in turn? And in what way would this great unknown, which is itself part of human nature, so regulate this nature that it corresponds to the norm?

---

[34] VE 117; Gilson, op.cit. 171f; USE 53.

[35] *Grundlegung und Aufbau der Ethik*, 280. The thesis there defended is: "Indeterminism is the doctrine of the unfreedom of the will." See Kastil op.cit. 269. Brentano was not always a determinist. In the twenty-third "proposition" attached to his habilitation dissertation, he defended free will, see Zukunft 141, 180. In the 1869 article on Comte, he left open the possibility that God performs miracles. But later he realized that true philosophy proceeds from the exclusion of contingency, Zukunft VIIff; Vier Phasen 123, see also 164; Kastil, *Die Philosophie Franz Brentano's*, 227.

In summary we could say that the later philosophy of Brentano faces three great problems. The solving of these problems at the same time marks the two most important phases in the development of Husserl's thought.

(*A*) First there is the impasse in Brentano's theory of knowledge, i.e. the gulf between the (physical) "thing in itself" and the immanent intentional object.

(*B*) The second difficulty concerns the founding of a priori truths. Husserl believed that he had solved this difficulty with his doctrine of the intuition of essences, which he defended in LU.

(*C*) The third problem arises from ascribing equal value to the positivistic and phenomenological modes of treatment. Husserl first found a solution for this around 1908. By way of the doctrine of the transcendental reduction, he made a radical criticism of the *roots* of naturalism. The natural world in which positivism is caught up is nothing other than the correlate of the "natural attitude," which is in turn rooted in a process of self-alienation within the absolute mind. This idealism at the same time represents a radical solution to the epistemological problem.

CHAPTER SIX

PRELIMINARY CONCLUSIONS

PARAGRAPH ONE. PHILOSOPHY AS DESCRIPTIVE PSYCHOLOGY –
FORMS OF PSYCHOLOGISM

When we examine the early work of Husserl, we encounter the dominant influence of his teacher Brentano. It appears that Husserl also read the British empiricists, but that they did not determine the framework and background of his philosophy. All of Husserl's earliest publications were inspired by the later Brentano's descriptive analyses of origins.[1] Husserl was certainly a very independent and gifted student of Brentano. In his doctrine of acts of a higher order, he made his own contribution to descriptive psychology, though which it became possible to carry out descriptive analyses in the case of the fundamental concepts of Husserl's own academic field, i.e. mathematics.

What is more important is that in 1894, Husserl began to develop an entirely new concept of intentionality. The act is not a passive possession of a content but a sense-giving activity. The consistent application of this insight to all areas of consciousness was determinative for Husserl's own style of descriptive analysis.

Husserl had not yet arrived at new insights with regard to the founding of the a priori sciences. His descriptive analysis was a priori but not yet "eidetic." Furthermore, he had not yet broken through the naturalistic picture of the world. Descriptive psychology was not yet a transcendental phenomenology.

---

[1] For other views of the influence of Brentano on Husserl, see Cahiers de Royaumont. Philosophie no. III 1959, 29f, 65, 70. I do not agree with Spiegelberg's claim that Husserl borrowed the "tools" for his analysis in PA from John Stuart Mill, *The Phenomenological Movement* 92. At two central places in PA, Husserl proceeds from distinctions made by Brentano, 72, 215.

We can best characterize this first period as *descriptive-psychological*. This period is often characterized as psychologistic. The term 'psychologism' can be used in various different senses and thus should not be applied without further specification. By 'psychologism' one could mean the following.

(1) In the first place, one could speak of psychologism when the object of the act is identified with the act – as in British empiricism.[2] No distinction is made between the sound and the hearing of the sound. Both Brentano and Husserl reject this psychologism from the outset.

(2) The term 'psychologism' could refer to the *immanence* of these contents. It is in this sense that Frege speaks of psychologism (or idealism).[3]

(3) Husserl's theory of number is called psychologistic because he regards formal properties or categories as predicates of reflection. This is a different and separate form of psychologism because it does not involve a psychologizing of the content to an act; the reduction concerns only the formal aspect of a content.

(4) One could speak of psychologism when genetic psychology is regarded as the fundamental discipline and the basis for the normative sciences.[4] A logical law would then be nothing but a particular kind of psychological law. We have seen above that Husserl was never guilty of this kind of psychologism.[5]

(5) When the normative sciences are founded in descriptive psychology, we can speak of psychologism only insofar as the inadequate *founding* of logical (and other a priori) laws is concerned.[6] No distinction is made at this point between the psychical phenomenon and its eidos, between the sense-giving act and the ideal meaning-content.

(6) Finally, in the spirit of the later Husserl, one could call this initial phase psychologistic because no distinction is made between conscious-

---

[2] See above 19.

[3] Primary contents *remain* immanent for Husserl, also in LU and Ideen. But they are no longer the object of the intention. The intentional act is then seen as a sense-giving which – with the help of these content, as the material of sensation – constitutes the transcendent object; see below 134 and 162.

[4] See above 62.

[5] See above 93.

[6] In the analysis of number, psychologism in senses 3 and 5 go together. In LU, Husserl also overcomes psychologism in arithmetic in two phases. First the objectivity of number is recognized as a correlate of categorial perception. Then, on the basis of this recognition, the idea of number is inspected in categorial abstraction; see below 279.

ness as "mind" (*Seele*), as a stratum of "natural" reality (the object of psychology), and transcendental consciousness as the "all of absolute being" (the object of transcendental phenomenology).[7]

In the next paragraph we will see how important it is to distinguish these various meanings of 'psychologism.' It is impossible to gain insight into Husserl's early work if the vague term 'psychologism' is used without further specification.

PARAGRAPH TWO. SOME CRITICAL OBSERVATIONS

(1) The earliest study of the development of Husserl's thought, *Die vor-phänomenologische Philosophie Edmund Husserls und ihre Bedeutung für die Phänomenologie*, by Werner Illeman (1932), is of little importance. Illeman apparently assigns the publications which I have discussed above to a non-phenomenological or genetic-psychological period which he calls psychologistic. He even includes an article of 1897 entitled "Bericht über deutsche Schriften zur Logik aus dem Jahre 1894." He does so despite the fact that Husserl himself regarded this early work as descriptive psychology; in his "Selbstanzeige" describing PSL, he characterizes this article of 1897 as "a piece of purely descriptive psychology"![1] Illeman's view is probably derived from Husserl's polemic in LU against genetic psychology as the foundation for logic. But it is a misconception to think that at this point Husserl had his own earlier work in mind.

(2) A.D. Osborn's work *The Philosophy of Edmund Husserl in its Development from his Mathematical Interests to his First Conception of Phenomenology*, appeared in 1934. It was reprinted unchanged in 1948 under the title *Husserl and his Logical Investigations*. Osborn's work includes many bibliographical givens, based partly on interviews with people who knew Husserl personally, but it contains little philosophical analysis. Osborn devotes considerable attention to the influence of Frege and calls Husserl's reaction to Frege the great turning point in his career.[2] It is true that Frege's criticism did have a great influence on Husserl – insofar as it contributed to his acceptance of ideal Numbers. But we have already seen that Frege did not take much trouble to try to

---

[7] See below 407.
[1] Illemann, op.cit. 6of.
[2] Osborn, op.cit. 43.

penetrate Husserl's philosophy. Furthermore, he used the term 'psychologism' to refer to various different things. (What Frege really did was to confuse 'psychologism' in senses 1, 2, 3, and 5 outlined in the preceding paragraph.)

(3) The most extensive study of the early Husserl, which virtually gives a translation of LU, is Marvin Farber's the Foundation of Phenomenology. Farber calls this first period "psychologistic." The psychologistic element in Husserl's thinking is his attempt to clarify arithmetical concepts with the help of descriptive psychology (psychologism in sense 3).[3] My objection to Farber is that he follows Frege in identifying this psychologism with the doctrine that contents are immanent (psychologism in sense 2). Furthermore, he makes a mistaken attempt to defend Husserl on this point against Frege's objections. It is Farber's view that what Husserl meant by 'content' is somehow really the extra-mental object (Gegenstand). He bases this reading in part on Husserl's use on the expression 'numbers in themselves.'[4] According to Farber, Husserl could better have avoided the term 'content' and used 'object' instead.[5] A critical revision of the text would have eliminated many objections. He admits that there is "some degree of confusion" of "the objective and subjective orders, including even an expression of a form of psychological idealism," but in principle there is "no confusion."[6] Thus Farber more or less reduces the question to one of semantic sloppiness.

[3] Farber, op.cit. 16, 18. According to Farber, the psychologistic period lasted until 1895.
[4] See above 27 note 17, 64.
[5] Farber, op.cit. 27 note 2.
[6] Farber, op.cit. 26, 57f. Farber defends Husserl against Frege's reproach to the effect that Husserl confuses the moon with the presentation of the moon, making it appear that objects are reduced to subjective ideas, 55. We have already seen that it is incorrect to reproach Husserl for making things products of the mind. But this does not mean that contents are extra-mental, as Farber would have it. The mistake results from a failure to take account of three terms: act, content, and real object. The content is neither an act (Frege) nor an extra-mental object (Farber) but an immanent content.

In general, the arguments of Frege and the complicated themes of Husserl have been too little analyzed in the secondary literature. An analysis of these matters is indispensable if the relation between Frege and Husserl is ever to be clarified. Such an analysis is not present in D. Föllesdal's article 'Husserl und Frege, Ein Beitrag zur Beleuchtung der Entstehung der phänomenologischen Philosophie.' As a result, Farber and Föllesdal are not in agreement on the question what Frege's critique meant for Husserl's development (compare Farber, op.cit. 5, 16, 57 and 98 with Föllesdal, 52). An analysis of Frege's critique is necessary in order to determine on what point Husserl was really affected by Frege: as I interpret Husserl, it was in his sensualistic theory, which forces us to reduce an object that is not sensorily perceivable to a property of acts. As Farber correctly argues, this does not conflict with the possibility of Husserl's maintaining some other analyses.

Farber also attaches a good deal of weight to the argument in "Ziegenfuss," according to which a correlative mode of treatment is already present in PA. This retrospective interpretation was already discussed in Chapter 1. I must object even more strongly to Farber's suggestion that in PA, Husserl was already aware of the distinction between psychological judgment and logical judgment.[7] This is in fact the new discovery of LU; it became necessary precisely because of the problems which had come up in the earlier work (in connection with psychologism in sense 5).

(4) A recent publication on the development of Husserl's thought, which also devotes extensive attention to PA, is the lecture given by Walter Biemel at the third phenomenological congress at Royaumont on "Les phases décisives dans le développement de la philosophie de Husserl." According to Biemel, the seeds of Husserl's later phenomenology are already to be found in PA. In this work Biemel claims to see the concepts of production and reflection, as well as the clarification of the origin of a thing by going back to the source of its meaning in consciousness.[8] Biemel derives his orientation primarily from Husserl's view that formal relations are not to be met with in the things but are established by the mind itself. It is true that collective relations are produced by an act (i.e. an act of a higher order). But this implies for Husserl in PA that these relations *do not exist on the side of the object*. As I have pointed out more than once, the act of a higher order has no correlate of its own; there is no object of a higher order. On my view, any attempt to regard the collecting act as a constituting act must run aground on this point, for constitution implies that the act has a correlate which it constitutes. In PA we simply do not find any object which could serve as the "clue" in a constitutive analysis. *It is precisely because of this absence that reflection is necessary.* Because the object is not without, it must be within. This is the only reason why reflection is necessary in PA, where there is no trace of correlative analysis. When Husserl speaks of "origins" in PA, he does not mean an object arising from an act but a concept arising from an object or "denotatum" (*Begriffsgegenstand*), i.e. an object which in the case of the concept of number is to be found only in reflection.[9]

---

[7] 26, 57f: Here too he relies on the article in Ziegenfuss, which speaks of the "characteristic doubling of logical and psychological analyses" 570; see above 26.

[8] Biemel, op. cit. 39f, 49; see above 26.

[9] It is especially because of the importance of the question of the origin of the concept

Furthermore, we have seen that the concept of constitution (and the necessity of correlative analysis) was not discovered by Husserl in connection with the analysis of number; this discovery was made in PSL (1894) in connection with meaning-conferring acts. After this, from 1897 on, it was applied to perception and categorial abjects.

(5) Herbert Spiegelberg, in his history of the phenomenological movement, distinguishes three periods in Husserl's thought: (i) a pre-phenomenologicai period, which includes the early writings plus the "Prolegomena to Pure Logic" in LU, (ii) a period in which phenomenology is seen primarily as the subjective correlate of pure logic, and finally (iii) a transcendental-idealist period beginning about 1906.[10] What is noteworthy about Spiegelberg's division is that the break between the first and second periods runs right through LU. The "Prolegomena to Pure Logic" making up the first volume of LU are assigned to the first, pre-phenomenological period, although Spiegelberg is well aware that a radical change took place between PA and LU.[11] In Part II, I will go into the relation between the "Prolegomena to Pure Logic" and the six investigations which together comprise LU.

of constitution that Biemel has been discussed here. Biemel's view on this matter has since been accepted by Joseph J. Kockelmans in: *A First Introduction to Husserl's Phenomenology*, 12ff and R. Sokolowski in *The formation of Husserl's concept on constitution*. Sokolowski's book devotes a good deal of attention to PA, which is a hopeful sign of a renewed interest in this too much forgotten early work of Husserl, but it does not give us a new point of view. Sokolowski follows Husserl's self-interpretation in FTL, and therefore, like Biemel, he comes up with an anachronistic interpretation of PA op.cit. 2, 13, 16ff, see also 35, 65, 109, 203 note 1. The following quotation is characteristic. Sokolowski claims that there is a close similarity between Husserl's theory of psychical relations in PA and his theory of categorial objects in LU. He then continues: "In both cases, we have a reality which is somehow objective, but which owes both its existence and its structure to subjective mental processes. Since the process that results in categorical objects is called constitution in the Investigations, it seems the same name could be given to the 'mental activity' described as the source of psychic relationships in the Philosophy of Arithmetic. In the latter, Husserl already calls the concepts of such relationships 'categories,' and in his own reference to this work in Formal and Transcendental Logic he adds the phrase 'categorical objects as formed objects,' to describe the concepts treated her," 18. In this quotation Sokolowski manages to make all the mistakes that one could make in interpreting Husserl's PA. He follows the self-interpretation found in Husserl's FTL (a work of almost 40 years later). The presence of categorial objects, which was first defended in LU, is projected back into PA. The forming of these objects is then interpreted as constitution, and this constitution is explicated in the sense of the later correlative analysis.

[10] Spiegelberg, The Phenomenological Movement, 74, 91, 114, 119f, 124.

[11] Spiegelberg speaks of a "radical shift," op.cit. 93. Husserl breaks with the psychologistic founding of logic and arithmetic, see also 74.

The question whether it is correct to group Husserl's early writings together with LU under one head and regard them as making up Husserl's early period can be raised independently of this discussion. This is what Eugen Fink does. Contra Spiegelberg, he assigns all of LU to Husserl's first phase, on the grounds that this work belongs to his pre-transcendental period.[12] I can agree with Fink insofar as the major dividing line in Husserl's thought is the turn to transcendental idealism. Nevertheless, there is still reason to give LU a place of its own, for in this work descriptive psychology is deepened to become an eidetic psychology, thanks to the new doctrine of the intuition of essences (disregarding for the moment other new elements, such as the theory of perception). Of course one could always argue further about the question whether this justifies a new division. But it is out of the question to follow Spiegelberg in assigning "Prolegomena to Pure Logic" to a first period and the rest of LU to a second. According to Spiegelberg, what is new about the six investigations which make up volume 2 of the German edition is that they transform psychology into eidetic psychology, describing not psychical facts but essential structures.[13] But if this is sufficient reason to speak of a new period, then the first volume of LU ("Prolegomena to Pure Logic") also belongs to this period. Pure Logic, which is defined in the first part of volume 1, is – as we shall see – nothing but a branch of the eidetic psychology of the rest of LU.[14]

In conclusion, there are no good arguments for calling this period pre-phenomenological. Descriptive psychology, which characterizes this phase, was already called phenomenology by Brentano.

---

[12] 'Vorbemerkungen des Herausgebers' in Entwurf 107. The division of the German edition into two volumes does not correspond to the division of the English translation by J.N. Findlay into two volumes. Volume 1 of the German edition includes only the "Prolegomena to Pure Logic." Volume 2 is divided into two parts. Part 1 (cited here as LU II) is made up of the first five investigations, while Part 2 (cited here as LU III) includes only the sixth investigation. Volume 1 of the English edition includes the "Prolegomena" plus the first two investigations, while Volume 2 includes investigations three through six.

[13] Spiegelberg, op.cit. 101f.

[14] See below 289.

PART TWO

PHILOSOPHY AS DESCRIPTIVE EIDETIC
PSYCHOLOGY

INTRODUCTION

Husserl published his *Logische Untersuchungen* in 1901, when he was still an almost unknown university lecturer (Privatdozent). According to Landgrebe, who was later to become Husserl's assistant, this event was "one of the greatest changes ... that German philosophy had undergone since the end of the age of idealism."[1] Before long, a dispute about the interpretation of this work broke out, a dispute that continues to this day. One of the central points in this discussion is the question of the relation between the two volumes. Husserl's sudden fame was due mainly to his refutation of psychologism in logic, which he accomplished – in unparalleled masterly fashion – in the first volume (the "Prolegomena to Pure Logic").[2] The second volume followed up this defense of pure logic with a philosophical clarification of this logic. For the most part, this clarification consisted of a piece of descriptive psychology.

I will begin Part II with an analysis of this descriptive psychology and its most important results. In particular, I will examine the new concept of perception and the methodological framework within which it stands.

In the second chapter, the relation of this psychology to genetic psychology will be discussed. It appears that descriptive psychology is in fact an a priori ideal science. The principles of the new form of a

---

[1] Landgrebe, *Der Weg der Phänomenologie* 9.

[2] Ueberweg observes: "It was LU that opened the struggle against psychologism, and it was through its effects that psychologism was overcome." Also: "The influence of Husserl was so important that LU can be called the most influential and consequential philosophical work to have appeared in the new century. Its struggle against psychologism, in particular, has had its effects especially on the younger generation of investigators." *Friedrich Ueberwegs Grundriss der Geschichte der Philosophie*, fourth Volume, 506, 512.

priori analysis (i.e. the "intuition of essences") will be set out in Chapter 3 – in contrast with Husserl's earlier theory and in their new form.

In Chapter 4 it will be shown that the construction of a pure logic is now possible. In the process I will already touch on the thesis to be defended in Chapter 5, namely, that pure logic is ultimately nothing but a deductive elaboration of certain fundamental concepts of *eidetic* descriptive psychology.

CHAPTER ONE

ACTS, OBJECTS, AND THE RELATIONS BETWEEN THEM

If it is true that each philosophy has only one "original intuition," then Husserl's is the discovery of the mystery of consciousness, the "wonder of all wonders."[1] Husserl's student Fink, who has characterized his teacher as a "genius of reflection and analysis," speaks of a "gigantic vivisection of consciousness" which Husserl carried out, with ever more subtle analyses and with an eye to even the smallest nuances.[2] In LU we see that Husserl for the first time tries to describe the inexhaustible riches of consciousness. Later, after 1908, he also discovered the ontological absoluteness of this mystery that bears the entire world.

SECTION ONE.
ACTS

PARAGRAPH ONE. INTRODUCTION – THE NATURAL AND PHENOMENOLOGICAL THOUGHT-STANCES

In LU, Husserl develops his own style of psychological analysis. He begins from the descriptive psychology of Brentano, but he manages to deepen it considerably. His goal is a fundamental analysis of all "modes of consciousness" in which we are aware of objects.

In connection with his purpose in LU, which will be discussed later, Husserl limits himself to presentation and judgment. Within the cognitive area of consciousness, Brentano had recognized only two "modes of consciousness," i.e. "mere presentation" and "judgment" or

---

[1] Id III 75; see also Spiegelberg, *The Phenomenological Movement* 87.
[2] 'Die Spätphilosophie Husserls in der Freiburger Zeit,' *Edmund Husserl 1859–1959*.

positing. But Husserl describes a great variety of modes of consciousness. We distinguish not only between positing and non-positing acts but also between significative and intuitive acts. Within the latter category we must again distinguish between perceptual and imaginative acts (fantasy, memory and "pictorial" presentation). Furthermore, alongside sensory perception Husserl also recognized a categorial perception. Finally, he introduced the "intuition of essences" in LU.

Perceiving and describing these acts requires a separate "phenomenological attitude" which is "unnatural," for this kingdom of structures of consciousness is concealed at the outset. Once the phenomenologist has hit upon the proper attitude, an inexhaustible terrain of fundamental discoveries lies open before him. It was Husserl's view that only the steadfast co-operation of a generation of investigators entirely dedicated to this great task would suffice to solve the most important questions in this area.[1] I will begin with a provisional sketch of the new thought-stance. Husserl first speaks of the "natural thought-stance" in the introduction to the second volume of LU. Paragraph 3 of this introduction bears the title "The Difficulties of Pure Phenomenological Analysis."[2] By pure phenomenological analysis Husserl means descriptive psychological analysis. At this point phenomenology and descriptive psychology are still identical concepts,[3] and therefore the terms 'purely phenomenological' and 'descriptive psychological' are used interchangeably in the first edition.[4] What, then, are the difficulties of descriptive psychological analysis? They lie in the "unnatural direction of intuition and thought" demanded in phenomenological analysis.

Whereas in the normal thought-stance we are directed through-the-acts toward the objects of the acts, in phenomenology we must turn toward the acts themselves in order to analyze them. Husserl speaks of this as a direction of thought which "is contrary to the firmest of practices, practices which grow ever stronger from the beginning of our

---

[1] II, 12. As already indicated, I will be quoting frequently from LU in part II. Because the first edition is no longer available, I will take most of my quotations from the second edition. Part II of the second volume will be cited as LU II, and part II as LU III. When I refer to the first edition, I will make this explicit; wherever possible, the corresponding pages in the second edition will also be listed, see above 121 note 12.

[2] II (ed. 1) 10ff (ed. 2, 9ff).

[3] II (ed. 1) 18 (ed. 2, 17).

[4] II (ed. 1) 42 (ed. 2, 42).

psychical development on." The normal thought-stance, which takes shape in every individual and can only be broken through with difficulty, is called by Husserl "straightforwardly objective." Elsewhere he speaks of it as "naively objective."[5] The naiveté consists in this, that the objects are indeed seen, but not the acts by means of which these objects appear to us. One might observe that Husserl is here maintaining little that is new. Is he doing anything more than contrasting reflection, as a turning back toward, with direct experience? What is there really new, as Husserl saw it, in what is brought forward here? This question is all the more important because Husserl had already made use of the concept of "inner experience" in PA, and had appealed in the process to Locke's concept of "reflection."

It is Husserl's view that in Locke and the other English psychologists there is indeed talk of reflection, but that this is not yet an actual analysis of acts. These psychologists in fact remained mired in the natural thought-stance. Therefore they were not in a position to analyze the typical character that belongs to consciousness. Reflection is more difficult than one might think at the outset, and for the psychologist there is an almost ineradicable tendency to fall back from the phenomenological thought-stance into one that is straightforwardly objective.[6] *We think that we are analyzing acts, but in fact we are describing subjectivized objects.* In Paragraph 8 I will return to Husserl's view of this English "data-psychology," which, he believes, has led to a number of fundamental errors in psychology and theory of knowledge.[7] A certain hiddenness is inherent in consciousness, then. The mapping out of this *terra incognita* requires training. A "practiced ability" is necessary "to place oneself in the unnatural attitude of reflection and reflective investigation and to allow phenomenological relations, undisturbed by any admixture of intentional objectivity, to work upon oneself in full purity."[8]

In this introduction, Husserl already refers to a certain aspect of this hiddenness: the instrument of *language* is inadequate for describing consciousness. To refer to the subjective acts, we have at our disposal only a few multivocal expressions such as 'sensation,' 'perception' and

---

[5] II (ed. 1) 42 (ed. 2, 42); II (ed. 1) 75 (ed. 2, 75); see above 63, 64.

[6] II (ed. 1) 10 (ed. 2, 9).

[7] II 128.

[8] II (ed. 1) 11, 12, (ed. 2, 11); II 390; on this hiddenness, see below 159; on the hiddenness (anonymity) of transcendental consciousness, see 371.

'presentation.' Further we must make use of expressions which indirectly describe the corresponding acts.[9] Ordinary language is completely attuned to the sphere of normal interests, i.e. to objects, and can describe adequately only this primary objectivity. The phenomenologist must use words that are attuned to the natural attitude. In other words, the unnatural, reflective thought-stance is forced to speak the language of the natural direction of thought. This, of course, causes certain difficulties in communication. One condition for understanding a phenomenological analysis is that one must be able to transpose himself into the typical phenomenological attitude and thus see the phenomenological relations "purely."

In the following paragraphs I will discuss further the five most important kinds of acts that Husserl now distinguishes. Then I will return to the phenomenological thought-stance and its opposite.

PARAGRAPH TWO. SIGNIFICATIVE ACTS

In this theory of significative or meaning-conferring acts, Husserl further develops the ideas of his article of 1894.[1] I have already indicated that in this article he takes the first step toward a phenomenological analysis of consciousness. Husserl points to the importance of the "modes of consciousness" in which we are aware of objects. This was a discovery that gave rise to "amazement." In the article of 1894, the analysis of these "representations" had a bearing only on so-called "founded" acts. i.e. on acts that rest on a founding perception. What is new in LU is that this concept is also applied in the case of perception itself, as we shall see in Paragraph 4.

A comparison with the article of 1894 shows that the theory of significative acts had undergone no essential changes, although Husserl had become more aware of the methodological importance of this discovery for the analysis of consciousness. The analysis of acts is sharply delimited vis-à-vis the "objective" direction of thought, which seeks to explain the reference of the word to the object signified exclusively on the basis of an analysis of "contents." The term 'founded act' is now used for the first time.[2]

---

[9] II (ed. 1) 11 (ed. 2, 10, 11); on the problem of language in transcendental phenomenology, see below 373.
[1] See also above 13.
[2] II 76; III 75, 96.

The founding act is a normal perception. It does not have an immanent object (as in 1894) but a transcendent object (see Paragraph 4 below). The act in which this object constitutes itself is called the "act involving the appearance of an expression (*Akt der Ausdruckserscheinung*). Here the physical side of the expression appears, i.e. the physical phenomenon or sound.[3]

An act of meaning is now built on this normal perception. In contrast with the perceptual act, this act of meaning in which the physical object becomes a sign, a "sense-bearing expression," is an entirely new mode of consciousness. Husserl again illustrates this with the example of the sound which is first heard simply as a sound and is then understood as a word with a meaning.[4] When this happens, a change takes place in consciousness. The act in which the physical object appeared is *modified*. This modification, as part of the descriptive character of the act, must be described by the phenomenologist.[5] That the sign as sign can only be understood is this way is evident from the fact that the physical object does not change when it becomes an "expression." Therefore Husserl can say: "To be a sign is not a real predicate." Something becomes a sign only through a new, sense-giving act.[6] The "sense" can be grasped only through reflection on this act.[7]

The two acts together form a "phenomenological unity," which cannot be understood as a pure coexistence of "contents." This is apparent from the fact that we carry out both acts even though our interest is entirely in the founded act. The founding presentation is merely a "support" or "vehicle" (*Stütze, Anhalt*). Husserl speaks here

---

[3] II 37, 39, 40, 407, 508; As a "sound-complex," the word is also called a natural object III, 89. In LU, this founding perception is already an act of sense-giving. From a systematic standpoint, this act would have to be discussed before the significative acts founded in it. I have chosen to move in the reverse direction in order to do justice to the historical origin of the new concept of perception.

[4] II 39f, 68, 384.

[5] II 384. Here Husserl literally quotes from his study of 1894. He does so in a paragraph in which he explains the new concept of intentionality and defends it for the first time. At this point, the conferring of sense in the case of language is only an example of the universal phenomenon that is now called intentionality. The new context in which this quotation stands is again an indication that the concept of intentionality originated in the analysis of linguistic meaning, as established in the article of 1894.

[6] II 41, 424; III 89.

[7] II 183, 344. Husserl was later to say that the "sense" does not lie in the sensorily perceivable content but is nonetheless something objective. See below 171 and 443.

of a certain "asymmetry." Also rooted in this structure is the peculiar reference of the sign to what is signified.[8]

PARAGRAPH THREE. "IMAGINAL" OR IMAGINATIVE ACTS

In LU, Husserl also gives a more detailed analysis of a representative act already mentioned in 1894, i.e. presentation via an image. He now speaks of this as imaginative apperception. He regards this "image-apprehension" as present in fantasy and in presentation via a "physical" image. I will limit myself to the latter.[1] As in the case of significative apperception, I will distinguish between the founding act and the founded act.

The founding act is a normal perception. For example, we see a photograph or something made of marble simply as a physical thing, as a piece of paper or a quantity of marble.[2] In a new apperception, the thing made of marble "constitutes itself" as an image or statue, and the piece of paper constitutes itself as a photograph.[3] That the thing made of marble (the image as object, as Husserl calls it) refers as image to the imaged thing (i.e. that of which it is an image) is due solely to the new "mode of apperception." As a physical thing, the statue has remained the same. To be an image is not a perceivable property; it is not a "real predicate" like redness or roundness. The marble becomes a statue through the observer, who, through a new apperception, gaves the physical thing the "meaning" of statue.[4] We can only understand this new function by relating it to the modification of consciousness during observation.[5]

---

[8] II 39, 406.
[1] In LU, these two forms of apperception were still placed on the same level. Later this was corrected. Only presentation via an image is a founded act. Compare II (ed. 1) 364, 394, 398, 466f, 526, 714 with (ed. 2) 385, 419, 423, 503f; II 54ff, 243. See also II 442, 490f and Id I 79, 186, 209, 211.
[2] II (ed. 1) 414 (ed. 2, 443); II 510; III 54; see also Id I 226.
[3] II (ed. 1) 397, 466f (ed. 2 resp. 423, 502f).
[4] II 422f; see also III 82, 89f, 93 on the identity of the foundation.
[5] II 386, 488. In the transition from a perceptual act to an imaginative act, there is a qualitative modification that takes place in addition to the imaginative modification (which is called "representative" modification in the first edition of LU). The "quality" of the founding act changes from one of positing to one that is neutral (see Paragraph 5 below). In "imagine-apperception" it makes no difference whether the image exists as object or not. Only later did Husserl discover this second modification II 487 (ed. 2) 491; Id I 226.

PARAGRAPH FOUR. PERCEPTUAL ACTS

We turn now to the analysis of perception, which functions as the founding act for significative and imaginative acts. In 1894 Husserl saw perception as the intuition of an immanent content. The new modes of consciousness which he had discovered at that time had a bearing on the acts founded in this perception *but not on perception itself.*

In LU, perception itself is also a "representation."[1] Husserl maintains that in perception there is also a typical new mode of consciousness at work. On closer analysis, perception appears to consist of two elements: the "experiencing" (*erleben*) of an immanent content and the perceiving of an object via the content. The immanent content is a representative of the perceived object. It now appears that we can apply to perception the definition earlier given of representations, namely, that "by means of certain contents given in consciousness, they aim at (*abzielen*) others not given."

Perhaps this new concept of perception can best be explained by means of a comparison with that of Brentano, for the latter's view was originally shared by Husserl. Husserl believed that Brentano did distinguish the act from the content – the hearing of a sound is not the sound itself – but that he had not discovered the act's own typical character. Brentano did not see that there is an essential difference between the passive possession of a content and the "apperception" of that content. Therefore he was blind to the particular "functional" or form-giving aspect of intentionality. In FTL, Husserl says that Brentano had discovered intentionality but not its objectifying function.[2] The intentional act is active; it does something with the sensation. This immanent sensation-content is its material; it is what is apperceived. Through the act, the immanent content is conceived of as a transcendent property. To use Husserl's examples: "I do not see color sensations but colored things; I do not hear sound sensations but the song of the singer, etc. "Here it may suffice to point out that when we have a presentation or a judgment about a horse, for example, it is a horse – and not our sensations of the moment – that is presented and judged about."[3]

---

[1] II 500, 503; III 79, 95, 234.

[2] FTL 187 see also 231. Husserl raises an analogous objection against Brentano's concept of inner perception. This "inner consciousness" or "experiencing" (erleben) is not yet an objectifying, making an object of something, III 239, see also EU 63.

[3] II 161, 374, 382, 385.

The possession of perceptions must not by itself be called an act. For Husserl, this "sensing" is "the mere fact that a sensory content, which, furthermore, is an utter non-act, is present in the experienced complex." Unlike Brentano, Husserl does not want to distinguish here between a content of sensation and a sensory act. He regards such a distinction as purely verbal, as a tautology. The "experiencing" of a perception is nothing but the presence of an immanent content in consciousness.[4]

On this point too, Husserl's "Selbstanzeige" (Author's Abstract) of 1897 about his PSL gives us some insight into the gradual evolution of his thinking. At that time he already drew attention in a footnote to the difference between the presence of a content and the apperception thereof. But he stuck by the old way of speaking and still called this presence of the content to consciousness an act. This forced him to accept two kinds of acts: (1) acts that are representations and are directed toward an intentional object, and (2) acts that are related to non-intentional immanent contents. The latter include, for example, "sensory pleasure and displeasure."[5] In LU, Husserl realized that the latter can no longer be called acts but are components out of which acts are built.

Husserl calls the sensation, which is immanent, a "real" (*reell*) content; it is a real component of consciousness. From then on, 'real' (*reell*) is used as a technical term to refer to that which is itself present in consciousness.[6] Through the apperception of this immanent content, the transcendent object appears. The acoustic sensation is conceived of as a transcendent sound. In the light of this new theory of perception, we must distinguish carefully between the immanent sensation and the transcendent property, which appears through the apperception of the sensation and *is the actual object of the intention*. Against this

---

[4] III 243 note 1; see also II 394 note 1: In "inner consciousness," in which the immanent data of sensation are given, "being" and "being inwardly present to consciousness" coincide. Of every content we are *ipso facto* conscious. Thus we cannot distinguish the content from the consciousness of the content, as though the content would somehow be "unconscious" if there were no consciousness, see ZBW 471, 473.

[5] Bericht über Deutsche Schriften zur Logik aus dem Jahre 1894, 226 note 1. In LU, Husserl says that only apperception can be called an act. Together with sensation, it forms the "full act," of which the sensation is the "sensory kernel," II 128, 365 note 1, 383; III 170; see also Id I 170, 172.

[6] II 352, 399. Husserl makes a distinction between 'real' and 'reell.' 'Reell' refers to that which really exists: consciousness. 'Real' is used to refer to a certain apperception of what is "reell," i.e. as a stratum founded in a thing, see below 456. The term 'real' is used in connection with the reality of the natural attitude, of which the thing (*res*) is the cornerstone.

background, Husserl sharply criticizes Brentano's talk of an immanent or mental object. His well-known critique of Brentano's definition of intentionality is directed particularly toward the terms 'immanent objectivity' and 'intentional' or 'mental inexistence.' According to Husserl, these terms further the misconception that the intentional object to which each act is related is immanent. They give rise to the impression that the relation of the act to the object is a "real relation" between two "things to be found in consciousness in like manner, i.e. the act and the intentional object." If we say that the object is given "in" the experience, we must understand this in a figurative sense. The same holds for Brentano's expression 'is contained in.'[7] These expressions do not mean that the object of consciousness is a "real constituent."[8] Husserl appeals here to the evident fact that in perception we perceive things – transcendent things.[9] Without discussing further the nature of this transcendence (see Section 2), I must at least establish that the perceived thing manifests itself as an object transcendent to consciousness. Therefore this thing cannot be identified with the sensations that are present in consciousness itself.[10]

Although Brentano had discovered intentionality, he still paid tribute to the presupposition introduced by Locke, namely, that a perceived content must be immanent. The same is true of the early Husserl, who also held that the perceived content is immanent. In LU, Husserl remarks – correctly – that he has given up his earlier concept of "intuition."[11]

I have repeatedly used the term 'apperception' to describe the new concept of intentionality. Synonymous terms for Husserl are 'interpretive (auffassende) intention' or simply 'interpretation' (Auffassung). It is this apperception that "animates" sensation. By

---

[7] II 269, 271, 350, 375. See also Krisis 245 (E 242).

[8] II 128.

[9] II 97 note 1, 372.

[10] It is presupposed in Husserl's theory of perception that this matter of sensation is present and can be pointed out. This aspect of Husserl's theory has been rejected by many of his followers; it has been regarded as something left over from his empiricist past. See, for example, J.P. Sartre. L'être et le néant, 23–27, 378; M. Merleau-Ponty, Phénoménologie de la perception 278, 281, 464; A. Gurwitch, Théorie du champ de la conscience 215. At this point, I cannot go into the contention that Husserl later gave up this theory about sensations.

[11] III 32 note 1.

itself, sensation is "blind."[12] In apperception the immanent content is received into a new "mode of consciousness." In contrast with the pure presence of sensation, the latter is a totally different form of consciousness.[13]

Here Husserl points out a shortcoming of the traditional theory of apperception, which seeks to explain perception exclusively on the basis of sensations. By 'apperception,' the traditional theory means the phenomenon that one and the same stimulus does not always rise to the same sensations. This is said to be the result of the actualizing – through this stimulus – of dispositions present within us as deposits of earlier experience. This theory, says Husserl, can provide no account of the given and does not penetrate to the heart of the matter. What is here described as apperception has to do exclusively with sensations. The various ways in which the sensations are apprehended is completely ignored.[14] The objectifying of sensations cannot be explained by the addition of new sensations.[15] Here we come upon a completely new dimension of perception as compared with pure sensation. What makes this apparent is that different objects can appear through the same contents. This happens, for example, when I believe I am perceiving a person moving about in the dark, but it turns out to be a shrub.[16] The reverse also occurs. Furthermore, the sensations can change constantly, as they do, for example, when I perceive a small box that I turn in my hands. I continue to perceive the same thing while this is going on.[17]

For Husserl, then, the term 'apperception' is not opposed to 'perception'. Every perception comes about through an apperception

[12] III 176.

[13] II 352, 374, 381.

[14] II 318. Here Husserl quotes literally from the "Selbstanzeige" (Author's Abstract) mentioned above, Archiv. f. system. Phil. 1897, 226 note 1. In this "Selbstanzeige," he presents the content of his article of 1894 and adds in a critical note that perception cannot be explained as a pure collection of contents. In the article itself, Husserl still referred to the traditional theory of apperception without criticizing it PSL 169. Thus the new concept of perception was born in Husserl's mind after 1894. This too makes it apparent that the new concept of intentionality arose in connection with the analysis of the "representative" function of consciousness, as he called it in 1894.

[15] II 385, 504; III 54.

[16] II 381, 419. The example is borrowed from Id I 215, see also 206.

[17] II 382. In the light of the further analysis of Ideen I, I must point out that the example requires additional commentary. In this case, the noematic "modes of appearance" would also change, see below 441. The "object referred to" (Gegenstand welcher) or identity pole remains unchanged.

of sensations. Because of the false opposition to the term 'perception,' argues Husserl at one point, the term 'apprehension' might better be used.[18] Through this "apprehension" of sensations, in which the sensations undergo an "objectifying interpretation," objective *Gegenstände* (objects) appear to us;[19] they are "constituted" in this act. Here Husserl uses the much discussed term 'constitution' for this first time.[20]

This constitution is further described as a *sense-giving*. Also synonymous with 'apperceive' is the term 'interpret' (*interpretieren, deuten*).[21] The sensations are apprehended in a particular "sense." This is the "material" of the act, the "appercipient sense" (*Auffassungssinn*).[22] Husserl himself tells us that when he seeks to describe perception, he cannot resist the temptation to use terms borrowed from the analysis of significative acts. He does so in a passage in which he suggests the possibility of a consciousness that has sensations but cannot apperceive or apprehend them. "If we imagine a consciousness prior to all experience, it may very well have the same *sensations* as we have. But it will intuit no things and no events pertaining to things; it will perceive no trees and no houses, no flight of birds or any barking of dogs. One is at once tempted to express the situation by saying that its sensations *mean* nothing to such a consciousness, that they do not *count as signs* of the properties of an object, that their combination does not count as a sign of the object itself. They are merely lived through, without an objectifying interpretation derived from experience. Here, therefore, we talk of signs and meanings just as we do in the case of expressions and cognate signs."[23]

The analogy with meaning-conferring acts is indeed striking. In the case of the meaning of a word, we speak of a meaningless content that is "animated" by an act and thereby receives a "mental" side. The physical sound functions only as a "vehicle" (*Anhalt*) for a new act directed entirely toward the signified object. All these terms recur in the

---

[18] III 91.
[19] II 194, 349, 365; III 232f.
[20] II 165, 247; III 219.
[21] II (ed. 1) 704f. On page 232 of the second edition, 'interpretation' is replaced by 'apperception.'
[22] See below 144.
[23] II 75.

discussion of perception. The sensation is simply a "vehicle" that gets its "sense" through apperception.[24] This content is "informed" or "animated" through an interpretive act, and in the process an object is constituted.[25] As in the case of the significative act, there is a certain "asymmetry," for in perception we are directed entirely toward the perceived object. "*Sensations*, and the acts 'interpreting' them or apperceiving them, are alike experienced (*erlebt*), *but they do not appear as objects*: they are not seen, heard, or perceived by any sense. *Objects*, on the other hand, appear and are perceived, but they are not *experienced.*"[26]

The interpretation of sensations, like the interpretation of sounds in language, is ultimately learned through experience. A young child cannot yet apperceive.[27] The following schema can be used to illustrate the analogous structure of the two acts.

                                        interpretation
signification   "vehicle" ─────────────────→ signified
(a founded act)   (perceived   object
                             object)

                                        interpretation
perception   "vehicle" ─────────────────→ perceived
(founding act)   ("experienced"   object
                             sensation)

Thus the terms 'meaning' and 'sense-giving' are now applicable to all objectifying acts – and not just to linguistic meaning. In Ideen I, Husserl calls this an "extraordinary and yet in its own way permissible enlargement of the concept of 'sense' (*Sinn*)." Here for the first time he gives an explicit account of this enlargement. "Originally these words have reference only in the linguistic sphere, the sphere of 'expression.' However, it is virtually unavoidable and at the same time an important

[24] II 374, 383, 385.
[25] II 385, III 24, 26. Husserl sometimes speaks of "evaluating" the sensation, a process whereby it becomes a property of the object III 57, 78.
[26] II 385.
[27] In PSL 175f. Husserl wrote that a child has "intuitions" but no representations. Thus, what applied there to founded representations now applies to the founding perception itself. Perceiving must be learned as well as speaking. On this "primal instituting (Urstiftung), see II 75 and "Selbstanzeige." Archiv. f. syst. Phil. 1897, 226 note 1; see also CM 141 and FTL 277.

step forward in knowledge to enlarge the meanings of these words and to suitably modify them, whereby they find application in the entire noetic and noematic spheres, that is, in all acts, whether they are bound up with acts of expression or not."[28] In order to be able to distinguish between the two concepts of "linguistic sense" and "perceptual sense," he uses the term 'meaning' (*Bedeutung*) for the narrower concept ("expressive meaning") and the term 'sense' (*Sinn*) for the broader concept.

It is clear that this analogous structure does not exclude important differences. I will discuss this matter at greater length in the next paragraph. For the present, I must draw attention to the following two points.

In the first place, the relation of the sense-giving act to the "sign" is much different in perception than in language. In perception there is an intrinsic bond between the sensation and the object constituted via the apperception of the sensation. The sign is not arbitrary, as it is in language. Connected with this is the fact that perception can "fulfill" a significative meaning, for in perception an object is constituted, which object, through its presence, makes "present" the merely significatively meant object.

Secondly, a signification is only possible on the basis of a perception that constitutes the physical word as sound. The object of perception is the "vehicle" of the significative meaning. In the significative act, then, there are two objects. The first is the present sign, and the second is a merely meant object that is not itself present. The latter point is important in connection with Husserl's polemic against the image theory of perception.[29] Although in perception there is mention of representation – an object is represented through a sensation – there is no mention of two objects, as in significative and imaginative apperception;[30] there is no mediation through an image or sign. Husserl expresses this concisely as follows: what is called apperception with reference to immanent contents is *the same* as what is called perception

---

[28] Id I 107 and 256.

[29] See below 192.

[30] The 1894 definition of "representation," which was quoted at the beginning of this paragraph, is now applied to perception itself. For the same reason, it no longer holds for significative and imaginative acts. The founding content of these acts is no longer immanent.

in relation to the intentional object.[31] Therefore Husserl usually calls perception a "presentation," for the object is "itself" present here.[32]

In this exposition I have limited myself to apperception, by which things are constituted. In the case of sensations of touch and so-called "feeling-sensations," two separate and different interpretations are possible. First, a feeling of pleasure can be interpreted objectively. A particular event then appears as "pleasingly painted" or "as if bathed in a rosy gleam." Secondly, such a feeling can be related to one's own body. Here we find the first traces of the "constitution of the body," which will be discussed at a later stage.[33]

This new concept of perception, which is based on the distinction between "erleben" (experiencing) and "auffassen" (interpreting), has two important consequences.

First, it shows that Husserl has broken with the presupposition *that everything of which we are aware must be "in" consciousness.* In connection with intentionality, we often hear of a "turn toward the object." By way of this alleged turn, Husserl is supposed to have executed his famous break with the Cartesian tradition of a closed consciousness. The subject does not remain enclosed within itself but is directed toward a transcendent world.[34] This perspective on Husserl seeks support in the new concept of intentionality, for perception is no longer the experiencing of an immanent content but the perceiving of a transcendent object. What does this directedness toward the transcendent mean? At the outset it means nothing more than this: it is impossible to deny that when I perceive, I experience the perceived as something transcendent. Any other theory would involve interference with the given. In the description of the given state of affairs, we must not be misled by presuppositions that seem to be obvious truths, e.g. that everything experienced is experienced in consciousness. As we shall see in Section 2, this recognition by itself prejudices nothing with regard to the question of a reality existing independently of conscious-

---

[31] II 385.

[32] See below 145.

[33] II 392ff; III 232 see also Id I 172; see below 385.

[34] See above 8, 50. That we perceive only what is immanent to consciousness is now called a Lockean presupposition by Husserl, see below 159. This presupposition must be distinguished from the Cartesian presupposition that Husserl had not yet overcome, see below 176. The Lockean presupposition is that all that is perceived is in consciousness. The Cartesian presupposition is that only what is in consciousness is actually given.

ness, nor does it prejudice anything with regard to our perception of it. The interpretation of Husserl mentioned above, which makes much of the "turn toward the object" and understands it in a *realist* sense, finds no support in this theory. For the present, nothing more is being maintained than this: the object is conceived of as a transcendent object. The given must not in any sense be interpreted away, for this would conflict with the "intuitionist" point of departure, i.e. the rule that every given "is simply to be taken as what it presents itself as being."[35]

A second consequence is of great importance for the further development of phenomenological analysis. The new concept of perception opens up the possibility of so-called "correlative investigation," an analysis in which the perception and the perceived object are investigated in close connection with each other. The perceived object corresponds to an aspect of the act, and vice versa, for *the object appears in the way the act apprehends it.* The act plays an active role in the constitution of the object. The perceived object thereby becomes correlated with the "sense" of the interpretation (or with the matter).[36] This correspondence later makes it possible to use the object as a "clue" in the analysis of consciousness, proceeding by the rule that to every kind of object there corresponds a particular mode of consciousness.[37] Because of the Cartesian presupposition to be discussed later, this correlative analysis was not developed in LU.[38] Certain inhibitions made it possible for Husserl to follow this new path at the time of LU.

PARAGRAPH FIVE. MORE ANALYSIS OF ACTS

The acts that have been discussed up to this point form a closed group, despite the differences between them. They are all acts directed toward "real" (*real*) objects. We shall see later that there are also acts that intend "categorial" and "general" objects. In the case of such acts, the differences in "modes of apprehension," which are to be dealt with now, recur. Therefore it is now in order to analyze further the acts

---

[35] Id I 43; see also Entwurf 120.
[36] See below 144.
[37] See below 319.
[38] See below 172 and 176.

discussed up to this point. I will do so by indicating first the elements common to all acts and secondly the differences between them.

I. The Essential Elements of Acts – Quality and Matter

An "experience" (*Erlebnis*) consists of two elements: the representative content (immanent content) and the act in the narrower sense, i.e. the apprehension. In this "apprehension" Husserl distinguishes between "matter" and "quality." Compare the following judgments: (1) "May there be intelligent beings on Mars!" (2) "Are there intelligent beings on Mars?" (3) "There are intelligent beings on Mars." They represent respectively a wish, a question and an assertion. They differ in quality. By the concept of quality, then, Husserl means emotional relations such as wishing, hoping, hating, liking, rejoicing, etc. and also attitudes on the cognitive level, such as questioning, supposing, etc. Finally, under the quality of an act he also includes its "belief" character – or, of course, its opposite, i.e. "mere presentation." Here Brentano's distinction between acts that "merely present" something and acts that affirm what is presented recurs. For Husserl, "belief" however is not an independent act but a non-independent aspect of an act that also includes matter. "Mere presentation" is also a component of an act; it is a qualitative determination of an act, and not a separate act.[1]

In addition to a difference in quality, the three examples of judgments above have something in common, i.e. the same "content." This is then the "matter" of the judgment. The matter thus indicates the determination of the act, that through which it is *this* act. It could easily happen that two judgments have different matter bu the same quality. The judgments "$2 \times 2 = 4$" and "Ibsen is the father of modern realism in dramatic art" have different matter but the same quality. Both are assertions (*Behauptungen, Setzungen*).[2]

One might be inclined to regard this difference in matter as a difference in the intentional object. Do the presentations Pope and Emperor not differ simply in this way, that in the one the Pope is presented and in the other the Emperor? But such a line of reasoning

---

[1] On this point too, the "Selbstanzeige" of 1897, 226 note 1 op.cit., offers us some insight into Husserl's development, for in it "mere presentation" is still an independent act, as it was for Brentano. In LU, this doctrine of Brentano's is considered and rejected in a very careful and extensive analysis 426ff.

[2] II 411, 435.

would be *unphenomenological*, for what is at issue is not a difference in objects but a difference in acts. It is not the case that every presentation simply has the general character of a presentation without further differentiation. The differentiation would then come in by way of the various objects toward which the presentations are directed. Husserl calls this a "Selbstverständlichkeit," a self-evident opinion that we are forced to maintain if we fail to draw the distinction between "object" and "meaning."[3] What he means by this is that there is a phenomenological, material difference between the acts. That the one act presents the Pope rather than the Emperor is a property *of the act itself.* It is this aspect of the act that stamps it as *this* act, directed toward this particular object. It is an inner determination of the experience. It is the aspect that "determines what we call this intention toward this object."[4] The matter indicates that every mode of "objective reference" is a particular one, that it has a particular "content." ("Content" thus refers here to the nature of the act; it is not the transcendent intentional object.)[5]

Naturally matter and "object" are closely related and parallel each other. The matter indicates that the act is inwardly determined by the property to intend a particular object. In the light of Husserl's theory of apperception, we could better say that the object is determined by the fact that it is apprehended through a materially determined act. The theme of correlativity is founded in the new concept of intentionality. We shall see later that in LU, Husserl preferred to devote his attention to the matter on the side of the act.[6] For the present, only this aspect of the correlation falls within the domain of descriptive psychology.

According to Husserl, matter is an aspect that all acts possess, regardless of whether they be significative or imaginative or perceptual. The same is true of quality. Therefore he speaks of matter and quality together as the "intentional essence" of the act.[7] The former gives us "what" we apprehend the object "as," and the latter "how" we apprehend it. The aspect of the experience that gives meaning or "sense" to the representative contents, the aspect that plays a role in

---

[3] II 407 (ed. 1) (see also 434 ed. 2). Thus this argument is aimed directly at Brentano, even though Husserl does not name him. See above 34.

[4] II 412f, see also 426, 478.

[5] II 413, 416, 478. On the term 'content' see below 253.

[6] See below 181.

[7] II 417; III 95f.

significative and perceptual acts, is thus referred to in further analysis as the "intentional essence."[8]

Meanwhile, Husserl also uses the term 'sense' with a narrower meaning, i.e. as referring exclusively to the matter. This determination of the apprehension or the "matter of interpretation" is also called the "Auffassungssinn" or "Sinn der Auffassung" (appercipient sense).[9] This anticipates Husserl's *Ideen*, where only the matter is called "sense," while the quality is called the "posited sense" (*Satz*).[10]

In this context I must again point out that the concept of sense (in both its broad and narrow meanings) is used analogically. It is derived from the sphere of language, that is to say, from the sphere of significative acts. The terms 'sense' is now used also to indicate a property of perception. It is then a "fulfilling sense" or "fulfilling meaning."

II. The Non-essential Elements of Acts – the Sensations

Matter and quality are essential elements which no act could lack. Husserl distinguishes them from "non-essential" components. Even if two acts are the same in matter and quality, they might still differ in other respects. Nansen's presentation of Greenland's icy wastes differs from the presentation that we have. Yet the "intentional essence" is the same in the two cases.[11] It is clear that these non-essential elements determine the difference between the various sorts of acts, i.e. significative, imaginative and perceptual. This new element is the "fullness." It is that by which an intuitive act (whether perceptual or imaginative) differs from an "empty" signification. This "fullness" is formed through the representative contents, through the sensations of the perceptual act.[12]

On this definition of the concept, the representative contents are regarded as non-essential because they do not occur in all acts, e.g. not in significative acts. Against this view one might object that significative acts do have a representative, i.e. the sound or the written sign. Yet this content gives no "fullness" to the act of meaning. Actually, it is a

[8] II 52; III 87. Thus the intentional essence is also called the "semantic essence" II 492, 417. See below 258.
[9] II 383, 385; III 91. See also FTL 120 note 1, 153.
[10] Id I 274; see below 438.
[11] II 38, 50, 61, 417ff; III 87.
[12] III 64ff, 75, 86ff, 171.

content that gives "fullness" to a founding act, to the act that perceives the sound *as* sound. It does not function as a fulfillment for the act of meaning itself.[13] From this it is apparent that what differentiates these acts is not so much whether they possess a representative content as what function this content has. Only in the case of certain acts is the relation of the act to its representative such that the latter at the same time gives it "fullness."

It is on the side of the relation to the representative content, indeed, that we can more precisely characterize the differences between the acts. Husserl calls this relation of matter and representative the "form of representation." Whether the act is intuitive or significative depends on whether the representative content functions intuitively or significatively. And whether a content functions significatively or intuitively depends on its relation to the matter of the act.[14] In the case of the significative act, there is no inner bond between the representative (the sound) and the meaning.[15] Thus the sign "assists" such an act as a "vehicle," but it has no intrinsic relation to what the act means.[16] This is apparent from the fact that the same thing is referred to in various different languages by means of entirely different signs.

This is not the case with regard to imaginative acts. Here the representative content is an image of the intended object that appears "in the image."[17] Thus there is an inner bond between the matter and the representative. The representative resembles that which the act intends. Hence it follows that in this case the apprehension is not entirely free. We can only intend something within a certain sphere of similarity. In the case of significative acts, any arbitrarily chosen sign could serve as a representative, but not in the case of imaginative acts. If we go outside the sphere of similarity, the act becomes significative and ceases to be an "image-interpretation" (*bildliche Auffassung*).

In perception, finally, the object is not represented by an image but is "itself" present "in person."[18] (In the second edition Husserl adds "bodily present.") This does not mean that the representative and the represented object coincide here, for the representative content is

[13] III 38, 87, 96.
[14] III 90f.
[15] III 55, 59, 88, 92.
[16] III 89. The meaning cannot hang in the air. On the question of thinking without words, see III 88, 92 and 6of.
[17] III 83, 56, 58f, 92.
[18] II 355, 442, 479, 491; III 56f, 116, 144.

immanent and the object transcendent. Yet the object *itself* appears via the representative which could therefore better be called the *presentative*; it is a "self-presenting content." We could say that the object appears by way of the apprehension; the latter makes the object present.[19]

III. The Connection between the Acts – Knowledge

Husserl had already pointed out in 1894 that a representation can become an intuition. He spoke of the consciousness of "fulfilled intention." This is now worked out further in the doctrine of the synthesis of significative and intuitive acts. In the significative act, the object meant is not given; it is "merely grasped putatively." Such an act is a "mere intention," which is to say that the intention is "empty."[20] There is indeed an "objective reference," but it is not "realized." The relation is actualized or fulfilled in a perception (or fantasy), which is therefore called a "meaning-fulfilling act."[21] "What the intention means, but presents only in a more or less non-genuine and inadequate manner, the fulfillment – the act attaching itself to an intention and offering it 'fullness' in the synthesis of fulfillment – *sets directly before us*. . . . In fulfillment our experience is represented by the words: 'This is the thing *itself.*'"[22]

The understanding of an expression does not require such a perception. We can understand an expression even if we do not perceive what is meant. The expression even remains meaningful if a perception is impossible. If an "intuitive illustration" of a meaning is possible, if the relation to the meant object is realized, then we know that the meaning has "reality" and is not imaginary.[23] Thus it is perception that determines the validity of a meaning. We could also say that in such a case, there is a "fulfilling sense" corresponding to the "intended sense." The intentional essence of the act of meaning fits the intentional essence of the intuitive act.[24]

Since the quality of these acts can vary, the aspect that actually fuses here is the matter. Matter is the bearer of synthesis.[25] We may take it

[19] III 83, see above 140.
[20] II 37f.
[21] II 37, 50.
[22] III 65.
[23] I 240; II 54, 67, 96; III 29, 92.
[24] III 32.
[25] III 64.

that it is partly because of this possibility of synthesis that Husserl also speaks of matter or sense in the case of intuitive acts. From the comparison of significative and perceptual acts, it appears that what we call meaning in the case of the former is also to be found in the case of the latter. In such an act of fulfillment, the object is given to us – and given in the same way in which it is meant in a pure act of meaning. Both acts have the same meaning (matter). There must be something in the perceptual act that corresponds to the "sense" of the significative act.[26] In both acts the same object is intended with exactly the same properties. Thus both must have the same material determination. *The transfer of the term 'sense' from the significative sphere to that of perception rests on this possibility of identification, of a "coincidence" (Deckung) of the two acts.*[27] That "sense" as the meaning of a word is something other than "sense" as the meaning of a sensation is emphasized by Husserl himself in the sixth investigation, when he claims that only a significative act can confer meaning on a word. A perception cannot do this; it can only fulfill a meaning.[28]

Whenever a signification passes into an intuitive act, we can speak of "recognition." The unity that arises here through fusion is a "unity of knowing."[29] This synthesis between two acts comes about via a "transitional experience." Thus the unity comes about through a new mediating act, which connects the two acts with one another. This synthetic act is a knowing act, an act of "identifying coincidence" (*Deckung*), in which one and the same object of meaning and intuiting appears.[30]

Now, it is also possible – and this is new in relation to the article of 1894 – for this unity of identification to pass into an explicit act of identification, in which what is intended is not the one object of intuiting and meaning but the identity of both. In other words, what happens is not that we experience an *adequatio rei et intellectus* in a synthetic act of evidence but that we make this *adequatio* itself the object. In that case we would perceive not a "real object" but a

---

[26] II 50f; see also Zusatz II (ed. 1) at 180 and 286 on 717f. (ed. 2 par 31); III 35, 64, 87.

[27] II 52, see also 131f, 137, 141, 145ff, 150, 165f, 169, 183, 189.

[28] III 14ff, 19, 87, see above 139.

[29] III 25ff, 51, 65.

[30] III 35, 50. The synthesis that comes about is a *continuous* synthesis through direct fusion III 148f.

"categorial object." In PA, such a perception of identity was impossible.[31]

PARAGRAPH SIX. CATEGORIAL ACTS

Categorial acts occupy an important place in LU. The task which Husserl had set for himself in the second volume culminates in the analysis of these acts i.e. the clarification of logical categories and of the logical laws founded in them. In the theory of categorial acts, we find the real philosophical complement of pure logic. This clarification forms the goal toward which all six investigations work. Thus the connection between the first volume (defense of the necessity of a pure logic) and the second volume (clarification of pure logic) is strongest in the sixth investigation, which, according to Husserl himself, is the most important of them.[1] In particular, in its second section (entitled "Sense and Understanding"), Husserl redeems his promise to provide a philosophical supplement to pure logic. Thus we find there a first "theory of reason." Because of the task which Husserl had set for himself, this theory remained limited to "formal logical reason."[2]

We have already encountered these categorial acts under the name 'acts of a higher order.' We have seen that in the second edition of LU, Husserl complained – partly unjustly – about how little attention PA, his first work, had received. Over against Cornelius and Meinong, he claimed priority in the analysis of the "apprehension of plurality."[3] An analysis of PA makes it apparent, however, that Husserl recognized acts of a higher order but not objects of a higher order. The act of a higher order has an object only indirectly, because the lower constituent acts have an object. The total act (*Gesamtakt*) has an object only in a secondary sense. It is not the case that out of the objects of the constituent acts, this act constitutes an object of its own (through a "total performance") to which it is primarily related.[4]

---

[31] See below 169; III 35, 124, 150.

[1] Vorwort I, (ed. 2) XVI.

[2] Vorwort III (ed. 2) V.

[3] II (ed. 2) 282. Kraus speaks of a "struggle about priority" between Husserl and Meinong PES II 313f. In a letter to Kraus, Husserl denied this. With reference to this letter, Kraus remarks that although there was no actual struggle, there was nevertheless a claim to priority on Husserl's part PES III, XXIII note 2. See also above 11, 25.

[4] II 401ff. This passage in LU can thus be read as an implicit self-criticism. It is a correct analysis of the position of PA.

In LU, Husserl upheld the standpoint of PA in that categorial properties cannot be ascribed to "real" objects. The collective relation is not a sensorily perceivable property. The same holds for the relation "property of" or inherence. I can see a color, but I cannot see being colored; I can feel smoothness, but I cannot see being smooth. In the narrower sense, only that which we see with our eyes or hear with our ears is perceived.[5] The collective connection, which is referred to by way of the word 'and' (just as the disjunctive connection is referred to by way of the word 'or'), "is not anything, as we rather roughly put it above, that can be grasped with one's hands or apprehended via some sense." We cannot paint it. "I can paint A and I can paint B. . . . I cannot, however, paint the both, nor can I paint the A and the B."[6] Therefore we would be totally mistaken if we sought such forms in what can be sensorily perceived.[7] The relation of part and whole, for example, cannot be found back completely in a perceived whole. I can perceive the part and the whole, but not the part as part; in other words, I cannot perceive the fact that it is a part.[8] Thus a sensory form of unity, the perceivable "form-quality" (Gestaltqualität), must not be confused with a categorial form of unity. I can perceive a row of trees. This is a "sensory unity."[9] The plurality as such is not perceivable. The perceived unity can, of course, represent a merely intended process of counting that has not been carried out.[10] If this collecting is actually carried out, then the plurality is constituted. But this plurality is not perceivable as a property in things.

In LU, Husserl also approaches this non-sensory perceivability as follows. Every meaning is fulfilled by an intuition. The meaning "whiteness" finds its fulfillment in the perception of whiteness. But what about the meaning "and" and other formal concepts? There is no intuitive moment in the realm of "mere seeing" that gives this meaning "fullness." This is also apparent from the fact that many different judgments can be made on the basis of the same "real" object, e.g. "This paper is white" and "This white paper."[11]

[5] III 137f.
[6] III 160.
[7] III 135.
[8] III 152, 155.
[9] III 156; II 277f, 282 note 1; see our criticism of Szilasi below 168.
[10] See above 12, 23 note 4, 31 note 39.
[11] III 131.

This non-sensory perceivability raises a problem for Husserl, namely, where the origin of concepts is to be sought. All concepts – formal concepts not excepted – must have a foundation in intuition. After all, we say that the judgment as a whole – and not just the "terms" – expresses a perception.[12] In PA, Husserl had answered that these concepts arise from inner perception. The concept of a "collective relation" arises from reflection on an act of collecting. In LU, Husserl calls this a "fundamentally mistaken doctrine" that has been in general circulation since Locke. The origin of the concept of "collective connection" lies not in the connecting but *in the object of the connecting act*. Just as we find the origin of the concept of "table" in the table and not in the perception of the table, we find the origin of the meaning "and" in the collective connectedness and not in the collective connecting. We must indeed carry out a collecting act in order to "perceive" a collective, but this does not mean that we perceive the collecting act itself. Such a perception would give us something entirely different, namely, the simple concept of a "collecting act." The perceiving of a collecting act is a normal "sensory" perception (of the "inner sense"),[13] while the collecting act itself is a categorial perception. The origin of the concept of "collective connection" is to be sought, then, not in a connecting act but in the object of a connecting act.[14] This is to say that Husserl accepts a *non-sensorily perceivable object*, which is a categorial object or an "object of a higher order." In the connecting act, a new object is constituted. It is not a "real object" but an "ideal object," a "thought-object."[15]

Collecting is nonetheless called a categorial *perception*. Husserl chooses to use the term 'perception' here because this act manifests characteristics that correspond to those of normal sensory perception. In this act, the collective connection is not just intended in an empty way but is "itself" given. Therefore the use of terms like 'perception'

---

[12] III 128, 142.

[13] III 139ff; see also 167f, 179. Here Husserl fails to mention that the sharp criticism also applies to the standpoint which he himself had defended. Does this perhaps have something to do with him claim to priority over against Meinong?

[14] III 142, 151. This given collective is again the object of categorial abstraction (intuition of the essence of a category on the basis of a categorial perception); see below 279.

[15] In II 164, 166 Husserl speaks of the "objects of our thinking" (gedankliche Objekte); III 145, 147, 156, 177.

and 'intuition' is unavoidable. This perception is not "sensory" but "super-sensory."[16]

By introducing this ideal, super-sensory object. Husserl *breaks out of a dilemma* in which he was trapped in PA. He speaks of the traditional sensualist pattern according to which an object must be either physical or psychical.[17] From the fact that the collective connection is not a physical object, he had to draw the conclusion that it is therefore a psychical object, and that the origin of the corresponding concept is to be sought in inner perception. There was no other possibility. I have already shown in Part I what tensions this led to in Husserl's theory of numbers. Therefore it should not surprise us that when Husserl wrote an "Entwurf einer Vorrede" (sketch toward a preface) in 1913, he observed that doubts about the correctness of this theory tormented him from the very outset. Since he put forward this theory despite these doubts, we may take it that there were some powerful factors blocking the way to a better understanding of this matter.

The step Husserl takes here is indeed a major one, for he now posits the existence of objects that are not sensorily perceivable. Thereby he breaks with the sensualist pattern he had picked up early in his career. We find this pattern not only in his teacher Brentano but also in all the other thinkers that Husserl studied at that time and quoted frequently, i.e. the British empiricists Locke, Berkeley, Hume, and especially John Stuart Mill. All concepts find their basis in perception – if not in outer perception, then in inner perception. But in number Husserl encountered a concept that actually finds its origin in neither of these. He sought an origin for it in inner perception, but this led to difficulties. Hence, *the current philosophy had let him down* in his effort to provide a philosophical founding for mathematics.

These difficulties induced Husserl to take the radical step of introducing "ideal objects" in LU. The origin of number is to be sought in the object of a collecting act, an object that is ideal. Thus Husserl is no longer forced to take refuge in reflection. It is because he raises the possibility of the perception of super-sensory objects for the first time here that this step is so important. It is true that categorial perception is not the same as the "intuition of essences." Yet both acts have *the same structure*, and therefore Husserl discusses them in the same breath. In

[16] III 142, 165.
[17] Entwurf 127; see above 27.

both, what is perceived or intuited is not a real object. Categorial perception has opened the door, as it were, to a new ontology, to a realm of ideal objects. In the light of Husserl's empiricist past, this is a revolutionary development. Husserl himself spoke of it as a "Platonism" that was not pleasing to his contemporaries, who wanted to base philosophy and science solely on facts, on "realities."[18]

In connection with these categorial acts, the question could easily arise whether we must interpret this constitution of the object of a higher order as the deed of a creative consciousness. The making of connections, after all, is dependent on our choice. In PA, Husserl emphasized the freedom with which we can collect any possible objects. We can connect a number of sensorily perceivable objects into a collective, but we can also refrain from doing so. Furthermore, numerous combinations are possible. If we now accept an ideal correlate for every collective connection, is this correlate to be regarded as a product of consciousness?

This question is important because some interpreters of Husserl argue that the constitution of these ideal objects (in particular, objects of number) served as a model for Husserl's idea of constitution in general. Thus the constitution of real objects would also have to be interpreted on this basis. In this way, the interpretation of categorial perception is drawn into the debate on the question whether Husserl's concept of constitution tends toward realism or toward idealism. I will return to this question later in the chapter and limit myself here to a closer analysis of categorial acts. A correct description of these acts will give us what we need to answer such questions.

When we compare categorial perception with ordinary perception, it becomes apparent that the way in which these two acts make an object appear (constitut) differs inwardly. When we look at a real object, it appears "at one stroke." The thing is not perceived as a sum of aspects that are observed in a number of separate acts. It manifests itself all at once, just as the perceiving act is a homogeneous unity.[19] Husserl calls this perception "straightforward" (schlicht) and "simple." It is as though we pointed to the object "with one finger."[20] A categorial

---

[18] On Brentano's objections against these objects, which he regards as fictive, see PES II 238, 158.

[19] III 146f.

[20] II 473.

object, by contrast, first appears in a synthetic act, in a "many-rayed" consciousness.[21] This synthetic consciousness presupposes the straightforward consciousness.[22] Thus the relation between the two acts is the following: *the categorial act makes explicit what is contained implicitly in the straightforward act*.[22] For example, in one glance we can observe a particular whole. In a closer explication of this perception, we can focus on the various parts as well as the whole which they form together. It is in this act that the parts first appear *as* parts and the whole *as* whole. The same point could be illustrated by way of a row of trees. Although the trees are perceived at one glance when we first look at them, they can later be analyzed in a many-rayed act. In such an act, not only must the various constituents be observed one after the other, but they must be held fast and embraced in one total act. In this total act, the new object, which is founded in the real object, is then given.[24]

The spontaneous character of these acts has been pointed out above. It depends on us whether or not we make a perceived object explicit. And if we do decide to do so, we must still choose between various standpoints. Thus freedom and choice are possible here. Although the categorial act is impossible without the straightforward act as its foundation, we are nevertheless free in our categorial formation. But our freedom is not without limits. Here I must point to two limits. (1) It is not possible to explicate a particular real object in an arbitrary way. We cannot apprehend a part as a whole, and vice versa, nor can we apprehend a unity as a property.[25] (2) Categorial formation is bound to laws that are founded in this formation itself. These laws determine which variations and transformations are possible when an object once has a particular form.[26] Arithmetic, for example, represents such a morphology, for it formulates the laws possible on the basis of the "and" relation. Algebra gives us formulas for the possible (i.e. valid) combinations.

[21] II 473 (ed. 2) (ed. 1, 442). The term "many-rayed" (mehrstrahlig) (from Ideen I) does not occur in LU.

[22] III 146, 166, 175.

[23] III 150ff.

[24] III 154f, 187.

[25] III 188. See also A. Messer, *Empfindung und Denken* 75.

[26] III 188ff; see below 252.

These formal laws also include the laws of pure apophantic logic. *It is at this point that phenomenology, i.e. the analysis of consciousness, is tied up with pure logic.* The intuitive basis of formal fundamental concepts is to be found in categorial acts. The combinations which are possible on the basis of these forms are then worked out further by logic. Phenomenology is interested primarily in the forms themselves and in the acts in which they "realize" themselves.[27] In conclusion, therefore, I must make a few observations about the founding relation between form and "stuff" and about the possibility of formalization.

A categorial act is not possible without a perception as its basis. The notion of a "pure mind" apart from all sensibility is "nonsense."[28] Nonetheless, it remains true that we can abstract from the founding act. We can see the property (e.g. whiteness) *as* a property only when we perceive a concrete piece of white paper and on this basis predicate whiteness as a property of the paper. We express this by way of the judgment "This paper is white." But we can separate the form from the particular content. The inherence relation can be applied to any possible concrete thing. Thus we can vary the content, the "stuff." In the expressed judgment, we substitute symbols for the "terms." The formalized judgment reads: S is p. In this way the founded object is separated from the particularities of the contents. It is clear that any law holding for such a form is independent of the content. Therefore Husserl calls such laws purely analytic. The symbols in such laws are to be regarded as freely variable.[29]

PARAGRAPH SEVEN. GENERAL PRESENTATIONS OR ACTS OF IDEATION

Husserl deals with categorial acts and acts in which we intuit something general at the same time. General presentations are themselves called a special kind of categorial act. The objects of both of these kinds of acts are "thought-objects" or "objects of a higher order."[1] As I see it, it was because of this analogy in structure that the discovery of categorial acts with their correlates acted as a catalyst for the doctrine of the intuition of essences.[2] This new doctrine, which was to provide a foundation for pure logic and the other a priori sciences, will be dealt with in a chapter III within the framework of the problem of abstraction.

In this paragraph I will concern myself only with the typical *new mode of consciousness* in which we intend these general objects or "essences." What is noteworthy about the doctrine of "general objects"

[27] See below 292.
[28] III 183.
[29] II 253f.
[1] III 147, 162, see Fink, 'Die phänomenologische Philosophie Edmund Husserls in der gegenwärtigen Kritik' 324f; II 164, 166: "gedankliche Objekte" (object of our thinking). In EU, the two are also dealt with at the same time, see 231 and 381.
[2] See above 29, 90, 151.

in LU is that it is *on the basis of an analysis of consciousness* that Husserl defends the legitimacy of the notion of an "ideal" world beyond the "real" world. His point of departure is the undeniable, phenomenologically given fact that while there are acts in which something individual is intended, there are also acts of a different nature in which something general is presented.[3] Just as in the case of categorial presentations, this distinction cuts across the division into significative and intuitive acts. Thus there are acts in which something general is intended in a merely significative way (*A*) and other acts in which something general in intuited – the intuition of essences (*B*).

(*A*) In his defense of the existence of ideal general objects, Husserl takes his point of departure in general meaning. There are significative acts that mean something individual and others that intend something general. This descriptively given difference between acts that "mean" something in an individual way and others that "mean" something in a general way can be phenomenologically established.[4] We must then pay attention to their "sense" or "substance of meaning," i.e. to their "content."[5] At the very beginning of the second logical investigation (entitled "The Ideal Unity of the Species and Modern Theories of Abstraction"), Husserl already goes to work in this way. He writes: "The question as to whether it is possible or necessary to treat species as objects can plainly only be answered by going back to the meaning (the significance, the sense) of the names standing for species and to the meaning of assertions claiming to hold for species."[6] If these names can be interpreted in such a way that the actual objects of the intention are individual (which is what the empiricist theory of abstraction of Berkeley, Hume and John Stuary Mill maintains), then there are clearly no general objects. But if this is not the case, and if it is apparent from an analysis of the meaning that these expressions and their direct intentions are directed toward general objects – toward "species," as Husserl calls them – then the empiricist theory must be false.

It is immediately clear that such meanings as "Socrates" and "all men" refer to empirical things. But in the case of "two," "round square" and "all purely logical propositions," it is evident that we are confronted with general objects or ideal entities – ontological and

[3] II 142.
[4] II 130, 140, 222.
[5] II 88, 172, 145, 147f, 202.
[6] II 110f.

apophantic respectively.[7] This differrence in modes of consciousness must not be interpreted away. No one can deny that when we speak of "the pitch C" or "the color red," we have a general object before us, even if it is "before our logical regard."[8] Over against meaning an individual object, this is a "new kind of mode of consciousness," a "new mode of apprehension"; it represents a "new character of act."[9]

(*B*) What is only presented symbolically in the general meaning now finds its fulfillment in the intuition of essences. "Basing ourselves on intuitive presentations, we carry out the fulfillments of meanings corresponding to our merely significational intentions; we realize their 'genuine' purport (*Meinung*)."[10] Here something general is *itself given*. Thus we can speak of a clarification "of the meaning of general names by recourse to fulfilling intentions." This clarification is at the same time an "evident confirmation."[11]

To many, Husserl writes, the term 'universal intuition' will sound as strange as 'wooden iron.'[12] Invariably we think of intuition as sensory perception, which is always individual. But the time has come to speak of the perception of an "idea" – in a founded perception built on normal sensory perception. When we look at an individual red thing, we are directed toward the "redness,"[13] or – to use an example important for Husserl's founding of arithmetic – when we speak with evidence about the number four, we have a group of four things before our eyes but are mentally directed entirely toward "fourness," "the species four."[14] The idea is the object of our "logical regard." This act of universal perception differs specifically from a sensory perception, as a reflective analysis of it will bear out.[15] On the foundation of an individual perception, a new mode of intuition develops, and in it a "new kind of objectivity appears."[16] It is a "new mode of reference," a "new kind of mode of consciousness," a "reference of a fundamentally new sort."[17]

[7] See below 252.
[8] II 145f, 156, 171.
[9] II 170, 109, 183, 381.
[10] II 141, see also 153.
[11] II 120, 216.
[12] III 162.
[13] III 161ff, 132ff, 141, 146f.
[14] II 140.
[15] II 141, 144, 153, see also I, 136, 221.
[16] III 162.
[17] II 171, 175, see also 122f.

PARAGRAPH EIGHT. THE NATURAL AND PHENOMENOLOGICAL
ATTITUDES – A PROVISIONAL SUMMARY

When Husserl inaugurated a new form of analysis of consciousness in
LU, he did so in a continuing polemical confrontation with what he
called the "English theory of knowledge." He was thinking, of course,
of the British philosophers Locke, Berkeley, Hume, and the younger
Mill. In PA, Husserl already appeared to be thoroughly acquainted
with the latter's work. His relation to these thinkers deserves a closer
look, for in a certain sense he saw their work as preparatory for
phenomenology. Even after Husserl went over to transcendental
idealism, this British philosophy continued to interest him strongly,
despite the great objections he had against it. Of what nature were these
objections at the time of LU? Husserl nowhere gives a sketch
summarizing this British psychology. Yet it is possible to grasp the
heart of his critique on the basis of his detailed analysis of the various
acts. In a certain sense, these philosophers had attempted the same
thing as Husserl, i.e. an analysis of consciousness in all its forms. But
their endeavor went wrong at the very beginning because of a
fundamental misconception about the nature of consciousness.

These psychologists regard consciousness as a receptacle containing
"impressions" that are gathered through sense perception. In the
course of time, these impressions fade and "ideas" arise. These
impressions and their shadows form the only material from which
consciousness is built up.[1] Perception is then explained by way of these
givens, as, for example, in the traditional theory of apperception.
Because these immanent givens stem from sense perception, Husserl
also characterizes this theory as "sensualistic."[2] Everything is reduced
to sensibilia – hence the term 'data-psychology.'[3] Because everything
must be visible and/or tangible, as it were, this psychology from the very
outset leaves no room for categorial objects or essences (so-called
"thought-objects" or "conceptual objects").[4] The sensualist psychology makes of these objects a play of associations and external

---

[1] II 187, 504; see also Id I 227.

[2] II 163f; see also 131, 143, 182, 188. See also PSW 317 and FTL 186f, where Husserl
speaks of "Lockean sensualism," which "has become almost all-pervading in modern
philosophy." Compare Id I 178, 192 note 1, 227; CM 13, 76, 114; Krisis 87 (E 85).

[3] Krisis 245 (E 242).

[4] II 164, 175. 'Thought' is here opposed to 'real' rather than to 'intuitive.' This
thought-object can be properly *perceived*, III 202; see also PSW 315.

connections of ideas.[5] Furthermore, the significative act is then interpreted as the association of a sound with a "fantasy image"[6] and the imaginative act as a faded shadow of an "impression."[7] The difference between positing and mere presentation is reduced to a difference in the intensity of ideas.[8]

What Husserl reproaches this psychology for is reducing all differences in modes of consciousness to differences between contents and combinations of contents. Apperception, which creates sense in the sensations and brings about unities that are more than a mere "togetherness" or "succession" of contents, is ignored.[9] Consciousness is regarded as a kind of space in which contents become connected through similarity and contiguity in time and space. Husserl compares this associative mechanism with a calculating machine's way of operating with numbers.[10] It would take me too far from my path to describe in detail the consequences of this "data-psychology." I will concentrate on the theory of perception, in which the results of the naturalistic thought-stance can most clearly be demonstrated.

The fundamental shortcoming of the empiricist theory of perception, according to Husserl, is its "unclear idea of idea." Here he points out that the concept of idea, upon which all these thinkers rely, is ambiguous. The English word 'idea,' like the German 'Vorstellung' (presentation), can mean either the subjective presentation or the presented object. We find this confusion in Locke, in his opponents Berkeley and John Stuart Mill, and in Hume.[11] With reference to all of these thinkers, Husserl speaks of an "ideological psychology." By

---

[5] II 178ff, 181 (ed. 1) (see also ed. 2, 182), 189ff.

[6] II 76, 131, 143, 217.

[7] II (ed. 1) 364, 397, 466 (see also ed. 2, 385, 423, 501f, respectively); see also Id I 227 where fantasy is called a "pale sense-datum." Husserl says, on the contrary, that in the material of sensation there need be no difference between perception and imagination. The "fantasy image" is only constituted in imaginative apperception.

[8] II 187. According to Husserl, intensity applies only to sensations and not to acts II (ed. 1) 374 (ed. 2, 396); see also FTL 187, 231.

[9] See also Id I 176. Intentional functions are given just as well as immanent sensations II 183, 450, 473; III 153, 157, 160; see also PSW 318 and Entwurf 315. Even on the lowest level of consciousness, that of perception, a unity is more than the sum of its parts II 29f; III 148; compare CM 83 on the phenomenological unity of association. Here we see the points of contact between Husserl and Gestalt psychology; they were later worked out by Aron Gurwitsch in 'Beitrag zur phänomenologischen Theorie der Wahrnehmung.'

[10] II 175, see also EP 92, 100; for Locke, consciousness is "something like a plain or a room." Husserl also observes: The famous *tabula rasa* metaphor is significant . . . ."

[11] II 128, 143, 160, 187, 195, 197.

'idea' they mean a content of consciousness. This content of consciousness is not an act but a *subjectivized object*. It is the perceived thing. According to Locke, the subjectivity of the objects of consciousness is a necessary consequence of the fact that we are conscious of them. "It seems completely self-evident that an act of consciousness can act immediately only on what is actually (*wirklich*) given in consciousness, on the contents that constitute it."[12] This is the well-known "principle of subjectivity" or "principle of immanence." This "principle," which forces us to regard the properties of things or even the things themselves as contents of consciousness is unmasked by Husserl as a "presupposition," as a "supposedly self-evident conclusion." *This presupposition is closely bound up with the so-called natural attitude*, a connection that explains something about its persistence. Husserl speaks of this as a concept falsification almost without equal in philosophy and also as an error from which epistemology "suffers to the present day."[13] It has caused immeasurable harm and "errors that have dragged on through the centuries."[14]

What, then, is this link with the natural objective direction of thought, and how can we understand this presupposition on the basis of it? The concepts of natural man and natural thought were already used by Husserl in 1894. At that time he meant a thinking which does not reflect and makes the mistake of regarding the appearance as the thing itself.[15] The ideological psychology had become aware of the relatedness of all objects to subjectivity, and to this extent it was not naive. It was a step ahead in comparison to pre-scientific naive thought. Yet here too Husserl speaks of an "objective" thought-stance and of naiveté. He can do so because as he sees it, consciousness and the being characteristic of it (*Eigensein*) remain just as hidden for these psychologists as for the natural man who never reflects. The "principle of subjectivity" does not go beyond the formal, general claim – which is made *without a further analysis of consciousness* – that everything of which we are conscious is in consciousness. It does not become a theme but remains an empty title.[16] What get analyzed under the heading of psychology are in fact subjectivized objects. Thus we are confronted with the

[12] II (ed. 1) 159 (ed. 2, 160).
[13] II 165, 129.
[14] II 161, 182, 187, 424.
[15] PSL 178.
[16] Krisis 245 (E 242).

noteworthy fact that this philosophy reduced everything to psychology but still failed to actually discover the psychical – two shortcomings that hang together. Precisely because nothing was known of intentional acts that apprehend and interpret sensations, all objects were reduced to immanent data. This psychologism is actually an objectivism. It did not discover the apperceiving acts; they did not become the object of reflection. We "live through" them, just as the pre-scientific man does.[17] The subjectivizing of the objects and the blindness toward intentionality are two aspects of the same outlook.

These psychologists proceed on the basis of the adage that everything of which we are directly "conscious" (*Bewusst*) is in consciousness (*Bewusst-sein*), without asking what consciousness really is. A phenomenological analysis teaches that the term 'conscious' or 'aware' (*bewusst*) refers to something different in the first part of the preceding sentence than in the latter part. In the first part, it points to the typical mode of consciousness that Husserl calls "apperception," i.e. the intending of a transcendent object. In the latter part, it is an immanent "experiencing" (*erleben*).[18] As a matter of course, every consciousness of something is interpreted as an "experiencing." "*To have an experience and to experience a content* – these expressions are often used as equivalent."[19] Yet there is an evident difference between the two. We hear the song of the singer and thereby "experience" acoustic sensations. Because Locke and company interpret every consciousness as an "experiencing," every perceived object must be a subjective content of consciousness. Consciousness as such is not investigated. These psychologists actually analyze objects and – under the influence of the presupposition mentioned above – posit what they establish "in" consciousness without any further ado.[20] Consciousness remains a fully undifferentiated concept. It is a passive receptacle, a box: the contents "are simply there."[21] Over against this, Husserl shows that consciousness consists of a finely branched out system of intentional functions. The sensations are only the raw material with which

[17] II 39, 376, 385.
[18] II 161.
[19] II 505.
[20] II 10 (ed. 2, 10), 161, 183 (ed. 1).
[21] II 165, see also Id I 227 where Husserl refers to these contents as "miniscule things" (*Sächelchen*).

consciousness weaves the pattern of a transcendently constituted world full of sense. [22]

Over against the natural thought-stance, Husserl calls for consistent and radical reflection. We must not become lost in the performance of acts (*im Vollzuge aufgehen*) but must make these acts themselves our object. [23] In LU, this reflection is not yet accompanied by a suspension of existential judgment with regard to the intended objects – at least, not in Husserl's methodological reflections. At the end of this chapter, we will see that such an epoché does indeed surface in LU, provided that we pay attention not only to what Husserl says he is doing but also to what he actually does.

SECTION TWO.
THE TRANSCENDENT OBJECT

When Husserl's LU are compared with his earlier publications and with the views of Brentano, it appears that he has opened the way to a new, "modern" conception of intentionality. Whereas intentionality was originally a direction toward an immanent object, the object of the intention is now transcendent. [1] We hear the song of the singer rather than sensations present within us. The animals and trees we perceive are not, as Locke believed, "ideas" or combinations of "ideas"; they are not immanent. [2] These statements seem clear and could conceivably be interpreted in the sense of a "turn toward the object." This is done by J.H. van den Berg, among others, who describes the perceived tree as "the tree out there in the garden." The perceived things are the "things of reality." "There *is no* difference between the intentional object . . . and the object really present there. There is only one object, i.e. the one out there. *There is only one world: the world in which we live.*" [3] The subject, according to this interpretation, has finally broken out of the

---

[22] Husserl calls consciousness a "web" of acts II 42 or an "interweaving" of acts II 405, 418.

[23] II 9, see also 39, 376, 409. In the second edition 18, this "im Vollzuge aufgehen" is given the deeper meaning of the execution of the "general positing" (*General-thesis*), i.e. the implicit affirmation of existence that accompanies the objective attitude. There is no trace of this in the first edition. See below 36.

[1] See above 40 and below 185.

[2] II 129, 374.

[3] J.H. van den Berg 'Het menselijk lichaam' II 279, 281, 283.

caged existence in which a real relation to reality would be inconceivable. Van den Berg also speaks in this context of the "evasion" of the subject and of "ex-istence," by which he means finding ourselves outside. The arrow of intentionality extends to the world.[4]

In support of this interpretation, one could also point to Husserl's sharp rejection of any image or sign theory of perception. In perception we do not see a sign or image but the thing "itself," which is "bodily present." Must this expression not be interpreted to mean that in perception we reach the real thing outside?[5] Before we give our assent to any such interpretation, there are two questions to be raised. First, what is this transcendent object? And second, how does Husserl justify this jump to an external world?

(1) When Husserl utters these strong statements about the perception of the transcendent, he is contrasting the experiencing of sensations with the perceiving of the object. What he objects to is the identification of the sensation with the perceived objective property.[6] Here too he appeals to the mode of givenness. The objective color, which is necessarily bound up with a spatial shape, can never be given in the form of a psychical content, for color is inseparable from an extended surface of which it is the color.[7] A three-dimensional spatial form can never be the object of an adequate inner perception.[8] The thing is always given in "adumbrations" (Abschattungen). (This adumbration itself, as the "intuitive substance" of the act, can be adequately perceived.[9]) Making use of Brentano's terminology, we could formulate this as follows: in principle there is a difference between two kinds of "physical phenomena." We must distinguish the one, as an aspect of the experience, from the other, as a property of things.[10]

---

[4] Op.cit. 313, 319, 321, 324, 338, 340. A similar realistic interpretation of perception (which could then be in agreement with the "realism of concepts" of LU – see below 260) is to be found in other writers. Lévinas, for example, writes: "It appears that in the realistic attitude of LU, the objectifying acts reach a being that exists independently of consciousness . . . ." La théorie de l'intuition dans la phénoménologie de Husserl 87, 98. The intentional relation is also interpreted in this sense by R. Sokolowski in The formation of Husserl's concept of constitution 46.

[5] Spiegelberg believes that the term 'bodily present' suggests a realist theory of knowledge, see his essay 'The "reality phenomenon" and reality' 87f.

[6] III 128, 194, 204, 220.

[7] II 76, 162, 195, 253, 277; III 226.

[8] II (ed. 1) 337 (this paragraph was dropped in the second edition).

[9] II 349, 76; III 57, 79, 117.

[10] See above 18. Compare A. Messer, Empfindung und Denken 48 note 2 and Id I 179

From this it already follows that there is a close relation between the two, despite the principial difference. *Ultimately, the transcendent property is nothing but the transcendently interpreted sensation.* It is a sensation which is "objectively" apperceived; that is to say, it is apprehended as a property of an object. Therefore the act of apperception is also called an objectifying act[11] which provides a presented object through an objectifying interpretation.[12] Husserl also gives expression to this close relation between sensation and property when he claims that the sensation gives us *analogous building material*, as it were, for the constitution of the object. The things that appear to us are constituted from the same matter as the immanent contents.[13] Although they are not identical, they are "generically related."[14] There are certain "kinds" (*Gattungen*) of sensations, e.g. sensations of sight and of touch. When these "kinds" now appear to us as transcendent things (via their objective interpretation), we can refer to them by way of the same name, and herein lies their relatedness. In both cases we speak, for example, of "color" or "smoothness."[15] We are faced here with the ambiguous use of a term, which has contributed to the identification of the two (i.e. sensation and property).

This equivocation can be particularly troublesome in the case of the concept "spatial." When we speak of spatiality in connection with sensations, we mean the aspects that help to constitute objective space, which are not themselves in space. Therefore it is confusing when Husserl also speaks of "extension," "position" and "size" in connection with immanent objects. In the second edition he adds by way of warning that the "presentative moments" of extension, position and size are meant.[16] In another passage in which he speaks about immanent contents, he replaces the expression 'spatial extension' with 'quasi-spatial extension.'[17] This is indeed a clarification, for it is characteristic of "experiences" (of which immanent contents are a part) that they are not spatial. In his analysis of inner time consciousness, Husserl was to contrast

for Stumpf's concept of 'appearance,' which, according to Husserl, coincides with what he (i.e. Husserl) understands by 'sensation.'

[11] II 401, 500, 441, 494.

[12] II 30, 184, 349, 364, 494.

[13] II (ed. 1) 707. In the second edition, this was changed to 'analogous matter.' III 234.

[14] II 75f. In the first edition II 707 we read 'gleichartig' (homogeneous); in the second edition, this was changed to 'analogous matter' III 234; see also Id I 75.

[15] II (ed. 1) 706f (see also ed. 2 III 234f); II 129.

[16] II 257 note 1 and 2.

[17] II 289 (see also ed. 1, 281); in the first edition, Husserl had already warned against this identification 241 (more extensively in the second edition 247).

inner time, which cannot be measured by a chronometer, with external time or "space-time."[18]

Meanwhile, we should note that Husserl's ideas with regard to space are more consistent in LU than they had been earlier. In PA, he had maintained that acts are in time and contents in space. This raised the difficulty of how there could be spatial contents in a non-spatial psyche. This difficulty is now resolved. Only the sensations are immanent. Via an objectifying interpretation of the sensations, a spatial transcendent object appears to us.

Thus there is an inner bond between the transcendent object and the presentative contents. Here 'presentative' is even narrowed down to "self-presenting."[19] The perceiving of an object, then, is nothing but the objective interpretation of the material of sensation.[20] It is clear that the transcendent object is not a "thing in itself" standing outside consciousness. What appears in perception is an "appearance." *We do not know whether it actually exists.*[21] In principle, there is no change in Husserl's thinking on the question of the external world from PA to LU. We perceive objective colors. These colors are objectifications of immanent "colors." How do these sensations come about? Must there be some external cause evoking this material of sensation in us? This question is not explicitly raised in LU and thus not answered. Husserl simply takes it for granted that we have sensations and then describes our apperception of them. The reason for his silence on this question is to be sought in his point of departure, i.e. descriptive psychology.[22] Ultimate causes of the described phenomena lie completely beyond consideration. The question whether Husserl accepts such cause and whether we can speak here of a "thing of physics" will be discussed separately later. For the moment I am content to establish that the transcendent object is *not* this real thing.

(2) All of this is confirmed when we inquire into the justification of this new theory of perception. The epistemological problem is usually formulated as follows. There is an object, a "thing in itself" independent of consciousness. The psychical act is directed toward this object. The question is then how consciousness can know this thing as it

---

[18] See below 462. Like objective space, objective time originally comes about through an objectifying interpretation.

[19] II 382; III 79; see above 145.

[20] II 351.

[21] Therefore there must be an epoché with regard to existence, see below 178, 199.

[22] See below 167, 177.

really is. To answer this question, we must be able to adopt a standpoint that lies within and outside consciousness at the same time, which is an evident impossibility.

Husserl does not pose the problem in this way.[23] In descriptive psychology he recognizes no problem of "bridging the gap." He takes consciousness, the sphere of "experiences" (*Erlebnisse*), as his point of departure and maintains that there are certain experiences that are directed toward something transcendent. The experience constitutes in itself a relation to something which it is not. That a transcendent object appears means "that a certain act is experienced in which certain sensory experiences are 'apperceived' in a certain manner."[24] With the presence of a certain act, a transcendent object is thus given at the same time.[25] There is indeed something "over against us,"[26] but this is not the "over against" of a metaphysical thing in itself but of an appearing object which makes the act itself appear by objectifying certain sensation material. Husserl does use the term 'thing in itself,' but "in the only sense relevant and understandable in our context, the sense which the fulfillment of the perceptual intention would carry out."[27] In other words, it is the object that appears when the act in question is a perceptual act, i.e. an adequately perceiving act. The definition of 'real object' is thus that it is "the possible object of a straightforward perception."[28] From then on, the object is defined through the relation to perception. It is the object "*as* it appears in perception, and *as what* it appears in perception" and not "the object existing in objective reality ... which is only later to be brought out through experience, knowledge and science."[29]

The claim that certain acts perceive a transcendent object is thus a *descriptive psychological* claim. The difference between Husserl and

---

[23] This is a metaphysical problem, according to Husserl I 114; see below 195.

[24] II 407, 412. Compare what Husserl says in 435: "That a presentation refers to a certain object in a certain manner is not due to its acting on some external, independent object, 'directing' itself to it in some literal sense, or doing something to it or with it, as a hand writes with a pen. It is due to nothing external to the presentation but solely to its own inner peculiarity." See also 371 (ed. 1, 351) and 376 (ed. 1, 355) and Id I 64. The intentional relation is not a "real relation" between two things.

[25] II 337 (ed. 1, 462).

[26] II 350.

[27] III 57.

[28] III 151, compare 149 and 154 on the contrast between the phenomenological object and the object of physics; see below 195.

[29] III 154.

Brentano, then, is not that Brentano limits himself to what can be established on psychological grounds while Husserl breaks out of this circle toward a world transcendent to consciousness. *Both remain within psychology.* What Husserl can reproach Brentano for is not seeing the difference between the "mere having" of a content and the objective interpretation of a content. Anyone who confuses these two falls prey to an equivocal concept of "conscious" (*bewusst*) and to such ambiguous expressions as 'in consciousness' and 'immanent to consciousness.' Husserl's most important argument is this distinction between two different "modes of consciousness." When he speaks in LU about acts that perceive the object "itself" and posit it as "existing," this too is psychological language.[30]

In LU, indeed, the intentional object is not immanent, as it is in earlier writings of Husserl. Nevertheless it remains an *intentional* object in the *Scholastic meaning* of the term 'intentional,' in which it is opposed to 'actual' (*wirklich*).[31] The theme of intentionality in LU does not as such give us any reason to apeak of a realist theory of knowledge. We shall see later that we can speak of realism in LU despite this, but for reason *outside the theme of intentionality.*

At present this conclusion is still premature, for we have not yet taken the "ideal object" into the scope of our consideration. The realism of LU is often based squarely on the intuition of essences. At this stage in our investigation, however, we are not yet in a position to make judgments about the ontological status of these essences. I will return to this matter at the end of Chapter 3.

SECTION THREE.
THE RELATIONS BETWEEN ACTS AND CONTENTS

PARAGRAPH ONE. THE CONCEPT OF CONSTITUTION

There has been a great deal of dispute among interpreters of Husserl about the import of the concept of "constitution." The realist and idealist interpretations here stand opposed. Proponents of the former view maintain that the relation of consciousness to the object is one of

[30] See below 180 and 321.
[31] See below 194.

"encounter." Constitution, on this view, is letting an object independent of consciousness appear. Husserl is often interpreted in this
sense by "existential" phenomenology (e.g. Biemel). Other interpreters
of Husserl, by contrast, are of the view that constitution must be
conceived of in a transcendental idealist sense. Finally, it has also been
argued by some that Husserl's writings are so ambiguous on this point
that the dispute cannot be resolved.[1] It is my conviction that this
question can be discussed meaningfully only in the light of Husserl's
development. When this is done, we will see that this disputed question
can actually be resolved, and that the two interpretations mentioned
above do not exclude one another but represent different phases in
Husserl's thinking.

I will limit myself here to an analysis of the concept of constitution in
LU. First I will discuss acts of the first order, and then categorial acts.

(A) We have seen above that in LU, long before Husserl went over to
transcendental idealism, he already used the concept of "constitution."[2] What he meant by it in this period was indeed sense-giving in
Biemel's sense; it is the interpretation of a sensation, through which an
object appears. Thus, constitution as we find it in LU must not be
conceived of as a creating. Therefore we can say, as Husserl had said in
PA, that creative acts are "psychological absurdities." Constituting is a
"making something appear," in the sense that a given immanent
material is apprehended as an objective property.[3] The question of the
origin of these sensations can only be answered by a genetic explanatory psychology. For descriptive psychology, it is enough to observe
that we encounter these sensations in consciousness.

This non-idealist concept of constitution was retained by Husserl
when he went over to transcendental idealism. It is true that within
transcendental phenomenology, constitution means bringing forth, as
Fink contends in the article authorized by Husserl. Yet this does not
alter the fact that the non-creative concept of constitution lives on, i.e.
in so-called phenomenological psychology. This psychology, which is a
continuation of the descriptive psychology of LU, is a stage preparatory for transcendental phenomenology, a stage in which the transcendental turn has not yet taken place. Thus, even after Husserl's
conversion to transcendental idealism, it remained true from the

[1] See below 410.
[2] See above 137.
[3] II 194, 349, 365, 481, 494, 500, 503.

psychological standpoint that creative acts are absurdities. As Fink argues, the psychological experience of man in the world is receptive. Psychological intentionality is a "constituted" mundane intentionality and, as such, is powerless.[4]

(*B*) I alluded above to the possibility that constitution might have to be interpreted on the basis of acts of a higher order.[5] There are actually two questions involved here: (1) the interpretation of these acts themselves, and (2) whether categorial perception served as a model for the concept of constitution.

Opinion is divided on the first of these questions. Szilasi believes that what characterizes Husserl's philosophy is that consciousness does *not* create relations; he appeals to the term 'categorial *perception*' in support of this claim. On this point he contrasts Husserl with Kant and argues that one could hardly imagine a more radical break with the philosophical tradition. The forms are not brought forth by the understanding but are given in perception.[6] But little can properly be derived from Husserl's use of the term 'perception.' After his conversion to transcendental idealism, even a normal perceiving of a thing can have a creative character. Furthermore, Szilasi neglects the point that is really at issue here, i.e. the difference between sensory perception and categorial perception. That relations are properties of the things themselves is by itself nothing new. In opposition to Kant, Husserl had already maintained this in PA with regard to physical (material) relations. The question now is whether this is also true in the case of *categorial* relations which arise from our *spontaneity*. Szilasi neglects this difference. This is apparent when he points to the perceiving of a "row" of trees as an example of a categorial perception. Thereby he does exactly what Husserl warns against, i.e. confusing a sensorily perceivable unity with a categorial unity.[7] The perceiving of a row of trees is a normal sensory perception. "Being a row" is a "form-quality," i.e. a perceivable property, a quasi-quality, as Husserl calls it.

The possibility that Szilasi ignores arises when we proceed to actually count the row of trees and say, "There are fifteen trees." Is this number a property of the things or a product of our counting? In PA, Husserl

---

[4] 'Die phänomenologische Philosophie Edmund Husserls in der gegenwärtigen Kritik' 358, 364, 370, 372.

[5] See above 152.

[6] W. Szilasi, *Einführung in die Phänomenologie Edmund Husserls* 28f, 37, 41.

[7] III 161. See above 23 note 4, 149.

answered this question by maintaining that the acts are brought forth by us but not the numbers: the numbers do not exist objectively outside us. In LU, however, Husserl accepts the view that the act of counting has its own correlate, i.e. the collective as an "ideal object." Is this object not a product of the mind? Is the number as a categorial object not brought forth by categorial perception? I believe that this question must be answered in the negative. We can speak of spontaneity in connection with these acts, but this does not yet mean that consciousness is creative here. We have seen above that categorial perception is a founded act. It cannot exist without a founding sensory perception, the object of which it more fully *explicates*. It uncovers what is implicitly given on the pre-categorial level, e.g. a part-whole relation or a relation of inherence. [8]

Thus we must think of a "making something appear" rather than of a producing. This is also apparent from Husserl's doctrine of the "categorial representative." Husserl sees categorial perception – like sensory perception – as the objective interpreting of an immanent content, which in this case is a psychical bond formed on the founding level. Continuous synthesis through fusion in perception is the condition for the possibility of an "articulated" or explicit synthesis on the categorial level. [9] Here we have a true analogy between sensory perception and categorial perception.

This really answers my second question also, i.e. whether categorial constitution served as a model for perceptual constitution. [10] My analysis does not support this hypothesis. In Part I we already saw that Husserl did not discover the sense-giving activity of consciousness in connection with his analysis of acts of a higher order; he discovered it when examining significative acts. In LU, Husserl also sees perception as sense-giving. He then applies this new concept of perception to categorial perception, which is seen as an objective interpreting of a categorial representative. Thus it turns out that the reverse is true; that is to say, it was perceptual constitution that served as a model for

---

[8] On the relation between the spontaneous categorial synthesis and the continuous synthesis of perception (also called 'sensory' or 'aesthetic' synthesis), see Id II 18ff. "Indeed, one could say that no analysis can bring out anything that was not already hidden in a certain way and implied in implicit synthesis" 21; see also Id I 42.

[9] III 150, 154, 172. Husserl later dropped this theory of the categorial representative III, V.

[10] This is Fink's opinion; see also his article 'Les concepts opératoires dans la phénoménologie de Husserl' 224ff, 240.

categorial constitution. Thus, the decisions with regard to the interpretation of the doctrine of constitution must be made on the basis of the doctrine of perception. In Part III we shall see that the "Phenomenological Fundamental Consideration" of Ideen I is based on an analysis of these acts. Only such a consideration could properly lay claim to the title "fundamental," for sensory perception is the basic act of consciousness. Actually, it would be completely un-Husserlian to interpret sensory perception on the basis of categorial perception instead of the other way around, for Husserl always wanted to return to the final, founding groundwork of our knowledge – from "judgment" we must go back to "experience."[11]

PARAGRAPH TWO. THE CORRELATION BETWEEN THE ACT AND THE OBJECT

I have already pointed out the importance of the new concept of perception for correlative analysis.[1] In this paragraph I will elucidate certain aspects of this correlativity insofar as they bear on the rest of my exposition.

(1) The "*object as referred to*" and the "*object referred to.*" An important distinction is that between the "object as it is intended" and the "object which is intended" or the "object in the strict sense (*schlechthin*).[2] This distinction recurs in Ideen I as that between the properties of a thing and the bearer of the properties (the identity pole).[3] Correlated with these two aspects on the act side are the matter and the "objective reference" (which we could call an identity pole within the material direction of the act). Husserl gives the following example. I can intend the German Kaiser as such, i.e. in his function as Kaiser, but I can also intend him as the grandson of Queen Victoria and the son of Kaiser Frederick III. In these three intentional acts, the "object as referred to" differs, but the "object referred to" remains the same – hence the name 'identity pole.' In these acts we are directed toward the same, identical figure, who is presented in each case with different properties.

---

[11] EU 21, 38; FTL 150, 182, 185.
[1] See above 141.
[2] II 400, 415, 434, 499.
[3] See below 438, 447.

Husserl's remark at a certain point that the matter can change while the object remains the same must be interpreted in the light of this distinction.[4] It does *not represent a breaking of the correlation* between act and object. What is meant is that the object reference remains the same. Husserl would have made himself more clear if he had said (noetically) that the matter can change while the "objective reference" remains the same or (noematically) that the "object as referred to" can change while the "object referred to" remains the same.

(2) *The matter: stuff and form.* Within the matter, we can again make a distinction between stuff and form. This holds for categorial acts. The "stuff" or the "terms" of such an act stem from the founding perception. The sensorily perceived objects can be formed in various different ways. Thus the terms in the judgments "S is p" and "S which is p . . ." are identical, but the two judgments differ in form. These formal differences recur in the matter of the act. Stuff and form in the act correspond completely with stuff and form in the categorial object.[5]

(3) *No noematic significance.* The theme of correlativity was raised in connection with perceptual acts. This is not an accident, for in LU, this *correlativity does not apply to significative acts.* We must pay special attention to this fact, for it is of the greatest importance for any effort to get a grasp of Husserl's development and of the significance of correlative analysis in *pure logic.*[6] In LU, the theme of correlativity is limited to perception ("straightforward" and categorial), a limitation that was only overcome later.[7] In the case of significative acts, indeed, there is also a directedness to a meant object, but that is not to say that the act *as such* has a correlate. The meant object is actually the correlate of the perception that fulfills the meaning. In the case of the significative act, this relation to the object is not "realized."

The same state of affairs can also be explained as follows. When an act of meaning gives meaning to a physical sound, the meaning is not an objective correlate but lies exclusively in the act.[8] When H speaks of "meaning" in the LU, he means the meaning-giving aspect of the act (or its eidos)[9] and not the noematic correlate of the act.

[4] II 47, 49. J. Thyssen draws from this the unjustified conclusion that Husserl makes the meaning independent and severs the relation to the object 177. Thyssen himself maintains – to the contrary – that meanings differ only insofar as they name different things. But this is also what Husserl holds.

[5] II 475, 478, 480, 483f, 492, 506; III 128, 182, 187.

[6] See below 285, 296 and 492.

[7] Vorwort (ed. 2) XIV, XV; see below 319, 443.

[8] See above 131.

[9] See below 253.

(4) *Correlativity and the phenomenological point of departure.* In LU, we face the noteworthy fact that the correlative relation is fully recognized – at least in the case of perception – even though correlative analysis has not yet been developed. Phenomenological analysis prefers to direct itself toward acts. The intentional objects are really not regarded as legitimate subject matter for phenomenology. "In a phenomenological treatment, objectivity itself counts as nothing; to speak in general terms, it transcends the act."[10] Husserl presupposes that in phenomenological (i.e. descriptive psychological) analysis, only consciousness itself can properly be described, for it alone is given. But if the intentional objects also appear, if they are phenomena, does it not conflict with the "principle of all principles" to exclude them from phenomenological description? Before we can answer this question, Husserl's theory of perception must be discussed.

PARAGRAPH THREE. THE THEORY OF PERCEPTION

I. Adequate and Non-adequate Perception

Husserl's distinction between adequate and non-adequate perception is closely bound up with his new theory of perception. It is completely determined by the distinction between the "experiencing" (*erleben*) of a content and the objective interpretation of it. By adequate perception, he means a perception that takes its objects as what they are, that "simply takes them in as what they are." Over against this stands non-adequate perception, which does not "simply take its object as it actually is" but goes beyond it interpretively. This perception takes its objects not "as what they *are*" but "as what they are *interpreted* as being."[1] I will elucidate this by reference to inner and outer perception.

(1) *Outer perception* consists of an interpretation of sensations. In consciousness that are color sensations, for example, and these are now apprehended as the color of an intentional object. But this color, which is an "appearance," is not adequately perceived, for it is a product of interpretation. We cannot be certain that it is in reality the way it appears to be. But we do have this certainty in the case of the sensations themselves. These contents are perceived in (inner) perception as they

[10] II (ed. 1) 387 (see also ed. 2, 412); In 1913 Husserl wrote concerning LU: "The method of the intentional analysis of the correlates consciousness and objectivity is developed." We shall see that at most, this is the case only implicitly.

[1] III 232, 238ff (see also ed. 1, 710).

really are, as they are "experienced" (*erlebt*). In this case we must disregard the transcendent interpretation of these immanent contents and simply take them "as what they are." We can then be certain that what is perceived really exists as it is perceived, that it is "really at hand" (*reell vorhanden*). "Adequate perception involves ... that in it the perceived, just *as* it is perceived (as the perception thinks or conceives of it), is experienced."[2] Only that which is "experienced," which is "in" consciousness, can be adequately perceived, i.e. acts and immanent contents. In this regard Husserl has not departed from his earlier standpoint, according to which acts and contents are adequately perceivable. The difference is that Husserl now distinguishes between the experienced content and the property that is objectively perceived via the content. Brentano's term 'physical phenomenon' now has two meanings: it can mean the immanent sensation but also the objective property. Only the former can be perceived as it actually is.[3]

It is clear that an outer perception is always in essence an interpretation, and that therefore it can never be adequate. Husserl does say that we can make the transition to adequate perception here, but this is only possible when we disregard the interpretation. Thereby, however, the perception would *ipso facto* cease being an outer perception and would become an inner perception of a sensation. Now, Husserl does posit adequate perception as the final goal of outer perception; outer perception attains its ultimate fulfillment in adequate perception.[4] Whereas normally there is a distinction between the sensation and the phenomenon appearing, in such a case the two would coincide,[5] and that toward which every perception strives would be realized.[6] This fulfillment has the character of a "relation admitting of degrees"(*Steigerungsrelation*), of which adequate perception is the "ideal limit," the absolute goal. Every outer perception, as a "self-presentation," points to this perception in which the "absolute self" is given.[7] This absolute self is also called the "object in itself" or "the thing itself."[8]

On Husserl's view, then, the adequate perception of a representative is in line

---

[2] III 240; II 30, 199, 398.

[3] This difference between the objectively interpreted phenomenon and the "experienced" content likewise manifests itself in the case of the perception of one's own body (which was already mentioned above 140), e.g. in a toothache, which is perceived as *localized*. "The perceived object is not the pain as it is experienced but the pain as it is transcendently interpreted and even attributed to the tooth" II 392, 395; III 232, 240.

[4] III 118.

[5] II (ed. 1) 707 (ed. 2 III 83, 117f).

[6] III 57.

[7] II 354f; III 66, 117.

[8] III 57, 119.

with the interpretation of the representative. This implies that in perception, the intention is directed ultimately toward the sensation. The interpretation would terminate in the intuiting of that which is interpreted. It is in this sense that we must understand Husserl's remark in the first edition of LU that the perceptual intention finds partial fulfillment in the present content and thus has to do partially with an existing object.[9] This too presupposes that in perception there is an intention directed toward the interpreted content. The fulfillment of this intention is then the final fulfillment. As long as perception is a self-presentation, it always remains supposed or presumptive (*vermeintlich*). Even if the apperceived object itself is given, it remains an intention, for the "absolute self" is identical with the representative.[10] As long as there remains a difference between the perceived color and the sensation of color, perception has not reached its final goal.

What is unsatisfactory about this theory is that what Husserl sees as the final fulfillment of outer perception in fact constitutes a denial of outer perception as outer perception. The interpretation that is essential to outer perception is then undone. It is difficult to accept the view that the intention of a perception is ultimately directed toward the immanent content which, as the "object in itself," is what is ultimately intended or meant. It is much more in agreement with Husserl's view of apperception to see "self-presentation" as the final stage. Perception, after all, is the instant of fulfillment for signification or "empty" meaning. When we make the transition from outer perception, i.e. the interpreting of the representative, to the perceiving of the representative itself, an end is brought to the interpreting and a transition is made in principle to *inner* perception. In the appendix to the second edition of LU (1920), Husserl changed his standpoint. The perceptual intention is no longer directed in part to the representative itself.[11] This is in agreement with the teachings of Ideen I, where there is a principial gap between transcendent and immanent perception.[12] What is perceived outwardly can never become immanent, and thus it can never be adequately intuited.

This theory of perception is illustrative of Husserl's point of departure in LU, which I will examine separately. He was tied to it so firmly that he held that in outer perception, only the sensation can count as given. But he repeatedly broke through this methodological point of departure in the analysis itself.

(2) An objective interpretation is also possible when the perceptual

[9] II (ed. 1) 711, 713; see also ed. 2 III 57 and 117.

[10] II 349ff, 362f, 34. Perception is an "intuitive putative grasping," a "supposed grasping" (*anschaulich vermeinen, vermeintlich erfassen*) II 479; III 50.

[11] Compare II (ed. 1) 711 and 713 with (ed. 2) III 239. In the second edition this was not corrected in III 57 and 117. See the foreword to the second edition VII, where Husserl says that he has revised especially the appendix.

[12] Id I 76. In Ideen I, outer perception is "supposed" in the sense of presumptive; see below 335.

intention is directed toward consciousness. Thus *inner perception* need not always be adequate. Interpretation is possible here, resulting in a spatial, localized apprehension of something in consciousness. An "experience," says Husserl, is then perceived with "physical" determinations. As an example, one could mention the "fear that tightens our throat." In an adequate perception, this interpretation would be undone.

This remark is interesting because there is a certain analogy between this localizing apperception and what Husserl later called psychological (or mundane) apperception. This is the apperception that apprehends consciousness as a part of the world, as "psyche." The analogy nicely manifests the difference between LU and the transcendental idealism of Ideen I. Husserl now has no objections against psychological apperception. Like Brentano, he calls attention to the incorrect localization of consciousness, which is non-spatial in nature. But in Ideen I, Husserl sees this spatializing as a consequence of a much more fundamental error, i.e. the view of consciousness as the higher level of a psycho-physical unity. Husserl had not yet seen through this error in LU. In the second edition, he states that this "psycho-physical apperception" is the deepest root of the spatialization of consciousness.[13]

II. The Phenomenological Point of Departure – "Presupposition-lessness"

Although the perceiving of psychical "experiences" (*Erlebnisse*) is not always adequate, it is nevertheless true that we can adequately perceive only these "experiences." In the case of "experiences," it is possible to perceive that which we perceive as it actually is. The perception is adequate "when the object really is 'there' (*da*) as what it is, when it is bodily present, thus when it is itself present in the perception and is one with it. Thus it is obvious, indeed, evident from the mere concept of perception, that adequate perception can *only* be inner perception, and that it can only be trained upon experiences simultaneously given and belonging to one single consciousness."[14] It

[13] III 232, 241; see also II (ed. 1) 713; see also below 462 and above 39.

[14] II 333 (ed. 1; see also ed. 2, 355); 357. The notion that "experiencing" is itself a perceiving like the "inner consciousness" of Bretano (see above 38) is rejected by Husserl explicitly. Consciousness is not automatically perceived II 371, 339 (ed. 1), 353, 357, 361. It is perceived only in a separate act, which makes it an object. III 227 note 1; compare Id I 83 where consciousness is "ready to be perceived," perceiv*able*.

is of the essence of adequate perception "that the intuited object itself really and truly dwells in it."[15] As we have seen, it is necessary for such a perception, which grasps its object as it really is, that we not allow ourselves to be misled by transcendent interpretations, e.g. when we perceive a pain "in the tooth" or speak of a "happiness that makes me shudder" (*mich durchschauernde Seligkeit*).

But if we perceive experiences as they are actually "experienced," then inward evidence in the pregnant sense of "knowledge in the strict sense" is possible.[16] Every relativism runs aground on this inward evidence. It would be irrational to doubt the existence of experiences "while we are experiencing them."[17] Here we arrive at what Husserl himself calls the Archimedean point of his philosophy. On this basis, the world of "unreason" and doubt "may be levered on its hinges." Anyone who gives up this inward evidence also gives up all reason and knowledge. "If we were to lose faith in inward evidence, how could we rationally make and sustain assertions?"[18] *Here Husserl deliberately declares his adherence to the starting point of Descartes, namely, the inward evidence of the "I am."*[19] The "Cartesian treatment of doubt" rests on the consideration that it would be evidently irrational to doubt inner perception, which simply takes its objects as they are. Here the "evidence of existence" is indisputable.[20] Therefore phenomenology must limit itself to the "only regulative sphere of immediate consciousness." Only that which can be adequately perceived is actually given.[21]

In the introduction to the second volume of LU, Husserl devotes a separate paragraph to "the principle of the presuppositionlessness of epistemological investigations." Every epistemological investigation that lays claim to being scientific must satisfy this principle. *In concreto*, this presuppositionlessness means for Husserl that the epistemologist must limit himself to the realm of inner perception.[22] In LU, phenomenology is identical with descriptive psychology; it is a description of experiences. This sphere of experiences is called by Husserl

---

[15] III 240.
[16] III 121, 225.
[17] III 225.
[18] I 121, 143, 152.
[19] I 121; II 356; III 225, 240.
[20] III 240, 238.
[21] II 120 (ed. 1; see also II ed. 2, 121); II (ed. 1) 369 note 1.
[22] II 19f (ed. 1); see also 387.

the "phenomenological inventory of the ego."[23] Phenomenology must never make statements that go beyond this sphere.

When Husserl – on this basis – binds himself entirely to the given, the question arises how a theory of knowledge is possible, for what a theory of knowledge bears on is exactly the question of the relation to the object. It must answer the questions that have to do with the "legitimacy of the claim to objectivity." According to Husserl, psychology can abstract from this question.[24] I do not need to be certain that the object exists in order to possess inward evidence that I am perceiving this particular object. My "relating myself to the object" is given. If, for example, I form a presentation of the god Jupiter, the phenomenological given is simply my forming a presentation of Jupiter. Whether or not Jupiter exists is irrelevant to the description of this experience. *It makes no difference in psychical respects.* If the presented object does not exist, this means that only the intention exists. If the object does exist, then both the intention and what is intended exist.[25]

This theory of knowledge must be characterized as a psychology of knowledge – and a descriptive psychology at that. Thus it is not a genuine "theory"; that is to say, it does not "explain." Theory of knowledge still had this meaning for Brentano; on his view, it went beyond the bounds of psychology. It tried to explain how the contents described arose in consciousness. By means of causal reasoning, Brentano then arrived at the hypothesis of a world existing outside us. In descriptive psychology, the question of transcendence is eliminated on methodological grounds. But in LU, Husserl also wanted to limit theory of knowledge to the psychological standpoint, i.e. by restricting it to the sphere of "experiences" (acts and immanent contents). This means that in theory of knowledge, the question of the existence of the external world cannot arise either.[26] The question of the existence and nature of an ultimately external world is a metaphysical issue.

---

[23] II 397 note 1 (ed. 1; see also ed. 2, 17, 398), 345.
[24] II 348, 382, 413.
[25] II 373, 425.
[26] When Husserl speaks of causality, he means a phenomenal causality as intentional object. Thus it shares the intentional character of the phenomenon and implies nothing about actual existence II 369 note 1 (ed. 1; see also ed. 2, 391).

III. The Suspension of the Question of Existence (Epoché)

The purely descriptive character of analysis comes to the fore methodologically in the demand for a "suspension of the external world." We shall see that the famous *bracketing of reality*, which has achieved a certain notoriety since the publication of Ideen I in 1913 and has become something of a shibboleth among followers of Husserl's, is already to be found in LU. Moreover, we shall also see that *only in LU does it occur in the strict sense of a suspension of the external world.* It is in LU that Husserl first places reality between brackets – and not in Ideen I. What is at issue in the latter work is a suspension not of reality but of a particular vision of reality. A real theory of knowledge solving the problem of the "thing in itself" would be impossible in LU.[27] As to the background of this "epoché," it is only on the basis of adequate inner perception, which does not go interpretively beyond the given, that an existential judgment is possible. The sphere of "experiences" is also called the real (*reell*) by Husserl.[28] It is that which actually exists. In the case of all other perception, it can be doubted whether the object actually exists and whether it exists just as it appears.[29]

Everything that is transcendently interpreted thus falls outside phenomenology – not only things, then, but also the body,[30] and even one's own experiences, to the extent that they are localized and interpreted transcendently. Finally, the consciousness of the other also falls outside the phenomenological sphere. The psychical phenomena of an other cannot be perceived as they are. Only our perception of our *own* experiences is evident.[31] Thus it is completely consistent on Husserl's part to abstract from the existence of the public in the introduction to LU. Presuppositionlessness, he says, is in no way undermined by the many expressions which the author directs toward his public, for the existence of this public is not presupposed in the content of his work. The analyses have their value regardless of whether any other persons exist.

The only demand that must be satisfied is that all statements be phenomenologically justifiable.[32] Only judgments about acts can be

---

[27] See below 397.

[28] II 347, 352f; III 244.

[29] III 238, 240.

[30] II 226. The existence of our "sense organs" must also be left unconsidered; see below 210.

[31] II 34; III 240. Here lies the root of the later egological reduction.

[32] II (ed. 1) 22.

justified phenomenologically. This is the reason for Husserl's *one-sided preference for the description of acts* in the correlation between act and object. There is a constant movement backwards, as it were. Instead of analyzing the object correlate, we analyze the directedness of consciousness to this object. Characteristic of this method is the statement: "The object is an intentional object: this means there is an act having a determinate intention – determinate in a way that makes it an intention toward this object."[33] The schema by which Husserl works is this: "*The object is . . . that is to say, there is an act.*" The phenomenological turn is possible exactly because the determinations of the object are mirrored in the determinations of the act. The correspondence, as I have already pointed out, is complete. In the matter as an aspect of the act is mirrored not only which object is intended but also with what properties it is intended. Therefore we can see that when the matter is the same in two acts, their object is the same, and vice versa.[34]

PARAGRAPH FOUR. THEORY OF KNOWLEDGE AS A "PSYCHOLOGY OF REASON"

In this paragraph, Husserl's theory of knowledge will be worked out in greater detail, within the methodological limits imposed. In the process we will discover something interesting, namely, that there is a tension – sometimes latent and sometimes manifest – between Husserl's concrete analyses and the methodological framework within which they are carried out. The Cartesian point of departure binds Husserl strictly to the sphere of experiences as the sole given, but in practice he transcends the officially avowed point of departure continually. This brings about a noteworthy tension between the methods actually used and methodological reflection on these methods. In practice Husserl repeatedly broke through the narrow Cartesian framework – but without any explicit discussion of what was going on.[1]

The question how a theory of knowledge is possible on the level of psychology is really answered by Husserl in two ways – explicitly and implicitly. The latter answer transcends the sphere of experiences and

---

[33] II 412f.

[34] II 412f, 415, 418f; III 88.

[1] This discussion occurs in 1907, *Die Idee der Phänomenologie.* See below 314f. According to Kern Husserl introduced the concept of noema for the first time in 1904, *Husserl und Kant,* 180f.

recognizes the intentional object too as subject matter for phenomenological investigation. Because these two answers run through one
another, the question we are now considering is a rather complicated
one. Yet the effort to untangle this knot and lay bare the two levels in
Husserl's description will be amply rewarded, for what we face here is
the birth of the extremely important concept of "noema" or the
perceived as such, which played a central role in Husserl's later
phenomenological psychology, i.e. the descriptive psychology that
then served as a preparatory stage for phenomenology.

I. Two Questions

By way of two questions, I will now try to bring to light the two strata
in Husserl's reflection.

(*A*) The existence of the perceived object must be placed between
brackets, according to Husserl. The question could well be raised
whether this conflicts with some of his other statements. I think
particularly of Husserl's distinction between "mere presentation" and
"positing as something" (*setzen als etwas*). [2] In any objectifying act, it is
possible either to posit that which is presented as existing or to merely
form a presentation of it. Only in the former case can we speak of an act
of belief. In such an act, a position is taken with respect to the question
of existence or non-existence. But in mere presentation, consciousness
adopts a neutral attitude. [3]

Husserl also describes this attitude as a "leaving in suspense" (*dahingestellt
lassen*), [4] an "understanding without taking a position" (Dahinstehend
haben). [5] As an example he cites "mere imagining" or fantasy, [6] and also "mere
understanding," e.g. when we listen to someone speak without taking a
position of "belief" or "disbelief" with regard to the existence of what is being
spoken about. [7] It is possible to pass from an act of positing to an act of mere
presentation, and vice versa. Such a change, which leaves the matter untouched, would be a so-called qualitative modification. Thus memory, for
example, finds its neutral "counterpart" in imagination. [8]

[2] See above 142.
[3] II 429, 459.
[4] II 487, 479; III 120.
[5] II 456 (ed. 2).
[6] II 431.
[7] II 446, 448, 490, 499.
[8] II 442, 444, 454, 465, 487.

The following question can now be formulated: if in outer perception we must refrain from judging about the existence or non-existence of what is perceived, does it make sense to draw a distinction between objects posited as really existing and merely presented objects?

(B) A second question bound up closely with the first concerns Husserl's analysis of significative and perceptual acts. Was it not the typical difference between the two that the former intends its object in an "empty" way whereas the latter, the intuitive act, either fulfills or does not fulfill the intention? In the latter event, the meaning would have to be rejected as impossible, for then it could not be "realized."[9] It is the perceptual act that determines whether or not we are correct in positing an object. If we see something itself, we can say that it *is*. If we must abstain from judgment about existence as a matter of principle, what are we to make of this? Is a genuine theory of knowledge that takes a stance on the *justification* for positing objects possible at all?

II. A First Answer

(A) Our first question, which concerns the distinction between acts of "mere presentation" and acts of judgment, is answered by Husserl firstly in a way that we could characterize as purely phenomenological; that is to say, his answer is based purely on an analysis of acts. His view is that we do not need to express ourselves about whether or not the intentional object exists in order to be able to ascertain (in inner perception) that we intend such an object as existing. Given is an intentional act of the quality "positing" (*Setzung*), an act in which the object is intended as "actually existing."[10]

But this does not mean that the object does in fact exist. Its actual existence is just as real a possibility as the reverse, i.e. that we have merely formed a presentation of an existing object.[11] The difference between mere presentation and positing is an immanent descriptive difference between acts; it is a difference that concerns their "quality." It makes no difference to *psychological* description whether there is an actually existing object corresponding to the act of positing.[12] Such description does not concern itself with whether an act of positing is justified, i.e. with the relation of such an act to an actually existing

---

[9] See above 146.
[10] II 451, 463.
[11] II 479.
[12] II (ed. 1) 353 (see also ed. 2, 373).

object. There appears to be no criterion to judge such matters – unless perception as a "self-giving" act is a criterion.

(B) The difference between a mere "empty" act of meaning and a perceptual act is that the latter presents the object "itself." On the basis of a perception, we can therefore determine whether a meaning is "possible," i.e. realizable. But a closer look reveals that this difference between significative and perceptual acts is also a purely descriptive psychological difference. That an object is "itself" present means nothing more or less than that an act with the immanent character of "self-givenness" is present. It may sound paradoxical, but from a psychological standpoint this tells us nothing about the existence of the perceived object. We maintain only that there are descriptive differences between the acts. *These differences are described in a purely phenomenological way according to the form of representation, i.e. according to the relation between matter and representative*, the two immanent aspects of the act.[13]

The same is true of the relation of fulfillment.[14] As the title of the sixth investigation indicates, this description of knowledge is a "phenomenological elucidation of knowledge."[15] Now, that acts of signification and perception can enter into such a relation of fulfillment with one another is a "primitive phenomenological fact." This does not in any way prejudice the question of the existence or non-existence of the object perceived. The description must remain phenomenological.[16] Even when the object is "itself" present, the epoché with regard to existence is maintained.

The preceding can be summarized as follows. (A) First, that a particular object is presented means (purely phenomenologically) that there is a particular act of mere presentation. Second, that an object is posited as existing means that there is an act of positing. (B) That an object is "itself given" means that there is a self-presentative act.

---

[13] III 92; 116. Husserl speaks of "an *internal* difference of acts"; see also II 384ff. See above 145.

[14] II 344; III 24; "Disappointment" (*Enttäuschung*) is also a phenomenological fact III 41.

[15] Compare the title of the third chapter of the sixth investigation and also III 15, 26ff, 30, 32ff, 38, 40, 42, 47, 63, 75, 52ff, 80, 92.

[16] III 25, 33; "Although the fullness of a presentation . . . varies, the intentional object which is intended and as it is intended remains the same; *in other words*, its matter remains the same" III 88 (italics mine); "Physical things are given to us and stand before us . . . *that is to say*, we have certain perceptions . . . which 'are directed toward these objects'" II (ed. 1) 337 (italics mine).

III. The Possibility of a Second Answer

When I distinguish here between a first and a second answer, I mean that there is an "official" answer and an "unofficial" answer. The former is really *the* answer of LU. Nevertheless, there are various passages in which the object is taken into consideration.

Husserl speaks, for example, of two different standpoints from which one could look at the synthesis between a significative act and a perceptual act. From the standpoint of the object (the objective standpoint), we can speak of knowledge or identification. From the phenomenological standpoint, we speak of "fulfillment" or "coincidence" (*Deckung*). Thus, while the acts (the matter) coincide, the objects are identified.[17]

We find the same duality of viewpoint in the description of "forms of representation." They are described on the one hand according to the relation between matter and representative and on the other hand according to the relation between object and representative.[18] This duality also surfaces in the case of the concept of "fullness." On the one hand it is described as a "fullness of presentation"[19] and on the other hand as a "fullness of the object."[20] There is a correspondence between the two.[21]

I could put it in even more general terms by asking whether the givenness of the object is not presupposed in the entire argument. *Otherwise, how could we speak of an exact correlation between the two?* If it is true that the apprehending of the content is *the same* as the perceiving of the object, and that with the apprehending of the content an object is *eo ipso* present,[22] is it not inconsistent to claim that only the act and the immanent content are given? Husserl's answer is that the two mean "exactly the same."[23] When an act is present, then, an object is "intentionally present" – and that *eo ipso*. This is fully in agreement with Husserl's theory of perception, in which he claims that an

---

[17] II 33, 38, 52, 59, 64; see above 147.

[18] III 55, 59, 89.

[19] III 77. "Fullness" is called "intuitive substance" *in* and *with* the apprehension II 57, 79, 117. We do not perceive the sensations in themselves III 78; we perceive them insofar as they are apprehended III 85. The concept of pure perception developed by Husserl in this connection is also defined in a purely phenomenological way III 80, 82.

[20] III 74, 76.

[21] III 78ff, 97, 100, 234, 243.

[22] II 372.

[23] II 372, 377, 473.

intentional object is constituted via the apprehension of a content. Of course it is not the case that the two are given in the same way. The apprehension and the immanent content, which together form the experience, are "present"; the object is "presented."[24] Nevertheless, the object is also given in some manner or other. What else could the expression 'intentionally present' mean?

This intentional presence does not mean that the object also exists in reality. Suppose the object does not exist (which cannot be determined on phenomenological grounds). Then, says Husserl, the act of presentation exists – in any event – but not the object.[25] Actually, we must fill this out and say: not only the object exists but also *the object that – eo ipso – is present*. By 'object' is meant not the real object but the object constituted through the apprehension of the content, i.e. the *phenomenon*.[26] In other words, "within" the *sphere of consciousness* we must yet accept a certain correlation between the act itself and the object appearing to it.

Yet we can well understand why Husserl says that all that exists in this case is the act, i.e. the intention. The mode of being of the intentionally present object, after all, cannot be specified easily. Forming a presentation of the god Jupiter can again serve as an example. Jupiter exists neither outside the mind nor in the mind. That he does not exist outside the mind is a matter of definition. But neither is he immanent. We may not say, "He *exists*, but only in the intention," for this was the mistake of Brentano and others.[27] All that exists immanently is the act.

Are we then to conclude that Jupiter as a presented fantasy image does not exist at all? To this we must answer – and Husserl was later to give this answer – that there is a third possibility, a *tertium datur*. The fantasy image can exist as a transcendently objectified phantasm, as a "fantasy appearance as such," as an object whose mode of being is intentional in the sense of Scholasticism but is nevertheless not immanent. In LU, this answer is in fact already given *where perception is concerned*. Even when the "real" object does not exist, perception still has a transcendent intentional object.

"Is" the appearing object then outside the mind? Yes, insofar as we

[24] III 116f, 82f.
[25] II 399 (ed. 1; compare edition 2, 425).
[26] III 235 (ed. 2).
[27] II 352 (ed. 1; ed. 2, 372).

do not mean by 'is' the "real existence" of extra-mental things, which Husserl calls "the objective being, the true being-in-itself of the world."[28] The existence of this being is independent of whether we form a presentation of it or not. The intentional object is completely dependent on the existence of the act; if the act disappears, the object also disappears. This is the case with regard to fantasy images, for example, but it also holds for perception. When the act disappears, the phenomenon also disappears. It is the act that constitutes the object; that is to say, it "makes it appear." It is necessary to carry out the act if the object is to appear. I already reached this conclusion in connection with my analysis of the concept of "constitution." The act does not bring forth the object, but it does bring forth its phenomenality, its being-for-us. The intentional object thus enjoys a peculiar mode of being. It is not dependent on the existence of an extra-mental object – *thus the elimination of this object does not affect it* – although it is dependent on the act. Yet it is apprehended as "outside the mind," as a correlate. *It has the mode of being that Husserl was later to attribute to the noema: the noema is "an objectivity that belongs to consciousness and yet is a unique, peculiar object."*[29]

In Ideen I, the noema is also called the "sense" or the "presented as such." The term 'perceived as such' already occurs in LU.[30] Yet at this stage, we still find no explicit reflection on the mode of existence of this intentional object. Husserl simply observes that it makes no difference from a psychological standpoint whether or not there is an actually existing object. What is most important is that we always have an act. He did not yet dare to draw the consequences of his theory of apperception and claim that there is also an intentional object given – *meaning by 'intentional' not real*. Yet this step was taken again and again in a clandestine manner, as it were. It seems as though Husserl was afraid that the intentional object would (wrongly) be taken to be the actually existing extra-mental object. Judging by the number of interpreters who have interpreted LU as a "turn toward the object," we could conclude that he was not careful enough about this matter!

For the careful reader of LU, there can be no uncertainty about this point, for Husserl warns expressly against this identification. When he observes – contra Hume and all the other "ideological" psychologists –

[28] II 387, 435. Husserl speaks of an "object existing outside it, in and for itself."
[29] Id I 265, see also 202.
[30] III 16.

that there is a difference between immanent sensations and perceived properties (i.e. between the experiencing of immanent sensations and the apperception of the sensations and perceived properties of an object), he goes on to say: "We must note here that nothing scientifically or metaphysically transcendent should be substituted for this object; by the 'object' we mean the object as it *appears* in this *intuition*, as it *counts for* this intuition, so to speak."[31]

The intentional object is thus the phenomenon that appears when a sensation is interpreted transcendently. An ultimately metaphysical or natural scientific "thing in itself" as the cause of the sensation, then, is beyond consideration. The question of the origin of sensations comes up only in explanatory psychology. Phenomenology concerns itself only with the "appearance." This is not only the case in this passage but in any passage in which Husserl is concerned with the intentional object as the correlate of the act (the "object referred to" and the "object as referred to").[32] This is the object that "counts" for us, as Husserl says repeatedly.[33]

The intentional object is "merely grasped putatively."[34] We do not know whether it actually exists as it appears. This does not make it impossible for it to be given *as* appearance. Husserl himself attests to this inward evidence of the appearance *qua appearance* when he speaks of an "objective evidence" in contrast with an existential evidence. In "objective" evidence we lack the certainty that what is intended actually exists, but it is a genuine evidence nevertheless. "I may be deceived as to the existence of the object of perception, but not as to the fact that I perceive it as determined in this or that way, that my percept's target is not some totally different object, a pine tree, e.g. instead of a cockchafer." This evidence concerns "the intentional object as such."[35] Such evidence is likewise presupposed in inner perception, but in inner perception we know also that the appearing object really exists

---

[31]   II 197, see also 194.

[32]   For instance II 362, 435, 375; III 47 and 149.

[33]   See also II 30, 165, 197, 398, 423; II 10 (ed. 1) has "appear of count" (compare ed. 2, 9). Husserl used the term 'phenomenon claiming validity' (*Geltungsphänomenen*) in 1907. See below 321.

[34]   II 218 where the intentional object is "merely intended." Compare 362 where perceiving is a "presumptive apprehension"; see also above 174 note 10.

[35]   II 197, compare III 121 on "inward evidence in a somewhat looser sense."

just as it appears. The inward evidence with regard to existence is included.[36]

Thus we see that Husserl repeatedly says things that go beyond the methodological framework which he has established. According to the Cartesian point of departure, only the sphere of experiences, the adequately given, can be accepted as given. This is the phenomenological "residue," to use a term from *Ideen*. The "principle of all principles," however, demands that every givenness be recognized as such. Therefore, if Husserl wishes to be self-consistent, he must admit that this residue embraces more. But this cost him considerable pains. Later, in the *Krisis*, he explained (correctly) that only after completing LU did he arrive at an "express self-consciousness with regard to its methods, which even then was still incomplete."[37]

IV. A Second Answer

The questions that were raised can now be answered once more.

(*A*) What can it mean phenomenologically that – after suspending the question of the existence of the perceived object – a particular object is posited as existing? In order to achieve a proper understanding of Husserl's psychological reduction (which would contribute greatly to an understanding of Ideen I), it is of the greatest importance to realize that an answer to this paradoxical framing of the question is possible. The first answer is: there is an act of positing. The second answer, which flows from it logically and is equivalent to it, must be: there is an act of positing and an intentional correlate of this act, which correlate is posited as existing. *The predicate 'existing' as the correlate of a "positing" must thus be ascribed to the intentional object.* This does not mean that this object actually exists but only that it is intended as actually existing. To use a term borrowed from Spiegelberg, it is not a reality but a "reality-phenomenon." It is "supposedly real," which does not mean that it is "really real."[38]

---

[36] II 199, 203, 205. The preference for this existential evidence sometimes determines the course of the argument. An example is when Husserl switches from the abstract appearing content to the "experienced" content in an argument directed against Hume, who denies the existence of abstract contents.

[37] Krisis 246 (E 243).

[38] H. Spiegelberg 'The "reality phenomenon" and reality' 84. H. Conrad-Martius makes use of similar terminology in her description of the psychological reduction, which she, like Spiegelberg in the article mentioned above, wrongly sees as *the* reduction (see below 199). She distinguishes between reality as grasped putatively and real reality. The

It is now clear what dangers the ambiguity of the term 'merely intended' poses for an understanding of Husserl's purposes. In a certain sense, it is true of every object that it is "merely intended"; insofar as its mode of being is intentional, this holds by definition! 'Merely intended' is then opposed to 'real' in the sense of existing independently of consciousness. Here 'merely intended' is a synonym for 'only intentional' or 'phenomenal'[39]

On the other hand, 'merely intended' can also mean "correlate of an act of mere presentation." In this sense, its opposite is 'existing,' i.e. the correlate of an act of positing. The object that is merely intended in the first sense could in the second sense be either posited or merely presented. In other words, the latter opposition represents a distinction *within the realm of merely intentional objects in the former sense.* Only in this way can we understand how it is possible for Husserl to give a "psychology of reason" after putting the question of existence between brackets.[40]

In the introduction to the second edition of LU, Husserl wrote that it is impossible to describe acts without bringing in intentional objects. "One then readily forgets that such subsidiarily described 'objectivity,' which is necessarily introduced into almost all phenomenological description, has undergone a change of sense, in virtue of which it now belongs to the sphere of phenomenology."[41] Here Husserl admits that the object belongs to the sphere of phenomenology, and that as intentional object, i.e. as modified – in Ideen I Husserl calls it "noematically modified" – and not as "object in itself." But I also detect a self-correction in this. What Husserl's admission means for the concrete question before us is that we must speak not only of positing (and not positing) but also of its correlates. In other words, the concept of "quality" must also be used noematically.[42]

---

former is the noematic reality-moment, "the *supposition* of being which belongs to any noematic sense," and the latter is a "real reality" abiding in itself and independent of consciousness. "It is not possible to characterize this peculiar problem in any other way than through a terminological doubling of expression: *real* reality": 'Die transzendentale und die ontologische Phänomenologie' 179.

[39] II 218; III 225.

[40] On this psychology of reason, see also Husserl's *Encyclopaedia Britannica* article, Husserliana IX 245, 327, from which this phrase is borrowed. Husserl's "phenomenology of reason" in the fourth section of *Ideen I* can also be conceived of psychologically. See below 445.

[41] II (ed. 2) 7, 11 (see also ed. 2, 199).

[42] Husserl explicitly introduced the noematic concept of "positing" (*Setzung*) in 1907.

As far as "merely presentative" perceiving is concerned, there are no clear examples of the "merely presented as such" to be found in LU. As I see it, this has something to do with the fact that Husserl only later discovered the qualitative modification of perception that takes place in the constitution of images.[43]

In *reproductive* consciousness, i.e. memory and imagination, there is indeed a clear difference between positing and non-positing consciousness. In the case of fantasy, Husserl does not yet recognize an intentional correlate. The 'intentional existence' of the object is another formula for the non-existence of the object. In the first edition of LU, Husserl wrote: "The forms of reproductive fantasy . . . exist only phenomenally and intentionally; that is to say, *properly* speaking, they do not exist at all. Only the relevant *acts of appearing* exist." Husserl later filled out this sentence by adding: "with their real (*reell* = immanent) and intentional contents."[44] This is in agreement with Ideen I, where Husserl maintains that the centaur exists neither outwardly nor inwardly (as Brentano maintained). Nonetheless, the fantasy is a phantasm *of* (about) something. "to this extent, 'the centaur as meant' actually belongs to the experience itself." Husserl was close to this recognition in LU – how else could he speak of a "phantasm of the mind that floats before me"? – but he did not yet take this step.[45] I have already pointed to the same hesitation with regard to the significative level.[46]

(B) As far as the concepts of "matter" and "fullness" are concerned, I have already shown that a one-sided understanding of them does not fit in with the tenor of Husserl's theory of apperception. If the matter is the sense of the apprehension, then there would be a constituted sense corresponding to it as its correlate.[47] If the relation between the matter and the representative is such that the object "itself" appears, then there is no reason not to ascribe this character of "self-appearing" to the intentional object and no reason to define perception exclusively according to the form of representation, i.e. according to the relation between the two moments of the act (the matter and the sensations).

When in descriptive psychology there is talk of an object that is "itself present," this could mean either that there is an act with the character of self-presentation or that there is an object that is "itself"

He also used it in Ideen I, where he called it "thetic character" (see my analysis of IP below 316 and 438).

[43] See above 132 note 5.

[44] II (ed. 1) 715 (see also ed. 2, III 244).

[45] Id I 42; see also LU II 357.

[46] See above 171.

[47] In the second edition, Husserl uses the term 'perceptual sense' to refer to the appearing object III 235.

given. This character of self-presence can be the basis for the validity of the positing; it founds the "justification" of the positing. Through an investigation of the presence of the posited object, a "rational appraisal" (*Rechtsprechnung der Vernunft*) becomes possible. This is a phenomenology of reason judging whether the object is rightly posited.

Meanwhile, we must not forget that this is no more than a *psychology* of reason. It remains within the bounds of psychology and speaks about the world only as phenomenon; that is to say, it speaks only of intentional objects. It makes no claims about a reality existing independently of consciousness. Whether or not such a reality exists is irrelevant to the existence of the phenomenon *as* phenomenon. Because no judgment about the actually existing world is possible, *this theory of knowledge is caught in an impasse*. It was only later that Husserl saw that a theory of knowledge on a psychological basis is a "transcendental circle":[48] it seeks to clarify the relation to the world despite the fact that the world is itself presupposed as the supporting ground of consciousness. In Part III we will see how Husserl overcomes this impasse in his psychological theory of knowledge by way of a transcendental transformation or reinterpretation of this psychology of reason.[49]

PARAGRAPH FIVE. THE INTENTIONAL OBJECT AND THE "REAL" OBJECT

In Brentano we already encountered the distinction between the intentional object and the real object. The distinction as such stems from Scholasticism, but Brentano himself used it in a way entirely different from that of the Scholastics. In principle, Husserl uses these two terms in the same sense as Brentano. What should draw our attention is that Husserl, like his teacher Brentano, agrees with the Scholastic distinction in a certain respect but yet rejects it in essence. Discussing this question will enable me to complete an important aspect of my picture of Husserl's philosophy.

I. Husserl and the Scholastic Schema

I will begin with Husserl's critical remarks about the "traditional schema" (i.e. inner image and outer object), which, according to

---

[48] Husserliana IX 292.
[49] See below 402f.

Husserl, is the cause of "errors that have dragged on through the centuries."[1] In the first place, he objects to the notion of the immanence of the intentional object. Husserl, after all, sees the intentional object as the result of a transcendent objectification. In the second place, he criticizes the use of the term 'image,' for the intentional object appears as an image only in so-called imaginative apperception. In perception, the intentional object "itself" appears.[2]

In the third place, Husserl says that it is not correct to make a distinction between the intentional object and the real or actual object of perception. He writes: "It need only be said to be acknowledged *that the intentional object of a presentation is the same as its actual object, and on occasion as its external object, and that it is absurd to distinguish between them.*"[3] This passage has often been used to support a realist interpretation of Husserl's theory of intentionality, for Husserl here appears to deny the distinction between the intentional object and the real object. The intentional object, which was still immanent for Brentano, appears to be identified here with the real object – and in no uncertain terms. Indeed, it appears that Husserl here executes the famous turn toward the object: the subject breaks out of its immanence and directs itself toward the real world. Is this interpretation justified? In opposition to this reading of Husserl, I could conceivably point out that it conflicts with his other statements (as well as with what I have written above about his theory of apperception). In that case, I would have to maintain that there is an internal contradiction in Husserl. But it is my view that we need not accept such a contradiction, and that the statement quoted above can and must be interpreted in an entirely different sense. What Husserl was writing in the passage in question was not a polemic directed against Brentano; Husserl himself maintained Brentano's distinction between the intentional object and the "real" object. What, then, does he mean when he says that the intentional object and the real object of the intention are one and the same?

Husserl's polemic here is directed not against Brentano but against the Scholastic conception of intentionality. In order to understand the statement in question, we must bring to the fore the thinker who forms

[1] II 374 note 1, 424.
[2] See above 140. In the second edition and in Id I 224 Husserl went on to point out that this image theory leads to an infinite regress. He also wanted to avoid the term 'perceptual picture' to refer to the perceptual "adumbration," III 57, 83.
[3] II 425 (see also ed. 1 398).

the background of this discussion, i.e. Twardowski.[4] Twardowski was a member of Brentano's school who, following Höfler, brought about a certain broadening of Brentano's doctrine of intentionality in the direction of the Scholastic doctrine; perhaps I could better say that he returned it to the Scholastic mold. Brentano spoke of an intentional directedness and of its content. Höfler and Twardowski operate with three terms: act, intentional content, and object.[5] Now, "behind" the content Brentano also recognized an object existing in itself, which is posited by physics. But this is not what Twardowski meant. On his view, the object existing in itself, which is to be distinguished from the psychical image "in" us, is *the object of the intention*. Thus he returns to the Scholastic doctrine that we can intend the object outside us. Consequently, he again ascribes to the intentional object its mediating function. It is again an "id quo" – and not an "id quod," as Brentano maintained. It forms a point of transition to the real object in the external world. For Brentano, who departed completely from Scholasticism on this point, the intentional object is the terminus of the intention. Any inner relation between the intentional object and the "real" object is eliminated.

For Twardowski, the "actual object of the presentation" is not the "psychical image of the object" but rather "the object itself."[6] Yet the image is also presented, but in an entirely different way. Forming a presentation of an object does not mean the same as forming a presentation of a content. Twardowski illustrates this by using the work of a painter as his example. When a painter paints a landscape, in a real sense it is the landscape that is being painted, but we could also say that it is the painting that is being painted. For the painter, the image is a means for depicting the landscape. The landscape is the

---

[4] Twardowski's *Zur Inhalt und Gegenstand der Vorstellungen* has drawn too little attention from interpreters of Husserl. Husserl himself paid considerable attention to it. From a letter of April 5, 1902 to Meinong, we learn that Husserl had written an essay in the same year that the book appeared; the essay, which dealt with the intentional object, was never published. *Philosophenbriefe, Aus der wissenschaftlichen Korrespondenz von Alexius Meinong.* In LU, Husserl repeatedly makes critical remarks about Twardowski's book, which he nevertheless calls "a most careful and thorough work" 202 note 1, see also II 50 note 1, 124, 134, 217 note 1, 280, 297 note 1, 506. In Ideen I he returns to this book and speaks of it as a "beautiful work" 267.

[5] Twardowski cites the *Logik, Unter Mitwirkung von Dr. Alexius Meinong* verfasst von Dr. Alois Höfler, op.cit. 4.

[6] Twardowski op.cit. 5.

primary object of the painting activity, and the painting is the secondary object.

We encounter a similar state of affairs in presentation. "Someone forms a presentation of an object, e.g. a horse. In doing so, he is forming a presentation of a psychical content. The content is the likeness of the horse in much the same way that the picture is the likeness of the landscape. Thus, when someone forms a presentation of an object, he at the same time forms a presentation of a content relating itself to this object. The presented object, i.e. the object toward which the presentative activity, the act of presentation, directs itself, is the primary object of presentation; the content through which the object is directed is the secondary object of the presentative activity."[7] When we say that the content is "presented," we mean that something is presented *through* the presentation. *In* the presentation, the object is presented: "the content is the means, so to speak, through which the object is presented."[8]   For Twardowski, then, there are two objects of the intention, both of which are presented, albeit in different ways. Husserl frequently directs sharp criticism against this "presentative activity moving in two directions."[9] This doctrine is also the background to the controversial and critical passage quoted above. When Husserl says that there is no difference between the intentional object and the real object, he means that the intentional object *is the real object of the intention.* He opposes the doctrine that regards the intentional object only as a mediating term that is presented secondarily, while the primary intention is directed toward another object. There are not two objects in perception, and there is no presentative activity moving in two directions. The intentional object is the direct and only real object of the perception. There is no difference between the *intentional* object and the *intended* object. That this is what Husserl means is apparent from a statement that follows the controversial passage: "The transcendent object would not be the object of *this* presentation if it was not *its* intentional object. This is plainly a merely analytic proposition."[10] From this quotation it is apparent that Husserl equates the "object of

---

[7] Twardowski op.cit. 18.

[8] Twardowski was probably aware of his departure from Brentano. In any event, he writes that he uses the term 'secondary object' in a sense somewhat different from that of Brentano. For the latter, the act itself is the secondary object (of "inner consciousness").

[9] II 50, 506.

[10] II 425; III 81.

the presentation" with the "intentional object."[11] Part of what 'intentional' means for Husserl (as for his teacher Brentano) is "intended." What Husserl is saying, then, is nothing other than that the intended object is intended. This is indeed a purely analytic statement, a foregone conclusion. For Husserl it is absurd to draw a distinction between the intentional object and the object that is *really* intended, which is what Twardowski does. But this does not mean that the intentional object is "real" (*wirklich*) in the sense of "existing in itself." For the present, this claim on the part of Husserl is a *descriptive psychological* claim which seeks to do justice to the fact that perception clearly represents a *direct* perceiving of the object without any intermediate term.

This passage, then, is not a polemic against Brentano but rather a declaration of adherence to Brentano's rejection of the notion of the intentional object as mediating term. This "adaptation" (*Umwertung*) of the Scholastic conception of intentionality did not escape Husserl's attention; he was aware of it and approved of it.[12] (When he did criticize Brentano, it was on other points: (1) that he conceived of the intentional object as immanent,[13] and (2) that he called this object a "sign." He raised analogous objections against the term 'image;' it furthers the confusion between perceptual and significative appercep-tion. Unlike the word, the perceived thing is not a sign that refers to what is signified.[14])

If there is nevertheless a point of agreement between the Scholastic theory of the intentional object and that of Husserl and Brentano, it concerns the ontological status of this object. For Husserl, the term 'intentional' has a Scholastic meaning alongside the meaning men-tioned above. The intentional object is dependent on consciousness and can exist even if the "real" object does not exist.[15] What this means for Husserl, for whom the intentional object is the end-term of perception, is that we can abstract from the existence of the ultimate real object

[11] Husserl adds-I quote from the second edition: "The object of the presentation, of the 'intention,' *that is and means*: the presented, the intentional object."

[12] Husserliana IX 247, 249.

[13] See above 135.

[14] II 424.

[15] In LU, Husserl sometimes uses the Scholastic term 'immanent,' but he always either uses quotation remarks or adds the word 'so-called' II 202, 350, 391, 423. In Ideen I we find an explicit comparison with the Scholastic conception with regard to the ontological status of the immanent object, see below 427.

without thereby losing anything. This is the background of his phenomenological epoché.

II. The "Real" Object and the Physical Object

Brentano and Husserl also agree that "behind" the perceived intentional object there is still a really existing object. The question that remains is whether Husserl, like Brentano, regards this object as the object of physics. Does this object, which is beyond the scope of intentionality, lie within the domain of natural science? In LU, we find only a few passages about the thing of physics. The scarcity of these passages is understandable, for this thing comes up for discussion only in an explanation of the phenomenon (something which falls completely outside the sphere of phenomenology, as we have seen).[16] Yet we do find a few givens on this matter when Husserl speaks of "the presupposition of an existing world," which physics accepts. The starting-point of physics is an appearance given to us directly, i.e. the intentional object.[17] When the physicist explains subjective phenomena in their lawful succession, he presupposes a world existing outside consciousness, the lawfulness of which is determinative for that of the phenomenal world. Like Brentano, Husserl speaks here of a "metaphysical presupposition."[18] This presupposition is metaphysical because the physical object is not given in intuition.[19]

Husserl's definition of natural science as the science of the physical phenomenon is misleading. The phenomenon is only the *starting-point* of physics; the actual object of this science is the presupposed physical thing which is independent of consciousness – the "thing of physics," as Husserl was to call it later. *In LU, it is this physical thing that plays the role of the "real" object over against the intentional object.*[20] 'Real' must

---

[16] See above 165, 167.

[17] II (ed. 1) 340. This passage was dropped in the second edition.

[18] I 11; II 20; see above 48.

[19] Husserl therefore calls it a metaphysical transcendence III 224, 226. On the term 'metaphysical,' see II 361 note 1 ("corrupt forms of a metaphysics of the ego"). On the metaphysical realism of Plato, see II 121, 124. On the metaphysical problem of our knowledge of the "thing in itself," see I 113; II 123, 387; III 200 and 203 (only in the second edition; compare ed. 1, 675).

[20] II 197; III 154.

The respective standpoints of Scholasticism, Brentano and Husserl could be represented schematically as follows. The arrow is that of the intention.

here be understood in the sense of independent of consciousness. Husserl therefore contrasts the natural scientific or metaphysical thing with the intentional phenomenon. It is true that this phenomenon is also transcendent to consciousness, but its transcendence is the result of the transcendent interpretation of an immanent given; it is not a natural scientific or metaphysical transcendence.[21]

Husserl also raises the question of the nature of this natural scientific thing. He does not give an a priori answer to this question but leaves it to the future development of science. He wants a "natural science without bodies."[22] What he means by this is that we must not proceed a priori from a division of reality into body and soul. He calls for a division of the sciences that is "not binding metaphysically."[23] Therefore he wants to base it on the distinction between the act and the intentional object appearing in it. Thus a division of the sciences according to the type of phenomenon dealt with, i.e. physical or psychical, can be defended phenomenologically; such a division is purely descriptive and does not presuppose anything about a metaphysical difference between "matter" and "mind."[24]

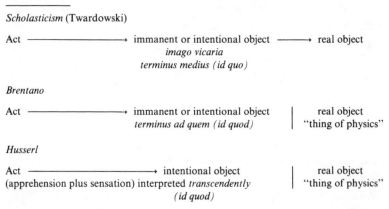

Scholasticism (Twardowski)

Act ⟶ immanent or intentional object ⟶ real object
imago vicaria
terminus medius (id quo)

Brentano

Act ⟶ immanent or intentional object | real object
terminus ad quem (id quod) | "thing of physics"

Husserl

Act ⟶ intentional object | real object
(apprehension plus sensation) interpreted *transcendently* | "thing of physics"
(id quod)

[21] In LU, Husserl gives no account of how concepts are formed in the explanatory sciences. He makes a few casual observations, which were not worked out further until PSW. Science, he says, seeks unity in change and finds it in causal lawfulness. This unity (also called substance) is not of a phenomenological character but of a natural scientific or metaphysical character. Both physics and explanatory psychology operate with some such metaphysical concept of substance II (ed. 1) 332, 248, 250 (all these passages were later dropped), further II 124, 218, 197 (ed. 1; see also ed. 2, 198). The soul is a metaphysical reality but not a "mystical" reality, for this substance is a product of science. It is "not a mystical 'in-itself' but rather an empirically grounded 'in-itself'" II (ed. 1) 332, 336. On this view on the concept of substance, see below 229.

[22] II (ed. 1) 339. This passage too was dropped from Husserl's revised version. See below 485.

[23] III 226, 145.

[24] II (ed. 1) 332, 338. Both passages were later dropped. See also below 229.

Despite the cursory nature of these references to the physical thing, we are in a position to draw some important conclusions. The very fact that most of these passages were dropped in the second edition of LU demonstrates their relevance to the question of Husserl's development.

It appears that *Husserl proceeds from the hypothesis of a reality existing in itself,* a hypothesis that he himself characterizes as a metaphysical presupposition. Of course he does distantiate himself from any naive metaphysics that proceeds uncritically from the existence of such disputed transcendent realities as the soul and the body.[25] *Yet this does not alter the fact that their existence remains presupposed.* To use the language of Ideen I, Husserl bases himself on the firm ground of the natural world. This is apparent from the way in which he speaks of the "real" metaphysical or natural scientific thing. It is even clearer, as we shall see in a later chapter, in his psychology. The *abstracted* phenomenological sphere is regarded as a particular stratum of reality founded in a body.[26]

On the basis of this analysis, I feel justified in concluding that Husserl's philosophy in LU is indeed realist. *This realism is not based on the doctrine of intentionality,* as is often erroneously supposed, *but is based on reasons outside the theme of intentionality.* It is bound up with the concealed "metaphysical presuppositions," which are not a factor in psychological analysis. The intentional psychological analysis of intentional consciousness as such is neutral with regard to the problem of realism and idealism.[27]

PARAGRAPH SIX. THE NATURAL AND PHENOMENOLOGICAL ATTITUDES IN LU – CONCLUSION

In his sketch toward a preface to LU, Husserl wrote in 1913: "There is indeed a big difference between making theoretical statements of a new

[25] III 145, 222f.

[26] It was in 1907 that Husserl first took a critical position with regard to this "psychological apperception," see below 310.

[27] When Gaston Berger in his book *Le cogito dans la philosophie de Husserl* says that it is a legend that Husserl gave up his original realist standpoint to turn toward idealism, he is correct insofar as this realism – as usually understood – is based on Husserl's theory of intentionality. There is in fact a realism in Husserl (in the background of his descriptive psychology), a realism that is usually overlooked. (Berger is no exception.) As Berger says, the later works represent a natural culmination of the earlier works. Yet, as we shall see, this natural development consists in a radicalization of the phenomenological standpoint; it is directed toward overcoming the realist counterpole in Husserl's thinking and incorporating it into phenomenology.

kind on the basis of inner necessaity and in pure devotion to the demands of the things, and becoming clear in reflection about the particular sense of the method used."[1] This is a good characterization of what actually goes on in LU, a work outstanding because of its overwhelming riches in concrete analyses but providing little information about the methods actually used. We have seen that its one and only methodological prescription boils down to a revolution of focus: in carrying out the act, we must not lose ourselves but must re-flect and turn back.

Meanwhile, it has become clear that there is something more at issue here. Although the term 'epoché' was not used in LU, that which Husserl was later to apply it to was fully present there, i.e. the suspension of the question of existence. In fact, he used the epoché in practice without any reflection on it as a mental operation. Later he became aware of what he had done. In the *Krisis* he wrote that the epoché "as an explicit methodological basic requirement could be the focus of subsequent reflection only on the part of someone who, with a certain naiveté and through a certain historical situation, was already pulled into the epoché, so to speak." Thus it was not untill four years after the completion of LU that Husserl came to an explicit – if still imperfect – self-consciousness with regard to its method.[2] In his later work, this methodological reflection – in the form of a "phenomenology of phenomenology" – was to play a large and almost dominant role.

Such a discrepancy between actual analysis and methodological awareness is also present in the case of the residue of this reduction. Although the choice of the Cartesian starting-point (the sphere of experiences) as basis actually excluded intentional objects from the domain of phenomenology, these objects were in fact frequently brought into the analysis – at least in the case of perception. It was only later that Husserl expressly claimed that the phenomenological residue takes in not only the *cogitationes* but also the *cogitata qua cogitata*.[3] The latter are "inseparable" from the sphere of acts. Furthermore, this

---

[1] Entwurf 109; see also LU I 5.
[2] Krisis 246 (E 243); see below 308, 312. This is also the case in eidetic psychology, see also below 207.
[3] In IP, see below 315. Husserl later wrongly ascribed the recognition of *cogitata qua cogitata* to LU, Krisis 237 (E 234).

is no more than a consequence of Husserl's theory of perception, which regards transcendent objects as sensations interpreted objectively.

A careful analysis of the possibilities and limits of psychological analysis as practices in LU is of the greatest importance for achieving a proper understanding of the development of Husserl's thought. Even after this psychology was superseded by transcendental phenomenology, it continued to play a major role in Husserl's thinking. Transcendental phenomenology is a revolutionized version of this phenomenological psychology, just as – conversely – phenomenological psychology appears to be a preparation for transcendental phenomenology. Thus this phenomenological psychology, which has now become better known through the publication of the *Husserliana* series, goes back to a certain period in the history of Husserl's thought.[4] As a historical phase, this period also illustrates Husserl's epistemological *impasse* and shows us the problems and presuppositions he tried to overcome by way of transcendental idealism. In this regard, LU is indispensable for understanding Husserl's later development.

Husserl's solution to the problem of knowledge is not so much a solution as an evasion of the actual problem. *The method of the suspension of the question of existence illustrates the perplexity in Husserl's thinking.* We shall see later that the transcendental epoché of Ideen I has the function of rendering this pseudo-solution superfluous; it solves the problem which the psychological epoché evades. In LU, the suspension still is only negative in character; it is a movement back to consciousness but without the idea that from there the world "in itself" can again be reached. *Thus we see that the famous bracketing of the "external world," which is often ascribed to Ideen I, is actually already to be found in LU.* In Part III, moreover, I will defend the thesis that the reduction in this form occurs *only* in LU. We will then see that the issue in Ideen I is a suspension not of the world but of a particular interpretation of the world, i.e. exactly that interpretation of the world as world "in itself" that the psychological reduction of LU makes necessary as a solution.[5]

[4] We find this phenomenological psychology in Krisis, in EP and especially in PP. This psychology also plays a role in Ideen I, in a not directly apparent way, as the transitional stage to transcendental phenomenology; see below 432.

[5] In the Husserl literature, the transcendental-phenomenological reduction of the first chapter of Ideen I is often described as a psychological reduction, as a reduction of reality to the phenomenon of reality (of being to sense). See, for example, H.U. Asemisen *Strukturanalytische Probleme der Wahrnehmung in der Phänomenologie Husserls*, 18,

Husserl called the problem of the relation of consciousness to a reality existing in itself a metaphysical problem out of place in psychology. Thereby he admitted that it is insoluble – at least in the terms in which it is posed. But he was not yet in a position to be able to undermine the presuppositions which govern this statement of the problem. In his sketch toward a preface (1913), he formulated this problem in a very clear way in connection with his criticism of Lotze. Lotze's error, Husserl wrote, is that he accepts a reality "in itself," a "metaphysical world of things existing in themselves"; this world stands over against human consciousness, which must depict it and strives in vain to establish agreement between itself and this world.[6] Lotze's acceptance of a "system of preformation" is completely arbitrary. Lotze speaks of an "abyss of the marvelous" in connection with the problem of knowledge. Husserl calls this "the public confession of a theory of knowledge that has failed. A real theory of knowledge clears things up, and something that has been cleared up is something that has become understandable and is understood; thus it is the utter opposite of something marvelous." This is doubtless a fine statement. But the question that could be raised is whether it is entirely fair on Husserl's part to direct this criticism against Lotze in a 1913 preface to LU when Husserl himself had not gotten much further in that very work. The one thing of which Husserl can be proud, however, is that he did not offer some merely apparent solution, e.g. along the lines of a pre-established harmony on an ultimately theological basis.[7] He kept the problem open, and to that extent he is to be commended for not blocking the way at the very outset to the radical solution of Ideen I.

The paradox that man is in the world and is part of the world but at the same time constitutes the world is not cleared up in LU.[8] Husserl draws back to the sphere of experiences, an operation reminiscent of Descartes, *to whom Husserl was closer at this point than during any other*

52ff, 58ff. I would defend the thesis that such a reduction occurs only in LU, and that it represents a stage that Husserl tries to transcendent in Ideen I; see also below 397ff.

[6] Entwurf 324f; see also LU I 113f and III 199.

[7] See also Krisis 184 (E 180). Such a solution, which is characteristic of the naiveté of positive religion, is unacceptable in philosophy, see also LU I 195.

[8] 'Ber. üb. deutsche Schriften z. Logik i.d. Jahr. 1895–99,' 399. Compare the *Krisis* on the paradox: 'How can one of the world's components, namely, human subjectivity, constitute the whole world-constitute it as an intentional formation?" 183, see also 184, 186 (E 179, 180, 182). See also E. Fink 'Die phänomenologische Philosophie Edmund Husserls in der gegenwärtigen Kritik,' 350.

phase of his development. One could argue that the psychological theory of knowledge of LU in a certain sense remained stuck in "representationism," provided that this is not understood in the sense of the image or sign theory of perception. The reduction of being to sense is not a reduction to an image of reality. Perceptual sense appears as "itself." But Husserl shares with representationism the idea of a closed consciousness which can achieve no connections with a reality existing in itself.[9]

The methodological observations of LU – when compared with those of Ideen I – are of particular importance with regard to Husserl's development for what they do *not* say. Through a consistent reflective attitude, Husserl discovered the characteristic nature of consciousness and unmasked the natural attitude of "ideological" psychology. Only later was he to realize that even after the discovery of this "being characteristic of consciousness," (Eigensein) a natural attitude is still possible, i.e. an attitude that apperceives this consciousness as a mundane region, as a particular stratum within the world. The insoluble metaphysical problem of knowledge is then seen as involving an intra-mundane relation, i.e. a relation between an absolutized world in itself and a consciousness that is part of this world (as a region founded in a body). The impasse of the psychology of "reason" arises because of the alternation between empirical consciousness and transcendental consciousness. Husserl later discovered the priority of constituting consciousness and thereby became aware of its transcendental power. Consciousness is not one region alongside others but the *primordial region*, the source of all being. A so-called world "in itself"

---

[9] See also A. de Waelhens *Une Philosophie de l'ambiguité*, 89ff who claims that in this period, Husserl maintained the idea of an "interior consciousness," *closed and pure*, which *pictures for itself* something outside, which is inaccessible in itself." The question whether there is a reality corresponding to this representation would then be insoluble.

[10] PSW 340; see also below 357. My genetic analysis of Husserl's phenomenology also casts some light on well-known controversy in Husserl interpretation. It has often been argued that Husserl's phenomenology is neutral with regard to the problem of realism versus idealism. Because of methodological considerations, it is maintained, Husserl's phenomenology limits itself to a description of the phenomenon of reality. Husserl then became unfaithful to this neutrality when he defended idealism in Ideen I. Reality (being) was then identified with phenomenality (sense). This was a dogmatic, metaphysical step on Husserl's part. See for instance M. Farber *The foundation of phenomenology*, 490, 519ff; H.U. Asemisen *Strukturanalytische Probleme der Wahrnehmung in der Phänomenologie Husserls*, 60, 69, 87; H. Reiner 'Sinn und Recht der Phänomenologischen Methode,' 140.

As the case of Héring illustrates, this psychological conception of the phenomenologi-

existing outside it is a fiction of the natural attitude. Consciousness is to be regarded as the source of all being, the *rhizōmata pantōn*. "the mothers," as Husserl calls it, borrowing a phrase from Goethe.[10]

cal reduction is characteristic of the so-called early Husserl school, which was concentrated in Göttingen and Munich. *These Husserlians wanted to freeze phenomenology at the stage of LU*; see Héring's article 'Edmund Husserl, souvenirs et réflexions' 27. This psychological concept of the reduction is also to be found in H. Conrad-Martius 'Die transzendentale und die ontologische Phänomenologie' 180; in A. Pfänder *Logik* 166 and in his student H. Spiegelberg 'The "Reality-Phenomenon" and Reality' 93. This view also exercised some influence on Spiegelberg's *The phenomenological Movement* 137, 144. The view that phenomenology as such permits no conclusion on the question of realism versus idealism is also defended – in a brilliant way – by Ph. Merlan in his essay 'Idéalisme, Réalisme, Phénoménologie' 289, 402, 407. As I see it, Merlan is completely correct as far as a *psychological* phenomenology is concerned, i.e. a phenomenology at the stage of LU, but not as far as phenomenology as such is concerned. When Husserl defends an idealist phenomenology after 1908, psychological phenomenology (or phenomenological psychology, as he usually calls it) becomes only a preparatory stage for actual transcendental phenomenology. See below 434.

CHAPTER TWO

GENETIC AND DESCRIPTIVE PSYCHOLOGY

In the preceding chapter, I have tried to convey an impression of the new kind of analysis of consciousness that Husserl brings into play in LU. This descriptive psychology has a definite function in LU: it is intended to clarify the fundamental concepts of pure logic and thereby serve as a philosophical complement to this logic. The specific task of descriptive psychology with regard to logic will be discussed in Chapter 4 and 5.

In this chapter I will examine descriptive psychology as such. Just as in Part I, I will compare it with genetic or explanatory psychology. I will bring out the differences between the two types of psychology by examining three pairs of oppositions. The concepts "explanatory," "inductive" and "psycho-physical" stand over against "descriptive," "a priori" and "pure."

PARAGRAPH ONE. GENETIC PSYCHOLOGY

(1) Empirical psychology, according to Husserl, is an explanatory natural science.[1] "*Theoretical explanation* means an ever increased rendering intelligible of singular facts through general laws, and of general laws, in turn, through a fundamental law."[2] Actually, there is no theory but explanatory theory, for we can only speak of theory when there is a *systematic coherence* in our knowledge, when a number of "grounded validations" are combined to form a higher "interweaving" of such "validations."[3] An explanatory theory is possible in a factual science as well as in such an a priori science as mathematics. In psychology, which is a factual science, explanation involves showing

---

[1] I 211 note 1.
[2] II 20, 18.
[3] I 15ff, 230ff.

that "what happens under given groups of circumstances happens *necessarily*, i.e. according to *laws of nature.*"[4] Prediction and a certain "domination of nature" thereby become possible.[5] The facts in psychology are experiences. They are the "real events" that come and go in time. Cognitive acts are also psychological facts of this kind, and we can also trace causes for their coming about and passing a way in time.[6] In this sense, psychical acts belong to "nature."[7]

To explain a particular fact is to see its "ground," i.e. to see that it is necessary. By 'ground' Husserl always means "law-ground." It is a law of nature that when particular circumstances are realized, a particular effect necessarily follows. Thus the necessity of the effect always has to do with a particular causal succession of facts. That everything in nature is subject to causality is a "metaphysical presupposition" from which every science of "actual reality" (*reale Wirklichkeit*) proceeds.[8] This means that psychology must proceed from the causal determination of psychical facts and then try to trace the laws in accordance with which particular psychical facts, e.g. correct judgments, occur.[9] If this law is found, the psychical fact is understood in its necessity.

(2) Empirical psychology is a "science based on experience" and as such is committed to *induction*. We do not have a priori insight into the laws which it formulates; these laws are generalizations of connections that have been factually ascertained. This implies that these laws are not exact and apodictic, as the laws of mathematics are. They are "vague generalizations of experience," "statements about approximate regularities of coexistence and succession."[10] This lack of precision is not provisional but a matter of principle. Induction never brings us any farther than probability. It is true that these laws are usually formulated as exact laws, but this is only an idealizing fiction – albeit a fiction *cum fundamento in re.*[11] The empirical laws of psychology (e.g. the laws of association) share in this provisional character.

(3) Psychology, which seeks to explain the causal genesis of events in

---

[4] I 71, 76, 148, 231; II 20.
[5] I 10, 73, 195; II 167.
[6] I 128f, 66, 139, 150.
[7] I 168, 186f.
[8] I 10, see also 108.
[9] I 108, 187, see also 66, 139; II 120, 145, 189, 191, 204.
[10] I 61, 74, 187, 108.
[11] I 72f.

time and space, also takes physiological causes into account.[12] Thus psychological explanation is at the same time *psycho-physical* explanation. A physiological psychology of this sort relies on psychophysical experiments.[13]

PARAGRAPH TWO. DESCRIPTIVE PSYCHOLOGY

(1) For Husserl as for Brentano, the *descriptive* character of this psychology implies first of all its concepts are intuitive in character. A descriptive concept is one that can be checked *directly* against intuition. Husserl contrasts such concepts with the hypothetical concepts of the explanatory sciences. The objection he raises against many explanatory sciences is not that they explain but that they confuse the results of explanation with the given phenomenon. In an explanatory science, a concept is a theoretical supposition for explaining the given – but it is not the given itself. As an example, Husserl himself points to the theoretical concept of an "air vibration" or a "stimulation of the auditory sense" whereby the phenomenon of "sound" is explained. Such explanation by itself is unobjectionable. But it is a mistake and an expression of "common materialism" to maintain that sounds are "in truth" only air vibrations. "Here theoretical hypotheses that explain the given genetically are substituted for the given."[1]

The same holds for psychical phenomena. Here descriptive psychology tries to describe the phenomenon as it shows itself and does not concern itself with theories about the *origin* of the phenomenon.[2] A genetic theory works with causes in the unconscious and in the physiological processes. These causes are used as hypotheses to explain the given. Such an explanation, says Husserl, may well be very enlightening, but it does not affect our "immediate descriptive findings, which alone have relevance for the clarification of our concepts and acts of knowing."[3] Descriptive psychology is interested only in that which is directly given. Insofar as it represents a description of acts of

---

[12] II 21, 210, 384.

[13] II (ed. 1) 12 (in the second edition II Husserl speaks of experimental psychology and psychological experiments, 11).

[1] II (ed. 2) 210 (compare ed. I, 208) 398. See also II 129. The primary qualities of Locke (the "powers," etc.) are not the things that appear to us.

[2] II 210, 384.

[3] II 200.

knowing, the name '*theory* of knowledge' cannot properly be applied to it, for it is not a theory at all. The descriptive psychology of acts of knowing does not explain knowledge as an actual event in a psychological or psycho-physical manner; it "clears it up." Here, then, it has the function of "inquiry into origins"; what it investigates in the first place – but not exclusively – is the origin of the fundamental concepts of formal logic.[4]

(2) Descriptive psychology is an *a priori* science, just as it was in Brentano and in Husserl's earlier phase. It establishes laws that are "grounded purely in concepts." On the basis of intuitive concepts, it is possible to formulate a priori laws that hold for all objects falling under such concepts.

Despite the agreement between LU and the earlier work, there is a fundamental difference with regard to the *founding* of these a priori judgments. Husserl had earlier believed that an apodictic, evident insight is possible on the basis of the perception of an individual fact. At the end of Part I, I presented an analysis of the difficulties of this theory. In LU, Husserl's thinking on this point underwent a fundamental change. Alongside "actual reality," he now recognized an "ideal being." The a priori sciences are founded in this ideal being, in "essences." This introduction of the "intuition of essences" is the second new element in his thinking. (The first is the new theory of perception, i.e. the concept of constitution.) Later in this chapter and in the next chapter, I will deal with Husserl's new theory of the a priori sciences. Her I will elucidate the analysis of essences only by way of a few examples.

It is an a priori law (which we already encountered in Brentano) that a desire without a presentation is impossible. An intention in which something is desired without an objectifying act presenting that which is desired is "inconceivable."[5] The conjunction of these two is just as much an a priori matter as the conjunction of color and extension.[6] In an objectifying act, it is inconceivable that a quality could exist apart from matter, and vice versa.[7] It is also an a priori truth that in any judgment, the quality could change from positing to non-positing

---

[4] See below 283.
[5] II 428.
[6] II 423, 435.
[7] II 436, see also 441.

without a change in the matter.[8] This is an "ideal lawful" coherence. There is also such a coherence between propositional and nominal acts. It is true a priori that there is a propositional act corresponding to every nominal act, and a statement (*Aussage*) to every name.[9] None of these laws have to do with actual events in reality. They do not claim that something takes place in reality; their only claim is that an event of such-and-such a kind is possible.[10]

From these examples, to which I could add others, it is sufficiently clear that descriptive psychology is *in fact* an analysis of essences. To use a term of the later Husserl, descriptive psychology is an eidetic psychology. But on this point – as is often the case with Husserl – there is a certain incongruity between what he in fact does and what he says he is doing. As in the case of the phenomenological reduction, methodological reflection lags behind the actual use of a method.[11] Here we face a remarkable fact of which Husserl himself was not aware at the time of LU, namely, that descriptive psychology is an *eidetic* science. This is apparent, for example, from the introduction, where Husserl describes phenomenology as descriptive psychology, saying nothing about the eidetic character of this psychology. He writes simply: "Phenomenology is descriptive psychology."[12] It is not likely that Husserl wrote many sentences he regretted more than this one. If we define phenomenology in this way, then it does not differ from the descriptive psychology of Brentano and of PA. It would then be a psychology that works with "inner experience" rather than with the intuition of essences.[13] All that is gained in LU would thereby be lost. In particular, it is not clear how an analysis of essences is possible on the basis of "inner experience." Yet it must be possible, for the pure logic demanded by Husserl in his Prolegomena is such an eidetic science; this

---

[8] II 446, see also 480.

[9] II 466, 470, 473.

[10] II 470; III 153, 155, 188, 199.

[11] See above 198.

[12] II 18 (ed. 1).

[13] I (ed. 1) 211 note 1; II 440 (ed. 2). In the second edition of LU, we find an explicit critique of the attempt to derive eidetic truths from inner experience. "This cardinal error infects that style of psychologism which thinks it has satisfied the requirements of pure logic, ethics and epistemology, and that it has gone beyond extreme empiricism merely because it speaks of 'apodictic evidence' and even of 'a priori insights,' without ever leaving the ground of inner experience and psychology. "We may read this as a critique of Brentano, who, as we have seen, represents exactly this "style of psychologism." LU (ed. 2) 440. See also below 274.

eidetic science, as I hope to show in Chapter 5, is a division of descriptive psychology *as far as its fundamental concepts are concerned.*[14]

Furthermore, this statement in the introduction is not a slip of the pen, for it is in agreement with the methodological remarks in the text. In the case of the examples mentioned, Husserl does speak in the first edition of "ideal lawful" and a priori coherences, but nowhere does he show that these coherences are founded in an eidetic psychology. The idea that the analysis of experiences is an analysis of *essences* is first introduced in a systematic way in the second edition. Phenomenology is then called a "theory of the essences of experiences."[15]

At first glance, Husserl appears to be strikingly inconsistent in speaking of certain a priori laws but not of an a priori science. Yet this can readily be explained. It appears that in LU, Husserl still thought of a priori science in very definite terms, i.e. as a deductive system in which less general statements are understood on the basis of more general statements, which are in turn understood on the basis of a few very general laws and axioms.[16] Every (material and formal) mathematical eidetic science (e.g. geometry, arithmetic, pure logic) forms such a system.

It was only later that Husserl realized that a non-deductive eidetic science is also possible. He then began to distinguish particular "types" of ideas, as he remarked in the preface to the second edition.[17] The most important distinction between essences is that between mathematical or

---

[14] See below 291.

[15] I (ed. 2) 211 note 1; II (ed. 2) 2, 9, 18f. In addition to these important references, we should also take note of the following: The terms 'essential' and 'essence'-which Husserl already used in the first edition in connection with the analysis of experience, e.g. in his definition of intentionality II 249 (ed. 2, 368) and in the term 'intentional essence' II (ed. 1) 403 and 456, see (ed. 2, 429 and 492) – are placed between quotation marks in the second edition II 481, 426, 474 (compare ed. 1, 393, 400, 442 respectively). Furthermore, 'distinction' II (ed. 1) 329 becomes 'essential distinction' (ed. 2, 351); 'Law' II (ed. 1) 401 becomes 'eidetic law' (ed. 2, 428). 'Lawful' II (ed. 1) 421 becomes 'eidetically lawful' (ed. 2, 450). 'Analysis' II (ed. 1) 214, 412 becomes 'analysis of essences' (ed. 2, 216, 439), and an entire passage about the analysis of essences is added. 'Treatment' II (ed. 1) 426 becomes 'eidetic treatment' (ed. 2, 455). To 'analysis of acts' II (ed. 1) 364, 406, 440, is added 'ideally grasped' in edition 2 (386, 432, 470). 'Essence' or 'pure essence' is also added (compare II (ed. 1) 120, 174, 329, 333, 379 with (ed. 2) 121, 175, 351, 355, 403). Another new passage about the analysis of essences is found in II (ed. 2) 369 (compare ed. 1, 349).

[16] II 21.

[17] Vorwort XV.

exact essences and inexact essences. Husserl also calls the latter morphological essences. They have to do with the things given to us in intuition, e.g. the spatial form of a perceived petal. Such an essence can be described only in a vague way, e.g. through such concepts as "notched" and "faded." This is not a shortcoming, for it belongs to the essence of *descriptive* concepts. Descriptive psychology also operates with such inexact concepts. Over against these morphological essences stand the so-called "ideal essences" or "ideas in the Kantian sense" or simply "ideas." They are the result not of a direct intuition of the essence of the given but of a peculiar "idealizing." This ideation intuits ideas as ideal limits, as "ideals" that can never be found in perception.

Bound up with this distinction between types of essences is a distinction between eidetic sciences. Mathematical essences can be ordered in a deductive theory, but descriptive essences cannot. A mathematics of experiences is not possible – although a rigorous fixation of these essences, and thus a rigorous science of them, is possible.[18] This distinction between types of eidetic sciences was not yet made by Husserl in LU. As for the a priori sciences, he still thought exclusively of their mathematical forms. This is the background of his definition: "Phenomenology is descriptive psychology." What does not come to expression in this definition is that psychology is an *eidetic science* – albeit *not a deductive science.*[19]

(3) Husserl had already spoken of *"pure* psychology" or "pure phenomenology" in LU, although he did not mean "pure" in the sense

[18] II (ed. 2) 245; Id I 6, 139ff. See below 452.

[19] This train of thought on my part is supported clearly by what Husserl writes in Ideen III 44ff. There he points out that rational psychology, unlike the mathematical sciences, is not deductive in the sense that the whole theory could be derived from a small number of basic statements of direct insight. Rational psychology presents us with an endless field of eidetic truths to be grasped directly by intuition. "But it is bound up with the nature of the eidetic insights demanded here that the beginner is inclined at first to allow descriptive psychology and phenomenology to shade into one another without separation." This "beginner's" standpoint is characteristic of LU.

In a review of the (Dutch) first edition of this book, Rudolf Boehm remarked that my contention that the second volume of LU contains descriptive psychology conflicts with Husserls corrective declaration, see 'Philosophische Rundschau' 286f. From what has been established above, it is apparent that this claim on the part of Boehm is completely wrong. What I have tried to show is exactly that Husserl's later *correction*, which I have discussed repeatedly, see above 207 and below 275, 284, 288, 309 note 3, was completely justified. What Volume 2 contains *de facto* is an analysis of essences, and therefore I have spoken of a descriptive *eidetic* psychology. Not only have I shown this, I have tried to explain why Husserl continued to cling to the old name in 1901.

in which he was to speak of "pure phenomenology" after the turn to transcendental phenomenology.[20] Pure consciousness and pure experiences were then the result of a *transcendental* "purification." In LU, the term 'pure' did not yet have this meaning. This is apparent from Husserl's comment in the second edition that there was no transcendental purification in the first edition.[21]

On the question of the "purity" of phenomenology, then, Husserl's thought underwent some important development. Yet, as I hope to show, there is a significant connection between the earlier and later conceptions. On this point, the turn taken by Husserl's thinking after 1908 is not so much a break as a radicalization of tendencies already present, something that led to greater inner unity and consistency in his conception. The inner split in the early Husserl's ontology, which manifested itself concretely in the juxtaposition of explanatory psychology and descriptive psychology, was then overcome. Although Husserl's thinking in LU still moves on two tracks – despite his manifest preference for descriptive psychology – his thinking after the transcendental reduction is unfolded radically from one principle or one root, i.e. transcendental consciousness.

What does Husserl mean in LU by 'purity'? My analysis of the passages in which he speaks of purity leads me to conclude that in LU, the purely phenomenological substance of an experience is the purely descriptive substance.[22] The purity thus lies in the measure in which phenomenology refrains from theoretical explanation and limits itself to pure description. Furthermore, Husserl also speaks of the purely psychical as the result of an abstraction. When we proceed from the empirical ego, i.e. the ego as a concrete, individual object, we must abstract from the body in order to retain only the purely psychical sphere. "If we separate the ego-body from the empirical ego," the result is "the purely psychical ego" or the phenomenological ego.[23] Later Husserl describes this process as follows: "We excluded the body-ego, whose appearances resemble those of any other physical thing, and dealt with the mental ego, which is empirically bound up with the

---

[20] II (ed. 1) 4, 12, 15 (ed. 2, 2, 11, 20); II (ed. 1) 226 (ed. 2, 229); II 183, 190, 200.

[21] See the title of Ideen I and 4. In the second edition the LU are adapted to this standpoint. See the second edition II 347 note 1, 373 note 1, 375, 382, 350 note 1, 357, 369, 382, 397 note 1, 397f, 439, 180. See also the introduction 11, 17f, 21; III 232, 235, 241, see also below 454.

[22] II (ed. 1) 4, 16, 18 (ed. 2, 2, 11, 18); 183, 190, 229.

[23] II (ed. 1) 331 and 325 (ed. 2, 353 and 346).

former and appears as belonging to it."[24] These passages are particularly interesting in the light of the later development, for in both cases Husserl calls this abstraction a "reduction."[25]

Both references to purity come down to the same thing, i.e. not considering the physical or physiological. A psychology that tries to remain purely descriptive has nothing to do with causes that lie in the physiological or the unconscious. It does not deny the existence of such causes, but neither does it concern itself with them.[26] Husserl's complete silence with regard to the genetic origin of sensations is rooted in the same motive.[27] If these causes remain unconsidered, the physical thing that causes the sensations is left out – and thus the human body is left out as well. The latter is expressly emphasized in connection with the abstraction that is called "reduction." In a certain sense, this abstraction is already included in the suspension of the physical thing, for Husserl also sees the human body as a "Körper" (body).[28] On the other hand, the human body occupies an exceptional position, for it is the bearer of a sphere of experiences. We must go into this matter more deeply, for this relation of consciousness to the physical thing to which it is empirically bound is a central aspect of what Husserl was later to call the natural attitude. It is also a ground-motive for the transcendental reduction, i.e. the transcendental purification.[29]

Like Brentano, Husserl tries to place all phenomena in a schema which requires that the human body be given a status equivalent to that of other physical objects. The foundation for this division of the sciences remains the distinction between experiences (acts plus sensations) and the non-experiences presented in experiences. The sciences must be divided on a purely phenomenological basis. The most satisfying division would therefore be one that proceeds from the most fundamental phenomenological distinction, i.e. the distinction between the descriptive content and the intended object of the perceptions. Psychology would then be the science of the psychical phenomena, and natural science that of the physical phenomena.[30]

[24] II (ed. 1) 342 (ed. 2, 361).
[25] In the second edition 357 this is interpreted in the sense of the transcendental reduction; see below 454.
[26] II 200, 213, 384; see above 165, 167, 177, 195.
[27] II 381.
[28] II (ed. 1) 342 (ed. 2, 361); see below 309, 385.
[29] Therefore the transcendental reduction is discussed in connection with these passages in the second edition II 361, 357.
[30] II (ed. 1) 339 (later dropped). The physical phenomenon here is not the sensation, as for Brentano, but the objective interpretation of it.

This simple schema leads to simplifications on both sides. On the side of the act, all acts (cognitive, ethical and aesthetic) and sensations are brought under the general concept of experience. On the objective pole, there is the physical phenomenon, which is the point of departure of all natural sciences.[31] Even the human body is a physical phenomenon; to use Husserl's own words, it is a body "whose appearances resemble those of any other physical thing." Over against beings with "experiences" stand perceived outer objects or "bodies."[32] (Körper) Thus the perceived things outside us – already a simplification, for this group includes not only physical things in the narrow sense but also plants and animals[33] – must indeed be placed on the same level as the human body.

What I have established here is important, for *this equivalence in status*, as we shall see later, *is one of the conditions for the possibility of carrying out the transcendental reduction.*

In opposition to this, one could conceivably point to what I have written above about the constitution of the "body." (Leib) There is, however, no mention of a theory of the "constitution of the body" in LU. All we find are certain remarks that were later developed in the direction of such a theory. In both of the passages cited, Husserl does speak of the "Leib," but it is apparent from the context that he is using this term interchangeably with 'Körper.' The question whether Husserl's doctrine of the "constitution of the body" breaks in principle with the schema mentioned above can only be dealt with later.[34]

When Husserl speaks of the "empirical ego," he means the unity of a "body" (Körper) and a sphere of experiences. He also speaks of such a unity as a "person" or an "empirical person."[35] In a pure description of the sphere of consciousness, the human body cannot be considered.[36]

PARAGRAPH THREE. THE TWO FUNCTIONS OF DESCRIPTIVE
PSYCHOLOGY

For Brentano, descriptive psychology originally had no other function than preparing the way for explanatory psychology.[1] But about fifteen

---

[31] See above 54.
[32] II (ed. 1) 345f (ed. 2, 365); I 194f.
[33] In addition to things, Husserl mentions plants and animals e.g. II 75, 129, 161.
[34] See above 140 and below 385.
[35] II 350, see below 473.
[36] See below 309.
[1] See above 54.

years after the publication of PES, it appeared that this psychology was no longer solely a descriptive stage preparing the way for empirical psychology; it became an autonomous science and was assigned a second task, i.e. tracing a priori laws for human conduct – in the first place in the area of ethics, but also in the areas of logic and aesthetics. Descriptive psychology, which *in fact* was already an a priori science in 1874 as far as the structure of the psychical is concerned, was now to lay the a priori foundations for the normative sciences of ethics, logic and aesthetics.

In LU, Husserl immediately placed full emphasis on this second function of descriptive psychology (in connection with the question of pure logic). But the first function of descriptive psychology was by no means forgotten. Descriptive psychology is first of all a "preparatory stage" preceding theoretical psychology; it describes the empirical objects that theoretical psychology seeks to investigate and explain causally in their genetic context.[2] Unless it is preceded by proper description, theoretical explanation can make no claim to definitive validity.[3]

But for Husserl, descriptive psychology is much more important insofar as it plays a role in the founding of the normative sciences, i.e. logic, ethics and aesthetics. The "experiences" it describes form the concrete "substratum" for the abstraction of concepts used to build up ideal laws in these sciences.[4] Of these normative sciences, it was pure logic that drew Husserl's special attention; he hoped to "clear it up" with the help of descriptive psychology. In a later chapter I will discuss Husserl's new theory of the abstraction of ideal concepts and his founding of pure logic as an ideal science in a descriptive psychology.[5] This second function of descriptive psychology is so important to Husserl that he reaches for a new term and speaks for the first time of "phenomenology." This term is used to refer to the description that is intended not as a preparation for explanation but as a clarification of the fundamental concepts of the a priori sciences.[6]

---

[2] II (ed. 1) 18 (compare edition 2, 18); I 211 note I and II, 336 ed. 1 (later dropped).
[3] II 190, see also 212.
[4] II (ed. 1) 18 (ed. 2, 18); II 365, see also 1, 6 and II (ed. 1) 214 (ed. 2, 216).
[5] See below 283, 289.
[6] II (ed. 1) 18. See above 57.

PARAGRAPH FOUR. HUSSERL'S CRITICISM OF EXPLANATORY
PSYCHOLOGY

Explanatory psychology with its inductive empirical method forms the
heart of Brentano's positivism. The application of the natural scientific
method to psychology was based on his belief in progress and his
optimistic outlook on the future. Even when he later came to recognize
that there is a place for an autonomous descriptive psychology
alongside this empirical psychology, he did not give up this ideal.[1] At
the time of LU, what was Husserl's position with regard to these
positivist ideals? This question must be raised in connection with his
sharp criticism of explanatory psychology. To what extent does this
criticism signify a principial rejection of the natural scientific method?
Does his heavy emphasis on descriptive psychology imply a renunciation of positivism?

Husserl's logical investigations have indeed been interpreted to mean
that he opposed the natural scientific study of consciousness. It is
argued that the disturbing consequences of naturalistic positivism –
especially as they apply to subjectivity and the realm of the "mind" –
had become apparent to Husserl. His opposition to psychologism
would then be a protest against the dominant natural scientific method
of his time, against the "calculative thinking" (to use Heidegger's term)
that results in a "psychology without a psyche."[2] This interpretation
appears to find powerful support in all the passages in which Husserl
seems to oppose an explanatory method in psychology and seems to
oppose any psychological "theory." Indeed, does the Prolegomena to
Pure Logic not imply a rejection of such a psychology as skeptical and
absurd? It is clear that what we face here is a central problem in Husserl
interpretation. As I see it, it is the key to understanding Husserl's
development after 1901. I will return to this matter at the end of this
paragraph.

First we must inquire into the background and meaning of Husserl's
opposition to the explanatory method in psychology. His complaint
comes down to this, that neither of the two functions of descriptive
psychology has been properly appreciated. On the one hand, explanation has been attempted without a thorough description of the

[1] See above 108.
[2] Compare J. v.d. Hoeven *Kritische ondervraging van de fenomenologische rede* 20ff.

phenomena to be explained, and on the other hand, attempts have been made to use this explanatory psychology in the founding of the normative sciences (e.g. logic).

(A) With regard to the first complaint, Husserl's criticism was later to grow into the formal demand that experimental psychology be totally reformed. In LU, where the second aspect comes especially to the fore, Husserl did not yet place heavy emphasis on the significance of descriptive psychology for the reformation of empirical psychology, as he was later to do in PSW.[3] Yet in LU, we do find the premises on which this criticism is based. Husserl's complaint about the British empiricists (e.g. Hume) is that their explanation lacks a descriptive foundation and thus can make no claim to being scientific.[4]

Husserl later elaborated on this criticism in a certain way, although the conditions for this elaboration were already present in LU. He pointed out that this descriptive psychology not only analyzes the concepts used by empirical scientists but also establishes general laws normative for empirical investigation – some of them already been mentioned – on the basis of a descriptive analysis of the essences of psychical phenomena. This psychology then forms the basis of empirical psychology, just as geometry (and phoronomy) form the foundation of explanatory natural science. "Of course eidetic insights about perceptions, volitions and any other type of experience hold also for the corresponding empirical states of the animal organism, just as geometrical insights are valid for the spatial figures of nature."[5] Thus the development of descriptive psychology as a preparatory stage for explanatory psychology receives a fundamental significance which is determinative for the scientific character of the latter. In his sketch toward a preface to LU, Husserl praises Dilthey and Wundt for recognizing the importance of LU for the reformation of psychology despite the fact that Husserl had not as much as mentioned the reformation of psychology in that work and first raised this prospect in PSW.[6]

Finally, Husserl's criticism of explanatory psychology can be elucidated by means of a concrete example. The universal concept plays a central role in logic. Husserl recognizes this concept in two forms: as

---

[3] See below 477.
[4] II 190; see also 212.
[5] Entwurf 337; II (ed. 2) 18.
[6] Entwurf 332f.

the general meaning of a word and as the intuition of something general, in which the meaning of a word is fulfilled.[7] By describing this phenomenon that cannot be explained away, phenomenology provides a clarification of one of the fundamental concepts of logic, i.e. "general presentation." The mistake of such thinkers as Mill and Hume was that they sought to elucidate this process of abstraction through explanation; instead of describing that which is characteristic of this consciousness of the universal, they gave an explanation of its genesis. They pointed to the empirical context in which this "experience" occurs in the stream of causes and effects.[8] As a result, the "descriptive state of affairs" (i.e. the consciousness of the universal) comes to light in a distorted way at best, and we get lost in a hypothetical play of associations.

We see this in John Stuart Mill's theory of abstraction. According to Mill, we can only perceive individual things. Yet there is such a thing as a general concept. In Mill's writings we do not find a genuine description of the particular kind of consciousness in which something universal is intended; we only find an explanation of the genesis of the general concept. On his view, it is because we associate certain features of an individual thing with the sound of a word that we are able to think something general. When we hear a sound (or see something written), we associate with it a certain property, a property that only occurs *in concreto*. This thinking of a property in general, which is made possible by the word, is called a concept by Mill.[9] Husserl writes that such a theory can be very enlightening with regard to the causal conditions for the genesis of the consciousness of something universal, and thus for the genetic *psychology* of abstraction. (He particularly praises Hume in this respect.) But it does not get around to describing the consciousness of something universal as an evident given. Indeed, it is the express intention of this theory to "prove the nullity" of such a consciousness.[10] Thereby this psychology explains away a phenomenological given – a procedure that Husserl compares to the "materialism" that regards sounds as "vibrations."[11] All the same, it is apparent that Husserl has no principial objection against this sort of genetic explanation of abstraction. He expresses himself unequivocally on this score.[12] The thrust of his argument is rather that a preparatory descriptive study is indispensable for explanation.[13]

---

[7] See above 155.
[8] II 200.
[9] II 137, 139 (Mill); 191 (Hume).
[10] II 142, 144, 146 (Locke); 170, 175 (Berkeley); 187ff, 192 (Hume).
[11] II 210.
[12] II 145.
[13] See below 479.

(*B*) Husserl's main attack was against "*the naturalizing of ideas* and thereby of all absolute ideas and norms," as he called it in PSW. In theory this naturalism is an absurdity, and in practice it is a growing danger to our culture.[14] It manifests itself not only in logic but also in ethics. The area in which Husserl chose to do battle with it was not ethics (Brentano's choice) but logic; this choice was doubtless bound up with his mathematical education. Husserl explained in the introduction to LU that difficulties in the founding of mathematics had led him to logic. This was a natural progression, for pure logic and formal mathematics form a unity from the standpoint of formal analysis.[15] His struggle against naturalism in logic, which reduces all laws of thought to "laws of nature governing thought," is significant for all other areas of human endeavor as an example (in part because formal axiology is founded in this logic).[16]

This naturalism must lead to an absolute relativism and skepticism, for ideal, super-temporal laws are made dependent on empirical facts. The largest part of the Prolegomena – perhaps the most read part and in any event the most applauded part of this entire work – consists of a brilliant refutation of this form of naturalism. Husserl never tires of pointing out in detail the absurd consequences of this standpoint and focusing his spotlight on its skepticism, both open and hidden.

Husserl's attack is a typical example of what he himself was later to call a "negative criticism based on consequences."[17] He tries to show that this naturalism leads to absurd consequences in every respect. The criticism proceeds through three phases.

(1) In the first place, Husserl maintains that psychologism is unscientific by its own criteria. If it is the case that mutually contradictory propositions cannot coexist in the human mind (as Mill maintains), where are the empirical investigations that would justify this induction? Have there not always been people who maintain contradictions as true (e.g. the insane)? There have even been normal people who denied the validity of this principle (e.g. Hegel). Thus it does in fact happen that the human mind affirms mutually contradictory propositions. Mill's so-called empirical law is nothing more than a "rough generalization from pre-scientific experience," a plausible supposition.[18]

---

[14] PSW 293, 295.

[15] Vorwort I, VI. See below 252.

[16] Id I 304, 197f, 237ff; FTL 121, 88 note 1; EP II 24.

[17] PSW 293, 296f; compare LU I 78: "One might almost say that it is only inconsistency that keeps psychologism alive: to think it out to the end is already to have given it up . . . ."

[18] I 81, 83, 87f, 97, 197. On Hegel 141.

(2) But if we were to assume that such empirical evidence had indeed been gathered, we would still have only probable results rather than universally valid results (a limitation of all empirical science). We get no further than "vague generalizations from experience" or "statements about approximate regularities of coexistence and succession."[19] This inexactness of psychological laws cannot be attributed to the immaturity of psychology in comparison with other experiential sciences (e.g. chemistry, which knows a great deal about the reactions that will take place under given circumstances[20]). This lack of precision is not temporary but a matter of principle. Induction never gets us further than probability or approximations. There are no exact laws in the experiential sciences; the way laws in these sciences are formulated sometimes creates an impression of exactness, but this is due only to an "idealizing fiction." The theoretical ideal of understanding all the facts on the basis of a number of exact laws – and ultimately on the basis of one fundamental law, i.e. the ideal of "unity on the basis of lawfulness" – is beyond the reach of the experiential sciences.[21]

If the laws of logic were nothing but a particular brand of psychological law, they would share in this inexact and provisional character. But this is clearly not the case. The principles of logic, the laws of the syllogism, etc., are absolutely exact and valid. Their "lawfulness" is not an ideal but a realized possibility. These laws are justified not by induction but by apodictic evidence.[22] A psychological founding of logic would demand as a consequence that logical (and mathematical) laws also be regarded as only probable. But we see immediately that this is absurd.

If logic rests on a shaky foundation, all the other sciences threaten to collapse. This would mean not only that the premises from which we reason are provisional, which is the case in every empirical science, but also that the principles in accordance with which we reason are provisional. The principles of logic are the conditions for the possibility of science; they are the "ideal conditions for knowledge." Logic, as the science of these ideal conditions for knowledge, is the sciences of sciences or the theory of theories. It investigates the categories that form the constituents of all sciences (such as truth, conclusion, proof, theory), the forms of the connection of judgments (i.e. conjunctive, disjunctive, hypothetical), and finally – on a still lower level – the subject and predicate forms.[23] The laws founded in these forms determine the validity of each theory. It is clear that every science – including psychology – must stand or fall with the science of sciences.[24] If logic were to fall, the psychologistic theory itself would be undermined.

(3) Let us go on to suppose – moving still further in the direction of the proponent of psychologism – not only that empirical investigation into his

---

[19] I 61, 108, 187; compare Id I 37.
[20] I 108,187.
[21] I 63, 72, 150, 177; compare 15, 236.
[22] I 63, 73.
[23] I 122, 139, 160, 166, 179, 187, 241, 243.
[24] I 245, 253ff.

thesis has been done but also that it has yielded incontestable positive results supporting his view. Only then does the untenability of his position become fully apparent. The proponent of psychologism has confused empirical causes with justifying grounds; he has confused facts with norms. From the standpoint of a genetic theory, every judgment is "necessary" because it is "naturally conditioned." If the law of nature were at the same time a logical law, then a judgment would be true if it were empirically necessary. This implies that the truth of a judgment is dependent on natural causes, i.e. on prior psychical facts causing the judgment. But this is absurd.[25] An argument that lays claim to being true appeals to a norm, i.e. agreement with reality. Ascertaining how a train of thought in fact originated cannot tell us whether it is true.[26] In order to attain formal truth or consistency – which is the focus of our attention here – all thinking must appeal to the validity of this norm. Without this, no striving for truth would be possible. The proponent of psychologism, making use of these principles, now argues that they rest on empirical generalization and are thus a description of actual thought processes. If this were indeed the case, it would be impossible to use these principles to criticize thinking, for criticism presupposes a principle that transcends the facts. Thus the proponent of psychologism denies the principles on which his own thinking – and with it his argument – rests. Husserl here speaks of skepticism in the pregnant sense. In brilliant fashion he applies the argument of self-contradiction to the skeptic. If the skeptic is right, then he is wrong. Only if he is wrong is it possible to determine whether he is right.[27]

(C) It follows from the preceding that we cannot speak of a rejection of explanatory psychology in LU. This is obvious as far as the first part of Husserl's criticism is concerned. The laying of a descriptive foundation as a preparatory stage makes little sense if the explanation to follow is to be rejected. Husserl's intention is rather to place this explanation on a higher scientific level. His objection is against blindness to descriptive

[25] I 76, 119f, 128, 131; see also below 271.

[26] In a certain sense, the proponent of psychologism recognizes the difference between an empirical science (psychology) and a normative science (logic). Logic, he says, is a "Kunstlehre" (theory of an art) that gives us directions for making correct judgments. But the question is: on what do we base these directions? The proponent of psychologism answers: on the laws of psychology. Logic uses certain laws, namely, the laws of *correct* thinking, as norms. "Thinking as it should be" is nothing but a "special case of thinking as it is" I 54f. Thus the norms are still borrowed from factual processes. This is also apparent from the psychologistic conception of a "Kunstlehre," which is not a theory of how one must learn to apply rules but a technology! If we have learned that correct lines of reasoning are produced under certain circumstances – just as a chemical reaction is produced under certain conditions, see I 105ff – then we must strive for the realization of these circumstances. (On the concept of a "Kunstlehre," see above 92 and below note 29 and 224f).

[27] I 84, 86, 110, 112, 237f, 255.

states of affairs, for this leads to attempts at explanation without knowing properly just what it is that is to be explained. Although Husserl had the greatest admiration for certain achievements of explanatory psychology (especially those of Hume), and although he rejected in the blossoming of psychology and took the "liveliest interest" in it, he saw clearly that we must not expect any help from empirical psychology when it comes to clarifying concepts.[28]

Roughly the same is true with regard to the second point. What Husserl rejects is not the causal method but the founding of ideal laws in this method. These laws can be discovered only through descriptive eidetic analysis of psychical phenomena, which are then subjected to ideational abstraction or the intuition of essences. But this does not alter the fact that the same phenomena can be objects of a causal explanation. The criticism of a certain presumptuous pretention of empirical psychology is *not a criticism of psychology itself*. No rejection of empirical psychology can be deduced from Husserl's plea for a pure logic independent of all empirical psychology. *The reverse could better be argued*, for it is one of Husserl's arguments that psychologistic logic sets not only logic but also the empirical sciences – and thus empirical psychology itself – on a shaky foundation. His assault on psychologisme protects not only logic but also the empirical sciences, for formal logic is the instrument of every science, and thus also of the inductive sciences. The rescue of logic from the relativistic tidal wave of psychologism is at the same time the rescue of the empirical sciences![29]

Indeed, it is a misconception to suppose that Husserl ever attacked the legitimacy of the empirical sciences. In his transcendental idealist period, as we shall see in Part III, he did not do so either. But thus does not alter the fact that at a basic level, there is a clear difference operative between Husserl's attitude toward the sciences in LU and his attitude in later works. In Ideen I, he regards a fundamental philosophical criticism of the sciences as necessary. It is true that this criticism does not touch on the internal workings of science – as Husserl had already pointed out in LU, the progress of science is not dependent on

---

[28] I 211 note I.

[29] Over against the misunderstandings of certain critics, Husserl accentuated his appreciation of empirical psychology. He argued than an empirical study of logical thinking in the style of Mill, Sigwart and Wundt is indispensable for logic as a "Kunstlehre," (theory of an art). As a "Kunstlehre" logic has its theoretical foundations in *two* sciences, i.e. pure logic and empirical psychology; see his review of Melchior Palàgyi, 288.

philosophy[30] – but it does present us with a fundamental reinterpretation of its results in the light of the transcendental idealist ontology. The sciences in themselves are "dogmatic"; that is to say, they proceed from the presupposition of a world existing in itself. This implicit naturalistic ontology must be removed from science. Husserl calls this step a "metaphysical interpretation" that is at the same time a final epistemological founding making possible a transformation of the dogmatic sciences into philosophical sciences. In LU, we do not find a radical critique of the sciences along such lines. Therefore the roots of the naturalistic ontology remain untouched.[31]

In LU, Husserl sees two tasks for philosophy. In the first place, philosophy is the theory of science in the sense of a formal logic and methodology. The man of science does not concern himself with the principles according to which he thinks, and he has no explicit insight into his symbolic methods. In this regard, science needs a philosophical supplement. The second, complementary task is the clarification of the concepts used in science. In this connection, I could point to Husserl's philosophical elucidation of the concept of number in the first part of PA: the mathematician, says Husserl, operates with concepts like "number" and "quantity" without definite insight into the essences of these concepts.[32] These two complementary tasks hold for both the empirical sciences and the formal, logical sciences. (The philosophy of the latter will be elucidated in Chapter 5.) The investigation of the special scientist and the "critique of knowledge" of the philosopher are "complementary scientific activities."[33] Thus philosophy does not present a radical critique that throws open to discussion the world as the "foundation" (Weltboden) on which the sciences base themselves. Their task is "complementary" (ergänzend).

In the light of Husserl's later development, it is surprising how favorably he speaks of the "formerly undreamt-of mastery of nature" that has become possible because of modern science with its refined mathematical instruments.[34] His words sound Comtean. By tracing causal laws, it is possible to predict events and orient ourselves better and better in the world around us. Even on the level of savages and on

---

[30] Compare LU I 253 with Id I 46.
[31] Compare below 1481ff.
[32] I 10f, 252ff. See above 63, 67.
[33] I 254.
[34] I 10, 73.

the level of "everyday people," there is a certain adaptation and dominance. But their world is still "a system merely approximate in its regularity and shot through with countless accidents." This picture of the world develops into that of the man of science, for whom the world is "a nature ruled throughout by absolutely strict law."[35] Blind thinking has replaced scientific thinking. "Man's superiority lies in his intelligence. He is not solely a being who brings perception and experience to bear on external situations: he also thinks and employs concepts to overcome the narrow limits of his intuition. Through conceptual knowledge he penetrates to rigorous causal laws, which permit him to foresee the course of future phenomena, to reconstruct the course of past phenomena, to calculate in advance the possible reactions of the things around him, and to dominate them physically – all of this to a vastly greater extent and with with vastly more confidence than would otherwise be possible. From science, foresight, and from foresight, action, as Comte tellingly remarks."[36]

In his later publications, Husserl says that although science has taught us how to dominate nature, it has made no contribution to "understanding" nature. This understanding, which in LU is only complementary,[37] is then the sole genuine form of knowledge of reality: "transcendental understanding" of the world on the basis of achievements of consciousness is the only real "explanation."[38] The belief that the natural sciences clear up the riddle of the reality in which we live, move and have our being stands revealed as a superstition to "those with a deeper insight," according to PSW. "Calculating the course of the world does not mean understanding it," as Lotze correctly pointed out.[39] The Husserl of LU cannot yet count himself a full member of the company of those who enjoy a "deeper insight." To reach this insight, an entirely new, eye-opening operation is necessary – the transcendental reduction.

PARAGRAPH FIVE. TWO KINDS OF METHODS (ONTOLOGIES) – NATURALISTIC AND PHENOMENOLOGICAL

Husserl remained true to the positivistic science ideal, as we have seen.

[35] I 201, 205.
[36] I 195.
[37] See I 206, 254.
[38] Krisis 193 (E 189); compare Id III 95f.
[39] PSW 336.

But on the other hand, he did object vigorously to the positivist claim that ideal laws can be reduced to laws of nature. In psychology, the science of consciousness, he therefore placed a descriptive, a priori and "pure" phenomenological method next to the explanatory method. The *juxtaposition* of these two methods, which is characteristic of Husserl's standpoint in LU, implies an ontological dualism. He could not remain content with this dualism. I will try to demonstrate that it was exactly the inner problematics of this juxtaposition that drove Husserl's thinking in the direction of transcendental idealism. In principle, two standpoints clash here – a naturalistic-positivistic standpoint and a phenomenological standpoint. How is it possible to grasp consciousness by way of these two points of view at the same time?

(*A*) First I will work out the problematics of these two standpoints somewhat further. I will begin by raising the question how it is possible to place consciousness under ideal norms while *at the same time* grasping it as part of a determined system. Husserl distinguishes sharply between "ideal" possibilities of knowledge and "real" possibilities.[1] The former determine validity, and the latter determine factual realization in spatio-temporal reality. The latter are dependent on the actual existence of causal conditions. The problem, now, is how a norm can be realized within a naturally lawful process. Does the placing of an ideal norm not presuppose breaking out of this causality? Does it not presuppose a certain freedom as the field for its possibility? Nowhere in LU does Husserl make it apparent that he is aware of this problem. In the very paragraph in which he mentions the ideal conditions for the possibility of knowledge, he writes: "Naturally the possibility of knowledge in a psychological regard embraces all the causal conditions on which our thinking depends."[2] Thus the same psychical acts which must satisfy ideal norms are subject to strict natural lawfulness. (Furthermore, insight into the norm is itself a natural fact.)

The two points of view and the difficulties inherent in maintaining both can be illustrated with reference to knowing acts. What Husserl reproaches thinkers like Sigwart for is that they fail to make a sharp distinction between the subjective necessity that belongs to every

---

[1] I 111, 236f; III 152, 155, 188, 199; II 164f "Laws of nature" stand over against 'ideal laws.'

[2] I 237, see also 209.

"experience" as an element in a causally determined series and the "apodictic necessity" which belongs only to apodictically *correct* judgments.[3] From a psychological standpoint, *every* judgment is necessary. But a judgment is only logically necessary if it is the realization of an ideal law. In other words, the act of judging is a psychical fact and is causally determined, but the "content" of the judgment derives its validity from an ideal norm.[4] It is clear that a psychological cause is something entirely different from a logical ground.[5] If logical laws are regarded as laws of nature, we can no longer distinguish between true and untrue judgments. Every conclusion would be psychologically necessary, but only a true conclusion would be necessary in the sense of "ideal lawful validity."[6] Logical commitment is not a psychological "thought-compulsion," Husserl maintains – contra Sigwart *cum suis*.[7]

Nevertheless, all judgments, including evident judgments, are subject to the causal law, according to Husserl. We could, for example, undertake an investigation of the psychological conditions for the appearance of an evident insight. The insight would then be understood in its natural necessity.[8] Thus Husserl can agree with the statement, "Thinking as it should be is merely a special case of thinking as it is."[9] His objection is against making this standpoint exclusive, i.e. against degrading the logical laws of correct judgment to laws of nature. The same facts can also be viewed from an entirely different standpoint, i.e. as concretizations of a norm. The latter standpoint is necessary if we are to avoid falling into a relativistic and absurd psychologism.

The problematic aspect of Husserl's view comes to a head in the question of the possibility of logic as a "Kunstlehre" (theory of an art), for such a discipline is supposed to teach us how obedience to logical norms is to be realized in practice.

Husserl distinguishes between a pure theoretical logic, a normative logic, and a practical "Kunstlehre." Pure logic develops free of any bond with a possible

---

[3] I 134. Brentano had already criticized Sigwart on this point in USE.

[4] I 119.

[5] I 75.

[6] I 107.

[7] I 142.

[8] I 183ff, 186; see the examples on 108 and 187.

[9] I 54, 207. That every "experience" has a cause is universally accepted II 189 (ed. 1, 188 has "is certain"); II 145 (compare ed. 1, 144); III 92.

normative influence of purely logical "ideal laws."[10] Logic as a normative science arises from a fundamental valuation (*Werthaltung*). The logical laws developed in pure logic becomes norms through this "valuation." They represent the *goal* toward which all thinking strives and by which any method or science can be measured. If it is pure logic that develops the idea of science, it is normative logic that gives us the properties which a science must possess if it is to correspond to this idea.[11] Logic as a "Kunstlehre," finally, gives us directions for applying the norm in practice.[12] We find similar distinctions in ethics. Alongside pure ethics there is also a normative ethics and a practical ethics – the latter as a "Kunstlehre" of "ethical conduct."

Husserl claims – rightly – that any "Kunstlehre" is dependent on a normative science, but that the reverse is not the case. A normative science tells us only when an action is correct, i.e. under what conditions. But a "Kunstlehre" is concerned with realization in practice. This is the reason why a thinker like Schopenhauer developed an ethics as normative science but – because of his doctrine of in-born character – rejected any practical moralizing as a matter of principle! Schopenhauer's problem could also be raised with regard to Husserl himself as far as his view of explanatory psychology as a natural science is concerned. It is characteristic of Husserl's standpoint in LU that he sees no difficulties here and regards the possibility of a "Kunstlehre" as self-evident."[13]

The development of a logical "Kunstlehre" implies the possibility of striving after this norm as a goal. When Husserl speaks of the teleology present in human thinking,[14] he affirms not only the possibility but also the reality of such goal realization. But it seems that this teleology too fails to break out of causal thinking. What at first glance appears to answer to a teleological principle turns out ultimately to be in need of causal explanation. Husserl claims that it can be useful and instructive to undertake a teleological investigation of certain achievements of

---

[10] I 164f, 227ff.

[11] I 26, 41, 44. The unity of a normative science therefore lies not in the actual unity of its statements but in a "highest goal"; see I 36, 46, 48, 236 and A. Roth's *E. Husserls Ethische Untersuchungen* 70. For a wholly analogous theory, see Windelband's *Präludien* Volume II 131f, 167ff. According to Windelband, a normative science moves between the two poles of a highest goal and reality. The "matter" of this highest goal is derived from a fundamental "valuation." With this highest goal before its eyes, normative science tries to derive formally a number of duties, in the light of reality.

[12] I 26ff, 31, 47, 50; FTL 28, 39.

[13] I 30, 47.

[14] I 25, 73, 201, 208, 196.

(pre-)scientific thinking by looking to see how a certain goal – in this case, the formation of a scientific method making possible a practical domination of nature – is in fact realized. Sometimes a method of this sort is formed instinctively and mechanically, as it were, without insight into the rational principles involved (e.g. the decade system of numbers). But we cannot remain content with ascertaining that such a goal has been realized, for the teleological principle is not a "final explanatory rational principle" but only the summary of a number of "adaptive facts." The goal realization ascertained in this way is regarded as a wonder or as the result of a creative deed on the part of a divine intelligence (which amounts to the same thing). Science cannot rest content with this. It must show how such goals-directed action arises "from itself" on the basis of "purely natural grounds." Nothing can be explained via a teleological principle. It only creates confusion to regard certain phenomena as the necessary result of such a principle. "A psychological or epistemological law concerned with an *endeavor* to achieve as much as *possible* in this or that respect is a chimera. In the pure sphere of fact, there is no maximum possibility; in the sphere of law, there is no endeavor. What happens in each case, as a psychological matter of fact, is quite definite: there is so much of it and no more."[15] The pre-scientific picture of the world arises in accordance with psychological laws, but the same is true of the scientific picture of the world. "Naturally all scientific grasping and explaining proceed according to psychological laws."[16]

Thus scientific thought too must be explained by natural scientific means. On the one hand, it derives its validity from its relation to ideal laws. While the ideal law presupposes striving for a goal of the greatest possible rationality ("unity on the basis of lawfulness," the ideal of all scientific thought), the psychology of this thinking can only regard such striving as an absurdity or chimera![17]

If we think this through *in extremo* – and it would be entirely in Husserl's spirit to do so – we see that in the final analysis, science as human striving does away with itself as human striving. In other words,

---

[15] I 204.

[16] I 209. Husserl sometimes speaks of a psychical mechanism I 83, 201. He also uses the image of the calculating machine for the psychical process I 68 and does not restrict its application to 'ideological' psychology as in II 175.

[17] For Husserl's later view of teleology (and theology!), see below 355, 390 and 504.

physics renders the physicist superfluous, and psychology renders the psychologist superfluous.

(B) After this explication of the philosophical problem, we will see in the second half of this paragraph how much the Husserl of LU is in fact still caught up in a picture of the world that he himself later sought to overcome through the transcendental reduction. That the explanatory method is not only incompetent with regard to the founding of norms but even excludes all normativity does not become a problem in LU. The defence of ideal norms against all relativism therefore assumes a somewhat isolated position within the framework of Husserl's total conception. There is no inner unity between the ideal realm of ideas and the realm of nature which is normed by it.[18] Only later was Husserl to see that the defense of this ideal realm requires a thorough revision of ontology. The naturalism that naturalizes norms is supported and fed by the naturalism that naturalizes consciousness. Only an attack that address itself to the latter point could produce real results. By referring to the text of LU (particularly the first edition), I will show concretely (1) that there is still talk in LU of a naturalistic apperception of consciousness, and (2) that the purity of descriptive psychology is not yet a transcendental purity.

(1) Consciousness, together with the body as a physical thing, forms the unity of psycho-physical nature. The "sphere of experiences" is founded in a body by which it is influenced and which it in turn affects. Thus we can speak of an interaction between "body" (Körper) and "mind" (Seele), just as Brentano had done. The dependence of the body is investigated by physiology or psycho-physical psychology. Thus man is part of the physical world – that is, the world as "the unified objective totality corresponding to and inseparable from the ideal system of all factual truth." The world of (ideally complete) science is the "world in itself." According to Husserl, even the ego and its contents of consciousness belong to this world. The relativity of the existence of the world thus implies the relativity of the existence of the ego.[19]

---

[18] Compare I 207ff where it appears that speaking of teleology amounts to embracing a "philosophy of as if." In actuality, reality is determined by natural forces-and not by ideals. No doubt Husserl was acquainted with Hans Vaihinger's book *The Philosophy of As if*, for Vaihinger was a professor at Halle from 1884 to 1906.

[19] I 121; II (ed. 1) 337 (later dropped); III 200. The passage about the relativity of mundane existence, a relativity in which consciousness shares, is in sharp contrast with Ideen I, where Husserl says that consciousness is only modified by an annihilation of the world, see below 340.

This bond between the "mind" and the physical world also comes to the fore when Husserl discusses the theory of evolution, according to which man is a product developed by the world. Husserl calls it a generally accepted doctrine and speaks favorably of the results of teleologically directed investigations along evolutionary lines.[20] In this context he mentions the hypothesis that the world had already existed for a long time before there were human beings and calls it a presupposition that is not absurd by any means. The teleological principle plays a role in the biological sciences. These sciences deal with man as an "animal being."[21] Husserl speaks of physical and psychical biology and also physical and psychical anthropology; the principle of division is whether man's physical side or psychical side is studied.[22]

Man, to use one of Husserl's later expressions, is a "being on two levels," with a physical constitution and a psychical constitution.[23] Of course these two sides are different in character; nevertheless, the one is "nature" just as much as the other, insofar as the two are investigated by one and the same method. Husserl bases the differences between the two realities first of all on their different modes of givenness. The psychical is immanent and is therefore adequately given. The physical thing is given in three-dimensional space and can never be adequately perceived. Thus Husserl does not want to commit himself to the existence of two totally different substances ["body" (corpus) and "mind," (mens)]. The two differ in their respective modes of givenness; whether the realities are actually correspondingly different – that is to say, in their true "nature" – is a question that can be decided only by the progress of science. Husserl himself wants to leave open the possibility that the realities which we postulate on the basis of the given phenomena ultimately turn out to be the same – which would bring about the collapse of the entire distinction between mind and matter. Therefore it cannot be determined whether the two sciences of physics

---

[20] I 121, 147 note I 195, 203.

[21] I 5, 121.

[22] I 194, 196, 203; II 168. As a human phenomenon, science is a biological fact, I 210, or an anthropological fact I 173f. The physical part of man is a "body" (Körper) like any other. Thus it comes under consideration in explanatory physics ór in physical biology, which looks at it from a teleological point of view. Physical biology is thus a (non-scientific) preparatory stage for physics, see the Encyclopaedia Brittannica article in Husserliana IX. In physics, "animal bodies" (Leiber) are regarded as "mere bodies" (Körper).

[23] I 163f; see also 162, 120f. As a fact, man is part of the "real world."

and psychology will remain separate "in their complete development." It depends on whether the realities involved in the two sciences are actually separate, or at least independent of one another. Husserl points out that independence does not mean that the two realities "must be separated by some mystical abyss, by completely unheard-of differences."[24]

From this entire discussion, it seems clear that Husserl sees the task of explanatory psychology as completely analogous to that of physics. The psychologist undertakes investigations which "are aimed, like physical researches, at elementary laws."[25] By tracing the causal laws of the formation and transformation of psychical experiences, this explanatory psychology determines the "real essence of the ego (not a mystical essence but only an in-itself to be grounded empirically), the binding together of psychical elements to form the ego, and then their development and dissolution." Husserl even expressly compares the determination of this abiding element in the change to the same procedure as applied to the appearing physical phenomena. The ego as a "subsisting object" is a unity transcending the many changes; it is a unity in the sense of a lawful causal bond bringing about a thingly unity in the metaphysical sense (not in a mystical sense).[26] After the preparatory description explanatory psychology has a task analogous to that of explanatory natural science. The schema of description and explanation, after all, is itself derived from the natural sciences.[27] Every explanation proceeds from the phenomena and must look for a unity deeper than the phenomenological unity.[28] Explanation must seek the "in-itself" of the phenomena. This is a metaphysical unity, for it transcends the given, but it is not a mystical unity, for it is the result of scientific investigation. Husserl was later to say that science seeks the "nature" of the phenomena, a procedure permitted only in the case of physical phenomena.[29] Thus it is no accident that both passages in

---

[24] II (ed. 1) 338, 332 (later dropped). No passage better illustrates the gulf between LU and Ideen I, where Husserl speaks of an "abyss of sense" between the thing and consciousness, which are "in no sense co-ordinate forms of being" 93, 92. See below 360, 485.

[25] I 196; compare 'Ber. üb. deutsche Schriften zur Logik in den Jahren' 1895–99, 389.

[26] II (ed. 1) 336 and 332 (later dropped).

[27] See above 55; compare Krisis 226 (E 223).

[28] In LU, Husserl already sees phenomenological unity as a unity in time (ed. 1) 332. The phenomenological unity in the case of physical phenomeno serves as a comparison, III 226 note 1.

[29] PSW 310f; see 319f. Compare I (ed. 1) 206, 256 where Husserl claims that science

which he speaks of this "nature" of the physical were dropped from the second edition of LU.[30]

It is true that empirical psychology was not rejected by Husserl after 1908, but it was nevertheless subjected to a fundamental ontological re-evaluation.[31] The view of the world developed up to this point is characteristic of what Husserl was later to call the "natural world." Man is a "being on two levels" who, on his physical side, takes part in the physical world existing in itself. His mental side is empirically bound up with this world and is even the object of a natural scientific investigation. To this extent, the philosophy of LU is still caught up in what Husserl was later to call the "prejudice of the centuries."[32]

(2) But Husserl also speaks of the "purity" of descriptive psychology. In this psychology we abstract from the connection with physical nature and do not explain it. Does this not represent a break with the natural view of consciousness? We have already seen that the purity of this psychology only comes about through abstraction from the (psycho-)physical. It is a temporary disregarding of the connection that actually exists. The purity is *artificial*; it is the result of a methodological device and has only *methodological meaning* – and *no ontological meaning*. The sphere of purely psychical "experiences" is an artificial island, as it were, within a positivistic-naturalistic world. If we disregard this artificial limitation, there remains only nature governed by causal laws; man and his consciousness are part of this nature.

This conception of purity will undergo a radical change when Husserl begins to regard consciousness not as a region founded in a body but as the primordial region. Then purity will not be the result of a limiting abstraction and isolation of consciousness from the whole of reality. Purification will be the liberation from an interpretation which wrongly conceives of consciousness as a part of reality, whereas it is in fact the origin of all being and also constitutes the physical world in itself.[33]

seeks the "true essence" behind the appearance. On this "substance," see also above 196 and below 480.

[30] The conclusion of Paragraph 4 and all of Paragraph 7 of the fifth investigation.

[31] See above 196 and below 484.

[32] Krisis 216 (E 212). Husserl here opposes the conception of psychology as a "parallel science": "The mind (its theme) is then something real in the same sense as the bodily nature." "Beforehand, the world, viewed naturalistically as a world of two levels of real facts, was governed by causal lawfulness; minds, accordingly, as real annexes to their corporeal bodies, were also thought of in an exact scientific manner . . . ."

[33] When Husserl in LU refers to the neo-Kantian use of the word 'transcendental,' he regards it as a predicate applying to *human* consciousness. "For even transcendental psychology is also psychology" I 93 note 3; compare 123f and 214.

In LU we find a *limiting* of the competence of the positivist method – but not a principial critique of the naturalist ontology. From the standpoint of explanatory psychology, intentionality, as a sense-giving function of consciousness subject to norms as such and calling for a "rational appraisal" (*Rechtsprechung der Vernunft*), remains subject to a determinism of the laws of nature.[34] This *dualism* of methods without an attempt at synthesis or reconciliation is characteristic of LU. The dualism of methods is grounded in a deeper conflict in ontology. On the one hand, this ontology sees consciousness as a sphere of its own requiring its own methods of analysis and investigation, but on the other hand, it founds and incorporates this sphere in a positivistically and naturalistically interpreted physical reality. It was this dualism (in such thinkers as Dilthey, Brentano, Windelband, and Rickert) that Husserl was later to characterize as a half-way measure and a lack of radicalism. He then spoke of a "modern dualism in interpreting the world" and of the noteworthy split in modern consciousness, according to which man on the one hand is part of the universe of natural facts but on the other hand is a person and a bearer of norms. When he lectured to the Vienna "Kulturbund" on the crisis of man, Husserl declared that there is a burning need to understand the mind, and that "the unclarity about the methodological and actual relation between the natural sciences and the mental sciences (*Geisteswissenschaften*) has become almost unbearable." Dilthey devoted his whole life to clarifying the relation between nature and the mind; alongside psycho-physical psychology, he placed a descriptive psychology. Neither he nor Windelband nor Rickert was able to produce the clarification desired. Such a clarification can only be achieved when the dualistic conception of the world in which nature and the mind count as realities in the same sense is given up.[35]

This characterization of the situation also applies to Husserl's own earlier work, including LU. This analysis of LU reveals something of the personal background of Husserl's struggle against this dualism. It is a worldview of which he himself had to break free. In the lecture mentioned above, Husserl sees the recognition of the independence of the mind and the dependence of nature as the radical solution to the problem of nature and the mind. There can be no thought of "equality"

---

[34] See Id I 176ff. Seen naturalistically, intentionality too is nothing more than a "real relation"; see also LU II 350 and Id I 64 and 182.

[35] Krisis 318, 341, 345 (E 273, 293, 297).

between the natural sciences and the mental sciences. As soon as we accord a certain independence to nature, we fall prey to dualism. Later (in Part III), we will see how Husserl overcame this dualism through a radical vision of unity that proceeds from the ontological priority of the mind.[36]

PARAGRAPH SIX. CONCLUSIONS OF CHAPTERS ONE AND TWO

(A) In Chapter 1, I showed how Husserl's ontological dualism led to an impasse in his theory of knowledge. Within the phenomenological sphere, which is brought by isolating the physical, we can study acts and ultimately their intentional objects as well. But this gives us no knowledge of the world in itself. Behind the intentional object is the real object, as the hypothetically presupposed object of physics. This theory of knowledge on a phenomenological basis remains purely immanent and is a *psychology* of reason.

(B) Chapter 2 dealt with Husserl's struggle against the naturalizing of ideas. Although this polemic is very penetrating, it remains stuck in what Husserl himself was later to call a "negative criticism on the basis of consequences." The naturalizing of ideas leads to absurd consequences. It is a "hopeless attempt," said Husserl (using Kant's words), "to establish by an empirical theory what is itself presupposed by every theory."[1] The phenomenological sphere must provide the foundation for these ideal laws. But this sphere itself remains part of the natural world; it is a link in the system of natural necessity governing all of psycho-physical nature. I have analyzed the inner problematics of this standpoint with reference to logical experiences. It is not made clear how ideal norms can function within the realm of natural necessity.[2]

The methodological abstraction that gives us the purely psychical sphere is merely a methodological device and is unable to turn back the "tidal wave of positivism." Only later did Husserl realize that a radical critique of the naturalizing of ideas is possible only after the naturalizing of consciousness has been overcome. A radical critique of naturalism requires not only an attack on the basis of consequences but first and foremost a positive critique of the implicity ontology. Apparently

[36] See below 389, 395.
[1] I 84 note I.
[2] See below 301.

Husserl had to experience for himself how little effect a purely negative critique has. Presuppositions make us blind, he says, and anyone who considers only the experiential sciences will not be deterred by absurd consequences. Therefore, in order to break through this naturalism, the natural scientific philosophy must be attacked in a radical manner.[3] A truly presuppositionless analysis of consciousness will demonstrate that the naturalistic ontology is absurd. This will lead ultimately to an overcoming of naturalism and a *total* phenomenological outlook. As Husserl was to say in the Krisis, psychology is the "decision center" for philosophy. *In 1901, the decisions had not yet been made!*[4]

---

[3] PSW 296, 295, 293, 297; Entwurf 114.

[4] Krisis 218; see also 207, 212. Thus Fink is completely correct in assigning LU, together with PA, to Husserl's first period see his "Vorbemerkung" Entwurf 107; See above 121.

CHAPTER THREE

THE NEW THEORY OF ABSTRACTION

The most important anti-psychologistic thesis that Husserl wished to defend in the Prolegomena is that logic, as an a priori science, is not a real science but an ideal science. In this work he already observed that a proper conception of the distinction between these two kinds of sciences is only possible when the empiricist theory of abstraction is given up.[1] The question of abstraction is indeed the central problem in the founding of the ideal sciences. Therefore I will begin this chapter by taking up the new theory of abstraction. Then, in Chapters 4 and 5, I will deal with the question of the task of the philosophical analysis of origins in connection with the formal a priori sciences.

PARAGRAPH ONE. RECAPITULATION OF THE PROBLEM

The standpoint with regard to abstraction and general concepts defended by Husserl in his earliest publications can be summarized as follows. (1) There are acts in which something general is presented in a non-intuitive way. These are the acts in which we intend something general in a non-genuine way, with the support of a linguistic sign. Husserl calls this non-intuitive presentation a concept, which for him is the same as the meaning of a word. In the article of 1894, this act of meaning is regarded as one of the kinds of acts which "represent" something. He contrasts these acts with intuitive acts. (2) Husserl sets this view off against what he calls nominalism. Nominalism is blind to the concept as the meaning of a sign; it sees only the sign. Thus it reduces the meaning to the sensorily perceivable "vehicle" (*Anhalt, Stütze*). Like Brentano, Husserl makes it clear that he is a believer in the Scholastic adage "Voces significant res *mediantibus conceptibus*." It is

---

[1] I 178.

only via the concept that the sign receives meaning. Therefore we can call this standpoint conceptualism. (3) Every concept finds its origin in intuition; this is the basic principle of Husserl's intuitionism. What, then, is the intuitive basis of the general concept? This question comes up especially in the case of a priori concepts, which form the basis of laws that are "grounded purely in concepts." Yet they are *the only general concepts in the full sense of the word*, for the empirical concepts that rest on induction are not universal but are limited in their extension to the perceived instances and the contingent state of the research. (4) According to Husserl, the general concept is abstracted from that which a number of objects have in common. Abstraction is an act of attention in which we disregard the differences and focus exclusively on similarities. That which a number of things have in common is the *fundamentum-in-re* of the general concept. Like his teacher Brentano, Husserl rejects any Platonizing conception of the universal as a separate reality beyond the things.

In Chapter 4 of Part I, I tried to point out the inherent difficulties of this standpoint. It is apparent from later publications that Husserl was intensely concerned with these problems. In a "Selbstanzeige" of 1897, he indicates that there was a fundamental change in his position, and that in principle he had already discovered the intuition of essences.[1] Husserl writes: "Since the appearance of this work [i.e. the article "Psychologische Studien zur elementaren Logik" of 1897], I have become aware of the essential distinction between abstract contents (as intuited parts) and abstract *concepts* – a distinction which, unfortunately, has not be regarded as essential." Thus Husserl now distinguishes between the abstractum as perceived and as concept. Under concept, then, we must understand not the meaning of a word but the eidos;[2] it is the general object, the essence. The central problem of the theory of abstraction embraced by Brentano and the early Husserl is thereby solved, i.e. the problem how a universally valid concept can find its origin in the perception of individual things.

A problem closely bound up with this, namely, how we can establish a priori laws on the basis of these concepts, is raised and solved in a principially new way in an earlier footnote. There Husserl mentions a

---

[1] 'Bericht über deutsche Schriften zur Logik aus dem Jahre 1894,' 225 note 1; Compare II, 201. In the foreword to the second edition, Husserl says that the Prolegomena goes back to lectures of the year 1896, I (ed. 2) XII.

[2] See below 241.

priori laws that hold for the relations between independent and non-independent contents. In the article dealt with in the "Selbstanzeige" (i.e. PSL, of 1894), Husserl had written that we possess evident certainty about necessary truths. But it was not made clear how these necessary truths are justified. We make assertoric judgments about facts. Assertoric evidence is based on perception. But what is the basis for apodictic evidence? The basis is a concept, Husserl was to answer. But then the problem shifts to the question of the origin of this concept. How do we find an intuitive foundation for such a concept if reality consists only of individual things? In the footnote in question, Husserl remarks that such a truth does not depend on a contingent evident "experience." This evidence must be anchored objectively. "Objectively valid is the law that a content of the kind in question can exist only as part of a whole, that is, as connected with other contents." It is not the evident "experience" that makes such a content non-independent. Husserl thus criticizes the definition which he himself had given: "A content is non-independent if we have evidence that it is thinkable only as part of a more encompassing whole, whereas this evidence is lacking in the case of independent contents." Indeed, this does not in any way tell us what the basis of this evidence is. The definition must therefore undergo an "objective turn." Thus the new definition starts out: "Objectively valid is the law . . . ." The new theory of abstraction, which was only set out in passing in this "Selbstanzeige," was worked out further in LU.

PARAGRAPH TWO. GENERAL PRESENTATION: MEANING AND INTUITING

In the article of 1894, Husserl regarded the general concept as the meaning of a general name. He introduced an entirely new element when, in LU, he recognized a descriptively given difference between acts in which something general is presented and acts in which something individual is intended. In the first chapter, I dealt with this distinction between "modes of consciousness" as a subdivision of descriptive psychology. There is a descriptively demonstrable difference between significative acts in which the individual is intended and acts in which something general, the "specific," is intended. If we focus our attention simply on this given and take it as it is without explaining it away, then we see that the difference between general and individual significative acts is just as evident as the difference between a color and a sound.[1]

There is also such a difference, however, in the case of perception. In addition to the perception of something individual, there is also the perception of something general, of the essence. As we shall see, this given of descriptive psychology becomes the cornerstone of Husserl's new theory of abstraction.

In connection with the above, Husserl also changes his views on nominalism. Up to this point, he had regarded nominalism as an attempt to reduce the concept to a mere linguistic sign. The universality of the sign is then explained on the basis of the associative connections between the sign and the objects intended. Conceptualism, by contrast, sees the sensorily perceived sign only as the basis of the concept. Husserl now regards this conceptualism, too, as a nominalism and calls it a conceptualistic nominalism. What is characteristic of nominalism is not that it explains the universality of a concept on the basis of the associative power of the name as sound but that if fails to recognize that the consciousness of universality has a character of its own. Therefore nominalism includes conceptualism, insofar as the latter does not distinguish between individual and general acts of meaning. Thus, alongside extreme nominalism there is a conceptualistic nominalism.[2]

PARAGRAPH THREE. COMPARISON: IDENTITY AND SIMILARITY

The general concept, like any other concept, has its origin in intuition. Husserl had pointed to that which a number of things have in common as the basis for abstraction. In LU, however, he calls this an attempt to reduce the "ideal unity" to the "dispersed manifold." It is a conception that "splinters the unity of the species in the manifold of objects falling under it."[1] Husserl means by this that most philosophers object to an "ideal object" as the object of a general intuition and believe that they can get by in their theory of abstraction with the individual things that make up the extension of the concept. He raises the following arguments against this approach.

(1) It is maintained that the universal corresponding to the universal meaning can be found by comparing objects that fall under the concept. But such comparison is only possible, Husserl argues, if one first

---

[1] See above 154ff; Entwurf 335.

[2] II 122, 137, 143, 144, 151.

[1] II 100, 113, 116. Compare PA, 108, where Husserl expounds his early standpoint with regard to similarity and identity.

accepts an ideal object. Thus this procedure presupposes something that was to have been avoided. We might, for example, compare a number of objects that have one thing in common, i.e. being red. We then speak of *the same* color. This similarity of color does not mean *identity*, for the color of each individual thing is different. Yet, establishing similarities presupposes a certain identity, i.e. of the *respect* in which the similar things are similar. We can only compare the members of the extension of a concept if we first recognize – as an ideal object – the respect in which they are being compared. In all red things, one ideal object (i.e. "redness") is realized; it is through this redness that they are similar to one another. Husserl writes: "'Alikeness' is the relation of objects falling under one and the same species. If one is not allowed to speak of the identity of the species, of the respect in which there is 'alikeness,' talk of 'alikeness' loses its whole basis."[2]

(2) If the intention directed toward the general object is to be explained by the presentation of individual objects included in the extension of the concept in question, it must be remembered that the extension is infinite, and that therefore only a small part of it can be taken into consideration. Even if it were possible to compare all the members of the extension with one another, it would be of no avail. It is the ideal object that first creates the unity of the extension and thereby the ideal possibility of comparing all the objects it includes.[3]

(3) But the most important argument is that this theory overlooks what is clearly the sense of the general intention. When we describe acts that intend something general just as these acts are given, we see that their direct intention is focused on the general object, and that their relation to the members of the extension is indirect. There is a clear difference between the meaning "redness" and the meaning "all red things." In the former case, we grasp an attribute as the respect in which things are similar. This is an ideal unity. In the latter case, we intend a number of objects that are alike in a certain respect. If there were only these individual objects, a general name would have no general meaning at all. Thus Husserl returns here to the argument of the different "modes of consciousness," which has already been mentioned.

---

[2] II 109, 112, 113, 211ff.; Compare Id I 27 on the extension as "ideal total aggregate."
[3] II 110, 113, 114, 115, 117. It is noteworthy that Husserl refers to PA without mentioning his critique of his earlier standpoint (114).

PARAGRAPH FOUR. ATTENTION AND THE INTUITION OF
ESSENCES

In a general intuitive act, something general is not only meant but is itself given. In these acts we see what is actually meant in significative acts, what their genuine meaning is. Here a "clarification of a general name" takes place, through a "recourse to fulfilling intuitions," by "plainly establishing their intention in the sense of their fulfillment."[1] I have already discussed the phenomenological analysis of acts in Chapter 1 of Part II. At this point I will limit myself to two examples.

When we intuit "redness' (also called "redness in the species"), we do so in a founded act that is based on the sensory perception of an individual red thing, e.g. a piece of red paper. But this does not mean that we also intend the individual objects that appear. No, for although these objects appear, "we are rather 'meaning' the single identical 'redness' (das Rot), and are meaning it in a novel mode of consciousness, through which precisely the species and not the individual becomes our object."[2]

The second example is borrowed from geometry. Here, too, we have to do with a founding sensory perception and a founded ideal intuiting (Schau). If we construct a proof about a triangle, we are directed toward the triangle in general, and not toward the triangle which we have drawn on paper. It would be a great mistake to think that the proof is about the triangle on paper, for the figure on paper is only a means to make possible something general which we intuit.[3]

On the basis of this new conception, Husserl criticizes the thinkers who see abstraction as an achievement of attention. He speaks of this as an influential theory that was first defended by John Stuart Mill. We have seen that Husserl himself was not able to escape the influence of this theory. Thus the criticism of Mill is at the same time a form of self-criticism, although Husserl did not admit this in the passage in question. Given Husserl's earlier claims about abstraction, we see that a statement of Goethe's which he had cited in the foreword is also applicable here: "We oppose nothing as strongly as the errors which we ourselves have overcome."

[1] II 120, 145, 153, 216.
[2] I 101, 128, 129; II 106, 107, 100.
[3] II 157, 158, 180.

According to this theory, there are in reality no general ideas in the sense of Plato (or Locke). In every concrete case, what we see is a property which, as an aspect of a thing, as a part-phenomenon, shares in the individuality of that concrete thing. How, then, do we find the universal? This question is answered: by an act of concentration of attention, which has a positive effect and a negative effect. Negatively we disregard the "individualizing connection," and positively we focus on the universal. "*Abstraction as exlusive concern eo ipso produces generalization.* The abstracted attribute is *de facto* an element in the appearance of the individual complex of attributes that we call the phenomenal object. But the 'same' attribute, i.e. one fully agreeing with it in content, can occur in countless such complexes. What distinguishes the repetitions of this same attribute from case to case is uniquely and solely their individualizing association. Abstraction, therefore, as exclusive concern, causes the distinctness or individuality of what is abstracted to vanish. It is the ignoring of all individual aspects, which is the reverse side of our concentrated concern, and it yields the attribute that is everywhere one and the same."[4] This is a terse summary of the theory of abstraction in question. It is attention directed toward a property of an individual thing that is able to de-individualize this property and thus make possible a fulfillment, an intuiting of the universal.

According to Husserl's criticism, this achievement cannot be credited to attention. Even the most intense concentration on a particular property cannot nullify its individual character. An attribute that is a constitutive element of an object is just as individual as the object itself. Paying exclusive attention to a part of something does not rob that part of its individuality. In short, we cannot change objects via attention. If there were only individual things,[5] and if abstraction demanded the concentration of attention, the intending of something general would be impossible. Because it cannot be denied that something general is meant again and again in our thought and speech, this theory collapses.

It seems to me that Husserl was influenced by Frege not only in his positive solution to this question but also in his rejection of the theory of attention. The agreement between Frege's criticism of Husserl's theory of abstraction and

---

[4] II 137, 151, 153, 158, 216.

[5] This presupposition is bound up with the concept of "idea." If every object is an immanent thing, an inner image, it is of course individual (see also II 143, 217).

Husserl's own critical remarks at this point is striking – despite all the differences in style! Frege's objection to Husserl's theory of the abstraction of the concept of unity was that this abstraction involves a real transformation. Husserl had said that in this abstraction, we must disregard the particularities of the content in order to arrive at the concept of "something." Frege calls this a "purification in the psychological washtub" in which attention functions as a kind of detergent to wash away all differences between the objects. The lye used on the things in this washtub must not be too diluted, on the one hand, for then it would not change the things sufficiently, but on the other hand, it must not be too concentrated, for then it might dissolve the objects entirely. In this manner, the objects would really be changed. Frege here sees a confirmation of his view to the effect that Husserl believes that we ourselves bring forth the objects.[6] The psychologism that reduces the world to presentations (which Frege also calls "idealism")[7] First throws the things into the washtub to soak. Lye, in the form of attention, does the rest.

I have already established that Frege repeatedly misses the mark in his criticism of Husserl. This is also the case in connection with Husserl's supposed "idealism." Husserl does not reduce the world to presentations. Frege actually makes two mistakes, for the external world is not reduced to an immanent content, and the latter *a fortiori* is not reduced to a presentation in the sense of an act. Yet Husserl must have felt that Frege's criticism of the function of attention hit home. This criticism concludes with the words: "Attention is a highly effective logical power; this probably accounts for the absentmindedness of scholars."

PARAGRAPH FIVE. "GROUNDED PURELY IN CONCEPTS" –
EVIDENCE

What is forgotten by the theory of attention (i.e. the theory of abstraction after Locke) is that the determinative factor is not the concentration of attention but rather the *mode* thereof. There is a demonstrable difference between concentration on something individual and concentration on something general. Only in the latter case do we have abstraction in the sense of concept formation; this is an act in which "we are evidently aware of a species."[1] It is already apparent from this quoted phrase that Husserl here uses the term 'concept' in the sense of "general object." Here, then, it is not a meaning (the meaning of a word) but an ontic essence, that in which a general meaning finds its fulfillment. We must give this our attention, for

---

[6] 'Dr. E.G. Husserl: Philosophie der Arithmetik' 324, 326, 329, 216, 318. See above 32 note [1].

[7] *Grundgesetze der Arithmetik* XIX.

[1] II 164, 216.

through this explication of the term 'concept', the expression 'grounded purely in concepts' becomes understandable in the new meaning which it now has for Husserl. He uses the following terms to distinguish an individual thing (e.g. a red thing) from redness as a general object: over against the individual moment, the singular moment or the single case,[2] he speaks of the attribute in the species, or simply the attribute.[3] The attribute is also called the content of the concept, or simply the concept. The individual object is then the denotatum (*Begriffsgegenstand*). Concept is thus opposed to denotatum as eidos to fact![4]

Thereby the expression 'grounded purely in concepts,' which Husserl takes over from Brentano, assumes an entirely new meaning.[5] Brentano used this expression to refer to a priori truths, which are analyzed out of concepts. But he left unsolved the problem how we can abstract these concepts. Thus their validity remained open to question. From this point on, when Husserl uses the expression 'grounded purely in concepts,' he means "founded in essences." Thus an analysis on the basis of concepts is an analysis not of the concept as meaning but of the object of the meaning; it is an analysis of the reality itself, i.e. the ideal reality. Thereby the objectivity of the concept is objectively anchored. A justification of this concept in an intuition – an intuition of an essence, at that – is indeed possible.[6]

For Brentano, all a priori truths are analytic. Husserl goes along with this, but he regards them as *ontological*-analytic. Such truths represent the analysis of a concept in the sense of the analysis of an essence. For Brentano, a priori judgments are logical-analytic judgments. But he left unanswered the question how these judgments could imply cognitive claims. The logical concept was not justified on the basis of an ontological origin. For Husserl, the logical concept (the meaning) finds its origin in the ontological concept (the species). 'Purely on the basis of concepts' means purely on the basis of ideal objects.

When Husserl speaks in Ideen I of "obscurities on the idealist side," this also applies to Brentano, even though he is not mentioned. As in LU, Husserl here means by 'idealism' any philosophy that recognizes a priori judgments. Thus, although these philosophies are on Husserl's

---

[2] II 114, 130, 128.
[3] II 157.
[4] II 134, 136, see also 221, 151.
[5] I 99 et passim.
[6] II (ed. 1) 72 (compare ed. 2, 72, where the text is somewhat clearer).

side, they are not clear in their defense of this position. "Indeed, they accept pure thought, an 'a priori' thought, and thereby reject the empiricist thesis; but they do not reflectively bring to clear consciousness the fact that there is such a thing as pure intuition, a mode of givenness in which essences are given in an original manner as objects, just as individual realities are given in experiential intuition. They do not recognize that *every insight involving judgment*, and in particular the insight into unconditional *universal* truths, also *falls under the concept of presentative intuition.* . . ." Here Husserl also criticizes the theory of evidence held by these idealists. "It is true that they speak of evidence, but instead of pointing out the *essential relations* between insight and ordinary seeing, they speak of a 'feeling of evidence' which, like a mystical index of truth, lends the judgment an affective coloration."[7] I am convinced that it is very enlightening to read this passage as a criticism of Brentano and thus as an implicit self-criticism. What Husserl here describes is exactly the shortcoming of Brentano's theory with regard to the a priori sciences. Brentano does speak of the analysis of concepts, but he is not able to make it clear how these concepts are verified in intuition. Thus he is not faithful to the intuitionist principle that every concept must be justified by experience. The doctrine of "ideation" or the intuition of essences makes it possible for Husserl *both to maintain a priori judgments and to remain faithful to intuitionism.*

Brentano remained a positivist as far as his theory of reality is concerned. Positivism recognizes only the experience of individual facts. Husserl calls this blindness toward ideas a pre-supposition. Because positivism claims to reject all presuppositions, it becomes unfaithful to itself. Anyone who does not close his eyes to the seeing of essences and does not argue such seeing away must recognize ultimately that essences are given as well as facts. It testifies to prejudice to regard all experience as the experience of something individual. The seeing of essences, like the experiencing of facts, must be recognized as a source for the justification of judgments.[8] "The intuition of essences includes no more difficulties or 'mystical' secrets than perception,"[9] Husserl writes in PSW. Positivism is driven by honorable motives. Against all the forces of tradition and superstition, it recognizes only

---

[7] Id I 39, see also LU II 108. See also Husserl's critique of the old rationalism in Id III 56, 70: Entwurf 320; Krisis 14, 337 (E 16, 290).

[8] Id I 35, 36.

[9] PSW 315.

autonomous reason as authoritative. But in recognizing only one form of this reason, i.e. the experiencing of facts, it is itself traditional. By the "Sachen selbst" (things themselves), it understands only "Tatsachen" (facts). It regards "essences" and "ideas" as Scholastic entities, as metaphysical specters from which the new natural science has freed mankind.[10] Husserl calls this positivism a superstition of facts.[11] "To the things" (*zu den Sachen*) must mean the recognition of *all* givenness, including that of essences. To this extent, Husserl can call himself the true positivist. "If by 'positivism' is meant the absolute, unprejudiced grounding of all the sciences on the 'positive,' i.e. on that which is grasped in an original manner, then it is *we* who are the genuine positivists."[12]

Now we also understand why Husserl objected so sharply to the reproach that he practiced a Scholastic analysis of concepts. Here one might conceivably seek a point of contact in the expression 'grounded purely in concepts.' But what is overlooked is that for Husserl, this expression does not mean a hollow analysis of concepts in the sense of Scholastic ontologism, in which it is believed that truths about facts can be derived from an analysis of the meanings of words. For Husserl, the meanings of words only form the point of departure for the investigation: the intention of the investigation is to check these meanings against intuition. It is an analysis of the phenomena that answer to these concepts, in order to give these concepts a well-defined meaning.[13] In Entwurf, Husserl includes a special paragraph on "dismissal of slogans: phenomenology as the analysis of the meanings of words."[14] When we consider this charge in the light of Husserl's development, we must conclude that it can be applied with a certain amount of justification to writings *before* LU. The a priori analysis was not yet equipped with an adequate self-justification. But when it is applied to LU, this charge represents a serious misunderstanding of Husserl's position. The analysis of essences is an analysis of that which is given in experience in an original manner.

[10] Id I 35, 36.
[11] PSW 336.
[12] Id I 38; PSW 340.
[13] PSW 304, 305; see also Id I 301.
[14] Entwurf 328, see also 112, 115, 333, 334.

It would be instructive to compare Husserl's doctrine of a priori judgments with that of Kant, for Husserl himself saw the problematics connected with a priori knowledge as the actual point of agreement between Kantianism and phenomenology.[15] Thus the comparison with Kant must concentrate on this point. Husserl reproaches Kant for not making a clear distinction between the concept as meaning and the concept as essence.[16] Kant's problem was the cognitive import of synthetic a priori judgments. From the standpoint of experience, they represent an "arbitrary elevation of validity."[17] Husserl appeals to the perception of essences in order to justify such judgments. In a certain sense, Kant's synthetic a priori judgments could be called synthetic a posteriori for Husserl, insofar as the intuition of essences is also a form of experience.[18] In this way Husserl "saves" these judgments, which his teacher Brentano, in sharp criticism of Kant, had characterized as arbitrary presuppositions.[19]

This matter can also be explained as follows. For Husserl, all a priori judgments are analytic, in the sense of ontological-analytic (eidetic-analytic). But in relation to the subjective concept, these judgments are synthetic, for they enlarge our knowledge. They are synthetic in the logical sense, to use Pfänder's phrase.[20] (Within this class of eidetic-analytic judgments, Husserl then distinguishes between analytic and synthetic judgments, according to whether the judgment in question has to do with the content or with the form of the essence.[21]) It is clear from the preceding that Husserl does not follow Kant's path when he justifies synthetic a priori judgments, the judgments that form the point of departure for Kant's transcendental turn. Kant's narrow concept of experience forced him to seek the solution in "transcendental deduction," but Husserl can here appeal to the intuition of essences. Later we will see that the problem of transcendental constitution in Husserl finds its origin in an entirely different problematics – and not in that of a priori judgments. The problem of synthetic a priori judgments is only a mundane problem for Husserl, a problem that can precede the problem of transcendental constitution both historically

---

[15] E. Fink, 'Die Phänomenologische Philosophie Edmund Husserls in der gegenwärtigen Kritik' 379, see below 327/8.

[16] II (ed. 1) 675 (see also III ed. 2, 203).

[17] Kritik der reinen Vernunft, Einleitung II and IV.

[18] This eidetic experience is also valid for ordinary sensory experience. The eidetic laws developed in formal and material ontology can be applied to individual reality. On this "application," see below 258.

[19] Vier Phasen 20; VE 27: Vom Dasein Gottes 82.

[20] 'Logik,' 339; see also 273, 274. Stumpf, too, defends the thesis that for Husserl, a priori propositions are actually analytic, "for when he characterizes insight into regional axioms as an intuition of essences, this means that it arises from an immersion in the essence of the judgment-material in question, which in a broader and likewise more pregnant sense must be called an analytic insight." Erkenntnislehre I 201. Like Pfänder, Stumpf wants to argue that judgments which are synthetic from a logical standpoint are analytic from an ontological standpoint.

[21] See below 251.

(LU is earlier than Ideen I) and systematically (in the structure and composition of Ideen I). This means that from the standpoint of Husserl's
transcendental idealism, Kant had remained stuck in a pre-transcendental (i.e.
dogmatic) position. He did not see through the "natural attitude," and
therefore he accepted the natural world as his basis (*Weltboden*). It is within this
world that the problem of synthetic a priori judgments, which Kant tried to
solve in his *Critique of Pure Reason*, arises. Since Husserl was concerned with
the same problem in LU and had not yet transcended the problematics of
mundane a priority by way of his transcendental idealism, one could defend the
thesis that Husserl was never closer to Kant than in LU.[22]

We have apodictic evidence about necessary truths. What is the basis
of this evidence? In PSL (one of his earliest works), Husserl was
satisfied with the observation that it is impossible to think the opposite
of such a truth: for example, we cannot think a non-independent
content as an independent content. The criterion is that the opposite is
"unthinkable." In a remark in a notice about this article, Husserl
already appears to have realized what is unsatisfactory about this
standpoint. Such evidence must be objectively anchored.[23] When we
say that it is impossible to think something, we are giving expression to
a subjective aspect of an objective state of affairs. It is an distinction
rooted in the pure essence of the matter that forces us to declare that a
judgment denying this must be false. The inability-to-think-otherwise is
not a "subjective necessity, that is, a *subjective incapacity*-to-represent-
things-otherwise but an *objective necessity* reflecting an inability-to-be-
otherwise."[24] In a note to the second edition of LU, Husserl adds that
the "decisive ontological transformation of the notion of evidence into
one of pure eidetic lawfulness" expressed in this passage was already
carried through in a penetrating way in the article of 1897 mentioned
above.

In the third logical investigation, which deals with independent and
non-independent objects, the earlier doctrine is again taken up and
worked out in this new spirit. Every a priori law is now called a pure
eidetic law. Insight into such an eidetic law (i.e. a law analyzing an
essence) is evidence in the pregnant sense, or apodictic evidence.[25] It is

[22] From the transcendental phenomenological standpoint, the problem of the a priori
is a pre-philosophical problem of the natural attitude. Fink a.a., 379ff. See also below 277
and 488.

[23] See above 236.

[24] II (ed. I) 235 (ed. 2, 239).

[25] I 91.

the "final authority in all questions of knowledge."[26] In this evidence, we have an "experience" of the "idea."[27] Therefore it must be distinguished from assertoric evidence, in which we recognize a fact as existing (in inner perception). We could well say that an eidetic truth cannot be "thought" otherwise, but this expression is then an application of an objective eidetic law to subjective judgments.[28]

Whenever we have apodictic certainty about an eidetic law, this essence is given to us in a manner just as original as the adequate perception of individual experiences. Consequently we can speak here, too, of "insight" or simply "seeing," of "ideal fullness," and so on, just as in the case of perception. The analogy that connects all "originary presentative experiences" justifies such language.[29]

PARAGRAPH SIX. THE EIDETIC REDUCTION

Apodictic judgments are indeed based on experience, but not on individual experience. Yet, ideation is accompanied by an individual perception. The intuiting of redness, for example, is founded in the perception of an individual red thing. But this does not mean that knowledge about the general essence arises from this experience. "All knowledge 'begins with experience,' but it does not therefore 'arise' from experience," declares Husserl, quoting Kant.[1] If the eidetic judgment is not based on facts, neither does it imply the existence of facts. It makes a claim not about actual reality but only about possibility. We cannot derive an existential judgment from an eidetic judgment. Brentano had already realized this; he maintained that every apodictic judgment is equivalent to a negative existential judgment. 'The sum of the angles of a triangle = 180 degrees' means that there is no triangle of which this is not true. What we can deduce from this judgment is not that there is at least one triangle but only that if there is one, then it has these properties.

It is noteworthy – and likewise illustrative of the growing misunderstanding between Brentano and his student Husserl – that Brentano

---

[26] II 100.

[27] I 101, 128, 190.

[28] I 183, 185.

[29] I (ed. 1) 190 (compare the somewhat different text of the second edition); III 123, 144.

[1] I 75.

(and particularly his student Kraus) reproaches Husserl for deriving an existential judgment from an apodictic judgment. Husserl, of course, speaks of essences as ontic entities, and even of a supra-temporal realm of ideas. According to Brentano and Kraus, he conceives of the apodictic judgment as an affirmative existential judgment and thereby introduce fictive entities.[2] Certain passages could have given rise to this interpretation of Husserl. The latter does say that ideal objects exist: "Ideal objects truly exist." This interpretation is also furthered by Husserl's claim that we can make true judgments which have such entities as their subjects. If I see that 2 is an even number and that this predicate actually pertains to it, "then this object cannot be a mere fiction, a mere *façon de parler*, a mere nothing in reality."[3] The ideal object 2 is then "before my logical regard."[4] Is this not a confirmation of Brentano's reproach that Husserl introduces absurd realities like essences?

Yet Husserl is in fact fully agreed with Brentano that an apodictic judgment is equivalent to a negative existential judgment. The apparent contradiction is resolved when we bear in mind the different meanings that the concept of being has for Husserl. Within the "unified conception of being" there is a fundamental categorial difference between being as species and being as individual. When we make a judgment about an essence, we posit an ideal existence. No "interpretive skill in the world" can eliminate this "ideal object."[5] Brentano's attempt to reduce these judgments to negative existential judgments is one of these interpretive skills. It may be true that they are equivalent to negative existential judgments, but this does not mean that they are identical with them. On the contrary, their direct meaning is that they intend a general object. Brentano's theory is governed by the dogmatic presupposition that only "real being" can exist. Therefore he must also conceive of essences and ideas as realities and must interpret Husserl's doctrine in the sense of a metaphysical Platonic realism. But Husserl, too, holds that it is absurd to regard essences as realities in space and time.[6] Yet, he argues that we must not deny their

[2] WE 157; see also Spiegelberg, *The Phenomenological Movement* 96 note 1; for Marty's critique, see Entwurf 120.

[3] II 125, 111.

[4] II 140.

[5] II 125/6.

[6] See below 264.

"objectivity"[7] (*Gegenständlichkeit*) together with their reality. We can make judgments about these essences. When such judgments are formulated in the form "There is" or "There exists," then what is meant is not a "real" existence but a "mathematical existence."[8] Examples of such judgments are: 'There are algebraic numbers' and 'there are regular solids.' 'There is' (*Es gibt*) here means 'It is true that' (*Es gilt*). But this is not to say that such numbers or solids exist in reality. But if we say, "There are cakes," we mean that cakes exist, here and now – to eat as we drink our coffee![9]

Although this paragraph is called "The Eidetic Reduction," this term does not occur in LU.[10] Yet, what it names is fully present. The intuition of essences – or better, "ideation," for Husserl uses the latter term in LU – is a disregarding of the individual fact (to this extent an abstraction) and an insight into the essence. It hardly needs to be argued – although it is not superfluous to mention it, unfortunately – that this disregarding of individual existence has nothing to do with the phenomenological reduction, which disregards the actual object. In the former case we abstract from the individual fact, and the general essence is the reductum. In the latter case we disregard the real object, and the intentional object is the "residue."[11]

---

[7] II 110; III 104.

[8] I 71, 74; II 87, 94, 101; III 103, 105, 106. Against the misconception that he attributed actual existence to ideas, Husserl defended himself two years later; see his Literaturbericht Palàgyi, 287–294.

[9] II 135f, 87, 94; compare further Id III 47 en 82.

[10] This term is first used in Id I 4.

[11] The failure to distinguish sharply between essence and sense is one of the greatest causes of confusion in Husserl interpretation. Even those who realize that the eidetic and phenomenological reductions are two different operations often describe them in a manner that does not exclude confusion. Thus Quentin Lauer, for example, identifies the result of the two reductions by describing essence as sense in 'La philosophie comme science rigoureuse,' 14, note 4, 15, 46, 48 and the notes 90, 120, 233; see below 268 note 41. Husserl himself warns expressly against the confusion of essence and sense in Id III, 85. The two operations can only be brought into relation with one another if we proceed from the vague expression 'putting being between brackets.' But something entirely different is meant by this phrase in the case of the one reduction than in the case of the other. In the phenomenological reduction, we disregard the existence of the perceived object on the basis of epistemological considerations. This limitation is bound up with the psychological point of departure (which Husserl only overcame in the transcendental reduction). The eidetic reduction is concerned with the founding of a priori judgments. Here we speak of a disregarding of "being in the sense of individual existence. But this by no means takes place in an attitude of resignation, as in the phenomenological reduction. Therefore, although such terms as 'epoché' and 'neutrality' are sometimes used in connection with the eidetic reduction, this practice is not to be recommended. Max Scheler, who saw the

It must be maintained that both of these reductions are present in LU in fact, but not in terminology. As is the case more often with Husserl, his methodological reflection lags behind what he actually does. In the preceding paragraphs, I have dealt with Husserl's theory of abstraction in confrontation with his earlier standpoint. I will now continue my analysis by way of a more positive explication.

PARAGRAPH SEVEN. TWO KINDS OF ABSTRACTION

Corresponding to the basic schema of Husserl's philosophy, i.e. the relation between act and object, we can also distinguish two kinds of abstraction, an abstraction directed toward acts and another directed toward their objects. In the former case we intuit "meanings," and in the latter case "species." The realm of ideas is thus bipartite. It includes ideas about acts (meanings) as well as ideas about objects, e.g. redness, the pitch c, numbers, and geometric shapes.[1] The relation between meaning and species is thus analogous to that between act and object.

Meanings are abstracted in a reflective ideation. Whereas in a normal act of reflection, attention is directed toward an individual act that arises and passes away in time, in reflective ideation this individual experience is only the "substratum" for the intuiting of the idea. Husserl continually compares the relation between meaning and act to that between redness and the individual red thing.[2] Just as the individual thing is the basis for abstraction in the latter case, in reflection the individual act is the basis.[3]

Let us take as example an act that has the number four as its object. Two kinds of ideation are then possible. When we have a group of four things before us, we can focus our mental regard on the ideal object four. But in reflective ideation (or ideational reflection) we can also intuit the idea of the act-of-forming-the-presentation-four. The result

intuition of essences as a suspension of the life impulse (*Entwirklichung*), is probably partly responsible for this confusion; see *Die Stellung des Menschen im Kosmos*, 55, 90. The term 'reduction' is certainly in order here, and it was indeed used by Husserl.

[1] II 101, 102, 184. When the act is significative, the corresponding idea is simply called the "meaning," but if it is a perceptual act, the essence is called the "fulfilling meaning" or the "intuition in specie" III 97. The latter is thus the idea of the "fulfilling sense" II 50. See above 144.

[2] II 100, 106; see also I 101, 128, 129. We will see in Chapter 5 that this comparison is particularly important for the relation between pure logic and descriptive psychology.

[3] I 71, 74, 101, 186, 229; II 39, 43, 103, 104, 106, 94, 100, 150, 183.

of the abstraction is then the meaning: "four." An identical meaning is realized in all acts that mean four. Thus there are two kinds of general objects in this example: the species four and the meaning: "four."[4]

ideal identical meaning "four"	species four
act of intending four things	group of four things

In this example we proceeded from an act that intends a general object. Of course there are also acts that intend something individual. These acts also have an ideal correlate. This means that an ideal meaning (as the eidos of the act in question) could be either general (in the sense of specific) or individual, depending on the object to which it is related.[5]

PARAGRAPH EIGHT. TWO KINDS OF CATEGORIAL ABSTRACTION
– TWO KINDS OF LOGIC

Not only regular perceptions but also categorial perceptions can be the "substratum" of ideation. Thus we distinguish between "sensory" and categorial abstraction. If a sensory perception is the foundation for an ideating act, then such concepts as "color" and triangle arise via external abstraction, and concepts like "judgment" and "wish" by reflective abstraction (in the inner sense). From categorial abstraction arise such concepts as unity, plurality, collective, identity, etc., or such reflective concepts as conjunctive and disjunctive connection, subject and predicate forms, etc.[1]

Categorial perception itself is already a founded act. Thus categorial abstraction is doubly founded. As we noticed in Paragraph 6 of Chapter 1, Husserl also speaks of the object of categorial perception as "ideal." Here 'ideal' has only the negative meaning of not "real." It is not a supra-temporal idea like the species. The ideal object of the categorial perception is itself individual. Only the category in species, as the eidos of the form, is universal. As we have seen, categorial perception, together with the recognition of the objective existence of "objects of a higher order," contributed to the doctrine of the intuition of essences, insofar as it negatively broke through the presupposition that all perception is sensory perception.[2]

[4] II 103, 140. Both can be called the "concept." See above 241.
[5] II 103, 106, 111, 112, 141, 136, 222.
[1] I 171, 243, 244; II 163; III 184.
[2] III 184, 141, 142, 144, 147, 162. See above 151.

The categorial forms are the subject matter of formal logic. Corresponding to the division into "objective" categories and "meaning" categories, thus, are two kinds of logic: a logic of the ontological forms, which Husserl was later to call formal ontology, and a logic of the forms of meaning, which he was later to call apophantic logic.[3]

This science of pure forms develops the implications of the forms of objects and meanings, while abstracting fully from their content. The results, according to Husserl, are purely analytic a priori judgments.[4] In this concept of form lies the unity of the pure logic of meanings and the pure logic of the species (i.e. formalized mathematics). Pure logic in the broad sense includes both. In this way Husserl was able to combine the formal analysis of the mathematicians, the non-Euclidean geometry (both of which had arisen in his time) and mathematical logic with apophantic logic to form one whole.[5]

PARAGRAPH NINE. EIDOS AND FACT

In this paragraph I will examine further the identity (I) and universality (II) of the eidos. In the process I will presuppose a division of the realm of ideas into objects (species) and meanings. Then I will turn to the application of eidetic knowledge (III) and the extent of the realm of ideas (IV).

I. The Identity of the Eidos

(*A*) The general *object* stands over against the individual things as the ideal unity over against the "dispersed manifold." Earlier I gave the example of the one species "red" over against the many red things. It is the species that makes possible a "comparative survey of a manifold of individual cases." The many red things are indeed "the same," but not in the strict sense of identity; otherwise they would have become one thing. Only the essence is identical.

---

[3] Husserl sometimes speaks of both simply as logic II 184. In Ideen I, he calls the doctrine of material essences, which is developed in non-categorial abstraction, regional ontology. In this context he sometimes also speaks of "logic," that is, a material logic, Entwurf 123, see also 333.

[4] II 251.

[5] I 200, 244, 248 cf. Entwurf, 121, 130, 320. See also above 66. See as well the Literaturbericht Palàgyi, 288. Husserl here argues that he does not wish to reduce apophantic logic to mathesis in the ordinary sense (formal ontology). Over against the logic of extension, he shows that the quantifying method need not be limited to objects. Here he appeals to his articles of 1891.

(*B*) The same holds, *mutatis mutandis*, for the *ideal meanings* in relation to the many acts of meaning. I will work this out more fully in connection with the real problem of LU, i.e. the possibility of a pure logic.

Presentations, judgments and acts of meaning are psychical experiences that arise and pass away in time. Over against these many acts stands the one ideal meaning that is realized in all of them. "My act of judging is a transient experience: it arises and passes away. But what my assertion asserts, the content *that the three perpendiculars of a triangle intersect in a point*, neither arises nor passes away. Whenever I, or anyone else, make this same assertion in the same sense, it is judged anew. The acts of judgment can be distinguished in each case, but *what* they judge, *what* the assertion asserts, is always the same. It is one and the same geometrical truth."[1] Archimedes and Newton both had their own individual concepts of circle, but the one ideal meaning was realized in these two instances. Herbart had already distinguished between the one identical concept and the many subjective concepts in which we make this concept our own. The ideal concept of circle belongs to no one in particular; it is a "supra-empirical unity," an "ideal unity of meaning."

The individual act is made public. The hearer finds out that someone has uttered a particular judgment. In this judgment the ideal meaning is "asserted."[2] This ideal identical meaning is also called the "content" or the "objective" meaning by Husserl.[3] Both expressions are potential sources of misunderstanding.

If the ideal meaning is called the "content" of the act of meaning, then the misconception that the ideal meaning is the object of the act could easily arise. Husserl himself says that Palàgyi, misled by the double meaning of the word 'content,' confused "meaning" with "state of affairs" (*Sachverhalt*).[4] The object of the act of meaning is the meant thing toward which the intention is directed. The ideal meaning is the idea of the act of meaning itself and can ally be grasped in *reflection*. In our example, it is the ideal meaning "four," not the meant ideal four itself. Husserl makes the correct relation between the content and the

---

[1] II 44; see also II 93, 95, 150, 217; I 100, 216; Literaturbericht Palàgyi 290.

[2] II 42, 43, 45, 46; On the individual act of meaning over against the identical meaning, that is, on the act of meaning *in concreto*, see II 417, 421, 433, 435, 492.

[3] II 94, 95, 146.

[4] Literaturbericht Palàgyi 291.

act completely clear when he compares it to that between the ideal redness and the individual moments of red. The individual act is a "singularization" of the ideal meaning; it is the meaning *in concreto*.[5] When Husserl speaks of content here, he does so in the same sense in which the matter of the act can be called content. The ideal content is the eidos of this real content, of the material determination of the act.[6]

The ideal meaning is called "objective" by Husserl – not because it stands over against the act as its object, but because it is not subjective in the psychical sense (as it is for Brentano and his student Marty, for example).[7]

There is yet another misunderstanding, related to that of Palàgyi, which I must point out here because it has had great influence on the interpretation of LU. The ideal meaning, on this view, is interpreted in the light of Husserl's position in FTL – an anachronistic interpretation which stands in the way of any attempt to get a proper insight into the relation between the Prologomena to Pure Logic and the six investigations. When Husserl in FTL posits "the" judgment over against judgments (plural), he means the judgment-noema, the objective correlate of the judgment that is constituted in the act of judging. In LU he uses the same way of speaking: "the" judgment is contrasted with the subjective judgments (plural). But in LU, Husserl means something different, namely, the eidos of the subjective act. As we have already seen, the concept of neomatic meaning is not present in LU. The act of meaning has no objective correlate, and the "content" is nothing other than the act itself – but then "ideally apprehended in *reflective* ideation.[8] It is not an intended content, as Husserl explicitly remarks.[9]

---

[5] The logical judgment is given *in concreto* in the psychological judgment I 66, 71, 101, 119, 132, 139, 142, 143, 150, 176 note 1, 216, 237; II 42, 43, 52, 96, 97.

[6] II 414, 434, 454. Both matter and the eidos of the matter are called "content" – Husserl himself uses the quotation marks II 436, 455. Sometimes Husserl offers an analogous line of reasoning with regard to the relations between matter and the object and between ideal meaning and object II 47, 421.

[7] I 134, 135; II 8, 9, 10, 52, 77, 95, 143, 146; compare 150 and 181 with regard to the categorie of meaning; see Referat Marty, 1108.

[8] From the analysis Husserl gives in paragraph 34 of the first investigation of how we become conscious of a meaning in reasoning and in returning to a certain line of thought, it is clear that *in fact* he must already have had the later concept of noema in mind. This is all the more remarkable because of his explicit declaration that we *reflect* when we bring a meaning before the mind.

[9] II 97 note 1; In FTL, Husserl realized that the one judgment over against the many acts in which it is judged need not be an "idea": he called it an ideal unity but not an idea 138, 147, 192. In a letter to Ingarden of April 5, 1918, he wrote: "The mistake lay above all

The same is true of the famous concept of "truth in itself." This truth is not an objective correlate of a true judgment. The truth is an idea of which an individual true judgment is a "singularization." Many true judgments as such can "realize" the one truth. "Truth is an idea whose individual instance is an actual experience in the evident judgment."[10] Note also the often quoted passage in the introduction to the second volume, where Husserl speaks of the question how "the 'in itself' of objectivity comes to presentation and thus in a certain sense may again become subjective." This passage, too, has to do with the relation between eidos and individual realization.[11]

What we face here is an anachronistic interpretation similar to the one already uncovered with regard to the acts of a higher order in PA.[12] There, too, a correlate was accepted on the authority of FTL, although in fact there was none. Therefore, just as in the case of the acts of a higher order in PA, we cannot speak of constitution in the sense of "production" (Leistung) in connection with significative acts. A constitutive analysis that clarifies objects on the basis of acts is only possible, of course, if there are objects that could then serve as "clues" for such an analysis. Thus the analysis of origins with regard to meanings is something entirely different in LU than in FTL. It is not an analysis of acts which aims to clarify the judgment that is constituted within them as noema; rather, it is a description of these acts undertaken because the idea is "realized" in them.[13]

II. The Universality of the Eidos

(A) The ideal object stands over against the many individual things not only as a unity over against plurality but also as the universal over against the individual. The ideal object is at the same time a "general object." But this universal is not an aspect of things. It stands apart from individual things belonging to spatio-temporal reality. The eidos is supra-temporal. It is not a universal in re but rather a universal supra

in conceiving of 'sense' and asserted proposition ⟨...⟩ as essence or 'idea' in the sense of essence (species). The independence of the sense of a proposition from the contingent judgement and those who judge it does not mean that the ideal-identical is something specific," ZPF 1959, 349, also published in Briefe an Roman Ingarden, 10. See above 171 and below 443 and 493.

[10] I 190. See further I 77, 117, 128, 187, 229, 231 note 1; II 50; III 123, 125. The correlate of this "truth in itself" is "being in itself," I 228; II 90, 125; III 5, 118, 122.

[11] II (ed. 1) 8, compare II 141 and I, VII.

[12] See above 26. Ryle also interprets ideal meanings as intentional objects (accusatives), 'The Theory of Meaning,' 260.

[13] See below 290.

rem.[14] This universal *supra rem* finds its concrete realization in the universal *in re*, for things are not purely individual but also have a universal aspect. This is the "common," the "similar," the "alike," or whatever else Husserl chooses to call it.[15] This common element in things is the individualized foundation for an act of ideation.

Husserl makes a terminological distinction between the two types of universality, i.e. the "general" (= the idea) and the "universal" (= the common element). On this basis we can understand what Husserl means by the unusual expression 'individual-universal'; it refers to the universal in reality, or the "universal generality" (*universelle Allgemeinheit*), which is distinguished from the "general generality" (*generelle Allgemeinheit*).[16] Universal judgments about reality are also possible, e.g. "All men are mortal." Husserl calls this a universal-individual judgment. A "general" Judgment is a judgment about a species.[17] The possibility of "applying" an eidetic a priori judgment to reality is rooted in this relation between the species and the universal *in re*.

(*B*) Analogous relations are valid, *mutatis mutandis*, for the relation between the *ideal meaning* and the act of meaning. Meanings – as opposed to acts of meaning – are general.

This generality is not to be confused with that of their object. Depending on whether meanings intend something general or something individual, we speak of general or individual meanings.[18] The latter are also general as far as the relation to the act is concerned. Take the name 'Hans' as an example. There is only one individual object to which it is applied. To that extent it is individual. But it is general with

---

[14] I avoid the term 'ante rem' because Husserl rejects any theological founding of universals. He does speak of a supra-temporal realm of ideas, I 130, but these ideas are not thoughts of God, as they are for Bolzano, II 101; I 127. By using the expression 'supra rem,' I am emphasizing Husserl's "Platonism," which separates the idea from reality. The essence is not immanent to the fact, as Merleau-Ponty maintains in *Phénoménologie de la Perception*, I and X. The essence is still above reality in Ideen I 10 – before the transcendental reduction, which relates the ideas to transcendental consciousness and thereby overcomes Platonism, is carried out, Id I 322, 323. See below 490.

[15] II 109, 118.

[16] II 111.

[17] An individual-universal judgment states a general fact, e.g. "All southerners are hot-blooded," or "All ravens are black" I 136, 178. These are contingent factual generalities. In Literaturbericht Palàgyi Husserl gives the example "All spheres are red," 293. See also I 171, 173, 174, 178, 186 on the difference between a merely universal class concept and a general (ideal) genus concept or eidetic concept.

[18] I 76, 77, 121; II 102, 103; see above 251.

regard to the many individual acts in which Hans is meant. An infinite multitude of acts realizing this same identical meaning is possible.[19] Even such a meaning as 'here' is one ideal unity over against the many acts that mean "here."[20]

Every act of meaning is a singularization in time of the one general meaning. The acts change from individual to individual, and in one individual from time to time. They have their endless individual "peculiarities" (both on the mental side, the "animation with sense," and on the physical side, the act of making a word "appear"). Yet the same meaning is realized in all the acts.[21] The meaning belongs to the eternal realm of the idea, which stands in exclusive opposition to the individual reality, the individual "experience" here and now. The concepts of reality and temporality have the same extension.[22]

But the act is not merely individual; it is an individualized universal. The common element in the acts corresponds to the ideal meaning.[23] Correlated with the strict identity of the ideal meaning, which first makes comparison possible, are the acts that are "the same." They have a certain "similarly determined" (*gleichbestimmt*) "tincture," whereby they differ materially from others. Similarity is not identity. Only the ideal meaning is identical. If the acts were identical, they would have grown together to form a unity.[24] The common aspect have grown together to form a unity.[24] The common aspect in the acts is the basis for ideation: "to meanings *in specie* correspond acts of meaning, the former being nothing but ideally apprehended aspects of the latter."[25] The act is "the real (reell) phenomenological correlate of the ideal

---

[19] III 26, 29, 31f. The same is true of ideal fulfilling meaning with regard to the many perceptions of the same individual object II 51; see also 158f; compare Id I 257, 259, 261.

[20] II 109ff. Husserl later gave up the view that contingent truths or truths about facts are also ideal entities. Only eidetic truths are ideal entities. In the letter to Ingarden mentioned above 254 note 9, he writes: "For some time now I have recognized that the position of the Prolegomena with regard to eidetic truths is mistaken and have made clear the grounds of the fundamental difference between eidetic truths and factual truths." But this does not mean that Husserl has given up the doctrine of "truths in themselves," as De Waelhens maintains, *Phénoménologie et vérité*, 7, 15. De Waelhens appeals to the foreword to the second edition of LU, XII, XIII. But what Husserl there admits giving up is not the doctrine of truths in themselves but only the one-sided orientation of this doctrine toward "truths of reason."

[21] I 100, 132, 150, 175; II 42, 43, 97, 98.

[22] I 99, 171, 216; II 44, 102, 123, 141; III 133, 144, 187.

[23] II 411, 420, 426, 427, 442, 453, 462, 465, 467, 487; III 18.

[24] II 155, 418.

[25] II 343, see also 312.

meaning" If matter and quality are alike (i.e. the "significational essence" or "intentional essence"[26]) then we can speak of a singularisation of the same ideal meaning. Conversely, this act can become the basis for an ideative reflection.

Thus the ideal meaning is the eidos of the matter, plus quality. Husserl says that he wondered for a long time if he should not equate meaning with the eidos of the matter alone. The objection against this was that the assertive aspect (*Setzung*) of the meaning was excluded.[27] But Husserl makes it clear repeatedly from his use of language that he sees the ideal meaning first and foremost as the essence of the matter, for both are called *sense*. The meaning is thus the ideal sense, and the matter the sense *in concreto*, the moment of the act.[28]

III. Application

Ideal eidetic truths can be applied to facts. Everything that is true with regard to an eidos is also true of the facts of which this eidos is the essence. That three books is more than two books is an application of an eidetic truth about the ideal entities "two" and "three."[29] To have insight into a fact on the basis of an eidetic law means to have insight into the ground of an actual event. In a factual science, this means that we have insight that something happens necessarily under certain circumstances.[30]

Here we touch on the difficult problem of the relation between eidetic laws and inductively discovered laws of nature. With regard to nature, a priori ontologies hold respectively of physical nature[31] (geometry, chronology and phoronomy) and for psychical nature[32] (rational psychology). What is the relation of empirical facts (e.g. Newton's law) to these a priori laws? One gets the impression that Husserl sees the empirical law, the "general fact," as a provisional approximation. The ideal law would then be the limit of all empirical laws.[33]

---

[26] II 417, 421, 433, 435, 492; III 2, 95. See above 144.
[27] III 85, 87, 35.
[28] Literaturbericht Palàgyi 298, 290.
[29] I 74, 172; see also II 215; III 198; Id I 20, 23. This is the basis of synthetic and analytic a priori judgments about facts, Id I 38.
[30] I 231, 323; II 255.
[31] I 149, 156 note 2, 251, 232.
[32] See above 206.
[33] On Newton's law, see I 63, 72, 127/8, 149, 150, 179, 145, 234, 255; see above 52f.

Ideal laws about "meanings" can also be applied. An individual truth is a "single instance" of a "truth in itself."[34] An ideal truth can be converted into an equivalent statement about the possibility of evident judgments.[35] This is of particular importance in connection with Husserl's topic (i.e. pure logic), for the laws about the ideal forms of meanings regulate the formal truth of thought. The possibility of a theory in general rests on these laws. Here the Kantian question about the possibility of science – as far as formal "reason" is concerned – is answered.[36]

IV. The Extent of the Realm of Ideas

One of the most important questions that can be asked with regard to essence is that of the extent of the realm of ideas. This question is left open in LU. Plato's followers already argued about the question whether there is an idea of a hair, of a bed, and so on. When we compare Husserl with those who have followed him in his so-called ontological realist phenomenology,[37] we are struck by how parsimonious he is in LU with regard to essences. In fact, we always find the same examples borrowed from the mathematical sphere, i.e. numbers, geometrical figures. He also uses colors and sounds (probably under the influence of Lotze and Stumpf), and sometimes (under the influence of Frege and Bolzano) he uses essences about the many forms of signifying consciousness, i.e. ideal meanings (in which those about categorial acts play a central role).

It is important to note that according to Husserl, not all general concepts are eidetic concepts. In EU he distinguishes explicitly between empirical general concepts (such as "dog") and pure general concepts.[38] This distinction is also present in LU, as the difference between class concepts and genus concepts.[39] We have seen that only the latter are truly general.[40] With regard to Husserl's theory of essences, a fundamental mistake is often made, namely, that of identifying

[34] I 91, 99ff, 107, 129, 167f, 187 compare the definition of the concept of truth in II 122ff.

[35] I 89, 183, 185ff, 239; II 293 (ed. 2).

[36] I 236ff; II 471; III 187–199; see also below 277.

[37] See below 260ff.

[38] EU 398, 409; see also PP 72, where the difference between empirical generalization and ideation is already worked out.

[39] See above 256 note 17.

[40] See above 235.

essences with general concepts or universals in the sense of traditional conceptual realism. Actually, Husserl's essences can better be compared with the transcendentalia of Scholasticism or the categories of Kant. Later, Husserl himself made it clear that the issue with regard to essences is the basic structure of a certain area or region. He then called these concepts material categories.[41] The misunderstanding to the effect that all general concepts are eidetic concepts was furthered in part by the fact that Husserl developed his doctrine of the intuition of essence in LU within a polemic against the empiricist theory of abstraction, which does indeed apply to all concepts. An experience of essences is completely impossible according to this theory, and therefore Husserl first had to defend himself on this score. Only later did a positive explication under the heading of "eidetic variation" follow.

PARAGRAPH TEN. HUSSERL'S "PLATONISM" OR "REALISM"

I am now in a position to fill in a gap in my argument of Section 2 of Chapter 1, where I discussed the transcendence of the object without exhausting the topic. I dealt exclusively with the transcendent object of sensory perception, the "real" object. But this is not the only transcendency, as we have seen since. Husserl also speaks of an "ideal" object which is transcendent with regard to the intuition of essences or founded perception.

This issue is of special importance for Husserl's development, for here we again encounter the question of his so-called "realism," which has been the subject of much discussion. This "realism" here concerns not the real object but the essence. (Therefore it is often referred to by way of the misleading term 'conceptual realism.') What is independent of thought is the essence or idea, rather than the object of normal sensory perception.[1] Most references to Husserl's realism at the time of LU mean this kind of realism. This conceptual realism would then fit in with the standpoint of LU, which is also interpreted as realist in another respect.[2] This matter has become a highly controversial issue, parti-

---

[41] See I. Kern, *Husserl und Kant*, 142ff. See also U. Claesges, *Edmund Husserls Theorie der Raumkonstitution*, 15 and my article 'Edmund Husserl,' 99.

[1] P. Thévenaz speaks of a "realism of ideal essences," 'Qu'est ce que la phénoménologie,' 1952, 13, 21. See also R. Ingarden, *On the Motives which led Husserl to Transcendental Idealisme*, 4ff.

[2] See above 162, 166.

cularly through the work of the so-called "Göttingen Husserl school," made up of a number of followers who gathered around Husserl during his Göttingen period.[3] They were fascinated by his method of analyzing essences and saw the revival of ontology as the chief new element in phenomenology. By 'ontology' they then understood the eidetic analysis of objects existing independently of our thought, i.e. essences. They have also been called "realist ontologists."[4] Husserl's later conversion to transcendental idealism must have been a complete surprise to them[5] and also a deep disappointment,[6] for in Husserl's later period, ideal objects are also constituted by consciousness. While Husserl's earliest followers saw the turn toward idealism in part as a turning away from the original intentions,[7] his later followers instead maintained that the so-called realist ontologists had not "understood" Husserl.[8]

[3] See H. Spiegelberg, The Phenomenological Movement, I 169ff; J. Héring, 'La phénoménologie d'Edmund Husserl, il y a trente ans.' Héring reports that Husserl's followers practiced analysis of essences in such an enthusiastic – and at the same time wilful – fashion that it threatened to become a mere intellectual sport. Husserl warned them against "picture book phenomenology" and urged them not to lose sight of the great philosophical problems, 370 note I. See also his article 'Edmund Husserl, souvenirs et réflexions,' 27; on the method-less intuitionism and ontologism of the early Husserl school, see also Landgrebe in Der Weg der Phänomenologie, 21, 23 and La phénoménologie, Journées d'études de la société Thomiste. As realist followers of Husserl, Koyré names: Scheler, Reinach, Hildebrand, Conrad-Martius, Edith Stein, and Ingarden op.cit. 72. Stein herself says that the older Husserl school took over the doctrine of essences and applied it to psychology and the mental sciences.

[4] According to Fink, 'Die phänomenologische Philosophie Edmund Husserls in der gegenwärtigen Kritik' 237 note 1.

[5] Héring says that Husserl did maintain that he had taken this step earlier but that this "to our knowledge escaped all of his hearers" 371.

[6] This is true, for example, of Hedwig Conrad-Martius. See her article 'Phänomenologie und Spekulation' 195, 116ff. She sees the significance of Husserl in the step he took from fact to essence. See also her article 'Die transzendentale und die ontologische Phänomenologie,' 175ff. A similar reaction came from the so-called "Münchner," a group of followers in Munich. Spiegelberg says of them: "...they followed Husserl's development in Freiburg with growing reserve. The major cause of their displeasure was Husserl's phenomenological idealism ...." The reserve was mutual. Husserl reproached the "Münchner" for remaining stuck in ontologism and realism. See Spiegelberg, 'Perspektivenwandel: Konstitution eines Husserlbildes,' 60.

[7] This certainly does not apply to Edith Stein, who did not go through the transition to idealism with Husserl but did see the connections with his previous work La Phénoménologie, Juvisy 1932, 102ff. See below 376.

[8] Fink writes that the realist ontologists fell into the same mistake as the neo-Kantians, op.cit. 237. They interpreted LU as a "turn toward the object" and considered the later Husserl to be under the influence of neo-Kantianism. They would have preferred the reverse development. According to Fink, both the realist ontologists and the neo-

In the previous chapters, I tried to show that Husserl's alleged realism – at least as far as sensory perception is concerned – rests on a misunderstanding. The so-called self-given object is a phenomenon with an intentional mode of existence. Existence is put between brackets, and "self-givenness" is regarded as a psychological characteristic. When I spoke of realism despite this consideration, I did so for reasons *outside the theme of intentionality*. It represents the motives in his thinking that are not specifically phenomenological. It is the counter-pole that maintains its validity *alongside* descriptive analysis. (To speak in the language of Ideen I, it is left outside consideration but is nevertheless presupposed.)

Now the arguments for conceptual realism appear to be much stronger, for Husserl lays great emphasis on the existence of these idealities "in themselves." They have an "ideal existence" that is independent of our thought. Borrowing an expression from Brentano, Husserl says that being thought is "non-essential" (*ausserwesentlich*).[9] Ideal being does not mean "being in our mind." Neither the general meaning nor the ideal object may be reduced to "something psychical."

As far as *meanings* are concerned, this independence is another formulation of the irreducibility of eidos to fact, which was discussed above.[10] This is the background of the famous expression 'meanings in themselves' or 'truths in themselves.'[11] The objective unity of meaning "is what it is, whether anyone actualizes it in thought or not."[12] It is a "unity in the manifold," which must be distinguished from the fleeting experience.[13] The meanings together form "an ideally closed set of general objects, to which being thought or being expressed are alike contingent."[14] Within the area of meanings in themselves, "truths in themselves" form a separate group. They are the meanings which are true and which admit of an intuitive illustration. Their truth, of course, is also independent of whether anyone has insight into it. "What is true is absolute, true 'in itself': truth is one and the same, whether men or non-men, angels or gods apprehend and judge it."[15]

Kantians make the mistake of interpreting ideal being ontologically, as a thing in itself; see also 325. See further H. L. van Breda, 'La Réduction phénoménologique' 1959, 312 and the discussion on this point with Ingarden, 329ff.

[9] Literaturbericht Palàgyi, 291.
[10] See above 253, 256.
[11] II 92, 104.
[12] II 94, 100.
[13] II 44.
[14] II 105.
[15] I 117, see also 116 note I, 121, 128, 232, 238.

As far as the *general object* is concerned, we have to do with another form of anti-psychologism. Here psychologism is said to identify the correlate (or object) of thought with thought itself. Locke, for example, does this when he speaks of the universal triangle within our minds.[16] Husserl discusses this psychologizing at greater length in Ideen I. Such thinkers appeal to the fact that the formation of concepts is a psychical activity and therefore call the concept a "psychical formation" (*Gebilde*). In opposition to this, Husserl claims that we do spontaneously produce the consciousness of something general or universal, but not the universal itself. The universal can be called a concept, but then we must understand 'concept' as "general object" or essence. In this sense, the ideal number is a concept.[17]

Every essence is independent of the existence of anything actual, and the realm of ideas is likewise independent of the existence of an actual consciousness. This is Husserl's so-called "Platonism." The enthusiasm of some of his followers helped to bring about sharp opposition to this doctrine at the time that LU was published; "Platonism" and "logicism" quickly found enemies. Husserl, as a "Platonic realist," was accused of a grammatical and metaphysical hypostatization of concepts and meanings.[18] Whatever value one might ultimately accord to Husserl's doctrine, my main concern here is the historical question to what extent we may indeed attibute such a Platonism or realism to him.

First I must make an observation of a terminological nature. Husserl was always sharply opposed to calling his doctrine of ideas "Platonic realism" or "conceptual realism." He took this name to represent a doctrine that regards ideas as *realities*, that is to say, as things that have the same mode of being as "real" things in space and time. In opposition to this view, Husserl always emphasized the *ideal* mode of being of essences. Therefore he called himself not a realist but an "idealist."[19] The essence can never be a reality, for ideality is the "complete opposite of reality."[20] The essence and the thing have only this in common, that both can become the object of a perception or

---

[16] II 123, 133, see also 118.

[17] Id I 41, 43, 117, 195.

[18] Id I 40, 117.

[19] II 108.

[20] II 102. We can speak in Husserl's case of a χωρισμός between idea and fact, see also 133 and 159 note 1. He rejects only an absurd *chōrismos* that would bring about a split *within reality* between the individual and the universal. J. Wahl's comment that Husserl separates essences from existence, which Merleau-Ponty criticizes, is correct. See *Phénoménologie de la perception* X.

judgment, but in no case do they share the same mode of existence. The thing is temporal and the idea eternal. The arising and passing away of an essence would be "simple nonsense" and "pure absurdity."[21]

This hypostatizing of an essence (which thereby becomes a reality) occurs in two forms. It can be a hypostatizing of something *outside* thought or of something *within* thought. In the former case, Husserl speaks of *metaphysical* hypostatizing.[22] He accuses Plato, who attributed "real existence" to ideas, of this.[23] The misconceptions connected with this Platonic realism or conceptual realism are regarded by Husserl as "disposed of long ago."[24] But this is not the case with regard to *psychological* hypostatizing. Here the essence is hypostatized to form a reality *within* consciousness, i.e. a "real existence of the species in thought."[25] We find this in Locke, who accepts a universal triangle *within* thought. This doctrine is just as absurd as that of Plato. There is no more a universal triangle within consciousness than one within the "real world" outside consciousness. What is absurd in reality is also absurd "in the mind," for "psychical being" is also "real being."[26]

When Husserl rejects Platonism, he means this metaphysical hypostatizing. When he calls himself a Platonist despite this rejection, he usually places the name in quotation marks. His is a revised Platonism that conceives of the essence as an ideality and not as a reality.[27] Thus the name 'realism' or 'conceptual realism' is unfortunate from the terminological point of view. We can use it only insofar as we mean by it that Husserl accepts a *being independent of consciousness*. But, as we will see later in connection with this question, the cardinal distinction between reality and ideality must somehow be taken into account. For the moment I will disregard this distinction and ask whether Husserl is a realist in the broader sense mentioned immediately above. It appears that this question must be answered in the affirmative. The intentional object has only an intentional mode of being, but the ideal object is independent of consciousness. Thus, in a consciousness of a un-

---

[21] II 155, 44, 119, 141, 148.
[22] II 121, 122.
[23] II 119, 135, 136.
[24] II 123, 110.
[25] II 101, 110, 121ff.
[26] II 115, 123, 133.
[27] Husserl says that he arrived at this interpretation of Plato's thought through Lotze (Literaturbericht Palàgyi 290), whose interpretation of the theory of ideas exercised a "deep influence" on him. Sometimes Husserl himself interprets Plato in this sense, see EP I 10, 11ff. Plato then functions as the discoverer of the "intuition of essences."

iversality, an object which is not merely intentional is indeed present. "Presence" would have to be understood in a realist sense here. The same holds with regard to the concept of constitution. When Husserl speaks of constituting a general object[28] or an ideal meaning,[29] this would have to be understood in the sense of "encounter." The existence of the object is not dependent on our understanding it.

Two factors indispensable for judging this realism, however, must be taken into account here. In the first place, I must point out that Husserl *tries to remain true to the phenomenological point of departure* in the doctrine of the intuition of essences. This is apparent in his argumentation against nominalism. His primary argument against nominalism is not that in addition to individual things, essences are also given, but that *in addition to acts that intend something individual, there are also acts that intend something general.* The givenness to which Husserl appeals is the givenness of the *consciousness* of a universality.[30] His reasoning in LU is *descriptive psychological*. In this regard there is a striking difference between LU and later writings. In later publications Husserl says: essences are given as well as facts, and the refusal to recognize this testifies to a prejudice. But in LU Husserl points to the givenness of the consciousness of an essence. This is in agreement with the noetic point of departure of LU, which regards only the Cartesian sphere of *cogitationes* as given.[31]

This state of affairs is of particular importance, but attention has seldom been focused on it. The framework within which the doctrine of the intuition of essences stands clarifies certain tensions in Husserl's thinking and at the same time casts light on his later development. If only the acts are given, then we really must abstract from the object – from the ideal object as well as from the real object. Husserl is consistent in this respect when he makes the (implicit) epoché with regard to existence apply not only to acts directed toward something individual but also to acts in which an essence is presented. "In a phenomenological treatment, objectivity counts as nothing... It makes no difference what sort of being we give our object, or with what sense or justification we do so; whether this being is real or ideal . . . the

---

[28] II 109, Zusatz, 142, 145, 175, 181, 188; III 161.
[29] II 45, 106, 181.
[30] See above 154, 236 and 238.
[31] See above 175. Here I would point to the introduction, where Husserl appears to mean the *acts* when he speaks of the "things themselves," Einleitung II 6.

act remains 'directed toward' its object."[32] Whether I form a presentation of something intelligible or of a physical thing, ". . . it makes
no difference whether this object exists. . . ."[33] Because the act of
ideation is itself individual,[34] this standpoint is not self-contradictory.
On the other hand, it appears that Husserl repeatedly goes beyond this
framework. Thus, what happens in the case of sensory perception also
happens here: Husserl does not confine himself to the limits imposed by
his phenomenological point of departure. If he had done so, he would
have been able to make no eidetic statements – neither about things nor
about consciousness itself, for the sphere of *cogitationes* is strictly
individual. If we limit ourselves to this sphere, the only statement we
can make is: "This there." We can only make experiential judgments.
Husserl himself later admitted this and corrected his theory on this
point. In 1907 he declared that we must recognize as given not only
cogitationes but also essences, and that he had actually presupposed
this givenness earlier.[35] Thereby he brought the phenomenology of
phenomenology into line with phenomenology itself. In this case too,
methodological reflection lagged behind the use of a method *in actu
exercito*.

This tension between point of departure and actual analysis also manifests itself
in Husserl's concept of evidence. Actually, evident assertions are possible only
in the case of "experiences." In immanent perception, the object is "phenomenologically realizable." An essence can never coincide with an experience, and
thus no adequate evidence with regard to an essence would be possible.
Nevertheless, Husserl speaks repeatedly of the adequate givenness of an idea
and compares it to the givenness of an individual thing.[36] In a certain passage,
he speaks of this evidence as the means by which the world of unreason and
doubt may be "levered on its hinges."[37] But when he summarizes all his
arguments against relativism, the argument takes an important turn: he then
says that the evidence of inner perception is what makes any relativism
impossible.[38]

[32] II 412.
[33] II 425.
[34] II 133, 141, 148.
[35] See below 314.
[36] I 190.
[37] I 143.
[38] I 121.

Only when we take these methodological limitations into account is a proper light shed on the so-called conceptual realism of LU. I do not deny that there is mention in LU of a certain realism of this nature.[39] But this realism is only implicit. Given Husserl's point of departure, it is not present *de jure* but only *de facto*; it lacks a philosophical justification. To this extent, this doctrine of the intuition of essences is a precarious matter. Thus, it is apparent that the last thing Husserl intended to do was to inaugurate a breakthrough to a realist philosophy by means of it. His firm ground on this point is: it is established phenomenologically that there are acts in which something general is intended. As for the ontological status of the latter and its relation to consciousness, there are many problems that remain. The followers of Husserl who greeted this doctrine enthusiastically were not sufficiently aware of the methodological framework within which it had been developed. As is more often the case, there were more uncertainties on the part of the master than on the part of the disciples.[40] To them, Husserl's later development represented a break, but to Husserl himself, it was the fruit of a consistent elaboration of motives already

---

[39] Fink himself admits this when he says that the emphasis on the independence of the being of essences is somewhat overdone in LU op.cit. 329, 236. In Fink we see an understandable inclination to interpret LU in the light of Ideen I. This is to be explained on the basis of his reaction against the "ontologists." Taking advantage of historical distance, a more balanced judgment should be possible. Fink already sees latent in the six investigations a change from the "naive-ontological question of the being of the ideal" to the "phenomenological-*constitutive* problem of the ideal objects" of FTL. We saw above 254 (compare below 292) that the basis for such an interpretation is not to be found in LU. We also encounter an inclination to minimize the Platonism of LU in Husserl's assistant Landgrebe, see *Der Weg der Phänomenologie* 17, 18. Three years before Fink's article, Lévinas had already interpreted LU on the basis of Ideen I, see *La théorie de l'intuition dans la phénoménologie de Husserl* 143, 147. According to Lévinas, the Prolegomena to Pure Logic stand implicitly on the level of Ideen I. Underlying LU is the conviction that "the origin of being is in life," 148. Husserl "takes logic as it occurs in the life that occupies itself with logic." Lévinas correctly points out that there is something general given in general intentions. However, this relation must not yet be conceived of in a transcendental idealist sense in LU. In Lévinas' book, which is otherwise excellent, Husserl is interpreted on this point too much on the basis of his later position. There is indeed a certain Platonism in LU.

[40] Some notes in Husserl's diary illustrate these uncertainties: "... while I was working at the sketches toward the logic of mathematical thinking and particularly of the mathematical calculus, I was tormented by incomprehensible new worlds: the world of pure logic and the world of act-consciousness, or, as I would now call them, of the phenomenological and also the psychological. *I did not know how to unite them, yet they had to have some relation to one another and form an inner unity*" (italics mine), PPR 1956, 294.

present. From the neo-Thomist side, too, some have been too quick to recognize beloved themes drawn from Scholasticism. We have already seen that this was the case with regard to the theme of intentionality. The typically modern framework within which these considerations stand, i.e. the "principle of subjectivity" which recognizes only subjective consciousness as point of departure, was thereby ignored.[41]

My second remark is closely bound up with the previous observation and also concerns the framework within which Husserl's "Platonic realism" stands. Here I would like to raise the principial question whether it is correct to characterize Husserl's philosophy by way of the act of ideation. The latter, after all, is a *founded* perception. In response to this question, I refer the reader to what I have written above about categorial perception.[42] It also applies here *mutatis mutandis*. *In Husserl's case, the decisions on the question of realism versus idealism fall within the analysis of sensory perception.* It is a basic law, so to speak, of Husserl's phenomenology – and thus also of Husserl interpretation – that we must proceed from founding acts. We will see later that in Ideen I, the definitive clarification of the relationship between being and consciousness also takes place in an analysis of sensory perception. The basic relations that are laid bare here have repercussions for all other relations that rest on this foundation. In FTL, Husserl speaks of the "ontic priority (*Seinsvorzug*) of real objects vis-à-vis irreal objects."[43] All ideal and categorial objects are founded in real objects. The critique of experience in Ideen I therefore implies a re-evaluation of the being of ideal objects. They are then regarded as entities constituted by transcendental consciousness. Every ontological a priori is related to a

---

[41] For the Thomist point of view, see *La Phénoménologie*, Juvisy 1932. Edith Stein writes: "The strongest element that phenomenology and Thomism have in common appears to me to lie in the objective analysis of essences. The procedure of eidetic reduction, which disregards factual existence and anything accidental in order to make the essence visible, appears to me – from a Thomist standpoint – to be justified by the separation between essence and existence in everything created" 109. Although the differences between Husserl and Thomas Aquinas are kept in mind, this analysis of essences is still interpreted as a "turn toward the object," e.g. by Von Rintelen 103 and Söhngen 105. Husserl's concept of knowledge, according to them, is realist. See also Koyré, 70, on this matter. Husserl's conversion to transcendental idealism is likewise understood on the basis of the doctrine of the intuition of essences. The suspension of being in the phenomenological reduction is identified with the suspension of existence in the eidetic reduction. Transcendental idealism is seen as giving up individual existence. See below 470 note 24.

[42] See above 170.

[43] FTL 150.

phenomenological a priori. This reinterpretation is based on a reinterpretation of sensory perception and its correlate.[44]

Thus, when I speak of realism in LU, I do so in connection with the
problematics of sensory perception – and then not on the basis of
intentionality, but because of realist metaphysical presuppositions! As
far as the object of founded perception or ideation is concerned, there is
a certain realism insofar as the realm of ideas is independent of
consciousness, but this realism is not justified philosophically by
Husserl and, furthermore, awaits a definitive interpretation as far as its
ontological status is concerned.

[44] See below 487ff.

CHAPTER FOUR

LOGIC AND PSYCHOLOGY

In this chapter I will raise the question what consequences the new doctrine of the intuition of essences has for logic. The development of Husserl's thought can be traced *in concreto* in connection with this formal a priori science. I have already devoted a paragraph to this matter in Chapter 4 of Part I. Husserl hoped to achieve two things in LU. In the Prolegomena to Pure Logic, he sought to place logic on a firm, non-psychological basis, and in the six investigations, he tried to clarify its fundamental concepts. In this chapter I will examine how Husserl carried out the former task. Then, in Chapter 5, I will discuss the philosophical analysis of origins.

PARAGRAPH ONE. STATEMENT OF THE PROBLEM

In LU, Husserl defines logic as the theory of the art (*Kunstlehre*) of correct scientific judgment. This definition fits in with what has been established above.[1]

Nor did Husserl change his mind about the task of this logic. Logic bears not only on logical deduction but also on calculation and the formation of constructs, both of which play a part in science. However, logical deduction is primary. In fact, all science consists of "grounded validations" (*Begründungen*). We can certainly make use of algorithmic methods in science, but these methods are ultimately nothing other than "abbreviations and surrogates for grounded validations" and derive their validity from the grounded validations which they spare us.[2] In a "logic of the logical calculus," as Husserl calls it, it must be shown that the operation in which we engage as well as the formation of constructs is based ultimately on logical deduction.

---

[1] I 14, 28, see above 91.
[2] I 23, 24.

As the theory of an art, logic must teach us in what way we can construct scientific theories. This theory of an art is based on *a normative* discipline in which the properties that any correct theory must possess are listed. The latter science in turn presupposes a discipline in which the criteria for truth are unfolded. This is done by logic as a *purely theoretical* science. It establishes laws which thought must conform to if it is to apprehend truth.[3] In this formal logic, truth must be conceived of as formal truth.[4] Husserl's struggle in the Prolegomena is against psychologism, against the logicians who want to derive logical laws from psychology. Logic, they reason, has to do with judgments, conclusions, proofs, etc., all of which are psychical activities. Logic, which deals with correct judgment, is thus a psychology of this correct judging.

This attempt to base logic on psychology is generally called psychologism. Husserl himself speaks of "logical psychologism."[5] Now, we have already seen in Part I that the term 'psychologism' should not be used without further specification, for it makes a great deal of difference on which psychology logic is alleged to be dependent. Someone like John Stuart Mill sees psychology as an explanatory natural science, and the logical law as an inductive law of nature. The absurdity of this standpoint was already pointed out by Brentano. Thus, when Husserl makes his celebrated attack on this psychologism, he could not have had his teacher Brentano or his own earlier position in mind. How is this to be reconciled with the widely accepted view that in LU, Husserl denied his own past position (among other things) and retracted his earlier mistakes? Does Husserl himself not cite Goethe's saying – in the foreword to LU – that we oppose nothing as strongly as the errors we have just abandoned?[6] Moreover, he openly retracts his criticism of Frege. Such an open self-criticism is unusual for Husserl and has rightly drawn a great deal of attention. If Husserl condemns an earlier standpoint of his own, he must have an entirely different psychologism in mind from that of Mill. Of what nature is this psychologism? Only a comparison with Brentano's standpoint can yield an answer to this question.

Before I take up this matter, I must touch on yet another problem,

[3] See above 224f.
[4] I 140 note 1, 144; II 93, 96.
[5] I (ed. 2) Vorwort XIII.
[6] I, VIII.

which is bound up with it. Perhaps no statement of Husserl has occasioned more surprise than his remark in the introduction to the second volume of the original German edition of LU to the effect that he proposed to base the "pure logic" defended in the Prolegomena on a descriptive psychology. For many of Husserl's readers, this remark was a stumbling block. In the Prolegomena they had read an overwhelmingly strong brief against psychology as the foundation for logic, together with a plea for a pure logic. This ideal science must become the foundation for normative and practical logic, they read. To their dismay, they then heard Husserl declare in the continuation of LU that he wanted to found pure logic, whose a priori character he had already demonstrated in such convincing fashion, on psychology. Many saw this as a relapse into psychologism.[7] But such an interpretation is completely untenable. Any such hypothesis condemns itself when applied to a thinker of Husserl's stature. We must take it that Husserl knew what he was doing when he wrote this controversial statement. Here, too, a great deal of misunderstanding will be avoided if we take the difference between explanatory and descriptive psychology into full account. The Prolegomena does not attack psychology as such but only explanatory psychology. It is this psychology that is incompetent to serve as the foundation for logic. Must we then conclude that Husserl sees descriptive psychology as the foundation for logic? This is indeed his intention. But then we again face the question: what is the difference between Husserl and Brentano, between the Husserl of LU and the Husserl of the earlier publications? Thus we are directed anew to a closer study of the differences between Husserl and Brentano. *How could Husserl follow Brentano's lead by proceeding from descriptive psychology and yet distantiate himself for Brentano?* This was also unclear to Brentano. As we have already seen, the latter felt that he had not been done justice in LU. He sensed an attack on himself in the attack on the empirical psychological founding of logic, and he countered this – rightly! – by pointing out that he, Brentano, had demonstrated the absurdity of such an undertaking long before Husserl. Brentano, after all, had called Mill's view an "astounding error."[8] Thus, when we analyze the differences between LU and Husserl's earlier position, we can clear up a misunderstanding between Husserl and his teacher at the same time.

[7] See below 287.
[8] See above 94.

PARAGRAPH TWO. THE PSYCHOLOGICAL CONCEPT AND THE
LOGICAL CONCEPT

*Husserl's answer in principle to logical psychologism is to be sought in the
distinction between eidos and fact, between the ideal meaning and the act
of meaning (meaning in concreto). It is also an answer to psychologism à
la Brentano,* which does not, of course, put logical laws on the same
level as empirical psychological laws, but does seek to derive these laws
from the psychical fact. The principle of contradiction is a law which is
"made obvious" to us *ex terminis.* The concepts of these terms are
abstracted from the inner perception of "a" judgment, "a" difference in
the quality of judgments, "an" evident experience.[1] For Husserl, too,
these concepts arise from inner perception – but then in the sense of
inner *ideation* on the basis of a "sensory" inner perception. In this
ideation we intuit not the individual act but its idea. Husserl also
distinguishes between meaning something *in concreto* and the ideal
meaning as between the *psychological* concept and the *logical* concept.
Psychologism rests on a confusion of these two meanings of 'concept.'
The proponents of psychologism claim that terms like 'presentation,'
'judgment,' 'conclusion,' etc. refer to psychical activities, and this is
certainly obvious. But attached to all these words is a fundamental
ambiguity, which Husserl regards as one of the "most dangerous
equivocations" by which logic is corrupted. These terms can refer either
to the act or to the eidos of the act.

'*Concept*' means not only the act of meaning but also the one ideal
meaning. When we speak in science of concepts like "force," "mass,"
"integral," etc., we mean not the individual acts through which the
practitioners of science think these concepts but the "concepts in
themselves" as ideal unities. These unities are maintained as such, even
though individual experiences and individual expressions come and
go.[2] When we speak in logic of the content and extension of concepts,
we mean not the individual presentations but their eidē. "Meanings in
the sense of specific unities" form the "domain of pure logic," i.e.
meanings as a subdivision of the realm of ideal objects.[3]

---

[1] See above 95, 207 note 13.

[2] II 101, 102, 214 note 1, 218, 210, 211. This is even the case for meanings like "here"
and "now" II 84, 85, 91. Husserl calls this the "boundlessness of objective reason." Later
he gave this up, compare EU 43 and above 257 note 20.

[3] II 91, 92, 101, 107, 343.

What I have established about concepts holds also for judgments, which are built up out of concepts. Here, too, we distinguish between the psychological judgment and the logical judgment or (asserted) "proposition." The "proposition" as an ideal unity "is what we have in mind when we say that 'the' judgment is the meaning of 'the' declarative sentence – only, the fundamental equivocity of the word 'judgment' at once tends to make us confuse the evidently grasped ideal unity with the real act or what the assertion intimates with what it asserts." When the logician speaks of the judgment "s = p," he means not the act through which this judgment is thought but the identical "propositional meaning" which is realized in the many individual "real acts" as contingent facts.[4]

The same is true in turn for *inferences*, which are built up out of judgments. Over against the many individual acts in which a particular conclusion is drawn stands the one identical conclusion.[5]

Finally, the same opposition occurs in the series of foundings that we call a *theory*. Over against the "tissue of knowing acts" stands the one "ideal theory" as an "ideal complex of meanings." In the case of each science, therefore, we must distinguish sharply between two kinds of connections: on the one hand, "a pattern of connections (*Zusammenhang*) of *cognitive experiences*, in which science is subjectively realized, a *psychological pattern of connection* among the presentations, judgments, insights, surmises, questions, etc.," and on the other hand, the "*logical pattern of connection*, i.e. the specific pattern of connection of the theoretical ideas, in which the unity of the truths of a scientific discipline – in particular, those of a scientific theory or a proof or an inference – is constituted."[6]

I can now answer the question with which I concluded the previous paragraph. It is the analogous structure of the thinking of Brentano and Husserl on logic that enables us to determine precisely on what point they differ. They are agreed in virtually all respects, but on one fundamental point concerning the founding of the a priori judgments of pure logic they differ. Husserl realized that an inner perception of logical acts is not sufficient. Therefore he speaks not of inner perception but of inner ideation or inner abstraction. The origin of the concept must be sought not in an (inner) fact but in its essence. Thus Husserl here draws the conclusions implicit in his theory of abstraction, which I

---

[4] I 117, 119, 167, 175, 177, 191; II 45, see also 93, 94, 99, 100, 104.

[5] II 2, 26, 94, 175.

[6] II 94; 1, 12, 178, 179, 228. In addition to the equivocity of the concepts "presentation," "judgment," "inference," and "theory," Husserl also points out the equivocity of "psychological" and "logical impossibility" 1, 90, 103, 141; "psychological" and "logical necessity" 134, 148; "understanding" and "reason" 124, 173, 214; "laws of thought" 148; "truth" 148, 190. All these ambiguities are rooted in the duality of eidos and fact, of the ideal meaning and the act of meaning.

dealt with in Chapter 3. Because he had introduced a realm of ideal entities together with all the consequences of such a doctrine, Husserl could rightly speak of a "new grounding of pure logic."[7] In Entwurf (1913), he says that it was from Lotze and Bolzano, with their doctrine of "truths in themselves" and "presentations in themselves," that he learned to see the difference between the psychological judgment and the logical judgment. Before that time he regarded these essences as "metaphysical monstrosities" (Abstrusitäten).[8] We know that Brentano shared this assessment and never changed his thinking in this respect.

When Husserl engages in sharp self-criticism in the foreword to the Prolegomena, his criticism is not directed against an inductive founding of logical laws: Husserl had never maintained such a theory. Neither is his criticism directed against descriptive psychology as such. Husserl's target is the view that this science is an *experiential* science, an analysis of *actual* conscious structures. This view, he says, prevents any clarification of the relation between the "logical unity of the thought-content" and the subjective psychological act. This drove him to reflect more and more on "the relationship between the subjectivity of knowing and the objectivity of the content known."[9] In addition to Lotze and Bolzano, Natorp helped Husserl along on this point. And it was in this context that Husserl retracted his criticism of Frege.[10]

The difference between Brentano and Husserl can thus be summed up briefly as follows: Brentano wished to proceed from descriptive psychology as an empirical science, while Husserl saw this psychology as an eidetic science. In his characterization of this science, unfortunately, Husserl did not directly and clearly indicate that he had *eidetic* analyses in mind, and this may well have contributed to the misunderstanding between himself and his teacher. In Chapter 2 I gave the reason for this inadequate self-characterization, which Husserl later regretted deeply. He seized the very first available opportunity to correct this "misleading characterization."[11]

[7] I, VII. Logic, as the science of ideal meanings, is now an ideal science I 178, 188, with apodictic evidence, I 101, 134, 163.

[8] Entwurf 129.

[9] I, VI/VII.

[10] I 169 note 1, see also 57 note 3 and 156 note 1.

[11] In a review of a book by Elsenhans, in 'Archiv f. system. Phil. 1903.' How important Husserl regarded this correction is apparent from how often he returned to it, I (ed. 2), XIII; PSW 318 note 1; Id I, 2 note 2. In particular, pp. 316–8 of PSW represent a brief

PARAGRAPH THREE. THE LAWS OF LOGIC

The new standpoint has certain consequences for logical principles. These consequences will now be worked out somewhat further. It is true of logical laws that they are "grounded purely in concepts."[1] The "concepts," here, are also "essences" – the essences of presentations, judgments, etc. The validity of these laws, of course, is not dependent on the inductive procedure of gathering facts. "They are grounded and justified not by induction but by apodictic evidence."[2] Neither does it rest on concepts which arise from an empirical description of facts of consciousness. Because these laws do not rest on facts, neither do they say anything about the existence of facts: no existential judgments can be derived from them.[3] From a logical law, then, we could not determine that there are certain presentations; these laws have no "existential content." This point can again be elucidated by means of the principle of contradiction, which says nothing about real experiences but states only that two ideal judgments or "propositions" with the same matter and opposed quality cannot both be true. It "contains no shadow of an empirical assertion about any consciousness and its act of judgment." It would maintain its full validity even "if there were no psychical processes."[4]

In the laws of *formal* logic, furthermore, we are concerned with lawfulness rooted in the *forms* of concepts and judgments.[5] In the process we abstract from the content of knowledge. These laws are based on the *categories* of meaning.[6] They determine not the material truth but the "formal consistency" of a theory. In the case of these laws based on categories, we can again distinguish two groups.

In the first place, there is the so-called morphology of meanings.[7] Morphology investigates what connections between meanings are possible without lapsing into nonsense. An assertion like "If is green" conflicts with morphology, which

against the confusion of empirical and eidetic description in descriptive psychology. Husserl admits that his own inadequate characterization in the introduction to LU II is partly responsible for the confusion.

[1] I 43, 73, 74, 78, 97, 99.
[2] I 62; II 26.
[3] I 71, 139.
[4] I 97, 149.
[5] I 100, 101, 162, 166, 174f, 179.
[6] I title par. 68, 163, 239, 245; II 92, 95, 96; see above 251.
[7] I 243, see also 111, 115, 117, 129, 139, 159, 184, 187, 239, 241, 255; II 317ff, 335; III 193, 194.

determines that a non-independent word like 'if' cannot function as the subject of a sentence. Such a judgment be "meaningless." Husserl also calls morphology, which guards against nonsense, pure grammar. This pure grammar is a kind of substratum or "basement" of pure logic.[8]

We can only speak of logic in the proper sense of the word when we investigate not the possible but the *valid* forms.[9] Agreement with these formal laws determines the truth of a theory in the sense of formal correctness. The judgment "All A's are B, but some are not" conflicts with these laws.[10] Such a judgment is not "nonsense" (*Unsinn*), for we understand it well enough; it is an "absurdity" (*Widersinn*). It is an analytic contradiction, that is to say, a contradiction rooted purely in the form of the essence.

I have already pointed out that the ideal laws of pure logic can be applied to subjective acts.[11] The laws of pure logic are called by Husserl the purely logical conditions for the possibility of knowledge. When applied to acts, they delimit the sphere of possible acts satisfying these conditions. They are the noetic conditions for the possibility of knowledge and science.[12] Through the founding of pure logic as an ideal science, a normative and practical logic, which operates with ideal laws as criteria, now becomes possible. Thereby the possibility of science is guaranteed.

Husserl deliberately formulates this problem in the terminology of Kant. Logic deals with the "conditions for the possibility of science as such." He correctly adds that this is a universalization of Kant's question of the "conditions for the possibility of experience."[13] Kant sought to deal with the possibility of natural scientific experience by way of this question. For Husserl, this problematics is dealt with in *material* logic (or material ontology).[14] In LU, we already find the first traces of this material ontology, which is analogous to Kant's transcendental logic. Although Husserl raises the question of the validity of knowledge in a much more universal manner than Kant,[15] i.e. as a question applicable to *every*

---

[8] II 333ff, 340. Referat Marty 1108.

[9] I 245; II 92, 96, 329. See Bar-Hillel, 'Husserl's Conception of a purely Logical Grammar.' According to Bar-Hillel, Husserl's distinction between pure grammar and pure logic anticipates Carnap's distinction between rules for formation and rules for transformation.

[10] See also FTL 98; LU III 192; S. Bachelard, *La Logique de Husserl*, 56, note 2 and 58.

[11] See above 258, 218.

[12] I, 111, 237 note 1. These conditions function as *norma normata*.

[13] I 236f; III 199.

[14] Especially in the third investigation. See also II (ed. 2) 120.

[15] This is bound up with Kant's "unspeakably inadequate" conception of formal logic, which prevented him here, too, from posing transcendental questions I 214, III 203; FTL 228, 235.

science, it is nevertheless a typically Kantian problematics. Natorp, in his review of the Prolegomena, pointed out that the task which Husserl assigns to pure logic is the same task which the Kantian school assigns to the critique of knowledge.[16] Husserl agreed with this observation. In a letter to Albrecht he declared: "Natorp correctly remarked that the goals which I assign to pure logic coincide essentially with those of the Kantian critique of knowledge."[17] In the Prolegomena, too, Husserl declared that he was close to Kant, although he rejected his "mythical" concepts of "understanding" and "reason."[18] Kant needed those concepts because he was blind to ideas. Understanding and reason had to found the a priority of knowledge because Kant did not see the possibility of an "experience" of essences. But Husserl's greatest objection to Kant was that he conceived of understanding and reason as psychical powers. This is Kant's "anthropologism." "Consciousness as such," as a *fact*, founds knowledge for Kant. Thus Husserl's objections against Kant are analogous to his objections against Brentano. This "consciousness as such" or "intellectus ipse" or whatever we choose to call it must be seen as the noetic conditions for knowledge, as a possible realization of the ideal laws of logic, which laws it thus presupposes. Husserl accepts the term 'consciousness as such' – but then conceived of as "timeless normal consciousness," so that it coincides with his realm of ideas.[19]

---

[16] 'Zur Frage der logischen Methode,' 270; see above 245.
[17] EP I, XIX.
[18] I 214, see also III 203 (ed. 2).
[19] I 88, 124, see also 173f; III 197f.

CHAPTER FIVE

PHILOSOPHY AS ANALYSIS OF ORIGINS

SECTION ONE.
THE PHILOSOPHICAL CLARIFICATION OF ARITHMETIC

The actual task of the six investigations that make up the second volume of the German edition of LU is to clarify the concepts of pure logic. Nevertheless, Husserl also speaks of the analysis of the origins of arithmetical concepts, usually when explaining his intentions. Therefore I will begin with a short explication of this philosophical clarification of arithmetic. This will give me another opportunity to compare LU in detail with PA.

Compared with PA, there are two important changes in Husserl's theory of number. (1) A number, he says, can only be given in an act of counting.[1] The origin of the concept of number, however, lies no longer in the act itself but in the object of the act. We do not reflect on the act of collecting; instead we grasp its correlate, i.e. the collective.[2] (2) But this categorial perception cannot provide the foundation for arithmetic as an a priori science, for arithmetic deals with ideal numbers.[3] The categorial perception of a collective must therefore become the foundation for a categorial abstraction. Categorial perception makes the collective *in concreto* (e.g. a group of four object) appear. Categorial abstraction then apprehends the universal in this. Its object is the species "four."[4]

Husserl describes this process very clearly in the Prolegomena. The concrete collectives are "instances" of ideal numbers. "If we make clear to ourselves what the number five really is . . . we will first achieve an

---

[1] I 105, 168, 185.
[2] III 141, see also 139 and 193; II 314, 173.
[3] I 172; II 110f, 115, 318.
[4] II 125, 141.

articulate, collective presentation of this or that set of five objects. Thereby a collective is intuitively given in a certain articulated *form* and so as an instance of the number-species in question." Then follows the second stage. "Looking at this intuited individual, we perform an 'abstraction,' i.e. we not only isolate the non-independent moment of the collective form in what we intuit, but we apprehend the idea in it: the number five as the species (of the form) enters our referring conscious-ness." What is before us is the "*ideal (form-)species*, which in the sense of arithmetic is absolutely *one*, in whatever act it may be individuated for us in an intuitively constituted collective . . . ."[5] Thus we must seek the origin of the concept of number not in the collecting act (which gives us only the concept of "collecting act") nor in the correlate of this act (which cannot give us a foundation for an a priori concept), but in the eidos of this correlate.[6]

When we speak of the objectivity of the number, we must therefore distinguish between two levels of objectivity, corresponding to the two forms of psychologism which Husserl overcomes in two stages.[7] In the doctrine of categorial perception, he recognizes that the act of a higher order has an object of its own. It is in categorial abstraction that Husserl first arrives at the doctrine of ideal numbers. Here, then, lies the real point of contact with Frege. Through the doctrine of numbers as ideal entities, Husserl honors Frege's criticism of his 'psychologism." Although Frege did not distinguish the various forms of psychologism and unjustly accused Husserl of reducing contents to acts, Husserl must have felt that here Frege's criticism really did apply to his philosophy of arithmetic. Arithmetic concerns itself not with psychical facts but with ideal entities. The mathematical and the psychological belong to "such different worlds that the very thought of interchange between them would be absurd." Thus Husserl retracts his criticism of Frege.[8]

---

[5] I 171. The words 'of the form' and 'form' were added in the second edition.

[6] Husserl sometimes speaks of the psychological origin but then apparently goes on to confuse the founding substratum and its eidos, see below 284 note 6; I 170 and Vorwort VII.

[7] See above 90, 116. The confusing of the two levels is furthered by the fact that Husserl also calls the categorial object an "ideal" object. The whole debate in Royaumont (Biemel, Fink, Ingarden) takes on an air of unreality because of the failure to distinguish between two kinds of objectivity, Cahiers de Royaumont III 63, 67, 70.

[8] I 169.

Section Two.
The Philosophical Clarification of Pure Logic

PARAGRAPH ONE. THE PHILOSOPHY OF PURE LOGIC

Philosophy's task with regard to pure logic is analogous to its task with regard to arithmetic. Here, too, we are concerned with a clarification of the central concepts. Pure logic deals with meanings as ideal objects, but these meanings are not directly given in full distinctness. For example, think of the changing meanings attributed to concepts like "presentation," "judgment," "general concept," etc. The eidetic laws formed in connection with these ideal objects then share in this inexactness. An unnoticed ambiguity in the terms can lead to an ambiguity in the purely logical laws. It is the task of philosophy to clarify these laws, to make them "clear and distinct," as Husserl remarks, probably alluding to the Cartesian "clare et distincte." We must therefore unlock the sources from which these concepts arise, in order to be able to fix them in full sharpness. Like all concepts, logical concepts arise from intuition; they arise from abstraction directed toward particular objects. In this case, these objects are the logical "meanings" (plus the "substratum" of these "meanings," i.e. the significative acts and their fulfillments).

Thus philosophical clarification really seeks to repeat this abstraction. We cannot remain satisfied with a purely significative-symbolic understanding of these terms but must go back to the "things themselves" – in this case, the logical acts and their ideal superstructure (the "meanings"). "Through sufficient repeated checking against reproducible intuition," we must hold fast the meaning of a word "in its inalterable identity."[1] We discover that a logical term has various meanings when it is capable of fulfillment in various intuitions. Thereby the unclarity of the concept, which is one of the major causes of logic's lack of progress, can be overcome. Husserl's distinguishing of the thirteen meanings of the concept of "presentation" is an example of this.[2]

---

[1] II (ed. 1) 1, 4, 7, 15, 21, 56, 61, 77, 120, 190, 145f, 217, 343, 365 note 1; III 200; I 29, 172, 245. Selbstanzeige LU in 'Vierteljahrschr. f. wiss. Phil 1900/1901 (quoted in Entwurf, 125).

[2] II 500.

Husserl speaks of this clarification as an "epistemological clarification."[3] Ueberweg correctly observes that Husserl uses the term 'theory of knowledge' in a peculiar sense of his own.[4] Nevertheless, it is not entirely correct to equate this term with pure logic, as Ueberweg does. Although pure logic does deal with formal categories that determine the validity of any theory and with the validity of all knowledge, only the philosophical clarification of these concepts can really be called theory of knowledge.[5] It is in this clarification that the concepts of pure logic first find their "justifying grounding." Clarification, as a checking against intuition, is at the same time a verification. Thereby it is proven that the concept has "reality," that it is possible. When the "possibility" or the "existence" of the concepts and laws of pure logic is proven in this way, the formal possibility of subjective knowledge is guaranteed. The term 'possible' is then applied to individual instances (in this case, acts) that fall under an ideal law. This anchoring of knowledge in ideal laws is Husserl's "idealism" at the time of LU.[6]

This theory of knowledge, then, must be sharply distinguished from the "metaphysical" theory of knowledge, which proceeds from the problem of transcendence.[7] Husserl wants to remain free of any and all metaphysical presuppositions; he wishes to base his clarification exclusively on the given, i.e. the sphere of acts. Indeed, logical concepts can only be clarified on the basis of the sphere of acts. Ideal meanings are the eidetic superstructure of the acts. Matters are somewhat different in the clarification of arithmetical concepts, for there the correlate is taken into consideration – the formal relation as the objective correlate of the categorial connection. Husserl must then make use of the givenness of the intentional object, which is still only implicitly recognized in LU.[8]

In dealing with the relation between pure logic and philosophical clarification, I am touching on the problem of the relation between

---

[3] II 21; I 254. The term 'theory of knowledge' is already used in this sense in PA, VI.

[4] Ueberweg 508.

[5] I 8, 203, 205, 211 note I 214, 236; II 9, 16 (ed. 1) (ed. 2: 8, 16, 109 (ed. 1), 170, 380, 384, 507; see also PSW 298.

[6] I 73, 241; II 3, 16, 120; III 101, 107. On the term 'idealism,' compare I 236 and II 107.

[7] I 113f, 219; III 199. 'Ber. üb. deutsche Schriften z. Logik-i.d. Jahr 1895–99.' When Husserl speaks of the "object in itself," he does not mean the "thing in itself" but the ideal object I 228; II 90; III 5, 9 (ed. 1) (ed. 2: 8), 118.

[8] As far as this categorial object is concerned, Husserl sometimes comes to an explicit recognition, compare III 189, 190, 193.

philosophy and the special sciences, which was to play such an important role in Husserl's later thought.[9] In order to get a proper perspective on the place of LU in the total *oeuvre* of Husserl, it is important to emphasize the *limited* meaning of philosophy for these sciences (in this case, pure mathematics and logic). This function is limited in comparison with the later central position of philosophy as "first philosophy," embracing and founding all the sciences. Philosophy then makes true sciences (i.e. philosophical sciences) of all the other sciences. It does so by unmasking the natural "world as basis" (*Weltboden*) on which these sciences rest as a presupposition, and by revealing transcendental consciousness as their true ground. Not only the factual sciences (e.g. physics and psychology) but also the ideal sciences (including the *mathesis universalis*) rest on this basis, and to that extent they are "sciences of the world."[10]

Against the background of this later development, it is striking what a modest task Husserl, in the introduction to the six investigations, assigns to philosophy in connection with this *mathesis universalis*. Philosophy still has the same task as in PA, i.e. the clarification of concepts through recourse to the intuition of the "denotatum" (*Begriffsgegenstand*). The clarification of concepts concerning ideal entities takes place simply – the later Husserl would day "naively" – through intuiting them. It does not yet require recourse to the acts of consciousness in which these ideal entities are constituted.[11]

PARAGRAPH TWO. THE ORIGIN OF THE FUNDAMENTAL
CONCEPTS OF LOGIC

It is already implicitly clear from the preceding that the concept of origin has the same meaning in LU as in Husserl's earliest work. In this regard there was no principial change. Origin means "denotatum" (*Begriffsgegenstand*). An analysis of origins is an analysis of the objects from which the concepts are abstracted. Meanwhile the doctrine of the intuition of essences and the extension of ontology by way of an ideal superstructure must be taken into account in connection with the

[9] See above 220.
[10] See below 488.
[11] In Entwurf Husserl gives an interpretation of the philosophical task with regard to the *mathesis universalis* on the level of Ideen I 121ff, 130ff. This is also the background of the criticism of Bolzano Id I 196 note 1.

concept of origin, for general concepts no longer arise from the comparison of individual objects: they arise instead from the intuiting of an ideal object. The individual object can only be called the origin in an indirect sense, insofar as it functions as "substratum" or example in the intuition of essences.

Now, there is something unclear about Husserl's discussion of the analysis of the origins of fundamental logical concepts – at least in his methodological reflection – for he speaks of the descriptive psychology of "inner experience" and not of eidetic psychology.[1] Later he rightly called this a "self-misunderstanding" and added: "The analyses were carried out *de facto* as eidetic analyses, but not always in a constant, clear reflective consciousness."[2] Now this unclarity also appears in the tracing of origins. Husserl says, for example, that purely logical concepts find their origin in acts of thinking and knowing, in thought-functions.[3] Actually, these are the only foundation for abstraction: these thought-concepts originate in an ideation of the essence of these thought-functions. Concepts, after all, do not *arise* from (inner) experience but only *begin* with this experience.[4] The source of the concept is not the act but its eidos. If the origin of concepts lay in acts, clarification could not at the same time be a "justifying grounding" which guarantees the "reality" or validity of logical laws. We must reflect on the act in order "to have a seeing grasp in ideation of the general in the singular, of the concept in the empirical presentation."[5] A logical justification of a logical category is first accomplished through "recourse to its intuitive ... essence." The concept is then "real" (*wesenhaft*). Therefore Husserl is more correct at the end of LU when he speaks of the "logical" origin, for the object of the reflective clarification is the "logical" concept, the ideal meaning, and not the "psychological" concept which realizes the meaning subjectively.[6]

Thus the analysis of the origins of the fundamental concepts of the a priori sciences (in this case, logic and arithmetic) is further an "ideal analysis," i.e. an analysis of ideas.[7] This is where PA and LU differ. But in neither work do we find a constitutive analysis of origins in the sense of the later Husserl. I emphasize this because the interpretation of these

---

[1] I 211 note 1 (ed. 1); II 18 (ed. 1); see above 207, 274.
[2] Entwurf 329 see also 321, 330, 333, 337.
[3] I 244; II 7, 29, 343.
[4] I 75. Husserl here uses the Kantian formula that knowledge begins with experience but does not arise from experience.
[5] I 101, 228.
[6] I 240, 244. The essence or abstractum in the logical sense (not as the individual moment) is the origin. Compare II 157, 172, 192.
[7] II (ed. 1) 5.

works is all too often guided by Husserl's later self-interpretation, which gives rise to an anachronistic view of Husserl's early philosophy. It has already been pointed out that such an interpretation is incorrect as far as the analysis of number in PA is concerned.[8] The same holds for LU. We must not read Husserl's talk of the "sources" of concepts through the spectacles of Ideen I or other later works.[9] These sources are simply the essences from which the concepts are analyzed. This analysis does not yet refer to performances of consciousness in which these essences are constituted.

Such an analysis, in which the essence serves as the clue to the disclosure of conscious structures, requires a much deeper penetration of the idea of constitution and correlation than is in fact present in LU. We have seen that only the first traces of such an idea are to be found there, in connection with sensory perception. We do find mention of sense-giving, and to that extent the possibility of a correlative analysis is present. Yet there is certainly no mention of such analysis as a program. This would presuppose a much more developed awareness of the consequences of this discovery. Limiting ourselves now to the perceptual level of consciousness, this would require first of all that the intentional object be recognized as legitimate subject-matter for phenomenology. A fortiori there could be no mention of such analysis on the significative level of consciousness, for here an intentional correlate of consciousness is completely lacking.[10] Therefore we must try to develop a sense of the gradual growth of Husserl's philosophy. (The analyses in the previous chapters have prepared us for this.) This requires first of all that the term 'analysis of origins' be given the meaning that it really has in LU. The only respect in which this analysis differs from what we read in PA is that the origin of the a priori concept is sought in the essence – in accordance with the altered theory of abstraction. In the analysis of number, this origin is the ideal number (as the eidos of the categorial object). In logic this source is the ideal meaning (as the eidos of the sense-giving act).

---

[8] See above 26, 72.

[9] Therefore it is very important to examine the first edition of LU. In the second edition, clarification on the basis of the sources, II (ed. 1) 3, is explained as a philosophical understanding "on the basis of primordial phenomenological sources" II (ed. 2) 16. The introduction to the second edition is on the level of Ideen I: See also our article 'Das Verhältnis zwischen dem ersten und zweiten Teil der logischen Untersuchungen Edmund Husserls.'

[10] See above 131 note 7, 171, 189, 254.

Now the question can be raised why the six investigations, which were to clarify logic, give analyses of subjective consciousness. Do we not, in fact, find in them a first beginning of a constitutive phenomenology?

PARAGRAPH THREE. THE PROBLEM OF THE RELATION BETWEEN
THE PROLEGOMENA AND THE SIX INVESTIGATIONS

I. The Problem

With this question we have arrived at the famous problem of the relation between the first and second volumes of the German edition of LU. Even since the appearance of LU, this relation has been a problem and a *crux interpretum*. Landgrebe correctly notes that when this work appeared, the apparent contrast between the anti-psychologism of the Prolegomena and the psychological analyses of the six investigations was regarded by Husserl's critics as a stumbling block. In general, the six investigations were seen as a relapse into psychologism.[1] What accounts for this impression? It was recognized that in the Prolegomena, Husserl had defended the ideality of meanings with all his strength. He argued that logic, as the science of these meanings, is an ideal science, and launched his devastating attack on psychologism, which regards the study of correct presentations and judgments as a subdivision of psychology. In the second volume, which was announced by Husserl at the end of the Prolegomena and published a year later, a philosophical clarification of pure logic was to be given. In the introduction to this second volume, Husserl spoke of "laying an epistemological foundation for pure logic," of "preparatory studies to make possible a formal logic," and of studies "toward an epistemological clarification and future construction of logic."[2]

A start on the construction of a pure logic, for whose necessity Husserl had pleaded in the Prolegomena, was now generally awaited. But analyses of the kind that could serve in the building up of this ideal science are to be found only in the first four investigations. The remaining two investigations, which together exceed the first four in length, are made up merely of psychological analyses. They deal with

[1] L. Landgrebe, *Der Weg der Phänomenologie* 9, 18. See also my article 'Das Verhältnis zwischen dem ersten und zweiten Teil der Logischen Untersuchungen Edmund Husserls.'
[2] I 254; II 3, 5, 16 (ed. 1).

the intentionality of consciousness and discuss its many forms. In the first chapter of Part II, I have given an impression of the wealth of analyses of consciousness which these investigations embrace. In place of a pure logic as an eidetic science, thus, there followed a psychology. And did Husserl himself not characterize these "Investigations Toward a Phenomenology and Theory of Knowledge," as the second volume is entitled, as a "descriptive psychology"? Is psychology, then, the science in which pure logic must be founded? This was regarded as one of the many paradoxes in which the work of Husserl abounds: the thinker who seeks to cut every tie between logic and psychology still wants to found logic in an analysis of consciousness.[3]

The result of this "paradox" was that Husserl more or less fell out of favor with both camps. The idealists, whose side he had chosen in the Prolegomena, saw in the six investigations a relapse into psychologism. The proponents of psychologism, who had been attacked in the Prolegomena, discovered to their surprise that in the six investigations, psychology again appears on the stage as the foundation for logic – albeit in their eyes a poor Scholastic psychology (so-called analyses of words instead of empirical investigations). This misunderstanding, like many other so-called paradoxes in Husserl's work,[4] is the result of careless reading (in this case, manifested by a non-differentiated use of the term 'psychologism'). Any hypothesis in this direction is unworthy of a thinker like Husserl. He himself rightly says of these critics: "That one and the same author who in the first volume manifested an acuity which they praised highly should seek his salvation in open and simply childish contradictions in the second they do not see as mistaken."[5] He complaints that the idealists read the second volume poorly and

[3] See, for example, F.H. Heinemann: "Here arises the first paradox of his teaching. On the one hand he rejects psychology as the basis of logic and stresses the autonomous ideal character of logic, on the other hand he holds that meaning of logical propositions can only be revealed by going back to the subject, i.e. to those acts of our consciousness in which this meaning is 'constituted.' To do this, he stresses, is the task of phenomenology, but not of psychology. But what is the difference between the two? In spite of Husserl's strong anti-psychological bias, his phenomenology often appears to be nothing more than a specific sort of psychology, very similar to Kant's transcendental psychology and to Brentano's 'intentional' psychology," *Existentialism and the Modern Predicament*, London, 1958, 49. See also P. Thévenaz, 'Qu'est-ce que la phénoménologie?,' 21; Heidegger, too, declares that he did not understand the relation between the Prolegomena and the six investigations, *Zur Sache des Denkens*, 83.

[4] For example, the paradox that Husserl brought about a turn toward realism and yet wound up in idealism himself.

[5] Entwurf 115.

hastily, and really did not take it seriously. This was contrary to Husserl's intentions, for he regarded the fifth and sixth investigations, with their analyses of consciousness, as the most important of all.[6] In Chapter 4 we saw that a great deal of misunderstanding could have been avoided if the distinction between the two kinds of psychology (i.e. empirical and descriptive) had been taken into account properly. It is exactly the supposed "scholastic" character of these analyses that should have put the critics on the right track. All that we can rightly reproach Husserl for is not laying sufficient emphasis on the eidetic character of his analyses. Even though he himself called his investigations "descriptive psychology," they were nevertheless de facto "eidetic analyses," as he himself rightly remarked in Entwurf.[7]

As I see it, the question of the relation between the Prolegomena and the six investigations still remains unresolved. In general it is realized – in part because of Husserl's own testimony on this point – that there can be no talk of a relapse into psychologism. But this does not mean that clarity about the relation between the Prolegomena and the six investigations now exists. What is the nature of the positive relation that apparently exists between pure logic and descriptive psychology? At present a solution is usually sought in an anachonistic interpretation which is equally unacceptable, on my view. Attempts are made to understand the subjective investigations on the basis of Husserl's later work, particularly FTL. This interpretation has been generally accepted because Husserl himself, with his assistants Fink and Landgrebe, led the way in promoting it. The analysis of consciousness is seen as a revelation of subjective acts in which the ideal entities of logic are constituted.[8] As I see it, it is because of this anachronistic in-

---

[6] Entwurf 112, 323, 332.

[7] See above 207, 274, 284.

[8] See Landgrebe op. cit. 9: "Looking back thirty years later, Husserl in his FTL gave it [i.e. the question of the relation between the Prolegomena and the six investigations] the definitive interpretation and thereby closed the discussion of this question once and for all." Fink, too, in his well-known article in *Kantstudien* (1933), interprets LU on the basis of Husserl's later transcendental idealism, albeit in a more cautious manner than Landgrebe. In LU he already sees "beginning" and in latent form "the phenomenologica-*constitutive* problem of ideal objects." He writes: "For after the naive-thematic attitude toward the formations (*Gebilde*) of pure logic in the first volume, the objectivity of the logical formations already becomes a problem in the second volume; the 'correlative' approach to subjective experiences already lays claim to the dignity of a philosophical grounding of pure logic" 329 and 329 note 1, see also 321, 325. LU is also interpreted in this spirit in Fink's article in the *Philosophen-Lexikon* of Ziegenfuss. The inner unity lies in the "correlative manner of consideration." The Prolegomena establishes the objec-

terpretation, which finds no support in LU, that there has been so little progress in solving this problem. In fact, it still awaits a solution. In what follows I will first give a positive explication of my own interpretation and will then confront it with the currently accepted interpretation.

II. Pure Logic and Descriptive Psychology

In what follows I will defend the thesis that the pure logic of the Prolegomena – *as far as its fundamental concepts are concerned* – is nothing but a subdivision of descriptive (implicitly eidetic) psychology. This is the reason why psychology can describe and clarify the fundamental concepts of logic. Thus the Prolegomena and the six investigations are concerned with the same fundamental concepts. These concepts, on which all of pure logic rests, are the so-called categories. In the Prolegomena Husserl defends the ideal character of these categories, and in the six investigations he describes them further.

On my view, it is possible to describe the relation between the Prolegomena and the six investigations in such a way that their unity and the coherence between them becomes visible. What was established in the preceding chapters gives us the premises for such an undertaking. It appears to be unnecessary to postulate contradictions, tensions and paradoxes. Here I will briefly sketch the arguments that led to this conclusion. The links in the chain of reasoning are the following.

(*A*) In Chapter 4 it became apparent that pure logic is a science concerning itself with ideal meanings, more specifically, with the formal aspects of these meanings, i.e. the so-called meaning categories. The ideal laws of logic are founded in these ideal categorial forms. They are purely analytic laws that determine the validity of thought independently of the content (the "stuff") of thought.[9]

(*B*) Ideal meanings, furthermore, are related to individual acts of meaning as eidos to fact. A proper interpretation of this relation gives us the key, as it were, to the solution of our problem. This is why I devoted so much attention to it in Chapter 3. The ideal meaning is not an objective correlate of the act of meaning but its idea. *It is the act itself – but then "ideally apprehended."* We must not allow ourselves to be

---

tivity of logical entities, while the second volume represents the "recourse to the subjective sources from which the logical formations arise . . . ." Every a priori is referred back to "the primordial field of all a prioris," i.e. pure consciousness 570ff.

[9] See above 154, 171 and 276.

misled here by the term 'content.' The content in question is not a content over against consciousness, such as the later "noema," but the eidos of the conscious act. It is the essence of the act.[10]

The ideal meaning-*category* is the eidos of the "form" of the act. Thus it is the eidos of the categorial act – especially of the aspects that Husserl distinguishes from the "stuff" or "terms" and calls "form."[11]

(C) The ideal meaning is the essence of the acts of meaning (whether they be significative or perceptual). The essence of the acts is studied by descriptive psychology. Thus the fundamental concepts of logic are "at home" in descriptive psychology; they find their "Heimat" there, as Husserl says elsewhere. What logic – because of its special interests – studies is an isolated way is here re-inserted into the broad connections of consciousness.[12] The categories of meaning are the essences of a certain group of acts.

(D) In LU, origin means "denotatum" (*Begriffsgegenstand*). Thus, when Husserl seeks to clarify the origin of fundamental logical concepts, he must analyze the essence of categorial acts. Naturally, such an analysis is at home in descriptive psychology.

(E) Finally, I could raise the question with which Paragraph 2 ended: if the analysis is eidetic in characters, why is the subjective individual consciousness involved? Husserl himself raises this question in the introduction to the second volume of the German edition, and gives the following answer. What is at issue in logic, he says, is the idea, the logical judgment – and not the psychological judgment in which the idea is realized as in an "instance." Thus, although the goal is ideal analysis, phenomenological analysis is nevertheless indispensable – and that because the logical or ideal meaning is only given to us in subjective realizations: "they are given, so to speak, as embedded in concrete psychical experiences."[13] The answer that Husserl gives is in agreement with his theory of abstraction: we cannot describe an essence

---

[10] See above 253.

[11] See above 251f.

[12] Id I 276. Phenomenology investigates the a priori of logic together with all the other a prioris of consciousness. Thereby it is again "embedded" in the broader connections, 278. In this way, the morphology of logic (pure grammar) is rescued from isolation. In Ideen I the clarification of "formal reason" is placed within the broad framework of a universal phenomenology of reason, 304ff. What the logician studies in isolation can only be comprehended in the broader connections of consciousness (for example, on logical principles compare LU III 113 and Id I 301). In Entwurf, Husserl characterizes the logic of Meinong, from whom he distantiates himself, as "homeless," 322.

[13] II 4, see also III, 189 and A. Reinach, 'Ueber Phänomenologie,' 381f.

without the help of an "instance" or example. To use the Kantian formula again, knowledge of essences does not arise from the experience of something individual, but it does begin with it. Because of this "beginning," a psychological analysis is necessary.

My conclusion that the fundamental concepts of logic form a subdivision of the arsenal of concepts of eidetic descriptive psychology is demonstrated *in concreto* in a particularly clear manner in the final paragraphs of the sixth investigation, which should be regarded as the high point of LU and are in fact so regarded by Husserl.[14] There he shows that the laws of genuine thought which function as norms for non-genuine thought are based on categorial intuitions, that is to say, on the essence of categorial intuitions.[15] Insight into a law of thought comes about in abstraction directed toward a certain categorial perception. I then have insight as to what categorial intuition is possible at all and what connections can eventually come about as ideal possibilities. Merely significative or non-genuine thought must subject itself to these possibilities as norms.[16] It is a universal law that whatever is eidetically impossible is also impossible in reality. The laws of ontologies delimit certain actual possibilities. In the same way, the laws of categorial intuition delimit the individual thought-acts which are possible or valid in formal respects.

The laws of formal logic, then, are nothing but a particular group of

[14] I (ed. 2) XVI; III, IV. In the introduction to the six investigations, Husserl makes it clear that all the analyses of acts to follow culminate in the description of categorial acts. Compared with this description, everything else is preparatory work, II 15; see also Id I 258 note 2.

[15] "The laws are grounded ... in the purely specific character of certain acts," III 197. The doctrine of the valid forms is a "general doctrine of the pure forms of the intuitions of states of affairs," III 193. The laws of "genuine thought" are "laws of categorial intuitions in virtue of their purely categorial forms," III 191. These laws can be used as norms for non-genuine, non-intuitive, significative thought. They delimit "the purely ideally founded possibilities or impossibilities of the adequation of variously formed acts of non-genuine thought in relation to corresponding acts of genuine thought" III 199.

[16] The passage corresponding to III 189 in the first edition reads as follows: "To gain insight into these laws, therefore, we need not actually carry out a categorial intuition: any categorial imagination which puts before our eyes the possibility of the categorial complex in question would suffice. In the generalizing abstraction of the total complex possibility, unitary intuitive 'insight' into the law is achieved; and this insight has, in the sense of our doctrine, the character of an adequate general perception. The general object, which is itself given in it, is the categorial law." This law, which determines that a certain categorial synthesis can be carried out, at the same time says that the complex object of the act is possible. This is why a significative synthesis in agreement with it can lay claim to "objectivity" or truth.

eidetic psychological laws. This insight enables us to understand Husserl's declaration in Entwurf that the real refutation of psychologism lay in the eidetic character of descriptive psychology. "The whole refutation of psychologism" is based on this, that the analyzes in LU "be taken as eidetic analyses, thus as apodictic, evident analyses of ideas."[17]

If this is the case, then the question arises: what is the difference between pure logic and descriptive psychology (or philosophy)? The difference lies on the one hand in the method and on the other hand in the direction of interest. As far as the latter is concerned, logic in a certain sense proceeds uncritically from some fundamental concepts or categories of meaning. On the basis of these concepts, it establishes certain axioms and then concerns itself exclusively with the purely analytical consequences of these axioms. In long, drawn-out *deductive* analyses, all the implications and complications of these forms are worked out. Thus, in a purely mathematical way, there arises a formal theory comparable in all respects to a purely mathematical theory. Husserl calls the mathematician an "ingenious technician" or "constructor."[18]

The philosopher, by contrast, is interested exclusively in *fundamental concepts*, more specifically, in their basis in intuitive abstraction. He seeks to clarify and "understand" the basic forms of logic; his interest is epistemological. He analyses the origin in eidetic analyses of categorial acts. Thus the philosopher concerns himself with the starting point for formal theory, with the basis of deductive theory. The analysis is not deductive but morphological.[19]

III. Some Critical Observations

I now propose to deal with the question whether we should follow the lead of Husserl's later interpretations of himself as we seek to understand LU. This problem already arose when we saw that Husserl tries to interpret PA as a phenomenological-constitutive investigation.[20] Later in his career, Husserl also offered various self-interpretations of LU and of the relation between the Prolegomena and

---

[17] Entwurf 329.
[18] I 253; see above 208.
[19] See also Id I 278; see below 453.
[20] See above 26, 119.

the six investigations.[21] These self-interpretations naturally exercised a great influence – all the more, as Fink observes, because the relation between the two parts of LU originally remained hidden from Husserl's contemporaries.[22] Landgrebe maintains that in FTL, Husserl provided the definitive interpretation "and thereby closed the discussion of this question once and for all," I cannot agree with this judgment. The purpose of my observations here is to open up this discussion again. Perhaps greater historical distance will make it possible to do justice both to Husserl's later intentions and to what determined them historically.

The view that Husserl proposes in his later works is, of course, significant and revelatory with respect to his own view of his past and especially for an understanding of his later ideas. Thus we can well see why his assistants Landgrebe and Fink, who had a hard time setting off Husserl's later philosophy against the interpretation of the so-called "realist ontologists," promoted this interpretation. Thereby they wanted to show that the heart of the transcendental problematics was already present in LU, and that Husserl's later turn toward transcendental idealism did not signify a denial of his own "realist" past, as the members of the early Husserl school generally saw it. I agree with the view that the philosophy of LU naturally leads to transcendental idealism, and I hope to demonstrate this later. But this does not mean that Husserl's early work must now be raised to the transcendental level. However important the view promoted by Husserl, Fink and Landgrebe may be for achieving insight into the systematics of Husserl's "later philosophy," it is unacceptable for the historian. It is my view that insight into the later philosophy will be hindered rather than furthered by such anachronistic interpretations of the earlier philosophy. If Husserl's philosophy is to be understood on the basis of its genesis, we must not allow ourselves to be led by a conception that precludes insight into this development by projecting a later standpoint into the earlier works. We have already seen that rejecting Husserl's self-interpretation of PA opens new perspectives on the development of such central themes as constitution and the intuition of essences.

Let us listen to some representatives of the currently accepted interpretation. Alwin Diemer says in his chapter on Husserl's develop-

---

[21] Especially in FTL 135ff, 153ff; PP 20ff and the article in the Philosophen-Lexikon of Ziegenfuss; compare also Id I 320ff and CM 94.

[22] Ziegenfuss 570.

ment that PA is not concerned with the description of numbers and other logical entities (*Gebilde*). "His investigations are always *analyses of origins*, that is, intentional analyses, which begin with intentional formations – here of a higher order – and inquire back into this constituting production of consciousness." As Diemer sees it, the formulation of the problem in LU can be understood on this basis, and the so-called discrepancy between the Prolegomena and the six investigations can be recognised as a misconception. "The point of departure here is the following: the intentional analysis demands for its recourse to consciousness a priori clarification of the 'clues' with which we begin in inquiring back." After the objectivity of the logical entities is established in the Prolegomena, the six investigations follow, in which, "on the basis of the respective intentional logical productions, we can inquire back into the 'logical acts' of transcendental subjectivity."[23]

Joseph Kockelmans also allows his interpretation to be led by Husserl's later view of LU. In the Prolegomena, the ideality of logical and mathematical entities is defended. In the six investigations, the typical correlation that exist between the "ideal objects of pure logic and the subjective experiences in which they are constituted" is explained. What is in need of explanation is how these entities are given to consciousness. The task of phenomenology is to describe the psychical activities in which these entities are constituted. It was not Husserl's intention to separate pure logic entirely from psychology, as many have maintained. "The impossibility of this position is precisely the main point brought home by the second part of the *Logische Untersuchungen*. In *Phänomenologische Psychologie* Husserl says that the most fundamental problem of the *Logische Untersuchungen* consisted in the question of how the hidden psychic experiences which are in mutual relationships with the ideal entities of formal logic manifest themselves; and, in particular, how these experiences can come about as corresponding and completely determined 'achievements' in such a way that the knowing subject is able consciously to grasp these ideal

---

[23] A. Diemer, *Edmund Husserl, Versuch einer systematischen Darstellung seiner Phänomenologie,* 59. The same interpretation is given by J.M. Broekman, *Phänomenologie und Egologie,* 12, 24. See also R. Sokolowski, *The formation of Husserls concept of constitution,* 38, 168; E. Levinas, *En découvrant l'existence avec Husserl et Heidegger,* 128; see also above 267 note 39; E. Tugendhat, *Der Wahrheitsbegriff bei Husserl und Heidegger,* 16.

entities in a knowledge which, at least in principle, is genuinely evident."²⁴

It is striking that neither of these authors appeals to the *only authority in this question*, i.e. *the text of LU itself*, in defense of his interpretation. When we consult the text, it becomes apparent that these interpretations are far removed from it. Is it really Husserl's intention that the ideal object serve as a "clue" for inquiring back into the "productions" of transcendental consciousness (Diemer)? What Husserl says about the analysis of origins in the Prolegomena is the following. Pure logic develops the implications of certain fundamental concepts or categories. The origin of these concepts must now be established. The question is not one of explaining their genetic origin but rather of "a logical origin or – if we prefer to rule out unsuitable talk of origins, which is bred in confusion – we are concerned with *insight into the essence* of the concepts involved, looking methodologically to the fixing of unambiguous, sharply defined verbal meanings."²⁵ The analysis of origins, then, is simply an analysis of the concepts used by logic, via an analysis of the "denotatum" (*Begriffsgegenstand*), which is in this case the essence. Husserl says exactly this in the introduction to the six investigations. Because such concepts of logic as "presentation" and "judgment" are so ambiguous, we must check them against the "things themselves," i.e. the essence of these acts (for which, as we saw, we need the acts themselves as examples). The purpose of the analysis is "to give fixed meanings to all fundamental logical concepts."²⁶ On the necessity of describing the psychical activities that correspond to ideal entities and constitute them (Kockelmans), we find not a word.

The same anachronistic interpretation is the background of the so-called spiral theory of Spiegelberg.²⁷ In PA, according to Spiegelberg, Husserl begins with a description of subjective phenomena. In the Prolegomena, an objectivistic pure logic follows as a reaction. Then there is another turn toward the subject as the source of objective entities. The six investigations represent "a descriptive study of the

---

²⁴ J. J. Kockelmans, *Edmund Husserl's Phenomenological Psychology: A Historico-Critical Study*, tr. Bernd Jager, 90f.

²⁵ I 244 (ed. 1). In the second edition 'logical' has been replaced by 'phenomenological.'

²⁶ II 6 (ed. 1).

²⁷ Spiegelberg, The Phenomenological Movement, 102f, see also 74. Such a spiral theory was defended earlier by H. J. Pos in 'Descartes and Husserl' 23–38 and in his lecture 'Valeur et limites de la Phénoménologie' 33–52.

processes in which the ideal entities studied in pure logic are presented."
It is a description "of the ideal types of logical experience corresponding to the ideal logical laws." In this way we are in a position to justify
epistemologically our knowledge of logical objects. He then continues:
"The relationship between pure logic and phenomenology, understood
as the study of the experience corresponding to the logical entities,
illustrates an insight which pervades the whole of Husserl's work . . .
the insight that there is a parallelism between the structure of the
subjective act and of its objective referent. This parallelism forms the
basis for a correlative investigation under which both aspects of any
phenomenon are to be studied and described in conjunction. . . . This is
what Husserl later on came to call the parallelism between the 'noetic'
(act) and the 'noematic' (content)." Thus Spiegelberg also sees in the
descriptive psychology of the six investigations a return to the subject, a
description of the acts that are correlated with ideal objects, as noeses
are correlated with noemata.

In general it can be said that these interpretations proceed from two
incorrect presuppositions.

(A) They proceed from a view of ideal meanings inspired by
Husserl's FTL. But the concept of "noematic meaning" in the sense of
objective concept or judgment is not present in LU.[28] In FTL, this
noema, which is also spoken of as "ideal," is the identical over against
the many acts that intend it. When Husserl speaks in LU of one
meaning over against the many acts, he means not this noema but the
ideal meaning in the sense of idea. It does not stand "over against"
consciousness as the noema does. The relation between the ideal
meaning and the subjective act is not comparable to that between the
noema and the many noeses, and thus the former relation is not suitable
for "correlative analysis." The ideal meaning is the eidos of the act of
meaning; it is a superstructure (universal *supra rem*). The relation is

[28] See above 171, 254. Illustrative of the absence of the concept of noematic meaning
in LU is the use of the term 'noetic,' I, 111, 237ff. Husserl there speaks of noetic logic. This is
not the subjective correlate of noematic logic, as in Ideen I. The term 'noetic' refers to the
functions of subjective consciousness, to which the ideal law of the logical "content" are
applied (see 218, 258 and 277, note 12). The relation of ideal meaning to noetic
consciousness is not that of noema to noesis but that of eidetic structure to actual
subjective consciousness. These subjective functions as concretizations of ideal standards
are also called ideal conditions for knowledge, for they participate in the normative
power of the ideal objective laws (they function as *norma normata*). As such, they are
distinguished by Husserl from the causal or "real" (*real*) conditions for knowledge (see
above 224).

that of eidos to fact; it is comparable to that of "redness" to the individual red thing.

(*B*) If there is no noematic meaning, there is naturally no place for a subjective analysis that discloses the acts in which noemata are constituted. Furthermore, such an analysis would be possible – without falling into a new form of psychologism – only on the basis of transcendental idealism, which is not present in LU! When Husserl speaks of the analysis of origins, he does not mean such a constitutive analysis. An analysis of an origin is an analysis of the essence from which the concept is abstracted, of the "denotatum" (*Begriffs-gegenstand*). In this case, the essence is the ideal meaning, particularly its formal aspects.

The currently accepted interpretation falls with these two premises. The descriptive psychological analysis undertaken in the six investigations is not a return to the subject, to the subjective correlates of logical entities, but a *description of the logical entities themselves*. This clarification comes about by drawing the individual "realization" (the concrete individualization) of the idea into the description. These "realizations" (the individual acts of meaning) function as examples in eidetic analysis. In the transition from the Prolegomena to the six investigations, then, there is no alteration of focus or change of attitude. In both parts of LU, Husserl is interested in *the same* logical structures. In the Prolegomena he defends their ideality, and in the six investigations these structures are further described and clarified. Thus the two parts forms a solid unity. The first part of LU is rightly called "Prolegomena" in the sense that it is only in the second part that the actual philosophical task can be undertaken. As Husserl had learned from Brentano, a descriptive psychological clarification of the fundamental logical concepts is the real task of philosophy. But this analysis

---

[29] That it was to the second part of LU that Husserl looked for the definitive refutation of psychologism rather than to the first is also apparent from a letter he wrote to Meinong on August 27, 1900, when the manuscript was still at the printer's; "Yet I now hope that the second part will provide the proof that my struggle against psychologism is not an empty struggle about principles, a struggle that disputes about things superficially, but that it rests on an earnest elaboration of a phenomenology of cognitive experiences," *Philosophenbriefe, Aus der wissenschaftlichen Korrespondenz von Alexius Meinong*, 102. The end of this sentence makes it apparent that Husserl looked especially to the sixth investigation for the refutation of psychologism. Twenty years later, in the foreword to the second edition, he confirms this. The radical conquest of psychologism takes place in this investigation's chapter on the laws of genuine and non-genuine thought. Husserl rightly complains about the superficial reading of this chapter, which led to the

ran into difficulties with regard to the founding of these concepts. Therefore the clarification had to be preceded by an earlier inquiry that would establish the ideal character of this foundation. Only then could Husserl begin with the task he had actually set for himself. It probably never occurred to him as he was thinking out LU that there could be so much misunderstanding and strife about the relation between its two parts. [29]

"grotesque reproach" that he had lapsed into psychologism in the second part of LU III, V. The chapter in question is nothing other than a piece of eidetic psychology about categorial acts. Therefore Husserl could also say in Entwurf (as we have seen) that the whole refutation of psychologism lay in the eidetic character of descriptive psychology. The Prolegomena really does nothing more than demonstrate the absurd consequences of psychologism. If Husserl had done this, we could indeed say that the struggle against psychologism was an "empty struggle about principles," as he put it in the letter to Meinong. The second part of LU gives the positive theory, in the form of a most "earnest elaboration of a phenomenology of cognitive experience."

CHAPTER SIX

CONCLUSION

PARAGRAPH ONE. PHENOMENOLOGY AS DESCRIPTIVE EIDETIC
PSYCHOLOGY

In characterizing the second period in Husserl's thought, the first thing
that must be established is that he still sees the task of philosophy
entirely within the framework of the descriptive psychological analysis
of origins, as he had learned it from Brentano. This form of analysis is
now applied not to arithmetic but to pure logic. The extensive analyses
in the six investigations are undertaken for the sake of the clarification
of pure logic. All forms of presentation and judgment must be
investigated in a descriptive psychological manner.

Meanwhile, this analysis has been placed within a new methodological framework which is bound up with Husserl's most important
discovery, i.e. the new concept of intentionality. Thereby the intentional object receives an entirely different status: it is no longer
immanent but transcendent. Nevertheless, it still belongs to the domain
of phenomenology, even though we noted many hesitations in this
regard. The new concept of intentionality is also the root of the
phenomenological reduction, which we encounter here for the first time
– albeit not as a reflective methodological meditation but as a method in
use. The transcendently interpreted object is a noema or sense which is
not lost when existence is suspended or disconnected. The epoché here
has the character of a psychological reduction; it is a methodological
limitation to the psychical sphere.

The second important change is Husserl's new concept of abstraction
and the birth of the concept of "intuition of essences." From this point
on, the a priori sciences are ideal sciences. Retaining the intuitionist
principle, Husserl now succeeds in breaking through to a satisfying
founding of the a priori sciences. Not only the deductive mathematical

sciences but also descriptive psychology are ideal sciences of this sort. Only later did Husserl achieve greater methodological clarity about the typical, morphological character of ideal analysis in the latter sciences. Nonetheless, psychological analysis already functions fully as eidetic analysis in LU. Thus Husserl's philosophy at the time of LU could also be characterized as descriptive eidetic psychology.

PARAGRAPH TWO. FORMS OF PSYCHOLOGISM

With regard to the six forms of psychologism, I am now in a position to affirm the following.

Husserl has overcome the second and third forms of psychologism insofar as he sees the content of the act as a transcendent object and now also accepts a transcendent correlate in the case of acts of a higher order. In this connection, we often hear talk of the "realism" of LU. We have seen that we must be careful with this term. This realism cannot be derived from Husserl's doctrine of transcendent perception. When I speak of realism despite this reservation, I do so in connection with the framework within which this descriptive psychology stands. It is a separate, isolated sphere presupposing a world within which it forms a separate region. We have seen that this realism brings Husserl to an impasse in his theory of knowledge. The phenomenological reduction, in the psychological form in which it appears here, can almost be seen as an answer born of desperation, and thus as something provisional in character.

Husserl has definitively overcome the fifth form of psychologism as well, for his sharp distinction between the psychological concept and the logical concept enables him to develop a logic not based on psychical facts. His thinking with regard to the a priori problem achieves a certain completion in the doctrine of the intuition of essences. Husserl never denied his eidetics. In this sense, his Prolegomena can be read as pro-legomena to the whole of his later work. What Husserl later brings forward with regard to these problems can be viewed as specification, extension and reinterpretation.[1]

---

[1] We find a specification in the doctrine of eidetic variation in fantasy, PP 72ff (that fantasy can serve as basis is already apparent from LU III 164, 189, 195) and in the distinguishing of "types" of ideas, I (ed. 2), XV. Furthermore, a very important specification is the determination of essences as material categories, see above 260. The distinction between the noetic idea and the noematic idea, see below 445, is an extension of the doctrine of essences. The most fundamental change is the reinterpretation of ideal

The sixth form of psychologism is closely bound up with the impasse in theory of knowledge and the problematics of the two kinds of methods. I have shown in Chapter 2 that Husserl overcomes the naturalizing of ideas but not the naturalizing of consciousness. Therefore the phenomenological sphere remained ultimately embedded in a naturalistically interpreted world governed by causal relations. In this regard, Husserl did not – in essence – get beyond Brentano. It defies comprehension how the phenomenological sphere can be subject to both ideal norms and natural causality. Naturalism makes not only the founding of ideal norms but also the normative effect of these laws impossible. This "idealism" with regard to ideal laws must be complemented by an "idealism" with regard to consciousness. Husserl takes this step in 1908: he sees through the "natural world" of positivism as a prejudice of the natural attitude and founds all of reality in transcendental consciousness. The phenomenological sphere is then no longer *a* region but becomes the source of all being, the primordial region.

But in LU we do not yet find anything of this. Husserl himself spoke of LU in this context as a "breakthrough work, and thus not an end but a beginning." By breakthrough he then means a breakthrough to transcendental idealism.[2] I can agree with Husserl here insofar as the problematics of LU does call for a more radical solution, and insofar as a radicalizing of the method of descriptive psychology will give Husserl the solution. At the time of LU, there was a tension in Husserl between a phenomenological ontology and a positivistic, naturalistic ontology. Later he realized that he would only be able to overcome the impasse in his theory of knowledge and the dualistic view of the relation between the natural sciences and the mental sciences (*Geisteswissenschaften*) by way of a radical revision of ontology in a phenomenological direction. This was brought about in the transcendental reduction, which reveals consciousness to be the ground and basis of all reality and ideality. Husserl saw this as a definitive overcoming of psychologism in the sense of transcendental psychologism, i.e. the psychologism that naturalizes consciousness by conceiving of it as part of the world.[3]

entities in transcendental idealism, see below 487ff. After 1908, the most important opposition is no longer between ideality and reality but between the transcendental attitude and the natural attitude (compare LU I 6, 145, 170 with Id I 115 on the metabasis *eis allo genos*; and LU I 99, 188; II 141 with Id I 76 on the heterogeneity of being).

[2] LU I (ed. 2), VIII: Entwurf 110, 117, 124, 330, 338.

[3] FTL 136, 221ff; see below 396 and 458.

FROM DESCRIPTIVE PSYCHOLOGY TO TRANSCENDENTAL PHENOMENOLOGY

INTRODUCTION

Husserl's little book *The Idea of Phenomenology*, which appeared in 1947 as the first work drawn from his *Nachlass*, has rightly attracted a great deal of attention. It is of particular significance for any attempt to gain an understanding of his development, for it is an important source for our knowledge of the period 1901 to 1910.[1] The book includes five "lectures" delivered by Husserl under this title from April 26 to May 2 of 1907. These lectures were an introduction to a broader cycle of addresses which Husserl characterized as "main parts of a phenomenology and critique of reason."

The publication of these lectures is of particular interest because of the point in time at which they were deliverd. From Husserl's diary we learn that he underwent a severe crisis during the year 1906.[2] Although personal disappointments formed part of the reason for this crisis, it was mainly determined by philosophical difficulties. By 1906 Husserl had reached a critical point in his attempt to achieve a "critique of

---

[1] These five lectures form the introduction to Husserl's lectures on "thing and space," which have since appeared ("Ding und Raum," *Husserliana* XVI). When the reduction is discussed in this context, it still has a psychological flavor 9, 16, 22, 31f, 144, even though the introduction mentions a disconnection of psychological apperception, 139ff.

Since 1966, we can make use of Husserl's *Vorlesungen zur Phänomenologie des inneren Zeitbewusstseins* in the new *Husserliana* edition vol. X. In this edition, the period from which each passage stems is indicated. It appears that the passage on the reduction in Paragraph 1, which is in full agreement with LU, stems from 1905. This would confirm what Fink wrote in the article in Ziegenfuss, namely, that Husserl followed the method of the consistent suspension of transcendencies in these "lectures" of 1905 but did not yet make a principal distinction between psychological and transcendental subjectivity. This also fits in with my own analysis of IP (1907) and with Husserl's statement that the decisive distinction between descriptive psychology and transcendental phenomenology was made in 1908. On the analysis of time, see below 462. PSW 1910, which is on the transcendental level, will be dealt with in my analysis of Ideen I.

[2] VII. Page references in the Intermezzo are to IP unless otherwise indicated.

reason." On September 25 of that year he wrote the following dramatic words in his diary: "First of all, there is the general task which I must carry out for myself if I am to be able to call myself a philosopher. I mean a *critique of reason*, a critique of logical and practical reason, of valuational reason in general. Unless I become clear in general outline about the sense, nature, method, and principal features of a critique of reason, unless I succeeded in thinking through, planning, stating, and grounding a general sketch for this critique, I will really and truly not be able to live. I have felt enough of the torments of unclarity, of wavering to and fro in doubt. I must achieve an inner firmness. I know that this involves something enormous, that great geniuses have failed at it, and if I were to compare myself with them, I would have to despair at the very outset..."

In the five lectures as they have been preserved, we see Husserl busy with his struggle toward a critique of reason. He even calls it a "new beginning" and adds in his diary: "... unfortunately not understood as such by my students and not taken by them as I had hoped. The difficulties, also, were too great and could not be overcome on the first attempt."[3] As Husserl himself admitted, the lack of understanding which he encountered here – and which was to remain tragically characteristic of his relations with his students from that time on – stemmed in part from obscurities on the part of the master. At this point, Husserl's thinking had not yet become ripe. It was not until six more years had passed that he finally published something about his thinking since LU – and then at the insistence of his students. The five lectures give us a look at this process of ripening; they present a transcendental phenomenology in the making. The form of the lectures betrays the fact that they represent an experimental stage. The composition is weak. The argument strays from one subject to another and lapses repeatedly into repetitions. Husserl himself seems to have felt the need of a summarizing overview, for on the evening of May 2 he wrote an account of the "train of thought in the lectures," in which he divided his argument into three stages.[4] This overview will help us a great deal in interpreting IP.

What is especially interesting about IP is that it represents a much more extensive reflection on the methodological starting-point of LU than the latter work itself includes. After Husserl had written LU, he

[3] XI.
[4] 87.

apparently felt a much stronger need to justify (from a methodological standpoint) what was posited in it. Thus, he shed some light on the framework within which LU must be read.

CHAPTER ONE

THE NEGATIVE ASPECT OF THE REDUCTION – THE EPOCHÉ

PARAGRAPH ONE. THE SUSPENSION OF ALL TRANSCENDENCIES

Husserl begins with a clear explication of a problem which in LU remains in the background of the methodological limitation to the sphere of experiences, namely, how we can know something beyond consciousness.[1] How can perception's claim to "give" us something transcendent be justified?[2] If we are to base our knowledge on an absolutely sure foundation, then we must see to it that we find an area in which this problem does not come up. As in LU, Husserl seeks this area in the sphere of experiences, but he now devotes much more attention to the *method* by which this area is to be found. *He speaks here for the first time of "reduction,"* an operation with a negative aspect and a positive aspect. Negatively it is a suspension of all judgments concerned with something transcendent, and positively it is a return to the absolute given. Husserl introduces the term 'epoché' for the negative aspect.

But this does not mean that what the term refers to, i.e. abstaining from judgment about transcendencies, first occurs in 1907! Throughout my analysis of LU, I have made it clear that Husserl *in fact* already applies the method there. But the abstention from judgment had not yet become an explicit object of methodological reflection. Therefore I would point out once again how important it is in assessing Husserl's work to distinguish between what he in fact does and what he claims to be doing. The question whether the phenomenological epoché already appears in LU must be answered as follows: it appears in fact but not in terminology.

Let us first observe how Husserl formulates this negative aspect of the phenomenological reduction. The reduction is the result of the

---

[1] 5.
[2] 36f, 43, 46, 49, 83.

epistemological impasse. Only the genuinely immanent is "beyond question"; I can "make use" of it. "That which is transcendent (not genuinely immanent) I may not use. Therefore I must carry out a *phenomenological reduction: I must exclude all that is transcendently posited.*"³ This means that ". . . everything transcendent (that which is not given to me immanently) is to be assigned the index zero. . . ." This index indicates that ". . . the existence of these transcendencies, whether I believe in them or not, is not here my concern; this is not the place to make judgments about them; they are entirely irrelevant."⁴

This formulation fits in very well with Husserl's procedure in LU. The existence of the transcendent object must be put between brackets – even if the object is posited in "belief." In the latter case, the positing itself is absolutely given, but not what is posited.⁵

PARAGRAPH TWO. THE IMPLICATIONS OF THIS SUSPENSION

All sciences that "make use of a transcendence thesis" are affected by the suspension of the transcendent. The sciences based on the existence of transcendent objectifications which they accept as "given beforehand" must thereby be assigned an "index of questionability." Through the epoché, all sciences become *phenomena* of science.¹ We already encountered this suspension of the sciences in the introduction to LU. In phenomenology, no use may be made of physical or psychological hypotheses about transcendent realities like the "body" and the "mind." The only new element is that Husserl now sees this as a direct consequence of the epoché. All disconnections that flow from the phenomenological principle that only the given is to be accepted are now brought under one heading. This includes the "abstraction" of one's own body, which is implied in the disconnection of all transcendencies.²

Husserl already drew these conclusions in an article of 1903, in a passage that deserves close attention. He himself attached great importance to it and referred to it repeatedly in later writings.³ I cite

---

³ 5, 6.
⁴ 29, 39.
⁵ 50, see above 181.
¹ 6, 24, 36.
² See above 210f.
³ The text in question is from Husserl's 'Bericht über deutsche Schriften zur Logik in den Jahren 1895–1899,' 398ff. Husserl refers to it in PSW 318 note 1 and Id I 2 note 2. In

this passage here because it is of great importance for Husserl's development. It shows us that only a few years after the publication of LU, Husserl had already begun to reflect on his methodological starting-point. In an important respect, he goes beyond LU here, insofar as he rejects "psychological apperception" and therefore also the name 'descriptive psychology.' In this passage of 1903, Husserl calls physics and empirical psychology the sciences of bodily (corporeal) and mental facts respectively. Both sciences proceed from "the world in the ordinary sense before any criticism," i.e. before any "division of facts into corporeal and mental. Both remain uncritical, however much they may modify the content of the original conception of the world. As explanatory sciences, they presuppose the pre-given objectification, whose sense and whose clarification according to its possibility they can do without – as the fact of the great blossoming of these sciences without the assistance of the critique of knowledge shows. Meanwhile, from these pre-critical objectifications – with their divisions between egos and non-egos, between 'one's own' ego and 'other' egos, with their interpretive attributions of immediate data as 'psychical states and activities' in one's own ego, and their interpretive transfer outside the ego of physical things and states, of other persons, experiences, etc. – from such objectifications, I say, arise the difficulties of the metaphysical problem of the possibility of knowledge . . . ."

Thus, conceiving of consciousness as "psychical activities and states" of an empirical person, of one's own ego or some other ego, is seen by Husserl as going beyond the given, as an "interpretation" (*Deutung*). Phenomenology does not deal with the "experiences or classes of experiences of empirical persons, for it knows nothing of persons, of the ego of others, of my experiences and the experiences of others. It raises no questions about such matters and attempts no statements; it forms no hypotheses." Here Husserl speaks for the first time of psychological apperception, by which he means conceiving of the phenomenological sphere as a certain stratum of the psychophysical unity "man." He regards this as a conception that transcends the given and must therefore be suspended.

It is not hard to see that this is indeed a consequence of the phenomenological point of departure. If I am not allowed to presuppose the existence of the body, then I also know nothing of

particular, he expresses regret at having characterized phenomenology as descriptive psychology in the introduction to the second volume of the German edition of LU.

empirical persons – including myself as a unity of mind and body. This means that I may not conceive of consciousness as "psyche," for 'psyche' is Husserl's technical term for a certain stratum of the psycho-physical unity. The term 'psyche' already includes a reference to the body as its bearer. Thus this conception of consciousness as psyche, this doctrine of "psychological apperception," must be excluded. Therefore Husserl now also rejects the term 'descriptive *psycho*-logy.'

Here Husserl certainly carries the consequences of the phenome-nological starting-point farther than in LU. When he speaks in LU of the disconnection or suspension of psychological presuppositions, he means presuppositions about the nature of consciousness, about an ultimate substance behind the appearances, which could serve as a principle to explain the phenomena. Sometimes he also has in mind an interpretation that spatializes consciousness and attributes physical properties to it.[4] At the same time, the body must remain unconsidered. But now, however, the epoché concerns not the body but the de-pendence on the body (and implicitly of all physical reality) of consciousness – thus a characteristic of consciousness itself (its being part of the psycho-physical unity). Also important is what Husserl says about the re-connection of psychological apperception. When we again "connect" (*einfügen*) this apperception, the phenomenological ana-lyses then receive the character of descriptive psychological analyses; they then function as substrata for the theoretical explanations of psychology, of the natural science of mental phenomena." Here we already encounter the first traces of the later "conversion" (*Umwendung*) of transcendental phenomenological analyses into de-scriptive psychological analyses.[5]

In the lectures of 1907, this disconnection or suspension of of psychological apperception is worked out more fully in the context of a criticism of Descartes. Like the Husserl of LU, Descartes had conceived of consciousness as part of the empirical person considered as a psycho-physical unity. The Cartesian ego is in need of a purification. "First, the Cartesian *cogitatio* already requires the phenomenological reduction. The psychological phenomenon in psychological apperception and objectification is not a truly absolute datum. The truly absolute datum is the *pure phenomenon*, that which is reduced."[6] Descartes did not

[4] See above 175.
[5] See below 450ff.
[6] 7.

discover the genuine, pure *cogito*, although he came close to it; "... for Descartes, to discover and to abandon were the same."[7] He confused the pure phenomenon with the psychological phenomenon. He conceived of consciousness as a state of the "experiencing ego, the object, man in time, the thing among things." This consciousness can be the object of a natural scientific psychology, for it is a part of nature. We can, of course, abstract from this in descriptive psychology, but doing so would not detract from the fact that consciousness actually remains part of the "real world." Thus description is also a preparation for explanation. By disconnecting or suspending psychological apperception, we also transcend descriptive psychology. "We finally abandon the standpoint of psychology, even of descriptive psychology."[8]

This criticism of Descartes can also be read as a self-criticism. Husserl admits that this new step is not simple, and that it encounters strong resistance. Our natural inclination is to interpret consciousness in a psychological way. "If I, as a person thinking in a natural way, look at the perception which I am experiencing, then I immediately and almost inevitably apperceive it – that is a fact – in relation to my ego. It stands there as an experience of this experiencing person, as his state ... and integrates itself with this objective time."[9]

PARAGRAPH THREE. CONCLUSIONS

With regard to the negative aspects of the reduction, there are three new developments in 1907. (1) Husserl now uses the terms 'epoché' and 'disconnection' (*Ausschaltung*). He has developed a technical terminology for an operation already applied in LU. (2) He creates more internal unity among the disconnections that flow from the phenomenological starting-point. (3) By far the most important of the new developments is his approach to psychological apperception. I will return to this matter in the third chapter.

---

[7] 10, 43, see also 49 and 75.
[8] 7.
[9] 43; see also 18 and 29.

CHAPTER TWO

THE POSITIVE ASPECT OF THE REDUCTION – THE RESIDUE

PARAGRAPH ONE. CONSCIOUSNESS – REAL IMMANENCE

There is only one area in which the riddle of transcendence does not surface and certain knowledge is possible. We discover this area by applying the "Cartesian method of doubt." Husserl writes: "the being of the *cogitatio*, of the experience, is beyond doubt during the experience and in simple reflection on it. The seeing, direct grasping and having of a *cogitatio* is already a knowing. the *cogitationes* are the first absolute data."[1]

When I attempt to doubt everything, it quickly becomes clear that it is impossible to cast everything into doubt: "in every case of a definite doubt, it is indubitably certain that I have this doubt." This now holds for *every cogitatio*. Whatever the object of my perception, presentation or judgment may be, "as far as the perceiving itself is concerned, it is absolutely clear and certain that I am perceiving this or that, as far as the judgment is concerned, that I am judging of this or that, etc."[2] Thus it appears that doubt is indeed possible with regard to the validity of perception, for example, but *that* I am perceiving is beyond doubt. The experience is given as something "whose being cannot sensibly be doubted."[3] We stand here on an absolute foundation, that is to say, on an absolute given. When we ask ourselves why this knowledge is not subject to doubt, the answer is: because of its immanence. It is a foregone conclusion that the cognitive act can "reach" (*treffen*) an object within consciousness.[4]

Husserl now goes beyond this Cartesian reduction to the immanent, which is already to be found in LU. In the "train of thought" this is

---

[1] 4, 33.
[2] 30.
[3] 31.
[4] 5.

called a "first level" of phenomenology. The result of the first consideration was that only the really immanent, the sphere of *cogitationes*, is given to us. This is the "first level of clarity," as Husserl calls it. But a closer examination will reveal that this first result is not tenable. Husserl even calls it a "fatal mistake."[5] The belief that only the subjective sphere of *cogitationes* is given is a prejudice.

PARAGRAPH TWO. ESSENCES – PURE IMMANENCE

If only the sphere of individual experiences is really given, we immediately face a difficulty: in that case we could make only individual judgments, and no a priori judgments would be possible. We could only say: "This here." Consciousness would form a strictly individual Heraclitean stream.[1] But in the preceding, we have *in fact* already gone beyond this sphere, for we made the a priori judgment of the absolute givenness of an experience.[2] Thus we proceeded implicitly from the givenness of immanent *essences*. Thereby the transcendent returns, for we find no essence *in* the stream.[3] Here we face an impasse. The Cartesian sphere does not get us any further, for with this transcendence, doubt also returns.[4]

At this point Husserl asks why we accept consciousness as given at all. What is the criterion? The criterion is not so much immanence as givenness, the possibility of a "clear and distinct perception." Well then, the intuition of essences satisfies this criterion. Thus it is a *prejudice* not to regard essences as given. "Could a deity, an infinite intellect, do more to lay hold of the essence of redness than to 'see' it as a universal?"[5]

This is an important conclusion, for with the help of the Cartesian criterion, Husserl has now broken out of the Cartesian closed consciousness. The given for him now includes not only that which is immanent in a real sense but also the transcendent, provided that it is given. Thus the suspension of transcendencies no longer means the suspension of all that is transcendent to consciousness; it now means

[5] 36.
[1] 47.
[2] 50.
[3] 8, 25, 56.
[4] 20, 48.
[5] 8, 49, 57, 10, 51, 56.

the disconnection of *whatever is not given*. Thereby the reduction takes on "a more profound determination and a clearer meaning."[6]

This second step into phenomenological meditation can also be seen as a *methodological clarification and justification of the analysis already carried out in LU*. In the first place, Husserl now declares with great emphasis that descriptive psychology is an analysis of essences.[7] Secondly, from the standpoint of the "principle of all principles," it is a prejudice to limit the sphere of the given to what is immanent in the real sense. The (theoretical) standpoint of LU is that of a "beginner." The sphere of the given is conceived of too narrowly. To be absolutely given is not the same as to be really immanent. The immanence of acts must therefore be seen as a special case of immanence in the broader sense, in the sense of "*pure* immanence." All that is given is the "purely immanent."

PARAGRAPH THREE. THE GIVENNESS OF THE NOEMA

I. The Second Extension of the Phenomenological Sphere
We now come to the third level of Husserl's meditation. We have learned that we must accept everything that is itself given. Now the question is how far this sphere of givenness extends. We have already encountered – as a prejudice – the limitation to that which is immanent in the real sense. On the second level, phenomenology appears to be an *eidetic* description of immanent experiences. This looks like a "simple matter," but things are "less pleasant" when we see what is really given. The *cogitationes*, "which we regard as simple data and in no way mysterious, hide all sorts of transcendencies." More specifically, it appears that in a *cogitatio*, e.g. an experience of a sound, "the *appearance and that which appears stand over against each other* – and this *in the midst of pure givenness*, hence in the midst of true immanence."[1] Husserl says here – not without reason – that we are "taken aback." The transcendency that was initially suspended now seems to reappear within the sphere of the given. It is a prejudice that we must limit ourselves to inner perception and to the intuition of essences based upon it. The phenomenological sphere embraces *all* data, and it is

---

[6] 9.
[7] 51, 58. These passages contain some clear criticism directed toward Brentano. See above 266.
[1] 10f, 61.

not to be denied that something transcendent is itself given in perception,[2] even if it does not appear in an adequate way.[3]

As we consider this step taken by Husserl, we must bear in mind the principle by which he was guided, namely, to recognize as given all that shows itself as given. Well then, when we perceive the given in an unprejudiced way, we see that not only subjective experiences (and their essences) but also correlative objects are given. Our theme is *all* self-givenness – thus not only that of acts and essences. When the prejudice that essences fall outside the sphere of the given (of pure immanence) is eliminated, the prejudice that the intentional object is not given is also cleared away.[4] And this intentional object is given in many ways, corresponding to the many modes which consciousness can assume.

Here we face an important moment in Husserl's development. The recognition of this state of affairs had a startling significance for him. Therefore I will let Husserl himself speak at this juncture. After he has established the many forms of intentional "objectivity" (*Gegenständlichkeit*), he goes on to say: "But is this not an absolute marvel? Where does this constitution of objectivities begin, and where does it end? Is it not the case that in every presentation and judgment, a datum is given in a certain sense? Is not every objectivity a datum, and an evident datum, insofar as it is intuited, presented, or thought? In the perception of an external thing, that thing, e.g. a house before our eyes, is said to be perceived. The house is a transcendency, and it forfeits its existence after the phenomenological reduction. The house-appearance, this *cogitatio* emerging and disappearing in the stream of consciousness, is given as actually evident.... But is it not also evident that a house appears in the house-phenomenon, and that it is exactly on this account that we call it a perception of a house? And what appears is not only a house in general but just exactly this house, determined in such-and-such a way and appearing in that determination. Can I not make an evidently true judgment as follows: on the basis of the appearance or in the content of this perception, the house is thus and so, a brick building with a slate roof, etc.?"[5]

Thus we see that after the suspension of the perceived house, not only does an act remain (i.e. the house-perception) but in the act an object

---

[2] 10, 73.
[3] 13.
[4] 57, 60, 62.
[5] 72. See also *Ding und Raum*, 17ff, 30ff.

appears – in this case, a *purified object*. The same thing happens in imagination. What we imagine need not exist. But even if it does not exist, we would still be left not just with an act of imagining but also with an imagined object.[6]

I have quoted Husserl at some length because what we confront here is the birth of the concept of "noema," of the "intended as such," of the "cogitatum qua cogitatum." The noema is that which remains when the existence of the transcendent object is excluded from our consideration. It is not the metaphysical object but the intentional object. It is immanent in the sense of "purely immanent." Here Husserl again uses the old term 'intentional inexistence.'[7]

What is true of the second phase of Husserl's meditation is also true of the third: it can be regarded as a piece of *methodological reflection on what Husserl in fact already does in LU*. That there remains an intentional object after the suspension of existence is an official recognition of a standpoint already adopted in LU. We see again that Husserl's actual analyses outstrip his reflection on his method. Apparently it was painful for him to recognize that the Cartesian starting-point is incorrect for methodological reflection. In the second edition of LU, Husserl revised the introduction to make it agree with the actual content of the book. We wrote that the object "has undergone a change of sense, in virtue of which it now belongs to the sphere of phenomenology."[8] When we disregard extra-mental existence, what remains in addition to the act is the intentional object. It is *extra mentem* in the sense of "purely immanent."

The standpoint that the reduction to the given limits us to what is immanent in the real sense is the standpoint of a "beginner." We must learn to see the phenomena as they are instead of speaking about them "from on high."[9] Then the judgment (*Urteil*) that nothing general is given to us will be recognized as a pre-judice (*Vor-urteil*) that is not based on intuition.[10] This we already learned on the second level of phenomenological reflection. The inclination to allow ourselves to be

---

[6] 14, 69, 72.

[7] 55, 74. Insofar as the noema was recognized, *implicitly* in LU, Husserl says in Krisis 237 (E 234) – rightly – that the "cogitatum qua cogitatum" was first introduced there. Husserl explicitly introduced the noema for the first time in 1904, see Kern, *Husserl und Kant*, 180f.

[8] LU II 11, 397 note 1; II 244.

[9] 5, 7.

[10] 56.

led by prejudices is even stronger in the case of the intentional object. Husserl admits that the extension of the phenomenological sphere cost him more pain here and heaves a sigh: "We are once again led somewhat deeper, and in the depths lie the obscurities, and in the obscurities the problems."[11] Out of faithfulness to the phenomenological principle of "giving free rein to the seeing eye," we must also reject the second prejudice, which limits eidetic analysis to acts. No inclination is more dangerous to seeing cognition than "to think too much, and from these reflections in thought to create supposedly self-evident principles." We also read: "'*Seeing' cognition is that form of reason which sets itself the task of converting the understanding into reason.* The understanding is not to be allowed to interrupt and to insert its unredeemed bank notes among the certified ones.... Thus, as little understanding as possible, but as pure an intuition as possible (*intuitio sine comprehensione*)."[12] It is certainly clear from these revealing quotations that Husserl sees this reflection of phenomenology on itself, this phenomenological awakening to self-awareness on the part of consciousness, as a consequence of the "principle of all principles."

Husserl had already revealed the noema in perception and imagination, but he now goes further: *symbolic thinking also has an intentional object.* "Let us say that without any intuition, I think that 2 times 2 equals 4. Can I doubt that I am thinking this arithmetical proposition, and that what is thought does not concern today's weather, for example? If this is evidently so, is there not something like a datum here? And if we go this far, nothing can prevent us from recognizing that the nonsensical, the completely absurd, is also 'given' in a certain way. A round square does not appear to me in imagination as a dragon appears, nor does it appear in perception as some external thing, but an intentional object is still obviously there. I can describe the phenomenon 'thinking of a round square' in terms of its genuine content, but the round square itself cannot be found there; still, it is evident that it is thought in this mental act, and that roundness and squareness as such are thought in the object so thought, or that the object of this thought is both round and square."[13] here for the first time Husserl uses the concept of significative meaning in the objective sense. In Ideen I, where he distinguishes between noetic and noematic meaning, this is worked out.[14]

[11] 10.

[12] For Husserl, then, understanding and reason are related to one another as thought and intuition or as "signification" and "intuition." See LU III 201. When an empty reference (*Meinung*) is fulfilled by becoming intuition, understanding becomes "reason." See also FTL 16, 25, 143.

[13] 73.

[14] See below 443.

II. *The Correlativity Theme and the Problem of Transcendence*

An important consequence of the incorporation of the intentional object into the phenomenological sphere is that the analysis now becomes correlative. In LU Husserl had already distinguished between two meanings of the term 'phenomenon': it refers on the one hand to the subjective appearance (the act) and on the other hand to the appearing object. Yet the description was directed one-sidedly to the objective phenomena. Now, however, the phenomenology of cognition "is the science of cognitive phenomena in two senses, of cognitions as appearances..., acts of consciousness in which this or that object is presented or is an object of consciousness..., and on the other hand of these objectivities themselves as presenting themselves in this manner."[15] In Part II, I pointed out that this theme of correlativity is potentially present as soon as Husserl begins to regard perception as "sense-giving," for what the object appears as is dependent on the "sense" in which the material of sensation is apprehended.[16]

We can now understand why this theme was not developed explicitly. Husserl was still under the sway of the prejudice that only subjective *cogitationes* are given. This prejudice already caused tensions in LU: there was a tension between the actual analyses and the methodological starting-point. On the one hand, the intentional object was (officially) not part of the phenomenological sphere, but on the other hand, the phenomenological sphere did (unofficially) include it. Now, however, the inner obstacles to the development of correlative analysis are removed. From this point on, the correlative manner of analysis, which has become characteristic of the phenomenological view of consciousness and reality, could occupy the foreground. The "wondrous correlation" between object and consciousness must be subjected to a universal analysis that embraces all forms of consciousness, for to every form of consciousness corresponds a form of objectivity (*Gegenständlichkeit*) suited to it.[17]

Just as he had done in LU, Husserl now opposes the view of consciousness as a uniform seeing, as "a mental inspecting without a character of its own, always one and the same, undifferentiated in itself: the seeing just sees the things (*Sachen*), the things are simply there ... in consciousness, and seeing is simply

[15] X 14, 55. See also LU III 223f.

[16] See above 141, 172.

[17] See 67f, 71 on the correlation between temporal consciousness and the temporal object, and 71, 74 on the consciousness of something general and the general object.

to look at them."[18] Things are not in consciousness as in a vessel or a case but rather constitute themselves in acts, which, in their varied structure, "create objects in a certain way for the ego, insofar as we need appearances of just such a sort and just a construction, so that what is called 'given' lies before us."[19] In another passage Husserl writes that the object is not a thing which is "put into" cognition as into a sack, "as if cognition were a completely empty form, one and the same empty sack in which now this and now that is placed. Instead we see in what is given *that the object is constituted in cognition*, that a number of different basic forms of objectivity are to be distinguished, as well as an equal number of different forms of presentative cognitive acts."[20]

The problem of transcendence can only be solved when this problematic relation is "brought to givenness in a seeing way." Writes Husserl: "What I seek is *clarity*. I want to understand the *possibility* of this reaching (*Treffen*), but that means that I want to be able to see the nature of this reaching. . . ." I must "be able to see the seeing itself."[21] I must not construct any theories about this matter. "A seeing cannot be demonstrated. A blind man who wants to be able to see will not be enabled to do so by scientific demonstrations. Physical and physiological theories about colors yield no seeing clarity about the sense of color like that possessed by those who see."[22] It is characteristic of Husserl's phenomenology of reason that he seeks to describe concretely how the knowing of the many kinds of objects takes place. Thus the analysis of correlation coincides with the phenomenology of reason.[23] Now that the intentional object is also given, such a description is possible. But this does not yet mean that Husserl has essentially transcended the psychological starting-point of LU, for we must not forget that this object is not the thing in itself. It is the intentional object as "inseparable" correlate of consciousness, which remains given even if the real thing does not exist. This means that *the original question is not answered*. Husserl solves the problem by stating it in a different way. "Originally the problem concerned *the relation between subjective psychological experience and the reality in itself grasped therein* – first of all actual reality and then also the mathematical and other sorts of ideal realities. But first we need the insight that the

---

[18] 11f.
[19] 12, 71.
[20] 74f.
[21] 31, 37.
[22] 6, 33, 38.
[23] See below 445.

radical problem must have to do rather with the *relation between knowledge and object*, but in a *reduced* sense...." This is the true problem, and it can be solved in an evident manner.[24]

Here, then, the question immediately arises whether Husserl's thinking on this point is stuck in the same impasse as his thinking in LU. The solution to the epistemological problem offered there is really not so much a solution as an elimination of the problem. The question how the "thing in itself" is to be reached cannot be answered. We draw back to the immanent sphere of experiences and "phenomena claiming validity" (*Geltungsphänomene*). The sphere of the immanent is now – explicitly – seen as broader than the Cartesian sphere of consciousness, but this does not yet mean a principial breakthrough out of a closed consciousness, for the intentional object is not yet the real object. And describing the correlation between this object and consciousness gives us no solution to the question how we can actually know existing reality.

As long as it does not become clear how this originally excluded world can again be integrated in one way or another into the sphere of the given, it will not be apparent how Husserl transcends the problematics of LU. Is this "critique of reason," too, nothing more than a "psychology of reason"? Here I have reached the point in the analysis at which I must devote some attention to the passages in which Husserl does go beyond LU in essential respects.

[24] 7, 75.

CHAPTER THREE

FROM DESCRIPTIVE PSYCHOLOGY TO TRANSCENDENTAL PHENOMENOLOGY

Husserl's lectures of 1907 come chronologically halfway between LU and Ideen I. Their content could also be characterized as intermediate. In large measure, these lectures consist of a reflection on the method of LU. Husserl claimed that they deal with the "final clarification of insights . . . which already dominate my LU," as every "reader of that incomplete and imperfect work who sees more deeply" can establish for himself.[1] On the other hand, new insights are also brought to the fore.

In the final analysis, how Husserl's reduction in its negative and positive aspects is to be interpreted depends on these new insights. We shall see in Part III that the terminology of the reduction is ambiguous and can be conceived of in either a psychological or a transcendental sense.[2] How the suspension is interpreted is determinative here. In LU, the epoché is something of a desperate solution; it testifies to a certain resignation. In Ideen I, Husserl discovers that this interpretation rests on an improper absolutizing of the world. What we suspend in the epoché is not the thing but an absurd interpretation of the thing. The epoché, then, is not a limitation; nothing is lost. Therefore the question is: has Husserl in 1907 already seen that the assumption of a "thing in itself" rests on an absolutizing? The epoché would then be an undoing of this absolutizing, and the thing would recur in the phenomenological sphere in purified form. The same question could be raised with regard to psychological apperception. Has Husserl already seen that this apperception is rooted in the same absolutizing of the thing, and that regarding consciousness as a certain region within a psycho-physical unity therefore represents an unjustified interpretation?

If the answer is yes, then Husserl has reached the watershed between

---

[1] 90f.
[2] See below 429.

descriptive psychology and transcendental phenomenology. There is a subtle boundary between the two, which is crossed when psychological apperception is not just suspended but *seen through*, revealed to be an illusion.

Now, there are clear indications that the answer to our question is yes. The absolute givenness of consciousness guarantees absolute existence.[3] The theory of knowledge therefore opens the possibility of a metaphysics (or ontology) as a theory of absolute being. Does this theory of absolute being also have as its counterpart a theory of relative being, as in Ideen I? Indeed it does, as is apparent from the critical function of epistemology with regard to the sciences. In the natural thought-stance arise "*interpretations* of the being known in the natural sciences, which interpretations are fundamentally mistaken because they contain inner contradictions." Thus materialistic, spiritualistic, dualistic, and psycho-monistic interpretations stand alongside one another. Phenomenology can give a "metaphysical interpretation" (*Auswertung*) of the being known in these sciences.[4] Thereby a metaphysics of nature rises alongside the metaphysics of the mind.[5]

It first became clear in the Fundamental Consideration of Ideen I how this ontology, which represents a reversal of the naturalistic hierarchy of being, is carried through *in concreto*.[6] Via this ontology, the psychological terms of the reduction finally receive their *philosophical* meaning, whereby they are converted into their opposites. It is because Husserl's position in 1907 stands on the boundary between psychology and transcendental phenomenology that it is of such great interest.[7] It gives us an insight into the historical growth of transcendental phenomenology out of psychology. We shall see that this is part of the reason why phenomenological psychology could later serve as a pedagogical preparation for transcendental phenomenology.[8]

[3] 8, 30f. In the lecture on "thing and space" Husserliana XVI 287ff we already find mention of the experiment of world-annihilation. It is not necessary that the world exist; it could well dissolve itself into a "whirl of sensations." The harmony is only a matter of fact; it is an irrational fact. (This lecture is dated August 3, 1907.)

[4] See below 482ff.

[5] 3, 23, 32, 59. See also PP 237 and a text from 1908 included in EP 381ff. This text of a year later speaks of the absolute as the basis of nature.

[6] Compare 23f; here Husserl speaks in a highly critical way of the hierarchy of being, which we already encountered in Brentano.

[7] In Entwurf, Husserl dates the discovery of the difference between rational psychology and transcendental phenomenology as "about the year 1908," 337. Compare I. Kern, *Husserl und Kant*, 31 note 1.

[8] See below 432.

PART THREE

PHILOSOPHY AS TRANSCENDENTAL PHENOMENOLOGY

* Without further indication we quote in part II from LU, in the Intermezzo from IP, and in part III from Id I.

INTRODUCTION

In Part II we saw that the problematics of LU drove Husserl further in the direction of a radical solution – and that in two respects. In epistemology and philosophy of mind, his thought moved along two tracks. The problem caused by this dualism could be overcome only provisionally by means of a methodological abstraction from the realistic and naturalistic standpoint.

In Part III we will move in an opposite direction. By way of an analysis of the Phenomenological Fundamental Consideration of Ideen I, I will show in the first chapter that Husserl broke through to a radical, consistent phenomenological outlook. The analysis and interpretation of this classic text will give us sufficient ground under our feet for the subsequent chapters, in which I will try to show, on the basis of this new view, how radical solutions are given for epistemological problems and for the question of the problematic relation between empirical psychology and descriptive psychology.

AN ANALYSIS OF THE PHENOMENOLOGICAL
FUNDAMENTAL CONSIDERATION

PARAGRAPH ONE. THE INTRODUCTION OF THE
TRANSCENDENTAL EPOCHÉ

Husserl begins his Fundamental Consideration with a sketch of the natural attitude and how it is to be disconnected. The first chapter occupies a special place within the whole. In a few pithy words we are told what the natural attitude is and how it is to be disconnected or suspended. There is no prior statement about the possibility and necessity of such an operation.

A person who lives in the "natural attitude" is directed toward a world. In perception, material things are "simply there" for him; they are present whether he is actually directing his attention toward them or not. The same is true of other persons. Although I myself perceive only a part of the world, I "know" that it is there – a knowledge that has nothing to do with "conceptual thought." I regard it as infinitely extended in space and time. I myself am a member of this world, and I also see other persons as subjects directed toward the same world and belonging to it.

It is characteristic of the natural attitude that it sees the world as "existing," as "reality." Husserl calls this the general positing of the natural attitude.[1]

"*Instead of remaining in this attitude, we now propose to alter it radically,*" he continues. The natural attitude, which is a pre-predicative positing, is to be subjected to an *experiment* of doubt in the Cartesian sense. Such an experiment is a possibility that we may choose freely, because the doubt in question is not real doubt. We are not free to doubt whatever we choose. We can doubt only if our experience gives

[1] 48–53. In part III, all page references without titles are to Ideen I. The pagination of the first edition has been used.

us some occasion for doing so. (We should note here that this represents an important difference between Husserl and Descartes: Husserl does not regard the world as a *dubitandum*.) The *attempt* to doubt, however, is even possible when something is adequately given. Such an attempt brings about a certain cancellation (*Aufhebung*) of the positing, but not in the sense that it is transferred into the opposite of a positing, i.e. a negation. Although it remains what it is, it undergoes a modification. This modification is described as putting the positing "out of action" and, correlatively, as "bracketing out" what is posited. It is already apparent from the way in which Husserl introduces these concepts that the epoché represents something *sui generis*. It does not represent a real doubt, for it is compatible with an unshaken belief in what has been disconnected. Neither is it an attitude of neutrality, the "mere thinking" already analyzed by Brentano.[2]

What, then, is the object of the natural positing that is disconnected in the epoché? With regard to what are we to suspend our judgment? This only becomes clear in the course of the Fundamental Consideration.

PARAGRAPH TWO. PHENOMENOLOGICAL MEDITATION – ITS PROBLEM, GOAL AND METHOD

The second chapter of the Phenomenological Fundamental Consideration bears the title "Consciousness and Natural Reality" and occupies a central place in the Fundamental Consideration. At the end of this chapter, Husserl says that his reflection has reached a climax. All that follows can be regarded as conclusions (the first six paragraphs of Chapter 3), additions (the rest of Chapter 3), and further elaboration (Chapter 4). Later I will discuss the relation of this second chapter and the chapter before it. In the paragraphs that follow, I will analyze the content of this second chapter.

"We have learned to understand the sense of the phenomenological epoché, but by no means what it can do," writes Husserl at the beginning of the second chapter. The problem that concerns us after reading the first chapter is formulated by Husserl as follows: "*What, then, will be left when the whole world is disconnected, including ourselves with our thinking (cogitare)?*"[1] This is indeed a burning problem when

[2] 53–57.
[1] 57.

we recall that the purpose of the epoché is the discovery of a new sphere of being and of a science of this being. In the first chapter Husserl had already written: "Our design is ... just to discover a new scientific domain, such as might be won ... *through the method of bracketing.*" [2] What is characteristic of this operation, which at first glance looks entirely negative, is that it has a positive goal. There must be a sphere of being that remains because it is not affected by this epoché. Thus the epoché is the means to discover this sphere of being, this remainder. In connection with this, Husserl already introduced a *limitation* of the epoché in the first chapter. The suspension must not be universal, for then nothing would be left over. Now, there are great problems contained in this limitation of the epoché, and Husserl rightly begins his second chapter with the remark that it is certainly not yet clear what remains afterward. How can the epoché be limited when Husserl nevertheless states expressly that it applies to the *entire* world, including ourselves? And the problem does not become any simpler when we see how Husserl introduces the limitation.

After pointing out the necessity of this limitation in connection with the positive goal toward which he is striving, Husserl says: "This limitation can be characterized in a word." Then comes this passage: "*We put the general positing which belongs to the essence of the natural attitude out of action;* we put in brackets anything and everything that it includes in ontic respects: *this entire natural world, therefore,* which is continually 'there for us' or 'present' and will ever remain there as 'reality' for consciousness, even if it pleases us to put it in brackets." [3] This continuation is somewhat perplexing and has often caused interpreters of Husserl to rack their brains. How is it possible to seek the *limitation* of the epoché by putting in brackets "*anything and everything,*" this "*entire* natural world"?

Thus it is no wonder that Husserl begins the second chapter by formulating this problem. What could the remainder be, and what does this limitation mean? He does not give a provisional solution; as we shall see, a solution only becomes possible later. Husserl does give an indication of what remains, what the residue might be. The first paragraph of the second chapter is entitled "Intimation (Vordeutung) Concerning 'Pure' or 'Transcendental Consciousness' as Phenomenological Residue." At this point he already announces that

[2] 56.
[3] 56.

the domain sought is "pure" or "transcendental" consciousness; it is the sphere of pure experiences with its pure correlates of consciousness.[4]

At first glance this residue strongly resembles that of the epoché in LU. There, too, the remainder that was left after this suspension was the sphere of experiences (plus the intentional contents). Does the limitation of the reduction perhaps mean that it affects only reality outside consciousness? It is clear that something more, something different, is at issue here than in LU. This is immediately apparent from the fact that *all* of reality, including our consciousness, is disconnected, and that the residue is now called "pure" or "transcendental consciousness."

What Husserl must now show is that transcendental consciousness is a sphere not affected by the disconnection of all of reality; to formulate it in his own words, we must come to the insight "*that consciousness in itself has a being of its own which, in its absolutely unique nature, remains unaffected by the phenomenological disconnection.*" Only with this insight can we understand the meaning of the epoché. It then appears to be an operation that makes a new area accessible to us, an area that can become the field of a new science.[5]

After indicating the final goal of the Fundamental Consideration in this way, Husserl says that we must seek this sphere of pure experiences through an analysis of the consciousness given in the natural attitude. We proceed from experiences as "real occurrences in the world, even as experiences of animal entities." We act for the present as though we have never heard of the phenomenological epoché and focus our analysis on consciousness as it occurs in the world, that is, as a certain stratum or region of man, a region that is a "real object like so many others in the natural world," whose acts, therefore, are "occurrences in the same natural world."[6] This argument appears to move through two phases. First it is shown that consciousness has a character and unity very much its own, and then that this consciousness has an absolute mode of being, which is not affected by the epoché.

---

[4] 58.
[5] 59.
[6] 60, 58.

PARAGRAPH THREE. THE FIRST PHASE – CONSCIOUSNESS AS A
MONADOLOGICAL UNITY

The reflection on the character peculiar to consciousness is not new. It
goes back to Brentano, who took extensive account of the differences
between physical and psychical phenomena, and it was worked out by
Husserl in LU. In this work he showed that consciousness includes a
wealth of differentiations and modifications that were completely
neglected in the "data-psychology" *à la* Locke. This immersion in the
essence of consciousness is now concentrated on the theme of the unity of
consciousness.[1]

Husserl's point of departure is the distinction between acts directed
immanently and acts directed transcendently. It belongs to the essence
of immanently directed acts that their intentional objects – if they exist
– belong to the same stream as the acts themselves. This is always the
case when an act is related to an act in the same stream. Consciousness
and its object then form an "individual unity brought about solely by
experiences." This is not true of transcendently directed acts. Such acts

---

[1] Husserl already spoke of the unity of consciousness repeatedly in LU. He called
consciousness a real phenomenological unity and further characterized it as a "bundle"
or an "interweaving" (*Verwebung*). The parts of consciousness together form a
'connected unity' which Husserl still identified with the Ego. See below 474. LU II (ed. 1)
325/6 (cf. ed. 2, 346/7); (ed. 2) 353, 358, 361. Furthermore, in LU Husserl distinguished
between a phenomenological unity and a causal unity. The latter is not something
descriptive, but is assumed by explanatory science, LU (ed. 1) 332 and 338. Both passages
were later dropped, see above 229 and below 480. This unity was not further investigated
in LU. This had been done previously by Husserl's teacher Brentano, whose PES
included a noteworthy chapter on the unity of consciousness, a chapter that was admired
by James, among others. Brentano called this unity the "most consequential and disputed
fact" of psychology, PES I 136, see also 232. When we compare Husserl and Brentano on
this point, two respects in which Husserl's analysis transcends that of Brentano stand
out: the themes of the pure ego and of time as factors creating unity. Brentano could
actually find unity only among contemporaneous acts. He could find no indication that
the perceived group of momentary acts again froms a unity with a group of remembered
acts from the past. We do assume this when we say, "I hear," and "I heard," but this unity
of the ego is not demonstrable, PES I, 132, 237, 239, 244. Husserl, however, sees time as a
principle of unity and shows how the identification of the pure ego takes place in time. In
PSW he calls time a "continuing intentional line which is, as it were, the index of the all-
pervading unity." In this connection, then, he also speaks of the "monadic" unity of
consciousness, which forms a stream enclosed within itself, see below 467; PSW 312f; Id I
163, 165, 245. See also appendix XI Husserliana III.

The themes of immanent time and the pure ego will be discussed in another context. In
the analysis of the Fundamental Consideration, this matter can be provisionally
disregarded, for Husserl himself does so as well.

are directed toward objects outside the stream, e.g. essences or things.[2]

Husserl points out that what he means by 'transcendent' here is transcendent in the principial or absolute sense. But this concept can also be used in a relative sense.[3] It would then mean transcendent in relation to the many acts in which we are aware of something. In this sense an experience can also be transcendent. Thus a remembered experience, for example, is transcendent in relation to the many acts in which we are aware of it. This kind of transcendence is irrelevant here. Husserl is concerned with that which in essence can never occur in the immanent sphere.

That Husserl does not mean transcendence in the relative sense is also apparent from the conclusion toward which he moves. Such a transcendence also occurs in intra-psychical relations and is missing only in the case of immanent perception. Act and object here form a direct unity of one concrete *cogitatio*. The perception cannot be isolated from its object; it is a non-independent aspect of this unity. (Thus Husserl sees this as a unity that comes about when independent aspects or abstract parts are founded in one another.[4] Later he was to draw important conclusions from this.) Such a unity is not present in an immanent recollection. Therefore it is possible for the act of recollection to exist when the remembered experience does not (which is impossible in the case of immanent perception, as we shall see). But this does not alter the fact – and this is the point in this context – that the remembered experience, if it does exist, together with the act of recollection, "belongs necessarily to one and the same uninterrupted stream of experience which continually mediates both through various experiential concretions." This is not true in the case of the transcendent thing, where there is no essential unity between the act and the transcendent object. The thing is transcendent to consciousness in a principial sense. It can never from a part of consciousness. Husserl concludes: "*A pure unity determined by the nature characteristic of experiences themselves is exclusively the unity of the stream of experiences;* in other words, an experience can only be united with experiences

---

[2] 68.

[3] 76f. In PP 175, 176 Husserl is very clear on this transcendence in a relative sense over against transcendence in a genuine or absolute sense. See also FTL 148.

[4] Husserl X 48, 85, 316.

in a whole whose total essence encompasses the essences belonging to these experiences and is founded in them." [5]

PARAGRAPH FOUR. INTERMEZZO – TRANSITION TO THE SECOND PHASE

Husserl writes that this thesis about the unity of consciousness will take on an important meaning in the course of the argument. This is immediately apparent from the following paragraph, in which he examines the question how this stream is bound to the body. Here the argument takes an important turn, for Husserl now takes up a theme that affects the starting-point of the natural attitude. Up to now it was accepted as a foregone conclusion that consciousness is a certain stratum of the concrete person; it is an entity bound to the body and supported by it. In LU, Husserl abstracted from the body and thematized only consciousness as the phenomenological given. At the beginning of the second chapter of the Fundamental Consideration, he expressly chooses the same starting-point. The consciousness analyzed is the consciousness of the "animal being," of the concrete psycho-physical unity, of the "person." This unity with the body was not considered explicitly, but it was nevertheless presupposed throughout. Now Husserl raises the question how such a unity is possible.

That this unity is problematic can be made clear by comparing the starting-point of the natural attitude with the insight into the essence of consciousness that we have now achieved. According to the natural attitude, consciousness rests on the foundation of a material substratum. Matter (or thing) and consciousness thus form "an interconnected whole, connected in the individual psycho-physical unities that we call animals...." Via this body, consciousness is then connected with the rest of the world. Husserl asks whether such a unity does not presuppose a certain "community of essence" (*Wesensgemeinschaft*) between matter and consciousness. Principial heterogeneity is excluded here.

Now, from the analyses above we have learned that experiences only

---

[5] This unity of the stream of experience is given as an idea in Kant's sense. Of course we can never embrace the whole stream in reflection and thereby intuit its unity. But we can see that this reflection would continue endlessly, for "the stream of experience cannot begin and end," 163. We then have an insight into this never-ending possibility as such, 166/7, 298.

form a whole with one another. A thing can never form part of the stream of consciousness. Consciousness has an "essence of its own"; with other consciousnesses it forms "a self-contained *connective whole (Zusammenhang) determined purely through this, its own essence,* i.e. the connective whole of the stream of consciousness." Matter is "in principle different in kind" from consciousness, and therefore it is *"excluded from the experiences' own essence."*[1]

This problem raises important questions which drove the investigation further in the direction desired by Husserl. In order to reach clarity here, we must undertake a further inquiry into the mode of being of consciousness and of things. Here the transition to the second phase of the Fundamental Consideration takes place. At the end of the second phase, Husserl returns to the problem posed here.[2] By that point a totally new insight into the mode of being of material reality has been gained, whereby the problem of the relation between consciousness and matter (thing) can be stated in terms entirely different from those used when the problem is formulated on the basis of the natural attitude.

PARAGRAPH FIVE. THE SECOND PHASE – THE PRESUMPTIVE
BEING OF THE THING AND THE ABSOLUTE BEING OF
CONSCIOUSNESS

The further analysis of consciousness and of material or "thingly" reality begins with outer perception, an act in which the thing and the consciousness of it are connected. If we want to know more about the mode of being of the two realities, then outer perception is a suitable point to investigate the two in relation to one another.

Husserl first shows – entirely in agreement with the theory of perception of LU – that the object that appears in this perception is transcendent to the experience.[1] The color that appears is not to be

---

[1] 69f.

[2] 92f.

[1] It is true that the appearing thing is sometimes called "subjective" when compared with the thing of physics, but this does not mean that the appearance is "in" consciousness. In a short reflection on the thing of physics, Husserl claims that it is called the "true" thing because it has a greater measure of objectivity; that is to say, it is the same for everyone, and, unlike the perceived thing, it is not given to each perceiver in a different orientation. Only later does Husserl discuss the important question whether the world of physics has a reality independent of consciousness. See below 421.

identified with the sensation of color. Over against the one color stands a multiplicity of color sensations in which it is "adumbrated." "*The adumbration, in principle, is not of the same genus (Gattung) as what is adumbrated, although it is similarly named.* The adumbration is an experience. But the experience is only possible as experience, and not as something spatial. However, that which is adumbrated, in principle, is possible only as something spatial – it is even spatial in essence – and is not possible as an experience." On this basis Husserl comes to the conclusion that there is a fundamental and essential difference between "being as thing" and "being as experience."[2]

It is an eidetic law in the strictest sense of the word that a thing, because of its spatiality, is always given in adumbrations and therefore can never occur in the stream of consciousness. Husserl underscores this point by denying that a divine intuition would be capable of knowing the thing directly, that is, without the mediation of modes of appearance. We already know from LU that eidetic laws hold universally, that is, not only for men but also for angels and gods. Things are always given one-sidedly. In addition to the one side that is actually given, there is a horizon of co-givenness (*Mitgegebenheit*) that is as yet undetermined. This always makes new perceptions possible, in which the indeterminacies become determinate. In principle, the act of perception cannot be completed. "No divinity could alter this, no more than it could alter the fact that 1 plus 2 equals 3 or any other eidetic truth."[3] The givenness of the experience differs from that of the thing. The experience is not given in "adumbrations"; that is to say, "the perception of an experience is a straightforward seeing of something that is *given in the perception as 'absolute'* ... and not as something identical throughout adumbration in modes of appearance."

Here Husserl uses the term 'absolute' for the first time in Ideen I, as he describes the manner in which an experience is given in immanent perception. This means that a perceived experience does not point to other perceptions of the same experience, as is the case in the perception of things. It belongs to the essence of the immanent perception that it "gives us something absolute that cannot present itself in sides and adumbrations at all."[4]

[2] 75.
[3] 78, 81.
[4] 81f.

In addition to this difference in perceivability, there is also a difference in fitness for perception. It is true of the stream of consciousness as well as of the thing that it is not always perceived. And if this is the case, then this stream cannot be perceived in one glance, for in a glance we would only perceive the present. Yet, this transcendence is of an entirely different kind than the transcendence of the thing. Husserl had already made this point a number of times. The difference between the two kinds of transcendence is also apparent from the fact that an experience is always "ready to be perceived." We can reflect on it in a glance of "straightforward attention" – be it in reflective perception, which is what Husserl is thinking of especially here, or in reflective recollection. In the case of things, this is possible only in the "background field" of my perception, which actually makes up only a small part of the "world around me" (*Umwelt*).[5] The rest is only perceivable via a long chain of perceptions.

This is the basis for some important conclusions in the final paragraph of the second chapter. Every immanent perception necessarily guarantees the existence of its object. The "stream of experience" is never perceived as a whole. The past and future parts of the stream are always unknown – and to that extent transcendent. But when I reflect on life streaming through the given present, I can say without qualification: "*I am*; this life is; I live; *cogito*."

In the perception of things, on the other hand, there is always the possibility that the given does not exist. "*The existence of the thing is not a necessary requirement of givenness* but in a certain way is always contingent." It is always possible that further experience will alter or even "cross out" that which was already posited. It could be different than we thought, or even turn out to be an illusion. All of this is impossible in immanent perception. The sphere of consciousness is a "sphere of absolute positing."

From this it follows that the world of things has only a *presumptive* reality, whereas I myself enjoy an *absolute* reality. "*Over against the positing of the world, which is 'contingent,' stands the positing of my pure ego and ego-life, which is 'necessary'* and simply beyond doubt. *Any thing that is given bodily (leibhaft) could also not exist, but no experience given bodily could not exist;* that is the eidetic law defining this necessity and that contingency."[6]

After these conclusions, Husserl closes the second chapter with the words: "Here our consideration has reached a climax. We have gained the knowledge we need. The essential connections that have been

[5] 83f.
[6] 85f.

revealed to us contain the most important premises for the conclusions which we wish to draw about the separability in principle of the entire natural world from the domain of consciousness, the sphere in which experiences have their being." It is true that there are still a few supplementary discussions (*Ergänzungen*) needed to reach the final goal, but for the present Husserl disregards them. These discussions are found in Paragraphs 52–54. Now the most important conclusions already follow, "within the framework of a limited application."

These conclusions, then, will concern the "separability in principle of the entire natural world from the domain of consciousness." In this formulation Husserl alludes to the goal of the meditation as I described it in Paragraph 2 above. Thus the question of what remains after the suspension of the entire natural world must be answered in what follows immediately.

PARAGRAPH SIX. THE EXPERIMENT OF WORLD-ANNIHILATION

The conclusions Husserl draws from the second chapter include the famous experiment of world-annihilation. Thereby he seeks to show that the world of natural science and the world of perception are dependent on consciousness, for their existence. In the first place, Husserl wants to show that the world of experience "pure and simple" (*schlicht*) has indeed founded the world of physics and is the motive for it, but that the rise of natural science is not necessary.[1] The request for more exact determination issuing from the experienced world proceeds from experience as it actually is. It is certainly conceivable that the perceived world is the ultimate world "behind" which there is no world of physics. In that case, of course, experience would have to be other than it in fact is, for the motivation for undertaking physical investigations would not be present then, although we would continue to perceive "things," i.e. intentional unities that are constituted in a plurality of appearances.

But we can go still further. The perceived world, too, need not exist. This "real world" as a correlate of consciousness is only a special case of the many possible worlds and "Unwelten," which are "*correlates of the essentially possible variations of the idea of 'experiencing consciousness'* with more or less ordered experiential connections."[2] The

---

[1] See below 421.
[2] 88.

constituting of a real world is not necessary for consciousness. A real world is a fact dependent of particular actual connections in consciousness, i.e. connections that confirm one another. At this point Husserl throws into the argument a remark that is important because it is determinative for the conclusions drawn.[3] We must bear in mind, he says, that a transcendent thing is a correlate of a particular perception. The question "What is a transcendent thing?" can only be answered by pointing to the experience in which it is constituted. It is a correlate of "legitimating (*ausweisende*) experience." "Things are . . . what they are as things of experience." In other words: "*An object existing in itself is never such that is has nothing to do with consciousness and the conscious ego.*"[4]

A thing which, in principle, cannot be experienced would be "nonsense."[5] The idea of such a thing contains not a formal but a material contradiction.[6] Thus it can be compared to the idea of a square circle. As we have seen, an existing world is the correlate of *particular* conscious connections. It is not part of the essence of the perception of things that it *must* always be so. The perception of things leaves open the possibility that future experience will modify previous experience.

[3] E. Fink, probably not without justification, sees it as one of the most important presuppositions of Husserl's phenomenology that "being" is equated with "being for us," with the phenomenon. "To put it in a solid formula: whatever cannot be legitimated as a phenomenon cannot exist at all." He opposes this doctrine by arguing: "But the phenomenality of phenomena is itself never a phenomenological given. It is always and necessarily a theme of speculative determination. That only that which can be legitimated 'exists' and fulfills the full and valid extension of the concept of existing (*seiend*) cannot in turn be shown by legitimation. The appearing of an existent is not something that appears itself." *L'analyse intentionelle et le problème de la pensée spéculative* (with German text) 68, 70. In Part II we saw that Fink seeks to explain the identification of "being" and "phenomenon" on the basis of the constitution of number. See above 169.

Edith Stein also declares that this same "reinterpretation . . . which equates existence with legitimation for some consciousness" is not satisfactory. 'Husserls Phaenomenologie und die Philosophie des H. L. Thomas von Aquino,' 326. Elsewhere she writes: " . . . the fullness of essence and existence that breaks in on the experiencing subject in all genuine experience and transcends all possibility of being grasped by consciousness contradicts the reduction to a mere sense-giving on the part of the subject. Thus it appears to me that a faithful analysis of reality's givenness would lead precisely to a rejection (*Aufhebung*) of the transcendental reduction and to a return to the attitude of a believing acceptance of the world." *La phénoménologie*. Journées d'études de la société Thomiste, 110.

[4] 88f. See also FTL 147.

[5] Compare the addition in Husserliana III, 98.

[6] 90. According to Ingarden, 'Ueber den transzendentalen Idealismus bei E. Husserl' 193, Husserl formulated this as follows: The statements 'A exists' and 'A way to legitimate the existence of A is possible in principle' are equivalent.

The givenness of the thing, after all, is provisional and inadequate. Now, it is also *conceivable* that future experience will "cross out" previous experience. It is possible for an experience to dissolve in contradictions. Contradictory experience usually requires a correction through which the harmony of experience is restored. But this need not take place. It is possible for experience to "abound in conflicts that are irreconcilable, not for us but in themselves"; in short, it is possible "that there no longer be a world." It would then be the case that the plurality of experiences that constitute the thing do not fit together harmoniously. Experience "explodes." Then there would be no more thing, but at most raw "unity-formations."[7]

From this Husserl draws the conclusion "*that the being of consciousness, of any stream of experience at all, is indeed necessarily modified by an annihilation of the world of things, but is not affected in its actual existence.*" The annihilation of the world only modifies consciousness. Conversely, this means nothing else than that certain ordered experiential connections are lacking in the stream of experience. Consciousness itself continues to exist. This conclusion is expressed in the following Cartesian formula: "*Immanent being is doubtless also absolute being in the sense that, in principle, it nulla 're' indiget ad existendum.*" Husserl adds: "*On the other hand, the world of the transcendent 'res' is related unreservedly to consciousness, not indeed to something logically thought but to something actual.*"[8]

Thus Husserl's argument culminates in a number of conclusions about the mode of being of consciousness and of things. Between these two there is a "true abyss of sense. On the one hand we have a merely contingent and relative being in adumbration, never absolutely given, and on the other hand a necessary and absolute being which, in principle, is not given through adumbration and appearance."[9] Husserl also calls the relative being of the thing a "merely phenomenal" or "merely intentional being"; thus it is a being "that has the merely secondary, relative sense of being *for* a consciousness." Husserl declares: "It is not something absolute in itself, binding itself secondarily to something else, but in the absolute sense it is nothing at all; it has no 'absolute essence' at all but has the essentiality of something

---

[7] 91, see also 317 and above 323 note 3.
[8] 92.
[9] 93.

which, in principle, is *only* intentional, *only* conscious, presented to consciousness, appearing."[10]

Before investigating what role this reflection on being plays in the whole of the Fundamental Consideration and in what way it realizes its goal, I will undertake an inquiry into the meaning of some central terms. Husserl contrast the absolute and necessary existence of consciousness with the relative and contingent existence of the thing. In what sense are we to understand this? What do such terms as 'absolute,' 'necessary,' 'relative,' and 'contingent' mean here? And why can contingent existence also be called "merely intentional" and "merely phenomenal"?

PARAGRAPH SEVEN. THE MEANING OF THE TERMS 'ABSOLUTE' AND 'RELATIVE'

There is perhaps no concept more historically weighted than the concept of "being." Husserl was clearly aware of this, for his Fundamental Consideration is also a meditation on this concept. It represents "talk of being," as he himself says.[1] But one could well ask whether any clarity will be gained when the concept of being is tied to predicates like 'absolute' and 'necessary' in the course of the argument. What do these terms mean? When Husserl says that consciousness is absolute and exists necessarily, does this mean that existence and essence coincide here? Does it mean that what Husserl intends is a kind of deification of consciousness? Roman Ingarden, reacting against existentialistic interpretations of Husserl at the second international phenomenological colloquium at Krefeld, once more laid full emphasis on Husserl's idealism and his doctrine of the relativity of the world of things and the absoluteness of consciousness, but he, too, complained at the same time about Husserl's failure to clarify the concept of absoluteness – neither in Ideen I nor anywhere else. He also maintained that it is not clear what connection there is between the various senses in which this term is used.[2]

It seems to me that this reproach is not justified. First of all, it is

[10] 93f.

[1] 93.

[2] 'Ueber den transzendentalen Idealismus bei E. Husserl,' 199. In connection with what follows, see my article 'Die Begriffe "absolut" und "relativ" bei Husserl.'

impropable that Husserl would leave the meaning of such central terms in the dark, especially since he continually warned against understanding his terms in the traditional sense. They were only to be used in the sense which he himself had given them.[3] In fact, Husserl did define the terms 'relative' and 'absolute' at various times and tried to give them an *exact meaning*.

I. The Concepts 'Absolute' and 'Relative' in LU

Husserl presents these definitions in the third logical investigation, in connection with the distinction between independent and non-independent contents.[4] A content is independent if it can exist apart from other contents. This means that "the existence of this content . . . is not conditional at all on the existence of other contents, that it could exist just as it is even if . . . there were nothing in addition to it or if everything around it were changed arbitrarily, that is, in a non-lawful way."[5]

A content is non-independent if we have evidence that it can exist only in combination with other contents, that is to say, only as part of a more embracing whole. "The inability of a non-independent part to exist by itself therefore points to a *law according to which the existence of a content of this part's pure kind* (e.g. the kind, color, form, etc.) *presupposes the existence of contents of certain pertinent kinds. . . .*" "Color" is such a non-independent content. A color is only thinkable as the color of something.[6]

Husserl distinguishes further between relative and absolute independence. Absolute independence is an independence from all associated contents. But we can also speak of relative independence, that is, when a number of contents are independent with regard to one another (e.g. the parts of a table's surface) but together are dependent on another content (i.e. the table as a physical thing).[7]

When a content has non-independent parts or properties, it is called a concretum with regard to these non-independent or abstract parts. If this

---

[3] 60.

[4] According to the title of Paragraph 17 (LU II 266), Husserl seeks to given an "exact determination" of these concepts. As we have seen, the doctrine of independent and non-independent contents goes back to Husserl's earliest writings, and these in turn were influenced by Brentano and Stumpf. The concepts "relative" and "absolute" already occur in this sense in PA. See above 22.

[5] LU II 236. Here and in what follows, I will cite the first edition version but retain the pagination of the second edition.

[6] LU II 240.

[7] LU II 257; PSL 163.

concretum is itself non-independent, it is called an absolute concretum. What we usually mean when we speak of a "concretum" is an absolute concretum. It is also defined by Husserl in this sense in Ideen I: an absolute, independent essence, he writes, is a concretum.[8]

These analyses go back to 1894; some of them were taken over word for word in LU. In connection with his new founding of a priori truths, Husserl emphasizes fully that they are eidetic truths.[9] He then already says something about the method for discovering these eidetic lawfulnesses. The independence of a content means that we can keep it constant "in boundless (arbitrary, not prevented by any law rooted in the content's nature) variation of contents associated and given with it, so that it finally remains unaffected even by its elimination."[10] What Husserl describes here is nothing other than what he later called eidetic variation, which is always applied when we look for essential characteristics. When a certain object is subjected to variation in fantasy, we discover that there are limits to the variation. To go beyond such a limit is to rob the object of one of its essential characteristics. This invariable limit is therefore part of the essence. The aspects that can be altered in fantasy are non-essential or contingent.

In this case of variation in imagination, in which we are trying to discover the independence or non-independence of something, the variation is a thinking away or "annihilating." We already find examples of such "annihilating" in LU. In the quotation above, Husserl spoke of the boundless variation of all contents associated with a certain content in the sense that all are allowed to disappear in imagination. We discover that the object itself is not affected by this and consequently is independent (*selbständig, unabhängig*). It could exist "even if there were nothing else at all." Elsewhere Husserl says that an independent content is what it is "even if everything outside it is destroyed." If we imagine such a thing, then we are not referred to something else with which it is connected, "by whose grace, so to speak, it exists; we could conceive of it existing by itself alone without there being anything in addition to it."[11] This is exactly what Husserl characterized in Ideen I as "destruction in thought."

---

[8] 29; see also LU III 268.
[9] See above 235, 246.
[10] LU II 235f.
[11] LU II 238; see also Id III on imagination "annihilating" the world.

II. The Concepts 'Absolute' and 'Relative' in Ideen I

At bottom, the famous experiment in Ideen I about the possibility of annihilating the world is nothing other than an experiment in imagination that is supposed to lead to the discovery of independence or non-independence. It is important to view this discussion in this context, for then it loses some of its unusual character. What we are dealing with here is not an odd form of imagination but a procedure that is rigorously scientific, according to Husserl. It is an application of the method of eidetic variation. In this specific case, in which we are concerned with the relationship between consciousness and the world, Husserl applies the method to both inner and outer perception, for he hopes to investigate the mutual dependence of subject and object in the two cases.

(A) The Analysis of Inner Perception. (1) In connection with the *object* of inner perception, we speak of absolute givenness. When we look at what Husserl says here in context, we see that he means independence from other contents – in the first place from other (future) data of inner perception. This becomes clear when we compare inner perception with the perception of a thing. In the latter case, the datum can always be affected by a future datum and is consequently dependent on other contents. "It is indeed clear that . . . if we were to cut away the other varieties of appearance and the essential relations to them, nothing would remain of the sense of the givenness of things."[12] Here, then, we cannot think away future givenness. But in inner perception this is possible, and therefore it is independent of future givenness. Furthermore, the object of inner perception is also independent of perception itself. According to Husserl – who differs with Brentano on this point[13] – it is not necessary than an experience always be perceived; it can exist without being perceived.

(2) However, the reverse (i.e. being perceived without existing) is not

---

[12] Id 82, see also 286: "The positing act (*Setzung*) on the basis of the bodily appearance of the *thing* is indeed rational, but the appearance is never more than a one-sided 'imperfect' appearance . . . That which 'really' appears must be separated from the thing as though it were itself a separate thing; it constitutes a *non-independent* part within the full meaning of the thing, a part which can have unity of meaning and independence only within a whole that *necessarily* contains in itself components of emptiness and indeterminacy; see also Appendix XII and Husserliana X 105.

[13] II 356. In his analysis of time, Husserl shows that the temporal structure of consciousness makes possible a being-for-itself and thus founds reflection, Husserliana X 83; see also Id I 87 on the founding of reflection in consciousness.

possible, and therefore an "absolute positing" is possible. This "absolute positing," too, can be understood on the basis of the determination of concepts in LU. The *act* of inner perception is not independent. In immanent perception we speak of a direct unity between object and act. This unity is of such a nature that we cannot think the act without its object. "Here perception contains its object in such a way that it can be isolated from it only abstractively, only as something essentially non-independent." We are dealing here with two experiences; the higher of them, at least, is "non-independent and thus is not only founded in the lower but is at the same time intentionally directed toward it."[14] This is an eidetic law, then, which is founded in the essential characteristics of a content. Perception, as a non-independent content, cannot be thought without its object, just as a color cannot be thought without something of which it is the color. Now, we know from LU that a non-independent content's "inability to exist by itself" means that its existence essentially presupposes the existence of another content. In this case, the existence of immanent perception presupposes the existence of the perceived experience.

Thus immanent perception necessarily guarantees the existence of its object. "If my reflective grasp directs itself to my experience, I have grasped an absolute self whose existence in principle cannot be negated; that is to say, the insight that it does not exist is impossible in principle. It would be nonsense to regard it as possible for an experience *given* in this way in perception *not* to exist."[15] The object can be posited absolutely.

Now we can see why Husserl distinguishes within the sphere of immanently directed acts between immanent perception and other immanently directed acts such as the remembering of an "experience." It is possible for the remembered experience not to exist. In memory no absolute positing is possible. Only in immanent perception is absolute positing possible.[16]

(B) The Analysis of Outer Perception. (1) When we apply the same procedure to outer perception, we get the opposite result. The *object* is inconceivable without the objects associated with it, just as it is inconceivable without perception itself. Husserl demonstrated the first

[14] 68.

[15] 85.

[16] 69, 76f, Husserliana IX 175f; FTL 148. At bottom, only the present is apodictically evident. Later, in CM, this induced Husserl to raise the question how large this realm of the apodicticity of the *ego cogito* is, 61, 67. Answering this question is the task of a critique of transcendental self-experience.

point at length in the second chapter of the Fundamental Consideration. Every experience is part of a continuum of various appearances. It is given only presumptively, for it can again be "crossed out" by subsequent experience. This consideration was applied only noematically and had to do with the independence of any single noema from all other noemata. But the annihilation experiment showed that the object of outer perception is also dependent on perception itself. When we think away this perception in imagination, the world disappears as well. The world is nothing but a correlate of certain ordered connections of perceptions within consciousness, that is, connections that confirm one another. When the various experiences possible with regard to any spatial thing do not cohere harmoniously, the thing dissolves in irreconcilable conflicts. The same holds for the world as a whole.

From this Husserl draws the conclusion that the world of transcendent things is "completely dependent on consciousness, not on what is logically thought but on what is actually present." Therefore the being of the world is called a "merely phenomenal being"; it is "a being that has the merely secondary, relative sense of being for consciousness." It has no "absolute essence."[17] Because this harmony of experiences is not essential for consciousness and in this sense is contingent, the existence of the world is dependent on a contingent or factual characteristic of consciousness.

(2) I will now investigate the possible independence of *acts* of outer perception. It already follows from the nature of this givenness that it is not dependent on other, future modes of appearance (see A-1 above).

Moreover, when we vary the object, the correlate of consciousness, we establish that the non-existence of the world is not an invariable limit. We can go beyond this limit without affecting the essence of consciousness. Husserl carries out this experiment in two phases. First he shows that we can think away the physical world without thereby changing the world of straightforward experiences.[18] In the second phase he demonstrates that this life-world can be thought away without affecting the nature of consciousness. In this "destruction in thought of thingly objectivity – as correlate of experiential consciousness – we are constrained by no limits." It is not an essential necessity for consciousness that experiences harmonize. If they do harmonize, a phenomenal

[17] 92ff.
[18] 88.

"real" world comes about. If they do not harmonize, the world "explodes" and only "raw unity-formations" come about. The being of consciousness is "indeed necessarily modified by an annihilation of the world of physical things, but it is not affected in its own existence," Husserl concludes. The phenomenon "real world" is only one special case of many "possible worlds and non-worlds" (*Unwelten*). Because the failure of experiences to harmonize is conceivable in the case of the individual thing as well as in the case of the sum of all things (i.e. the world), it is quite well possible ". . . that there no longer be a world." Then follows the well-known conclusion that consciousness is an "absolute essence," which Husserl elucidates via a variation of a Cartesian expression, that is, that consciousness "nulla 're' indiget ad existendum."[19]

Because consciousness is conceivable here without an object, we come to a conclusion opposed to that of A-2. What is possible here is not an "absolute positing" of the object but only a contingent positing (*Thesis*). "Anything thingly that is given bodily could also not exist," writes Husserl. "*The positing of the world, which is contingent, stands over against the positing of my pure ego and ego-life, which is 'necessary'* and simply beyond doubt."[20]

The experiment of world-annihilation demonstrates a conclusion that Husserl already announced at the end of the second chapter of the Fundamental Consideration. There he said that his argument had "reached a climax," for the discussion up to that point already contained the "most important premises for the conclusions that we wish to draw about the separability of the entire natural world from the domain of consciousness." This separability is now demonstrated *in concreto*.

The terminology that Husserl uses here shows us again that this mode of argumentation is not new in his work. What we have here is an instance of what he calls "one-sided separability." In LU, Husserl had already given a definition of this. Following Brentano's lead, he distinguished between one-sided and mutual separability and in-separability. In the case of nutual inseparability, the founding relation between the two contents is reversible. Thus extension and color, for example, are inconceivable apart from one another and therefore are founded in one another. But in the case of the founding of a judgment

[19] 91f.
[20] 85f.

through a presentation, this relation is not reversible. Now we have established that this one-sidedness also applies to the case of the founding of the world in consciousness. It is clear that this concept of "separability" is already a technical term in the doctrine of independent and non-independent contents as we find it in LU. Husserl's doctrine of relative and absolute being is simply an application of a familiar theory that goes back to Stumpf and Brentano. At the same time, it is a piece of philosophy that Husserl could presuppose as known to the students closest to him. Because this background information has been lost, later interpreters have not understood the meaning of the concept "absolute," and this has given rise to murky speculation foreign to the lucid nature of Husserl's philosophizing.

That the appeal to Descartes is also to be interpreted in this context is obvious from another passage which was dropped from the second edition of LU. Husserl there maintains that the concepts "independent" and "non-independent" are applicable not only to contents but also to things (as unities of contents succeeding one another in time) and then says: "The independence is expressed directly, and, indeed, as independence in the absolute sense, in Descartes' definition of substance: *res quae ita existit, ut nulla alia re indigeat ad existendum.*"[21]

In the definition given in Ideen I, Husserl rightly omitted the words 'res' and 'alia,' for the consciousness to which the definition is applied is not a "res." The entire Fundamental Consideration is intended to prove that the gap between consciousness and reality is unbridgeable and that a "reifying" conception of consciousness (in psychological apperception) misconceives consciousness in its essence. Husserl then discovered that the only "res" which is absolutely independent in the sense of the definition, i.e. independent of all contents associated with it, is not a "res" at all! In Ideen III he writes that the thing is relative in principle, that it can only exist in connection with other things on which it depends causally. "A substance (in the sense in which everything objectively real is a substance) standing alone would be an absurdity. Thus a substance in the sense of the well-known distinctions of Descartes and Spinoza is something principially different from an objective reality in the sense of our demarcations."[22] Ideen I draws from this the positive conclusion that only consciousness is absolute. Only here is Descartes' definition actually valid.

[21] LU II (ed. 1) 251.
[22] Id III 4.

III. Provisional Conclusions

When we survey the various meanings of the word 'absolute,' it turns out not only that they are precisely circumscribed and even exact, but also that there are connections between them. What Husserl does, at bottom, is to apply the same method twice – to inner and outer perception respectively. When we try to think away one of the relata of the relation of perception, we are trying to establish the mutual dependence or independence of subject and object. The results, in summary, are as follows.

(A-1) In inner perception, the perceived experience turns out to be independent of future experience. Therefore we speak of it as "absolutely given." Furthermore, it is independent of perception itself.

(A-2) But the perception of an experience is non-independent. We cannot think it without thinking its object at the same time. Therefore the latter is "absolutely posited."

(B-1) The exact opposite is true of outer perception. The object is dependent on future data and is therefore spoken of as presumptively given. For 'presumptive' we can here read 'relative.' Furthermore, the perceived object is independent of its consciousness and is therefore "only intentional."

(B-2) The perception itself is independent of the object. It is fully possible to think this perception without the "real world" as object. Consciousness is an "absolute essence." Therefore the positing of this world is not necessary but contingent.

Consciousness appears twice in these positings: in the first as object of inner perception, and in the second as subject of outer perception (A-1 and B-2). Two conclusions about this are drawn. In the first place, consciousness is posited absolutely; that is to say, it is inconceivable for it not to exist. In CM, Husserl speaks of the "absolute inconceivability of the non-existence of consciousness." We have apodictic certainty about the existence of consciousness.[23] In this work, Husserl emphasizes explicitly that consciousness can therefore serve as the starting-point for an absolutely secure philosophy. Although this element is also present in Ideen I, Husserl does not make it central there.[24] This is

---

[23] CM 56.

[24] In the introduction to Ideen I, Husserl writes that the third book will be devoted to the idea of philosophy. "We will reach the insight that genuine philosophy, which aims to realize absolute knowledge, is rooted in pure phenomenology." Phenomenology makes possible a "first philosophy." In the "Nachwort" 146, Husserl lays great emphasis on this philosophical motive behind transcendental phenomenology. As "first philosophy" (a

bound up with the fact that the goal of the Fundamental Consideration is negative rather than positive; the negative side, the refutation of an incorrect, natural starting-point receives the most emphasis.

This becomes clear in the second conclusion, which is that consciousness is not dependent on the world. This claim on Husserl's part represents the opposite of the natural attitude, in which the world is absolutized. Husserl calls this attitude an absurd interpretation, for it contradicts the eidetic analysis of the thing, as we have seen. [25] It is not the case that consciousness is founded in the world (through bodies); rather, the world, in the words of LU, is dependent on the "grace" of consciousness. [26] "Thus the usual talk of being is completely inverted," Husserl rightly concludes. [27]

PARAGRAPH EIGHT. EIDETIC AND FACTUAL NECESSITY

On the basis of Husserl's statements about the absolute and necessary existence of consciousness, some interpreters have concluded that what we encounter here is some sort of deification of consciousness, in which existence and essence coincide. Such an interpretation is also the result of a misunderstanding of Husserl's intentions. We have seen that absolute positing is founded in a law of non-independence. [1] When a certain non-independent content is given, a founding content must be given with it. Because this is a purely eidetic law, it does not as yet say anything about the actual existence of these contents. We know that we can draw no conclusions about actual existence from an eidetic law. An eidetic law only says something about pure possibilities: *if* these contents exist, they must necessarily possess these properties.

This also applies to the eidetic law about inner perception. On the basis of this law, we cannot conclude that consciousness actually exists. A pure conceivability does not yet tell us anything about actual existence. An eidetic law does not imply existence, Husserl assures us in LU. Thus he does not by any means intend to make the mistake of the ontological argument for God's existence by deriving being from

philosophy that is absolutely founded and universal), phenomenology realizes the objective of all science and philosophy since Socrates and Plato; compare EP I 3 and CM 4.

[25] 98, 107.
[26] LU II 238.
[27] 93.

[1] Such laws found synthetic a priori judgments, LU II (ed. 2) 252.

thought. Absolute positing as an eidetic law can mean nothing more than that there is no consciousness that does not exist necessarily, or, to put it more precisely, that there is no immanent perception without its object.[2] This means nothing more than: if consciousness exists, it must exist necessarily, or, if it is perceived, it must be posited absolutely. This is not yet to say that it exists at all.

Nonetheless, it is certainly Husserl's intention to attribute the predicate of "necessary being" to an actually existing consciousness. We are concerned here with the "necessity of a fact," an "empirical necessity." This means that an eidetic law is here applied to a fact.[3] Such an application is analyzed by Husserl in Part I of Ideen I. A connection between eidetic judgment and the "positing of existence" appears. "Eidetic universality is here ... transferred to an individual posited as existing." Something similar takes place in geometry, for example. "The state of affairs (Sachverhalt) posited as real is then a fact insofar as it is an individual state of reality (Wirklichkeitsverhalt), but it is an eidetic necessity insofar as it is a singularization of an eidetic universality."[4]

It is such a state of affairs that we face here. The eidetic law reads: "no experience that is bodily present could fail to exist." But for this reason, the "necessity of being" of a *present individual* experience is not a pure "eidetic necessity, that is, not a purely eidetic particularization of an eidetic law: it is the necessity of a fact that is so called because an eidetic law is bound up with it – even here in its existence as fact."[5] The fact is necessary because it is bound up with the eidetic law applied to it. Husserl gives the following example of such an "empirical particularization" of an eidetic law: "this red is different from this green."[6]

In this case, the intuition of an essence has as its basis not something imagined but an actual perception. Therefore the judgment expressed also has an "existential meaning" alongside its "essential meaning."[7] Although we can derive no "positing of existence" from an eidetic

---

[2] An a priori judgment corresponds to a negative existential judgment.

[3] 86, 87, footnote 1. On this point, see Ingarden's article 194, 195, footnote 1. According to his review, the eidetic judgment then becomes a metaphysical judgment. He is of the opinion – and I cannot agree – that it is not certain that Husserl made this metaphysical judgment.

[4] 15, 16.

[5] 86f; see also J.P. Sartre, L'être et le néant, 22, 307.

[6] LU II 256.

[7] Id III 27.

perception, the perception of an essence can well go together with a "positing of existence." In the case of the apodictic judgment "I am," this positing of existence is an individual immanent perception. The eidetic judgment has a universal validity. The individual that serves as foundation has only empirical validity for my consciousness here and now. The combination of these two yields an apodictic judgment about *my* consciousness: "... *my* consciousness as such is given in an originary and absolute way, not only in its essence but also in its existence."[8] In agreement with this, Husserl says that the world is dependent not on a "logically conceived" consciousness but on an "actual" consciousness.[9]

What we are dealing with here is a "mixing" of two kinds of evidence: an apodictic evidence concerned with the essence and an assertoric evidence concerned with the fact. Such a mixture occurs in the "application of an insight to something seen assertorically and in general in the *knowledge of the necessity of the being thus (Sosein)* of a single something posited."[10] Husserl's argumentation could be summed up as follows in the form of a modus ponens argument (p → q; p; therefore q). The pure eidetic law forms the first premise. It maintains that if consciousness exists, it must exist necessarily. Actual perception provides us with a second premise: my consciousness exists *de facto*. The conclusion is then that my consciousness exists necessarily (in the sense that its non-existence is inconceivable).

This apodictic evidence about our own consciousness must be distinguished from adequate evidence about our own consciousness, for the latter has only assertoric meaning. This enables us to illustrate the difference between the evidence of the "I am" in LU and the evidence of the "I am" in Ideen I. In LU, an adequate perception of one's own consciousness was the Archimedean point on which phenomenology was based.[11] In Ideen I, however, consciousness is an apodictic point of departure. Now that the inconceivability of non-existence has been added to it, the evidence is even more firmly anchored.[12]

---

[8] 85. Here lies the root of what Husserl was later to call the egological reduction.

[9] 92.

[10] 285f.

[11] LU I 121, 143, II 356; III 225, 240.

[12] According to Husserl, an apodictic judgment is also possible when the object is not adequately given, 286. This even applies to experiences. An experience is never given completely. However, this inadequacy has an entirely different meaning in the case of an

De Waelhens, who analyzes Husserl's analogical train of thought in CM, rightly maintains that apodicticity is a matter of the necessity with which something is "thought" and not of the actual experience. But is he correct in taking this to mean a primacy of "thinking" over experience and therefore even a denial of phenomenology?[13] To begin with, we should note that Husserl does not make the classic mistake of rationalism here, namely, deriving being from thought. De Waelhens points this out himself when he observes in a footnote: "In fact, what compels us to think a certain being as existing necessarily is not an absolute logical necessity but a necessity which renders inconceivable the non-existence of a being whose existence was first factually established." Nonetheless, one could maintain that the first premise is a typical law of *thought*. Would that not represent an unphenomenological point of departure?

The answer depends on what we take phenomenology to be. I would argue that the conclusions mentioned above remain fully within the framework of Husserl's own presuppositions, insofar as we permit Husserl himself to determine what phenomenology is.[14] They do not directly contradict his other contentions. The phenomenological point of departure, the principle of all principles, is that "every intuition given in an originary way is a proper source of knowledge."[15] Now then, eidetic laws also rest on such intuitions. When Husserl speaks here of "thinking" and "conceivability," he means a thinking that rests on an intuition of its own, i.e. an intuition of essences (*Wesenschau*). A priori laws are also intuitively founded. Husserl's critique of traditional rationalism, we must remember, was that it does not justify a priori laws through intuition.[16] Thus, since he accepts no other criteria than the presence of the given, he does not go beyond the bounds of phenomenology. But he does recognize a broader domain of givenness than just individual experience. In addition to facts, essences can also be present – and in an originary way at that. Thus Husserl's phenomenology prepares a proper place for apodictic evidence.

experience than in the case of a thing. Compare 286, where Husserl expresses himself in a somewhat different vein about the corresponding givenness of an experience.

[13] A. de Waelhens, *Phénoménologie et Vérité* 33, 36, 38.

[14] See, for example, 285, where Husserl says: "It is a phenomenological realization of the greatest importance that both [he means apodictic and assertoric evidence] belong to *one* and the same essential genus . . . ."

[15] 43.

[16] 39; Id III 56, 70; Entwurf 320; Krisis 14, 337 (E 16, 290).

PARAGRAPH NINE. CONSCIOUSNESS AS THE NECESSARY
CONDITION AND SUFFICIENT REASON OF THE WORLD

We saw above that the existence of the world presupposes the existence
of consciousness, but that the reverse is not the case. Thus consciousness is described as a necessary condition for the existence of the world.
This does not yet imply that it is also a sufficient condition.[1] This fact
has sometimes been used to call Husserl's idealism into question. If
consciousness is not a sufficient condition for the existence of the world,
the world could also be dependent on other factors. "Consciousness is a
fundament for the world in the sense that the world cannot become
'real' (verum) unless there is a consciousness," writes Sokolowski, who
then adds: "There is nothing surprising about this assertion, nor is there
anything idealistic about it." Husserl's doctrine would only be idealistic
if consciousness were also a *sufficient* condition for the existence of the
world: "then subjectivity would actually 'make' or 'create' the sense of
phenomenal reality when it constitutes it."[2] According to Sokolowski,
this is not the case. In Husserl's theory, it is left open whether there is yet
another *necessary condition* for the existence of the world, a condition
outside consciousness. Thus Husserl is one-sided in that he deals with
only one source of constitution. In addition to consciousness, on this
interpretation, there is another ground, which explains the actual
content of constitution.

Sokolowski maintains that Husserl's concept of constitution is
purely formal. What he means by this is that constitution does not
explain why we are now conscious of *this* content and not of some other
content. This content is given as something factual; it is given as an
unexplained irrational fact that cannot be explained on the basis of
consciousness. "Therefore subjectivity does not cause or create senses
and objects. It merely allows them to come about. It is their condition,
not their cause: consequently, Husserl's doctrine of constitution should
not be interpreted in too idealistic a manner."[3] Therefore Husserl's
philosophy needs to be supplemented. "We suggest that it would be
necessary for him to complete his thought with investigation of another
'condition of possibility,' one which would encompass the facticity of
what is actually given in constitution . . . in other words, the fundament

---

[1] Ingarden reports that Husserl often used the following formulation in his lectures: if
we cross out pure consciousness, we cross out the real world, 193.

[2] R. Sokolowski, *The Formation of Husserl's Concept of Constitution*, 137.

[3] Op.cit. 159; ~e also page 60, 166, 192f.

in reality which allows reality to emerge in constitution has to be investigated. As long as this is not done, the content of constitution remains outside the sphere of philosophy. It has no principle of philosophical explanation and must be accepted as a brute irrational fact, something which philosophy is powerless to treat." Hence Sokolowski proposes to approach constitution on the basis of a "bilateral perspective." Constitution has two "sources" or grounds, one in subjectivity and the other in objectivity. The two must be dealt with in their mutual relation. "Constitution is not simply the evolution of subjectivity (the idealist extreme), nor only the evolution of reality as a closed process independent of consciousness (the empiricist position) but the development of reality and subjectivity in their fundamental relationship to one another."[4]

For the present I will leave Sokolowski's argument about the actual content of constitution untouched.[5] Instead I will raise the question whether Husserl's theory of consciousness as a *necessary condition* for the world permits these conclusions.[6] Is it really Husserl's intention to leave open the possibility of the existence of grounds outside consciousness for the origin of the world? As I see it, a proper understanding of the passage in question excludes such an interpretation. When Husserl says that the existence of consciousness does not imply the existence of the world, we cannot maintain that consciousness as such is a sufficient ground for the origin of the world. We cannot say: because there is

[4] Op.cit. 216–219.

[5] It is my conviction that these questions are answered by Husserl in his metaphysics as the science of transcendental facts. The world of facts, as a content of consciousness, points to an actual coherent system of connections within consciousness itself. This "irrational transcendent factity," as Husserl himself calls it, EP I 187 footnote 1, is ultimately explained in transcendental *theology*. See also EP I, 14, 194 and EP II, 248. Ideen I already makes this clear. The question of the "ground" of constitution consciousness leads back to God, 111. Husserl's idealism does not by any means conflict with this transcendental theology. The world remains dependent on consciousness in the first place, even if it were to turn out that this existence by the grace of consciousness is ultimately an existence by the grace of God; See I. Kern, *Husserl und Kant*, 298f, 424; S. Strasser 'Das Gottesproblem in der Spätphilosophie Edmund Husserls.'

[6] Sokolowski's misunderstanding is no doubt bound up with his view that Husserl has not demonstrated the relativity of the world. "Just as in the Logical Investigations, Husserl does not set before himself the task of showing the relativity of reality; this is not a thesis he tries to justify." He also writes: "If we were to analyze his argument logically, we would have to say that the relative, constituted nature of reality is an axiom, and not the conclusion of any argument," 133. In view of the great pains taken by Husserl in the Fundamental Consideration to demonstrate the relativity of the world in a rigorous and even apodictic manner, such a statement sounds strange.

consciousness, the world exists. But Husserl's reason for applying this formula is to demonstrate the independence of consciousness. It is the opposite of the reverse formulation (i.e. consciousness presupposes the world, or, the world is the necessary condition for the existence of consciousness). What Husserl means is that the *essence* of consciousness does not imply the existence of a world. Consciousness is "conceivable" without a world. But does this mean that the actual appearance of a world is dependent on factors other than consciousness? No, quite the contrary. What Husserl's proof of the independence of consciousness is based on is that any such fact is dependent on an *actual* structure of consciousness (see above, Paragraph 7, II, B-1). When consciousness manifests a certain arrangement, a world comes about. If consciousness does not do so, no world arises. (This non-existence means a "modification" of consciousness, i.e. the lack of a harmony of experiences.) However, if this harmony of experiences is present (Dei gratia!), the existence of a world follows necessarily. *This ordered experience is both the necessary and sufficient ground for the appearance of a world.* This is not just my own conclusion: it is explicitly stated by Husserl. He writes: "let us ... assume that the proper arrangements for consciousness [he means mutually confirming experiences, as is evident from the context] are in fact satisfied and that as regards the course of consciousness itself, there is nothing lacking which might in any way be required for the appearance of a unitary world and the rational theoretical knowledge of the same. Presupposing all of this, we now ask: is it still conceivable for the corresponding transcendent world *not to exist*? Would this not, on the contrary, be absurd?"[7]

Thus an actual, determined structure of consciousness is indeed a sufficient condition for the existence of the world that actually is. Husserl made this clear once more in a marginal note in his own copy of Ideen I. Alongside the sentence "Anything thingly that is given bodily could also not exist," he wrote: "Such sentences are not to be torn from their context. The thing must exist if the experiential coherence (*Erfahrungszusammenhang*) continues harmoniously without end. (Miss Stein believes that this has been misunderstood.)"[8]

Because consciousness is a necessary and sufficient ground for the world, we say that the world is "founded" in consciousness. Therefore

[7] Id I 92.
[8] Remark in 109, Husserliana III 473.

Husserl always speaks of transcendental consciousness as the ground or the basis (*Boden*) or – alluding to Part II of *Faust* – as the "mothers of knowledge" or – taking two of these ideas together – as the "Mutterboden."[9] Consciousness is the "ontic presupposition" (*Seinsvoraussetzung*) of the world.[10] Transcendental phenomenology is "presuppositionless" for exactly this reason, for it is aware that the world cannot be accepted as ground since consciousness is the true ground and basis. This great revolution, whereby consciousness rather than the world becomes the ground, is the "Copernican revolution" of transcendental phenomenology.[11] It is the only ground on which a rigorously scientific philosophy can be built, a philosophy that is not only absolutely founded but also truly universal. Consciousness is the ground of everything. In this way transcendental philosophy realizes the old ideal of "first philosophy" or "universal wisdom."

PARAGRAPH TEN. THE WORLD AS PRESUMPTIVE

There is another point that must be taken up briefly here, a point that also plays a role in the confrontation with existentialism. It is clear from the experiment of world annihilation that the presumptivity of outer perception does not apply to the individual thing only. It is conceivable for experience to "dissolve in illusion through contradiction, and not just in one particular case." Not only the individual thing but the "reality of the entire natural world" lacks independence.[1] The whole world is given presumptively – and is therefore object of the epoché. Husserl's thinking on this point is clear: what is true of the individual thing is true *a fortiori* of the totality of things.

This doctrine contrasts with that of Merleau-Ponty, who claims that we can be uncertain about an individual thing but never about the world as a totality. "There is absolute certainty about the world in general, but not about any thing in particular."[2] This conviction is

---

[9] The expression 'the mothers' already occurs in the 'phenomenologist's song,' which was born during the summer semester of 1907 out of a lecture on perception. This 'song' was included in A. Diemer, *Edmund Husserl. Versuch einer systematischen Darstellung seiner Phänomenologie*, 38. See also Id III 80. On the concept of 'Mutterboden,' see Ideen II 105; Krisis 156 (E 153).

[10] Nachwort 150; CM 189.

[11] CM 61, 173.

[1] 91, 93.

[2] *Phénoménologie de la perception*, 344.

bound up with a different conception of the concept of world. For Merleau-Ponty, the world is not a "sum total of things" that can always be cast into doubt but "the inexhaustible reservoir from which the things are drawn";[3] it is "an immense individual against which my experiences unfold and which dwells at the horizon of my life, just as the noise of a great city forms the background of all that we do there."[4] This world as horizon is the correlate of a primordial or originary belief.[5] In no way is this evidence about the world of less value than evidence about the *cogito*.[6]

Since I have limited myself to Ideen I in this study, I cannot go into the development which the concept of world underwent in Husserl's later thinking. Yet, I must point out that this development never gave him occasion to abandon the doctrine of the world as presumptive and relative.[7]

The doctrine of the relativity of the world and the absoluteness of consciousness remained the central point in Husserl's phenomenology even in his very last works. It is the heart of his transcendental idealism. If we give up this doctrine, Husserl was convinced, we fall back into the natural attitude and dogmatic, uncritical philosophy. We must bear in mind that the assumption of the world as the basis of being is the presupposition that every uncritical, pre-phenomenological philosophy accepts as a foregone conclusion. Anyone who falls back into

[3] Op.cit. 396.
[4] Op.cit. 378, see also 362.
[5] Op.cit. 50, 395, 454.
[6] Op.cit. 429, 432.
[7] Both Merleau-Ponty and De Waelhens appeal to Husserl's thinking in connection with this originary belief – particularly to the introduction to EU written by Landgrebe. For De Waelhens see *Une philosophie de l'ambiguité* 183 note 4; 215 note 2; 216 note 2, 323 note 3; (see also 264 and 401) and also *Phénoménologie et vérité*, 43, 45, 48ff. In this introduction, Landgrebe does indeed speak of the world as the universal basis of being. But this does not mean that Husserl gave up the doctrine of transcendental consciousness as the basis of being, for Landgrebe makes it clear that the return to the life-world is only a phase in the reduction to transcendental consciousness EU 49. Without this reduction, belief in the world and the correlate of this belief are naïve. Landgrebe later explained that he was still an idealist when he wrote this introduction. See "Lettre de M. Landgrebe sur un article de M. Jean Wahl concernant 'Erfahrung und Urteil de Husserl,' 282f. For Husserl, transcendental consciousness always remained the only basis of being. The most important texts on this point are: Encyclopaedia Britannica Artikel Husserliana IX 295; CM 56, 66, 189; FTL 144, 203ff; 208, 222, 241, 245, 248ff; Nachwort 153; PP 125; EU 12. In Krisis, his last work, Husserl also held on to the criterion of apodicticity, 78f, 117, 191f (E 77, 114, 187f). Measured by this criterion, only consciousness is an absolute sphere of being 80, 103, 117, 118, 169 note 1, 193, 202, 407, 408 (E 80, 100, 116, 166 note, 189, 199).

this position – and existentialism does so, according to Husserl – surrenders the claim that philosophy is a rigorous science.[8] The ultimate harmony of experience, which is necessary for the constitution of a world, remains an assumption for Husserl and not an apodictic certainty. This is the reason why the world cannot serve as the basis for philosophy. According to Husserl, consciousness is conceivable without the world.

Now, it is often argued that this view is in conflict with – and even a denial of – the concept of intentionality.[9] As I see it, this argument holds water only if we characterize consciousness (with Heidegger) as negativity or openness (*Offenheit*). But to do this would be to lose sight of what is characteristic of Husserl's position. For Husserl, the failure of experience to harmonize would not be a denial of the intentional structure of consciousness but only a denial of the harmony of certain intentions. If there is no harmony, then what we have is not a "real world" but a putative world that fails to be a world, an "Unwelt," a world of "raw unity-formations" that cannot lay claim to the predicate "real world" but are only "analogous" to it.[10]

PARAGRAPH ELEVEN. CONCLUSION OF THE SECOND PHASE

Earlier in this chapter we were able to determine just what the terms 'absolute' and 'relative' mean, without getting involved in abstruse speculation about absolute and necessary being. I now return to the problematics of Paragraph 4. Husserl chose his point of departure in the natural attitude, for which consciousness is a region of a psycho-physical unity. Consciousness and a thing together form an "animal entity." On first analysis, consciousness appeared to be a monadic unity of its own enclosed within itself in a very unique way. Husserl then raises the question how such a stream can be connected with a body. How is a psycho-physical unity possible? Does such a unity not

---

[8] Id III 138, 140. Finally, I would point out that Husserl's well-known lament in *Krisis* 508 (E 389). ("*Philosophy as a science*, as an earnest, rigorous, indeed apodictically rigorous science – the dream is over") does not represent his own conviction but only the judgment of his irrationalistic contemporaries. Spiegelberg also interprets this often misused passage in this way, *The Phenomenological Movement* 77 and supports his view of it with new arguments in the 1965 supplement to his book, 739. Other supporters of this interpretation are R. Boehm, 'Husserl et l'idéalisme classique' 378 note 81; H.G. Gadamer, 'Die phänomenologische Bewegung' 25.

[9] A. de Waelhens, *Phénoménologie et vérité* 38, 44.

[10] 88, 91.

presuppose a community of essence between the two parts? If we have a principial heterogeneity, such a connection seems to be impossible.

The second phase of the meditation indeed results in establishing such a heterogeneity. There is a "basic and essential difference" between "being as experience" (*Erlebnis*) and "being as thing"; it is "the most cardinal difference of all."[1] Returning to his point of departure, Husserl concludes from this that consciousness and reality do not form a whole. They are not "coordinate kinds of being living as friendly neighbors and occasionally 'entering into relations' or some reciprocal 'connection.'"[2] Thus a psycho-physical unity in which there is some sort of interaction between the parts must be excluded as a possibility. The goal of Husserl's reflection on the being of consciousness and of the thing, then, is to undermine a seemingly obvious conclusion drawn by the natural attitude. We cannot accept the view that a stream of consciousness is bound to a thing in the same manner in which two realities are connected.

This becomes even clearer from further definitions of this heterogeneity. "Between consciousness and reality there is a true abyss of sense. On the one side is an adumbrating, never absolutely given, purely contingent, relative being; on the other side a necessary and absolute being which in principle is not given through adumbration and appearance."[3] Material reality can only exist as a dependent correlate of consciousness. *This heterogeneity is of such a nature that it radically reverses "natural" relationships.* Consciousness is not founded in matter as the "fundamental stratum";[4] matter is instead supported by consciousness. It is not matter but consciousness that is absolute; in other words, it is not the case that consciousness is non-independent and founded in nature. The truth is rather that material nature is non-independent and depends on consciousness. "The usual meaning of the talk of being," Husserl rightly observes, "is reversed."[5]

Thus we see that the heterogeneity of being is not an argument against Husserl's idealism but rather an argument in favor of it.[6] Matter, which has a fundamentally different mode of being than consciousness, can exist only as a correlate of consciousness. The point

[1] 76f.
[2] 92f.
[3] 93.
[4] 70.
[5] 93.
[6] See above 334.

of Husserl's argument is that if a "real" relation between matter and consciousness is impossible, there can only be a transcendental relation between them. "Over against reality, however, the subjective is an irreality. Reality and irreality essentially belong together in the form reality and subjectivity, a form that excludes both and, on the other hand, as we said, essentially requires both."[7] If consciousness is called the "ground" of the world, then this is an entirely different founding from any we encounter *within* the world. Consciousness is not a cause. It is the unique relation whereby reality is grounded in irreality.

It must now be asked to what extent we have come closer to a solution of the problem posed in Paragraph 2. What remains when all of reality is disconnected? The experiment of world-annihilation leaves us with the impression that the answer must be: consciousness. But this answer in turn raises various questions. Does the epoché not mean that *all* of natural reality must be disconnected? Up to now, Husserl has spoken exclusively of the thing, which does indeed form the fundamental stratum of natural reality but not the totality of reality. Does the limitation of the epoché mean that only matter is disconnected, so that a kind of split between thing and consciousness is in fact brought about? These questions having to do with the interpretation of the epoché are doubtless among the most difficult questions that come up in Ideen I. We can only answer them by comparing the exposition of the first chapter of the Fundamental Consideration very carefully with the analysis of the modes of being of the thing and consciousness that follow it.

Husserl himself sees a close connection between the suspension of the general positing (*Thesis*) as described in the first chapter and the meditation on the modes of being in the second and third chapters. He claims that only through this reflection can we understand what is actually achieved by way of the epoché.[8] This reflection must demonstrate the possibility of such an epoché. When he arrives at the end

---

[7] Id II 64. Also important is what Husserl writes on Id II 21of. The fact that there are cardinal differences in modes of being between certain regions does not exclude the possibility that there are relations between these regions. As an example, Husserl takes the relation between the world of ideas and the experiential world. Another example is "the relation of the 'world' of pure, phenomenologically reduced consciousness to the world of the transcendent unities constituted in consciousness." See below 390, 404f and Fink, 'Die phänomenologische Philosophie Edmund Husserl in der gegenwärtige Kritik,' 369.

[8] 59.

of this meditation, Husserl once more underlines the necessity of these radical "preliminary consideration." If we think back to the first chapter, then "it in fact becomes obvious that over against the natural theoretical attitude, whose correlate is the world, a new attitude must be possible, an attitude which, despite the disconnection of this psychophysical total nature, retains something, i.e. the entire field of absolute consciousness."[9] Husserl himself will be our guide in what follows, as I seek to explain the first chapter on the epoché with the help of the transcendental "preliminary considerations" of the second and third chapters.

PARAGRAPH TWELVE. INTERPRETING THE TRANSCENDENTAL EPOCHÉ

There is perhaps no passage in the whole of Husserl's work that has caused more problems in interpretation than his introduction of the transcendental-phenomenological epoché in the first chapter of the Phenomenological Fundamental Consideration. Therefore a closer analysis of this introduction is needed. I will undertake this analysis without any preliminary discussion of particular interpretations that have been offered. My argument will be based exclusively on the text of Ideen I. In the process I will raise the following questions: (1) Which of Husserl's statements could have given rise to misunderstandings? (2) How are these statements to be interpreted within the context of the entire argument? The Fundamental Consideration, which is of central importance to Husserl's work, is fully worthy of this attention.

I. The Introduction of the Epoché

   (A) The negative aspect of the reduction. In the first chapter Husserl describes the negative aspect of the reduction as a suspension of the "general positing" (*Generalthesis*) and, correlatively, as a "bracketing" of "existing reality." The character of "existing" that we attribute prepredicatively to the world in the "general positing" must be put between brackets. Now Husserl quickly adds that consciousness is not affected by this disconnection. Although he leaves us in the dark about

---

[9] 95. See also 108. The purpose of the second chapter (and the conclusions and supplements of the third chapter) is to lay bare the insight that the phenomenological reduction is possible as the suspension of the natural attitude. See also a marginal note written after 1923 in 95 Husserliana III.

the motives behind this disconnection, we do get the impression that the epoché holds for the world outside consciousness. Was this not also the case for Descartes, with whose attempt at universal doubt Husserl here associates himself closely?[1] This impression is supported when we see how Husserl places the transcendent thing over against the immanent act. He speaks of the transcendent as doubtful and the immanent as beyond doubt.[2] The immanent is the object of an absolute positing, but the transcendent, by contrast, has only a relative existence. Seen in this light, the epoché appears to be a suspension of existential judgment with regard to the external world, a certain neutrality with regard to the question of its existence or non-existence.

But it appears that Husserl does not abide by this attitude. The original neutrality seems to turn into doubt and ultimately even denial. Is the final conclusion, i.e. that the world is only a correlate of consciousness and "beyond that nothing,"[3] not a negation of the wordl? If so, Husserl would then have broken out of his neutrality with regard to the external world in favor of a negative decision as to its reality character, as many interpreters maintain.

Furthermore, when LU is interpreted as a turn toward the object, whether on the basis of the existence in themselves of idealities or on the basis of the new theory of perception,[4] it is clear that Ideen I must be seen as a relapse into an immanentism of consciousness.[5] Husserl is then alleged to have given up the turn toward the object, under the influence of neo-Kantian thinkers. We know that this interpretation led to an estrangement between Husserl and many of his followers. It meant a break with the "realist" phenomenologists who had gathered around Husserl at the beginning of his professorship at Göttingen.[6]

(B) *The positive aspect of the reduction.* It appears that the reverse side of the exclusion of the world is a turn toward consciousness. In this respect, too, one might argue that what we encounter here is a renewed Cartesianism.[7] The limitation of the universality of the epoché seems to mean that consciousness does not fall under it. The region of

[1] See 53, 87, 118 and below 375.
[2] In the title of par. 46.
[3] 93.
[4] See above 161 and 260.
[5] See Fink op.cit. 327 note 1 and 321.
[6] See above 201 note 10, 260.
[7] In CM, Husserl speaks of a "neo-Cartesianism" 43 of a "Cartesianism of the twentieth century" 3.

consciousness need not be put between brackets, for it is given absolutely and is the object of an absolute existential judgment.

But this interpretation, which is sketched here in rough strokes, seems to conflict with two of Husserl's central theses, which is why the discussion about the reduction still has not come to an end. These two theses, which also seem to conflict with each other, are: (1) Nothing is lost in the reduction, and therefore the so-called "external world" is not lost. (2) The reduction applies to all of reality, including consciousness.

II. The Interpretation of the Epoché

(A) The epoché bears not on reality but on our interpretation of it. In the first chapter, in which the epoché is introduced, Husserl speaks without further reflection of "being" and the "positing of being." The rest of the meditation then concentrates on the meaning which this term 'being' can have, as Husserl establishes the principial difference between the modes of being of the thing and of consciousness.

He bases this difference first of all on the difference in givenness. When he now contrasts the presumptive givenness of the thing with the absolute givenness of consciousness, he does not mean to imply that the thing is not given. Indeed, this would be contrary to the phenomenological principle that every given is originally justified as such. The point is rather to characterize the *mode* of this givenness more precisely. Husserl does this by applying the criterion of apodicticity to it. It then becomes apparent that the givenness of a thing does not exclude an eventual correction in the future; that is to say, it is not inconceivable – as it is in the case of an inner experience (*Erlebnis*) – for future experience to alter the present experience. The intent of this observation is not to dispute the veracity of perception but simply to point out that this veracity is relative. Therefore Husserl's talk of the doubtfulness of transcendent being is especially misleading, for the doubt applies not to this givenness as such (as in the thought of Descartes and Brentano) but to the eventual claim to apodictic evidence. We have apodictic evidence only with regard to consciousness.

As a matter of fact, doubt does arise in the perception of things, for on closer examination the thing may turn out to be different than we thought. But as long as this is not the case and experiences confirm one another, there is no reason to doubt. In the course of experience, normally, no doubt would arise about the continuing harmony of experience, although there would be corrections of a subordinate nature. In fact, we do not doubt for a moment that there is an ultimate harmony by reference to which all illusion can be corrected – and we are right not to doubt this. To use the language of EU, there remains a universal basis of world-belief. This is justified because *actual* experience gives no support to the supposition of an explosion of the totality of experience that would make the world dissolve into irreconcilable conflicts.

In a later note on this passage, Husserl writes that the world has a certain "empirical indubitability" because it is impossible to doubt experiénce as long as it proceeds harmoniously.[8] Thus we see that the presumptivity of experience can well be paired with its indubitability. However, the actual continuity of experience in the same style, i.e. its consistency, remains a presumption or supposition from the apodictic standpoint. The ultimate annihilation of the world remains conceivable even if it is not a possibility suggested by experience.

I must point out once more that Husserl does not intend this as an undermining of outer experience. This experience must be described just as it is given. It is true that it is only justified relatively, but we must be sure to recognize this justification as a justification.[9] It makes no sense to criticize an experience simply because it is the way it is. In FTL, Husserl makes this complaint about Descartes, who allowed himself to be led by the idea of an absolute being hovering above the clouds of knowledge;[10] as a result, he was no longer able to see that the experience of things is also an original self-giving. (In Krisis, Husserl speaks of evidence as a rigid logical idol which makes it impossible to do justice to the evidence of experience.[11]) Hence Descartes arrives at the absurd idea of wanting to improve on the experience through a divine guarantee. Thus we see that Husserl's use of the principle of apodicticity in no way represents a failure to appreciate the data of experience. The epoché neither denies nor doubts the givenness of the world; what it denies is its claim to absoluteness. In the epoché, Husserl declares, "I *do not negate* this 'world' as though I were a

---

[8] 87. See also FTL 208, 222. Husserl's talk of the indubitability of outer perception must not be taken as evidence against his idealism. There are two kinds of doubt: empirical and apodictic. What is indubitable from an empirical standpoint could be dubitable from an apodictic standpoint.

[9] 159.

[10] FTL 249.

[11] Krisis 237 (E 234).

sophist, and I do not doubt its existence as though I were a skeptic."[12] In Krisis he therefore calls the epoché a *quasi*-skeptical epoché.[13]

That the epoché does not represent doubt is also apparent from the fact that it is always possible. The carrying out of the epoché belongs to "the realm of our complete freedom." Therefore Husserl can begin his explication with the remark: "*Instead of remaining in this attitude* [he means the natural attitude], *we now wish to alter it radically.*" The carrying out of this epoché is a *willed action*, but doubt is not. We can only doubt if experience gives us occasion to doubt.[14]

The following argument can be added to the preceding. If the suspension represented nothing more than doubt, it would be impossible to understand how the epoché is supposed to bring about such a revolutionary turn in Husserl's own thought and in the thought of mankind, as Husserl believed it would. Doubt, after all, is an act that occurs often in the natural attitude. Doubting does not make anyone a transcendental phenomenologist. No, we are dealing here with an act *sui generis* which cannot be compared to any known act (i.e. known from Husserl's pre-transcendental, psychological analysis of consciousness).

Therefore it is not identical with the so-called "neutral" stance of consciousness either, even though Husserl calls it a "not taking part" (*nicht mitmachen, keinen Gebrauch machen von*).[15] (The term 'disinterested spectator' does not yet occur in Ideen I.) The neutral stance of consciousness is contrasted with positing or belief; it was already analyzed by Brentano under the heading "mere presentation." We also encountered it as such in LU. It is an act known in the natural attitude and is not identical with the epoché, even though Husserl speaks of the two acts as closely related. The putting out of action of the general positing is not to be compared to any of the normal modifications of consciousness.[16]

The import of this act only become clear when we keep Husserl's meditation on the two kinds of being in mind. Contrary to all the so-called evidences of the natural attitude, this act brings about a reversal in our estimation of being.[17] Not matter but consciousness is the

[12] 56.
[13] Krisis 78f (E 77f).
[14] 56, 54.
[15] 94, 54, 223; compare FTL 52.
[16] 55.
[17] 58.

absolute bearer of reality. This re-evaluation came about through an eidetic analysis of outer perception, i.e. the perception that is the source of the natural attitude. In the natural attitude, perception is "something without essence in itself, an empty looking of an empty 'ego' toward the object itself."[18] This means that the naive person is not aware of the absoluteness of his own consciousness, and that he sees reality as "present," as "simply there" or "simply existing." We encountered all these expressions in the first chapter of the Fundamental Consideration.

The epoché, then, must be understood as a taking back of this absolutizing of material reality. Thus it is not directed toward transcendent reality as such but against the supposition that reality is simply there and present. "What happens is not that actual reality is 'changed' or denied but that an absurd interpretation of it, which thus contradicts its *own* sense clarified by insight, is disposed of."[19] *What is put in brackets is not the existence of the world* – this was already done in LU, as we have seen – *but a certain absurd interpretation of it.* (We shall see later that this absurd interpretation makes necessary an epoché in the sense of LU, and that seeing through this interpretation makes such an epoché superfluous.[20]) Therefore the epoché can also be described as a "changing of value" (*Umwertung*) which frees the thing from false interpretations, reveals it in its true being, and thus also fully recognizes it as such in this relativity. "The disconnection at the same time has the character of changing the value of the sign; thereby that which is changed in value is re-instated in the phenomenological sphere."[21]

If this "bracketing" (*Einklammerung*) does not mean putting existence as such between brackets, the suspension of the general positing, correlatively, does not mean putting belief as such or the positing of existence out of action. What is suspended is a certain kind of belief, a belief that absolutizes the world. The suspension of belief in the world is not a cancellation of this positing but only a cancellation of a certain "natural" quality it possesses. Husserl describes it as a "peculiar mode of consciousness which fixes on the original simple positing ... and transforms it in an equally peculiar way."[22]

---

[18] 70f., see also IP 11.
[19] 107.
[20] See below 432.
[21] 142.
[22] 55. See also CM 61, 188.

What happens is not that belief in an external world becomes disbelief or doubt but that a false mode of belief is corrected and thereby becomes a *belief founded in reality*, a belief that corresponds to the actual state of affairs. Thus Husserl can say that we do not give up the positing, and that the epoché is compatible with an uninterrupted belief in the truth of what is posited.[23] Thus it is a different kind of cancellation than normally takes place when belief becomes doubt or neutrality ("mere presentation").

Now we also understand why this epoché is within the range of our freedom. It follows from the meditation on being that the general positing is a certain interpretation – an interpretation that can always be suspended. We shall see that this view has far-reaching ethical consequences for Husserl, for it contains an appeal to the philosophers and, through them, to mankind in general for a liberation from the blinding effect of the natural attitude. This lies within the power of the philosophers and is therefore their calling.[24]

That this re-interpretation of being does not represent a negation is noted emphatically by Husserl himself. It is not a dissolution of being in consciousness or a subjective idealism. "To anyone who objects to our arguments by maintaining that this would amount to transforming the entire world into subjective illusion and embracing a 'Berkeleyan idealism,' we can only reply that he has not understood the meaning of our argument." Denying the absoluteness of reality is no more an injustice to reality than denying that a square is round is an injustice to the square, for an absolute reality is just an absurd as a round square.[25] The bracketing does not mean that that which is placed between brackets is "erased from the phenomenological blackboard."[26] It "continues to exist, just as that which is bracketed exists within brackets."[27] It is provided with a certain index, a different sign.[28] It is no longer absolute reality but a "unity of sense" which presupposes an absolute consciousness as the field for sense-giving.[29]

---

[23] 54, 55. See also CM 72. The epoché is a suspension of a "*natural* positing of being" and not of the positing of being as such. The correlate of perception retains the character of "really existing" 97.

[24] See below 506.

[25] 106f.

[26] 142.

[27] 54.

[28] 142. This expression can also be interpreted psychologically, as it is 183, 204, 278, 279, see below 427.

[29] 106.

In CM, Husserl also uses the terms 'phenomenon' and 'cogitatum qua cogitatum' to refer to the result of this changing in value. After the reduction, the world recurs as phenomenon.[30] We must not interpret these statements – as is often done – to mean that reality is lost while only the phenomenon remains. Those who make this mistake reproach Husserl for withdrawing from reality to a phenomenon and never returning to reality. This phenomenon is *reality itself* in the meaning which the reduction gives to being, for reality exists only as "merely phenomenal being" or "merely intentional being." The same applies to the concept of sense. When Husserl says that the world is sense (*Sinn*) and "beyond this nothing," he does not mean that reality is lost, for he also maintains that "the world itself has its entire being as a certain 'sense.'"[31] For Husserl, this bracketing of the object does not mean giving the object up but purifying it.[32] Actually, it is only *after* the transcendental reduction that we can speak of a turn toward the object, for the object is now known as it really is and need no longer be disconnected because of its supposed inaccessibility, as in LU.[33]

This new interpretation of being implies a radical solution to the epistemological problem of transcendence, to which I will return later. It also implies that consciousness as "residue" is not psychological consciousness but transcendental, absolute consciousness. With this we have arrived at the question of the interpretation of the residue of the reduction.

---

[30] CM 60, 71, 75. See also Krisis 177 (E 174). On this term 'phenomenon,' see below 375, 431.

[31] 107, see also CM 8, 123, 126, 164.

[32] The world does not disappear but loses its character as basis of being or 'Seinsboden,' see above 357. It is in this light that we must read Husserl's famous statement in CM, 183: "We must first lose the world by the ἐποχη in order to regain it by a universal self-examination." This is a New Testament way of speaking that Husserl used more often, see e.g. EP II 123. We read that through the reduction "the natural child or worldly child is transformed into the phenomenological child in the kingdom of the pure spirit," and that the "all (Seinsall) of the worldly child is not the all as such." The quotation from CM includes an appeal to Augustine's statement that we should seek not to go out of ourselves but into ourselves, for truth dwells in the inner man. This inner man is the absolute consciousness in which we "live and move and have our being," EP I 249. Here the world returns as a constituted correlate that we "understand," CM 164, on the basis of its rootedness in consciousness. Compare Fink, 'Die phänomenologische Philosophie E. Husserl's in der gegenwärtigen Kritik,' on the retaining (*Einbehaltung*) of the world 342, 370, 375, 383 and on the justification of realism 333, 335, 377f. See also below 405.

[33] See below 446f.

(B) The epoché as revelation of transcendental subjectivity. Is it the intent of the epoché to isolate a certain indubitable zone of the world from the rest of the world? We saw that Husserl does indeed fix on consciousness as a mundane region in his analysis. But at the same time it became clear that consciousness undergoes a radical reinterpretation in the course of the investigation. It becomes apparent that it is not a certain stratum of the person as a psycho-physical unity founded in matter but the bearer of material reality. *The corollary of this reinterpretation of matter is the reinterpretation of consciousness.* The two are actually facets of one and the same Copernican revolution. Insight into the relativity of the world implies the absoluteness of consciousness, and vice versa. If the world is a dependent correlate of consciousness, it would be absurd to make its being independent (= absolutize it) and then regard consciousness as one of its strata. Consciousness would then be founded in a product of its own constitution! It is clear that such an interpretation, too, must and *can* be suspended. The meditation on being makes the absurdity of this natural or naturalizing interpretation of consciousness as clear as day. Thus Husserl says repeatedly that the suspension of the world includes *myself.*

It is in this light that we must read the noteworthy statement about the limitation of the universality of the epoché. According to Husserl, the limitation is that we disconnect the *total* natural world. This claim loses its paradoxical character when we realize that the limitation is to be sought in the adjective 'natural.' What is disconnected is not reality but its natural character. The epoché limits itself to unmasking an absolutizing of the world (which implies a relativizing of consciousness). True reality is not affected by such a disconnection. Therefore the epoché is not so much a limitation (*Einschränkung*) *within* the natural world as a movement beyond the limits of the natural world as such (*Entschränkung*),[34] that is to say, an unlocking of its depth dimension, its transcendental "ground." We free ourselves from a certain view of the world. What remains is not a remainder or residue of the natural world but the totality of this world freed from a naturalistic interpretation.[35] Husserl already points out in the introduction to Ideen I that the reduction is a means by which "we push aside the cognitive

[34] Nachwort 153 and Fink op.cit. Kantstud. 342, 359.
[35] On the term 'residue,' see 94 note 1, 108, 109, 173, 202, and also Husserl's notes in 59 Husserliana III, and his self-criticism EP II, 432.

limitations belonging to the essence of all natural forms of investigation, deflecting the one-sided line of vision proper to it, until we
have finally attained the free horizon of 'transcendentally' purified
phenomena and, thereby, the field of phenomenology in our peculiar
sense."[26] Husserl begins his analysis with consciousness as a region of
the psycho-physical unity of the person because he hopes to undermine
the natural attitude gradually as he focuses on it. On the basis of
pedagogical considerations, he accommodates himself to the cus-
tomary way of thinking of the natural attitude in order to lay bare its
presuppositions.[37] In the course of the investigation it becomes
apparent that consciousness is not just some region but the *original*
region.[38]

Thus the epoché, as an unmasking of the natural interpretation, is at
the same time a way to radical self-knowledge, to an awareness of the
power of consciousness, a power that remains hidden in the natural
attitude. The view of consciousness as a mundane region is a self-
apperception that hides consciousness from itself. I do function as a
transcendental ego – thanks to whose intentional "productions" the
world exists – but I am not aware of this myself.[39] In a certain sense, a
revelation of consciousness is also possible within the natural attitude. I
can abandon the strictly objective (*gegenständlich*) attitude and reflect
upon myself. The analysis of consciousness in LU shows this
sufficiently. Yet this does not give us insight into the absoluteness of
consciousness. Such reflection continues to rest on the natural basis of
being. Therefore it cannot overcome psychologism in epistemology.
We will arrive at a radical insight into consciousness only via a special
phenomenological reflection, a reflection which does not participate in
the general positing of the natural world.[40]

Thus we come to the conclusion that the two claims of Husserl
mentioned earlier do not exclude each other but rather imply each
other. The suspension of a natural interpretation of *total* reality is at the
same time a *return* to total reality – now in purified form. Precisely
because everything is disconnected, everything can also return in
transcendental phenomenology. "We have actually lost nothing but

[36] 3.
[37] 3. See below 374, 432ff.
[38] 141.
[39] CM 164; Krisis 174, 209, 214 (E 171, 205, 214); Fink op. cit. 347, 366, 372f. See also
below 469.
[40] 94f. See below 431, 466ff.

have gained the entirety of absolute being which, rightly understood, contains all worldly transcendencies within itself and 'constitutes' them within itself."[41]

PARAGRAPH THIRTEEN. THE PROBLEM OF THE "WAYS" TO TRANSCENDENTAL PHENOMENOLOGY

When Husserl characterized his philosophy as transcendental idealism, he was well aware that his was not the first system to bear this name. Yet he insisted strongly that it was in his own thought that transcendental idealism was first justified in a rigorous descriptive manner strictly on the basis of intuition as source. He maintained that his idealism does not represent metaphysical construction. Transcendental conscious-ness is "indubitably manifest in its absoluteness and immediately given in intuition."[1] Not idealism but realism is "mythical."[2] We must remember that Husserl had already defended the doctrine of the intuition of essences against the charge of metaphysical construction. Essences are not metaphysical phantoms but given entities. We restrict ourselves rigorously to the given without any hypothetical or in-terpretive explanation, without making any appeal to accepted theories.[3]

This also applies to the transcendental reduction. Here the phrase 'to the things' (*zu den Sachen*) means a strictly descriptive analysis of consciousness in which we set out to do nothing more or less than to make manifest what is there.[4] Phenomenology strives for the "greatest possible presuppositionlessness" and "absolute reflective insight."[5] Writes Husserl, full of confidence in himself and his readers: "The reader experienced in scientific activity will be able to gather from the conceptual precision of the expositions that we have not plucked bold philosophical fancies out of the air but have concentrated carefully acquired items of knowledge in descriptions that are general in character, on the basis of fundamental systematic labor in this field," i.e. the field of consciousness.[6]

---

[41] 94, see also 59.
[1] 106, see also 313 and Fink op.cit. 378.
[2] 101.
[3] PSW 305; Id I 35, 33, 42, 53 and 157. See above 244.
[4] 58, 180.
[5] 121.
[6] 107; compare Fink op.cit. 339.

Peculiar difficulties present themselves when transcendental phenomena are described. Phenomenology does appeal to the given, but this appeal is not beyond dispute. At the outset it is not at all clear what is actually given. We have already seen that absolute consciousness is originally hidden in its absolute character, and also that the world shows itself as otherwise than it is. It appears that an extremely difficult operation, a phenomenological reduction, is necessary in order to open our eyes and uncover the field of the new apodictic science.[7] By nature our knowledge is darkened by deeply rooted habits of thought and mental limitations that are never cast into doubt but must first be broken.[8] Up until now, transcendental consciousness has never been seen. History shows us that there is indeed a certain longing for transcendental phenomenology, but this field nevertheless remained unknown and "hardly suspected."[9] This is because we are dogmatists by nature and are continually subject to the very strong temptation to fall back into the natural attitude.[10] If that which offers itself as obvious were the truly given, no "tiresome studies," no "complicated reduction with the accompanying difficult reflections" would be necessary to discover the truly given. We must first give ourselves to that which is given! As Husserl characteristically puts it, we have "laid it bare" (*herauspräpariert*) by means of the transcendental reduction.[11]

This situation now creates great difficulties for the transcendental phenomenologist who hopes to communicate his results to his fellow men in the natural attitude. Husserl's assistant Fink, with his well-known preference for striking formulas, has called this the "paradox of the situation of expression." This paradox occurs when transcendental phenomenology becomes a "philosophy making itself known to the world." The phenomenologist turns to the dogmatist to reveal transcendental consciousness to him. But is this possible? Is there any point of contact between them? The phenomenologist must speak the language of the natural attitude in order to be understood. This language is to be used to show that the natural attitude is not grounded. Even though he lives in the transcendental attitude and does not give it

[7] 108; 115.
[8] 3, 58.
[9] 59, 121, 118.
[10] 116f.
[11] 163.

up, the phenomenologist must transpose himself into the natural attitude in order to break through it from within. The transcendental insights are thus poured into a natural language. This is the "paradox of the phenomenological sentence" (*Satz*). This language will of necessity always fall short. All words have a mundane meaning, and we can only go beyond these meanings by using other mundane words. In the language of the phenomenologist, then, there is a necessary internal contradiction between "mundane word-meanings and their transcendental sense." Neither does the creation of a new artificial language represent a solution, for the intent is precisely to be understood by the dogmatist.[12]

This problem formulated so well by Fink is the problem of the "ways" from the natural attitude to transcendental phenomenology. It is not my intention to deal exhaustively with this much disputed problem, which plays a large role especially in the thought of the later Husserl. I will limit myself to Ideen I and try to make a contribution toward solving the problem within this framework. What does Ideen I teach us about the ways? First and foremost, I would argue that the preceding analyses suggest that all expressions must be interpreted in the light of the apodictic criticism of experience, which applies the criterion of the inconceivability of non-existence. This is what reveals the relativity and presumptivity of material reality as well as the absoluteness and necessity of consciousness. Only after this criticism can the possibility of the epoché and the meaning of the epoché be understood. Until the Fundamental Consideration reaches this point, all determinations remain provisional and – as Fink puts it – "bound to the starting point" (*einsatzgebunden*).[13]

As long as we are not aware that consciousness is the "all of being" that constitutes all transcendencies within itself, we do not understand that the region of consciousness is the *original* region, and that the residue is not a part of the world but the totality.[14] We see Husserl struggling with language when he says that the region sought is not a partial region. It is "principially separated" from the world and all other regions, "but not separated in the sense of a contiguity, as though

---

[12] Fink op.cit. 381f.

[13] Fink op.cit. 347.

[14] In a note to Husserliana III 57, Husserl speaks of the term 'übrig' as "dubious" (*bedenklich*). Compare his self-criticism with regard to the term 'residue' in EP II, 432; Id III 71ff.

it could extend itself by attaching itself to the world to form a more comprehensive whole together with it."[15] Consciousness is separated from the world, then, but not by a "boundary" (*Grenze*). This would in fact be impossible, for consciousness takes in everything and is "without boundaries."[16] In another passage, the term 'delimit' (*abgrenzen*) was therefore later replaced by 'point out' (*aufweisen*).[17]

Because it is natural to conceive of consciousness at first as psychological consciousness, as "mind" (*Seele*), as part of the psychophysical unity of the "person," a number of other expressions are also understood in the wrong way.[18] The description of reality as "sense" and "phenomenon," as "merely intentional" and "phenomenal being," is understood as a reduction of reality to psychical correlates of consciousness.[19] This speaking in the language of the natural attitude is the chief reason for the difficulties sketched in the preceding paragraph. This also applies to the description of the general positing and its suspension. At first this positing is automatically interpreted as a positing of reality as such, which suggests that its cancellation (*Aufhebung*) must indeed be some sort of doubt or neutralization. Only later does it appear that this positing represents some kind of absolutizing interpretation which is purified through the cancellation, a process that does not entail doubt about the posited reality as such.

As I see it, something similar must be said about Husserl's profession of agreement with certain views of Descartes. In general, these references to Descartes have been taken much too seriously and have in turn been used to criticize Husserl. In the first chapter, Husserl adopts Descartes' experiment of doubt but adds immediately that it is only a methodological device.[20] Descartes' attempt at universal doubt also had an entirely different purpose, namely, "bringing to light an absolutely indubitable sphere of being," which for Descartes is the immanent sphere of consciousness. Husserl's question is not *what* is given but *how* the given is given and what mode of being it has. Thus the two thinkers reach entirely different results. The point at which Descartes arrives is psychological consciousness (a so-called absolutely certain sphere), and from there he then attempts – in an absurd way,

---

[15] In a note to 59 Husserliana III.
[16] 96.
[17] In a note to 58 Husserliana III.
[18] Nachwort Id III 154.
[19] See below 430f.
[20] 54.

according to Husserl – to re-establish contact with a world that was at first shut out.[2] At the climax of the Fundamental Consideration, after the conclusion about the separability of consciousness has been drawn, Husserl says that thereby "a central, though not fully developed, thought of the . . . meditations of Descartes finally comes into its own." He even speaks of a certain impulse to transcendental phenomenology "in the wonderfully profound fundamental consideration of Descartes."[22] From these statements it becomes clear that Husserl's Cartesianism should not be overestimated. Edith Stein rightly claims that Husserl would have reached his transcendental idealism even without Descartes.[23] At most, the experiment of doubt and the discovery of the cogito are for Husserl an occasion for the unfolding of his own argument. The supposition that Descartes is mentioned only for the sake of the "scientifically schooled reader" whom we have already encountered seems to me to be justified. It is a suitable point of contact to begin an appeal to the "dogmatist" schooled in traditional philosophy!

Some commentators have expressed surprise that Husserl never gave up this Cartesian way. They forget too easily that at the very outset, Husserl adopted the Cartesian approach in a manner of his own – or "critically purified it," as he himself puts it.[24] When he criticizes this method in Krisis, his complaint is not about this way as such but about its generality at the very outset in speaking of consciousness (something for which he already offered his apologies in Ideen I).[25] Thus we do arrive in one leap at the transcendental ego, but because there is no preceding explication, this becomes apparent only in a certain "emptiness of content," so that at first we do not know what to do with it. A consequence of this is that we easily fall back into the natural attitude, as is also apparent from the reaction to Ideen I. Over against this Cartesian way, Husserl then places two other ways, one out of the life-world and the other out of psychology. The one from the life-world also

---

[21] In later writings, Husserl shows that for Descartes, the reduction to consciousness is only a detour in founding the natural sciences, their validity being accepted in advance. Thus, despite the return to the *cogito*, Descartes became the father of modern physicalistic objectivism. CM 4, 45, 48, 49, 63, 93, 182; Krisis 76, 83, 86, 94, 396f, 407, 423 (E 74, 81, 84, 91).

[22] 87, 118.

[23] *La Phénoménologie*. Journées d'études de la société Thomiste, 103.

[24] Krisis 156ff (E 153ff).

[25] 107.

begins from the natural standpoint, "with purely natural life in the world." After an analysis of this natural life, we come to the transcendental ego, but now "enriched by pieces of significant insight worked out along the way followed."[26] The advantage of this method is that when we reach transcendental consciousness, we already have a certain insight into its material structure. Husserl then follows a method which is the opposite of that used in Ideen I, as it were. In the latter work we were suddenly placed on the transcendental level; then came further analyses of the structures of transcendental consciousness. Apparently Husserl later thought it would be better to begin by giving concrete insight into the newly discovered field instead of going into principial questions immediately. We shall see later that a beginning of the "way from psychology" is already to be found in Ideen I.[27]

Returning to the problem of language, we see that the phenomenologist does indeed have a communication problem. Husserl reflected on this more and more as the years went by. This issue plays a particularly important role in understanding the difference between psychological and transcendental phenomenology, for all expressions are understood immediately in a psychological sense because the two types of phenomenology refer materially to the same thing.[28] The language of the people, in which the philosopher must express himself, simply has this "mundane" meaning.[29]

Yet we must be careful not to go too far in the opposite direction. It is not the case that what issues from the words is only an appeal whose meaning must be understood existentially, (as with Jaspers).[30] I would very much like to shield Husserl from such interpretations, for they are entirely in conflict with the spirit of his philosophy. Husserl did not intend to utter mystical words that must be appropriated in a personal way; he wished instead to teach a rigorous science into which we can gain apodictic insight. The heart of his argument, the basis for understanding everything, is the apodictic test to which inner and outer perception are subjected. Now then, such an analysis can be carried out by anyone. This analysis is no more mysterious than the analysis of an

---

[26] Krisis 157 (E 154).
[27] See below 432.
[28] See below 425ff.
[29] See Krisis 192, 213f, 252, 457 (E 188, 209f, 248) and Id I 6 and 123.
[30] EP II 182.

essence. The basis of Husserl's confidence is exactly this general human instrument that carries out a *repeatable thought-experiment*. The meaning of language is determined exclusively by what is seen. It is a "faithful expression of clear givens."[31] Thus there really is a "point of contact." Husserl's disappointment about the reception of his transcendental phenomenology is also to be understood against this background. It seems to me that Fink, who lays very little emphasis on Husserl's apodictic proof of the relativity of the world, has followed his preference for striking and paradoxical formulas too much. This can lead to interpretations that Fink himself could not have intended, for he emphasizes that phenomenology is not speculative: the pathos of phenomenology is characterized by the rejection of all systematic construction and the demand for rigorous science.[32] However strange it may appear, the problem of the origin of the world, this "legendary theme" of theology and dogmatic metaphysics, was first dealt with in human history in a scientific and theoretical manner by phenomenology.[33] The epoché is an "utmost exertion in the theoretical self-conquest of man."[34]

PARAGRAPH FOURTEEN. TWO INTERPRETATIONS – STUMPF AND RICOEUR

In Paragraph 12, I tried to sketch the possible misunderstandings to which the text of Ideen I might give rise. I avoided any reference to the many interpretations that have in fact been offered, for my goal is not to write a history of Husserl interpretation. However, I shall now make two exceptions to this rule. Among the many commentators on Husserl, there are some who have something of special importance to say, in my opinion. Stumpf and Ricoeur are certainly among them. I have chosen Stumpf because he represents the school of Brentano in a certain sense. Apart from Brentano, Stumpf was the one to whom Husserl felt most closely bound. Both honored the same teacher, and both reported their memories of him in Kraus's book on Brentano. Furthermore, Husserl studied under Stumpf, who was his senior by eleven years, and wrote his *Habilitationsschrift* under Stumpf in Halle.

[31] 123f.
[32] Fink op.cit. 345.
[33] Fink op.cit. 341, see also 339.
[34] Fink op.cit. 366.

On various occasions, I have pointed to the influence of Stumpf's ideas on Husserl. Husserl was aware of this influence and devoted his LU to Stumpf "in admiration and friendship." This work was written while Husserl was still Stumpf's colleague at Halle. Thus, we may take it that Stumpf meets all the conditions for understanding Husserl and his new ways.

Ricoeur, in addition, requires particular attention because of his French translation of Ideen I, complete with an introduction and a running commentary. Ricoeur is a representative of the French (existential) branch of phenomenology, which is one of the most important philosophical movements to which the work of Husserl has given rise. Furthermore, Ricoeur is a painstaking interpreter of the work of Husserl; he has a proper awareness of the difference between existential and transcendental phenomenology and strives for a historically faithful interpretation of Husserl.[1]

Each of these interpretations in its own way illustrates the problem of the residue that is left after the disconnection.

I. Stumpf

Stumpf's posthumously published *Erkenntnislehre* includes a critique of Husserlian phenomenology that bears on the phenomenology defended in Ideen I. Stumpf writes that despite the far-reaching influence of Ideen I, its actual thrust has seldom been understood. He continues: "Yet this presentation cannot lay unconditional claim to being in precise agreement with the intentions of Husserl either." Despite this note of caution, however, Stumpf does believe that he has indicated the overall direction of Ideen I: "we could not be mistaken in characterizing the quest for objective axioms as the most basis thrust – in particular, the axioms on which philosophy is based."[2]

By objective axioms, Stumpf means regional or material eidetic statements. Like Husserl himself, Stumpf distinguishes them from formal – "universal" in Stumpf's own terminology – axioms that bear on all objects without exception. Regional eidetic statements apply only to a particular area.[3] Husserl assumes – rightly, according to

---

[1] In a separate publication, I hope to show that what Merleau-Ponty writes about Husserl cannot be taken seriously as a *historical* interpretation. When he writes about Husserl, he does so not as historian but as mythologist.

[2] Erkenntnislehre I 186.

[3] Op.cit. I 155.

Stumpf – that such a regional ontology must be given for every area, and that such an ontology "seeks and formulates the a priori eidetic laws on which the special sciences are based."[4] In addition to this, Husserl also wants a "pure" phenomenology which is to become the eidetic basic discipline of philosophy. "It is required as the basic science of philosophy, analogous the regional phenomenologies as the basic sciences of the special disciplines."[5]

Stumpf regards such a pure phenomenology as "a phantasm, indeed, an internal contradiction." What could such a pure phenomenology be? Stumpf sees only two possibilities. Phenomenology as an a priori theory of objects is either regional or universal. Husserl does not mean that it is universal or logical, for he speaks of the new science not as universal but as "pure." If it were a regional ontology, we would understand what Husserl means, but then it would be nothing new.[6] Something of this sort had already been proposed by Brentano, Stumpf, Meinong, and even Husserl himself in LU. Thus Husserl apparently had something else in mind, for all the material-eidetic sciences are also to be disconnected. "But this is only to say what pure phenomenology *does not deal with*, not what it does deal with and what kinds of eidetic cognitions are left after this radical disconnection of all material-eidetic concepts and disciplines."

We see that Stumpf here poses the same question that Husserl raises: what can *remain* after the suspension of all of familiar reality and of the sciences, including the eidetic sciences? Thinking in Husserl's way would require calling Stumpf's answer a typical answer of the natural attitude. For someone who only sees and recognizes the natural world, of course, it is a complete riddle what could remain after the disconnection of this world. This also makes it apparent why Stumpf, who believes that he has grasped the general thrust of Ideen I, concludes his discussion of pure phenomenology as follows: "The pure ego that is to be seen through the pure 'ego-regard' is all too reminiscent of the Nirvana of Indian penitents whose gaze is fixed on their navels. I understand fully what the penetrating author of phenomenology meant by the intuition of essences, and I regard every thinking person as capable of this kind of knowledge – whatever name we may give it. But

---

[4] Op.cit. I 189.
[5] Op.cit. I 186, 192.
[6] Op.cit. I 188 note I, 190.

here we are staring into darkness, indeed, into absolute nothingness. (A dark field of vision would at least be something.)"[7]

II. Ricoeur

The noteworthy thing about Ricoeur's interpretation is that he warns earnestly against the Cartesian interpretation of Husserl's phenomenology on the one hand, but on the other hand sees important Cartesian elements in the argument of Ideen I. He believes that the Fundamental Consideration manifests a Cartesian style and that this style has given rise to mistaken notions about it. According to Ricoeur, Husserl himself is the main cause of these misunderstandings and must be protected against himself. (This is not necessary on my interpretation.)

According to Ricoeur, this Cartesianism is not just reflected in terms like 'region,' 'residue' and 'suspension' but is characteristic of the entire course of the argument in the second chapter. Consciousness is separated from the world and is characterized as indubitable. The experiment of world-annihilation is an eminently Cartesian step, even though Husserl gives other reasons for the separation than Descartes.[8] According to Ricoeur, the residue of this operation is an absolute being in the sense of the natural attitude; that is to say, a certain region *of natural reality* is posited as absolute.[9] In this context Ricoeur appeals to the passage where Husserl says that he wants to limit the epoché. He reads this as meaning that only a part of the natural world is subjected to the epoché, namely, the transcendent thing. Ricoeur is aware that this makes possible a dangerous interpretation of the reduction. It appears as though Husserl, remaining in the natural attitude, continues to want to separate a part of the world, i.e. consciousness.[10] According to Ricoeur, it is not made clear in the Fundamental Consideration itself

---

[7] Op.cit. I 192. This is reminiscent of a well-known passage in which Husserl says that the whole world is only a correlate of consciousness "and *beyond this* nothing." Did this perhaps make Stumpf think of the famous conclusion of the first volume of Schopenhauer's *The World as Will and Representation?* Schopenhauer wrote: "to those in whom the will has turned and denied itself [this is analogous to Husserl's 'change of attitude'], this very real world of ours with all its suns and galaxies, is – nothing (E.F.J. Payne translation). In CM, Husserl opposes an interpretation à la Stumpf: "therefore this *phenomenological* ἐποχη or this *bracketing* of the objective world does not leave us confronting nothing," 60.

[8] *Idées directrices* note 1 to page 54 and 80; note 2 to 85. For non-Cartesian motives, see note 2 to 80 and 86.

[9] Note 2, 85; note 3, 86 and 87, see also note 4, 92.

[10] Note 1, 56.

that this is not the intention. It is his view that the epoché as introduced here is psychological; it is a reduction to the psychological subject. The analysis of this subject in the second chapter is a piece of intentional psychology.[11] Does Husserl himself not say at the outset that he wishes to begin with an analysis of natural consciousness?[12]

Ricoeur sees this intentional psychology as a pedagogical aid that must prepare the way for the transcendental reduction.[13] This reduction itself, which must elevate psychology to the transcendental level, is not present in Ideen I, according to Ricoeur. The true transcendental phenomenology remains a pretence in Ideen I; it is a promise that is not fulfilled. That the residue is not a psychological consciousness, that it is not one region among others but the original region, is indicated in Ideen I but not explicitly established.[14]

Thus Ricoeur sees a close connection between the first two chapters of the Fundamental Consideration insofar as both stand on the same *pre*-transcendental level. In the first chapter, the epoché is described as something limited – limited to the suspension of the external world. In the second chapter we find a concrete analysis of consciousness carried out in the same spirit. A part of the natural world, i.e. consciousness, is separated from the rest.

The first point has already been discussed. By this limitation, Husserl does not mean a limitation of the reduction to a part of the natural world. What he has in mind here is really a transcendental reduction.[15] Husserl himself does not become a victim of the problems of language. The second chapter is also on the transcendental level. Husserl does begin with natural consciousness, but he does so only *provisionally*. In the course of the argument, it becomes apparent that consciousness must not be conceived of as a region. The contrast drawn between thing and consciousness is not a Cartesian step. What is cast into doubt is not the existence of the external world as such but its *mode* of existence. The result of the analysis is that the given thing has only an intentional mode of existence. *At the same time* it becomes clear that consciousness cannot be a region founded in matter. The discovery of transcendental consciousness is the corollary of the reinterpretation of the thing. Thus

[11] Note 3, 57; note 1, 48; XVI, XXVI.
[12] Note 2, 58.
[13] Note 1, 56, 85; and 118; XV, XIX, XXVI.
[14] Note 1, 48, 56; note 4, 87; note 3, 93; note 2 and 3, 94; note 1, 96, 106, 115; XVI–XVII.
[15] See above 362ff.

I subscribe fully to Boehm's view that the climax of the Fundamental Consideration is to be found at the end of the second chapter, where Husserl himself says that his meditation has "reached a climax."[16] All that comes later is simply addition and elaboration.

At this point in the argument, the transcendental level has been reached. Husserl has shown that the transcendental reduction of which he spoke in the first chapter is indeed possible. All terms that still testify to a certain contextual limitation or limitation to the starting point (*Einsatzgebundenheit*) are then seen through in their provisional character. Thus we must not regard the work of the second and third chapters as a piece of intentional psychology that must afterwards be brought to the transcendental level through a "change in attitude" (*Einstellungsänderung*). Husserl does speak of these chapters as a transcendental preliminary consideration," which is something different from the "pre-transcendental consideration" that Ricoeur makes of them. Husserl speaks of a "preliminary consideration" (*Vorbetrachtung*) because we can grasp the possibility of the transcendental reduction only after this analysis.

It is true that in later works – particularly the Encyclopaedia Britannica article and Krisis – Husserl presents transcendental phenomenology as following an intentional psychology that must prepare the way for it. But this is actually a much later view that originated from critical reflection on the argument of Ideen I. Husserl then regarded it as a *shortcoming* of Ideen I that it contains so little material psychological analysis of consciousness before the transcendental reduction. We find only a few traces of this "way from psychology" in Ideen I, and they occur not in the Fundamental Consideration but in the introduction of the concept of noema in Part III.[17]

PARAGRAPH FIFTEEN. TWO ASSUMPTIONS

The argument in the Fundamental Consideration, as I have analyzed it, rests on two assumptions whose validity is determinative for the outcome of the entire argument. In other words, the argument is only

[16] R. Boehm, "Les ambiguités des concepts husserliens d'"immanence' et de 'transcendence,' 507ff, 517.

[17] See below 425. This is also what Fink has in mind when he says that certain passages are neutral, as it were, with regard to the difference between phenomenological psychology and transcendental phenomenology.

conclusive if two conditions are satisfied. Husserl does not mention them, but he obviously presupposes them as justified. The first of these assumptions is that the relation to one's own body is identical with the relation to the perceived object. The second is that one's own body is also a thing like any other physical thing, although it is likewise more than a thing. The entire argument depends on these two claims. It is not my intention to criticize Husserl on this point, even though I am convinced that this is one of the areas where criticism would have to begin. For the present, my task is to understand Husserl's argument on the basis of his own presuppositions.

(A) *Perception and incarnation.* In Paragraph 38, Husserl claims that in the natural attitude, consciousness is bound to the world in two ways. In the first place, consciousness forms a psycho-physical unity together with a body. Secondly, it is a consciousness of the world. Following Ricoeur's lead, we could speak of these two aspects as incarnation and perception. Ricoeur rightly adds: "the second is the key to the first for Husserl."[1] We see that Husserl does not return to the first relation at all. The argument is made in connection with the perceived thing. Once it has been shown that the perceived thing is an intentional correlate of consciousness, it is accepted as a foregone conclusion that this holds for one's own body as well. One's body is also a dependent correlate of consciousness, and the incarnation that appears to bind consciousness and the body together into a unity is an illusion of the natural attitude.

We see, then, that Husserl simply presupposes the identity of the two relations. This supposition, which apparently seemed obvious to Husserl, is at first an occasion for surprise, for what we confront here is such a central point in the argument that we expect further explanation – and rightly so. But here, too, we must seek to *understand Husserl in terms of the basis schema of his philosophy.* In Part I, in a discussion of Brentano's view of the psycho-physical connection, I pointed out that

---

[1] *Idées directrices* note 1, 70 see also 1, 103. This subordination of incarnation to perception is the object of an interesting criticism of Husserl made by Ricoeur. An analysis of the boundness of consciousness to the body as revealed in the phenomenon of will (in the dialectic of the voluntary and the involuntary) breaks through Husserl's idealism, which is based on an analysis of "spectator consciousness," of "representation": ". . . the phenomenology of will dispels certain ambiguities of sense-giving (*Sinngebung*) which cannot be taken up on the level of a theory of 'representation.'" "Méthodes et tâches d'une phénoménologie de la volonté" 126. See also E. Levinas, *En découvrant l'existence avec Husserl et Heidegger*, 132ff, 140, 143, 156.

Brentano ultimately equates this connection with the relation to the perceived thing.[2] This is a consequence of the way that physical and psychical phenomena are distinguished from one another. A physical phenomenon must always be the object of outer objectifying perception. If it were not, it would not be a physical phenomenon. Here the classification schema leaves no other possibility open. Exactly the same is the case for Husserl, as I pointed out in Part II.[3] The physical phenomenon was defined by Husserl in terms of the (altered) relation of intentionality. Thus we can see why Husserl, in the Fundamental Consideration, bases the argument on the perception of things. The proof holds for *every* relation of consciousness to matter.

(B) The body as a thing. Equating these two relations further implies that the body is regarded as a thing like any other thing outside us. This, too, was pointed out in Part II. Nowhere in the Fundamental Consideration do we find an indication that Husserl changed his view on this matter.[4] Some have pointed out that when Husserl speaks of the body, he uses the word 'Leib' rather than the word 'Körper.' On the basis of modern anthropology, this is then seen as an overcoming of Cartesianism, which regards one's own body as nothing other than a *res extensa* like any other physical thing. This view seems to find support in the posthomously published works Ideen II and III, where Husserl speaks at length of the so-called "constitution of the body" (Leibeskonstitution).

But it is certainly questionable whether what Husserl writes there can be regarded as a principial change in standpoint. On an a priori basis this is highly improbable, for Husserl does not mention any distinction between "Leib" and "Körper" in the Fundamental Consideration.

---

[2] See above 53f.

[3] See above 211.

[4] That the body is a thing is also apparent from Husserl's regional ontology, in which thing and "mind" (*Seele*) count as concrete regions, 30, 133f. Husserl's cardinal division of reality is not broken through by the "Leib." See, for example, 71: "The world of things, and in it our body (*Leib*), is continuously present to our perception." In PSW 298 Husserl speaks of "certain physical things called bodies" (*Leiber*). Via the body, consciousness is related to the unity of physical nature, PSW 319 and Id I 70. The body, like any other physical thing, is a "unity of thingly appearance," PSW 320, a "spatial thing," Id I 61f. The physical thing called the "Leib" is something special because of its central position as bearer of consciousness – and not because of its inner structure. Therefore, the epoché with regard to the thing can function at the same time as an abstraction from the body, see above 309. What is then excluded as the counterpart of pure psychology is the object of pure physics, of "pure physical experience," Husserliana III, 393.

Thus the doctrine of the constitution of the body must be seen more as an addition on the basis of the same presuppositions than as a correction or revision. I hope to show that this is indeed the case in a separate treatment of our knowledge of the alter ego, a knowledge in which the body plays a central role.[5]

PARAGRAPH SIXTEEN. THE MEANING OF THE FUNDAMENTAL CONSIDERATION AS FUNDAMENTAL ONTOLOGY

In Paragraph 7 we saw that the import of Husserl's new ontology in Ideen I is first of all negative. The goal of this ontology is a radical disruption of naturalism, which Husserl had already pointed to in 1910 as a growing danger to culture.[1] The anti-naturalism of the Fundamental Consideration is obvious from its final conclusions. This radical reflection was necessary, Husserl informs us, "because of the philosophical poverty in which we labor in vain under the beautiful name of a worldview grounded in natural science."[2]

The natural attitude is not the same thing as the natural*istic* attitude. In Ideen I, Husserl does not reflect on the relation between these two. The description he gives in the first chapter is pre-scientific. The polemical remarks he makes later in the argument are directed not against the natural attitude as such but against a philosophy that takes this attitude as its basis. Husserl is well aware of the difference, for he writes that the "philosophical absolutizing of the world ... is completely foreign to the natural point of view on the world."[3] Thus there is hidden in the natural attitude an absolutizing that is first turned into a philosophy by naturalism. Naturalism is a philosophical stream bound up with the discovery of "nature" in the sense of seventeenth century natural science.[4] Overwhelmed by natural science, the naturalist comes to regard everything as nature.[5] Thus naturalism must be distinguished from both the natural attitude and natural science. But there is also a connection: via the rise of natural science, the natural attitude leads to naturalism. This has important consequences for

---

[5] On the theme of intersubjectivity, see my review of Theunissen's *Der Andere*.
[1] PSW 293.
[2] 95.
[3] 107.
[4] PSW 294.
[5] See below 483f.

Husserl's philosophy of history, for it now becomes apparent that the hidden absolutization of the natural attitude only becomes manifest in history. This means that both naturalism and phenomenology (as a radical overcoming of this naturalism) are dated and in a certain sense dependent on the rise of this naturalism.

In this paragraph I will attempt to reconstruct a picture of naturalism on the basis of the givens of the Fundamental Consideration, with a view to understanding Husserl's phenomenology as a reaction to naturalism. The sketch of the natural attitude which Husserl gives in the first chapter holds for "all persons in natural life." It is a piece of pure description "before any theory."[6] In Ideen II, Husserl calls this the "everyday world," the world of ordinary life;[7] it is the later life-world. In this attitude, science could originate. The natural attitude then became a natural-theoretical attitude.[8] In Ideen II, Husserl goes at length into the changes in the world-picture brought about by the influence of natural science. Included among these changes is the loss of cultural predicates that characterize the world of the natural attitude.[9]

As I mentioned, the transition from the natural attitude via natural science to naturalism is not explicitly discussed in the Fundamental Consideration, but in the course of the argument, Husserl does distantiate himself repeatedly from naturalism. The picture of naturalism he presents can provide a useful contrast with transcendental phenomenology, which Husserl sees as a radical refutation of naturalism.

I. The Naturalistic World-Picture

(A) The cornerstone of the naturalistic ontology is the thing. Matter or the thing forms the fundamental stratum of reality. Everything else is founded in this bottom level. It is the "supporting ground-stratum" (*tragende Grundschicht*).[10] This is nature in the first sense.

(B) The consciousness founded in this nature is conceived of on the analogy of the thing. In psychology an attempt is made to apply a method like that of physics. This is what Husserl opposed especially in

[6] 48, 52f.

[7] Id II 27, 208.

[8] 94.

[9] The natural world of the first chapter also includes cultural goods, utensils, etc., 50. In the natural attitude, we abstract from all of this, Id II 3, 14, 16, 282, see also 190.

[10] This expression was added in Husserl's personal copy Husserliana III 70. See further 97 Husserliana III and 103, 110 and 318 in first edition.

his article of 1910.[11] Consciousness and matter are bound up in a psycho-physical unity. They form a "connected whole, connected within the particular psycho-physical unities that we call animate beings and connected above all in the real unity of the world as a whole."[12] We do indeed abstract from these "real" relations, as is done in "pure psychology," but this does not detract from the fact that no area of reality is isolated, as every investigator of nature is well aware. The world as a whole is ultimately "one single 'nature,' and all natural sciences are branches of one natural science."[13]

(C) The relations within this world are of a causal nature. Causality, as a "relation of dependence between realities,"[14] also includes consciousness, which is connected to nature in two ways: via the body and via perception. The intentional relation is also seen as a real relation between two realities: a thing in nature (e.g. a tree) and a psychical state.[15]

(D) Consciousness and the thing together form the "psycho-physical totality of nature" (Allnatur), the "totality" (Weltall), the "whole of reality" (Allwirklichkeit), the "totality of realities," the "omnitudo realitatis."[16] To the natural man, this is the totality of being. Thus he does not realize that there is something left after the disconnection (Stumpf).

In this description, we recognize the world-picture of positivism. In the article of 1910, Husserl provides the following summary: "Whatever is, is either itself physical, belonging to the unified coherent whole (Zusammenhang) of physical nature, or is in fact psychical, but then merely as a variable dependent on the physical, at best a secondary, 'parallel accompanying fact.' Everything that is, belongs to psycho-physical nature and is univocally determined by rigid laws."[17] Husserl mentions Haeckel and Ostwald as representatives of this view. We could add to the list the young Brentano and – in a certain sense, with reservations in connection with the competence of the natural scientific method – the older Brentano and even Husserl in his earlier publications. Despite the demarcation of a phenomenological sphere,

---

[11] See below 478.
[12] 70, 103.
[13] 95f. 103 and Husserl's note to 103 in Husserliana III.
[14] 89 note 1, 93.
[15] 64, 182; see also LU II 391.
[16] 4, 94, 106 and Husserl's note to 57 and Paragraph 33 Husserliana III.
[17] PSW 294.

Husserl's philosophy in LU remained caught up in the basic pattern of naturalism. The naturalizing of ideas was combatted, but not the naturalizing of consciousness.[18]

II. The Phenomenological View

Husserl attacks this world-picture from two sides in the two stages of the Fundamental Consideration. In the first place, he shows that consciousness has an "essence of its own" (*Eigenwesen*) to which a natural scientific treatment is not at all suited. Consciousness is not something spatial but a flowing stream in immanent time. Husserl does not linger long over this point, for in this Fundamental Consideration he restricts himself to what is really fundamental.

The limitation of the method of physics, which is a consequence of the fact that consciousness has a nature of its own, is further worked out by Husserl in Ideen II and PSW. In PSW he contrasts the mode of givenness of consciousness and the thing and uses the term 'monad' for the first time.[19] Things manifest themselves as identical in many different appearances. Only in relation to other things is a unity in terms of causal lawfulness revealed. But consciousness is a unity in itself. Because it is a monad, any approach like that of physics would be inadequate, for geometry cannot be applied here.[20]

Yet this critique is not the essential motif of the Fundamental Consideration. Husserl's deepest intention is not revealed until the second stage. He wants to undercut a philosophical presupposition that remained unchallenged in the first stage. In the second stage, it is demonstrated that the basic supposition of every psychology (including descriptive psychology) is unjustified. Not only does consciousness have a nature of its own, it is also the supporting ground of reality. Thereby any naturalism is transcended definitively. "Thus the usual meaning of the talk of being is reversed," Husserl can point out rightly in conclusion. "The being that is first for us is second in itself; that is to say, it is what it is only in 'relation' to the first." This difference between "for us" (i.e. for us in the natural attitude) and "in itself" (i.e. after the unmasking) becomes clear when we examine the new view against the background of the old view.

(A) Not matter but consciousness is the fundamental stratum of

---

[18] See above 232 and below 502.
[19] Husserl probably borrowed this term from Lotze. See Entwurf 324f.
[20] PSW 310–312. See further below 477.

reality. "*All real unities are 'unities of sense.*' Unities of sense pre-suppose ... *sense-giving consciousness.*[21] Not the material world but consciousness is the true pre-supposition.

(*B*) Matter is founded in this consciousness; the world "is com-pletely dependent ... on consciousness."[22] This is not a "real" relation but a transcendental relation. Here Husserl really does reverse the natural relation radically. One could say that Husserl is an epi-phenomenalist just as well as the naturalists are – but then in the sense that matter is an epiphenomenon in relation to consciousness! It is a "parallel accompanying fact" that could well be absent.

(*C*) The world of consciousness is governed not by causal con-nections but by teleological connections.[23] There is causality, but it is confined to the correlate of consciousness, which is itself constituted in teleological connections. Consciousness is a "*self-contained system of being*, into which nothing can penetrate and from which nothing can escape, which has no spatio-temporal exterior and can be in no spatio-temporal system, which cannot undergo causality from anything nor exert causality on anything, it being presupposed that by causality we mean natural causality as a relation of dependence between re-alities."[24] Consciousness cannot be a component part of nature, for nature is constituted in consciousness. Therefore it is not causally dependent on nature in any way. "The existence of a nature *cannot* condition the existence of consciousness, since it arises as a correlate of consciousness; it *is* only insofar as it constitutes itself in ordered connections of consciousness."[25]

(*D*) This consciousness plus the correlate that is constituted in it is now called by Husserl the "totality of absolute being." It is a sphere "without boundaries."[26] Reality is not the totality of being; reality is only a correlate within absolute consciousness. The residue is not nothing but everything.

This view is radical because it attacks naturalism at its roots. The thing, the cornerstone of the naturalist ontology, turns out to be a dependent correlate of consciousness. Matter is not a ground (*Boden*). With this reflection on the being of the thing, Husserl has removed the

[21] 106.
[22] 93.
[23] See below 504.
[24] 93.
[25] 95f.
[26] 94, 96, 106.

basis for the hierarchical world-picture of naturalism. This is the deepest meaning of his "talk of being." It seems paradoxical that a meditation that disconnects being is in essence an ontology, yet this is indeed the case. This meditation seeks to show that not "reality" but "irreality" is the absolute being.

In Ideen I, Husserl promised to give an explication of the relation between the natural sciences and the mental sciences (*Geisteswissenschaften*) in a subsequent volume.[1] He never got around to publishing that second volume, but it did come out posthumously in the Husserliana series. Ideen II as we now possess it is devoted in its entirety to the so-called naturalistic and personalistic attitudes and the relation between them.

In this paragraph I will investigate the central thrust of Ideen II from the historical point of view. The relation between the natural sciences and the mental sciences (or phenomenology) played a central role in Husserl's earlier work. Ideen II discusses nature and the mind at length. It has been maintained that in the third section, which deals with the "constitution of the mental world," Husserl wanted to incorporate the mental sciences as they existed into phenomenology.[2] My own view is that there is more going on in Ideen II. Husserl wrestles here with a problem from his own past. The problem inherent in his own development give us the key to understanding Ideen II.

The naturalistic attitude, which was sketched in the previous paragraph in connection with the Fundamental Consideration, is discussed at length in Ideen II. I will limit myself here to a short summary. The area of nature in the sense of the natural sciences is defined by Husserl as "the totality of realities that are either themselves material nature or are founded in material nature."[3] In this attitude we carry out a "continuous fundamental positing" as a "positing of nature in the first sense, that of physical nature, according to which everything else called nature derives its sense from being something founded in

---

[1]   108, 115, 142, 318ff.
[2]   P. Ricoeur, 'Analyses et problèmes dans Ideen II de Husserl,' 14, 152.
[3]   Id III 21.

it."[4] In the midst of physical nature we encounter certain things possessing properties that are not physical in the strict sense. This is the "mind" (Seele) as a "stratum of real events in bodies," a "stratum in body-things."[5] It is founded in nature in the primary sense; Husserl calls it nature in the broader or secondary sense.[6] This view of consciousness is the "governing, sense-determining apperception" of naturalism.[7] Consciousness, including all valuation, willing and thinking, becomes a piece of nature. "That 'in' him, in that person over there, an 'I think' occurs, is a fact of nature which is founded in the body and in bodily events and is determined by the substantial-causal system of nature, which is not just mere physical nature, although physical nature is still what grounds and co-determines all other nature."[8]

Husserl also gives a sketch of the personalistic attitude, in which we recognize the (psychological) phenomenological standpoint of LU. This personalistic view is now described in terms strongly reminiscent of Dilthey.[9] The world toward which I am intentionally directed is a "surrounding world" (Umwelt) which is subjective, has a horizon structure, and is not explained but described. It is the later life-world.[10] The relation between this world and myself is not causal but intentional. There are tendencies in it which I can yield to or resist. The choice is a question of my free behavior.[11] There are relations of motivation between me, the world and my fellow men which we try to "understand" (verstehen) in the mental sciences.[12] The concept of motivation, which is originally derived from the sphere of willing – the willing of a goal motivates the willing of a means – is now regarded by Husserl as applicable to all of consciousness.[13]

---

[4] Id II 174.

[5] Id II 175.

[6] Id II 25, 27f.

[7] Id II 139; see also Id III 18.

[8] Id II 181.

[9] On Husserl's contacts with Dilthey after the writing of LU, see PP 6ff, 53; see also PSW 327, 329, 340.

[10] Id II 183ff, 195, 234, 288 note 1. In a text of 1917, Id II 374f, Husserl already speaks of the world of persons as the "life-world."

[11] Id II 215ff, 257ff, 268ff; see also LU II (ed. 2) 391.

[12] This understanding requires that I transpose myself into the other. I must "participate in" (mitmachen) his motives, Id II 275. In this respect, there is no difference between Husserl and Dilthey. The reduction's abstention from "taking part" (mitmachen) is an entirely different question.

[13] In Id I 89 note 1, Husserl says that the concept of motivation, as contrasted with causality, already occurs in LU, which is true. See LU II 28. In Ideen II, he uses this

There is a certain tension between the two views I have sketched here.[14] Man functions in one of them as mind and in the other as nature; he is a "double entity" (*Doppelwesen*).[15] This is a "puzzling state of affairs."[16] Anyone who is accustomed to thinking in the natural scientific manner is inclined to make man part of nature. The naturalistic psychologist, who wears blinkers as a matter of habit, sees only material nature, in which there are bodies with psychical correlates causally dependent on them. Nonetheless, the investigator of nature also lives as a person in a personal world.[17] There always remains the possibility of moving from the naturalistic attitude into the personalistic attitude, which is the attitude of everyday life. Without difficulty we glide from the attitude which sees only nature to the attitude in which we experience a "counterpart" or "Widerspiel" of nature, as it were.[18]

The tension between the two approaches can be illustrated in various ways. The cultural objects that man produces can at the same time be seen as natural objects.[19] The movement of my body that I, as a free subject, bring about is at the same time an event in physical nature that can be regarded from a purely mechanical standpoint.[20] The tension culminates in the double conception of man. The view of man as a person can turn into the view of man as nature.[21] How are these two approaches to be combined? How can man in his acts be both causally determined and function as a person, as a "*subject of rational acts*"? What the *autonomy of reason* means, after all, is that I am able to decide freely in theoretical and ethical respects; it means that I am responsible, for myself.[22]

This tension, according to Husserl, is characteristic of thinkers like Dilthey, Brentano, Windelband, and Rickert. They have recognized the one-sidedness of positivism, and Husserl attaches great value to their efforts. Nevertheless, they fail to break through to a *radical*

concept especially in his phenomenology of reason. An evident datum motivates a judgment of positing; the premises motivate the conclusion, and so forth Id II 220ff, 257.

[14] Id II 208.
[15] Id II 120.
[16] Id II 142.
[17] Id II 183, 288 note 1.
[18] Id II 180.
[19] Id II 282.
[20] Id II 218, 260.
[21] Id II 242f, 247.
[22] Id II 257, 269.

clarification of the opposition between the natural sciences and the mental sciences. Yet, such a breakthrough is the great need of our time. "Our entire worldview is determined in ground and essence by the clarification of these distinctions." [23]

It appears that the same tension characterized Husserl's own thought at the time of LU. One of the passages in Ideen II that makes this clear is the one in which he compares "real relations" and "intentional relations." In this passage, just as in LU, Husserl maintains that in the case of intentional relations, I am directed toward the perceived, judged, etc. *as such*; that is to say, I am directed toward the noemata. Here *it makes no difference whether the correlate really exists*. In the case of real relations, there is a causal connection between the two realities, i.e. the thing and the concrete person (as unity of matter and consciousness). This relation can only exist if the thing really exists. "The real relation falls away if the thing does not exist; the intentional relation continues to exist." The intentional relation is the relation that we encounter in the purely phenomenological sphere. We have seen that we abstract thereby from the ultimate existence of the intentional object. In LU, natural science is to decide on the question of reality as real existence. The real thing is called the "natural scientific" thing. This passage in Ideen II can be read as a commentary on LU, a commentary of particular interest because it discusses something about which Husserl is generally silent in LU and only mentions now and then in passing. In LU, he says that it makes no difference from a purely phenomenological standpoint whether a real object exists. He regards it as sufficient to observe that the existence of this object is the exclusive concern of natural science. In Ideen II, Husserl goes into this at greater length. If the real object exists, there is a real relation parallel to the intentional relation; that is to say, vibrations is space proceeding from the object affect my sense organs, and as a result, sensations arise in me. This process can be causally explained. According to Ideen II, a change of attitude has taken place when I do this: I have moved from the personalistic attitude to the naturalistic attitude. The relation of motivation changes into a real causal relation, and "the motivation-because becomes a real-because." [24]

What we encounter here is the double track on which Husserl moved in LU. Can these difficulties now be overcome? As long as both

---

[23] Id II 172, 313, 393.
[24] Id II 215, 232, 233.

attitudes stand next to each other as equally justified, no *radical* solution will be possible. We wind up in a vicious circle, as it were. In the naturalistic attitude, persons are "subordinate natural objects." In the personalistic attitude, "nature" as "mere nature" is an intentional object of consciousness alongside many others. Within this attitude we can take a particular interest in nature and thus make the transition to the study of natural science. The personalistic attitude then becomes the naturalistic attitude in which the person is seen as a piece of nature. But this naturalistic science always presupposes persons who carry out its work. Thus the practitioner of natural science can return to the personalistic attitude, and so forth.[25]

The *co-ordination* of these two methods is broken through in Ideen II. In the last chapter Husserl speaks of "the *ontological priority* of the mental (*geistig*) world over against the naturalistic world."[26] There are not "two equally justified, co-ordinate attitudes," two "apperceptions permeating one another." This illusion, says Husserl, comes about through a self-forgetting on the part of the person involved and an absolutization of nature.[27]

Consciousness is then conceived of as founded in this nature. This view, this "reifying" apperception, *is not broken through in the personalistic attitude* – neither in LU, as we saw Husserl himself admit, nor in thinkers like Dilthey. The absolutizing of nature and the apperception of consciousness as "mind" (*Seele*) is not undermined radically but only *left unconsidered*. Therefore the personalistic attitude is also a natural attitude, although it is not a naturalistic attitude.[28] The person counts as a "real" person, a reality, a "mental (*geistig*) reality." Mental science (*Geisteswissenschaft*) is a dogmatic science on a natural basis.[29]

A radical conquest of this dualistic standpoint only becomes possible when we see through this apperception via an artificial attitude, a phenomenological reduction, and discover the absoluteness of consciousness. Even the real person, i.e. a person seen as appearing within independently existing nature (which we presuppose but leave unconsidered) is relative and points to an absolute subject that constitutes

[25] Id II 210, see also 169, 193, 208.
[26] Id II 281 – italics mine.
[27] Id II 183f, see also 377, 170.
[28] See Husserl's notes to 95 and 96 of Id I in Husserliana III; Id II 180 and 312f.
[29] Id II 141, 143, 179, 202, 283; Id I 108 and 142.

nature within itself.[30] When we discover the relativity of nature and the absoluteness of mind, any view of consciousness as a "stratum of the body" becomes impossible *eo ipso*. How can consciousness be founded in a body that can exist only as the relative correlate of this consciousness?

The new view, which frees consciousness from the limitations of the natural attitude, *radicalizes* the personalistic standpoint and thereby confers a certain absoluteness upon it. It is the only standpoint that has *ontological* validity. Naturalistic thinking rests on an illegitimate absolutizing of nature that, *eo ipso*, implies a naturalizing of consciousness. Husserl has now broken through to a truly radical unified view. The root of all being is absolute mind. Only within absolute mind can nature – ultimately as physical nature – be constituted.[31]

Naturally this solution again raises new questions. The naturalistic view is now regarded as subordinate to the personalistic or phenomenological view. (The latter term is better because the person, on Husserl's view, is the real person, the mind that is still thought of as connected to a body.) The question that suggests itself at this point is: to what extent is the naturalistic view still justified? If it is mistaken in principle to conceive of consciousness as a reality, can such a view and a science supported by such a view have any meaning at all? I will deal with this question later.[32]

[30] Id II 171, 180.
[31] Id II 177f; 290, 297, 301f, 313, 325.
[32] See below 476ff.

CHAPTER TWO

PSYCHOLOGICAL AND TRANSCENDENTAL
EPISTEMOLOGY

PARAGRAPH ONE. HUSSERL'S TRANSCENDENTAL IDEALISM

In principle, the Phenomenological Fundamental Consideration contains the solution of all epistemological dilemmas that cannot be resolved in the natural attitude. If a phenomenology remains partly stuck in this natural attitude, as did the philosophy of LU, it cannot reach clarity in these matters. It then remains on the level of a psychology of reason unable to overcome the problematics of the thing in itself without falling prey to psychologism. In this chapter, I will show that Husserl, through the new transcendental turn, is able to produce the desired critique of reason that he struggled to formulate in his publications from LU on. His long struggle to achieve clarity in this area finally resulted in a principial solution in the form of a transcendental phenomenological idealism. As I see it, Husserl's thinking at this stage is definitive, despite the later modifications.

I. No "Thing in Itself"

In the Fundamental Consideration, a gradual reinterpretation of the concept of transcendent thing is carried out. In the natural attitude, the transcendent thing is conceived of as existing on its own, independent of consciousness. It has the character of being "present," being "simply there," "existing." In the course of the argument, it becomes apparent that this is an absurd interpretation. Husserl compares the concept of an independently existing transcendent thing to the concept of a round square. This definition is in conflict with the very essence of the thing. The thing is never something that has nothing to do with consciousness. It is not an independent entity but a dependent, merely intentional entity. The nonsense of an independently existing thing is the nonsense of the non-independent that is at the same time dependent (using these terms here in the technical sense which they have for Husserl from 1894 on). A non-independent thing is something whose independent existence would be inconceivable. The thing has "the essentiality of something that is in principle ['in principle' always means an eidetic necessity for Husserl] *only* intentional, *only* for consciousness, presented to consciousness, appearing."[1]

If this, then, is the essence of the thing, nothing can be lost by the disconnection of the natural world, which rests on an absurd absolutizing of the non-independent. Thereby Husserl banishes any problematics of a transcendent thing that cannot be reached by consciousness, which formed the point of departure for the lectures of 1907. Consciousness with its correlates is the totality of being; it is "without limits." There cannot be anything outside consciousness which it strives in vain to reach. This is the reason why Husserl speaks of consciousness as a closed system, as a windowless monad. This is not a closing off of the world but only an exclusion of an absurd interpretation of the world. Consciousness considered in its purity, that is, considered as it really is, is a "*self-contained system of being*," a system of *absolute being* into which nothing can penetrate and from which nothing can escape, which has no spatio-temporal exterior...."[2]

When Husserl says that objects are constituted "in" transcendental consciousness, he definitely does not mean that the object is immanent in the real sense, i.e. in the sense in which sensations are immanent. This would be to fall back into the "ideological" psychology of Locke and company, or into a Berkeleyan idealism. The entire Fundamental Consideration is based on a sharp distinction between immanent consciousness and the transcendent thing. Thus this immanence is of a principially different kind. It is the "pure" immanence of which Husserl had already spoken in IP. In this sense everything that is truly given is immanent. In later publications, Husserl uses the expression 'transcendence in immanence' to refer to this state of affairs.[3] Over against this stands the "natural" concept of transcendence, by which something outside consciousness is indicated.

This ambiguity in the term 'transcendent' is part of the reason for the

[1] 94, 77 note 1.
[2] 93, 165, PSW 312.
[3] Husserl speaks of "immanent transcendence" (CM 134, 138), of "ideal immance" (95), of the "transcendence of irreal includedness" (65), and of an "ideal being-within" (80).

problems in interpretation pointed out earlier. The epoché is often described as a disconnection of transcendencies. At the same time, Husserl talks about retaining the transcendent object, which recurs under another sign.[4] Such statements can only be understood if we keep the difference between natural and transcendental terminology in mind at all times.[5]

II. The Traditional Problem of Knowledge

This denial of the thing in itself is a step of great importance in Husserl's development; in fact, I believe it is the most important step of all. We first become fully aware of the meaning of this step when we view it against the background of the problematics of LU. The difficulties with which Husserl struggled there are now solved in a principial and radical way. The originality of Husserl's theory of knowledge is that it is neither realist nor idealist in the traditional sense. The new aspect of his theory of knowledge is that it undermines the traditional statement of the problem and therefore also transcends the traditional answers to this statement of the problem.

According to Husserl, the problem of transcendence has been the point of departure of all epistemology. We already encountered this problem in IP. At that point it was still Husserl's own problem, which he tried to solve in a provisional way through a Cartesian reduction. In CM, Husserl gives a sketch of the traditional problem – now from his new transcendental standpoint – which corresponds exactly to the problematics in IP. The problem is that I function as a person in the world and at the same time experience this world "in" my consciousness. Everything that exists for me in this world is there thanks to my cognitive consciousness. It is the "experienced of my experiencing, the thought of my thinking, the theorized of my theorizing, the intellectually seen of my insight." If we join Brentano in accepting intentionality as a property of my psychical consciousness, as "a real property belonging to me as a person as well as to any other person in virtue of his purely psychical being," then it is obvious that "everything that exists for me or for someone does so in my or his own conscious life, which, in all awareness of a world and in all scientific activity, keeps to itself. All distinctions that I make between genuine and deceptive experience and between being and illusion in experience are made

[4] 120, 142.
[5] 177f, 141.

within the sphere of my consciousness. . . ." All distinctions that I make between a priori necessity and absurdity, between truth and falsehood, etc., "all these are characteristics that occur within the realm of my consciousness, as characteristics of the intentional objects in question. Every grounding, every showing of truth and being, goes on wholly within myself, and its result is a characteristic in the *cogitatum* of my *cogito*." This sketch of the traditional problem of knowledge is interesting especially because it gives a statement of the problem of transcendence that corresponds exactly with the state of the question in LU. It is an excellent description of what I have called a "psychology of reason." There is talk of being and non-being, of truth and falsehood, but all these predicates remain within the psychical sphere. They hold for acts or their correlates, i.e. intentional objects. What, then, is the great problem that remains? Husserl formulates it as follows: "That I attain certainties, even compelling evidences, within the domain of my consciousness, in the nexus of motivation determining me, is understandable. But how can evidence (*clara et distincta perceptio*) claim to be more than a characteristic of consciousness within me?" In other words: "How do I get beyond my island of consciousness? How does that which appears within me as an evident experience acquire objective meaning?"[6]

The fact that human consciousness is both *in* the world and *before* the world is spoken of by Husserl in Krisis as the paradox of human subjectivity.[7] We could also formulate this paradox as follows: how can consciousness be founded in something that can only exist for consciousness? The paradox in this form underlies the argument in the Fundamental Consideration. On the one hand man is part of the world, and on the other hand the world is something that exists thanks to man. But how can a part of the world constitute the whole world? As Husserl points out in *Ideen* III, it is as though a part swallows up the whole: "The subject part of the world swallows up, as it were, the entire world and thereby itself. What an absurdity!"[8] Therefore this talk of man being a subject *before* the world and at the same time an object *in* the world has rightly given rise to continual philosophical amazement. In his later writings, Husserl shows that the tension caused by this position has been the hidden motor driving on the history of western philosophy

---

[6] CM 115f.
[7] Krisis 182ff, 251, 265f (E 178, 248, 262).
[8] Id III 71ff.

since Descartes. There was an oscillation between realism and idealism that did not lead to a radical solution. At the outset, even phenomenology stood before a wonder – the "wonder of all wonders."[9] Thanks to Descartes, philosophy has become aware of the universal relatedness of the world to consciousness.[10] We cannot nullify this awareness and accept the world as something obvious, as the naive person does. We must take the problem of subjectivity seriously and radicalize it. Therefore the beginning of philosophy, as Fink says, is "the awakening of a boundless amazement about the mysteriousness of this matter."[11] But we cannot stop here. This sense of wonder disappears, Husserl maintains, when the light of phenomenology falls upon it. "The wonder disappears because it is transformed into an entire science." The greatest of all riddles is comprehended and understood by phenomenology. In this respect, too, Husserl remains faithful to phenomenology's claim to the title of rigorous science. He concludes his remarks about this wonder of all wonders with a pathos characteristic of him: "A wonder is something incomprehensible, while something problematic is something comprehensible when formulated as a scientific problem; the latter is the uncomprehended that turns out to be comprehensible and is comprehended when reason solves the problem."[12] He also writes: "Genuine epistemology clarifies, and something clarified is something that has become understandable and has been understood. Thus it is the complete opposite of a 'wonder.'"[13] To what extent and in what way can Husserl make this claim good?

In the history of philosophy, two answers have been given to the problem of knowledge, neither of which is satisfactory. The first answer is the subjective idealism of Berkeley, which dissolves the world in conscious appearances. This is a "psychomonism."[14] This idealism thus allows the whole to be swallowed up by a part. The world is reduced to an appearance within a part of the world, i.e. the human psyche. This view is also called psychologism or transcendental psychologism, for it dissolves the world in a subjective event. Everything non-immanent is given the status of merely intentional

[9] Id III 71, 75.
[10] FTL 216; Krisis 82f (E 8of).
[11] Fink, 'Die phänomenologische Phil. Husserls' 350; Husserl speaks of the "great riddle of the modern period," FTL 34; Krisis 82 (E 80).
[12] Id III 75: see also Krisis 184 (E 181); EP II 442.
[13] Entwurf 324.
[14] Id III 74.

object: "esse" is "percipi."[15] Husserl calls such a psychologism absurd. Consciousness as the human psyche, i.e. as a certain region, can never function as the primordial region. Psychological consciousness is characterized by powerlessness; it is receptive vis-á-vis the world. On the psychological level, a distinction must be made between being for me and being in itself. To join Schopenhauer in regarding the world as a presentation (*Vorstellung*) of the world would be to deny man's "lack of importance and his insignificance in the cosmos."[16]

Over against this subjective idealism stands realism. Realism recognizes the subjectivity of the presentation of the world but tries to build a bridge from consciousness to the world outside. This is done via causal reasoning. The subjective presentation is an affect of the world outside; via this presentation, we can draw conclusions about an external world existing in itself. Descartes also solved the problem in this way: he tried to prove the existence of the external world by reasoning from the indubitable immanent sphere.[17] This realism occurs especially often in the following form. The world outside us is the object of physics (primary qualities). It is a world that we construe as behind the appearing subjective world (secondary qualities). The phenomena that appear to us are the subjective point of departure for the concepts of physics. It was this form of realism that Husserl himself learned from Brentano. It exercised an enormous influence on his thinking – hence his continual reflection on the problem of the relation between the world of physics and the life-world. This realism was also the (hidden) background of LU. When Husserl rejected this realism as absurd, a renewed reflection on the status of the thing of physics was required. I will return to this matter in a separate paragraph.

III. Husserl's Solution

When Husserl tries to solve the problem in a radical way, he does so by attacking its formulation. Thereby he does not mean to imply that being a subject *before* the world and at the same time an object *in* the world is only an apparent problem. It is certainly a real problem, but it is a problem *within* the natural attitude. Both traditional solutions are based on the same starting-point, namely, consciousness as the human psyche. Such a view leads necessarily to the problem of the thing in itself

[15] Fink 359; Id I 166f; Id III 150, 154; See also CM 119; FTL 224; Krisis 89 (E 87).
[16] Fink 377.
[17] CM 116, 33; FTL 114, 202, 203, 204, 223; Krisis 82 note 3 (E 80).

or to a psychological idealism. All of modern epistemology (including Kant) remained stuck in this dilemma because the difference between psychological and transcendental consciousness was not clearly seen.[18] The identification of the psyche with consciousness is a prejudice that can only be broken through via a radical reflection on the givenness of the thing and of consciousness such as we find in the Fundamental Consideration.[19] It then appears that consciousness is not a region within the world but the absolute of all being. *This* consciousness is not receptive and powerless. "Behind its naively supposed powerlessness flashes its transcendental might," as Fink fittingly puts it.[20] Thus transcendental idealism does not fall back into the absurdity of a psychological idealism that reduces the world to a part of the world. Traditional idealism has rightly pointed to the relatedness of the world to consciousness. Its mistake was that this consciousness was conceived of as the "mind (*Seele*) of a body existing in a pre-given spatio-temporal nature."[21] This made it impossible to understand the wonder of the relatedness of the world and consciousness to one another. But transcendental phenomenology, which changes all wonders into problems and understands them, also sees through the paradox of a consciousness that is *in* the world and at the same time *before* the world: it is a *paradox within the natural attitude.* When we break through the natural attitude and discover the true being of the world and consciousness as sense, then their relation is no longer a mystery but a concrete field for scientific analysis[22] "behind which, as the ultimate, there is nothing further that we could sensibly seek to inquire into and understand."[23]

Just as absurd as psychological idealism is its counterpart, i.e. realism. Realism proceeds from psychological consciousness as basis and then seeks to prove the existence of the world. That which is to be proven is presupposed in the process, for psychological consciousness is conceived of as part of the world and thus already presupposes the world.[24] From the outset we assume the natural world as the exclusive

---

[18] PSW 302, 321; Krisis 201ff; 207ff; 187ff (E 198, 204, 183); CM 118.

[19] Id III 74.

[20] 'Welt und Geschichte' 150.

[21] Nachwort 145.

[22] Krisis 185ff, 266 (E 182ff, 262).

[23] FTL 4, 214; see also Krisis 171, 192 (E 168, 188); PSW 317; CM 164; IP 6, 33, 37; Entwurf 325.

[24] CM 32, 116; FTL 204f.

basis. Since realism proceeds from the psychological ego and does not wish to reduce the world to it, it arrives naturally at the idea of the "thing in itself" as a reality independent of consciousness. We already know that the idea of an independent transcendent thing is just as absurd to Husserl as the idea of a round square. For consciousness, there is no outside. It is not the case that the world penetrates into my consciousness "from without," (θυραθεν) Husserl argues. "Everything outside is what it is within this inside and has its *true being* in the self-presentations and confirmations within this inside...."[25] Therefore it is an absurd enterprise to try to draw conclusions from this consciousness about a reality outside it. *"There is no conceivable place where the life of consciousness could break through or be broken through* so that we would encounter a transcendency that could have a sense other than that of an intentional unity appearing in the subjectivity of consciousness itself."[26] Such a causal inference confuses the intra-mundane causal relation with the transcendental relation between consciousness and the world.[27]

Thus, although transcendental idealism is neither a psychological idealism nor a realism, it does justice to the correct impulses in both. Idealism rightly proceeds from the relatedness of the world to consciousness. But Husserl argues that this being-for-consciousness must be understood not in a psychological sense but in a transcendental sense. In place of the "bad subjectivizing" of the "bad idealism," he calls for "transcendental subjectivizing."[28] The pre-phenomenological transcendental philosophy is a self-alienation, just as the psychological subject is a subject in self-alienation.[29] This subjectivism must be overcome by the most universal and radical subjectivism, i.e. transcendental subjectivism.[30]

The same goes for realism. Here, too, transcendental phenomenology honors the proper impulses. Transcendental idealism can also be called objectivism "insofar as it defends the legitimacy of any objectivity that can be shown through harmonious experience" without making the mistake of realist objectivism, which, in an absurd way,

---

[25] FTL 221, see also 204, 207.
[26] FTL 208; Id I 93.
[27] FTL 223; Id 93. On Descartes, see above 375.
[28] FTL 151f, 226.
[29] See below 469.
[30] According to the Encyclopaedia Britannica article Husserliana IX 253.

absolutizes this object experienced and makes it transcendent.[31] In his Nachwort, Husserl points out that his idealism does not deny the real existence of the world. It only seeks to "clarify ... the sense of this world, the very sense in which it counts for everyone as really existing – and that with actual legitimacy. That the world exists, that it is given in experience as an existing universe that coheres constantly in universal harmony, is completely indubitable."[32]

Earlier I pointed out that talk of a turn toward the object in Husserl's thought is only justified if it applies to the period after the transition to transcendental idealism, when, for the first time, Husserl's philosophy assigned the object a function and place of its own. Before this, the actually existing transcendent object was eliminated from philosophy in a psychologistic limiting to the psychological data: it was simply left unconsidered. This limitation was really an expression of powerlessness vis-á-vis the problem of transcendence. Husserl's idealist philosophy of the transcendent thing seeks to give this thing its proper place by avoiding two extremes. First, it is not an independently existing thing, as realism supposes. Secondly, it is not an illusion. Descartes, who believed it necessary to disqualify the value of the relative (under the influence of an apodictic ideal of certainty), fell back into the latter error. Hence Husserl believes that he has given objectivity fuller recognition than Descartes. Transcendent knowledge remains relative insofar as the continuous progress of experience in the form of a universal harmony remains a presumption and the non-existence of the world thus remains conceivable. This means that this experience is *not apodictic* – unlike the inner experience of transcendental consciousness. Nevertheless, it remains an experience with its own legitimacy, and it would be foolish to reject it just because it is the way it is. This would testify to a false ideal of absoluteness, insofar as absolute truth is sought where it is not to be found and relative truth is thus rejected.[33]

Here I must add a remark about modern existentialistic interpretations. When advocates of such interpretations observe that Husserl's philosophy transcends the traditional problem of knowledge and is therefore neither idealist nor

---

[31] Encyclopaedia Britannica art. 254; see also Krisis 190f (E 186f).

[32] Nachwort 152f; see also Fink op.cit. 377.

[33] FTL 144, 201, 241, 249. For Husserl, this recognition of relative truths is thus the *corollary* of his doctrine of apodictic truth, FTL 226. Merleau-Ponty totally mistakes Husserl's intentions when he observes with reference to these statements: "What FTL says in the main is that there is no apodictic evidence," Phénoménologie de la Perception XI note 2.

realist, I can agree fully. But when the conclusion is then drawn that his phenomenology must consequently be understood in an existentialistic sense in which the epistemic relation is seen as an "encounter," I must register an objection. Husserl overcomes the traditional opposition by means of an entirely new kind of idealism. The terms 'idealism' and 'realism' have many meanings, as Ingarden (among others) has pointed out. Husserl's rejection of the traditional forms of both idealism and realism does not automatically make him an existentialist.

IV. Comparison with Logische Untersuchungen

From the standpoint of transcendental idealism, one would have to say that the philosophy of LU moves within the natural attitude. Now, if the problem is indeed formulated there in natural terms, the question arises which of the two possible answers Husserl gives.

In Part II of this study, we saw that LU is certainly not a psychologistic or idealist work in the sense that it reduces being to consciousness. The distinction between the real object and the intentional object precludes such a view. The intentional object is indeed dependent on consciousness, but this does not prejudice anything about reality itself, for reality is left unconsidered on methodological grounds. Judgments are made only about experiences and correlates of experiences (intentional objects or "objects in quotation marks"[34]) or about the perceived "as such." But this means that the problem of transcendence is not solved: it is only set aside. Epistemology is then based exclusively on the psychologically immanent correlation. Husserl says that such a theory of knowledge has a certain legitimacy from his new standpoint, provided that it is not conceived of as transcendental philosophy.[35] It has a limited meaning. It can only become of philosophical importance when the view of consciousness as psychological consciousness is overcome and the results reached on the psychological level are reinterpreted (through a "change of attitude") as transcendental-philosophical results.[36]

But in LU, consciousness was still conceived of as "mind" (Seele), as a region founded in matter. Husserl had not yet discovered the absoluteness of consciousness. Therefore he was not in a position to undertake a principial clarification of the epistemological problem. His philosophy was not able to clarify the problematics of correlation in a

[34] See above 190ff; see also Id III 88f, 92.
[35] FTL 224.
[36] Nachwort 147; see below 437, 464.

radical way. As he himself admitted, the prerequisite for this was a "radical transformation of sense."[37] His standpoint in LU can best be characterized as a methodological psychologism. The point of departure is psychological consciousness, and therefore epistemology ultimately remains stuck in an impasse. On the basis of this standpoint, a consistent theory of knowledge can only be developed if we are prepared to reduce "esse" to "percipi," which is entirely contrary to Husserl's intent. In FTL, Husserl gave a clear explication of his standpoint at that time. He recognized that he had not yet overcome psychologism in LU. We must then read the term 'psychologism' as meaning transcendental psychologism, i.e. the view of consciousness as "mind." The psychologizing of logical idealities is indeed combatted in LU, but this represents only a limited concept of psychologism, which Husserl came to call "logical psychologism."[38]

In LU, Husserl was actually closer to the second answer, namely, realism. Behind the world of appearances stands the real world, which is methodologically put between brackets. Husserl later came to regard this separation between the presentation and the thing in itself as characteristic of the psychological standpoint of so-called phenomenological psychology, which analyzes consciousness on a pre-transcendental level.[39] Nevertheless, we must not simply identify his standpoint with that of Brentano, for nowhere in LU do we find an explicit statement about a causal inference from the appearance to the thing of physics. This reservation on Husserl's part is important. As I see it, his silence here testifies to a certain dissatisfaction. He did not close off his thinking prematurely by way of a solution à la Brentano. His great caution and the paucity of his statements on this point betray a certain fear of neatly formulated answers. Realism is certainly the background of his psychological theory of knowledge, but this realism appears to flow more from general considerations about the powerlessness and receptivity of psychological consciousness than from an explicit theory about a transcendent thing "behind" the phenomena.

V. The Concept of Constitution

In the light of the preceding, what meaning are we to attribute to the much debated concept of constitution? Opinion is still divided on the

---

[37] Krisis 169 note 1 (E 166).

[38] FTL 135f, 224; see above 116, 271, 300.

[39] Fink op.cit. 376f, 358, 364.

question whether constitution is to be conceived of as a "creating" or a "making something appear."

In Part II, I have already expressed my own view, namely, that a genetic analysis of Husserl's work shows that the question has two different answers, corresponding to different phases in his thinking. At the level of LU, constitution indeed means nothing other than making something appear. The constituted object is a phenomenon. The relation between consciousness and the object can be described (somewhat anachronistically) by way of the term 'encounter.'

But Husserl's thinking on this point did not stand still. The entire problematics of LU presses toward a principially different view. The history of Husserl's development should make it clear that the transcendental idealism of Ideen I is the necessary conclusion of a train of thought that had already commenced much earlier. As I see it, the interpretation of the concept of constitution in Ideen I as a "letting be" (*sein lassen*), which has become all too widespread under the influence of so-called existential phenomenology, represents a mistaken understanding of Husserl's development and of the deepest intentions of his phenomenology. It is an interpretation that cannot be documented from the historical text, and it actually brings Husserl's later development back to the level of LU.

We encounter this interpretation in Biemel (among others). He conceives of constitution by transcendental consciousness as a "constitution of sense."[40] His conception of the reduction fits in with this; the reduction puts an end to the naive attitude directed toward things and turns our attention inward in order to reveal consciousness in its constituting activity. Thus the reduction at the same time turns that which exists into a phenomenon; that is to say, we view that which exists only insofar as it exists for us. Hence, constitution is a constitution of the phenomenality of the thing – and not a constitution of the thing itself, which is placed between brackets.[41] De Waelhens is among those who use the term 'encounter' to describe the relation between consciousness and reality.[42]

[40] See above 119. W. Biemel, 'Les phases décisives' 53ff.

[41] W. Biemel, 69. Husserl's letter to Hocking, which Biemel quotes on page 46 and makes considerable use of in his argument against Fink's objections, bears on the concept of constitution in LU, as Husserl himself remarks in the letter. That this was no longer Husserl's view after the turn to transcendental idealism is apparent from his letter to Dilthey of July 5 and 6, 1911, which Biemel himself quotes on page 54, as well as from other sources. Thus Husserl sees the positing of being behind the phenomenon as an absurd hypothesis.

[42] *Existence et Signification*, 18 and 'Commentaire sur l'idée de la phénoménologie' 148. A similar view of the concept of constitution is presented in R. Sokolowski, *The formation of Husserl's concept of constitution* 60, 137, 195. This view is in conflict with Husserl's own view as stated on page 133.

But Ricoeur rightly observes that this term can only be used for the psychological level of phenomenology, which is characterized by receptivity.[43] This psychological phenomenology represents a historical phase in Husserl's thinking. After the turn to transcendental idealism, it continues to play a role on a lower, pre-transcendental level.

I must also comment here on the expression 'idealism of sense,' which has been used on occasion to characterize Husserl's standpoint.[44] This term can be used in different senses, depending on whether the context is psychological or transcendental phenomenology. One could argue that there is talk of an idealism of sense in LU rather than an idealism of being insofar as sense – and not being – is dependent on consciousness. This view, which leaves being unconsidered, was already abandoned by Husserl in 1910. In Ideen I, he equates sense and being: being is sense "and beyond this nothing." This, too, could be called an idealism of sense, but in that case this expression would have an entirely different meaning, for that which stands over against being would then no longer be (psychological) sense. The expression would then stand for an ontological idealism that reduces being to sense.[45]

On the basis of unambiguous statements in the Fundamental Consideration, I have tried to show what development Husserl's concept of constitution underwent. Via a historical analysis, we saw that transcendental idealism is the necessary outcome of this development. The famous transcendental-phenomenological reduction is not something that falls unexpectedly from heaven; it is the result of the preceding development of Husserl's thought.

The idealist interpretation of Husserl's phenomenology later received strong support from the article by Husserl's assistant Fink, to which I have already referred several times. Husserl himself signed this article and declared that it contained nothing with which he did not agree. Therefore Fink's article has rightly exercised great influence on Husserl interpretation.[46] Fink uses the strongest of expressions to characterize Husserl's idealism. Constitution, he writes, must be seen as a productive creation. "However harsh and doctrinaire it might sound

[43] Idées directrices pour une phénoménologie XXIX, XX.

[44] For example, in C.A. van Peursen, 'Phénoménologie et ontologie' 308f, 311.

[45] The terms 'sense' and 'being' are therefore used interchangeably by Husserl, especially in the claims that the world is constituted "in its being and sense" in consciousness, and that the world derives its "being and sense" from absolute consciousness, FTL 148; CM 117 et passim.

[46] There is a clear historical movement visible in the interpretations. After Fink's article of 1933, the idealist interpretation was accepted by virtually everyone. After 1945, existentialist interpretations following the lead of Merleau-Ponty began to appear. The influence of Merleau-Ponty is so strong at present that the historical Husserl threatens to vanish from sight completely.

to characterize the essence of constitution as productive creation, at least this characterization indicates the opposition to the mundane-ontic (psychical) experiential stream which is receptive in character and requires accepting being-in-itself."[47] Fink characterizes the world as "the surface of the transcendental life that allows the world to arise," as the "final objectification of absolute mind."[48] Now, Fink also says that the productive character of constitution only becomes clear at a later stage. He distinguishes the stage of Ideen I from a later stage in which the productive-constituting character of consciousness becomes more evident. The analyses of Ideen I are provisional in a certain sense. Via the reduction, transcendental consciousness is discovered in principle, but the definition of it given in Ideen I has a certain indeterminacy.[49] One could conceivably use this as partial support for the view that Ideen I represents a transitional stage in which the argument hesitates between two solutions[50] (an interpretation that Fink definitely does not support.) One would then have to maintain that the concept of constitution contains an ambiguity that permits both interpretations – a view reflected in the strange story of the index of Ideen I. The 1922 reprint includes an index prepared by Gerda Walther. In this index we find the following important note under the term 'phenomenological 'idealism': "'Phenomenological idealism' is not actually mentioned in Ideen, but certain statements made by Husserl in Ideen have become part of an extensive discussion under this heading. For purposes of orientation, therefore, it appeared useful to include in the index, under this term, all the passages pro and contra that are discussed." Then follows a list of passages under *Pro* and another under *Contra*. Thus it appears that a disagreement in which both sides can appeal to the text is possible.

A year later Husserl expressed his dissatisfaction with this index in the margin of his own copy of Ideen I.[51] In the index to the third printing (1928), which was prepared by Landgrebe, we find a much less ambiguous note under the term 'phenomenological idealism.' Landgrebe repeats that this expression was not used in Ideen I. Yet he adds that the entire argument could 'be characterized as 'idealist' in a

---

[47] Fink, 'Die Phän. Phil. E. Husserls in der gegenwärtigen Kritik,' 373.
[48] Fink op.cit. 378.
[49] Fink op.cit. 373f, 369.
[50] We encountered this view in Ricoeur, see above 381.
[51] In a note dating from about 1923 in Husserl's own copy, which is now in the Husserl archive at Louvain. See R. Boehm, 'Husserl et l'idéalisme classique,' 358.

correspondingly broad sense.... Therefore the passages in which the characteristic nature of phenomenological 'idealism' becomes visible have been listed."[52] For Landgrebe, then, it is a foregone conclusion that Husserl's position in Ideen I represents idealism. All that remains to be done is to point out the characteristic nature of this idealism. Now, this change, which was doubtless made at Husserl's request, could well have resulted from an impulse on Husserl's part to interpret an earlier work from a later standpoint. Here, too, the analysis of the text itself will have to be allowed the final say in our interpretation.

It is true that the term 'idealism' is not used in Ideen I, except to refer to the standpoint of those who accept ideas or essences. Thus Husserl uses the term there in the same sense as in LU.[53] Furthermore, he notes that his reduction of the thing to sense is not to be conceived of as an idealism in the style of Berkeley. He likewise rejects the speculative idealism of the early nineteenth century, which was "foreign to natural science." But from this we can deduce no more than that Husserl rejects certain kinds of idealism.[54]

If we are striving for a positive interpretation, it seems senseless to me to build up arguments for or against the alleged idealism of Ideen I on the basis of the use of certain isolated terms. Here again we must take the Fundamental Consideration as our point of departure, for it alone gives us a definite indication of what the basic intention of transcendental phenomenology is. When we understand the Fundamental Consideration as it ought to be understood, that is, as "talk of being" (Seinsrede) it seems to me beyond doubt that Husserl gives an idealist solution to the problem of knowledge. As evidence I would point to all the passages in which he speaks of matter as ultimately nothing but an intentional correlate of consciousness, a sense that sense-giving consciousness presupposes. I would also point to the absoluteness of consciousness, which constitutes the world within itself. Whether or not there is an existing world depends on the occurrence of certain connections in consciousness. It seems to me that Husserl's entire development becomes incomprehensible when this idealism is denied. Not only would the theory of knowledge be caught in an impasse, but psychology, as we shall see in a later chapter, would likewise remain

[52] This index is included in Husserliana III, see page 433.
[53] 116, 39; see also LU II 108.
[54] 106, 35.

partly stuck in naturalism – a naturalism that Husserl intended to overcome in Ideen I by attacking it at its very roots.

Furthermore, the arguments listed in Gerda Walther's index under the heading *Contra* do not stand up under close examination. Some rest on a misconception of the nature of Husserl's idealism, which is not a psychologism, and others rest on the passages in which Husserl speaks of the correlate of consciousness, or of the necessity of the existence of a world (under certain conditions), or of the phenomenology of the consciousness that constitutes a real object, etc. None of these passages represents an argument against Husserl's idealism. The reinterpretation of the thing and the world do not entail their denial.

The same must be said of a number of other arguments that still play a role in the discussion of Husserl's concept of constitution. Some point to the concept of intentionality, which as such implies a turn toward the object (the so-called "things themselves"). Others point to the primacy which Husserl accorded to perception, whereby an empty intention receives fulfillment. A favorite argument draws on the "bodily (*leibhaft*) presence" of the thing in perception. These expressions are referred to again and again as arguments for Husserl's realism, or at least for the realist tendencies in his otherwise idealist philosophy – as though Husserl were some sort of schizophrenic torn between realism and idealism! They occupy a prominent place, for example, in the long list of argument which Jean Wahl adduces in favor of a realist interpretation.[55]

As far as the concept of intentionality is concerned, a historical analysis makes it abundantly clear that the term as such does not in any way imply a turn toward realism. It appears that it was especially Heidegger's explication of this concept as "openness' (*Offenheit*) or "existence" that caused this awareness to be lost. It is forgotten all too

---

[55] 'Note sur quelques aspects empiristes de la pensée de Husserl,' 18ff and 'Notes sur la prémière partie de Erfahrung und Urteil de Husserl, 6, 7. The arguments of Wahl based on EU will not be discussed here. We find the same arguments in De Waelhens, 'L'idée phénoménologique d'intentionnalité' 125f. Ricoeur, too, points to the character of "personal presence" as a realist tendency. He sees in Husserl's work both an idealist tendency which comes to expression in such concepts as constitution and "production" (*Leistung*), and an intuitionist tendency, which is older than the phenomenological reduction. Like De Waelhens, he sees a dialectic between the concepts of sense (idealist moment) and presentation (realist moment). See his 'Etude sur les Méditations Cartésiennes de Husserl,' "C'est la conscience qui donne sense, mais c'est la chose qui se donne soi-même," 100.

quickly that the concept of intentionality had already undergone a long history before Heidegger's explication of it.

That the concept of perception as such represents the receptive moment in knowledge – or at least not the creative moment – is a Kantian view that does not apply to Husserl's phenomenology. How can this consideration be used as an argument for realism when Husserl himself, in the Fundamental Consideration, tries to prove idealism by way of an eidetic analysis of sensory perception? The characteristic element in Husserl's theory of perception is that the perceived object is dependent with regard to perception.

As far as the expression 'bodily presence' (*leibhafte Gegenwart*) is concerned, it was shown in Part II of this study that it is not even an argument for a realist view of perception in LU. When Husserl writes in LU that perception makes the thing bodily present, he is giving us an immanent psychological characterization of the way in which the intention apprehends the sensation. He is referring to a relation between the sensation and the sense (matter) of the interpretation. The actually existing object remains unconsidered here.[56]. In Ideen I, Husserl no longer makes the distinction between the existing thing and the perceived thing. When we interpret the perceived thing in the sense in which it is given, i.e. as relative and dependent on consciousness, then there is no reason for accepting the existence of a real thing "in itself" beyond it. Thus it is clear that the perceived object's character of bodily presence can in no way be used as an argument against an idealist interpretation of Husserl. The mode of being of the object which is itself present is of such a nature that it is dependent on consciousness. Here ontology is determinative for the epistemological question of realism versus idealism.

I must emphasize once more that Husserl's idealism is to be understood in the sense of this ontology. Many arguments that are used over and over in this debate must be ruled out because they do not settle the question on the basis on which Husserl settled it. This also applies to certain arguments *for* the idealist interpretation. Sometimes the term 'presentative (*gebende*) intuition' is used in such arguments. The typical difference between Husserl and Kant would then be that perception is already creative for the former.[57] But from the use of such a term,

[56] See above 182, 189.
[57] P. Ricoeur, *Idées directrices* XVIII, XIX, XXXVIII, note 6 to 7 in Id I; note 3 to 33; note 2 to 88; note 2 to 92; note 1 to 106; note 1 tot 282; note 1, 301; "This integration of

which already occurs in LU, nothing can be deduced. That we will not get anywhere in this way is apparent from the fact that Gerda Walther includes this term in her index under the *Contra* arguments! She is justified in doing so, for the term 'presentative intuition' was already used on the pre-transcendental level.[58]

Thus it is certainly not the case that the absence of the terms 'creation' and 'production' in Ideen I is to be regretted because it deprives us of an important argument in favor of the idealist interpretation of Husserl's thought. What Husserl teaches about the constitution of the transcendent thing is not at all ambiguous,[59] and it certainly makes things clearer than any reliance on a term like 'production,' for this term again gives rise to all sorts of problems of interpretation. In this context we should remember the discussion of the spontaneity of categorial acts, which likewise appeared to be of little help in this regard.[60] Fink points out that the German verb 'leisten' has many meanings. It can mean the manufacture of a utensil, the creation of a work of art, the production of an idea, etc.[61] Which of these meanings would we take, then, as the point of departure for our interpretation?

In contrast to this, the terms 'independence' and 'non-independence' give us Husserl's meaning exactly. When the idealism of the Fundamental Consideration is interpreted from this point of view, I see no principially insoluble difficulties in understanding Husserl's intentions. It is striking and at the same time unfortunate that Husserl's advice to his readers to understand his idealism as he would have it understood has been followed by so few. Many interpreters have preferred to approach his philosophy on the basis of traditional concepts. The result is an interminable debate without victors or vanquished. Does Husserl

---

seeing into *constitution* is without doubt the most difficult point of the phenomenological philosophy."

[58] 7, 34ff, 39, 42f.

[59] It is typical of Husserl's philosophy that the concept of constitution has different meaning in relation to different things, for to each type of object corresponds a unique form of experience. This is important for Husserl's theory of the constitution of the alter ego: if constitution means producing in relation to the thing, it need not have this meaning in relation to our fellow man. When we bear this in mind, it becomes apparent that Husserl's philosophy of the alter ego is less inconsistent than is generally supposed. See also FTL 243.

[60] See above 152f.

[61] Fink, 'Les concepts opératoires dans la phénoménologie de Husserl,' 228; for the German text, see ZPF 321–337. See also his article in Kantstud., 1933, 373.

himself not have the right to determine what he means by transcendental idealism?

Finally, I must add a comment about constitution in immanent time, a question connected with the problem of the *hylé* or material of sensation interpreted by the act.[62] In LU, Husserl left the question of the origin of sensations undecided, in agreement with his methodological limitation to descriptive psychology. After the transition to transcendental idealism, this question represents a major problem. Because there is no outside, we cannot take it that the sensation arises from a stimulus in the external world. Spiegelberg calls this material "a strong realistic element in the very heart of constitutive phenomenology."[63] It is accorded the same status in Wahl's interpretation. Fink claims that this problem is only solved in the doctrine of constitution in immanent time. The matter of interpretation is not a heterological moment, as in Kantian philosophy. "The *hylé*, too, which is regarded at first as a non-intentional moment of the act, is, like the intentional form of wholeness of the act itself, constituted in the depths of the intentional self-constitution of phenomenological time, a constitution not consisting in a process made up of separate acts."[64] This constitution in time is often regarded as a decisive argument for the idealist interpretation of Husserl's philosophy.[65] Within the framework of this methodological discussion, I would add that it does not seem right to transpose the decision with regard to the question of idealism to immanent constitution. Husserl himself does not mention this constitution of time anywhere in the Fundamental Consideration. Instead he makes the decision in connection with the apodictic criticism of experience. It is more justifiable methodologically to interpret the constitution of time on the basis of this criticism. Furthermore, it also seems possible to interpret this constitution in the realist sense, i.e. as meaning that the supposed physical stimulus is only disconnected, as Husserl in fact maintained in 1905.[66] Sokolowski, for example, who analyzes this immanent constitution at length, does not see it as a reason to change his interpretation of the concept of constitution. And in a certain sense he is right, for an analysis of time is always possible also on a psychological level. The decision about the level cannot be based on description itself but must instead be based on the framework within which the description stands. It depends on whether the natural attitude has been disconnected in advance, that is to say, on whether the reifying apperception of consciousness has been undone.

---

[62] See above 167.
[63] *The Phenomenological Movement*, 148.
[64] Kantstud. 1933, 376, see also 373, 375.
[65] Ricoeur, Idées directrices XXIII, XXXVI.
[66] ZBW 378f (E 34ff).

PARAGRAPH TWO. THE THING IN ITSELF AND NATURAL SCIENCE

The problem of the thing in itself is closely bound up with natural science. For Brentano, the unknowable thing behind the subjective appearance is identical with the thing of physics. This view was also accepted by the young Husserl. In LU, Husserl remains faithful to the distinction between the world of appearance and the world of physics. Although the appearance is not a part of consciousness, it is dependent on consciousness, but the thing of physics is not. He also speaks of the metaphysical thing in itself as the natural scientific thing. Husserl's idealist standpoint thus requires renewed reflection on physics. We already find this in PSW and also in a supplement to the Fundamental Consideration. With the help of this analysis of natural scientific research, we can better compare Husserl's transcendental idealism first with Brentano's theory of knowledge and then with Husserl's own theory of knowledge in LU.

I. The Thing of Physics in Ideen I

In the supplement mentioned above, Husserl gives a description of a natural scientific theory of knowledge. This description, like various others in his writings, is a statement of the *standpoint of Brentano*, although Brentano is not mentioned by name. This theory, which Husserl characterizes as "realist," posits the following: "That which is really perceived – and, in the first sense, appears – is to be regarded for its part as appearance, as the instinctive substructure of something else inwardly alien to it and separated from it. From a theoretical standpoint, the latter must be regarded as a reality which, for the purpose of explaining the way in which we experience this flow of appearances, is accepted as hypothetical and fully unknown, as a concealed *cause* of these appearances, a cause that can be characterized only indirectly and analogically through mathematical concepts."[1] Husserl regards this as a theory in conflict with the essence of the thing and of our experience of the thing. He therefore argues that it must be rejected as nonsense. He wants to show that the bearer of the "sensory determination-content" is *identical* with the bearer of the "physical determinations," that the experience of the physicist is *fully in line with* daily sensory perception, and that it is thus a mistake to see the thing of

[1] 97f; see also Krisis 54 (E 54).

physics as the *cause* of the perceived thing – especially as an *unknown* cause.

Husserl has already shown in the Fundamental Consideration that the subject of the predicates of physics is the same as the subject of the perceived determinations, and to that extent his further discussion of this point is certainly a "supplement." This identity does not mean that we must erase the distinction between the perceived thing and the thing of physics (which are also referred to respectively in Cartesian terms as the object of imagination and the object of the intellect).[2] Husserl himself wants to draw this distinction even more precisely than those who adhere to the doctrine of primary and secondary qualities are able to. Space is always regarded as one of the primary qualities, but this is a mistake. Color and space together form an inseparable unity. "Perceived space" (*Sinnenraum*) also belongs to the appearance and is not to be identified with the true or objective space of physics.[3]

This sharp distinction, however, is fully compatible with the identity of the bearer of the different properties, for there is no opposition between the perceived properties and the properties of physics. The latter represent a more precise determination of the former. The physicist proceeds from the same things that we experience in pre-scientific perception. "The thing which he observes, with which he experiments, which he sees continually, which he handles and places on the scale, which he puts in the melting-oven – this and no other thing is the subject of the predicates of physics, since it is what has the weight, mass, temperature, electrical resistance, and so forth. Likewise, the perceived processes and connections themselves are what the physicist defines by way of such concepts as force, acceleration, energy, atom, ion, and so forth."[4]

Husserl wants to show that what the natural scientist does has its point of departure in a process of constitution that already takes place on the lower level of the experience of things. Insofar as perception (*imaginatio*) already creates unity in the multiplicity of appearances, there is continuity: I experience the same property, but I see it in a different light. A number of properties are perceived as qualities of the same thing (the object referred to). It is probably no accident that

[2] 87f, 97, 100; Id II 207.
[3] 72, 315. Here we already find the famous distinction between the oriented intuitive space of perception and mathematical space, see also Id II 84f, 87, 77f.
[4] 100; see also *Ding und Raum*, 6f.

Husserl used the Kantian term 'relation to the object' in speaking of this relation of the many properties to the one thing.[5] That which Kant regarded as characteristic of natural science, i.e. the connection of the elements of the plurality to form a unity, already takes place on the level of perception.

In the constitution of the world of physics, a deeper unity is brought about. Things that are regarded as terminal points in daily experience are then taken to be appearances of the things of physics. This means that the physicist must subject the experienced thing to a causal analysis by bringing it into contact with all possible circumstances. In the flow of changing experiences, he seeks the identical, the abiding causal properties that manifest themselves in the appearances. Thereby things become appearances of underlying lawful connections.[6]

The sensory, intuitive level is left behind definitively in this higher type of constitution. The non-intuitive character of such theoretical concepts as atoms and ions is not the result of any imperfection in our perceptual apparatus; it is a matter of principle.[7] We could even say that the theoretical formation of concepts would become meaningless if the products of this thinking could be perceived, for the intent of this formation of concepts is to reach a deeper level of identity than the level of perception affords. In his interesting comments on so-called anomalies in Ideen II, Husserl shows that the intent of physics is to rise above the sensory realm as such. What one finger feels can be corrected by other fingers. Visual errors that result from squinting (e.g. seeing double) can be corrected via our sense of touch. But a *total* anomaly is conceivable. This brings us to the insight that the world of appearance is relative to our senses. Therefore we are driven to seek a non-relative world independent of the senses.[8] This step, which Husserl also refers to as a move from vague experience to exact experience, was first taken by Galileo.

In this exact determination, rational geometry and phoronomy are indispensable instruments preceding causal analysis. The decisive step forward in physics was taken when Galileo applied mathematics to physical phenomena.[9] This geometrizing, to which Husserl devoted

[5] See below 447.
[6] PSW 308, 311; Id I 146, Id II 84ff, 169ff, III 4, 65.
[7] 102, Krisis 130.
[8] Id II 65ff, 76, 87; Id III 67.
[9] Husserliana III 100, Id I 297, 299; Id III 36 note 1, 3, 43.

further attention in Krisis, is possible because things have a spatial aspect – even if the space in question is not a precise geometrical space.

At the time of Ideen I, Husserl already saw clearly the problem of the relation between "perceived space" and mathematical space. The former is directly given and is described via morphological concepts, while the latter is deduced from certain axioms. These axioms are grasped in a process of idealization that takes perceived space as its point of departure. In Ideen I, Husserl promises to deal with the unsolved problem of the relation between descriptive concepts and exact ideal concepts "in the continuation of these investigations."[10] This promise was later repeated.[11] In Ideen I, Husserl had already caught sight of the problem that he was later to discuss under the heading of life-world. His thinking on this point was not yet worked out, but we already find certain indications of an ontology of the life-world, particularly in the doctrine of morphological essences.[12] The description of morphological essences is the instrumentarium that makes an eidetic science of the life-world possible. Some commentators claim to see a tension between the theme of the life-world and the eidetic reduction, but we must remember that Husserl distinguishes types of essences. The morphological eidetic is simply an instrument that is accommodated to the non-exact aspect of the life-world. Besides that, he distinguishes ideas in Kant's sense, ideas that originate via idealization. This theme of idealization, which gives rise to exact geometrical space, also goes back to the early stages of Husserl's career. In LU he already speaks of "intellectio" in such terms: it is then a substratum for the apprehension of an idea.[13] It even occurs in Husserl's very earliest writings, but there it is not yet the foundation for an intuition of essences, for the doctrine of the eidetic reduction had not yet been developed.[14]

When we idealize, we imagine a process that in principle cannot be closed off. We construe the idea of an infinity – in which what is given is not the infinite itself, for this would be impossible, but an insight into this impossibility. In geometry this is a process in which the geometrical figure is thought on the basis of the intuited form. The geometrical figure is an ideal limit of this process. We already find all of this in Husserl's earliest writings, long before he gave an extensive account of this train of thought in Krisis.[15]

At this point we can draw five conclusions. First, it is incorrect to regard the things of physics as causes of perceived phenomena. We can indeed make an inference *from one appearance to another* as its cause, but this is not the same as inferring a cause *behind* the phenomena. The identity of

---

[10] 137.
[11] Id III 3, 44, 62.
[12] Id III 60, 63ff, 131ff; see below 453.
[13] LU II 65; LU III 133.
[14] PA 230, 249, 251, 264, 272; PSL 173.
[15] Krisis 23ff (E 26).

the subject of both the phenomenal predicates and the predicates of the physicist precludes any causal relation.[16]

Nor is the supposed cause unknown. The nature studied by the physicist is completely known. It is true that this nature is not perceivable via the senses, but it can nevertheless be thought. Our quest for an intuitive model is not an attempt to compensate for a shortcoming in our cognitive faculties; it is a practical method of conceiving of a conceptual unity via sensorily perceivable means. As such, these unities produced by thought have a "sense given in insight" (*einsichtige Sinn*).[17]

Because of the identity of the subjects of the two kinds of predicates, we are not to speak of the appearance as an image or sign. An image, as well as a sign, points to something else of which it is an image or sign. The sensorily perceived thing with its color, form, taste, and smell is a sign not of something else but of *itself*;[18] what is further determined in this thing itself.

Finally, it is clear that it is completely mistaken to describe the procedure of physics as an elimination of secondary qualities, of the "purely subjective,"[19] and it is likewise incorrect to characterize perception as a "taking as false" (*Falschnehmung*). The perceived world is indeed relative to our senses and is an appearance of the world of physics, but appearance (*Erscheinung*) is not illusion (*Schein*). Just as the lower stages are not crossed out as illusion when a deeper unity is discovered in the constitution of things, the lower stages (the level of things, of the *imaginatio*) are not crossed out in the constitution of the world of physics either. If we were to cross them out, we would give up the very ground on which we stand, for the world of the senses is the point of departure of physics, the medium through which thought proceeds and on which it rests. This makes it understandable why the phenomenal world can play a crucial role in the confirmation of theories – something that would be a complete riddle if this experience were pure illusion. Precisely because natural science constitutes a deeper level of identity in the world of appearances, it is possible for us to orient ourselves in the world more effectively by way of science.[20]

---

[16] 89, 101; IP 80, 81.

[17] 102.

[18] 100, 79. See below 442 note 33.

[19] PSW 311; Id I 72, 97. At this point, Husserl already bases 'epistèmè' on 'doxa,' to use terms borrowed from Krisis, cf. Krisis 128f, 131, 143, 158.

[20] 73; Id II 132.

The most important conclusion, however, is that *physics cannot affect the validity of the Fundamental Consideration*. If the experience of the physicist is nothing but an extension of our normal experience of things, then the thing of physics shares in the relativity and non-independence characteristic of the thing. Thus, although the Fundamental Consideration deals with the level of the sensory perception of things, the conclusions it reaches appear to be valid for the thing of physics as well. The facticity of the scientific world-picture was already pointed out in connection with the experiment of the annihilation of the world. [21] The actual course of our experience indeed gives us reason to construct such a "true" world, but this step is in no sense necessary. It is understandable that Husserl should return to the question of physics once more, for physics plays a very definite role in the naturalistic attitude. It is an important source of the absolutizing of the world of things, especially in the form of a so-called "natural scientific theory of knowledge."

In such a theory, the appearing things are first made contents of consciousness, with physical things then being regarded as causes of the merely subjective phenomena. Causality, which actually has meaning only within the constituted world, is thus turned into a mythical bond between the reality of the physicist and absolute consciousness. "Thereby a mythical, absolute reality is falsely attributed to the being of the physicist, while truly absolute, pure consciousness as such is not seen at all." [22] The absurdity of this way of thinking is that the world of physics, which is dependent on certain connections in consciousness, is made the cause of these connections. To think this way is to turn things inside out. When we stop mythologizing and inquire into the essence of our experience of things, such theories are seen to be untenable. The thing of physics is indeed transcendent to the perceived thing, but only in the sense of a higher correlate of consciousness that is founded in the former. "It is clear from the foregoing," Husserl's conclusion reads, "that *even the higher transcendence of the things of physics does not imply any reaching out beyond the world that exists before consciousness*, or before any ego functioning as the subject of knowledge (single or in the relation of empathy)." [23]

[21] See above 338.
[22] 101.
[23] 100.

II. *Comparison with* Logische Untersuchungen *and* Krisis

When we compare this standpoint with that of LU, we see that here Husserl does indeed draw the conclusions implied in his radical reinterpretation of being. In LU, the world of physics was still a world in itself. It is true that he already called this view a metaphysical or natural scientific presupposition that cannot be justified phenomenologically, but its validity as a supposition nonetheless remained unaffected. The phenomenological sphere that Husserl isolates in LU must be viewed against the background of this world in itself. It is an artificial island, as it were, in a natural scientific world.

In LU, Husserl moves along a double track epistemologically. He has seen that the world of appearances is not subjective in the sense in which sensations are subjective. He has also seen that the physical world is not an unknown world. (It is metaphysical but not mystical, for it is empirically founded.) Nonetheless, there is a noteworthy gap between the two. Appearances are intentional objects dependent on consciousness, whereas natural scientific things exists in themselves. The phenomenological sphere together with its correlates is projected against a "present" (*vorhanden*) world of natural science. Thus Husserl takes a halfway position between psychologism on the one hand – for although appearances are transcendent, they are still dependent on psychological consciousness – and realism on the other. What is essential here is that this realism and this psychologism condition each other. Looking at Husserl's position from the transcendental point of view, we could say that he is the victim of a dilemma that he himself later analyzed and outlined (i.e. objectivism vs. subjectivism or realism vs. subjective idealism) and regarded as characteristic of any theory of knowledge that remains stuck in the natural attitude.

This realism is also characteristic of Descartes. Descartes did wish to proceed from the *ego cogito*, but this was only a detour in the founding of natural science. He was convinced a priori of the validity of natural science. He, too, interpreted the world of physics as *metaphysically transcendent*.[24] His return to the *cogito* was only an attempt to found this world existing in itself, whose definitive validity was certain a priori.[25] Descartes' discovery of subjectivity was not truly radicalized until Hume, who was the first thinker to attack the foundations of objectivism (including scientific objectivism).[26]

[24] Krisis 76, 83, 86, 94, 407/8 (E 75, 81, 84, 91).
[25] See above 376 note 21, 402.
[26] Krisis 93, 99 (E 90, 96).

The radical phenomenological reinterpretation overcomes both horns of the dilemma at the same time. It shows that the thing (including the thing of physics) is a correlate of consciousness, and that any realism is therefore absurd. At the same time, it puts a radical end to any natural interpretation of consciousness and thereby to the necessity of withdrawing to an intentional object given to a powerless consciousness (a process that involves putting the question of being between brackets). The presupposition which the Husserl of LU prefers not to use is still maintained as valid. *It remains unconsidered, but it is not attacked.* The Fundamental Consideration has shown that this presupposition has no basis and rests on an absurd interpretation of the world as given to us in the experience of the physicist.

These Husserlian observations on the sense of physics have exercised great historical influence, particularly on so-called existential phenomenologists, who like to refer to the later Husserl, the Husserl of such works as Krisis and EU, where the theme of the life-world as the "hidden foundation of sense" for the natural sciences is developed. At this point, therefore, I will take a brief look at Husserl's later development. When we compare the standpoint of Ideen I with that of Krisis, it appears that the new element in the latter work is not so much the introduction of some new theme (e.g. the life-world as the foundation of the sciences) as a difference in accent and method. In Krisis, Husserl wishes to show that the scientific world rests on the life-world, and that the latter is an intentional correlate of transcendental consciousness. The argument proceeds in two phases.[27] Husserl uses the *opposite* procedure in Ideen I. The Fundamental Consideration shows that the thing of the senses is a correlate of consciousness. He then goes on to show that the thing of physics is only an extension of this perceived thing. In the second phase, the physical world is thus given its place as the correlate of transcendental consciousness.[28]

As I see it, this difference in method is bound up with different views regarding the origin of the natural attitude. In Ideen I, sensory perception is regarded as the root of the natural attitude, and Husserl points out that it also makes its influence felt in the sciences that remain in this attitude. Later, Husserl must have seen that these sciences

---

[27] Krisis 138, 151, 177, 154, 191ff (E 135, 148, 174, 151, 187); EU 49; Nachwort 139.

[28] Thus the so-called reduction of the natural scientific world to the life-world is already present in Ideen I; that is to say, it is in fact carried out. Here, too, Husserl's actual analysis runs ahead of his methodological reflection on it. See below 435f.

strengthen the natural attitude to an extraordinary extent. In PSW, he already speaks of the naiveté that seems to be immortal in natural science.[29] Furthermore, was Husserl himself not subject to the influence of this prejudice for a long time? His own past may have been one of the factors that convinced him of the unholy influence which the natural scientific positing of the world as something obvious is able to exercise, and it may have convinced him that the chief attack must be directed against this positing. The origin of the natural attitude is to be sought first and foremost in science and the scientific attitude.[30]

In Krisis, Husserl wishes to show that the world of appearance is not a suit of clothes (*Umkleidung*) covering a true, objective physical world, but that the system of physical concepts – on the contrary – represents a garment (*Kleid*) thrown over the life-world. In this connection he lays special emphasis on the geometrizing of the life-world, which first makes possible a mathematical treatment of it.[31] The method of Krisis and EU has the advantage of examining the natural attitude where it is strongest, i.e. in natural science. On the other hand, the path Husserl follows in Ideen I is clearer with regard to his ultimate intentions. We must remember that the reduction of the natural scientific world to the life-world in Krisis is only a *means* of ascending to transcendental consciousness via the reduction. The third part of Krisis bears the title "The Way into Phenomenological Transcendental Philosophy from the Inquiry into the Pre-given Life-world." The life-world is not a terminal point but a point of departure, and the analysis of this world is only a way into transcendental phenomenology. Husserl wants to show that the world is only a correlate of a transcendental constituting consciousness. This is the ultimate goal he had in mind in Krisis. The reduction of the physical world to the life-world is only a preparatory phase.[32] Thus it is a misconception to see the life-world as a final

[29] PSW 299; EP II 285.

[30] In Ideen II, all the emphasis already falls here, when Husserl distinguishes between the natural attitude and the naturalistic attitude. See above 386.

[31] Krisis 51 (E 51). The term 'Umkleidung' is used in Id I 99.

[32] Therefore, in his "Nachwort," Husserl says expressly that the second reduction, that of the life-world to subjectivity, is "the decisive step," 139. My historical treatment of the concept of the life-world should make it clear once more how mistaken it is to *play this theme off against Husserl's idealism*. Any effort to do so must run aground on the fact that in Ideen I, the life-world is already the point of departure for the proof of idealism. See J. Wahl, 'Cahiers de Royaumont, Philosophie' III, Husserl 429. A tension between the theme of the life-world and idealism can exist only if the life-world is given the ontological import which it *does* have for Merleau-Ponty but does *not* have for Husserl.

objective. A comparison with the Fundamental Consideration, which *begins* with the life-world, is useful here for purposes of correction. In this way, too, a genetic study of Husserl's philosophy can contribute to a better understanding of the later periods of his thought.

PARAGRAPH THREE. THE PSYCHOLOGICAL AND TRANSCENDENTAL CONCEPTS OF THE NOEMA

There has been such talk of a mixing of psychological and transcendental phenomenology.[1] This confusion is not characteristic of Ideen I as a *whole*, and certainly not of the Fundamental Consideration, but it is present in some passages in the last two sections. In particular, the passages in which the concept of the noema is introduced pose great interpretive problems. This matter requires our attention at this point, for more is involved here than the question how the concept of the noema is to be interpreted. The issue here is the fundamental difference between psychology and transcendental phenomenology. If the distinction between the two is vague at this point, the psychological interpretation of the Fundamental Consideration will always have something to appeal to. Thus there are three things to be done. In the first place, I must make an effort to define the difficulties. In what way does Husserl confuse the psychological noema with the transcendental noema? This will then give me an opportunity to formulate once more the fundamental distinction between the psychological epoché and the transcendental epoché. After this intermezzo, the question whether there is a satisfactory explanation for this confusion will seen even more pressing.

I. The Introduction of the Concept of the Noema

Among the general distinctions that must be made within the sphere of transcendental consciousness is the distinction between genuine and intentional components. Genuine components, which are also called "real" (*reell*) components, are the sensations and interpretive acts that Husserl now calls form and matter (*morphé* and *hylé*). He uses terms with which we are already acquainted from LU to characterize the intentional components, i.e. intentional object, sense, "the perceived as

See above 357. "Such a tension in fact does not exist," H.G. Gadamer rightly maintains, 'Die Phänomenologische Bewegung,' 31.

[1] See above 377, 383.

such." What appears to consciousness is the object – thanks to the sense-giving of the interpretive act (now called the "noesis"). As the correlate of interpretive noeses, this object is now called the "noema." This is the technical term used by Husserl from this point on to refer to the intentional object.[2]

Because it is apparent from the context that we are dealing here with a distinction within transcendental consciousness,[3] it would seem reasonable to conceive of this noema as the transcendental noema. That this is also Husserl's intention is clear from his comment that this analysis is *also* valid in psychological respects.[4] Furthermore, Husserl here repeats his assurance about the deep abyss between psychology and phenomenology. Thus the noema is to be conceived of first of all in a transcendental sense, which is also what Fink says in the article authorized by Husserl. The transcendental noema is the unity of sense of which the Fundamental Consideration spoke. It is reality itself. As Fink says, "it is the being (*das Seiende*) itself, and that in an as yet unknown depth of its hidden sense of being (*Seinssinn*) – as transcendental validity."[5]

Nevertheless, the passage referred to in the preceding paragraph contains a number of expressions that tend to further a psychological conception of the noema. What is peculiar about the introduction of the concept of the noema is that Husserl speaks anew of a phenomenological reduction. We get the impression that we have not yet reached the transcendental level, although in fact we have. This repetition, however, could be regarded as a short recapitulation. What is more confusing is that in this passage, Husserl uses a terminology that is psychological in many respects. Although these passages are meant in a transcendental sense, they manifest a certain "disturbing insensitivity" (to use Fink's words) vis-à-vis the difference between psychology and transcendental phenomenology. Fink adds that the difference between the psychological noema and the transcendental noema was not further worked out in Ideen I.[6] I will now make an attempt to accomplish this

---

[2] 179, 181, 185, 265, 201, 202.

[3] Transcendental consciousness is discovered in the second section. The later sections are explorations within this transcendental consciousness, as Husserl himself indicates, 121, 123, 139, 141, 144, 159, 162, 168, 177ff, 184, 187, 201f, 204, 266, 279, 306, 309, 313, 316, 319.

[4] 184.

[5] Fink, 'Die phän. Phil. E. Husserls in der gegenwärtigen Kritik,' 364.

[6] Fink op.cit. 364f.

myself in what follows. The analysis contained in the second volume of LU will providde the material required for comparison. First I will deal with the question in what respects Husserl's arguments on this score have a psychological flavor.

(*A*) What strikes us first of all is that the reduction has an expressly epistemological flavor. It reminds us of the reduction in IP carried out in connection with the problem of transcendence. Over against the thing outside we now have the "perceived as such."[7] We do read that the real experience is also disconnected, but nowhere do we read that we get absolute consciousness back. The sense that we get back therefore looks a great deal like the psychological sense of LU – all the more because Husserl himself points to LU.[8] The choice of illusion as an example points in the same direction, for it is a standard example for showing that the existence of the perceived is irrelevant in the psychological reduction.[9]

(*B*) More important is that the statements about disconnection and what we get back are not clear.[10] Nowhere is it made clear that the disconnection of reality represents the destruction of an absurd interpretation. Husserl does say that everything remains as it was, but this means something entirely different in the case of the psychological reduction. In the latter case, the residue is not reality itself but a psychological sense to which we retreat because true reality is inaccessible.

(*C*) A particularly strong argument for the psychological interpretation is the interesting comparison of the noema with the intentional object of Scholasticism. Husserl writes that it did not remain unnoticed in history that "the non-existence ... of the presented or thought object of the presentation as such cannot detract from ... the presentation itself. ... The difference is so striking that it had to come to literary expression. As a matter of fact, the Scholastic distinction between the '*mental*,' '*intentional*' or '*immanent*' object, on the one hand, and the '*real*' object, on the other, points back to this difference."[11]

In Part II of this study, I devoted considerable attention to the

---

[7] 187f.
[8] 182. See also 266f and LU III 16, 170.
[9] 183; LU II 348; PP 282.
[10] 182f, 187; see also 202, 142, and 278.
[11] 185.

similarities between the Scholastic concept of the intentional object and Husserl's concept of it. There is definitely some agreement, despite the fundamental difference. On the difference, of which Husserl made much, I refer the reader to Part II.[12] My concern at the moment is that the *tertium comparationis* or similarity furthers a psychological interpretation to a considerable extent. The comparison with the Scholastic concept is only meaningful if the psychological concept of sense is meant. Later this comparison was also used by Husserl in his phenomenological psychology.[13] The Scholastic concept of sense and the psychological-phenomenological concept of it do agree in this respect, that for both, the intentional object is not identical with the real object and is not dependent on the existence of this real object. If the latter did not exist, there would remain the act and its immanent content (Scholasticism) or the act and its transcendent object (Husserl). Here the non-existence of the object does represent a *loss*. What remains is an immanent sphere with intentional correlates 'representing'' reality.[14] Thus the comparison of the transcendental noema with the Scholastic concept of the intentional object is misleading. The same is true of the comparison of natural reality with the "object in the strict sense" (*Gegenstand schlechthin*) of Scholasticism, for the latter term refers to an outer real object and not to an absurd fiction, as it does for Husserl.[15]

(*D*) There are a number of expressions and arguments that could only apply to the psychological reduction. Thus Husserl contrasts the "object in the strict sense" (*Gegenstand schlechthin*) with the noema and then adds: "While objects as such (taken in the unmodified sense) stand under fundamentally different highest genera, all the objective senses (*Gegenstandssinne*) and all noemata taken as complete, however various they may be otherwise, belong in principle to a single highest genus." This means that there are no regional differences among the noemata. They all have the same psychical mode of being, even though

---

[12] See above 190ff.

[13] PP 176, 32.

[14] 279, 281.

[15] For Husserl, the term 'object in the strict sense' (*Gegenstand slechthin*) can also refer to the *reinterpreted* object *within* transcendental phenomenology. It is then spoken of as noematically modified. This modification is indicated by quotation marks. The "object in the strict sense" is then the identity pole or bearer of the properties. 265, 281f. See below 441, 447.

they are not immanent components of the psychical. Thus the definition of a noema is "an *objectivity* belonging to consciousness but possessing a *nature of its own*."[16] According to this outlook, the reality outside consciousness is regionally varied and is represented within consciousness by a psychical sense.[17]

In a paragraph on the "mode of being of the noema," we read: "Now, that which is given in the focusing of our regard [Husserl means the direction of our regard to the noema] is indeed itself an object, logically speaking, but one that is completely *non-independent*. Its *esse* consists exclusively in its '*percipi*' – except that the meaning of this statement is not to be taken at all in the Berkeleyan sense, for here the *percipi* does not include the *esse* as a real (*reell*) constituent."[18] The only reservation that Husserl makes here contra Berkeley is that the noema is not immanent in a "real" sense. Furthermore, it appears to be dependent on *psychological* consciousness and independent of reality. "The *tree itself (schlechthin)*, the thing in nature, is as different as it can be from the *perceived tree as such*, which, as perceptual sense, belongs inseparably to perception. The tree itself can burn up, resolve itself into its chemical elements, and so forth. But the sense – the sense of *this* perception, something necessarily belonging to its essence – cannot burn up; it has no chemical elements, no forces, no real properties."[19] Such a statement cannot be understood in a transcendental sense, for it transcendental consciousness is the totality of absolute being, this fire would certainly have consequences for the correlates of consciousness. In the spirit of the Fundamental Consideration, we must say that consciousness would be modified but not annihilated by a world-wide fire.

II. Intermezzo – The Psychological Epoché and the Transcendental Epoché

In Chapter I we encountered the transcendental concept of sense as reinterpreted reality. There we already noted the fundamental ambiguity of this concept, which can bear either a psychological meaning or a transcendental meaning. Now I am in a position to clear up this ambiguity by showing that this concept as well as the two (psychological and transcendental) technical operations that lead up to it have a totally different meaning – despite the identity of the terms. In both cases Husserl speaks negatively of putting being between brackets and positively of recovering it under another sign. The object we get back is

[16] 265.
[17] 279, 281.
[18] 206.
[19] 184. In Krisis, Husserl uses this argument only in connection with the psychological reduction, 245 (E 242).

then spoken of as "sense" or as a "phenomenon," which, although it is transcendent, has a certain ideal immanence.

(A) The disconnection of existence. In LU, this disconnection is an attempt to solve the difficult epistemological problem of transcendence. One could say of this reduction that it proceeds from the old idea of "representative" consciousness, i.e. the closed consciousness that faces the insoluble problem of reaching the external world. We could also say of this reduction that it proceeds from Kant's thesis that existence is not a predicate,[20] for when Husserl says that nothing is lost, he means that nothing is lost for consciousness or for knowledge. The concept (e.g. the intentional object) is not enriched by the predicate of existence, and therefore nothing is lost when existence is put between brackets. But from an ontological standpoint, there is indeed a loss of extra-mental reality.

In the transcendental epoché, only a certain interpretation is disconnected. Nothing is really lost. Insight into the relative mode of being of the thing *eo ipso* means an awareness of the absoluteness of consciousness.[21] Both are liberated at the same time from a naturalistic conception. Therefore the reduction is also *one movement*. It is not carried out in two phases, as though the thing were first disconnected, and then consciousness.[22] The reduction is sometimes conceived of as though a phenomenological epoché bearing on the world must be followed by a transcendental epoché bearing on consciousness. If the phenomenological epoché is then further interpreted as a phenomenological-psychological epoché, there is a Loss of reality after such an operation.

(B) The recovery of what was disconnected under another sign. What is recovered after the psychological epoché is the noematically modified object or simply the "object" (in quotation marks).[23] As we have seen in Part II, this sense can be described in all the aspects in which it occurs

---

[20] See A. de Waelhens, *Une philosophie de l'ambiguité*, 89. The adjective 'representative' might arouse objections precisely because perception, according to Husserl, is *pre*sentative ("*selbst*gebend"). As I have shown in Part II, the problematics of LU is the same as that of representationalism, despite all appearances to the contrary.

[21] Fink, 'Die phän. Phil. E. Husserl in der gegenwärtigen Kritik,' 350, 361.

[22] This is a widespread misconception that was already combatted by Fink. op.cit. 351. Husserl does speak of "steps" in connection with the reduction, but this concerns the presentation and working out of the consequences of this one epoché, 3, 59, 108.

[23] On this noematic modification, see 187, 189, 193, 207, 275; see also 161, 194, 198, 270.

in consciousness (merely meant, perceived, merely presented, posited, imagined, etc.) without thereby going beyond the immanent sphere.[24]

The sense that remains after the transcendental reduction is being itself. It is not the correlate of a mundane consciousness regarded as a region; it is rather the correlate of an a-regional consciousness that is the origin of all regions. Calling it a "phenomenon" or a "phenomenon claiming validity" (Geltungsphänomen) is no longer to limit it but to indicate that it is being itself.[25]

(C) Reflection. In both forms of the epoché, the disconnection is an act of the reflecting ego. We already encountered psychological reflection in LU as an interruption of the objective direction of our regard. It is a turning of consciousness toward itself.[26]

The psychological residue includes both noeses and noemata, and therefore Husserl distinguishes between noetic and noematic reflection in Ideen I. The latter is rightly called a "reflection of a peculiar kind," for it is reflection on something objective.[27] Husserl's denial that the noema is a product of reflection is a polemic against Locke, who does not recognize the objectivity of the noema and regards noematic properties as predicates of reflection. For Locke, reflection is noetic reflection.[28] Within Husserl's sphere of noematic reflection in the broadest sense, we can again distinguish between directedness towars the "object in the strict sense" (Gegenstand schlechthin) and reflection on the noemata in which it appears,[29] both of which are to be distinguished again from reflection on the noematic meaning.[30]

Transcendental reflection is not simply an interruption of the straightforward attitude. Anyone can carry out normal reflection, Husserl claims. But carrying out phenomenological reflection requires radical thinking like that of the Fundamental Consideration. In this reflection we undo the positing "through which the world exists for us." Husserl writes: "instead of living in them and carrying them out, we carry out acts of reflection directed toward them, and these we grasp as the absolute being which they are."[31] This is not a reflection of psychological consciousness on itself, but of a transcendental observer

[24] See above 187ff, 315ff.
[25] See above 369.
[26] See above 128, 160f and 201.
[27] 184, 185, 155.
[28] 220, 205.
[29] See below 441, 447.
[30] See below 443; 307.
[31] 94f, 104; CM 16, 73.

on transcendental consciousness. This ego of reflection is one of the three egos that play a role in transcendental phenomenology. It is the so-called transcendental phenomenologizing ego, the ego that is the subject of transcendental experience. [32]

III. The Way from Psychology

It appears that there is no easy way out of our difficulties. Apparently the opposition between the two reductions is unbridgeable. The psychological reduction is carried out within the natural attitude, while the transcendental reduction suspends this attitude. We could also put it as follows: the transcendental reduction eliminates the entire problem that made the psychological reduction necessary.

Nevertheless, there is a point of contact between the two reductions, namely, that both have the same consciousness as their theme. From a material standpoint there is no difference, even though consciousness is conceived of in two totally different ways, i.e. as a region and as the original region (*Ur-regio*). As I see it, an explanation for the confusion must be sought in this material identity. This explanation is supported by both the genesis of phenomenology and its later development. Husserl himself speaks in Ideen I of the "historical and natural route from psychology to phenomenology."[33] We saw further that in his argument resulting in the positing of absolute consciousness, he begins with the "real mind" (*reale Seele*). Thus there is indeed a line from psychology to phenomenology. Husserl's development enables us to describe this transition more precisely. In LU, consciousness is still conceived of as a region of the person, but that by virtue of which consciousness is human consciousness (i.e. the connection with the body) is left unconsidered. In this pure psychology, Husserl already reaches noteworthy results. A new insight into the essence of consciousness, which is seen to be a fine tissue of intentional acts, is achieved. In 1903 he takes a new step in methodological purification. If the body must be left unconsidered for methodological reasons (because it is not given), then any ground for a "psychological apperception" disappears. We go beyond the given when we conceive of consciousness as a stratum of an empirical person. We know nothing about the body, and hence we know nothing of any unity of body and consciousness or of

---

[32] Fink, 348, 355, 366, 383 and below 466f. The other two ego's are transcendental and psychological consciousness, CM 15; EP II 99.

[33] 266, 180.

any empirical person,[34] In 1907 this insight already grows into a clear criticism of Descartes. The Cartesian *cogito* is also in need of purification. Descartes' mistake was that he confused the evidence of the being of the *cogitatio* with the evidence that *my cogitatio* is, that is, with the evidence of the *sum cogitans*. Husserl points out how difficult it is to resist this inclination. I automatically conceive of consciousness as *my* consciousness, as a region of mine as a human being, as a person (= psycho-physical unity). Yet this purification must be carried out, and when it is, the basis of psychology is left behind definitively – "even that of descriptive psychology."[35]

As far as the negative aspect of the reduction is concerned, IP is already on the level of Ideen I. Furthermore, when we consider its positive reverse side, we see that Husserl has also broken through to a fundamentally new insight, for he speaks of the absolute givenness of consciousness, of its absolute existence, and even of a *revision of metaphysics* on this basis. This makes it apparent that the negative disconnection was already supported by an ontology of consciousness and the transcendent thing. Thus we see that Husserl, through a gradual radicalization in the process of purification, broke through almost automatically to transcendental phenomenology *from descriptive psychology*. The insight that consciousness has a nature and essence of its own (the first phase of the Fundamental Consideration) develops naturally into the insight that the existence of consciousness is absolute (the second phase of the Fundamental Consideration).

The disconnection of natural apperception is separated only by a thin wall from *seeing through* this apperception. Husserl broke through this wall in his apodictic criticism of experience. Therefore the latter is *the* center of the entire procedure of reduction. It makes possible the subtle transition from a negative disconnection to a positive acceptance of the world under another sign. However subtle this transition may be, it is of revolutionary significance. At that very moment, the naturalistic view of the world collapses. Consciousness is transformed from a region into the original region. We can imagine what the breakthrough to this insight meant to Husserl at a critical point in his philosophical career. The diary he kept during those years reveals that the issue for him was his very existence as a philosopher.

---

[34] See above 310.
[35] See above 312 and Krisis 80 (E 78f).

As I see it, this personal history, this "way from psychology" that Husserl himself took, was determinative for his presentation of transcendental phenomenology. Husserl himself was aware of what a long way he had come. How could the new insight that he had gained only after years of intense study and a personal crisis best be presented? In his many explications of this reduction, Husserl is never silent about the difficulties involved in this operation. In carrying out the reduction, we must fight a prejudice of the millenia strengthened in the modern period by the tremendous prestige of natural science.[36] The inclination to think in the natural attitude or to fall back into it cannot be rooted out completely. To Husserl, the entire history of western philosophy was an illustration of this struggle. This begins with Descartes. In 1907 Husserl already wrote: ". . . for Descartes, to discover and to abandon were the same." In Krisis, Husserl shows that because of this, Descartes could just as well have become the father of a beginning transcendental philosophy as the father of modern physicalistic objectivism.[37] The history of transcendental philosophy is then described as a falling and rising again, a continuous oscillation between genuine transcendental motives and a falsification of these motives by way of psychologistic interpretations of transcendental consciousness. The problem of German transcendental philosophy was the (material) identity of and radical difference between psychological and transcendental consciousness. Clarity on this point was not achieved.[38] This vision of the history of philosophy was also influenced very strongly by Husserl's personal life-history.

Could Husserl, who had gone through such a laborious struggle, expect his readers and students to understand this radical turn quickly and easily? If this was his original expectation, the way Ideen I was received by his students and his friends (Stumpf, for example!) must have stripped him of this illusion. Thus it should not surprise us that after Ideen I, Husserl devoted more and more of his attention to the search for "ways" to transcendental phenomenology. A pedagogical preparation is necessary if we are to be able to understand transcendental phenomenology. Husserl looked more and more to pure phenomenological psychology to accomplish this goal.[39] We must not forget

[36] See also Krisis 93 (E 90); Id I 1, 120.
[37] Krisis 74ff; 85ff (E 73ff, 83ff).
[38] Krisis 182ff; 207ff; 261ff (E 178ff, 203ff, 257ff).
[39] PP 278, 295, 270, 344.

that this psychology *by itself* was *already* revolutionary when compared to the psychology current at that time: in LU we find many
insights into the essence of intentionality that were unknown before
Husserl. Worthy of particular mention is the discovery (in principle) of
the noetic-noematic parallelism. If the gaining of such insights already
cost Husserl such extreme mental effort, was it reasonable to expect
that transcendental phenomenology would be directly understood? It
is certainly understandable that Husserl regarded the doctrine of the
psychological noema, according to which consciousness always has an
inseparable correlate, as some sort of preparation for achieving insight
into transcendental correlation.[40] A *material* analysis of consciousness
was to prepare the way for transcendental phenomenology. In this way
we become somewhat familiar with the wonderful theme of consciousness, which is inexhaustible even in the psychological attitude. We have
seen that Husserl complains in Krisis about the material emptiness with
which transcendental consciousness is made visible in Ideen I.[41]
Therefore he began searching for other ways. In Krisis he turned to the
way from the life-world and the way from psychology. In the way from
psychology, Husserl was following a route more or less the reverse of
that followed in Ideen I, in which the field of the new science is first
discovered and then explored. The chapters following the Fundamental Consideration deal with "general structures of pure consciousness."
As Husserl says, they gives certain basic directions for description to
follow. The "most general eidetic sorts" of the area in question are
revealed.[42]

   In Krisis and in the Encyclopaedia Britannica article, transcendental
phenomenology is preceded by a material analysis in the form of
phenomenological psychology. Because the material distinctions remain the same, we need "only" carry out the "change of attitude"
afterward in order to be able to give a transcendental interpretation of
what came before. The way from psychology, which by then was a
conscious method, had *in fact* already been followed by Husserl in the
last two sections of Ideen I. Here again we face a phenomenon that
surfaces repeatedly in the course of Husserl's development, namely,
that a method is in actual use before it becomes the object of conscious

---

[40] The expression 'inseparable' is used for both the psychological noema, PP 172, 175,
177, and the transcendental noema, CM 13, 15, 73, 97, 134; see further Id I 183ff, 188, 265.
[41] See above 376, 383.
[42] 141, 143.

reflection. "In the beginning was the deed," as Husserl puts it in Krisis, commenting on this matter.[43] Thus the so-called psychologism of Ideen I is not an incidental confusion but has a deeper ground. It is to be explained on the basis of the "route from psychology to phenomenology," which is "historical" as well as "natural."

Husserl was very anxious to show that phenomenology offers the possibility of concrete analysis, of "work with one's hands" (handanlegende Arbeit), as he put it in the foreword to the second edition of LU.[44] He wanted to offer not just a program but also some "fundamental work actually in progress." Therefore he believed that it was not necessary to adapt the second edition to the level of transcendental phenomenology in all respects. He wrote that readers rooted in some current philosophical stream, "like the work's author earlier in his life, at first can only gain access to what are preliminary steps" (italics mine). Thus Husserl expressly allows his approach to his readers to be determined by his own past! He continues: "Only when they have gained sure mastery over the style of phenomenological research do they see the fundamental meaning of certain distinctions which appeared previously to be insignificant nuances." Husserl first wants to acquaint his readers with intentional analysis and only introduce them afterwards to the "nuance" (rightly called fundamental) whereby psychology is transformed into transcendental phenomenology. From the "Nachwort" to Ideen I and the Encyclopaedia Britannica article, we know that what appears to the beginning reader to be an insignificant nuance is in reality a Copernican revolution.[45] Husserl's original silence about this nuance (on pedagogical grounds) only becomes dangerous when we proceed to interpret transcendental phenomenology on the basis of this provisional stage. To gain insight into Husserl's final intentions, we can better follow the way of the Fundamental Consideration.

PARAGRAPH FOUR. NOETIC-NOEMATIC PARALLELISM AND THE
PHENOMENOLOGY OF REASON

The theme of correlativity has already been taken up twice. It does not seem to have been present in Husserl's first period. It appears for the first time in LU, thanks to the new concept of perception. But its development was still hindered by the Cartesian prejudice that only subjectivity is to be regarded as given. In 1907 this limitation was already overcome. Correlative analysis could then be developed fully.[1] In a note to Krisis, Husserl writes: "The first breakthrough of this universal a priori of the correlation of the object of experience with the

[43] Krisis 158 (E 156).
[44] LU I, X, XI.
[45] Nachwort 147; Husserliana IX 327; see below 464.
[1] See above 34, 170, 319.

modes of givenness (approximately in the year 1898, while I was working on my LU) shook me so deeply that since then, my entire life's work has been governed by the task of working out systematically this a priori of correlation."[2]

After 1907, a distinction must be made in connection with this theme of correlativity: we must distinguish its elaboration on the psychological level from its elaboration on the transcendental level. In IP, Husserl moved mainly on the psychological level. But in Ideen I, it became clear that this psychological level represents a provisional stage. By a change of attitude, psychological consciousness is freed of a naturalizing apperception. After this purification, the correlation, which remains the same in material respects, receives a different, philosophical meaning. On the psychological level it is a relation between a psychical act and its intentional object. On the transcendental level it is a relation between absolute consciousness and the world that is constituted "in" it. On the latter level, a true phenomenology of reason is possible.[3] In this paragraph, I will compare a few concepts from Ideen I with corresponding concepts from LU to show how this phenomenology of reason was realized.

I. Noetic-Noematic Parallelism

(A) The quality of the act and the being of the object. In LU, matter and quality were two components that every act as such had to possess. The matter determined in what sense (i.e. with what properties) that material of sensation is conceived of, and the quality determined whether this happened in a positing or a non-positing way. In Ideen I, Husserl prefers the term 'thesis' to 'quality.' A thesis has a quality, but we would do well not to call it a quality.[4] If the thesis is positing, we speak of belief, and if not, we speak of neutrality.[5] More important than the change in terminology is the fact that the concept of quality is now interpreted in a correlative, two-sided way. As a property of the act, it is called "belief," and as a property of the correlated object, it is

---

[2] Krisis 169 note 1 (E 166 note); see also Id I 193, 269.

[3] Therefore Husserl adds the following comment to the quotation from Krisis: "The further course of reflection in this text will make it apparent that taking account of human subjectivity in the problematics of correlation necessarily entails a radical transformation of the sense of this entire problematics and must finally lead to the phenomenological reduction to transcendental subjectivity." This breakthrough took place "a few years after the appearance of LU."

[4] 268, 274.

[5] 222–235, 274 note 1.

called "being." Corresponding to the act of belief is an "actually existent" object. Husserl speaks of this being as "thetic character."[6]

The narrow noetic framework of LU is not just transcended in fact, for Husserl now *explicitly* recognizes the inadequacy of LU on this point: "However much the nature of the facts may have compelled us there to carry out noematic analyses, these were still considered more as indicators of the parallel noetic structures: the essential parallelism of the two structures was not yet clearly seen."[7] The analysis was one-sidedly noetic. Husserl writes that we must overcome this one-sidedness by interpreting the concepts of quality, matter and intentional essence in a noematic sense as well. We would then speak of "actually existing," of "sense" and "posited sense" (*Satz*).[8]

Husserl admits that noematic analyses were *in fact* carried out in LU too, even if it was done in a more or less clandestine manner. The actual analysis broke through the methodological framework. "To this extent, that which was regarded as analysis of acts, as noetic, was achieved when our regard was directed toward the 'meant as such,' and the structures thereby described were really noematic."[9]

(B) *The matter of the act and the object as sense.* In LU, matter is a subjective property of the act. In Ideen I, Husserl interprets this concept, too, in a noematic way, i.e. as the determination of the object that is constituted through the interpretation of a sensation. He speaks of this determination as "sense."[10]

In LU, there were two aspects to be distinguished in connection with matter, i.e. directedness toward the object in its full determination and an objective relation in a narrower sense. The latter can remain the same while the former changes in content. In connection with the correlative intended object, Husserl distinguishes between the "object *as referred to*" (*Gegenstand so wie er intendiert ist*) and the "object *referred to*"[11] (*Gegenstand welcher intendiert ist*). This distinction must now be further elaborated.

(1) *The object as referred to.* For the present I will abstract from the object referred to and analyze the sense. Husserl also calls this sense the

---

[6] 214–218.

[7] 266 note 1.

[8] 195, 267f, 216. The "cognitive (*erkenntnismässig*) essence" of LU (matter and quality plus fullness) is now called "fulfilled posited sense" (*erfüllter Satz*) 304, 298.

[9] 266; see also LU II (ed. 2) 397.[1]

[10] 268; see also 274 and Husserliana III to 269. See 144 and 258.

[11] See above 170.

noematic "core" (*Kern*), for the full noema also takes in the thetic character.[12] In connection with this noematic core (the object as referred to), we must again make a fundamental distinction between the core in the narrower sense and the full core. The latter is the "sense in the mode of its fullness."[13] Here the fullness, which, as we know from LU, is not present in every act, is taken into consideration. Thus the fulfilled sense occurs only in acts of intuition.[14] Husserl also uses two other terms in speaking of this difference. These terms bear on the expression 'object ás referred to.' Two things can be meant by this 'as': (a) a "meant as" (*Wie der Gemeintheit*) and (b) the *way* in which we are conscious of the object.[15]

(a) The determination with which the object is meant. By the "meant as," Husserl means the properties that remain the same despite the various ways in which we are aware of them. If what we intend is a blossoming apple tree, it can always be described by way of the same predicates, even though we are aware of the tree in various different ways. This is then a description that avoids all "subjective" expressions and limits itself to *what* we are aware of. Thereby a "fixed content in each noema" is delimited.[16]

(b) The way in which we are aware of an object.

(i) Attentional modification. The way in which we are aware of an object means first of all whether the object meant falls within the range of our attention or not. Husserl compares attention to the beam of a spotlight. That which we observe may be fully illuminated or half in the dark or completely in the dark. It is clear that these changes in ways of appearance affect and change the object of which we are aware. But this change in illumination changes the appearance not in its objective determination but in its way of appearing.[17]

(ii) Reproductive modification. An object also appears different depending on whether it appears in an "originary" way in perception or in an "imagined" (*phantasiemässig*) or "quasi-presented" (*vorschwebend*) way in imagination. In the latter case, it is not present "in person" but is represented. The re-presented object appears as a modification of that which is presented and points to it.[18]

(iii) Presentation via an image or sign. The presentation of an object via an image or sign belongs to another category of modification. A "depicting"

[12] 197, 213f.

[13] 273. The core in the narrower sense is often spoken of simply as the core, 193, 197, 199.

[14] This term already occurs in LU, but only in a noetic sense. See above 146.

[15] On the object as referred to, see 204f, 184; on the "way in which it is meant" (*Wie der Gemeintheit*), see 205, 270, 272; on the "way in which," see 270, 273, 279, 283.

[16] 188f, 269f.

[17] 127, 191, 193; ZBW 484f (E 178ff). This attentional modification does not coincide with difference in orientation, 190. On orientation, see 77f, 188, 203, 208, 270, 411.

[18] 188f, 196, 209.

(*abbildend*) presentation, as a founded act, is now distinguished from the simple act of imagination (recollection and fantasy).[19] The "pictorial" is also a property which is to be observed in the object itself.[20] The same applies to the character of sign.[21]

(iv) Clear and unclear presentation. We can be aware of the same thing with the same properties in the same mode of apprehension (e.g. perception) in a clear or un unclear way. In the latter case, there is a certain emptiness of intuition.[22] As in the case of reproductive modification and presentation via an image or sign, the difference concerns the fullness – but this time not the relation between matter and fullness (the reality level)[23] but the vividness (*Lebendigkeit*). We are aware of the object at various levels of clarity, of which absolute approximation is the ideal terminal point. This gradual difference is possible within intuition. Thus this clarification (*Klärung*) is not an "intuitive illustration" (*Veranschaulichung*) of what is represented or meant (in reproductive modification and presentation via an image or sign) but an "increase in the clarity of that which is already intuited."[24]

A special form of this clarification is that which takes place *within* merely significative presentation. When we read something, it may be that we are only conscious in a confused way of that which is presented significatively. Likewise, we may be conscious of a theoretical idea occurring to us in the elaboration of a theory in a generally confused way. But it is then possible to clear up this vague complex of thought by going step by step through what was articulated. By reviewing these acts of meaning, we achieve *logical* clarity. This clarity can again become vagueness when that which we have reviewed sinks away in consciousness. The sentence we have just read loses its articulation and becomes vague. Such a clarification of the meaning of a word can be achieved without returning to the corresponding intuition. It is even possible that there be no such intuition present to consciousness, but that such meanings are nevertheless clearly before us.[25] Husserl elaborated further on these analyzes in FTL.[26] Important for the relation between Ideen I and LU is the fact that this modification of clarity is also worked out *correlatively* in the former. Logical clarity is an evidence in which a *noematic* meaning is given (the meaning investigated by pure logic).[27]

All these modifications are now worked out in a consistent noetic-noematic way. The difference between actual and potential intentionality (attentional

---

[19]   79; see above 132.

[20]   209f, 213.

[21]   210, 213; See above 131 and below 443.

[22]   270 note 1; 273.

[23]   LU III 83. Nor is the issue the extent of the fullness that determines the emptiness of indeterminacy, 270 note 1, 127, but the difference in intensity where the extent is the same. This clarity is also different from the light that falls on something in attentional modification.

[24]   125f.

[25]   255, 195, 260f.

[26]   FTL 49ff.

[27]   See below under C.

modification) was already indicated in LU, but it was described there exclusively as a "mode of performing" (*Vollzugsmodus*) of consciousness.[28] Now Husserl shows that there are changes in the intentional object corresponding to it.

The forms of consciousness, i.e. the so-called "modes of perception" (*Auffassungsweisen*), namely, reproductive modification and presentation via images or signs, had also been described noetically only, as relations between matter and the representatives. It was the relation to the sensations that differentiated acts into the classes of signification, imagination and perception.[29] This description is now given its noematic completion. The concept of fullness, together with the concept of matter or sense, is now used objectively as well. If fullness is lacking, then the sense is empty. If it is paired with fullness, then we speak of sense in the mode of its fullness or of appearance.[30] Vividness (clear and unclear presentation) is now described noematically as well.[31]

Husserl assigns all of the modifications of the way in which we are aware of an object to the "subjective" mode of appearance.[32] The term 'subjective' is rightly put between quotation marks, for it does not mean that the noematic modifications are a part of the consciousness to which they appear. On the contrary, Husserl wants to show that they are modifications of the noema. The term 'subjective' must therefore be taken in a *relative* sense. All Husserl means by it is that these modes of appearance can vary while a certain component of properties remains the same. That which remains the same is the noema in the narrower sense, which is called matter in LU (see under a).

(2) *The object referred to*. The determinations of an object of which we are conscious can remain the same while its mode of appearance changes. But it is also possible for the determinations themselves to change. When we examine a spatial object from all sides, the object is *further* determined or – in the final analysis – may even prove to be *otherwise* determined. Nevertheless, it is the *same* thing that is perceived. Thus, an even deeper identity of that which is perceived is possible. This is the identity of the *bearer* of the properties. It is the central point of unity in a series of noemata, the identity, the "pure X in abstraction from all predicates," which remains the same while the

[28] LU II 160ff; 165, 372 note 1, 378 note 9, 405ff.

[29] See above 144.

[30] In the Husserliana edition, Husserl speaks of this as "apparency" (*Apparenz*), 'Randbemerkung' to 275. See also appendix XXIV 411, 412; ZBW 454; U. Claesges, *Edmund Husserls Theorie der Raumkonstitution*, 60, 70.

[31] See also LU III, 83.

[32] 269, see also 213.

predicates change.[33] Various cores can unite to form a unity, then. By way of all these changing noematic cores, we are directed toward the one object. This intending of the identical is not restricted to one changing perception but is also possible when we have two perceptions or when we have a perception and a recollection.

Even when we disregard the mode of appearance, we must still distinguish between two concepts of object. What remained identical through the changing modes of appearance was the "sense." Now then, this object, too, can change while the "object in the strict sense"

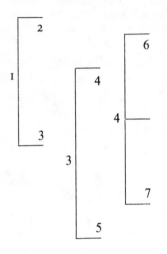

1. full noema
   fulfilled posited sense
   (cognitional essence in LU)
2. thetic character
   (quality in LU)
3. noematic core
   fulfilled sense
   sense in the mode of its fullness
   appearance (*Erscheinung*)
   apparency (*Apparenz*)

4. object as referred to

5. object referred to or "object in
   the strict sense"
   bearer of the properties
   the identity pole

6. core in the narrower sense
   that of which we are conscious or the pure objective
   sense
   (matter or sense in LU)

7. the way in which we are conscious of an object or the
   "subjective" appearance,
   e.g. fullness

---

[33] These properties can again be called subjective in relation to the object referred to. When we are directed toward the latter in the straightforward attitude, we only become aware in reflection of the changing properties, 313, 314; see also 180. Id II 5 note 1. The term 'subjective' is also used in this relative sense when the thing of the senses is called subjective in relation to the thing of physics, PSW 311 note 1; Krisis 129 (E 126).

(*Gegenstand schlechthin*) remains the same. Thus, various different senses can have the same "object in the strict sense."[34]

(C) The noematic significative meaning (Bedeutung). The noematic interpretation of the concepts of matter and quality can be regarded as a legitimatizing of analyses already carried out implicitly in LU. Yet, in another respect, Ideen I expands the conceptual apparatus of LU.[35] This expansion is of the greatest importance for Husserl's new concept of a transcendental logic. This new idea of a philosophical logic was first worked out fully in FTl, and to that extent, it falls outside the framework of this study. But what made this new development possible was a new understanding of the concept of judgment, a concept which was already present in Ideen and is therefore deserving of our attention. The new aspect of Ideen I is that Husserl now carries through the correlative approach on the *significative* level as well. In LU there was a correlation between act and object only in the case of intuitive acts, while acts of mere meaning really had no correlates.[36] There was no objective significative meaning corresponding to them. But In Ideen I, Husserl also accepts a correlate in the case of acts of mere meaning. This is the objective meaning. He now proposes to reserve the term 'meaning' (*Bedeutung*) for this noema. Thus this term, which was originally applied analogically in LU to all acts, gets its original meaning back. The word 'sense' – which, Husserl admits, also stems originally from the sphere of language and has the same meaning – continues to be used in a more encompassing way.[37]

Husserl now criticizes LU. In this work he sought to criticize the fundamental concepts of logic, e.g. the concept of judgment. By 'judgment' he meant the act of judging or the idea of the act of judging.

[34] 270f, 275.

[35] I will disregard another expansion of the conceptual apparatus, which is of less importance for Husserl's development. In Ideen I, Husserl also accepts correlates of non-logical or emotive acts. In an act of valuation we are directed toward a value. This being directed is not a "grasping," as in the case of logical acts, but an intentional "turning toward" (*Zuwendung*) that constitutes a correlate. Because it is not a grasping, it is not an objectifying act in the strict sense, although it is potentially or implicitly objectifying. At a moment when we are in a state of turning toward a value, we can make the transition to an act of grasping, a transition that would make an "object" of the value, 66, 102, 240ff, 197ff, 250ff, 305, 319. Beauty is now something in the object itself and no longer a predicate of reflection, as in LU. "Something is beautiful" no longer means "There is something that pleases me." See also Id II 14ff and PA 279; LU II (ed. 1) 713 (ed. 2, III); 241, II 428.

[36] See above 171, 285, 296.

[37] 275, 256, 259, 262.

Husserl now maintains that this way of thinking overlooks the fact that logic is really concerned with objective noematic judgments; that is to say, it is concerned with *the* judgment and not with jud*ging*. "The distinction already made in ordinary language between the *making of a judgment* and the *judgment made* can point us in the right direction, namely, that the judgment as such is related to the experience of judgment correlatively as noema."[38]

Husserl had already distinguished between *the* judgment and judging in LU. But when he spoke there of the one judgment of which we are conscious in many acts of judgment, he really meant the judgment as the *idea* of the judging act. In Ideen I he means the objective correlate of the judging act as well. When Husserl again takes up the theme of unity and the manifold, he is no longer dealing with the relation between idea and act; he is dealing instead with the relation between noesis and noema. In FTL he sees it as the task of subjective transcendental logic to describe how the one objective judgment can be constituted in many acts of judgment. *Only then does it become possible to view the clarification of this judgment as a correlative analysis.* In LU the relation between the objective judgment and the act of judgment was the relation between eidos and fact (which Husserl repeatedly compares to the relation between redness and the individual moments of redness). The correlative analysis that clarifies the noema of the judgment by describing the plurality of acts of consciousness in which it is con- stituted, and *which the Husserl literature invariably projects back into LU*, actually does not appear in LU at all. The history of the concept of intentionality shows that it could not have been present there, for the conditions for such an analysis had not yet been realized.

Of course this distinction between the act of judgment and its idea is by no means absent in Ideen I. This distinction is a lasting achievement. This idea of the act is now a fundamental concept of noetic logic (the logic that gives norms for subjective judgment).[39] Alongside this noetic idea, Husserl now recognizes a noematic idea as well (the idea of the judgment's noema). The distinction made in LU between the psy- chological judgment and the logical judgment (as eidos of the former) is correct, but we must also realize "that this one distinction is by no means sufficient, and that what is required is the fixing of many ideas which, in the essential nature of the judgment's intentionality, fall on

---

[38] 195, see also 306 and ZBW 430 (E 100f).
[39] 112, 196.

two different sides. Above all it must be recognized that here, as in the case of all intentional experiences, the two sides (noesis and noema) are to be distinguished in principle."[40]

Now that Husserl accepts two kinds of judgment concepts on the non-ideal level, he carries through this noetic-noematic correlation – entirely consistently – in the realm of ideas as well. In schematic terms we could depict this as follows.

	Act noetic idea (the ideal) meaning of LU)	Noema noematic idea
eidos		
fact	judging (significative) act	judgment's noema

II. Phenomenology of Reason

(A) From a psychology of reason to a transcendental phenomenology of reason. A complete description of the correlation between noesis and noema would at the same time include a phenomenology of reason. It would manifestly be "equivalent to a complete phenomenology of reason in respect of all its formal and material formations together with its anomalous (negative-rational) formations as well as its normal (positive-rational) formations."[41] The correlation between consciousness and the object, as laid bare by the transcendental reduction, is "the ultimate source ... for the only conceivable solution to the deepest epistemological problems, which concern the nature and possibility of objectively valid knowledge of that which is transcendent."[42] The riddle of our knowledge of the transcendent, which cannot be understood within the natural attitude, is now solved by means of a description of the way in which this object is constituted in transcendental consciousness. After this description there is nothing left to be asked, for the way in which consciousness constitutes an object can be "seen."[43] There is nothing left to reason about or deduce: "The only way to truly explain is to make something transcendentally understandable."[44]

---

[40] 195, 196 note 1; see also LU I, XIV/XV.
[41] 323.
[42] 204, see also 59.
[43] See above 320; cf. FTL 216 and Id 315.
[44] Krisis 193 (E 189); see also PSW 317.

Thus the phenomenology of reason must describe correlatively how a real object or an invalid object is constituted in consciousness, for according to fixed eidetic laws, the "existent object is a correlate ... of conscious connections of a fully determined eidetic content, just as, conversely, the being of connections of this sort is equivalent to the existent object."[45] In a negative instance we must describe how the harmony does not come about, causing experience to explode.[46] Thus the object is a "title for conscious connections"; it is a real object of rational connections or an invalid object of non-rational connections. In these analyses, the object functions as the "clue." The teleologically connected acts of consciousness that constitute this object are elucidated with this clue as guide.[47]

In the concrete implementation of this program, Husserl wants to show on what basis a rational positing corresponding to a real object is possible. To this end, the relation between positing (the quality) and the fulfilled sense must be investigated. A rational appraisal must then be possible. Thus a positing is only justified, for example, if it is a "positing on the basis of a fulfilled sense presenting itself in an originary way."[48] In the case of a transcendent thing, such a positing can only be presumptive, for the thing is given inadequately.[49] But in the case of the perception of an "experience," the givenness is a ground justifying a definitive positing.[50] Thus Husserl here returns to the arguments of the Fundamental Consideration – but this time with a refined system of concepts.

Thanks to such a description, the claim of consciousness to "reach" (*treffen*) an object is completely clear and is freed of all mystery.[51] With Ricoeur, we could call this a triumph of idealism.[52] Phenomenology

[45]   177; PSW 301, see also 315, 319 note 1.

[46]   176f, 287.

[47]   281, 300, 302.

[48]   281ff, 288, 298, 304. Between this matter and the "positing" (*Setzung*), there is a *motivational* relation. Husserl defines evidence as the "unity of a rational positing with that which essentially motivates it," 284.

[49]   287.

[50]   296, 298. Likewise, there is no difference between fulfilled sense and the "object in the strict sense" (*Gegenstand schlechthin*), although such a difference is characteristic of the perception of things, see below 448.

[51]   266.

[52]   'Etudes sur les Méditations Cartésiennes de Husserl,' 95. Ricoeur makes this comment in connection with the third meditation, which parallels the fourth section of Ideen I. (Furthermore, Ricoeur regards this triumph as a ruin, for that which is

can now speak of being and non-being. No longer is it necessary to put the question of existence between brackets, for the transcendental noema is not a psychological sense behind which we find an ultimate real object: it is being itself. The thesis of which we speak here is not the natural thesis (of the natural attitude) positing a world in itself (which makes a reduction to psychological sense necessary) but a purified thesis. Here 'real' does not mean existing in itself; it means correlate of a (presumptive) self-confirming act.

(B) The relation to the identical object. Finally, there is one barrier still to be overcome in the interpretation of the transcendental theory of knowledge, namely, the passages in the fourth section of Ideen I where Husserl speaks of the noema's "relation to an object." These passages have formed a true *crux interpretum* in the interpretation of Ideen I, leading Ricoeur to speak of "the most extreme difficulties of interpretation."[53]

When Husserl discusses the relation to the object in the introduction to the fourth section, which deals with the phenomenology of reason, he says of the noema that it "... relates itself to an object and possesses a 'content' by 'means' of which it relates itself to the object, the object being the same as the object of the noesis."[54] We get the impression that consciousness is directed toward a noema and via this noema is again directed toward an object. Writes Ricoeur: "Not only does consciousness go beyond itself to a sense aimed at, but the sense aimed at goes beyond itself to an object."[55] The noema "in turn aims beyond itself at an object which bestows the ultimate imprint of 'reality' on this sense...."[56] This impression is confirmed when Husserl says that the regard of the ego "goes through" the noematic core.[57] Ricoeur maintains – not without justification – that these statements make the reader somewhat uneasy, for it appears here as though transcendental consciousness suddenly breaks through its immanence and directs itself outwards. How can this be if consciousness is a closed monad and has

---

disconnected, as he sees it, returns. See the section below on the relation to the identical object.)

[53] According to Ricoeur, in a note to 265 *Idées directrices.*
[54] 266f, 269.
[55] P. Ricoeur, op.cit. note to 265.
[56] According to Ricoeur, 'Analyses et problèmes dans Id II,' 360 note 2.
[57] 268.

no outside?[58] After all, nothing can escape from consciousness[59] and nothing can penetrate it.[60] If it is now Husserl's intention to break through this immanence, there is definitely some confusion.

To some extent, I have prepared the way for the solution of this problem by means of the terminology 'object referred to' and 'object as referred to,' which I borrowed from LU. These terms are less confusing than those of Ideen I. When Husserl contrasts the noema with the "object" in Ideen I, one could easily be left with the impression that this object is something "behind" the noema. We think of the Scholastic opposition between the intentional object and the real object. This confusion is furthered when Husserl uses the loaded term 'object in the strict sense' (Gegenstand schlechthin) and speaks of the real object (the object that manifests itself as really existing, through the harmony of experience) just when he introduces this object.

What Husserl really had in mind is a relation *internal to the noema* itself (or internal to a number of noemata). The object is not an extra-mental object behind the noema but a central moment within the noema. The relation of the noema to the object is the relation of the object as referred to to the object referred to. Husserl wants to point out that the object referred to can remain identical while the object as referred to changes: we can be directed toward one and the same object as its properties are changing. The object is then the identity pole of a number of perceptions whose noema is changing; it is the bearer of the properties.

In LU, Husserl had already spoken of the "objective relation" as an identical beam that can remain the same while the material determination of the act is changing. *The difference between the noema and the object is a noematic interpretation of the same state of affairs.* The object of the identical beam is the object-referred to. Just as an identical directedness is maintained in the changing matter of the act, the many noemata point to one object of which they are properties. Here we have a noematic intentionality paralleling a noetic intentionality.[61] The

---

[58] Even if this analysis is conceived of psychologically, which is always possible, such a breakthrough to the outside is impossible. There is an outside in that case, but it is not to be identified with the "object in the strict sense" (Gegenstand schlechthin). As in LU, the "relation to the object" is, in psychological respects, also a relation to an inner moment of the noema. In 'Die Phän. Phil. Edm. Husserls in der gegenw. Kritik,' this is not brought out as clearly as it might be, 363f. See however Id III 85ff; PP 177, 431.

[59] 93.

[60] FTL 208.

[61] 202; ZBW 27, 364.

noemata refer to the identity pole as the "most inward moment" of each separate noema, which at the same time binds them together as properties of this one object.[62] Thus the object does not hide behind the noema but manifests itself *in* the noemata (just as the thing of physics, at a higher level of constitution, does not hide behind the appearances but "manifests" itself *in* them).[63]

It also makes sense that Husserl first discusses this object in the phenomenology of reason, for it is there that he deals with the justification for applying the predicate 'actually existing.'[64] A thing is always given in adumbrations, i.e. in a plurality of noemata. The question, then, is whether these noemata cover one another and thereby make an object appear. The claim of consciousness to reach an object is only justified when the relation to the same object can be maintained is a series of acts (or noemata, to use noematic terms). Whenever this is not the case and the noemata "cross each other out," the object explodes and dissolves into contradictory appearances.[65]

---

[62] 268f; see also CM 22, 90.

[63] On the intersubjective thing, see M. Theunissen, *Der Andere*, 76. The fifth stanza of the "Phaenomenologenlied" gives us a striking illustration of the relationship between the "objective relation" and the matter of the act (or between the noema and the object, to use noematic terms):

> "die neuen Schichten gleichen nur
> ner wunderbaren Perlenschnur.
> Die Perlen sitzen an nem Speer,
> der geht wohl mitten durch sie quer,
> und das ist die Intentio."

(The new strata are like a wonderful string of pearls. The pearls are strung on a thread that goes right through their middle, and that's the intention.) See A. Diemer, 'Edmund Husserl,' 38.

[64] 314, 316.

[65] See also 93, 176, 280, 287, 298.

PSYCHOLOGY AND TRANSCENDENTAL PHENOMENOLOGY

I have already touched on the contrast between psychology and transcendental phenomenology – as well as the relationship between them – a number of times. In this chapter I will deal with this relationship in a more systematic way. In the process we must bear in mind the fundamental difference between empirical psychology and descriptive psychology, a difference we already encountered in Husserl's early work. Thus the question of the relationship between psychology and transcendental phenomenology becomes two questions. First, what is the relationship of transcendental phenomenology to descriptive psychology? Second, what is its relationship to empirical psychology? I will take up these two questions separately.

SECTION ONE.
TRANSCENDENTAL PHENOMENOLOGY AND DESCRIPTIVE PSYCHOLOGY

When Husserl speaks of the close relation between psychology and transcendental phenomenology, what he has in mind primarily is descriptive psychology. Both descriptive psychology and transcendental phenomenology analyze consciousness's "own pure essence" (*reine Eigenwesen*) and are characterized by the same content.[1] The difference between these two sciences of consciousness is only one of "nuance," according to Husserl. But this nuance or change of attitude is of fundamental philosophical importance.[2] Because these two sciences have the same content, it is possible to use psychological analyses in

---

[1] 168.
[2] PSW 302; Nachwort 147; LU I, XI; Enc. Brit. article Husserliana IX 247 and 294.

transcendental phenomenology.[3] Conversely, transcendental phenomenological distinctions can also be used in mundane psychology.[4] In a certain sense, then, descriptive analysis is neutral with regard to this difference and is valid in both respects. In this section, I will investigate the nature of this material identity and look into what the fundamental change of attitude means.

PARAGRAPH ONE. THE AGREEMENT BETWEEN DESCRIPTIVE PSYCHOLOGY AND TRANSCENDENTAL PHENOMENOLOGY

The agreement between descriptive psychology and transcendental phenomenology is to be sought in the two primary characteristics of the former, i.e. that it is a priori and descriptive.[1]

(A) The A Priori Character of the Analysis of Consciousness. In Part II, I discussed the function of the a priori analysis in relation to empirical psychology. It is an indispensable condition for empirical investigation of facts. Because analyses of essences are carried out in both descriptive psychology and transcendental phenomenology, *either* can fulfill this normative function with regard to empirical psychology. When Husserl speaks of this, he does not expressly, mention the difference, for it is not relevant.[2]

When Husserl dealt with the reformation of empirical psychology by phenomenology, he left the transcendental character of the latter unconsidered. His reason is not hard to understand: it is not a direct concern of philosophy to provide leadership to empirical psychology. The psychologist qua psychologist can also carry out a priori analyses of consciousness. Brentano had already done this, as had Husserl in LU. What transcendental phenomenology represents primarily is a reformation of philosophy. It realizes the old ideal of every philosophy, i.e. a universal and completely founded knowledge of the origin of the

---

[3] 168 and 144. See also Beilage IX in Husserliana III 394; LU II 369[1].

[4] 143, see also 184. Husserl later spoke of this as becoming part of the stream (*Einströmung*), Krisis 212 (E 208); Nachwort 146.

[1] Among the passages on the a priority of transcendental phenomenology, see 5, 33, 153.

[2] PSW 314ff. This does not mean that this distinction is not made in PSW. Psychology, including descriptive psychology, is based on the natural attitude, and therefore it can never have philosophical meaning, 298, 299. In Ideen I, likewise, Husserl either makes no mention of the difference between transcendental phenomenology and eidetic psychology when it comes to this founding or explicitly places them on the same level, 151, 171; see also Id III, 43ff; see above 215 and below 476.

world. The reformation of psychology is only a "hidden implication."[3]
I already pointed out in Part II that the reformation of empirical
psychology by descriptive psychology in LU remained more or less
implicit.[4] The formal demand that all natural scientific psychology be
reformed was first stated in PSW. Therefore I will return to this subject
in Section 2.

(B) The Descriptive Character of the Analysis. Husserl first takes up
the unique character of the descriptive analysis of essences in Ideen I. he
raises the question whether it is possible to speak of a descriptive eidetic
science. When we hear the term 'eidetic science,' we think immediately
of highly developed eidetic sciences like geometry and arithmetic.
Because they are the only rational sciences that have been developed up
to now, and because they have acquired great prestige, the idea that an
eidetic science must manifest the same structure as these mathematical
sciences could easily arise. Since such a structure is not possible in
psychology, we might then be led to doubt the possibility of a rational
psychology.

We must view these comments *against the background of LU*. There
Husserl had already arrived at the insight that there must be an eidetic
theory of consciousness, but he was not yet willing to speak of an eidetic
psychology.[5] He now reveals what considerations held him back. He
had not yet achieved a clear insight into the unique character of this
eidetics. Thus he now devotes a number of paragraphs to the clarification of the opposition within the eidetic sphere between a mathematical and a descriptive analysis of essences.[6]

As an example of a mathematical science, Husserl mentions geo-

---

[3] Nachwort 146, 159; PP 247, 264, 267, 269, 295. See also below 477.

[4] See above 215.

[5] See above 207f.

[6] 133–141; see also LU II 245 (ed. 2). This doctrine of morphological essences is the
instrument by means of which the life-world is described. See above 419. In Krisis,
Husserl shows how the objective-logical a priori of physics is founded in the life-world a
priori, 143 (E 140). Although it is subjective-relative, the life-world has a fixed
"typology" (*Typik*), and therefore an ontology of it is possible. In PSW, Husserl speaks
of morphological structures in human cultural formations, which are described by
historians, 323. Dilthey is mentioned as the chief example; see also FLT 89, 257. In this
theory of types, Husserl was influenced by his former Halle colleague Benno Erdmann,
whose "theory of division into types" he discussed in 'Archiv für system. Phil.' 1897, 240.
A typical division is a division in which the members flow freely into one another. Husserl
mentions Erdmann in his discussion of vague expressions that indicate a flowing
transition, such as "signal-red" and "andante" (LU II, 89).

metry, which, like psychology, is a material-eidetic science. It is characteristic of geometry that it does not proceed descriptively, as a descriptive natural science does when it studies the empirical formations of nature. Geometry only focusses on certain fundamental concepts such as point, line and surface, deriving axioms from them. From this limited number of axioms, it is then able to derive all possible spatial forms deductively and determine the eidetic laws proper to them. The many geometrical spatial forms have the property of "definiteness"; that is to say, they can be derived from a finite number of axioms. From these primitive eidetic laws (which are themselves material-eidetic in nature), all other statements can be derived in a purely analytical way. A system of axioms that exhaustively defines a certain area in this way is a "definite system of axioms," and the respective science is mathematical in a pregnant sense.

If such a treatment is to be possible, the area of the science must measure up to certain requirements. One condition is precision in the formation of concepts. Husserl contrasts these exact concepts with non-exact, non-mathematical concepts. Again he takes his examples from descriptive natural science, which works with such concepts as notched, indented, umbelliferous, etc. These are morphological concepts of types and are unavoidably vague; that is to say, their sphere of possible application is flowing. This is not a shortcoming of these concepts; it is necessary because of the purpose for which they are used. Geometric concepts, on the other hand, are ideal concepts; that is to say, they are based on the analysis of ideas. The concept of idea has a specific meaning here. By 'idea,' Husserl no longer means essence, as in LU, but only a certain type, i.e. an idea in the Kantian sense.[7]

An example of a case where we form such an idea is the process in which a thing is given (which in principle cannot be completed). The thing itself is not adequately given in any one perception. But we can form an adequate idea of the endlessness of this process. In fact, we do so whenever we formulate the eidetic insight that a thing can be adequately given only in an endless perceptual process. This insight, i.e. that the endless process, in principle, is not given, presupposes the adequate givenness of this infinity itself as an idea. This idea dictates the rules about the perception of things not adequately given.

When he made this distinction, Husserl introduced a theme of great importance for the relation between the descriptive sciences and the

[7] 6, 138, 166, 296ff, 312.

exact, mathematical sciences. It is in this way, for example, that the relationship between descriptive natural science and exact, physical natural science must be clarified. Husserl already promised to make an attempt at this in the "continuation of these investigations." In reality, he did not do so until he wrote Krisis. Husserl's only purpose in this context was to distinguish clearly between the two forms of eidetic analysis and to defend the possibility of a descriptive eidetic science of consciousness. He even left open the possibility of developing an idealizing science of consciousness in addition.[8]

PARAGRAPH TWO. THE DIFFERENCE BETWEEN DESCRIPTIVE
PSYCHOLOGY AND TRANSCENDENTAL PHENOMENOLOGY

In a later discussion of the transcendental ego and the psychological ego, Husserl speaks of identity and difference.[1] The difference between them lies in what "purity" means; that is to say, the difference lies in the varying interpretations of this purity. Both descriptive psychology and transcendental phenomenology are called "pure."[2] In both cases, purity is brought about by a reduction. Pure psychology is the result of a psychological reduction (which is also called a phenomenological-psychological reduction).[3] Transcendental purity is attained through a transcendental reduction. In the preceding chapter, the relation between the two reductions was already discussed in connection with epistemology. We saw that the transcendental reduction offers a radical solution for problems that a purely psychological theory of knowledge either could not solve or dodged.

At this point I will take up the two reductions again, but with reference to a deeper set of problems, in which the epistemological impasse of LU is also rooted. The ultimate issue here is the conflict between a psychological approach and a radically phenomenological approach. The psychological reduction is two-sided in its application. As far as the relation to perception is concerned, it is a reduction to the intentional object or the sense, the *cogitatum qua cogitatum*. And as far as the relation to one's own body is concerned, we abstract from the

---

[8] In Ideen I 141, at least. Ideen II rules this out explicitly, see below 480.
[1] Krisis 205 (E 202); PP 292.
[2] The term 'pure' (*rein*) has a third use, i.e. the "pure ego." See below 473. I use the term 'ego' here in the broad sense that encompasses all of consciousness.
[3] Husserliana III 65, 183; Krisis 238 (E 235); PP 241, 243.

psycho-physical coherence. As Husserl later shows, this abstraction is actually implied in the first epoché, for the body, too, is a physical thing.[4] In both respects, leaving physical reality out of the picture results in a pure psychology. This psychology is a correlate of pure physics, which carries out the opposite abstraction and is to be contrasted with it.

This reduction is really the only one worthy of the name, for it is a *fencing in or enclosing.* A certain area is staked out by leaving another part of reality out of the picture. The coherences we disregard continue to exist; we simply ignore them temporarily. The immanent psychical sphere is the result of an artificial abstraction *within the natural world.*[5] In this sense, this psychology is still mundane. It is a science that continues to stand on the "basis of the world" (*Weltboden*) and brings about an artificial isolation within the world. We could also put it another way. Descriptive psychology is regional. It investigates a certain region of the world. Alongside this region is the region investigated by pure physics. The connection with the physical world is actually put between brackets. When we remove these brackets again, it becomes apparent that the psychical sphere is bound to a fundamental stratum that supports it, i.e. the material world. Explanatory psychology, which follows descriptive psychology, investigates the causal connections between psychical entities and between consciousness and the phys(iolog)ical contributing causes. Thus the phenomenological sphere is only an artificial island within a "natural world." It remains part of the chain of natural necessity that governs this world. Transcendental purification, on the other hand, "is something totally different from the mere abstraction of components of more embracing mutual coherences, whether necessary or factual. If processes of consciousness were inconceivable apart from their interlacing with nature in the very same way that colors are inconceivable apart from extension, then we could not regard consciousness as such as an absolute region of its own in the way we must. What we must realize is that *through such 'abstraction' from nature, we will only reach something natural* and never pure transcendental consciousness" (italics mine).

---

[4] See above 309 and appendices IX and X and 64 Husserliana III; PP 241, 243; Fink, 'Die phän. Phil. Edmund Husserls in der gegenw. Kritik,' 359.

[5] The expression 'delimit' (*abgrenzen*) and 'remove a part' (*wegtun eines Teiles*), which have brought about so much misunderstanding in connection with the transcendental reduction, are applicable *here.* The same applies to the term 'remainder' (*Rest*). See also 50 and 57 Husserliana III.

The result, likewise, is not a region but the *original region (Urregio)*. There is no independent natural sphere alongside and beneath the sphere of consciousness. In other words, the reduction is not "a mere restriction of judgment to a cohering portion of the totality of real being. In all the particular sciences of reality, the theoretical interest is confined to particular areas of the totality of reality; the others remain unconsidered except insofar as real connections between this and that may require mediating investigations. In this sense mechanics 'abstracts' from optical events, and physics 'abstracts' in general and in the widest sense from the psychological." But absolute consciousness knows no limits; it is not the product of a delimitation. "It is completely enclosed within itself, and yet it has no boundaries which might separate it from other regions, for anything capable of limiting it would have to share a community of essence with it. It is the whole of absolute being in the definite sense which our analyses have brought out."[6]

The difference between the psychological reduction and the transcendental reduction was already made apparent in connection with its relevance to epistemology. In an equally fundamental way, this difference is significant for the distinction between pure psychology and transcendental phenomenology. In pure psychology, the absolutizing of material nature is maintained. Matter is left unconsidered for methodological reasons, but it remains presupposed as the unquestioned ontic basis of consciousness. As we shall see, Husserl calls it a "mundane (*verweltlichend*) or "reifying" self-apperception.[7]

When consciousness is purified of all naturalistic interpretations, it turns out to be an absolute sphere within which natural reality is constituted. Once we have achieved this unobstructed view of transcendental consciousness, new questions arise. These questions have to do with the nature and possibility of the natural attitude. Once it is established that physical nature is only an intentional correlate of consciousness, how can this consciousness be conceived of at the same time as a region founded in matter? Husserl formulates this question neatly in a supplement: "Thus *on the one hand consciousness is supposed to be the absolute* in which everything transcendent is constituted, including ultimately the entire psycho-physical world, and *on the other*

[6] 95.
[7] Id II 90, 110f, 120, 124f, 139, 143, 169: Id III 5, 6.

hand consciousness is supposed to be a subordinate real event within this world. How does all this add up?"[8]

This question is our first explicit encounter with a certain central theme of Husserl's phenomenology, i.e. that of the relation between transcendental consciousness and mundane consciousness. We have already seen how important this distinction is for Husserl. It is the gateway to real solutions of all philosophical questions. For centuries philosophers have sought this gateway without finding it. In Ideen I, Husserl devotes only a few pages to this question. Despite his brevity, they present an outlook that was to remain decisive for his later reflection. "Let us make it clear to ourselves," he writes, "how consciousness enters into the real world, so to speak, how that which is absolute in itself can abandon its immanence and take on the character of transcendence." This character of transcendence can be assumed by consciousness only through a certain participation in transcendence in the first or originary sense, i.e. the transcendence of material nature. "Only through the empirical relation to the body does consciousness become real in the human and animal sense, and only thereby does it win a place in nature's space and time – the time that is physically measured." Thus, when Husserl here speaks of consciousness as transcendent, he means that it is founded in a transcendent thing. He also speaks of a founded transcendence.[9] What does this surrender of immanence mean? How does it come about? The answer to this question is: "A peculiar *kind of interpretation (Auffassung)* or *experience*, a peculiar kind of '*apperception*,' completes what is brought about by this so-called 'connection,' this reifying of consciousness." In this "interpretation," writes Husserl, "a peculiar sort of transcendence is constituted; a certain *state* of consciousness of an identical, *real* ego-subject now appears. In and through that sequence, this ego-subject makes known its *individual, real properties*, and we become aware of it as united with the bodily appearance, as a unity of properties manifesting themselves through conscious states. Thus, *on the plane of appearance*, the psycho-physical natural unity of man or beast constitutes itself as a unity *founded* in the body, corresponding to the founding of apperception."[10]

Thus Husserl uses the concept of apperception to explain this

[8] 103.
[9] See also LU II (ed. 2), 357 note 1, 373 note 1, 399 note 1; III 232, 236.
[10] 103f, PSW 302, 319.

"participation" in material nature. We are already familiar with this concept from LU. What it meant there in the first place was the interpretation of a linguistic sign and in the second place – by analogy – the interpretation of a sensation.[11] This concept is now pressed into service again, but in its new function it is accorded an important additional meaning. If we restrict ourselves provisionally to the original meaning (i.e. interpretation), we can take it as an important hint for understanding the *constitution* of the psychological ego by the transcendental ego. This self-constitution is generally regarded as the most precarious and objectionable theme in Husserl's transcendental phenomenology. At this point, I will withhold philosophical judgment and restrict myself to trying to understand the meaning of this self-constitution. Husserl seems to regard it as an *interpretation*. It is not the case that the psychological ego is produced by transcendental consciousness as a new entity. No, the mondane ego arises through a self-interpretation in which absolute consciousness views itself as psychological ego; that is to say, it views itself as bound to a material nature, as part of a psycho-physical unity. This is what brings about the remarkable situation in which transcendental consciousness, which constitutes material nature within itself, seems to be stricken with blindness as it views itself as dependent on this same material nature. The *original* region sees itself as a particular region within the natural world. Consciousness becomes the victim, as it were, of its own constitution of a material world; it loses itself in this world and becomes alienated from itself. Thus this apperception is a *falsifying* interpretation from which consciousness must be purified. The way in which Husserl describes the naturalizing of consciousness further buttresses my explication of the natural attitude and how it is to be overcome. The epoché is the undoing of a particular interpretation which – as we now see – transcendental consciousness itself has produced and which it can therefore also retract.[12]

The same fact of the natural interpretation is approached from two sides. Consciousness in the natural attitude – which Husserl now calls the psychological attitude – is the original starting point of the analysis, and in the Fundamental Consideration it is shown that this consciousness is not the true given. True consciousness can only show itself when this absolutizing of nature is disconnected. After we have created a path

[11] See above 137f.
[12] See above 370.

to the true phenomenon through this necessary operation, Husserl shows on the other hand how this datum is again lost through a certain apperception. In other words, *we now understand how our original point of departure*, i.e. natural consciousness, *came about* via a misleading self-apperception on the part of transcendental consciousness. The Fundamental Consideration and this supplement each other. The starting point of the former is the terminal point of the latter and vice versa.

The naturalistic interpretation of consciousness can be cast into doubt in the same way as the absolutizing of matter, i.e. by the experiment of world-annihilation. It is possible for our experience of nature to dissolve continually in contradictions. If physical nature were annihilated, there could be no body as bearer of a "mind" (*Seele*), and thus *the possibility of conceiving of consciousness as part of man, of a person, would be eliminated.* "Certainly an incorporeal and – paradoxical as it may sound – even an inanimate, non-personal consciousness is possible, i.e. a stream of experience in which the intentional empirical unities of body, mind and empirical ego-subject are not constituted, in which all these empirical concepts, and therefore also that of *experience in the psychological sense* (as experience of a person, of an animal ego) have nothing to support them and at any rate no validity."[13] This is indeed one of Husserl's boldest and most perplexing statements on the relation between the transcendental ego and the psychological ego, for he declares that it is possible for man as an empirical being, as a total *person*, not to exist. But this leaves absolute consciousness untouched. The existence of man as a psycho-physical unity appears to be sacrificed to the consequences of an idealist philosophy. It was at this point that Heidegger rebelled by making this mundane existence the center of his phenomenology. Husserl, from his standpoint, could only regard this as a relapse from phenomenology to a lower level, the level of LU, which transcendental phenomenology has left behind definitively.[14]

The disconnection of the empirical person is nothing more than a consequence of the reinterpretation of material nature. In this supplement, Husserl confirms once again that the disconnection of material nature *eo ipso* implies that of psychological consciousness, and that the reduction is *one* movement. It is because consciousness is bound to physical nature that it is thought of as psychological. But the

[13] 105.
[14] Nachwort 140.

Fundamental Consideration teaches that when we annihilate physical nature in thought, consciousness continues to exist. From this it follows that the consciousness founded in nature – *as founded* – can also be thought of as annihilated, without consciousness as such being affected. This can be shown by way of the same experiment of annihilation. If there were no longer any things, "then there would no longer be bodies, and thus no people." If there were no bodies, the possibility of conceiving of consciousness as *human* consciousness bound to a body would be eliminated. We now understand why the distinction between psychological consciousness and transcendental consciousness (which Husserl called the greatest of all discoveries) was for him bound up inseparably with the doctrine of the relativity of the world. The one implies the other.[15]

In this doctrine of a possible consciousness "free from the body" (*leiblos*) and therefore also from the "mind" (*seelenlos*) lie the premises for a phenomenological answer to the problem of immortality. At various points, Husserl lets the reader know that transcendental phenomenology is not purely theoretical in its significance but can solve existential questions. Questions about God, freedom and immortality are not banished from the arena of science in a positivistic narrowing of the task of philosophy. They, too, are "questions for reason" (*Vernunftvragen*).[16] Nowhere is the problem of immortality dealt with explicitly in the works of Husserl published up to now. Yet, we can attempt a solution in the spirit of his thought. If the existence of the thing is contingent from an apodictic point of view, then the bond between consciousness and the thing is also contingent.[17] But this means that death, too, is contingent. Thus, in CM, Husserl calls the problem of death a problem of contingent facticity.[18] The breaking of this bond is always conceivable. But it is not conceivable for the "experiential stream" (*Erlebnisstrom*) to cease to exist. In Ideen I, Husserl already wrote: "The experiential stream cannot ... come to an end."[19]

The clearest allusion to a transcendental doctrine of immortality is to be found in PP. When the body dies, that is, when it ceases to maintain itself in a certain organic style, the mind (*Seele*) also dies. "In the mundane sense, death is an annihilation (*Vernichtung*) of the mind – that is, as mind in the world."[20]

[15] See above 370.
[16] Krisis 7 (E 9).
[17] In this context J. Bednarski quotes a few noteworthy statements from Husserl's *Nachlass*. 'Deux aspects de la réduction husserlien; abstention et retour,' 59, 339 note 1, 2, 3,
[18] CM 182.
[19] 163.
[20] PP 109. Quotations on immortality drawn from the *Nachlass* are given by H. Drüe, *Edmund Husserls System der phänomenologischen Philosophie*, 317 and S. Strasser, *Het zielsbegrip in de metaphysische en in de empirische psychologie*, 47f. See also L. Eley, *Die Krise des Apriori in der transzendentalen Phänomenologie Edmund Husserls*, 72.

The one implies the other, for the body is the "apperceptive presupposition" of the mind; if there were no bodies, we could not conceive of consciousness as a structure built upon the body. Therefore the death of the body is the death of the mind – of the "mind in the world," as Husserl emphasizes. It means the death of consciousness in its self-apperception as a mundane region, but not the death of consciousness itself. We could also say that it means the *death of this self-apperception*. When we formulate it this way, reflection on death has the same consequences as the annihilation experiment. Both can help us see through the self-apperception of consciousness as "mind." When we think matter away, consciousness continues to exist. If this is so, we could also think away the "mind" without thereby affecting consciousness. At the same time, we discover that the "mind" is nothing but a certain mundane interpretation of consciousness. Thus the annihilation experiment can be conceived of as a meditation on the problem of death, and vice versa. We could then join Plato in describing the true philosophy as preparation for dying, as practice in freeing the soul from the body.[21] Husserl puts the emphasis on the consequences that such a meditation has for this life. I must recognize *now* that I am a transcendental consciousness and reinterpret the world as a correlate of consciousness.

In the passage from PP to which I referred, Husserl distantiates himself from the traditional doctrine of immortality. "Death as a real event in the world, then, does not mean a separation on the part of the mind (*Seele*), in which the latter becomes something real within this world." It is not the case that there is a splitting up within reality whereby the mind is separated from the body. I read this passage as a polemic directed against Husserl's teacher Brentano, who regarded the doctrine of immortality, of the separation of the mind from the body, as one of the most important branches of psychology.[22] Husserl gives this separation an entirely different meaning than Brentano. It is not an intra-mundane splitting up, as in a purely psychological reduction, but a separation of consciousness from the *entire* world.[23] The doctrine of immortality is not intended as a denial of the death of the mind (*Seele*). This death of the "mind" is the death of the mind that perceives itself exclusively as part of the world (*verweltlichter Geist*), and not the death of absolute mind.

Finally, I would like to focus attention on the consequences of this reifying apperception, which are threefold. The most important of them is that consciousness becomes part of a psycho-physical unity (*A*). Thereby consciousness is also drawn into the world of physical space and time (*B* and *C*).[24]

---

[21] In *Phaedo 67d*: See also the recollections of Schutz in 'Husserl's importance for the social sciences,' 87.

[22] PES I, 37. 'Religion und Philosophie,' 217ff.

[23] The climax of the Fundamental Consideration was the "principal separability of the natural world from the entire domain of consciousness," 87.

[24] 103.

(*A*) The link between consciousness and nature is discussed extensively by Husserl in Ideen II. This reifying apperception, which Husserl also calls "introjection,"[25] is the heart of the naturalistic view of man.[26] Through this founding in nature, consciousness itself becomes a kind of nature a nature in the broader sense, a quasi-nature,[27] a "stratum" or "annex" of the body.[28] That man is a psycho-physical unity is a foregone conclusion for both empirical and pure psychology. The only difference is that the latter abstracts from the relation to the body.[29]

(*B*) In the sketch of the natural attitude with which the Fundamental Consideration begins, Husserl emphasizes repeatedly that in this attitude, we regard the world as infinitely extended in space and time.[30] We place ourselves in this world. This implies that consciousness also takes on a certain spatiality because of its association with the body.[31] It is conceived of as if it were in space.[32]

(*C*) In the discussion of sensations in LU, Husserl had already warned against confusing phenomenological time, in which the subjective sensation is embedded, with the objective time of the spatial object, which is constituted in the transcendent apperception of this sensation.[33] The immanent analysis of time, which is brought up only once in LU,[34] came to occupy a greater and greater place in the later writings. The lectures on the phenomenology of inner time-consciousness, which were edited by Heidegger, include texts from 1905 on. In Ideen I, Husserl notes that his struggles with the problem of time, which "long remained fruitless," were "concluded in essence in 1905, with the results being made public in the lectures at the University of Göttingen." In Ideen I he published little of these results. He was of the opinion that he could ignore the problem of time for a while without

---

[25] Id II 161, 175.
[26] Id II 29, 174, 181, 209, 211.
[27] Id II 138.
[28] Id II 177, 183, 190, 228.
[29] PSW 298.
[30] 48, 52; PSW 298.
[31] PSW 319.
[32] On the non-spatiality of consciousness, see especially Id II 29, 33, 150, 153, 167f, 177, 187; in 162 Husserl speaks of a "secondary relation" (*Einbeziehung*) to space, see also Id II 33, 177f.
[33] See above 163f.
[34] LU II 336 (ed. 1); 358 (ed. 2).

affecting anything essential to his argument.[35] This immanent time, which is characteristic of the "experiential stream," is not to be confused with objective or cosmic time. Objective time is the time that can be measured by physical means. As in LU, Husserl compares the relation between this time and phenomenological time to the relation between an objectively extended color and a subjective sensation of color.[36]

Husserl gives a short characterization of immanent time; in a certain sense this characterization is a filling out of the Fundamental Consideration's sketch of the essence proper to consciousness. Every experience is part of an endless continuum of time, in which it has a certain duration. There is a certain mode of givenness bound up with this duration. Every lasting experience has a certain "now," after which it sinks away into the past. This succession of the "now" and the "just a moment ago" is a certain form to which all experiences are subject. But this abiding form always has a different content. There are always new impressions that have the form "now" and then become retentions (and retentions of retentions). The experiences together form a unity. In reflection I see that this unity is the product of the "form of the stream" that encompasses all experiences. I cannot take in all of this "experiential stream" in one act of consciousness, although I can grasp its unity – and that as an idea in the Kantian sense. When I direct my inward attention from one experience to the other, I grasp the boundlessness of the progression and thereby the unity of all experiences. It is a unity of such a nature that no single experience can be independent in the full sense.[37]

Through a reifying apperception, this immanent time is conceived of as "space-time" (*Raumzeit*). Because of the link with the body, consciousness has an in-direct relation to the "time of nature, the time that we measure by clocks."[38] But immanent phenomenological time cannot be measured by clocks or any other physical means.

---

[35] 162f; see also Nachwort 142. I will not take up this analysis of time, for it does not play a determinative role in the development of Husserl's thought. See above 415.

[36] ZBW 369, 419f, 422, 475 (E 22f, 86f, 90f, 165f).

[37] 162–167, see also 69, 77, 82 and PSW 312f.

[38] PSW 319, 313; Id I 161f. Husserl's contrast between "space-time" and immanent time parallels Bergson's contrast between "time-space" (*temps-espace*) and "duration" (*durée*) in a striking way. Inner time or "temps qualité" is projected by the intelligence into space and becomes spatialized "temps quantité." The intelligence considers this duration as extended because it applies to consciousness habits acquired in its contacts with matter. When this agreement was pointed out to Husserl, he is alleged to have answered, "It's just as though I were Bergson," according to Ingarden in 'Cahiers de Royaumont, Philosophie III, Husserl,' 264 note 5, see also 268, 269. To Héring, Husserl is supposed to have said, "We are the consistent Bergsonians," 'La Phénoménologie d'Edmund Husserl il y a trente ans,' 368 note 1.

PARAGRAPH THREE. THE RELATION BETWEEN PSYCHOLOGICAL
CONSCIOUSNESS AND TRANSCENDENTAL CONSCIOUSNESS (EGO)

In a discussion in CM of Descartes' discovery of the transcendental
cogito, Husserl writes: "It seems to be so easy, following Descartes, to
lay hold of the pure ego and its *cogitationes*. And yet, it is as though we
were on the brink of a precipice where advancing calmly and surely is a
matter of philosophical life and death."[1] The interpreter of Husserl
finds himself in a similar situation, for the ultimate decisions about the
meaning of Husserl's philosophy depend on this point. The differences
between psychological consciousness and transcendental consciousness are "seemingly trivial nuances," writes Husserl. These nuances
nevertheless "make a decisive difference between right and wrong paths
in philosophy."[2] He goes on to say: "In fact, it is here that the chief
difficulties of understanding are to be sought, for one cannot help but
regard it as a gross pretention that such a 'nuance,' which arises
through a change in attitude, is to have a great significance decisive for
all genuine philosophy."[3]

The risk involved in interpreting this nuance is unavoidable. I have
already been perched on this "precipice" for some time. In this
paragraph, I hope to bring this risky venture to a safe conclusion.

(A) Self-apperception and (ap-)perception of things. Self-apperception is also called self-constitution in Ideen I. Psychological consciousness is "constituted" in transcendental consciousness. He also calls this
psychological consciousness the "correlate of absolute consciousness."[4] It is important to analyze this state of affairs carefully, for it can
give rise to various misunderstandings.

When we deal with the concept of constitution, we must bear in mind
that it has a different meaning for each level of reality. We must be
aware of these differences, for although there is an analogy between
self-constitution and the constitution of things, there are also some
relevant differences. The similarity is that we can speak of a falsifying
interpretation in both cases. The difference, however, is that the
"mind" – *as mind* – owes its very existence entirely to this interpretation. This is not the case with matter, for when the absurd

---

[1] CM 63.
[2] CM 70f.
[3] Nachwort 147.
[4] 105f. Psychological consciousness is also called the intentional object of transcendental consciousness. LU II (ed. 2), 359 and 361.

interpretation is set aside, matter continues to exist in purified form. Yet, for the "mind," purification means the elimination of the "mind" *as* "mind." It is unmasked as a fiction. When we get right down to it (i.e. when we speak from a transcendental point of view), transcendental consciousness has no psychological consciousness whatever as its correlate. When Husserl speaks here of a "transcendence" or an "intentional unity," he means a fictive transcendence. In CM we read: "The ego as an ego in the natural attitude is also and always a transcendental ego, but it first comes to know this by carrying out the phenomenological reduction." Roman Ingarden observes with regard to this sentence that such an identity between the mundane ego and the transcendental ego only makes sense if the "real ego" is a fiction, and he immediately adds that Husserl would sharply reject such an interpretation.[5] Husserl's idealism, after all, is not an idealism in which what is constituted turns out to be a fiction. I am in full agreement with the latter claim, and in this context I would refer again to my interpretation of transcendental idealism, which rejects not reality but an absolutization of it. Ingarden is right when he says that what is constituted is not a fiction *as far as the constitution of things is concerned*. But when it comes to the constitution of the "mind," we face a different situation, for interpreting the product of this apperception as a fiction does not conflict with the view of the constitution of things expressed above. On the contrary, one can easily see that the two interpretations leave room for one another and even condition each other. If the constitution of the thing is the constitution of a relative reality, then it follows necessarily that the "mind" (*as* mind) is a fiction, for we cannot conceive of consciousness as a superstructure built on a correlate of consciousness dependent on it. Thus my interpretation of what constitution means in the two cases, is inwardly consistent.

If psychological consciousness is a fiction, then we can understand how Husserl can maintain the *identity* of psychological and transcendental consciousness.[6] Ingarden rightly asks how this is possible if the properties of the two are mutually exclusive. They appear to be mutually exclusive because the "mind" is contingent, relative, and so forth, while transcendental consciousness is absolute. "Only if we were to regard the constituted ego from the outset as an *illusion* – just like the entire constituted real world – could this difficulty be overcome, i.e. by

5 CM 213f.
6 See above 376, 432ff, 450, 454.

maintaining that only the pure ego exists and that the real ego is merely
... a *fiction* transcendent to the pure ego." I fully accept this
explanation that Ingarden rejects. The mistake in his line of reasoning
lies in the parenthetical phrase "just like the entire constituted real
world." What is true of the psychological ego need not be true of the
real world, and vice versa.[7]

(B) *Self-apperception and self-perception.* There is another respect
in which the constitution of things differs from self-apperception. In the
constitution of things, there is a correlation between thing and
consciousness, e.g. a house and a perception. These two stand over
against each other as that which is constituted and that which does the
constituting. When Husserl goes on to speak of the constitution of the
psyche, one is greatly tempted to conceive of this relation as well as an
intentional relation. The psyche would then be that which is constituted, and immanent perception would be that which constitutes it.
Thereby consciousness and the reflecting ego come to stand over
against each other as the two poles of constitution. The duality of the
psychological ego and the transcendental ego is then related to the
"bifurcation of the ego" (*Ichspaltung*). Consciousness as object stands
over against the (transcendental) observer or the reflecting ego. This
bifurcation of the ego is a phenomenon that fascinated Husserl. He
discussed it especially in connection with the problem of the identity of
the so-called pure ego as ego-pole.[8] Yet it is not correct to seek an
understanding of the problem of the relation between the psychological
ego and the transcendental ego on the basis of the structure of this
bifurcation of the ego. This would lead to insurmountable difficulties.[9]

That the duality of psychological consciousness and transcendental
consciousness is not the same thing as the duality in the bifurcation of
the ego is already apparent from the fact that this bifurcation occurs on
both the psychological level and the transcendental level. In the former
case we have to do with so-called natural reflection,[10] and in the latter

---

[7] I might add that the illusion meant here is not illusion in the ordinary sense but
"transcendental illusion," PP 295.

[8] See below 473.

[9] All the more when the pure ego as ego-pole is then identified with transcendental
consciousness. See below 475 note 47.

[10] See above 431; Husserl regards the modes of reflection as "matters of course"
(*Selbstverständlichkeiten*) of the natural attitude, 148. It is sufficiently clear from the
analysis of LU that the direction of regard in reflection does not by itself lead to
transcendental consciousness. Sometimes we find Husserl giving an explanation of the

case with transcendental experience. In both cases we can speak of self-perception or of self-experience and self-knowledge. Through reflection, the structures of consciousness are revealed. This analytical disclosure of consciousness is also spoken of by Husserl as self-constitution: in CM he speaks of "self-constitution" especially – but not only – when he is dealing with transcendental self-experience.[11] This constitution is further described as "self-explication" (*Selbstauslegung*) and culminates in the doctrine of self-constitution in immanent time.[12] This self-constitution (self-explication) in the broadest sense, which also includes the correlates of consciousness, then coincides with phenomenology itself. (Self-constitution in the pregnant sense shows how consciousness constitutes itself for itself, while self-constitution in the broader sense shows how this consciousness constitutes the transcendent world.) It hardly needs to be argued that this self-explication is not self-constitution in the sense of self-apperception or self-objectification (as Husserl also calls it often).[13] The latter is rather a self-alienation through which the transcendental self-explication becomes a psychological self-explication.

The structure of the bifurcation of the ego, furthermore, is not a basis for understanding the material similarity of the psychological and the transcendental, for there is no material identity between the subject of inner perception and the perceived stream of consciousness. Such an identity is lacking here, just as it is lacking in the case of outer perception. Just as he house differs from the perception of it, this perception is to be distinguished from reflection on it.

We can only speak of identity in connection with the so-called "pure ego" or ego-pole. There is identity between subject and object in an endless process of self-perception. This identity is possible precisely because the ego-pole has no content (see below, 473). In the relation between psychological consciousness and transcendental consciousness, we are concerned with the identity of the total stream of consciousness, the identity of the concrete monad. When Husserl speaks here of the "ego," he means the totality of experiences.[14]

transcendental reduction *after* he has discussed reflection 145f. On psychological reflection on myself as "person," see 50f, 95, 160 and especially EP II 79.

[11] CM 102.

[12] CM 25, 102f, 118, 179; FTL 241.

[13] On the term 'self-objectification,' see Krisis 116, 156, 183, 186, 190 (E 113, 153, 179, 182, 186); CM 130, 136f, 157, 159, 168; FTL 222ff, 243.

[14] See Gerd Brand, *Welt, Ich und Zeit*, 65–70, 97.

Thus the concept of self-constitution is highly ambiguous. We must distinguish here between self-apperception and self-perception i.e. self-explication or self-reflection. Self-apperception is an *act sui generis* in which all of consciousness is conceived of as a region within the world. Within this mundane consciousness, a bifurcation of the ego can appear in so-called natural reflection. Self-apperception can also be undone by an *act sui generis*, i.e. the *reduction*. This reduction discloses transcendental consciousness. Within transcendental consciousness there is a bifurcation of the ego in transcendental experience. The so-called bifurcation of the ego is a generally recognized phenomenon; self-apperception and reduction however, are very special acts that cannot be understood on the basis of the formal structure of the bifurcation of the ego.

I do not mean to deny that self-apperception and the epoché are linked with a bifurcation of the ego. As far as the epoché is concerned, Husserl says explicitly that it is an action of a disinterested observer.[15] Fink assures us that the epoché is an act of transcendental reflection. He also makes it known – something that is not yet to be found in Ideen I – that self-apperception, too, proceeds from the transcendental ego.[16] Thus we may also regard this self-alienation as a deed of the transcendental ego of reflection. The structure of self-perception is the formal framework within which the interesting and important dialectic of self-concealment and self-disclosure is played out. But it is the peculiar nature of this dialectic that this structure is materially broken through. What happens in self-apperception is that the reflecting ego itself goes under in the "mundanization" (*Verweltlichung*), which takes in all of consciousness. (Within the mundane sphere, the reflection-structure recurs in its totality as natural reflection.) But at the same time – and this is the great paradox of Husserl's phenomenology – consciousness in its totality still remains a transcendental consciousness. The ego of reflection, which conceals consciousness behind the curtain of the world (including itself), can also draw this curtain aside.[17] What is the ultimate sense of this drama? It is clear that we touch here on the outer limits of the "intelligibility" of transcendental phenomenology. Have we not reached the deepest motives of Husserl's thought, which set a final limit on understanding, "behind which it

[15] See above 431f.
[16] Fink 315, 372.
[17] See EP II, 77.

makes no sense to inquire" (to use a well-known expression of Husserl's)? In my opinion, an answer to this question can only be given on the basis of Husserl's philosophy of history.

(C) Self-apperception and self-alienation. The self-apperception of consciousness in which it conceives of itself as a mundane region, as a "mind," can be described as a self-alienation. Nature, after all, stands over against consciousness as "something alien," as the "being of the other."[18] Therefore consciousness has become an "other" through this apperception. Here we touch on a theme that plays a central role in modern philosophy, a theme tied up with the ultimate ethical-religious perspectives of Husserl's philosophy.

In Ideen I, this self-alienation has a meaning that is more Hegelian than Marxist. It is not a real change in consciousness but a self-concealing. Therefore it can be undone again by the eminently theoretical act of the reduction, by a "theoretical self-conquest," to use Fink's phrase.[19] The mundane apperception as interpretation is undone by a reinterpretation. The Fundamental Consideration has made it clear that a real interlacement of matter and consciousness is impossible. The two are heterogeneous to an extent that excludes this possibility. The so-called psycho-physical unity that originates through this psychological apperception is not a real unity, for unity is only possible between things that share a community of essence. In agreement with this line of thought, Husserl claims that consciousness does undergo a certain "change of value" through this interpretation, but "without a loss of its own content as consciousness."[20] He further explicates this apperception as follows: "Whatever this apperception may consist of, whatever special type of manifestation it may demand, this much is completely clear, that consciousness itself in these apperceptual interlacements, in this psycho-physical relation to the corporeal, *loses nothing of its own essential nature and can assimilate nothing that is foreign to its own nature* – which would indeed be absurd. Corporeal being is in principle a being that appears, that presents itself through sensory adumbrations. The consciousness that is naturally apperceived, the stream of experience given as human and animal and experienced in close connection with corporeality, does not, of course, through this apperception, become something that appears in adum-

[18] 70, 104.
[19] See above 378.
[20] 143.

brations"[21] (italics mine). Thus the "opposition," the "contrast," the "really essential difference" between the experience and the thing is fully maintained. When Husserl says that consciousness has become "other" in this self-interpretation, he goes on to say: "In itself, it is what it is; it is absolute in its essence. But it is not grasped in this essence, in its flowing thisness, but is 'interpreted as something.'"[22] Because the self-alienation is a self-apperception, this coming to itself is a theoretical "purification." It means that the self becomes *aware* of the transcendental consciousness that it *is* already.[23]

(*D*) *The transcendental ego and the eidetic ego*. In Part II, I drew attention to the necessary distinction between the eidetic reduction and the phenomenological-psychological reduction. This applies *a fortiori* to the eidetic reduction and the transcendental reduction. The two reductions are entirely different operations. The residue of the eidetic reduction is the eidos, while the residue of the transcendental reduction is pure consciousness. Therefore we must not describe transcendental consciousness as an eidetic structure. To do so is to fall prey to a peculiar misunderstanding of Husserl's intentions. It is not easy to see how this misunderstanding came about, for the two reductions are similar only in appearance. The most one could say – and this would involve very sloppy thinking – is that in both reductions, being (existence) is disconnected.[24] This particular interpretation is probably

---

[21] 103.

[22] 104.

[23] See also 16. Berger makes the interesting observation that Husserl described the state of mundane consciousness as follows: "We are partial (*befangen*) but not in captivity (*gefangen*)."

[24] See above 249, on the confusion between the eidetic reduction and the psychological reduction, which manifests itself in the identification of the results of the two reductions: essence is identified with sense. The same objections hold *a fortiori* for the identification of essence and transcendental sense. The residue of the transcendental reduction is not to be equated with the residu of the eidetic reduction, as happens in the Kantian interpretation. Even Fink's article has not succeeded in getting rid of this interpretation, which is defended by Pos in an article of 1949 entitled 'Valeur et limites de la phénoménologie.' In subjective interpretation, according to Pos, the subjective is the same as the ideal for Plato. The foundation for knowledge is sought in an a priori model, which for Plato is an ontological order and for Husserls transcendental consciousness that projects the a priori conditions for the possibility of experience into the world, 269, 273, 275. (I quote from the reprint in Beginselen en gestalten, Keur uit de verspreide geschriften van dr H. J. Pos, part II, 1958.) A comparable interpretation is to be found in T. Adorno's article 'Husserl and the problem of idealism.' According to Adorno, Husserl reduces transcendental consciousness to a mere possibility, 17.

This identification of the transcendental reduction with the eidetic reduction is to be found not only in the Kantians combatted by Fink but also among the earliest neo-

to be explained through the influence of a certain philosophical tradition dominant then, i.e. Kantianism. Fink, in his rejection of the Kantian interpretations, had already noted that the point of contact between phenomenology and Kantianism is to be sought in the doctrine of eidetic intuition.[25] Kantianism seeks the condition for the possibility of actual experience, but without subjecting this experience to fundamental criticism in the form of an apodictic critique of experience. In principle, therefore, Kantianism remains mundane and thus dogmatic.[26] Just as Husserl is read through Heideggerian spectacles today, he was interpreted on the basis of Kant in the 1930's. Fink points out that this conception identifies the transcendental ego of Kant with that of Husserl. "The 'irreality' of the transcendental ego in Husserl ... is misinterpreted along the lines of the Kantian concept of the 'irreal.' Thus it is equated with *pure form*."[27] Kantianism proceeds from the opposition between the empirical and the transcendental. For Husserl, the chief opposition is between the mundane and the transcendental.[28]

Thomist interpreters of Husserl. See *La Phénoménologie. Journées d'études de la société Thomiste Juvisy*, 1932. R. Kremer, in his contribution, identifies the two reductions because both put being (existence) between brackets, 63, 69, and he is followed in this interpretation by Koyré 72, Forest 77 and Söhngen 113, despite the careful distinction which the first contributor (Feuling) makes between the two reductions, 33, and Edith Stein's very accurate characterization of the difference between Husserl and the neo-Kantianism of Natorp, 102f. Because disconnected being is identified with factuality, the charge of "rationalism" is raised again and again, for the residue is pure rationality. See above 268 note 41.

The identification of essense and sense also plays a role in recent literature influenced more by existentialism. Here, too, the interpretation is based on particular presuppositions. If the Kantian interpretation misconstrues the transcendental reduction (sense becomes like essence) the existentialist interpretation makes the eidetic reduction fade into the background (essence is interpreted as sense). See G. Berger, *Le cogito dans la philosophie de Husserl*, 30 (see also 38 note 4, 69f); P. Thévenaz, 'Qu'est-ce que la phénoménologie?,' 22f; Tran-Duc-Thao, *Phénoménologie et materialisme dialectique*, 35ff. This confusion of sense and essence is furthered particularly by the philosophy of Merleau-Ponty, who uses the two concepts interchangeably. This is especially clear in *Les sciences de l'homme et la phénomenology*, 12. This misinterpretation is tied up with Merleau-Ponty's view that the transcendental reduction in Husserl is *at the same time* eidetic, *Phénoménologie de la Perception*, IX 430 note 1, a view also defended by De Waelhens in his 'Commentaire sur l'idée de la phénoménologie, 154 and in his article of Husserl in *Les Philosophes Célèbres*, 324. It is easy to show that this interpretation is in conflict with Husserl's own intentions. Here I would point out only that in CM, Husserl first carries out the transcendental reduction, 57, and only gets to the eidetic reduction much later, 103.

[25] Fink, 'Die phän. Phil. E. Husserls in der gegenw. Kritik,' 379f.

[26] Fink, op.cit. 332, 338, 340.

[27] Fink, op.cit. 345, see also 334ff.

[28] Fink, op.cit. 376.

The distinctions between the factual and the eidetic, on the one hand, and the mundane and the transcendental, on the other, *do not coincide.* The opposition between the factual and the eidetic can appear on the mundane psychological level as well as on the transcendental level.[29] Therefore it is not correct to speak of the relation between the transcendental ego and the factual ego in Husserl (as many have done). The correct opposition is between the transcendental ego and the psychological ego. Within both we can again distinguish between the factual ego and the eidetic ego.

Limiting myself now to the transcendental ego, I would point out that within this ego, Husserl always distinguishes between the individual and the eidetic. At the beginning of the Fundamental Consideration, he already writes that the new domain he seeks is not a world as eidos but a world of *individual* being.[30] This individual consciousness is subjected to an eidetic analysis in which the individual experiences function as examples or as "substratum."[31] Of great significance is his remark that the necessity of the existence of consciousness is an empirical necessity, that is to say, an eidetic judgment applied to an individual fact.[32] Furthermore, maintaining the purity of transcendental consciousness requires disconnecting not only individual realities but also transcendent essences.[33] Finally, I must draw attention to the fact that in an important "Note," Husserl raises the question whether a science of facts focusing on transcendental consciousness is possible alongside an eidetic analysis of this consciousness. This would be a "science of transcendental facts." In itself this is not impossible, for the phenomenological reduction does not disconnect individual existence. Yet, Husserl was of the opinion that we have no need of a science of transcendental facts. Everything we wish to know about transcendental facts can be learned from the dogmatic empirical sciences once they are subjected to a phenomenological "change in orientation" (*Umwendung*). In the last chapter, I

[29] The eidetic phenomenology at a mundane level, the rational psychology, is naive, 394 Husserliana III, or dogmatic, Id III 73ff, 80, 81.

[30] 58, see also 69. In the introduction, 324, he distinguishes sharply between the two reductions. In this context, Ricoeur wrongly interprets 'individual' as meaning "eidetic singularity," *Idées directrices* note 1 to 58. An individual, according to Husserl's definition on p. 29, is a "this there." Therefore, he can apply the expression 'flowing thisness' to transcendental consciousness, 104.

[31] 60, 125.

[32] 85, 87, note 1. See above 351.

[33] 111. See below 487ff; see also Theunissen, *Der Andere*, 37.

will return to this science of transcendental facts as "second philosophy" or metaphysics.[34]

One wonders whether the ego in Husserl's thought is perhaps super-individual or super-personal (an idea that would relate Husserl's philosophy to objective idealism).[35] But it is just as difficult to fit Husserl into the framework of objective idealism as it is to make him a subjective idealist. Transcendental consciousness is not super-individual but individual in an originary or absolute sense. The thing is only individual in a secondary sense.[36] When Husserl says that we disconnect the "person," he means the psycho-physical unity.[37] We get this unity back in a reinterpreted form,[38] for Husserl also speaks of personality in the transcendental attitude.[39]

(E) The transcendental ego and the "pure ego" (as ego-pole). Whenever I used the term 'ego' up to this point, I meant the concrete ego, the ego as a concrete monad, as the totality of the stream (paralleling the "mind" in the psychological sphere), i.e. the *cogito*.[40] But there is something missing in my argument, for in Ideen I, Husserl speaks for the first time of the so-called "pure ego." This pure ego is a unity-pole within the concrete monad. It is the identical point from which all acts arise. It is not an act itself, nor is it an aspect of an act. While all acts disappear in time, the ego is constant. It maintains its absolute identity as experiences succeed one another.[41] The "regard" of the ego is directed via the act to the object – which is why Husserl uses the phrase *"ego-cogito-cogitatum."* Related to the ego are not only the actual *cogitationes* but also the inactual *cogitationes*, which form the

[34] 119, see also 113, 4. On this "interpretation" of the empirical sciences see below 482. In the Nachwort 143, Husserl warns explicitly against the misconception that transcendental phenomenology is exclusively an a priori science. Alongside a priori phenomenology as "first philosophy," 5, 148, there is also a phenomenology of the factual as second philosophy or metaphysics; see also EP I, XVII.

[35] See P. Koestenbaum, '*The Paris Lectures*' XLV, LXXXII; Ricoeur note 1 to 105 *Idées directrices*.

[36] Id II 301; see also Krisis 222 (E 218f). The ego as ego-pole is also different in each experiential stream, Id I 109f.

[37] 105f. Husserl also speaks of the person as "human ego." We already found this definition of the person in LU. The same kind of definition is to be found in Stumpf, Husserl's friend and colleague at Halle, who defined the ego as "a whole made up of corporeal and mental states, the latter connected with the corporeal through the psycho-physical (causal) relation," *Erkenntnislehre* II 826.

[38] See below 485.

[39] CM 101, 191; Theunissen, *Der Andere*, 58, 148.

[40] CM 62, 99. Husserl first introduces this ego-pole in CM on p. 100.

[41] Id II 102. We must be especially careful not to confuse the identity of the pure ego as self-identity throughout repeated self-identification with another identity theme, i.e. that of transcendental and psychological consciousness, see above 465.

background of consciousness. These can have differing degrees of distance from or nearness to the ego.[42]

This theory of the pure ego requires our attention because Husserl had rejected such an ego in LU, in a polemic directed against Natorp. Now he retracts this criticism of Natorp.[43] In LU, Husserl says that consciousness has no unity other than that possessed by any other empirical object, namely, the unity formed by the connection of the properties. The ego is not something above the experiences but is simply identical with their unity of connection. This is all that can be shown phenomenologically. Husserl wants nothing to do with an ego principle that goes beyond this and unifies all experiences once more. He claims that he is unable to perceive or find any such "connection-center." But in the second edition, he declares that he has since learned where to look for the ego. His rejection of the ego had been all too much determined by his dislike of any "degenerate metaphysics of the ego."[44] If we wish to do justice to what is given, we see that the "*I* am" is indeed adequately given, and that therefore we may not reject the pure ego as the subject of experiences. Husserl calls this a "*peculiar . . . transcendence in immanence.*" We can only describe this ego in its modes of comportment; the ego thinks, fantasizes, makes judgments, rejoices, etc. "Apart from its 'modes of relation' or 'modes of comportmant,' it is completely empty of essential components and has no essential content whatsoever that could be explicated; in and of itself it is indescribable – pure ego and nothing more." [45]

The importance of this change in Husserl's standpoint, which by itself is remarkable, should not be overestimated, for it did not, in any case, play a role in his conversion to transcendental idealism. According to a comment made by Spiegelberg, Husserl already recognized the ego as given in 1905![46] Husserl himself claims that he discovered transcendental consciousness in 1908. This is likewise clear from his procedure in the Fundamental Consideration. In the first paragraph, in which the "proper essence" of consciousness is analyzed, Husserl says that he can leave the pure ego unconsidered. Thus the results he reaches

---

[42] 109, 160, 169, 192, 253.
[43] 110 note 1.
[44] LU II (ed. 2) 354 note 1, 357 note 1, 361 note 1, 363 note 1. In the foreword to LU I, XVI, Husserl writes that the new edition retains the original passages because of Natorp's interesting polemic in his *Allgemeine Psychologie* of 1913, 280, 290.
[45] 160.
[46] The Phenomenological Movement, 140 note 1.

are not dependent on it. The pure ego, like the problem of time, can remain in suspension. At the end of the Fundamental Consideration, he comes back to it once again and determines that it is an element of transcendental consciousness – a transcendence in immanence. A further treatment is promised in the second book.[47]

SECTION TWO.
TRANSCENDENTAL PHENOMENOLOGY AND EMPIRICAL PSYCHOLOGY

When we deal with the question of the relation between transcendental phenomenology and empirical psychology, we must distinguish care-

[47] 110; Nachwort 142. The adaptation of the fourth and fifth logical investigations to the level of Ideen I consists not in the acceptance of the pure ego but in other corrections (notwithstanding Ricoeur's opinion to the contrary, Idées directrices, note 2 to 182). See LU II (ed. 2) 347, 350 note 1, 357 note 1, 359, 361, 365, 369 note 1, 373 note 1, 382, 399, 439 and 2f, 7, 9, 17 and 19 of the introduction. Further in LU III 232, 235, 241f.

Thus the pure ego as ego-pole forms a separate theme that can be dealt with independently of the turn toward transcendental idealism. That the recognition of the pure ego is not inseparably bound up with the acceptance of transcendental idealism is also apparent from the fact that thinkers like Sartre and Gurwitsch are willing to apply the transcendental reduction but reject the pure ego. See J.P. Sartre, 'La transcendence de l'ego,' 85–123 and A. Gurwitch, 'A non-egological conception of consciousness,' 325, 338.

Husserl's transcendental consciousness is often identified with this formal, contentless ego-pole, and on this basis he is then criticized. See, for example, H. Asemisen, Strukturanalytische Probleme der Wahrnehmung in der Phänomenologie Husserls, 39ff, 50, 97: Fritz Heineman, Existenzphilosophie Lebendig oder tot?, 53ff, 58. It is not hard to see that the identification with this formal ego fits in well with the Kantian interpretation of transcendental consciousness, for Husserl compares this ego with the Kantian ego and applies to it the familiar formula "The 'I think' must be able to accompany all my representation," Id I 109. For Kant, this identical ego is the highest condition for the possibility of knowledge. Both Heineman and Van Peursen interpret transcendental consciousness in this sense, i.e. as a formal, empty ego that functions as the condition for the possibility of knowledge. See especially Van Peursen's 'Some Remarks on the Ego in the Phenomenology of Husserl,' 33f. Natorp, too, interprets Husserl's later recognition of the purely formal ego as a step in the direction of Kantianism, "Husserls 'Ideen zu einer reinen Phaenomenologie,'" 225. Also completely in line with this interpretation is the identification of the anonymity of transcendental consiousness, see above 371, with the anonymity of the ego of reflextion, see above 431f. The latter is the transcendental phenomenologizing ego, see also EP II 432, which, as active, precedes any self-objectification and thematization; see Van Peursen's article Die Phänomenologie Husserls und die Erneuerung der Ontologie, 494, 496f.

Contrary to all these interpretations, we should note that Husserl's 'I think' is only a moment within the totality of transcendental consciousness as a concrete monad. Furthermore, it does not have the function which the ego has for Kant.

fully between two levels on which the problem presents itself, for we can already speak of phenomenology without carrying out the change of attitude that transforms phenomenological psychology into transcendental phenomenology. On the pre-transcendental level, Husserl already directs sharp criticism toward the empirical (experimental) psychology current in his time. This criticism does not yet take account of the transcendental reduction. In principle, such criticism was already possible at the level of LU. Husserl's sharp attack on empirical psychology in PSW (1910) is simply an elaboration of tendencies present in LU (and already present in Brentano). It comes down to this, that we cannot explain without first describing what is to be explained. After his conversion to transcendental idealism, Husserl came up with a criticism different in principle, a criticism that moves in a different dimension, a philosophical dimension.[1] In one way this criticism is of less interest to empirical psychology, but in another way it is of greater interest. It is of less importance in that it is a criticism that does not touch psychology as such. It does not seek to move into the territory of the psychologist and call him back to order. The empirical scientist, as psychologist, can disregard this "criticism." On the other hand, it is of much greater importance because the issue at stake is philosophy and, with it, the destiny of man – including that of the psychologist as man.[1]

PARAGRAPH ONE. THE LIMITS AND POSSIBILITIES OF EMPIRICAL PSYCHOLOGY

In this paragraph I will take up the meaning of the a priori analysis of consciousness for empirical psychology. The difference between descriptive-psychological analysis and transcendental-phenomenological analysis will be provisionally disregarded.[1]

Empirical psychology sees consciousness as part of reality. This psychology is based on "reifying" apperception. Without discussing

[1] Entwurf 337/8. Husserl says here that he discovered the important difference between transcendental phenomenology and rational psychology around 1908.

[2] This difference is not of principal importance here. Yet it is not entirely without significance either. In descriptive psychology, the goal is to describe the purely psychical apart from any "natural meaning" which it receives through its connection with the physical body. Such a purification is indeed more *radical* in transcendental phenomenology, which sees the physical as a correlate of consciousness, than in pure psychology, which still proceeds from a psycho-physical unity and leaves the physical foundation of consciousness unconsidered. Falling back into the naturalistic outlook is easier in the latter case, Id I 143; see above 451; PSW 312/3.

this apperception itself (see Paragraph 2), I can already point out that there are limits to this naturalizing.[2] Consciousness is conceived of on the analogy of the thing;[3] we try to explain it causally.[4] But this explanation is bound to certain limits that preclude the same methodological handling which the thing receives. Reifying apperception binds consciousness to material reality. Thereby consciousness becomes nature in the broad sense, but it never becomes like a thing and can never lose its proper essence through this apperception. Indirectly it does receive a place in space, but it does not become spatial itself. This proper essence of consciousness can already be discovered by descriptive eidetic psychology. Therefore empirical psychology must be preceded by such an a priori psychology which is then to provide it with a rational instrument. What limits does the peculiar nature of consciousness impose on empirical method? What is the function of this preliminary rational psychology?

I would point out first of all that according to Husserl, every empirical science needs such an instrument. We first find a worked-out form of this doctrine of the a priori founding of any empirical science in PSW and Ideen I. Husserl argues that an empirical science does not arise only through experience and induction but also through the projection unto the phenomena of an eidetic theory about the phenomena.[5] In natural science, this function is fulfilled by geometry and phoronomy. It is true that there are physicists who deny the existence of essences and the possibility of an eidetic science, but this denial is in conflict with their own practice. Every physicist engages in eidetic analysis. We must pay more attention to what physicists actually do than to what they deny as philosophers. "The naturalist, one can safely say, is an idealist and objectivist in how he acts."[6]

The decisive step forward in discovering "true" physical nature, according to Husserl, was Galileo's application of an already long familiar geometry to natural phenomena.[7] In psychology, the application of a rational discipline concerned with the essence of experiences would likewise have meant a decisive step forward, but no such step was

---

[2] Id II 297, see also 291, 293.
[3] Id II 121, 125; PSW 310.
[4] Id III 3ff.
[5] Id IV 42, 43; see above 418f.
[6] PSW 295; Id I 44, 45.
[7] PSW 294, 308; Id II 65. On Husserl's philosophy of the thing, see Id III 4, 30; Id II 41–54; Id I 313–318; PSW 310, Ding und Raum XIX.

taken.[8] Psychologists who made an attempt at it, such as Brentano, Stumpf and Lipps, were not taken seriously and were dismissed as "scholastics." Their psychology was branded "armchair psychology."[9] Because of this, argues Husserl, psychology never became a genuine science.

This blindness to the real demands of a scientific psychology is the result of imitating the method of physics.[10] Following the example of physics meant reifying consciousness. The method of physics cannot be used in psychology, for consciousness is not spatial and is not given in the many subjective appearances in which the thing is given.[11] In consciousness, that which is identical does not show itself in a series of appearances; it is grasped instead in recollections and in repetitions of them. To find the proper method, we must not imitate physics but ask "what 'demands' being (in the sense of the psychical) makes on method *in and of itself.*"[12] It was precisely the influence of the example of physics that made psychology remain unscientific. So-called experimental psychology is still in a pre-Galilean state. The scientific instrument of psychology will only be found through the immanent eidetic analysis of consciousness. Without such a preliminary a priori analysis, the empirical psychologist is fumbling around in the darkness. How, for example, could one say anything about the relation between a stimulus and a perception or recollection without knowing from immanent analysis what a perception or recollection is? The experiences on which the experimenting psychologist bases his conclusions are in essence naive experiences. They are the recollections of the psychologist's own experiences and the empathetic re-living (*einfühlen*) of the experiences of the person being tested. The concepts by means of which these experiences are described, e.g. fantasy, recollection and expectation, remain without further definition and appear as such in the final scientific result. Does an exact psychology that fails to give an exact scientific formulation of the concepts *determining* its objects have any right to the title of science? It can no more claim such a right than a physics operating with pre-scientific concepts of heavy, weight, and mass could claim it. Only an eidetic analysis of these

---

[8] Id III 43.
[9] PSW 304, 320; on Lipps see also Id I 151.
[10] PSW 309.
[11] Id II 92, 133, 138.
[12] PSW 313f, 308.

concepts could turn naive psychological experience (experiential psychology) into a science.[13]

We must be careful not to misunderstand this criticism of the
empirical psychology current in Husserl's time. His intention was not
to undermine empirical psychology but to give it a foundation, to
elevate it to a science.[14] He complains in the introduction to Ideen I
that his PSW was regarded as an attack on empirical psychology as
such, an attack that betrayed contempt for experimental work. In
opposition to this view, he declares that it was instead his intention to
elevate empirical psychology to a higher level.[15] He repeatedly made
known his respect for the ingenuity and genius of those who have built
up the empirical sciences.[16] In Ideen III, these views are further
developed. Characteristic of the method of physics is the insignificant
role which description plays in it. Physics does explain the phenomenal
world, but it does not strive for a precise description of what it intuits. It
is interested in the colored, shining, sounding thing only insofar as it is
determinable in an objective and mathematical way. This can go so far
that physics finally forgets all about its "foundation of sense" in the
life-world.[17] The use of physics as a model has contributed to the
neglect of the role of the description of phenomena. This is fatal in the
case of consciousness – precisely because the rational foundation here is
descriptive.[18]

Once phenomenological analysis has created the instrument needed
by empirical science, what task and possibilities does this science have?
As a science of facts, this psychology seeks facts that cannot be derived
from essences.[19] The task proper to empirical psychology consists in
the discovery of all kinds of psycho-physical laws and regularities.[20]
We can go further and ask about the theoretical status of this empirical
science, but in Husserl's writings we will not find an answer to every
question. The rational foundation of this science is descriptive. Can we
deduce from this that empirical psychology does not go beyond

---

[13] PSW 303–320.
[14] 34, 159; PSW 304.
[15] 2; see also PSW 315.
[16] 56; PSW 290f, 308, 321.
[17] According to Husserl in Krisis 48 (E 48); see above 424.
[18] Id III 60ff.
[19] PSW 318. See also Id III 39f, 48. The a priori structure says nothing about
contingent truths.
[20] PSW 303f, 319, 321.

description? This conclusion would be premature. Is causal explanation possible? Can we not reduce phenomena to a deeper level of
reality that remains identical though the changing succession of
appearances? In his philosophy of natural science, Husserl describes
investigation as an exploration of changing appearances on the lower
level by postulating an identity on the higher level.[21] We always seek
something that remains the same while circumstances change. In
physics, this identical something is described in terms of mathematical
laws. Husserl calls it "substance." Is something like this also possible in
empirical psychology? Is it possible to develop a theory explaining that
which appears on a surface level on the basis of a deeper objectivity, and
could such explanation be formulated in terms of laws? Up to this
point, Husserl had only denied that geometrizing is possible here. In his
writings we find very few givens about the essence of such an empirical
psychological theory. But we can deduce a few things from his remarks
about empirical psychology in Ideen III. In fact, Husserl regards it as
possible to draw conclusions about certain properties from someone's
behavior. Thus we can get to know someone's factual structure, which
in turn renders a certain prediction of his behaviour possible.[22] If we
think of the concept of substance in mathematical terms, as Kant did,
then there is indeed no psychological substance, for no geometrizing is
possible here.[23] But Husserl regards it as possible to speak of substance
in a broader sense.[24] Thus there is an analogy between the experience of
things and the experience of "mind." A fixed structure appears in the
phenomena, a rule for possible conduct in similar circumstances.[25]
This rule, which gives us that which remains identical throughout the
change, is the "substance"; it is the analogue of the "true nature" of
physics.

Yet there seem to be a number of limits to this causal investigation –
limits imposed by the essence of consciousness. In the first place, it
appears that Husserl wants to speak of causality in the genuine sense
only in connection with dependence on the body. He does not want to
speak of intra-psychical relations and relations to other human beings
as causal (although they could conceivably be regarded as such).[26]

[21] See above 417ff.
[22] Id II 296.
[23] Id II 132.
[24] Id II 54, 120, 125, 131, 136. See also Id I 175 and PSW 310, 312f.
[25] Id II 121ff.
[26] Husserl speaks here of motivation instead of causality. Motivation is a fundamen-

Furthermore, this dependence on the body is limited to the sphere of sensations. Insofar as consciousness (the noetic) is causally determined, it is determined by the material of sensation.[27] Finally, this causal determination is not unequivocal. Because the other two relations in which experiences stand always play a role as well, a psycho-physical dependence is always co-determined by them.[28]

PARAGRAPH TWO. EMPIRICAL PSYCHOLOGY AND PHENOMENOLOGICAL PHILOSOPHY

In the criticism discussed in the preceding paragraph, I did not deal with the fundamental presupposition that every empirical psychologist accepts as basic. In the apodictic criticism of experience, which makes possible the turn to transcendental phenomenology, this presupposition is undermined. The psycho-physical unity is not a reality but the product of an interpretation, and it loses its validity when this apperception is suspended. If this is so, one could raise the question whether empirical psychology, which is essentially a psycho-physical psychology, is still possible. Does the move to transcendental phenomenology not mean an end to empirical psychology? What sense does it make to investigate "states" of an empirical person in dependence on psycho-physical circumstances when these states are the result of a kind of apperception in which we conceive of an experience that is absolute in essence as a state of a psycho-physical unity?[1] The very basis of psychology seems to slip away.

Now, it would indeed be strange if Husserl wished to elevate this science, in scientific respects, on the pre-transcendental level and then proceeded to deny it on the transcendental level. But this is not what he did. He continued to recognize the legitimacy of the naturalistic apperception (within the limits specified above). A science of consciousness in its "relations to nature" is possible.[2] In the Fundamental

tal rule governing the life of the mind, Id II 189, 220. On the naturalistic view, both intra-psychical relations and inter-psychical relations are regarded as causal – the latter as a kind of "inter-human causality," Id II 141, 184; Id III 20.

[27] Id II 132, 135, 276, 280, 285, 290ff; Id III 17. How far this direct dependence goes is a question to be settled by further empirical research, Id II 295; PSW 295, 319.

[28] Id II 135ff, 142, 295, 299; Id III 17. Husserl contrasts consciousness, which has an irreversible history, with the thing, which can appear again in the same state.

[1] 104ff, see also Husserliana III 86.

[2] PSW 314, 320.

Consideration, Husserl speaks of the "well-grounded talk of the real being *in* the world of the *human* ego and its conscious experiences, and of all that belongs to it in any way in respect of psycho-physical connections."[3] He says this despite the fact that consciousness is an absolute cohering system within which the world is constituted. Elsewhere he speaks of the legitimate truism to the effect that every consciousness is a state of a psycho-physical subject.

This claim on Husserl's part suggests that empirical psychology can discover truth despite the reifying apperception. It must be possible to "save" its results in some way or other. This can only mean that the results of this psychology allow of a "phenomenological revolution" or "interpretation" (*Umwendung*). This is indeed Husserl's view.[4] Not just all of phenomenological psychology but all of empirical psychology as well can be translated back into transcendental-phenomenological psychology.[5] How is this possible when the transcendental reduction makes consciousness lose its position as a stratum of a psycho-physical unity? If clarity is to be attained here, the situation of the empirical psychologist will have to be compared with that of the physicist, where this problem is somewhat simpler.

(*A*) The metaphysical "*interpretation of physics*." Like psychology, physics is based on the "pre-givenness" of an independent world. Therefore physics is a dogmatic science; it springs from the dogma of the absolute world. The epistemological attitude of the physicist is uncritical. Naturally, this does not mean that the physicist goes about his work in his own area in an uncritical way, for in drawing up a methodology he is particularly critical. The critical attitude of which Husserl speaks lies in another dimension: it is not a criticism within scientific experience but a criticism "that calls into question all of experience as such and all empirical scientific thinking as well."[6] This criticism is a product of transcendental phenomenology. As "applied phenomenology," it gives us a "metaphysical interpretation" of the special science.[7] In LU, philosophy's task with regard to the sciences was to complement them by clarifying their fundamental concepts.[8] In Ideen I, this task of philosophy was still acknowledged, but Husserl had

---

[3] 93.
[4] 119.
[5] Nachwort 147.
[6] PSW 299; Id I 118.
[7] LU II (ed. 2) 22; PSW 299.
[8] See above 220f.

broken through to a much deeper criticism. Philosophy calls into question the very foundation of the empirical sciences. These sciences proceed from the natural world, and to that extent they must be disconnected.[9] Their results can only be recognized by phenomenology after they have undergone a fundamental reinterpretation. This reinterpretation concerns the implicit ontology of these sciences. The cohering systems of physics must be traced back to the absolute consciousness that constitutes them. Thus phenomenology gives "the ultimate determination of the sense of the 'being' of their objects."[10]

In epistemological respects, phenomenology provides the final epistemological justification of physics. In Chapter 2 we already saw that phenomenology does not deny transcendent reality but recognizes it in the sense of its true being and justifies it as such. Physics itself cannot give us such a justification; it would be absurd to ask a science based on experience to solve a problem that calls experience as such into question, namely, the problem how well founded our knowledge of the external world is.[11] Transcendental phenomenology shows that the very supposition of a world "outside" us is incorrect and thereby solves the epistemological problem.

Now, Husserl has no objections whatever to the dogmatic attitude of the physicist as such. He regards this attitude as justified within the science of physics. But it is an entirely different matter when the physicist assumes the mantle of the philosopher, for then the premises from which he proceeds can only lead to errors. A *metabasis eis allo genos*, a non-sensical confusion of tasks, then takes place.[12] It is certainly understandable that Husserl raises strong objections to these philosophical pretentions. The dogmatic physicist approaches philosophical problems on the basis of his natural attitude. This means that he starts to philosophize without having gained access himself to the gateway to true philosophy. As a physicist, he cannot overcome the natural attitude, which is immortal, as it were, within the dogmatic sciences.[13] In epistemology this leads to absurd consequences, for causal explanation is then used. Cognitive acts are regarded as natural facts that can be explained in a natural scientific way.

[9] 48, 108.
[10] 118. Entwurf 122. On this basis, a science of transcendental facts is possible as second philosophy. See also Id III 77f and above 355 note 5.
[11] 46f; PSW 300; see also 333.
[12] 115.
[13] PSW 314f; see also 302, 294, 336, Id I 38.

This delimitation of tasks also entails that the physicist as physicist does not need the phenomenologist. He can go his own way calmly without concerning himself with the epistemological foundation. In fact, it is much better that he stay out of such things, for an epistemology on a dogmatic basis will only create confusion.[14] It is better to leave the physicist to his dogmatic attitude, for if he gets involved in philosophical questions, he will only get into trouble. That is the upshot of Husserl's approach. For him, the hidden riddle of naiveté is far to be preferred to the mysteriousness of a skeptical quasi-philosophy. One could borrow a phrase from D'Alembert and say to the physicist, "Go ahead, and faith will come later."[15] Thus this criticism of science is of a very special kind. It does not affect scientific activity as such. With regard to the sciences, philosophy is "a genus of investigation that in a certain sense gives them all a new dimension and thereby a final perfection. At the same time, however, the word 'dimension' indicates something else: rigorous science is still rigorous science, and doctrinal content remains doctrinal content, even when the transition to this new dimension has not been achieved."[16]

(B) The metaphysical "interpretation" of psychology. What applies to physics here also applies to psychology, for it, too, is based on the independent existence of the world, of which consciousness is only a certain dependent region. Psychology is likewise a dogmatic science.[17] Can empirical psychology, like physics, be reinterpreted ontologically by an applied phenomenology? This appears to be more difficult, since the psycho-physical unity from which psychology proceeds as such does not exist. Yet we must be careful not to misunderstand Husserl on this point. He maintains that consciousness is not interwoven with the body in a naturalistic way. But this does not mean that there is no relationship whatever between the body and consciousness. Although Husserl nowhere explicitly gives this metaphysical interpretation of empirical psychology, we can still form some idea of what such a reinterpretation would be.

As far as the body is concerned, it must be said that it is no more denied than is any other physical thing. Only the relationship to

---

[14] 46f. Husserl has nothing against physics as such, just as he has nothing against the natural attitude – as long as it stays out of philosophy, 107, see also LU II (ed. 1) 341.

[15] SAL 260.

[16] PSW 291 note 1.

[17] PSW 298f; see also Krisis 208 (E 204).

consciousness is viewed in a fundamentally different way. Consciousness is not based on the body: the body is dependent on consciousness. The body is constituted by consciousness – as a very special physical thing. We have an entirely different relationship to our own body than to any other physical thing. This is apparent, for example, from the fact that it is not given in orientations but is the center of all orientations.[18] For us, the body is the instrument through which we approach other things. Insofar as man's own body is a physical thing, it is naturally part of the causal chain in the physical world. Because consciousness has a special connection with the body, it is influenced by these relations, just as it in turn affects the physical world via the body. It is not impossible to reinterpret these psycho-physical facts in a transcendental phenomenology.[19] Only in such an attitude can one properly speak of *psychophysical* facts, for this term implies an ontological priority of consciousness.

According to Husserl, this reinterpretation must proceed from the gap between consciousness and the thing (matter). This implies a criticism of the ontology of LU. In LU, Husserl had left open the possibility that matter and consciousness ultimately have the same essence. In any event, he relegated the decision on this matter to the future development of science. The difference in givenness did not mean that the two "must be separated by a mystical abyss or by entirely unheard of differences." Husserl later dropped this passage. Now, according to him, there is an abyss in the difference in modes of being between the two. Indeed, the image of the abyss, as something naturalistic, is not even strong enough to express this difference.[20]

It seems to me that the central point in this "phenomenological revolution" in empirical science is that the phenomenological reinterpretation is not a denial. Once we gain the awareness that the body is not an illusion, there are no principial difficulties in recognizing the "phenomenological truth" of empirical psychology. That the body is not an illusion is also apparent from Husserl's doctrine of intersubjectivity. Mutual understanding between absolute monads first becomes possible through the connection of consciousness with the body in which it "expresses" itself. The experience of the alter ego

---

[18] Id II 158.
[19] See Id II 295 and PSW 295, 312f.
[20] Compare LU (ed. 2) 336, 338 to Id I 77, 93, 184. See above 229.

486   PHILOSOPHY AS TRANSCENDENTAL PHENOMENOLOGY

presupposes the experience of the other's body. It is the medium through which we perceive the consciousness of others.[21]

We can say the same of psychology as of physics. Husserl has no objection to this dogmatic science as long as the psychologist speaks as psychologist. Psychology only becomes dangerous when the psychologist develops philosophical pretentions, which was exactly what happened in Husserl's time. This inclination arises more quickly in the psychologist than in the physicist, for in the final analysis there is a certain inner affinity between psychology and philosophy. Both are concerned with consciousness.[22] Therefore some psychologists believe that they can build a truly scientific philosophy in the form of an experimental psychology. "This is supposed to be the long sought exact scientific psychology, that has at last become a fact. Logic and epistemology, aesthetics, ethics, and pedagogy have finally obtained their scientific foundation through it; in fact, they are already on the way to being transformed into experimental disciplines." In LU we are shown what results this leads to. Such a treatment of the normative sciences means the end of all normativity.[23]

In LU, Husserl limited the threat of this positivism.[24] The attack he now makes is much more effective. The metaphysical interpretation of nature pulls the rug out from under any positivism. Positivism is ontologically undermined and can exist only by virtue of an apperception that one does not see through in dogmatic naiveté. There will now come an end, Husserl hopes, to the "specious philosophical literature that flowers so luxuriantly today, claiming for itself the most serious scientific character and offering its theories of knowledge, logical theories, ethical theories, philosophies of nature, and pedagogical theories, all based on a 'foundation' of natural science and, above all, of 'experimental psychology.'"[25]

[21] PSW 312f; Id II 297.
[22] PSW 302, 321.
[23] PSW 297f.
[24] See above 232.
[25] PSW 321.

CHAPTER FOUR

TRANSCENDENTAL PHENOMENOLOGY AND THE A PRIORI SCIENCES

PARAGRAPH ONE. MUNDANE EIDETICS AND TRANSCENDENTAL PHENOMENOLOGICAL EIDETICS

In the preceding chapter, we saw that the positive sciences of physics and psychology are caught up in the natural attitude. Transcendental phenomenology changed these naive dogmatic sciences into philosophical sciences.[1] There is an analogous relationship between transcendental phenomenology and the a priori sciences. The eidetic attitude is also pre-philosophical. When we focus our attention on ideal numbers, for example, this world of numbers is also "there for us," just as the natural world is "there for us," even if it remains in the background.[2]

Therefore Husserl deals separately with the disconnection of the eidetic sciences, where disconnection at the same time implies a (re-)connection. Transcendental essences are disconnected, but immanent essences are retained.[3] Husserl means by this that the essences lose their relatedness to the natural world. In the naive attitude, these essences are regarded as the essences of natural realities, e.g. of a thing or of a mind. Rational psychology is a science that is practiced on this mundane level and works out of this attitude. In the eidetic analysis of consciousness, consciousness is conceived of as part of the world and thus as something transcendent (in this case, a founded transcendence). Thus we can refer to the essence of such a consciousness as a "transcendent" essence. It must lose this character of transcendence in the reduction. Such a purification of essences must be applied to any ontology that is constructed in the first instance as an ontology of the

[1] On the disconnection of the sciences in general, including the eidetic sciences, see 47, 56, 96, 108, 114, 118, 142.
[2] 51.
[3] 114, 116.

natural world. Hence this purification of the ideal world flows naturally from the purification of the real world, and to that extent it is secondary.[4] In later workd, Husserl speaks more extensively about this "mundane" character of all a priori sciences. They are all related to the natural world as instruments for the scientific study of it, and to that extent they are "sciences of the world." In FTL, Husserl shows this in connection with formal logic.[5]

In this light it again becomes clear why Husserl regards neo-Kantianism as a dogmatic mundane philosophy. Kantianism inquires into the a priori conditions for the possibility of the empirical sciences. Husserl assigns this task to mundane ontologies. In Kantianism, the world is investigated with regard to the condition for its possibility, but it is not subjected to an apodictic criticism as natural world and then disconnected. The a priori "world-form" of Kantianism is nothing other than the condition for the possibility of mundane experience.[6] It fulfills the same function as Husserl's realm of ideas. The reason why these a priori forms are sought in the transcendental functions of judgment is blindness to the givenness of ideas. According to Husserl, one must first recognize the givenness of ideas in order to be able to ask transcendental questions of these givens *afterwards*. Kant did not realize this.[7]

Husserl reports that this purification of essences was a very difficult step for him. What it meant was that all idealities would also be related to the transcendental consciousness in which they are constituted. This is a definitive conquest of the Platonism of LU. Actually, Husserl does not speak of this constitution of essences at all in Ideen I. It is something that only comes out clearly in the later works.[8]

In Ideen III, which was published posthumously, Husserl did take up the relation of rational ontologies to transcendental phenomenology. He says there that transcendental phenomenology devours all ontologies, as it were. All essences that are investigated dogmatically in

---

[4] 115, see also 108.

[5] FTL 197ff; see also CM 57.

[6] See also Fink, 'Die phän. Phil. e. Husserls in der gegenwärtigen Kritik,' 326, 332, 338, 340, 380; see above 471.

[7] See above 245. In Husserl's eyes, then, Kant's transcendental logic is nothing but a material ontology that projects into consciousness what it is not able to see in the "straightforward attitude."

[8] It is Ingarden's view, for example, that essences are still conceived of in Ideen I in a clearly realist manner. He first sees the new standpoint emerging in FTL and CM, where everything is "relative in being and essence to original, constitutive consciousness." See his review of CM in Kantstudien 1933, 206. Husserl does indeed speak very clearly in CM about the constitution of ideas, 111f, 155, 177.

the natural attitude can be found back in transcendental phenomenology as correlates of consciousness. Phenomenology then provides a philosophical foundation for this ontology by describing the acts of consciousness in which we are aware of ideas, a process in which the latter serve as clues.[9]

Insofar as we think of phenomenology as a purely descriptive science – and this is what Husserl does in Ideen I – it embraces only the *axioms* of the exact rational ontologies.[10] It then describes only the essences on which the fundamental concepts of a science rest. In the dogmatic attitude, many derived propositions are deduced from these fundamental concepts. Husserl sees this as *technical* work typical of mathematics with its long, spun-out deductions from fundamental propositions. Later he says that it is also possible to draw this indirect eidetic knowledge into phenomenology. Such an all-embracing transcendental phenomenology would then be a universal philosophy, and it would include the a priori foundations of all the sciences. Thus it would realize the Leibnizian and Cartesian ideal of a universal philosophy, but not in the form of a deductive mathematical theory, "as though all of being were unified through calculation."[11] The mathematical deductions are derived from some fundamental essences which phenomenology puts back into the broader cohering systems of consciousness, which itself is not mathematical in nature.[12]

Every essence is constituted in a particular fundamental form of consciousness. Thus, as an ontological a priori, it is related to a constitutive a priori in consciousness.[13] Ontological analysis is objectively directed in a one-sided way. Phenomenology supplements this one-sidedness by investigating noetic structures that constitute ontological essences. At the same time it provides the philosophical foundation for this ontology. In dogmatic ontology, the facts are understood out of their rational foundation, but a philosophical ontology goes on to confer a "transcendental intelligibility" upon them. The a priori of the world is then seen as "a 'stratum' in the universal a priori of transcendentality."[14]

---

[9] Id II 70ff; 84; see also Id I 302f, 323; CM 88.

[10] 113; see also EP I 187. On the reduction of all indirect knowledge to axioms as their sources, see above 453. These axioms are of direct concern to phenomenology, for they are immediately given in consciousness.

[11] CM 39, 181, PP 296.

[12] See above 292.

[13] FTL 291; Claesges, *Edmund Husserls Theorie der Raumkonstitution*, 28ff.

[14] CM 164; Krisis 177 (E 174).

PARAGRAPH TWO. PHILOSOPHY OF PURE LOGIC

Finally, I would like to apply these general remarks about the relation between transcendental phenomenology and ontology to the relation between transcendental phenomenology and pure logic in its two forms (formal ontology and apophantic logic).

(A) Overcoming Platonic realism. In Entwurf (1913), Husserl makes a number of remarks about the relation between pure logic and philosophy. These remarks cast an interesting light on his development after 1901. As in LU, he distinguishes between philosophy and mathematics as practiced by the specialists. In LU, the task of philosophy was to clarify fundamental concepts by checking them against intuition. Going back to the origin meant going back from the concept to the denotatum (*Begriffsgegenstand*). In Ideen I and in Entwurf, it means going back to the origin of the denotatum in consciousness. Thus the concept is clarified in a double way. Going back to the object, e.g. the number, is only a preliminary step. It is followed by a return to the consciousness of the number, by way of a description of the forms of consciousness in which the number is constituted.[1] It is only the second phase that gives us a philosophical clarification.

This clarification concerns the relation between being and consciousness. Husserl admits that in LU, this relation actually remained a mystery. In the Prolegomena, he writes, we find a powerful plea for the existence "as such" of ideal being: "Great effort was devoted to pressing the reader to recognize this sphere of ideal being and knowledge, or, as P. Natorp puts it, to side with 'the ideal in the true Platonic sense,' to 'confess idealism' together with the author."[2] The defense of the legitimacy of the eidetic in LU leves a certain gap – something that escaped Husserl's realist followers entirely. In Ideen I, Husserl says that it was only a first step that must be followed by a second. The second step had not yet been taken. Husserl found it "quite difficult."[3] In Entwurf, which was written at about the same time as Ideen I, Husserl praises Natorp for his sharp formulation of this gap. Natorp had outlined the situation in LU in a "masterful way." Husserl quotes Natorp as saying that the opposition between the a priori and

[1] 196 note 1.
[2] Entwurf 113.
[3] 116f.

the empirical, and thus also between the logical and the psychological, the objective and the subjective, remains unresolved in the execution of the Prolegomena. According to Natorp, there is a certain "logical uneasiness" that refuses to go away, despite the lucidity of the argument.

Husserl observes in this context that he does not deny the tension between the logical and the psychological. Only someone who has felt this uneasiness will be able to get further. Thus he defends the position of LU as a necessary phase that needs to be followed up by something else. His praise of Natorp is understandable when we compare the latter's reaction with the uncritical admiration of Husserl's realist students. Natorp deserves praise precisely because he has seen the difficulties involved in the doctrine of the intuition of essences. "Only someone who has felt the painfulness of this matter deeply and in a most intense form can go on to reach the insight that ... the 'being in itself' of the ideal sphere in its relation to consciousness brings with it a dimension of riddles ... which I believe must be solved through further investigations of a phenomenological nature."[4] The problem Husserl points to here is that of the "Platonism" of LU. In that work, Husserl had defended the existence of idealities without giving any clarification of the status of the being of this ideal, supra-temporal world. If this world is given in addition to immanent consciousness (Husserl's position in 1907), what could its relation to consciousness be? Is it an external world along with everything else that falls outside the phenomenological sphere? In that case, how could it still be known in its being in itself? What is the sense of ideal being? None of these questions are considered in LU. Platonism, Husserl says, contains no epistemology; it is "the simple inward reception of a completely manifest givenness."[5] When we speak of numbers or geometrical figures, we simply follow the evidence that gives us such ideas.[6] This is not yet an epistemology, but it is definitely a step that must be taken before posing epistemological questions. Anyone who does not *see* the ideal will never get around to justifying it philosophically.

(B) Formal ontology. When mathematics is pursued in the natural objective direction of regard, it is epistemologically naive, but when

[4] Entwurf 114f.
[5] Entwurf 131.
[6] Entwurf 115, 121. See also the critique of naive mathematical evidence, EP II 30ff; Krisis 80, 143, 192 (E 80, 140, 189).

mathematical entities are understood on the basis of constituting acts, logic becomes a philosophical science.[7] In Entwurf, Husserl claims that such investigations are conducted in the second volume of LU. But a little later he admits that this really is not so. In the second volume of LU we do find analyses of the acts in which we are aware of formal ontological entities such as numbers, but this awareness is still conceived of in a psychological way. It is impossible to understand ideal being as a constituted correlate of psychological consciousness. It is exactly this tension between the ideality of a priori ideas, on the one hand, and psychological consciousness, on the other, that gave rise to uneasiness about LU. This uneasiness can only be dispelled by distinguishing between descriptive psychology and transcendental phenomenology, for thereby both Platonism and anthropology will be avoided. Such a distinction makes it unnecessary to regard the ideal realm as "pre-given." A radical philosophy regards everything pre-given as a "prejudice." What counts as given in natural evidence, Husserl maintains in FTL, is, from a philosophical point of view, only a guide for inquiring back into constitutive performances of consciousness.[8] He had already said the same thing in Entwurf. A naive science like mathematics, which is directed toward the ideal in an objective way, can be founded only via a transcendental phenomenology. Only "a science grounded from the outset in 'transcendental phenomenology' and springing from it as a principial ultimate source" could satisfy the idea of fully justified knowledge. Husserl confesses that he first came to see this in "much, much later reflection."[9]

(C) *Apophantic logic*. What has been said of formal ontology also applies – with a few modifications – to apophantic logic or logic in the narrower sense. Here, too, the discovery of transcendental consciousness is presupposed in the clarification of logical entities on the basis of performances of consciousness. In still another respect, Ideen I contains a necessary condition for the possibility of a transcendental logic as a philosophical founding of naive logic, a condition that was still missing in LU. It was in Ideen I that Husserl first made the discovery of a noematic meaning as the correlate of an act in which something is meant. Thus it was at this point that correlative analysis, which clarifies the judgment as an identical unit on the basis of the

[7] Entwurf 132, 338. See also Id I 117.
[8] FTL 244.
[9] Entwurf 132.

many acts in which it is constituted, first became possible.[10] Husserl
began with this task in his FTL.

[10] See above 443. In FTL, Husserl no longer sees the ideal meaning intended in the
many acts as an essence. See above 254. This change in his view is bound up with the
discovery of the noematic meaning, which takes over the function of the ideal meaning as
essence in LU – at least its function as "unity in the manifold." In FTL, Husserl
continued to accept a distinction between the noematic meaning and the essence of that
meaning. See FTL 25, 31, 36f, 55, 63, 155, 160, 163, 170, 176, 189.

CONCLUSION

At the end of this study, I would like to look back. We have followed
Husserl from his first contact with Brentano's philosophy to his
conversion to transcendental idealism. We have seen that Brentano
also underwent a development. To compare his earliest philosophy
with that of the later Husserl is to study a most noteworthy and
interesting chapter in the history of philosophy. In barely 40 years, a
development took place which in all respects represents a break with
Brentano's original ideals. The gap between Brentano's positivism of
about 1874 and Husserl's transcendental idealism is indeed "deep as an
abyss," as Husserl put it.

The one thing these two thinkers had in common from the very
beginning was their elevated view of the task of philosophy. Both were
advocates of a radical reformation and renewal of philosophy as it then
existed. According to Brentano, a renewal of philosophy would lead to
a renewal of man and society. In Krisis, Husserl speaks of philosophers
as functionaries of mankind and of the rational organization of a new
humanity. The highest form of humanity is the "philosophical form of
existence," and therefore the function of philosophy is the humanizing
of man. "The completely personal responsibility for our own true being
as philosophers in our inward personal calling at the same time carries
with it the responsibility for the true being of humanity."[1] This
consciousness of calling shared by the two was paired with a radical
difference in their respective views of the true nature of philosophy.
Everything advocated by Brentano in 1874 was later seen by Husserl as
a deadly danger.

---

[1] Krisis 15, 72, 429 (E 17, 71).

In Part I, we saw how the young Brentano was gripped by the scientific ideal of the natural sciences. With great enthusiasm he defended the application of the natural scientific method to philosophy (i.e. to psychology). This, he believed, would lead to important results and the progress of humanity.

The following description of this positivism, which Husserl gives in PSW, could be applied in its entirety to Brentano. This philosophy works with a method "whereby it believes that it has definitely attained the rank of an exact science. It is so sure of this that it looks down on every other mode of philosophizing. [Think here of Brentano's opinion of such philosophers as Schelling and Hegel.] They stand in relation to its exact scientific philosophizing as the muddy natural philosophy of the Renaissance to the youthful and exact mechanics of a Galileo, or as alchemy in relation to the exact chemistry of a Lavoisier. If we ask about exact, though as yet scarcely developed, philosophy (the analogue of exact mechanics), we are shown psycho-physical and, above all, experimental psychology, to which, of course, no one can deny the rank of strict science. This, they tell us, is the long-sought scientific psychology that has at last become a fact. Logic and epistemology, aesthetics, ethics, and pedagogy have finally obtained their scientific foundation through it; in fact, they are already on the way to being transformed into experimental disciplines. In addition, strict psychology is obviously the foundation for all the mental sciences (*Geisteswissenschaften*) and even for metaphysics. With regard to the latter, of course, it is not the only foundation, since physical natural science has an equal share in supplying a foundation for this general theory of reality."[1] Even in its details, this description fits Brentano's views. Thus, Husserl must have had Brentano in mind. He could almost have copied this passage from the earliest writings of Brentano.

When Husserl wrote his famous article of 1910 entitled "Philosophie als strenge Wissenschaft," it was partly to warn against the practical consequences of the philosophy that wanted to lay a natural scientific foundation for the normative sciences of logic, aesthetics and ethics. But we know that Brentano later changed his position and no longer subscribed to the view sketched above. We must now seek an answer to the question to what extent Husserl's development is bound up with tendencies in Brentano's later philosophy. This again brings up the question of the relationship between LU and Ideen I. At the time of LU, there was still a close connection between Husserl's thinking and that of

---

[1] PSW 297.

the later Brentano. To what extent can we speak of a break with the past in connection with Ideen I, and to what extent is there continuity? Is it possible to regard transcendental idealism as the "triumph of intentions driving his thinking forward at the deepest level," as the fruit of a "struggle to achieve philosophical self-understanding"?[2]

We have already seen that Brentano limited the competence of the natural scientific method. Twenty-five years after the publication of his PES, he regarded the use of the natural scientific method to found the normative mental sciences as a mistake and abuse of this method. He was opposed to a historical inductive founding of these sciences as well as to a natural scientific founding. Natural science can only tell us what something *is* like and never what it *ought* to be like. Historical science can clarify a particular norm via its historical origin, but it can never justify it. The founding of the normative sciences is the exclusive task of descriptive psychology.

Husserl associates himself with these views in LU. In the Prolegomena, he shows with unparalleled acuity that the empirical sciences are not competent to found ideal norms. Any such effort leads to absurd consequences, and the empirical scientist who denies the existence of these norms contradicts himself. Insofar as he propounds a theory, he contradicts his own point of departure, which denies the presupposition of any theory, i.e. the ideal laws of logic. As Husserl remarks in PSW, this inner contradiction also characterizes the praxis of any such empirical scientist. "The naturalist teaches, preaches, moralizes, and reforms. But he denies what every sermon and every demand presupposes if it is to have a meaning." He believes that the natural scientific method elevates philosophy to a science, "and with all the enthusiasm that such a consciousness produces, he has installed himself as teacher and practical reformer in regard to what is true and good and beautiful 'from the standpoint of natural science.'" What Husserl reproaches these philosophers for – Haeckel and Ostwald are named – is not their activity as teachers and reformers or their wish to elevate philosophy to a science but their use of the wrong method. In their praxis, they themselves contradict this method, which recognizes no ideal norms. "One can safely say that the naturalist is an idealist and objectivist in the way he acts."[3]

Natural science cannot give us any fixed norms because empirical

---

[2] Fink, 'Die phän. Phil. Edmund Husserls in der gegenwärtigen Kritik,' 321 and 332.
[3] PSW 295.

generalizations are always provisional. Furthermore, it only establishes what is, and therefore it cannot give us any answer to the question
what ought to be. To use a formulation from Husserl's Krisis, it can
answer only "questions of fact" and not "questions of reason."[4] Mere
"fact-sciences make mere fact-people," he then remarks. But a true
human being cannot be a fact-person. Ancient man already strove for a
philosophical form of life. He wanted to "govern himself and all of his
life on the basis of pure reason, on the basis of philosophy."[5] The task
of philosophy is to make it possible for man to lead a rational life, i.e. a
life that can be justified rationally. As Husserl put it in PSW,
philosophy is "to teach us how to carry out the eternal work of
humanity." It must not only enlighten man about actual states of
affairs but also give leadership in ethical and religious matters. He
begins this famous article by observing: "From its earliest beginnings,
philosophy has claimed to be a rigorous science. What is more, it has
claimed to be the science that satisfies the loftiest theoretical needs and
renders possible – in ethical-religious respects – a life regulated by pure
rational norms."[6] In the latter respect, naturalistic philosophy falls
short: it cannot give leadership to life. (We shall see that it does not give
us satisfying knowledge in theoretical respects either.)

If natural science cannot teach us how we are to live, are we then to
look to some worldview (*Weltanschauung*)? Husserl discusses worldview philosophy in the second part of PSW. This philosophy is a
kind of historical skepticism in which the pretence of a scientific
philosophy has been given up. In a certain sense, Husserl thinks even
less of this kind of philosophy than of naturalism. In naturalism the
quest for a rigorously scientific philosophy has taken a wrong turn, but
in worldview philosophy, the very ideal of a scientific philosophy has
collapsed.[7] What is sought is not so much science as wisdom. This
wisdom is encountered in past philosophies, which are valued as an
indication of existential experience (*Bildung*). This wisdom can help us
in practical respects as we make our own decisions. The philosophy of
worldviews tries to work out this wisdom systematically and give it
theoretical form. It tries to achieve a formulation of the best possible
answer to the questions and riddles which life poses.[8] Husserl

---

[4] Krisis 6, 62, 65, 90 (E 9, 62, 64, 87).
[5] Krisis 4f (E 6f).
[6] PSW 289f.
[7] PSW 292f.
[8] PSW 329ff.

appreciates this effort as such, for he regards it as man's task to regulate his life in accordance with rational norms. Every step in that direction makes possible a more human, a more philosophical, indeed, a more "blessed" life.[9] As a striving for wisdom, worldview philosophy is an essential component of the ideal of a perfect humanity. "According to the idea, every man who strives is necessarily a 'philosopher' in the most original sense of the word."[10]

Precisely because man is in essence a philosopher, he cannot be satisfied with a worldview philosophy. What he seeks is not "wisdom about the world" but a "science of the world." The development of modern natural science teaches us that when science has spoken, wisdom has nothing more to say. Wisdom is valid only for a particular period, while science bears the marks of eternity. Philosophy must undergo a similar development. Husserl rejects any concession to the quest for a worldview as a "softening and weakening of the scientific impulse." It testifies to a lack of intellectual honesty and results in specious literature.[11]

It is historical investigation itself that makes such an attitude toward life impossible, for this investigation shows that all worldviews are historically bound and enmeshed in a crisis. As long as norms were not attacked, it was not impossible to live under the dominance and discipline of a worldview. But is it still possible now, "when each and every norm is combatted or empirically falsified and robbed of its ideal validity?"[12] In this context Husserl speaks of the spiritual need of his time, which had become unbearably pressing. How, in such a time, is a rational or philosophical or genuinely human life possible? We are repeatedly forced to make choices and to justify ourselves philosophically. "All life involves taking positions, and taking positions is subject to a must – that of doing justice to what is valid or invalid according to alleged norms absolute in their validity."[13] But how is such a justification possible? As we have seen, naturalistic philosophy is helpless in this respect, and worldview philosophy is unscientific.

[9] See EP II 16. We find true happiness and blessedness in philosophy: see also FTL 4.
[10] PSW 331, 336.
[11] PSW 339. In LU I, Husserl praises Bolzano for making a clear distinction between wisdom about the world and knowledge of the world, 226.
[12] PSW 336, see also 324. Here skepticism has a positive function, just as it does in epistemology. Living by a worldview represents a lower level of existence than living in a way that can be justified radically in a Socratic sense, EP II 8ff; FTL 5.
[13] PSW 336.

Meanwhile, life goes on, and ethical decisions cannot be postponed. "It is certain that we cannot wait."

When we compare Husserl's depiction of the situation in the 1910 article with his sketch of the situation some 25 years later in Krisis, we cannot deny that he had a certain talent for prophecy. His warnings about natural scientific philosophy in 1910 were probably inspired in part by the fear that dissatisfaction with exact philosophy would drive more and more students into the arms of some worldview or other. Unfortunately, Husserl's fear was borne out. In 1910 he still had to demonstrate that natural science is incompetent with regard to questions of life, for there was still a certain practical optimism. Because of the war, this situation changed radically. It was then generally recognized that science has nothing to say to us in this respect. Husserl observes that after the war, a certain enmity toward science began to manifest itself. "In our deep need – so we hear – this science has nothing to say to us." In science we seek facts alone and must abstain from any evaluation. All specific human questions are banished from the realm of science.[14] Thus science, particularly natural science, has achieved great successes in mathematics and physics and has brought us much further in our control of the world and in our effort to create prosperity, but it gives us no answer to existential questions. Thus, in the period between 1910 and 1936, natural scientific philosophy seems to have come to a certain self-awareness. It was discovered that the natural scientific method can indeed resolve no ethical dilemmas. The result of this realization was a certain impoverishment of the ideal of science. What came to be seen as science was a mere remnant in comparison to what the great renewers of science in the Renaissance era had in mind. Think of Husserl's definition at the beginning of PSW: the task of philosophy is to make possible a life that can be justified rationally and ethically. Now that science had defaulted in its task, it was no wonder that worldviews – in 1936 we must think particularly of the "myth of the twentieth century" – became more and more powerful. The attachment to worldviews represents an increasing

[14] Krisis 4f, 67 (E 6f, 66). The modern man of science no longer wants to be a practical reformer (Max Weber). When Husserl speaks in this context of the crisis of science, he does not mean in the first place that mathematical-deductive science has forgotten its foundation in the life-world. Placing it back in the life-world is only a means of indicating to natural science its limited place in the whole of a descriptive science of absolute consciousness: it is a condition for overcoming the crisis. The true crisis of science is its refusal to deal with life's problems.

renunciation of the human command to "live on the basis of pure reason." Thus we see that Husserl, like his teacher Brentano, was involved in a struggle on two fronts. He opposed both historical relativism and the effort to found the normative sciences in natural science. In both of these struggles, Husserl showed himself to be a worthy successor to his revered teacher, for he was facing an aggravated situation that threatened him personally.

I have chosen to go somewhat more deeply into the context of Husserl's philosophizing here because it becomes so clear what was at issue for him. It is against this background that we must view the pathos characteristic of Husserl when he speaks of the calling of philosophy and the philosopher. Now, Husserl has been reproached for a lack of engagement, for non-involvement.[15] While the world around him was collapsing, according to some critics, he led the life of a typical German philosophy professor, restricting himself largely to the study and the classroom. It is true that we do not find in Husserl the political engagement typical of his existentialist students. Husserl involved himself not in the affairs of a particular political party but in the business of European culture as a whole!

PARAGRAPH TWO. THE TURN TO TRANSCENDENTAL IDEALISM

When it comes to providing concrete answers to the problem sketched above, we see that Husserl actually lags behind his teacher Brentano. The founding of the normative sciences was to be sought in descriptive philosophy. In his book about the origin of our knowledge of right and wrong (*Vom Ursprung sittlicher Erkenntnis*), Brentano tried to develop an ethics of this kind that was scientific but not based on natural science. This book even contains the seeds of a philosophy of the state.

As far as foundations are concerned, Brentano lags behind Husserl. Both philosophers seek the founding of the normative sciences in a phenomenological analysis of consciousness. But Husserl justifies his analysis much more thoroughly in methodological respects – which is typical of him. His doctrine of the intuition of essences represents an

[16] H. Plessner, 'Phänomenologie, Das Werk Edmund Husserl's,' 47 and 58. Plessner speaks of the "sweetness of non-involvement" that manifests itself in the building up of the eidetic sciences. In his opinion, this testifies to an insufficient awareness of responsibility. Farber makes the same kind of reproach in *The foundation of phenomenology*, 94. A philosophy that does not concern itself with "actual historical needs" is "in effect a way of condoning dislocation in that world," 571.

attempt to provide a firm anchor for a priori insights. The growth of
this doctrine of the intuition of essences has been analyzed extensively
in this study. If we now ask what concrete results it led to, we must
admit that Husserl provided a foundation only for pure logic. He did
not provide a foundation for ethics. At the end of his moving article
PSW, he did refer to the possibility of an eidetic science, but in his
writings we find no concrete realization of this analysis or application
of it to questions of life.[1]

Husserl's caution in this respect is doubtless bound up with major
difficulties he envisioned. These difficulties made the turn to transcendental idealism necessary. After 1900, Husserl became aware of the
limitations and incompleteness of his way of combatting naturalism.
His criticism in the Prolegomena, he admitted, was in fact a criticism on
the basis of absurd consequences. It was directed against the naturalizing of ideas. Husserl became aware that such opposition had little
practical effect. This was apparent from the fact that the tidal wave of
positivism and pragmatism had continued to advance. Thus, Husserl's
argument on the basis of absurd consequences did not make much of an
impression and was unable to turn the tide. Furthermore, it may even
have had an unintended effect, namely, that some people lost all faith in
science under the influence of his refutation of the unjustified pretentions of science and sought salvation instead in a worldview
philosophy. What is needed, then, is a radical refutation of naturalism,
a refutation that opens up positive paths for a scientific philosophy.
Husserl tried to realize such a program in Ideen, the first volume of
which appeared during his lifetime and concentrated mainly on the
negative task. The projected third volume was supposed to be devoted
to the idea of a phenomenological philosophy as an absolutely founded
philosophy; it was supposed to deal with the possibility of metaphysics
as a science of transcendental facts.[2]

In Part II of this study, the difficulties that remained unresolved in
LU were discussed. The field delimited by the epoché within the
naturalistic world still remains part of this natural reality. Therefore
the epistemology given by Husserl in LU remains an ultimately
psychological epistemology that had to abstract from the being of the
objects known. The (natural scientific) "thing in itself" was pre-

---

[1] Even the *Ethische Untersuchungen* (The Hague, 1960) published posthumously by A.
Roth are disappointing in this respect.

[2] On this question *Ideen* I contains only a few remarks that point the way, 5, 119, 121.

supposed as something behind the intentional object; beneath the phenomenological sphere was the physical body, and via this body the rest of the physical world. This caused the tension in Husserl's ontology. Consciousness, which is isolated from the rest of reality through the epoché, remains as part of that reality. But how can this consciousness, which is subject to ideal norms, likewise be regarded as part of nature and subject to strict causal laws? Alongside the phenomenology of consciousness in LU, there is an empirical explanatory psychology. We saw that the positivistic element ultimately remains dominant; this is apparent, for example, from Husserl's rejection of any teleology. In the final analysis, the abstraction from causal reality in the epoché is artificial. The antinomy buried in the juxtaposition of the two methods (i.e. the descriptive-phenomenological and the positivistic-explanatory) is not clarified in LU. Therefore the struggle against naturalism was doomed to sterility and did not represent a radical critique. One could say that LU is characterized by a kind of Kantian division of tasks – with the difference that natural science is limited in its competence but *not in its scope*. To that extent, the difficulties remained greater for Husserl than for Kant. This was to drive him toward a more radical solution.[3]

In 1910 Husserl maintained that the way to combat naturalism is to oppose *not only* the naturalizing of ideas *but also* the naturalizing of *consciousness*. In the first chapter of Part III, we saw in what way Husserl attacks the roots of this naturalistic ontology. His approach leads to a radical purification of consciousness, a purification that is *not only methodological but also ontological*. Consciousness is not a superstructure built upon nature, for nature, on the contrary, is constituted within consciousness. Husserl realized that one cannot posit an ideal world like that of such neo-Kantians as Windelband and Rickert and maintain a positivistic theory of reality at the same time.[4] He did say in LU that these ideas, which form a supra-temporal realm, are "realized" in spatio-temporal causal reality, but it remains completely unclear how this is possible. We know that Brentano did not see this as a problem. It testifies to Husserl's greatness that he took this problem seriously and devoted all his energy to seeking a solution for it. These were persistent difficulties that would not go away. As a result,

[3] On Kant, see Krisis 103, 105, 112 (E 100, 103, 110).

[4] Husserl mentions them in *Ideen* II together with Dilthey and claims that they do not go about it in a sufficiently radical manner, 173. See above 231, 395.

there are certain important questions that Husserl never got around to dealing with. At the end of his life, he still thought of himself as a "beginner." Brentano had been too quick to look for results in his ethical theory. Husserl saw that positing an ideal realm requires a revision of ontology. An idealist philosophy of values cannot be combined with a positivistic ontology. In other words, Husserl realized that *the eidetic reduction must be supplemented by a transcendental-phenomenological reduction*. Here Husserl's philosophy, as he was well aware, finds a point of contact with post-Kantian idealism of freedom. Thus he carried through the phenomenological line in his thinking in a radical way. It is no longer the case that the phenomenological method is justified *along with others* in a certain area. Now it has become all-embracing. Natural science concerns itself with a non-independent correlate of consciousness, and its results must be metaphysically reinterpreted by phenomenology. Nature is a moment within absolute mind.

According to Husserl, it is natural science that isolates its area artificially from the cohering systems of absolute consciousness. This is an abstraction that must be overcome not by the physicist but by the phenomenological philosopher, who restores nature to the depths of transcendental consciousness where it is constituted. Natural science, which cannot serve as the foundation for an ethically justified life, *is not able to satisfy our theoretical needs either*. "Not in a single instance have the natural sciences unraveled actual reality for us, the reality in which we live and move and have our being." The belief that it is able to do so has been recognized as a superstition by "those who look more deeply." Husserl then quotes Lotze's statement that calculating the course of the world is not the same as understanding it. [5] The only true explanation, Husserl claims in Krisis, is "making something understandable in transcendental terms." He goes on to say: "Thus, natural scientific knowledge of nature does not give us a truly explanatory and ultimate knowledge of nature, for it does not investigate nature at all in the absolute coherence in which its real and genuine being is revealed in its sense...."[6] Nature is a clue for an analysis that lays bare the connections in consciousness by means of which nature is constituted. [7]

[5] PSW 335f. See also EP I, 249, where Husserl calls absolute consciousness the sphere in which we "live and move and have our being."

[6] Krisis 193 (E 189); see also Id I 319, 299.

[7] 296, 299.

These connections are unities of motivation[8] or teleological unities.[9] The real world is an index of this teleology. Husserl means that the transcendental reduction brings us closer to the traditional ideal of philosophy. Transcendental phenomenology is absolutely founded. It is universal and presuppositionless, for it denies the presupposition of the world on which all previous philosophy has been based. This rigorously scientific philosophy is not mathematical-deductive. It was the great error of the seventeenth century thinkers that they tried to build up philosophy "as if all being were unifiable through calculation."[10] Husserl put this classical *mathesis universalis* back into the context of a concrete, descriptive ontology of the mind.[11]

This philosophy and the metaphysics based on it are dealt with by Husserl in later writings. His intention in Ideen I was only to point the way to this philosophy. First we must show how to get to this new science. We do so by the difficult operation of the transcendental-phenomenological reduction. In this study I did not go into the later developments, for my goal was no more than to show how Husserl's transcendental idealism can be understood on the basis of his earlier work. I have argued that it can be seen as a culmination of all the earlier tendencies in his thought. In making this point, I might appear to be in conflict with Fink and thereby with Husserl himself, for they speak of the "transcendental unmotivatedness" of phenomenology. According to Fink, the reduction cannot be understood on the basis of any mundane problematics.[12] This is indeed correct insofar as transcendental phenomenology gives no mundane answers to mundane questions. We have seen that phenomenology solves tensions and riddles by altering the terms in which the problem is posed on a mundane level. To that extent, it can be said that phenomenology formulates its own questions. These questions are the true problems, and they allow of a solution. From the new standpoint, we see that the mundane problems cannot be solved, and in this sense we "understand" them. Therefore we may say that the mundane mysteries – as mysteries – are the motivation for transcendental phenomenology.

It was Husserl's fate that each solution he found again gave rise to

---

[8] 89 note 1, 93; see also CM 190.

[9] 176–303. See also Husserliana IX, 254.

[10] CM 39.

[11] See above 489.

[12] Fink, 'Die phänomenologische Philosophie Edmund Husserls in der gegenwärtigen Kritik,' 346.

new problems. Because of this, his philosophy took on a strongly preparatory character. The problem of the normative sciences drove him – like Brentano – to an a priori analysis of consciousness. This analysis raised the problem of the founding of a priori science, for which he found a solution in the doctrine of the intuition of essences. But this doctrine was not the terminal point either. The problems that remained led finally to a radical revision of ontology and a new idea of philosophy. In his efforts to found this philosophy, Husserl repeatedly had to engage in renewed reflection on the problem of the "ways" and the reduction. Thus, at the end of his life, Husserl felt somewhat like Moses, who had seen the promised land but was not allowed to enter it and cultivate it himself.[13]

This continual reflection on methodological problems should not cause us to forget that Husserl's original impulse or drive was of an ethical nature. I have already spoken of his elevated conception of the task of philosophy. Of Brentano, Husserl said: "I would characterize this straightforward conviction of his mission, which was not subject to doubt, as the most basic fact about his life. Without it, Brentano's personality cannot be understood or, consequently, properly evaluated."[14] One could say the same of Husserl himself. It is apparent from PSW that Husserl saw the struggle for a rigorously scientific philosophy as a matter of ethical obligation. This is clear especially from a certain passage that seems to me to have autobiographical significance. In this passage Husserl raises the question whether one should choose the development of a worldview philosophy or the development of a rigorously scientific philosophy as one's goal in life. This is a practical question that cannot be answered in a universally valid way when viewed from the standpoint of the individual. But when we bear in mind the interests of mankind as a whole, we look at this question differently. "For our historical influence and, with it, our ethical responsibilities extend to the utmost reaches of the ethical ideal, to those indicated by the idea of human development." When we recognize this, it is no longer difficult to decide for a "theoretical character." We must not sacrifice eternity to time because we want a system *now*. Yet, this is exactly what we are doing when we seek a philosophy that gives us a provisional solution to our problems but does not have universal validity. Husserl writes: "in order to alleviate

---

[13] Nachwort 161.
[14] 'Erinnerungen an Franz Brentano,' 160.

our need, we have no right to bequeath to posterity need upon need as an ultimately ineradicable evil."[15] Rigorous science gathers a treasure of eternal truths that are a blessing to mankind. This is the reason for the pathos with which Husserl speaks of the "will to science" (*Wissenschaftswille*). As long as there is no rigorous philosophy, the will to establish one is the most important thing. It is this will that has enabled the great geniuses of the past to achieve what they did. Husserl writes: "that which is so constantly desired in our age may repel the aesthetic sense, which finds the naive beauty of that which grows freely much more appealing; yet, what extraordinary values are present in the sphere of will, provided that the great wills find only correct goals."[16] All of Husserl's mental effort was directed toward finding these correct goals and developing an idea of philosophy which is able to "cultivate our minds and mobilize our energies."[17] The goal of philosophy is a genuinely scientific knowledge that can be justified from beginning to end. And anyone who wants to be a real philosopher must be filled with this "will to science": "I can only become a real philosopher through my free decision to want to direct my life toward this goal."[18]

[15] PSW 333ff.
[16] PSW 338ff.
[17] EP I, 7.
[18] CM 4. See also EP II, 17.

TRANSLATION TABLE

Ablösbarkeit	separability
Anhalt	vehicle
anschauen, Anschauung	intuit, intuition
anschaulich, unanschaulich	intuitive, non-intuitive
Auffassung	interpretation
Auffassungssinn	appercipient sense
Auffassungsweise	mode of apperception
ausschalten	disconnect, suspend
Begriffsgegenstand	denotatum, object of the concept
Bewusstseinsweise, Weise des Bewusstseins	mode of consciousness
Denkhaltung	thought-stance
eigentlich, uneigentlich	genuine, non-genuine
Einbegriff	collection
Enttäuschung	disappointment
Erlebnis	experience
Erlebnisstrom	experiential stream
gebende Anschauung	presentative intuition
Gegenstand an sich	object in itself
Gegenstand schlechthin	object in the strict sense
Gegenstand so wie	object as referred to
Gegenstand welcher	object referred to

Geltungsphänomen	phenomenon claiming validity
Ichspaltung	bifurcation of the ego
Inbegriff	aggregate
kolligieren	collect
Kunstlehre	theory of an art
natürliche Einstellung	natural attitude
realisierend	reifying
Rechtsprechung der Vernunft	rational appraisal
schlicht objektiv	straightforwardly objective
Seinsboden	ontic basis
selbständig, unselbständig	independent, non-independent
setzen als etwas	posit as something
Thesis	positing, thesis
Veranschaulichung	intuitive illustration
Verhalten	attitude
Verhaltungsweise	mode of comportment
vermeinen	grasp putatively
vermeintlich	supposed, presumptive
Weltvernichtung	annihilation of the world
Wesensschau	intuition of essences

BIBLIOGRAPHY

ABBREVIATIONS

Abbreviations used for Brentano's works

Letzte Wünsche   Meine letzten Wünsche für Oesterreich

PES   Psychologie vom empirischen Standpunkt

Psychologie des   Die Psychologie des Aristoteles, insbesondere seine Lehre
Aristoteles   vom νους ποιητικος

USE   Vom Ursprung sittlicher Erkenntnis

VE   Versuch über die Erkenntnis

Vier Phasen   Die Vier Phasen der Philosophie und ihr augenblicklicher
                 Stand

WE   Wahrheit und Evidenz

Zukunft   Ueber die Zukunft der Philosophie

Abbreviations used for Husserl's works

BZ   Ueber den Begriff der Zahl

CM   Cartesianische Meditationen und Pariser Vorträge

Entwurf   Entwurf einer 'Vorrede' zu den Logische Untersuchungen

EP   Erste Philosophie

Erinnerungen   Erinnerungen an Franz Brentano

EU   Erfahrung und Urteil

FTL   Formale und transzendentale Logik

Id	Ideen zu einer reinen Phänomenologie und phänomenologischen Philosophie
IP	Die Idee der Phänomenologie
Krisis	Die Krisis der europäischen Wissenschaften und die transzendentale Phänomenologie
Literaturbericht Palàgyi	Literaturbericht: Melchior Palàgyi, Der Streit der Psychologisten und Formalisten in der modernen Logik
PSW	Die Philosophie als strenge Wissenschaft
LU I	Logische Untersuchungen, Bd I Prolegomena zur reinen Logik
LU II	Logische Untersuchungen, Bd II, Teil I Untersuchungen zur Phänomenologie und Theorie der Erkenntnis (LU II can indicate both parts of volume II when the first edition is cited)
LU III	Logische Untersuchungen, Bd II, Teil II, Elemente einer Phänomenologischen Aufklärung der Erkenntnis, 2nd edition, 1921
Nachwort	Nachwort zu meinen 'Ideen zu einer reinen Phänomenologie und phänomenologischen Philosophie'
PA	Philosophie der Arithmetik
PP	Phänomenologische Psychologie
PSL	Psychologische Studien zur elementaren Logik
Referat Marty	Referat: Anton Marty, Untersuchungen zur Grundlegung der allgemeinen Grammatik und Sprachphilosophie. I Bd 1908
SAL	(Review) Schröder, Ernst, Vorlesungen über die Algebra der Logik
ZBW	Vorlesungen zur Phänomenologie des inneren Zeitbewusstseins

Journals

JPPF	Jahrbuch für Philosophie und Phänomenologische Forschung
PPR	Philosophy and phenomenological Research
RIP	Revue internationale de Philosophie
RMM	Revue de Métaphysique et de Morale

RPFE	Revue philosophique de la France et de l'Etranger
TP	Tijdschrift voor Philosophie
ZPF	Zeitschrift für philosophische Forschung

I. BIBLIOGRAPHIES*

A. Husserl's Works

BREDA, H.L. VAN, Bibliographie der bis zum 30. Juni 1959 veröffentlichten Schriften Edmund Husserls, in Edmund Husserl 1859–1959, 289–306, The Hague 1959

BREDA, H.L. VAN and PACI, E., Bibliographie I, Ouvrages de Husserl. Textes et traductions in Les grands courants de la pensée mondiale contemporaine, edited by F. Sciacca, Les tendances principales, Vol. I, Paris-Milano, 1961, 441–448

MASCHKE, G. and KERN, I., Husserl-Bibliographie II. Ouvrages de Husserl (textes et traductions) publiés de 1960 à 1965. RIP 19, 1965, 156–160

B. Works about Husserl

PATOCKA, J., Bibliographie, RIP, I, fasc. 2. 1939, 374–397 and 544

BRIE, G.A. DE, Bibliographia Philosophica 1934–1945, vol. I Bibliographia Historiae Philosophiae, Utrecht and Brussel 1950, 553–555

RAES, J., Supplément à la bibliographie de Husserl, RIP, 14, 1950, 469–475

BREDA, H.L. VAN, Bibliographie, in Institut international de Philosophie, La Philosophie au milieu du vingtième siècle, t. II ed. R. Klibansky, Firenze, 1958, 65–70

ROBERT, J.D., Eléments de bibliographie husserlienne, TP, 20, 1958, 534–544

ELEY, L., Husserl-Bibliographie, 1945–1959, ZPF, 13, 1959, 357–367

ELEY, L., Berichtigungen zur Husserl-Bibliographie, ZPF, 13, 1959, 475

CUCCHI,M., Studi su Husserl in Italiano, Aut-aut, 54, 1959, 431–433

BONA, I., Bibliografia in Omaggio a Husserl, II Saggiatore, Milan 1959, 291–316

BREDA, H.L. VAN and PACI, E., Bibliograpie, III Ouvrages et articles sur Husserl publiés de 1945 à 1959 in Les grands courants de la pensée

* For a Bretano bibliography, see The Philosophy of Brentano, edited by Linda L. McAlister, London 1976, 240–255.

mondiale contemporaine, edited by F. Sciacca, Les tendances principales, Vol. I, Paris-Milano, 1961, 449–464

MASCHKE, G. and KERN, I., Husserl-Bibliographie, part III: Ouvrages et articles sur Husserl publiés de 1951 à 1964, RIP, 19, 1965, 160–202

LELLIS, E. DE, Bibliografia degli studi Husserliani in Italia: 1960–1964, RIP, 19, 1965, 140–152

II. WORKS OF BRENTANO CITED OR CONSULTED

A. Works published during his lifetime

Ad Disputationem qua theses ... defendet ... invitat Franciscus Brentano, Aschaffenburg, 1866 (the quotations are taken from the new edition by O. Kraus in Ueber die Zukunft der Philosophie 133–142, see below under B)

Die Psychologie des Aristoteles, insbesondere seine Lehre vom νοῦς ποιητικος, Mainz, 1867

Auguste Comte und die positive Philosophie, in Chilianeum: Blätter für katholische Philosophie, Kunst und Leben (Neue Folge 2. Bd.) 1869. (We cite the new edition by O. Kraus in Die vier Phasen der Philosophie und ihr augenblicklicher Stand, 99–134, see below under B.)

Psychologie vom empirischen Standpunkt, Erster Band, Leipzig 1874. The chapters 5–9 of Book II were republished by Brentano under the title Von der Klassification der psychischen Phänomene, Leipzig, 1911. (We cite the new edition by O. Kraus of Book I and Book II, chapter 1–4 under the title Psychologie vom empirischen Standpunkt, Erster Band, and the new edition by Kraus of Book II, chapter 5–9 under the title Psychologie vom empirischen Standpunkt, Zweiter Band, see below under B.)

Ueber die Gründe der Entmutigung auf philosophischen Gebiete, Vienna, 1874. (We cite the new edition by O. Kraus in Ueber die Zukunft der Philosophie 83–101, Leipzig, 1929, see below under B.)

Was für ein Philosoph manchmal Epoche macht, Vienna, 1876 (we cite the new edition by O. Kraus in Die vier Phasen der Philosophie und ihr augenblicklicher Stand 33–60, see below under B)

Vom Ursprung sittlicher Erkenntnis, Leipzig, 1889 (we cite the new edition by O. Kraus, see below under B)

Ueber die Zukunft der Philosophie, Vienna, 1893 (we cite the new edition by O. Kraus, see below under B)

Die vier Phasen der Philosophie und ihr augenblicklicher Stand, Stuttgart, 1895 (we cite the new edition by O. Kraus, see below under B)

Meine letzten Wünsche für Oesterreich, Stuttgart, 1895

Zur Lehre von der Empfindung, Dritter internationaler Kongress für Psychologie (held in Munich in 1896), Munich 1897. This lecture has been republished by Brentano under the title Ueber Individuation, multiple Qualität und Intensität sinnlicher Erscheinungen, in Untersuchungen zur Sinnespsychologie, see below

Untersuchungen zur Sinnespsychologie, Leipzig, 1907.

B. *Posthumous works*

Vom Ursprung sittlicher Erkenntnis, edited by O. Kraus, 1921 (the quotations are taken from the new, expanded edition, Leipzig, 1934)

Psychologie vom empirischen Standpunkt, Erster Band, edited by O. Kraus, Leipzig, 1924

Psychologie vom empirischen Standpunkt, Zweiter Band, edited by O. Kraus, Leipzig, 1925

Versuch über die Erkenntnis, edited by A. Kastil, Leipzig, 1925

Die vier Phasen der Philosophie und ihr augenblicklicher Stand, edited by O. Kraus, Leipzig, 1926

Vom sinnlichen und noetischen Bewusstsein, (Psychologie Band III) I. Teil, edited by O. Kraus, Leipzig, 1928

Ueber die Zukunft der Philosophie, edited by O. Kraus, Leipzig, 1929

Vom Dasein Gottes, edited by O. Kraus, Leipzig, 1929

Wahrheit und Evidenz, edited by O. Kraus, Leipzig, 1930

Kategorienlehre, edited by O. Kraus, Leipzig, 1933

Grundlegung und Aufbau der Ethik, edited by F. Mayer-Hillebrand, Bern and Munich, 1952

Religion und Philosophie, edited by F. Mayer-Hillebrand, Bern and Munich, 1954

Die Lehre vom richtigen Urteil, edited by F. Mayer-Hillebrand, Bern and Munich, 1956

III. WORKS OF HUSSERL CITED OR CONSULTED*

A. *Works published during his lifetime*

Über den Begriff der Zahl, psychologische Analysen. Habilitationsschrift, Halle a.S., 1887

* Without further indication we quote in part II from LU, in the Intermezzo from IP, and in part III from Id I.

Philosophie der Arithmetik. Psychologische und logische Untersuchungen, erster Band, Halle-Saale, 1891 (see also below under B; we quote from the first edition)

Selbstanzeige (author's abstract): Husserl, Dr. E.G., Philosophie der Arithmetik, Vierteljahrsschrift für wissenschaftliche Philosophie, 15, 1891, 360–361

Der Folgerungscalcul und die Inhaltslogik, Vierteljahrsschrift für wissenschaftliche Philosophie, 15, 1891, 168–189 and 351–356

(Review): Schröder, Ernst, Vorlesungen über die Algebra der Logik (Exakte Logik). I. Band, Leipzig, 1890. Göttingische gelehrte Anzeigen, 1891, 243–278

A. Voigt's 'elementare Logik' und meine Darlegung zur Logik des logischen Calculs, Vierteljahrsschrift für wissenschaftliche Philosophie, 17, 1893, 111–120

Antwort auf die vorstehende 'Erwiderung' des Herrn Voigt, Vierteljahrsschrift für wissenschaftliche Philosophie, 17, 1893, 508–511

Psychologische Studien zur elementaren Logik, Philosophische Monatshefte, 30, 1894, 159–191

Bericht über deutsche Schriften zur Logik aus dem Jahre 1894, Archiv für systematische Philosophie, 3, 1897, 216–244

Logische Untersuchungen, erster Teil: Prolegomena zur reinen Logik, Halle a.S., 1900 (unless otherwise indicated, the quotations are taken from the second edition of 1913, see below)

Selbstanzeige: Husserl, Edmund, Logische Untersuchungen, erster Teil: Prolegomena zur reinen Logik, Vierteljahrsschrift für wissenschaftliche Philosophie, 24, 1900, 511–512

Logische Untersuchungen, zweiter Teil: Untersuchungen zur Phänomenologie und Theorie der Erkenntnis, Halle a.S. 1901 (unless otherwise indicated, the quotations are taken from the second edition of Bd I 1913 and Bd II, 1921, see below)

Selbstanzeige: Husserl, Edmund, Logische Untersuchungen, zweiter Teil, Vierteljahrsschrift für wissenschaftliche Philosophie 25, 1901, 260–263

Literaturbericht: Melchior Palàgyi, Der Streit der Psychologisten und Formalisten in der modernen Logik, Leipzig, 1902, Zeitschrift für Psychologie und Physiologie der Sinnesorgane, 31, 1903, 287–294

Bericht über deutsche Schriften zur Logik in den Jahren 1895–1899, Archiv für systematische Philosophie, 9, 1903, 113–132, 237–259, 393–408, 523–543; 10, 1904, 101–125

Referat: Anton Marty, Untersuchungen zur Grundlegung der allgemeinen Grammatik und Sprachphilosophie, I Band, Halle, 1908 Deutsche Literaturanzeiger, 31, 1910, 1106–1110

Philosophie als strenge Wissenschaft, Logos, I, 1910–1911, 289–341 (see also below under B, we quote from this first edition)

Logische Untersuchungen, erster Band: Prolegomena zur reinen Logik, zweiter Band: Untersuchungen zur Phänomenologie und Theorie der Erkenntnis, I. Teil, zweite, umgearbeitete Auflage, Halle a.d.S., 1913

Ideen zu einer reinen Phänomenologie und phänomenologischen Philosophie, JPPF, 1, 1913, VII; 1–323

Erinnerungen an Franz Brentano, in Oskar Kraus, Franz Brentano. Zur Kenntnis seines Lebens und seiner Lehre, Munich, 1919, Appendix II, 153–167

Logische Untersuchungen, zweiter Band: Elemente einer phänomenologischen Aufklärung der Erkenntnis, II. Teil, zweite, teilweise umgearbeitete Auflage, Halle a.d.S., 1921

Vorlesungen zur Phänomenologie des inneren Zeitbewusstseins, herausgegeben M. von Heidegger, JPPF, 9, 1928, VIII–IX; 367–498

Formale und transzendentale Logik. Versuch einer Kritik der logischen Vernunft, JPPF, 10, 1929, V/XIII; 1–298 (see also below under B; we quote from this first edition)

Phenomenology, in The Encyclopaedia Britannica, 14th ed., Volume 17, col. 699–702, London 1929 (the quotations are taken from the reprint of the German original in Phänomenologische Psychologie, Husserliana IX, 237–301, see below B)

Nachwort zu meinen 'Ideen zu einer reinen Phänomenologie und phänomenologischen Philosophie,' JPPF, 11, 1930, 549–570 (the quotations are taken from the reprint in Ideen III, Husserliana V, 138–162, see below under B)

Die Krisis der europäischen Wissenschaften und die transzendentale Phänomenologie. Eine Einleitung in die phänomenologische Philosophie, Philosophia, I, 1936, 77–176 (we cite the new edition in Husserliana, Band VI, see below under B)

B. Posthumous works

Erfahrung und Urteil. Untersuchungen zur Genealogie der Logik, redigiert und herausgegeben von Ludwig Landgrebe, Prag, 1939

Entwurf einer 'Vorrede' zu den 'Logischen Untersuchungen' 1913, TP, I, 1939, 106–133; 319–339

(Letter to Marvin Farber, in English translation) in Marvin Farber, The Foundation of Phenomenology, Edmund Husserl and the Quest for a Rigorous Science of Philosophy, Cambridge Massachusetts 1943, 17

Cartesianische Meditationen und Pariser Vorträge, herausgegeben und eingeleitet von S. Strasser, Husserliana, Band I, The Hague 1950

Die Idee der Phänomenologie, Fünf Vorlesungen, herausgegeben und eingeleitet von W. Biemel, Husserliana, Band II, The Hague, 1950

Ideen zu einer reinen Phänomenologie und phänomenologischen Philosophie, erster Buch: Allgemeine Einführung in die reine Phänomenologie. Neue, auf Grund der handschriftlichen Zusätze des Verfassers erweiterte Auflage, herausgegeben von W. Biemel, Husserliana, Band III, The Hague, 1950 (unless otherwise indicated, the quotations are taken from the first edition of 1913, see above under A)

Ideen zu einer reinen Phänomenologie und phänomenologischen Philosophie, zweites Buch: Phänomenologische Untersuchungen zur Konstitution, herausgegeben von M. Biemel, Husserliana, Band IV, The Hague 1952

Ideen zu einer reinen Phänomenologie und Phänomenologischen Philosophie, drittes Buch: Die Phänomenologie und die Fundamente der Wissenschaften, herausgegeben von M. Biemel, Husserliana, Band V, The Hague, 1952

Die Krisis der europäischen Wissenschaften und die transzendentale Phänomenologie, Eine Einleitung in die phänomenologische Philosophie, herausgegeben von W. Biemel, Husserliana, Band VI, The Hague, 1954

Erste Philosophie (1923/24), zweiter Teil: Theorie der phänomenologischen geben von R. Boehm, Husserliana, Band VII, The Hague, 1956

Persönliche Aufzeichnungen, herausgegeben von W. Biemel, PPR, 16, 1956, 293–302

Erste Philosophie (1923/24), zweiter Teil: theorie der phänomenologischen Reduktion, herausgegeben von R. Boehm, Husserliana, Band VIII, The Hague, 1959

Phänomenologische Psychologie, Vorlesungen Sommersemester 1925, herausgegeben von W. Biemel, Husserliana, Band IX, The Hague, 1962

Philosophie als strenge Wissenschaft, herausgegeben von W. Szilasi, Frankfurt, 1962 (we cite the first edition of 1910, see A)

Philosophenbriefe, Aus der wissenschaftlichen Korrespondenz von Alexius Meinong, edited by R. Kindinger, Graz, 1965

Zur Phänomenologie des inneren Zeitbewusstseins (1893–1917), herausgegeben von R. Boehm, The Hague, 1966

Briefe an Roman Ingarden, herausgegeben von R. Ingarden, The Hague, 1968

Philosophie der Arithmetik (1890–1901), herausgegeben von Lothar Eley, Husserliana, Band XII, The Hague, 1970 (this edition has a correlation table for the pagination of the first edition)

Ding und Raum, Vorlesungen 1907, herausgegeben von Ulrich Claesges, Husserliana, Band XVI, The Hague, 1973

Formale und transzendentale Logik, Versuch einer Kritik der logischen Vernunft mit ergänzenden Texten herausgegeben von Paul Jansen, Husserliana, Band XVII, The Hague, 1974 (this edition gives the pagination of the first edition in the margin)

Logische Untersuchungen Bd I, Prolegomena zur reinen Logik, Text der 1. und 2. Auflage, herausgegeben von Elmar Holenstein, Husserliana, Bd XVIII, The Hague, 1975 (this edition gives the original pagination of the first and second edition in the margin)

IV. ENGLISH TRANSLATIONS OF HUSSERL'S WORKS

Some of the English translations of Husserl's works give the original (German) pagination in the margin, namely, *Formal and Transcendental Logic*, *Introduction to the Logical Investigations*, *The Paris Lectures*, *Cartesian Meditations*, and *The Idea of Phenomenology* (all published by Martinus Nijhoff). For other works of Husserl Published in English without the original pagination we present correlation tables, namely, *Logical Investigations*, *Philosophy as a Rigourous Science*, and *Ideas*. In the case of works of Husserl not cited frequently, the page number of the English translation is given in addition, e.g. *Krisis* 237 (E 234). This has been done in the case of both *The Phenomenology of Internal Time-Consciousness* and *The Crisis of European Sciences and Transcendental Phenomenology*. In the (German) Husserliana edition, these works contain "Beilagen" that are not included in the respective English editions. Hence there are no references to English page numbers when quotations are drawn from these "Beilagen."

Ideas, A general Introduction to Pure Phenomenology, translation of Ideen zu einer reinen Phänomenologie und phänomenologischen Philosophie by W. R. B. Gibson, London, 1931, 1969[5]

Cartesian Meditations, An Introduction to Phenomenology, translation of Cartesianische Meditationen by D. Cairns, The Hague, 1950

The Phenomenology of Internal Time-Consciousness, translation of Vorlesungen zur Phänomenologie des inneren Zeitbewusstseins by J. S. Churchill, Bloomington, 1964

The Idea of Phenomenology, translation of Die Idee der Phänomenologie by W.P. Alston and G. Nakhnikian, The Hague, 1964

The Paris Lectures, translation of Die Pariser Vorträge by P. Koestenbaum, The Hague, 1964

Philosophy as a Rigourous Science, translation of Philosophie als strenge Wissenschaft by Q. Lauer, in: Phenomenology and the Crisis of Philosophy, New York, 1965

Formal and Transcendental Logic, translation of Formale und transzendentale Logik by D. Cairns, The Hague, 1969

The Crisis of European Sciences and Transcendental Phenomenology, An Introduction to Phenomenological Philosophy, translation of Die Krisis der europäischen Wissenschaften und die transzendentale Phänomenologie, Eine Einleitung in die phänomenologische Philosophie by D. Carr, Evanston, 1970

Logical Investigations, translation of Logische Untersuchungen by J.N. Findlay, London, 1970

A Draft of a "Preface" to the Logical Investigations, translation of Entwurf einer 'Vorrede' zu den Logischen Untersuchungen by Ph. J. Bossert and C.H. Peters, in: Introduction to the Logical Investigations, The Hague, 1975

Author's Abstracts to Volume One and Two of the Logical Investigations, translations of Selbstanzeigen in Vierteljahrsschrift für wissenschaftliche Philosophie Vol. 24 (1900) and Vol. 25 (1901) by Ph.J. Bossert and C.H. Peters, in: Introduction to the Logical Investigations, The Hague, 1975

CORRELATION TABLES

A. *Correlation Table for* Logische Untersuchungen

Unless otherwise indicated, the quotations are taken from the second edition (1913). This edition was published in three volumes. The first volume (LU I) is the Prolegomena. The second (LU II) contains the first five investigations, while the third (LU III) contains only the sixth investigation. The English edition includes this material in two volumes. The first volume of J.N. Findlay's translation (Transl. I) includes the Prolegomena and the first two investigations, while the second volume (Transl. II) contains the last four investigations.

Vorwort | 1st ed.		LU I	Transl. I	LU I	Transl. I	LU I	Transl. I
		27	71–2	77	110	127	147–8
LU I	Transl. I	28	72	78	111	128	148–9
		29	73	79	111–2	129	149
V	41	30	74	80	112–3	130	149– 50
VI	41–3	31	74–5	81	113–4	131	150–1
VII	42–3	32	75–6	82	114	132	151
VIII	43	33	76	83	114–5	133	151–2
		34	77	84	115–6	134	152–3
Vorwort	Foreword	35	77–8	85	116	135	153–4
zur 2.	2nd ed.	36	78–9	86	116–7	136	154–5
Auflage		37	79	87	117–8	137	155
		38	79– 80	88	118–9	138	155–6
LU I	Transl. I	39	80–1	89	119– 20	139	156–7
		40	81–2	90	120	140	157
VIII	43–4	41	82–3	91	120–1	141	158
IX	44	42	83	92	121–2	142	158–9
X	44–5	43	83–4	93	122	143	159– 60
XI	45–6	44	84–5	94	123	144	160
XII	46–7	45	85–6	95	123–4	145	161
XIII	47–8	46	86	96	124–5	146	161–2
XIV	48	47	86–7	97	125	147	162–3
XV	48–9	48	87–8	98	125–6	148	163
XVI	49–50	49	88–9	99	126–7	149	163–4
XVII	50	50	89– 90	100	127–8	150	164–5
		51	90–1	101	128–9	151	165
LU I	Transl. I	52	91	102	129	152	165–6
3	53	53	92	103	129– 30	153	166–7
4	53–4	54	92–3	104	130–1	154	167–8
5	54–5	55	93–4	105	131–2	155	168–9
6	55	56	94	106	132	156	169
7	55–6	57	94–5	107	132–3	157	169– 70
8	56–7	58	95–6	108	133–4	158	170–1
9	58	59	96–7	109	134	159	171–2
10	58–9	60	97–8	110	135	160	172
11	59–60	61	98–9	111	135–6	161	172–3
12	60	62	99	112	136–7	162	173–4
13	60–1	63	99–100	113	137	163	174
14	61–2	64	100–1	114	137–8	164	174–5
15	62–3	65	101–2	115	138–9	165	175–6
16	63	66	102	116	139– 40	166	176–7
17	63–4	67	102–3	117	140	167	177
18	64–5	68	103–4	118	140–1	168	177–8
19	65–6	69	104–5	119	141–2	169	178–9
20	66	70	105	120	142–3	170	179– 80
21	66–7	71	105–6	121	143	171	180
22	67–8	72	106–7	122	143–4	172	180–1
23	68–9	73	107	123	144–5	173	181–2
24	69	74	107–8	124	145–6	174	182–3
25	70	75	108–9	125	146	175	183
26	70–1	76	109– 10	126	146–7	176	183–4

LU I	Transl. I	LU I	Transl. I	LU II	Transl. I	LU II	Transl. I
177	184–5	227	224–5	17	260–1	67	303–4
178	185–6	228	225–6	18	261–2	68	304–5
179	186	229	226–7	19	262–4	69	305
180	186–7	230	227	20	264	70	305–6
181	187–8	231	227–8	21	264–5	71	306–7
182	188–9	232	228–9	22	265–6	72	307
183	189– 90	233	229– 30	23	269	73	307–8
184	190	234	230	24	269– 70	74	308–9
185	190–1	235	230–1	25	270–1	75	309– 10
186	191–2	236	231–2	26	271–2	76	310–1
187	192–3	237	232–3	27	272	77	311–2
188	193	238	233	28	272–3	78	312–3
189	193–4	239	233–4	29	273–4	79	313–4
190	194–5	240	234–5	30	274–5	80	314
191	195–6	241	235	31	275–6	81	314–5
192	197	242	235–6	32	276–7	82	315–6
193	197–8	243	236–7	33	277	83	316
194	198–9	244	237–8	34	277–8	84	316–7
195	199–200	245	238–9	35	278–9	85	317–8
196	200	246	239	36	279– 80	86	318–9
197	200–1	247	239– 40	37	280	87	319
198	201–2	248	240–1	38	280–1	88	319– 20
199	202	249	241–2	39	281–2	89	320–1
200	202–3	250	242	40	282–3	90	321–2
201	203–4	251	242–3	41	283	91	322
202	204–5	252	243–4	42	283–4	92	322–3
203	205–6	253	244–5	43	284–5	93	323–4
204	206	254	245–6	44	285–6	94	324–5
205	206–7	255	246	45	286	95	325
206	207–8	256	246–7	46	286–7	96	326–7
207	208–9	257	247	47	287–8	97	327–8
208	209			48	288–9	98	328
209	209– 10	LU II	Transl. I	49	289	99	328–9
210	210–1			50	289– 90	100	329– 30
211	212	1	248	51	290–1	101	330–1
212	212–3	2	248–9	52	291–2	102	331
213	213–4	3	249– 50	53	292	103	331–2
214	214	4	250–1	54	292–3	104	332–3
215	214–5	5	251–2	55	293–4	105	333
216	215–6	6	252	56	294–5	106	337
217	216–7	7	252–3	57	295	107	337–8
218	217	8	253–4	58	295–6	108	338–9
219	217–8	9	254–5	59	296–7	109	339– 40
220	218–9	10	255–6	60	297	110	340–1
221	219– 20	11	256	61	297–9	111	341–2
222	220–1	12	256–7	62	299–300	112	342–3
223	221	13	257–8	63	300–1	113	343
224	221–2	14	258	64	301–2	114	343–4
225	222–3	15	259	65	302	115	344–5
226	223–4	16	259– 60	66	302–3	116	345–6

LU II	Transl. I	LU II	Transl. I	LU II	Transl. I	LU II	Transl. II
117	346	167	387–8	217	427	264	465–6
118	347	168	388	218	427–8	265	466–7
119	347–8	169	389	219	428–9	266	467
120	348–9	170	389– 90	220	429– 30	267	467–8
121	349– 50	171	390–1	221	430	268	468–9
122	350–1	172	391–2	222	430–1	269	469– 70
123	351–2	173	392–3	223	431–2	270	470–1
124	352	174	393	224	432	271	471
125	352–3	175	393–4			272	472
126	353–4	176	394–5			273	472–3
127	354–5	177	395–6	LU II	Transl. II	274	473–4
128	355	178	396	225	435	275	474–5
129	355–6	179	396–7	226	435–6	276	475–6
130	356–7	180	397–8	227	436–7	277	476
131	357–8	181	398–9	228	437–8	278	476–7
132	358	182	399–400	229	438	279	477–8
133	359	183	400–1	230	438–9	280	478–9
134	359– 60	184	401–2	231	439– 40	281	479
135	360–1	185	402–3	232	440–1	282	480
136	361–2	186	403	233	441	283	480–1
137	363	187	403–4	234	441–2	284	481–2
138	363–4	188	404–5	235	442–3	285	482–3
139	364–5	189	405–6	236	443–4	286	483
140	365–6	190	406–7	237	444	287	483–4
141	366–7	191	407	238	444–5	288	484–5
142	367–8	192	407–8	239	445–6	289	485–6
143	368	193	408–9	240	446–7	290	486
144	368–9	194	409	241	447–8	291	486–7
145	369– 70	195	409– 10	242	448	292	487–8
146	370–1	196	410–1	243	448–9	293	488–9
147	371	197	411–2	244	449– 50	294	493
148	371–2	198	412	245	450–1	295	493–4
149	372–3	199	412–3	246	451	296	494–5
150	373–4	200	413–4	247	451–2	297	495
151	374–5	201	414–5	248	452–3	298	495–6
152	375	202	415–6	249	453–4	299	496–7
153	375–6	203	416	250	454	300	497–8
154	376–7	204	416–7	251	454–5	301	498
155	377	205	417–8	252	455–6	302	498–9
156	377–8	206	418–9	253	456–7	303	499–500
157	378–9	207	419– 20	254	457	304	500–1
158	379– 80	208	420	255	457–8	305	501
159	380–1	209	420–1	256	458–9	306	501–2
160	381	210	421–2	257	459– 60	307	502–3
161	381–2	211	422–3	258	460	308	503–4
162	382–3	212	423	259	460–1	309	504
163	383–4	213	423–4	260	461–2	310	504–5
164	384–5	214	424–5	261	463	311	505–6
165	385	215	425	262	463–4	312	506
166	385–7	216	426–7	263	464–5	313	507

LU II	Transl. II	LU II	Transl. II	LU II	Transl. II	LU II	Transl. II
314	507–8	364	552–3	414	588	465	626–7
315	508–9	365	553	415	588–9	466	627–8
316	509– 10	366	553–4	416	589– 90	467	628
317	510	367	554–5	417	590	468	628–9
318	510–1	368	555	418	590–1	469	629– 30
319	511–2	369	555–6	419	591–2	470	630
320	512	370	556–7	420	592	471	630–1
321	512–3	371	557	421	592–3	472	631–2
322	513–4	372	557–8	422	593–4	473	632–3
323	514–5	373	558–9	423	594–5	474	633
324	515	374	559– 60	424	595	475	633–4
325	515–6	375	560	425	595–6	476	634–5
326	516–7	376	561	426	597	477	636
327	517–8	377	561–2	427	597–8	478	636–7
328	518	378	562–3	428	598–9	479	637–8
329	518–9	379	563	429	599	480	638–9
330	519– 20	380	563–4	430	600	481	639
331	520	381	564–5	431	600–1	482	639– 40
332	521	382	565–6	432	601–2	483	640–1
333	521–2	383	566	433	602	484	641
334	522–3	384	566–7	434	602–3	485	642
335	523	385	567–8	435	603–4	486	642–3
336	523–4	386	568	436	604–5	487	643–4
337	524–5	387	568–9	437	605	488	644
338	525–6	388	569– 70	438	605–6	489	644–5
339	526	389	570–1	439	606–7	490	645–6
340	526–7	390	571	440	607–8	491	646
341	527–8	391	571–2	441	608	492	646–7
342	528–9	392	572–3	442	608–9	493	647–8
343	533	393	573–4	443	609– 10	494	648–9
344	533–4	394	574	444	610–1	495	649
345	534–5	395	574–5	445	611–2	496	649– 50
346	535–6	396	575–6	446	612	497	650–1
347	536–7	397	576	447	612–3	498	651
348	537	398	576–7	448	613–4	499	651–2
349	537–8	399	577–8	449	614–5	500	652–3
350	538–9	400	578	450	615	501	653–4
351	539–40	401	578–9	451	615–6	502	654–5
352	540	402	579– 80	452	616–7	503	655
353	541	403	580	453	617–8	504	655–6
354	541–2	404	581	454	618	505	656–7
355	542–3	405	581–2	455	618–9	506	657–8
356	543–4	406	582–3	456	619– 20	507	658
357	544	407	583	458	621–2	508	658–9
358	544–5	408	583–4	459	622		
359	545 548–9	409	584–5	460	622–3		
360	549	410	585–6	461	623–4	LU III	Transl. II
361	549– 50	411	586	462	624–5		
362	550–1	412	586–7	463	625	III	661
363	551–2	413	587–8	464	625–6	IV	661–2

LU III	Transl. II	LU III	Transl. II	LU III	Transl. III	LU III	Transl. II
V	662–3	47	705–6	97	745	147	788
VI	663–4	48	706	98	746	148	788–9
VII	664	49	707	99	746–7	149	789– 90
		50	707–8	100	747–8	150	790–1
I	667	51	708–9	101	748	151	791–2
2	667–8	52	709– 10	102	749	152	792
3	668–9	53	710	103	749– 50	153	792–3
4	669– 70	54	710–1	104	750–1	154	793–4
5	670	55	711–2	105	751–2	155	794–5
6	670–1	56	712–3	106	752	156	796–6
7	671–2	57	713	107	752–3	157	796
8	675	58	713–4	108	753–4	158	796–7
9	675–6	59	714–5	109	754–5	159	797–8
10	676–7	60	715–6	110	755	160	798–9
11	677–8	61	716–7	111	756	161	799
12	678–9	62	717	112	756–7	162	799–800
13	679	63	717–8	113	757–8	163	800–1
14	679– 80	64	719	114	758–9	164	801–2
15	680–1	65	719 20	115	759– 60	165	803
16	681–2	66	720–1	116	760–1	166	803–4
17	682–3	67	721–2	117	761–2	167	804–5
18	683	68	722	118	762–3	168	805–6
19	683–4	69	722–3	119	763	169	806–7
20	684–5	70	723–4	120	763–4	170	807
21	685–6	71	724–5	121	764–5	171	807–8
22	686	72	725–6	122	765–6	172	808–9
23	686–7	73	726	123	766	173	809– 10
24	687–8	74	726–7	124	766–7	174	810–1
25	688–9	75	727–8	125	767–8	175	811
26	689– 90	76	728–9	126	768–9	176	811–2
27	690	77	729	127	769– 70	177	812–3
28	690–1	78	730	128	773	178	813–4
29	691–2	79	730–1	129	773–4	179	814
30	692–3	80	731–2	130	774–5	180	814–5
31	693	81	732–3	131	775–6	181	816
32	694	82	733–4	132	776–7	182	816–7
33	694–5	83	734–5	133	777–8	183	817–8
34	695–6	84	735	134	778	184	818–9
35	696–7	85	735–6	135	778–9	185	819
36	697	86	736–7	136	779– 80	186	819– 20
37	698	87	737–8	137	780–1	187	820–1
38	698–9	88	738–9	138	781–2	188	821–2
39	699–700	89	739	139	782	189	822–3
40	700	90	739– 40	140	782–3	190	823
41	701	91	740–1	141	783–4	191	823–4
42	701–2	92	741–2	142	784–5	192	824–5
43	702–3	93	742	143	785	193	825–6
44	703	94	742–3	144	785–6	194	826
45	703–4	95	743–4	145	786–7	195	826–7
46	704–5	96	744–5	146	787–8	196	827–8

LU III	Transl. II	LU III	Transl. II	LU III	Transl. II	LU III	Transl. II
197	828–9	209	840–1	221	850–1	233	860–1
198	829	210	841–2	222	852	234	861
199	830	211	842–3	223	852–3	235	861–2
200	830–1	212	843–4	224	853–4	236	862–3
201	831–2	213	844–5	225	854–5	237	863–4
202	832–3	214	845–6	226	855	238	864–5
203	833–4	215	846	227	855–6	239	865–6
204	837	216	846–7	228	856–7	240	866
205	837–8	217	847–8	229	857–8	241	867
206	838–9	218	848–9	230	858	242	867–8
207	839– 40	219	849– 50	231	858–9	243	868
208	840	220	850	232	859– 60	244	869

B. Correlation Table for Philosophie als strenge Wissenschaft

PSW = Philosophie als strenge Wissenschaft, first edition, 1910
Transl. = Philosophy as a Rigourous Science, translated by Q. Lauer

PSW	Transl.	PSW	Transl.	PSW	Transl.	PSW	Transl.
289	71/2	303	92–4	316	111–3	329	130–1
290	72/4	304	94–5	317	113–5	330	131– 13
291	74/5	305	95–7	318	115–6	331	133–4
292	75– 77	306	97–8	319	116–8	332	134–6
293	77–8	307	98–9	320	118–9	333	136–7
294	78– 80	308	99–101	321	119–121	334	137–8
295	80–1	309	101–2	322	121–2	335	138– 40
296	81–3	310	102–4	323	122–3	336	140–1
297	83–4	311	104–5	324	123–5	337	141–2
298	84– 86	312	105–7	325	125–6	338	142–4
299	86–8	313	107–8	326	126–7	339	144–5
300	88–9	314	108–110	327	127–9	340	145–6
301	89– 91	315	110–1	328	129– 30	341	146–7
302	91–2						

C. Correlation Table for Ideen I

Id = Ideen Buch I
Transl. = Ideas, translated by W. R. B. Gibson

Id I	Transl.	Id I	Transl.	Id I	Transl.	Id I	Transl.
1	41	5	45–6	9	52–4	13	57–8
2	41–2	6	46–7	10	54–5	14	58–9
3	42–4	7	51	11	55–6	15	59– 60
4	44–5	8	51–2	12	56–7	16	60–2

Id I	Transl.	Id I	Transl.	Id I	Transl.	Id I	Transl.
17	62–3	67	122–3	117	181–2	167	240–1
18	63–4	68	124	118	182–3	168	242–3
19	64–5	69	125–6	119	183–4	169	243–4
20	65–6	70	126–7	120	187–8	170	244–5
21	66–7	71	127–8	121	188–9	171	245–6
22	67–8	72	128–9	122	189–90	172	246–7
23	68–9	73	129–30	123	190–1	173	247–8
24	69–70	74	130–1	124	191–2	174	248–50
25	70–1	75	131–2	125	192–4	175	250–1
26	71–2	76	132–3	126	194–5	176	251–2
27	72–4	77	133–5	127	195–6	177	152–3
28	74–5	78	135–6	128	196–7	178	253–4
29	75–6	79	136–7	129	197–8	179	254–6
30	76–7	80	137–8	130	198–9	180	256–7
31	77–8	81	138–9	131	199–200	181	257–8
32	78–9	82	139–40	132	200–1	182	258–9
33	90–1	83	140–1	133	201–3	183	259–60
34	81–2	84	142–3	134	203–4	184	260–1
35	82–3	85	143–4	135	204–5	185	261–3
36	83–4	86	144–5	136	205–6	186	263–4
37	84–5	87	145–7	137	206–7	187	264–5
38	85–6	88	147–8	138	207–8	188	265–6
39	87–8	89	148–9	139	208–9	189	266–7
40	88–9	90	149–50	140	209–10	190	267–8
41	89–90	91	150–1	141	210–1	191	268–9
42	90–1	92	151–2	142	212–3	192	269–70
43	91–2	93	153–4	143	213–4	193	271–2
44	92–3	94	154–5	144	214–5	194	272–3
45	93–5	95	155–6	145	215–7	195	273–4
46	95–6	96	156–7	146	217–8	196	274–5
47	96–7	97	157–8	147	218–9	197	275–6
48	97–101	98	158–9	148	219–20	198	276–7
49	101–2	99	159–60	149	220–1	199	278–9
50	102–4	100	160–2	150	221–2	200	279–80
51	104–5	101	162–3	151	222–3	201	280–2
52	105–6	102	163–4	152	223–4	202	282–3
53	106–7	103	164–5	153	224–6	203	283–4
54	107–8	104	165–6	154	226–7	204	284–5
55	109–10	105	166–7	155	227–8	205	286–7
56	110–1	106	167–8	156	228–9	206	287–8
57	111–2	107	168–9	157	229–30	207	288–9
58	112–3	108	170–1	158	230–1	208	289–90
59	113–4	109	172–3	159	231–2	209	290–1
60	114–5	110	173–4	160	232–3	210	291–2
61	115–6	111	174–5	161	233–4	211	292–4
62	116–8	112	175–6	162	235–6	212	294–5
63	118–9	113	176–7	163	236–7	213	295–6
64	119–20	114	177–8	164	237–8	214	296–7
65	120–1	115	178–9	165	238–9	215	297–8
66	121–2	116	179–81	166	239–40	216	298–300

Id I	Transl.	Id I	Transl.	Id I	Transl.	Id I	Transl.
217	300–1	244	332–3	271	365–5	298	397–8
218	301–2	245	333–4	272	366–7	299	398–9
219	302–3	246	334–5	273	367–9	300	399–401
220	303–5	247	335–6	274	369– 70	301	401–2
221	305–6	248	336–7	275	370–1	302	402–3
222	306–7	249	337–8	276	371–2	303	403–4
223	307–8	250	338–9	277	372–3	304	405–6
224	308–9	251	339– 41	278	373–4	305	406–7
225	309– 11	252	341–2	279	374–6	306	407–8
226	311–2	253	342–3	280	376–7	307	408–9
227	312–3	254	343–4	281	377–8	308	409– 10
228	313–4	255	344–5	282	379– 80	309	410–1
229	314–5	256	345–6	283	380–1	310	411–3
230	315–6	257	346–8	284	381–2	311	413–4
231	316–8	258	348–9	285	382–2	312	414–5
232	318–9	259	349– 50	286	383–4	313	415–6
233	319– 20	260	350–1	287	384–5	314	416–7
234	320–1	261	351–2	288	385–7	315	417–8
235	321–2	262	352–3	289	387–8	316	418–9
236	322–3	263	353–5	290	388–9	317	420–1
237	324–5	264	355–6	291	389– 90	318	421–2
238	325–6	265	359– 60	292	390–1	319	422–3
239	326–7	266	360–1	293	391–2	320	423–4
240	327–8	267	361–2	294	392–3	321	424–5
241	328–9	268	362–3	295	393–5	322	425–6
242	329– 30	269	363–4	296	395–6	323	426–7
243	331–2	270	364–5	297	396–7		

V. CONSULTED AND CITED LITERATURE

ADORNO, Th.W., Husserl and the problem of idealism, The Journal of Philosophy, 37, 1940, 5-18

ASEMISSEN, H.U., Strukturanalytische Probleme der Wahrnehmung in der Phänomenologie Husserls, Kantstudien: Ergänzungshefte, n. 73, Köln, 1957

BACHELARD, S., La logique de Husserl, Etude sur logique formelle et logique transcendentale, Paris, 1957

BAR-HILLEL, J., Husserl's conception of a purely logical grammar, PPR, 17, 1957, 362-369

BECKER, O., Mathematische Existenz, JPPF, 8, Halle, 1927

—, Über den sogenannten Antropologismus in der Philosophie der Mathematik, Philosophische Anzeiger, 3, 1929, 369-387

—, Die Philosophie Edmund Husserls, Kantstudien, 35, 1930, 119-150

BEDNARSKI, J., La réduction husserlienne, RMM, 62, 1957, 416-435

—, Deux aspects de la réduction husserlienne, abstention et retour, RMM, 64, 1959, 337-355

BERG, J.H. VAN DEN, Het menschelijk lichaam, een metabletisch onderzoek, Nijkerk, 1961

BERGER, G., Le cogito dans la philosophie de Husserl, Paris, 1941

BERGMANN, H., Brentano's theory of induction, PPR, 5, 1945, 281-292

BIEMEL, W., Husserls Encyclopaedia-Britannica Artikel und Heideggers Anmerkungen dazu, TP, 1950, 246-280

—, Les phases décisives dans le développement de la philosophie de Husserl, in Husserl, Cahiers de Royaumont, Philosophie III, Paris, 1959, 32-62. Also, abbreviated, published as 'Die entscheidenden Phasen der Entfaltung von Husserls Philosophie,' ZPF, 13, 1959, 187-213

BOEHM, R., Les ambiguités des concepts husserliens d'"immanence' et de 'transcendance,' RPFE, 1959, 481-526

—, Zum Begriff des 'Absoluten' bei Husserl, ZPF, 13, 1959, 214-242

—, Husserl, et l'idéalisme classique, Revue philosophique de Louvain, 1959, 351-396

—, Zijn en tijd in de filosofie van Husserl, TP, 21, 1959, 243-277

—, Elementare Bemerkungen über Husserls 'Phänomenologische Reduktion,' Bijdragen, Tijdschrift voor filosofie en theologie, 1965, 193-208

—, Vom Gesichtspunkt der Phänomenologie, Husserl-Studien, The Hague, 1968

—, Rezension, Th. de Boer, De ontwikkelingsgang in het denken van Husserl, Philosophische Rundschau, 15, 1968, 283–292

BOER, Th. DE, Das Verhältnis zwischen dem ersten und dem zweiten Teil der logischen Untersuchungen Edmund Husserls, Filosofia, Supplemento al Fascicolo IV, 1967, 837–859

—, Filosofie van de intersubjectiviteit, Algemeen Nederlands Tijdschrift voor Wijsbegeerte, 60, 1968, 101–112

—, Die Begriffe 'Absolut' und 'Relativ' bei Husserl, ZPF, 27, 1973, 514–534

—, Edmund Husserl, in Filosofen van de 20ste eeuw, Assen, 1976[6], 87–99

BRAND, G., Welt, Ich und Zeit, Nach unveröffentlichten Manuskripten Edmund Husserls, The Hague, 1955

BREDA, H.L. VAN, Husserl et le problème de Dieu, Actes du Xe Congrès international de Philosophie, Amsterdam, 1949, 1210–1212

—, Husserl et le problème de la liberté, Actes du IVe Congrès des Sociétés de Philosophie de Langue française, Neuchâtel, 1949, 377–381

—, Note sur: Réduction et authenticité d'après Husserl, RMM, janvier/mars 1951, 4–5

—, La phénoménologie, in La philosophie au milieu du vingtième siècle, Tome II, éd. R. Klibansky, Firenze, 1958, 53–65

—, La réduction phénoménologique, in Husserl, Cahiers de Royaumont, Philosophie III, Paris, 1959, 307–318

BROEKMAN, J.M., Phänomenologie und Egologie, faktisches und transzendentales Ego bei Edmund Husserl, The Hague, 1963

CAIRNS, D., An approach to phenomenology, in Philosophical Essays, in memory of Edmund Husserl, ed. M. Farber, Cambridge Massachusetts, 1940, 3–18

CLAESGES, A., Edmund Husserls Theorie der Raumkonstitution, The Hague, 1964

CONRAD-MARTIUS, H., Phänomenologie und Spekulation in Rencontre, Encounter, Begegnung, contributions à une psychologie humaine, dédiées au professeur Buytendijk, Utrecht, 1957, 116–128

—, Die transzendentale und die ontologische Phänomenologie, in Edmund Husserl 1859–1959, recueil commémoratif, The Hague, 1959, 175–184

DELBOS, V., Husserl. Sa critique du psychologisme et sa conception d'une logique pure, RMM, 19, No 5, 1911, 685–698

DIEMER, A., La phénoménologie de Husserl comme métaphysique, Les Etudes philosophiques, 9, 1954, 21–49

—, Edmund Husserl. Versuch einer systematischen Darstellung seiner Phänomenologie, Meisenheim am Glan, 1956

—, Die Phänomenologie und die Idee der Philosophie als strenge Wissenschaft, ZPF, 13, 2, 1959, 243–263

DRÜE, H., Edmund Husserls System der phänomenologischen Psychologie, Berlin, 1963

ELEY L., Die Krise des Apriori in der transzendentalen Phänomenologie Edmund Husserls, The Hague, 1962

ELSAS, A., Husserls Philosophie der Arithmetik, Philosophische Monatshefte, 30, 1894, 437–440

FARBER, M., The foundation of phenomenology, Cambridge Massachusetts, 1943

FEULING, D., La phénoménologie en elle-même, in La Phénoménologie, Journées d'études de la Société Thomiste, Juvisy 12 septembre 1932, I vol. Juvisy et le Saulchoir, s.d. (Société Thomiste)

FINK; E., Die phänomenologische Philosophie Edmund Husserls in der gegenwärtigen Kritik, Kantstudien, 38, Berlin, 1933, 319–383

—, Das Problem der Phänomenologie E. Husserls, RIP, I, 1939, 226–270

—, Vorbemerkung des Herausgebers zum Entwurf einer 'Vorrede' zu den 'Logischen Untersuchungen' (1913) von Edmund Husserl, TP, I, Leuven, 1939, 106–108

—, Husserl, in Philosophen-Lexikon, published by W. Ziegenfuss, Berlin, 1949, 569–576

—, L'analyse intentionnelle et le problème de la pensée spéculative, (texte allemand et français) in Problèmes actuels de la phénoménologie (Actes du Colloque international de Phénoménologie, Bruxelles, avril 1951), Paris, 1952, 53–87

—, Les concepts opératoires dans la phénoménologie de Husserl, in Husserl, Cahiers de Royaumont, Philosophie III, Paris, 1959, 214–230. Also published as Operative Begriffe in Husserls Phänomenologie, ZPF, II, 1957, 321–337

—, Die Spätphilosophie Husserls in der Freiburger Zeit, in Edmund Husserl 1859–1959, recueil commémoratif, The Hague, 1959, 99–115

—, Welt und Geschichte, in Husserl et la pensée moderne (Actes du deuxième Colloque international de Phénoménologie Krefeld, 1–3 novembre 1956), Den Haag, 1959, 143–159

FÖLLESDAL, D., Husserl und Frege, Oslo: I Kommisjon Hoe H. Asche houg en Co, 1958, Ein Beitrag zur Beleuchtung der Entstehung der phänomenologischen Philosophie, Avhandlinger utgist av Det Norske Videnskap-Akademi i Oslo II, Hist-Filos. Klasse, 1958, No. 2

FREGE, G., Die Grundlagen der Arithmetik, Breslau, 1884

—, Grundgesetze der Arithmetik, Bd I, Jena, 1893

—, Dr. E.G. Husserl: Philosophie der Arithmetik, Zeitschrift für Philosophie und philosophische Kritik, 103, 1894, 313–332

GADAMER, H.G., Die phänomenologische Bewegung, Philosophische Rundschau, 11, 1963, 1–45

GILSON, L., Méthode et métaphysique selon Franz Brentano, Paris, 1955

—, La psychologie descriptive selon Franz Brentano, Paris, 1955

GURWITSCH, A., A non egological conception of consciousness, PPR, 1940/41, 325–338

—, Phenomenological and psychological approach to consciousness, PPR, 15, 1955, 303–319

—, Théorie du champ de la conscience, Paris, 1957

—, Beitrag zur phänomenologischen Theorie der Wahrnehmung, ZPF, 13, 1959, 419–437

HAYEN, A., L'intentionnel dans la philosophie de St. Thomas, Paris, 1942

HEIDEGGER, M., Sein und Zeit, Tübingen, 1957

—, Zur Sache des Denkens, Tübingen, 1969

HEINEMANN, F., Existenzphilosophie, lebendig oder tot?, 2e Auflage, Stuttgart, 1956

HEINRICH, W., Review: Philosophie der Arithmetik, Vierteljahrschrift für wissenschaftliche Philosophie, 19, 1895, 436–439

HÉRING, J., La phénoménologie d'Edmund Husserl il y a trente ans, Souvenirs et réflexions d'un étudiant de 1909, RIP, I, 1939, 366–373

—, Edmund Husserl. Souvenirs et réflexions, in Edmund Husserl 1859–1959, recueil commémoratif, The Hague, 1959, 26–28

HILDEBRAND, F., Review: Philosophie der Arithmetik, Göttingische gelehrte Anzeigen, 1893, 175–80

ILLEMANN, W., Husserls vorphänomenologische Philosophie, Leipzig, 1932

INGARDEN, R., Review: Formale und transzendentale Logik, Kantstudien, 38, 1933, 206–209

—, Über den transzendentalen Idealismus bei E. Husserl, in Husserl et la pensée moderne (Actes du deuxième Colloque international de Phénoménologie Krefeld, 1–3 novembre 1956), The Hague, 1959, 190–204

—, Le problème de la constitution et le sens de réflexion constitutive chez Edmund Husserl, in Husserl, Cahiers de Royaumont, Philosophie III, Paris, 1959, 242–264

—, Edmund Husserl zum 100. Geburtstag, ZPF, 13, 1959, 459–463

—, On the motives which led Husserl to transcendental idealism, The Hague, 1975

KASTIL, A., Die Philosophie Franz Brentanos, Eine Einführung in seine Lehre, Salzburg, 1951

KELKEL, L., et R. SCHÉRER, Husserl. Sa vie, son oeuvre, avec un exposé de sa philosophie, Paris, 1964

KERN, I., Die drei Wege zur transzendental-phänomenologischen Reduktion in der Philosophie Edmund Husserls, TP, 24, 1962, 303–349

—, Husserl und Kant. Eine Untersuchung über Husserls Verhältnis zu Kant und zum Neukantianismus, The Hague, 1964

KOCKELMANS, A., Realisme en idealisme in Husserls phenomenologie, TP, 20, 1958, 395–440

KOCKELMANS, J.J., A first introduction to Husserl's phenomenology, Pittsburg, 1967

—, Edmund Husserl's phenomenological psychology, a historic-critical study (tr. Bernd Jager), Pittsburg, 1967

KOESTENBAUM, P., The Paris lectures, translated by P. Koestenbaum with an introductory essay, The Hague, 1964

KRAUS, O., Franz Brentano, zur Kenntnis seines Lebens und seiner Lehre, Mit Beiträgen von Carl Stumpf und Edmund Husserl, München, 1919

—, Geisteswissenschaft und Psychologie, Euphorion, 1927, Heft 4, 497–519

—, Einleitung des Herausgebers, to the following editions of Franz Brentano:
Psychologie vom empirischen Standpunkt, erster Band, 1924
Psychologie vom empirischen Standpunkt, zweiter Band, 1925
Die vier Phasen der Philosophie und ihr augenblicklicher Stand, 1926
Vom sinnlichen und noetischen Bewusstsein (Psychologie/Band III), 1928
Über die Zukunft der Philosophie, 1929
Wahrheit und Evidenz, 1930
Vom Ursprung sittlicher Erkenntnis, 1934

KUYPERS, K., La conception de la philosophie comme science rigoureuse et les

532 BIBLIOGRAPHY

fondements des sciences chez Husserl, in Husserl, Cahiers de Royaumont, Philosophie III, Paris, 1959, 72–82

—, Ursprung und Bedeutung der deskriptiven Methode in der Phänomenologie, Actes du dixième Congrès international de Philosophie, Bruxelles 20–26 août 1953, Amsterdam, 229–236

LANDGREBE, L., Husserls Phänomenologie und die Motive zu ihrer Umbildung, RIP, I, 1938/39, 277ff. Also published in German in Der Weg der Phänomenologie. Das Problem einer ursprünglichen Erfahrung, Gütersloh, 1963, 9–39

—, The world as a phenomenological problem, PPR, I, 1940, 38–58. Also in: Der Weg der Phänomenologie, 1963, 41–62

—, Die Bedeutung der phänomenologischen Methode für die Neubegründung der Metaphysik, Proceedings of the Xth international Congress of Philosophy, Bruxelles 1948, Amsterdam, 1949, 1249, 1219–1221

—, Lettre de M. Ludwig Landgrebe sur un article de M. Jean Wahl concernant 'Erfahrung und Urteil' de Husserl, RMM, 57, 1952, 282–283

—, Philosophie der Gegenwart, Bonn, 1952

—, La phénoménologie de Husserl est-elle une philosophie transcendantale?, Les Etudes Philosophiques, 9, 312–323

LAUER, Q., La philosophie comme science rigoureuse. Introduction, traduction et commentaire, Paris, 1955

LÉVINAS, E., La théorie de l'intuition dans la phénoménologie de Husserl, Paris, 1930

—, L'oeuvre d'Edmund Husserl, RPFE, 129, 1940, 33–85

—, En découvrant l'existence avec Husserl et Heidegger, Paris, 1967

LINCKE, P. F., Die phänomenale Sphäre und das reelle Bewusstsein, Halle, 1912

LOWIT, A., Pourquoi Husserl n'est pas platonicien, Les Etudes philosophiques, 9, 1954, 324–336

LÜBBE, H., Das Ende des phänomenologischen Platonismus. Eine kritische Betrachtung aus Anlass eines neuen Buches, TP, 16, 1954, 639–666

—, Positivismus und Phänomenologie (Mach und Husserl) in Beitrage zu Philosophie und Wissenschaft, Wilhelm Szilasi zum 70. Geburtstag, Munich 1960, 161–184

MARTY, A., Untersuchungen zur Grundlegung der allgemeinen Grammatik und Sprachphilosophie, Bd I, Halle a.S., 1908

MEINONG, A., Über Gegenstände höherer Ordnung und deren Verhältnis zur inneren Wahrnehmung, Zeitschrift für Psychologie und Physiologie der Sinnesorgane, 21, 1899, 205ff.

—, Selbstdarstellung, in Die deutsche Philosophie der Gegenwart in Selbstdarstellungen, Published by R. Schmidt, Leipzig, 1923, 101–160

—, Philosophenbriefe, Aus den wissenschaftlichen Korrespondenz von Alexius Meinong, herausgegeben und mit Anmerkungen versehen von R. Kindinger, Graz, 1965

MERLAN, P., Idéalisme, réalisme, phénoménologie, in Husserl, Cahiers de Royaumont, Philosophie III, 1959, 382–410

MERLEAU-PONTY, M., Phénoménologie de la perception, Paris, 1945

—, Le philosophe et son ombre, in Edmund Husserl 1859–1959, recueil commémoratif, The Hague, 1959, 195–220. Also in Signes, Paris, 1960, 201–228

—, Les sciences de l'homme et la phénoménologie, Les cours de Sorbonne, Paris, 1960

MESSER, A., Empfindung und Denken, dritte verbesserte Auflage, Leipzig, 1928

MÜLLER, W.H., Die Philosophie E. Husserls nach den Grundzügen ihrer Entstehung und ihrem systematischen Gehalt, Bonn, 1956

NATORP, P., Einleitung in die Psychologie nach kritischer Methode, Freiburg i. Br., 1888

—, Bericht über deutsche Schriften zur Erkenntnistheorie aus den Jahren 1894 und 1895, Archiv für systematische Philosophie, 3, 1897, 101–121 and 193–215

—, Zur Frage nach der logischen Methode, Mit Bezug auf E. Husserls 'Prolegomena zur reinen Logik,' Kantstudien, 6, 1901, 270–283

—, Allgemeine Psychologie nach kritischer Methode, I, Tübingen, 1912

—, Husserls 'Ideen zu einer reinen Phänomenologie,' Die Geisteswissenschaften, I, 1914, 420ff. Also in Logos 7, 1917/18, 224–246

NOËL, L., Les frontières de la logique, Revue néo-scolastique de Philosophie, 17, 1910, 211–233

OESTERREICHER, J.M., Walls are crumbling, seven jewish philosophers discover Christ, London, 1953

OSBORN, A.D., The philosophy of Edmund Husserl in its development from his mathematical interests to his first conception of phenomenology in his Logical Investigations, New York, 1934. The second edition was published under the title Edmund Husserl and his Logical Investigations, Cambridge Massachusetts, 1949

Peursen, C.A. van, Phénoménologie et ontologie, in Rencontre, Encounter, Begegnung, contributions à une psychologie humaine, dédiées au professeur Buytendijk, Utrecht, 1957, 308–317

—, La notion du temps et de l'Ego transcendantal chez Husserl, in Husserl, Cahiers de Royaumont, Philosophie III, Paris, 1959, 196–207

—, Some remarks on the Ego in the phenomenology of Husserl, in For Roman Ingarden, The Hague, 1959, 29–41

—, Die Phänomenologie Husserls und die Erneuerung der Ontologie, ZPF, 16, 1962, 489–501

Pfänder, A., Logik, JPPF, 4, 1921, 193–494

(La) Phenomenologie, Journées d'études de la Société Thomiste, I, Juvisy, 12 septembre 1932, Juvisy et le Saulchoir, s.d. (Société Thomiste)

Pietersma, H., Husserl and Frege, Archiv für Geschichte der Philosophie, 49, 1967, 298–324

Plessner, H., Phänomenologie. Das Werk Edmund Husserls (1859–1938), in Zwischen Philosophie und Gesellschaft, Bern, 1953, 39–59

Pos, H.J., Descartes en Husserl, Algemeen Nederlands Tijdschrift voor Wijsbegeerte en Psychologie, 31, 1937/38. Also published in Keur uit de verspreide geschriften van Dr. H.J. Pos, deel II, Beginselen en gestalten, Assen, 1958, 66–86

—, Valeur et limites de la phénoménologie, in Problèmes actuels de la Phénoménologie (Actes du Colloque international de Phénomenologie, Bruxelles, avril 1951), Paris, 1952, 31–52. Also published in Keur uit de verspreide geschriften van Dr. H.J. Pos, deel II, Beginselen en gestalten, Assen, 1958, 265–280

Rabeau, G., Species, verbum. L'activité intellectuelle élémentaire selon S.Th. d'Aquin, Paris, 1938

Reinach, A., Über Phänomenologie, 1914, Gesammelte Schriften, Halle, 1921, 379–405

—, Sinn und Recht der phänomenologischen Methode, in Edmund Husserl 1859–1959, recueil commémoratif, The Hague, 1959, 134–147

Ricoeur, P., Husserl et le sens de l'histoire, RMM, 54, 1949, 280–316

—, Idées directrices pour une phénoménologie. Traduction, introduction et notes, Paris, 1950

—, Analyses et problèmes dans Ideen II de Husserl, RMM, 56, 1951, 357–394; 57, 1952, 1–16

—, Méthode et tâches d'une phénoménologie de la volonté, in Problèmes actuels de la phénoménologie (Actes du Colloque international de Phénoménologie, Bruxelles, avril 1951), Paris, 1952, 111–140

—, Etudes sur les Méditations Cartésiennes de Husserl, Revue Philosophique de Louvain, 52, 1954, 75–109

ROTH, A., Edmund Husserls ethische Untersuchungen, The Hague, 1960

RYLE, G., The theory of meaning in British philosophy in the mid century, 1957

SARTRE, J.-P., La transcendance de l'Ego, Recherches Philosophiques 6, 1936/37, 85–123

—, L'être et le néant, Paris, 1948

SCHELER, M., Die Stellung des Menschen im Kosmos, Munich, 1928

SCHESTOW, L., Memento Mori, Anläßlich der Erkenntnistheorie von Edmund Husserl, in Potestas Clavium oder die Schlüsselgewalt, Munich, 1926, 307–457

SCHILLER, P. VON, Aufgabe der Psychologie, eine Geschichte ihrer Probleme, Vienna, 1948

SCHÜTZ, A., Husserl's importance for the social sciences, in Edmund Husserl 1859–1959, The Hague, 1959, 86–99

SIMONIN, H. D., La notion 'd'intentio' dans l'oeuvre de saint Thomas d'Aquin, Revue des Sciences philosophiques et théologiques, 19, 1930, 445–463

SOKOLOWSKI, R., The formation of Husserl's concept of constitution, The Hague, 1964

SPIEGELBERG, H., Der Begriff der Intentionalität in der Scholastik, bei Brentano und bei Husserl, Philosophische Hefte, 5, 1936, 72–91

—, The 'reality-phenomenon' and reality, in Philosophical essays in memory of Edmund Husserl, ed. M. Farber, Cambridge Massachusetts, 1940, 84–105

—, Perspektivenwandel: Konstitution eines Husserl-bildes, in Edmund Husserl 1859–1959, recueil commémoratif, The Hague, 1959, 56–63

—, The phenomenological movement (the second edition was accompanied by a separate Appendix), The Hague, 1960[1], 1965[2]

STEIN, E., Husserls Phänomenologie und die Philosophie des hl. Thomas von Aquino, JPPF, 10, 1929, 315–339

—, Contribution to the discussion, see above (La) Phénoménologie

STRASSER, S., Het zielsbegrip in de metaphysische en in de empirische psychologie, Nijmegen, 1950

—, Das Gottesproblem in der Spätphilosophie Edmund Husserls, Philosophisches Jahrbuch der Görres-Gesellschaft, 67, 1959, 130–142. Also published in Bouwstenen voor een filosofische anthropologie, Hilversum, 1965, 293–312

STUMPF, C., Zur Einteilung der Wissenschaften, Abhandlungen der Berliner Akademie, 1906

—, Erinnerungen an Franz Brentano, in Franz Brentano by O. Kraus, Munich, 1919, 85–149

—, Erkenntnislehre I, II, Leipzig, 1939

SZILASI, W., Einführung in die Phänomenologie Edmund Husserls, Tübingen, 1959

TALJAARD, J. A. L., Franz Brentano as wijsgeer, 'n bijdrae tot die kennis van die neo-positiwisme, Franeker, 1955

TANNERY, J., Science et philosophie, Paris, 1912

THEUNISSEN, M., Intentionaler Gegenstand und ontologische Differenz. Ansätze zur Fragestellung Heideggers in der Phänomenologie Husserls. Philos. Jahrbuch, Munich, 70, 1963, 344–362

—, Der Andere, Studien zur Sozial-Ontologie der Gegenwart, Berlin, 1965

THÉVENAZ, P., Qu'est-ce que la phénoménologie? Revue de Théologie et de Philosophie, 1952, 9–30 (translated by J. M. Edie, What is phenomenology? and other Essays, London, 1962)

—, La question du point de départ radical chez Descartes et Husserl, in Problèmes actuels de la phénoménologie (Actes du Colloque international de Phénoménologie, Bruxelles, avril 1951), Paris, 1952, 9–30

THYSSEN, J., Husserls Lehre von den 'Bedeutungen' und das Begriffsproblem, ZPF, 13, 1959, 163–186; 438–458

TRAN DUC THAO, Phénoménologie et matérialisme dialectique, Paris, 1951

TUGENDHAT, E., Der Wahrheitsbegriff bei Husserl und Heidegger, Berlin, 1967

TWARDOWSKI, K., Zur Lehre vom Inhalt und Gegenstand der Vorstellungen, Vienna, 1894

ÜBERWEG, F., Grundriss der Geschichte der Philosophie, Teil IV, Berlin, 1923

UTITZ, E., Franz Brentano, Kantstudien, 22, 1917, 217–242

VOIGT, A., Was ist Logik? Vierteljahrsschrift für wissenschaftliche Philosophie, XVI, 1892, 289–332

—, Zum Calcul der Inhaltslogik, Erwiderung auf Herrn Husserls Artikel, Vierteljahrsschrift für wissenschaftliche Philosophie, XVII, 1893, 504–507

—, Berichtigung, Vierteljahrsschrift für wissenschaftliche Philosophie, 18, 1894, 135

VOLLENHOVEN, D.H.Th., Geschiedenis der wijsbegeerte, Band I, Franeker, 1950

WAELHENS, A. DE, Une philosophie de l'ambiguité. L'existentialisme de Maurice Merleau-Ponty, Louvain, 1951

—, Phénoménologie et vérité, Essai sur l'évolution de l'idée de vérité chez Husserl et Heidegger, Paris, 1953

—, Husserl 1859–1938, in Les philosophes célèbres, Paris, 1956, 322–329

—, Existence et signification, Louvain, 1958

—, Commentaire sur l'idée de la phénoménologie, in Husserl, Cahiers de Royaumont, Philosophie III, Paris, 1959, 143–156

—, L'idée phénoménologique d'intentionnalité, in Husserl et la pensée moderne (Actes du deuxième Colloque international de Phénoménologie Krefeld, 1956), The Hague, 1959, 115–129

WAHL, J., Notes sur la première partie de Erfahrung und Urteil de Husserl, RMM, 1951, 6–34

—, Notes sur quelques aspects empiristes de la pensée de Husserl, RMM, 1952, 17–45

—, Clôture du colloque phénoménologique, in Husserl, Cahiers de Royaumont, Philosophie III, Paris, 1959, 428–432

WINDELBAND, W., Präludien, zweiter Band, Tübingen, 1921

ZIEGENFUSS, W., Philosophen-Lexikon, erster Band, Berlin, 1949

NAME INDEX

SUBJECT INDEX

presentative (bodily present), 16, 146, 162, 164, 173f, 182, 189
presupposition, 1) metaphysical – 41, 48f, 195f, 282, 309f
    2) naturalistic – 357, 371, 387, 389, 423, 456, 481
    3) Lockean – 17, 25, 33, 135, 140, 159f
    4) transcendental 357, 390
psychologism, *115*ff, *217*ff, 286, 297f; epistemological – (psychologism of objects) 20, 38,
    116, 241, 280, 300, 371, 407; logical – 92f, 96, 116, 207, *271*, 273, *300*, 407; transcenden-
    tal – 117, 300, *401*f
psychology, genetic – 52ff, 203f; genetic – and transcendental phenomenology 220f, *481*f,
    *484*f; descriptive – 54ff, 107ff, 205ff, 212ff, *452*f; descriptive – and transcendental
    phenomenology 167, 199, 305, 311; eidetic – 96, 121, *207*ff, 275, 284, 292, 298, 300, 451,
    477ff; pure – (phenomenological –) 59, 209f, 230; pure – and transcendental phenome-
    nology 210, 230, 322, 377, 382, 409, *425*, *432*ff, *450*, *454*ff; see the relation between
    psychological and transcendental consciousness
quality, see positing
real, 1) existing independently of consciousness 134, 185, 188, *190*ff, *195*ff, 388, 427
    2) existing as a component of consciousness (= reell) *134*, 173, 178, 189, 425, 429
    3) being a sensory object 141, 147, 149, 152f, 157, 165
realism, 46, 141, 152, 162, 166, 196, 201, 248, 260ff, 293, 363, *402*ff, 407, 416, 422, 490
reduction, egological – 178, 352; eidetic – *247*ff, 268, 470; phenomenological-psychologi-
    cal – 37, *49*f, 161, *177*f, 194f, *198*f, 211, 249, *268*, *308*ff, *361*ff, 406, *426*f, *430*f, 432, 454f,
    470; transcendental – 114, 210ff, *322*f, *328*ff, *362*ff, 409, *430*f, 455f; the relation between
    the phenomenological-psychological and the transcendental – 312, 375, 383, 429ff,
    432ff, *454*f
reflection, 10, 24, *39*, 128f, 159f, 201, 344; – and reduction *431*f, 466ff
relative, see absolute
representation, *13*ff, 130, 133; form of – 145, 182f, 189, 413, 441
Scholasticism, – and intentionality 7ff, 37, 43ff, 166, 184, 190f, 194, 427f, 448; – and
    intuition of essences 101, 244, *260*, 268, 287f, 478
sensation (Empfindung), 134ff, *144*, 160, *162*f, 172ff, 183, 336, 415, 462, 481
sense, 16, 131, *138*, 143f; – and matter *137*f, 141f, 147, 258, 438; – and noema 425f, 438
sign, 12, 14, 16, *131*, 138f, 144f, 237, 439f; – theory 40, 50, 54, 139, 162, 194, 201, 420;
    arithmetic – 64ff, 74
signification, 17, *130*ff, 138f, 144f
substance, 196, 339, 348, 480
synthesis, 1) fulfillment 15, *146*f, 183
    2) categorial – 153, 169
synthetic, see analytic
teleology, 225ff, 353, *390*, 446, 504
theology, 200, 355, 472f
thesis, see positing
thing in itself, see object in itself
time, 35, 163, 229, 255ff, 305, 332, 415, *462*f
transcendence, 17, 44, *161*ff, *314*ff, 339f, 397f; problem of – 46, *164*f, 147, 200f, 282, *308*f,
    320, 369, *399*ff, *437*ff, 483
turn to the object (Wende zum Objekt), 7ff, 50, 140f, 161, 185, 261, 363, 369, 405
understanding, 222, 392, 503f
unity of consciousness, 37, 332f, 359f